HANDBOOK
of CLINICAL
HEALTH
PSYCHOLOGY

Volume 2.
Disorders of Behavior and Health

HANDBOOK
of CLINICAL
HEALTH
PSYCHOLOGY

Volume 2.
Disorders of Behavior and Health

Editor-in-Chief
Thomas J. Boll

Volume Editors
James M. Raczynski
Laura C. Leviton

AMERICAN PSYCHOLOGICAL ASSOCIATION
WASHINGTON, DC

Published by
American Psychological Association
750 First Street, NE
Washington, DC 20002
www.apa.org

To order
APA Order Department
P.O. Box 92984
Washington, DC 20090-2984
Tel: (800) 374-2721
Direct: (202) 336-5510
Fax: (202) 336-5502
TDD/TTY: (202) 336-6123
Online: www.apa.org/books/
E-mail: order@apa.org

In the U.K., Europe, Africa, and the Middle East, copies may be ordered from
American Psychological Association
3 Henrietta Street
Covent Garden, London
WC2E 8LU England

Typeset in Goudy by World Composition Services, Inc., Sterling, VA

Printer: Sheridan Books, Ann Arbor, MI
Cover Designer: NiDesign, Baltimore, MD
Project Manager: Debbie Hardin, Carlsbad, CA

The opinions and statements published are the responsibility of the authors, and such opinions and statements do not necessarily represent the policies of the American Psychological Association. Any views expressed in chapter 5 do not necessarily represent the views of the United States government, and the author's participation in the work is not meant to serve as an official statement.

Library of Congress Cataloging-in-Publication Data
Handbook of clinical health psychology / edited by Suzanne Bennett Johnson, Nathan Perry, and Ronald H. Rozensky.—1st ed.
    p. cm.
  Includes bibliographical references and index.
  Contents: v. 1. Medical disorders and behavioral applications—
  ISBN 1-55798-909-5 (alk. paper)
  1. Clinical health psychology—Handbook, manuals, etc. 2. Health behavior—Handbooks, manuals, etc. I. Johnson, Suzanne Bennett. II. Perry, Nathan W.
III. Rozensky, Ronald H.

R726.7.H354 2002
616.89—dc21   2002018260

ISBN: 1-59147-091-9

British Library Cataloguing-in-Publication Data
A CIP record is available from the British Library.

Printed in the United States of America
First Edition

CONTENTS

CONTRIBUTORS

Phillip J. Brantley, Department of Behavioral Medicine, Pennington
Biomedical Research Center, Louisiana State University,
Baton Rouge

Ross C. Brownson, Department of Community Health, School of Public
Health, St. Louis University, St. Louis, MO; Alvin J. Siteman
Cancer Center at Barnes–Jewish Hospital and Washington
University School of Medicine, St. Louis, MO

Dawn Newman Carlson, Carlson Health Promotion, Gainesville, FL

Leslie F. Clark, Department of Health Behavior, University of Alabama
at Birmingham

Patricia M. Dubbert, G. V. (Sonny) Montgomery VA Medical Center
and University of Mississippi School of Medicine, Jackson

Timothy R. Elliott, Department of Psychology, University of Alabama at
Birmingham

Edwin B. Fisher, Departments of Psychology, Medicine, and Pediatrics,
Washington University, St. Louis, MO; Alvin J. Siteman Center at
Barnes–Jewish Hospital and Washington University School of
Medicine, St. Louis, MO

Robert J. Gatchel, Department of Psychiatry, University of Texas
Southwestern Medical Center, Dallas

Alex H. S. Harris, Center for Health Care Evaluation, Palo Alto VA
Medical Center, Palo Alto, CA

Susan M. Harding, Sleep/Wake Disorders Center, University of Alabama
at Birmingham

Shannon Hartley, Medical Psychology Program, Department of
Psychology, University of Alabama at Birmingham

Andrew C. Heath, Midwest Alcoholism Research Center, Department of
Psychiatry, Washington University School of Medicine, St. Louis,

MO; Alvin J. Siteman Cancer Center at Barnes–Jewish Hospital and Washington University School of Medicine, St. Louis, MO

Jean Harvey-Berino, Department of Nutrition and Food Sciences, University of Vermont, Burlington

Suzanne Bennett Johnson, Department of Medical Humanities and Social Sciences, Florida State University College of Medicine, Tallahassee

Abby C. King, Stanford Center for Research in Disease Prevention, Stanford University School of Medicine, Stanford, CA

Howard Leventhal, Institute for Health, Health Care Policy, and Aging Research, Rutgers University, New Brunswick, NJ

Laura C. Leviton, Robert Wood Johnson Foundation, Princeton, NJ

Nicole Liddon, Department of Health Behavior, School of Public Health, University of Alabama at Birmingham

Douglas A. Luke, Department of Community Health, School of Public Health, St. Louis University, St. Louis, MO; and Alvin J. Siteman Center at Barnes–Jewish Hospital and Washington University School of Medicine, St. Louis, MO

Ann Matt Maddrey, Department of Psychiatry, University of Texas Southwestern Medical Center, Dallas

Christopher M. Makris, Division of Pulmonary Medicine, Children's Hospital of Alabama, Birmingham; University of Alabama at Birmingham

Bess H. Marcus, Center for Behavioral and Preventive Medicine, Miriam Hospital/Brown University School of Medicine, Providence, RI

Pamela Davis Martin, Department of Behavioral Medicine, Pennington Biomedical Research Center, Louisiana State University, Baton Rouge

René Martin, College of Nursing, University of Iowa, Iowa City

John McBurney, Center for Disorders of Sleep and Fatigue, Spartanburg Neurological Services, Spartanburg, SC

Jesse B. Milby, Departments of Psychology and Medicine, University of Alabama at Birmingham

G. Vernon Pegram, Sleep Disorders Center of Alabama, Birmingham

James M. Raczynski, College of Public Health, University of Arkansas for Medical Sciences, Little Rock

Scott D. Rhodes, Department of Health Behavior, School of Public Health, University of Alabama at Birmingham

William Rogers, Department of Health Behavior, School of Public Health, University of Alabama at Birmingham

Dana Ross, Division of Preventive Medicine, Department of Medicine, University of Alabama at Birmingham

James F. Sallis, Department of Psychology, San Diego State University, San Diego, CA

Joseph E. Schumacher, Division of Preventive Medicine, University of Alabama at Birmingham

Richard M. Shewchuk, Department of Health Administration, University of Alabama at Birmingham

Katharine E. Stewart, Department of Health Behavior and Health Education, College of Public Health, University of Arkansas for Medical Sciences, Little Rock

Walton Sumner II, Department of Medicine, Washington University School of Medicine, St. Louis, MO; Alvin J. Siteman Cancer Center at Barnes–Jewish Hospital and Washington University School of Medicine, St. Louis, MO

Carl E. Thoresen, School of Education and Departments of Psychology and Psychiatry/Behavioral Sciences, Stanford University, Stanford, CA

Jalie A. Tucker, Department of Health Behavior, School of Public Health, University of Alabama at Birmingham

Delia Smith West, College of Public Health, University of Arkansas for Medical Sciences, Little Rock

INTRODUCTION TO THE SERIES

THOMAS J. BOLL

The history of psychology in medicine predates the formal development of psychology. For the many millennia in which medicine has made a contribution to humankind, most of its contribution was in fact psychological. Until sometime in the middle part of the 20th century, medicine had very little of either science or technology to offer. For example, no general anesthetic existed until the end of the 19th century, and no antibiotics were available until the 20th century. Most of the miracles of surgical intervention and restoration occurred sometime after that. Before this time, common sense, diet, rest, and bedside manner was the doctor's stock-in-trade.

With the advent of "miracle medicine," a great deal has been gained and much has been lost. What has been gained is obvious. Medicine has allowed us to "fix" many disorders and conditions and make many once-fatal illnesses curable. It has also, however, placed the emphasis on the role of the physician as the sole person responsible for healing. This thinking, in turn, has to a considerable extent removed not only the patient's role but also the role of the interaction between doctor and patient. In many instances, patients are essentially passive recipients of pharmacological, surgical, and other biomechanical interventions. It was not until the end of the 20th century and the beginning of the 21st century that what is now amusingly referred to as "alternative medicine" was rediscovered. Western allopathic procedures have become the mainstream, and all of the procedures that were for millennia the entire armamentarium of medicine are now only "alternative." Many of these procedures have roots in specific cultures and have continuously been in practice, whereas others are being re-recognized.

A positive effect of the biomedical revolution has been the prolonged life of many people with chronic illnesses. It is now common for individuals with diabetes, hypertension, hyperlipidemia, cerebral disorders, and coronary artery diseases to live not only long but also active and productive lives. At the same time, many early killers and limiters of life such as smallpox, whooping cough, and polio have been eliminated or largely controlled. However, this resulting longevity has led to the presence of increasing numbers of individuals with other illnesses of previously relatively small import (e.g., arthritis, dementing disorders), which has focused attention on the need for care of chronic illness and the elderly population.

Chronic care is an overbroad term that involves a return to nonbiomechanical interventions for individuals who simply cannot be "fixed." These individuals must, through their own participation as well as through the cooperation and active participation of significant others and a broad range of individuals in the "health care system," work to ameliorate symptoms, minimize dysfunction, increase capacity, and enhance quality in their lives. Much of this change was predicted by Nicholas Cummings and others in their seminal work at the Kaiser Foundation in the 1960s (Cummings & Follette, 1968; Follette & Cummings, 1962, 1967). Unfortunately, this knowledge is only recently gaining general acceptance with the health care community and general public. The remarkable work of Dean Ornish with end-stage cardiovascular disease demonstrates that behavioral interventions for "real" medical conditions work because they are "real" interventions (Ornish et al., 1990). Time in the hospital, time for recovery after surgery, and amount of medication required for seizure management and pain management can all be reduced with behavioral and biobehavioral techniques. This reality seems, all too slowly, to be seeping into the awareness of physicians, the general patient population, and—even more slowly—third-party payers.

The purpose of the books in this series is to detail the contributions of health psychology to scientific knowledge and effective evaluation and intervention. The last title in the series is *Models and Perspectives in Health Care Psychology*. The books covered by the *Handbook of Clinical Health Psychology* discuss the diagnoses contained in the *International Classification of Diseases, Ninth Revision* (World Health Organization, 1996) and the contributions of psychological and behavioral evaluation and intervention to each of these areas of medical disorder and dysfunction. Major systems of the body and the disorders attendant thereto are considered, as are lifestyle factors that affect health, in which health psychology has contributed to the development and implementation of effective methods for health promotion and for primary, secondary, and tertiary illness prevention. These books also discuss a wide variety of specific disorders and crosscutting medical conditions (e.g., sleep problems, obesity) and delineate techniques, results, and interventions that have been found to be effective and continue to be developed. Finally, the theoretical underpinnings for each of these scientific advances and clinical applications are discussed.

All of this information makes these handbooks the first comprehensive effort to characterize the field of health psychology. The three volumes seek to describe the scientific basis of the endeavor; to delineate the specific techniques, technologies, and procedures for evaluation and intervention in the field; and to demonstrate the applications of health psychology to the full range of diagnostic entities recognized in medicine today.

REFERENCES

Cummings, N. A., & Follette, W. T. (1968). Psychiatric services and medical utilization in a prepaid health plan setting: Part II. *Medical Care, 6,* 31–41.

Follette, W. T., & Cummings, N. A. (1962). [Psychiatry and medical utilization]. An unpublished pilot project.

Follette, W. T., & Cummings, N. A. (1967). Psychiatric services and medical utilization in a prepaid health plan setting. *Medical Care, 5,* 25–35.

Ornish, D., Brown, S. E., Scherwitz, L. W., Billings, J. H., Armstrong, W. T., Ports, T. A., et al. (1990). Can lifestyle changes reverse coronary heart disease? *Lancet, 336,* 129–133.

World Health Organization. (1996). *International classification of diseases, ninth revision, clinical modification.* Geneva: Author.

HANDBOOK
of CLINICAL
HEALTH
PSYCHOLOGY

Volume 2.
Disorders of Behavior and Health

INTRODUCTION TO VOLUME 2: DISORDERS OF BEHAVIOR AND HEALTH

JAMES M. RACZYNSKI AND LAURA C. LEVITON

Volume 2 of this three-volume series focuses on issues that cut across different disease outcomes and the promotion of health. These issues encompass risk factors, approaches to risk reduction, the maintenance of health, mediators of risk and risk reduction, and adaptation to health and disease. It is interesting to note that the medical model has often led to categorical thinking, not only when the treatment of a particular disease is being considered but also in the early (e.g., primary) and later (e.g., secondary and tertiary) prevention of diseases. Thus, although tobacco smoking is seen as a primary risk factor of a variety of disease outcomes—for example, heart disease, pulmonary disorders, and several types of cancer—research funding agencies and even private, nonprofit organizations (e.g., American Heart Association, American Cancer Society, American Lung Association) are rarely able to focus on the behavioral risk factor exclusive of a specific down-stream disease outcome. Switching to a public health model approach might lead to more integrated and coordinated primary risk reduction approaches across many agencies and health-related nonprofit organizations. After all, why should it matter whether or not we are focused on the prevention of cancer or heart disease, if the upstream risk factors of obesity or tobacco smoking are the focus of the primary prevention efforts? It does not matter which down-stream disease outcome is the particular *final* outcome of concern: The risk reduction prevention approach being implemented and evaluated is largely going to be the same. It is the refinement of the primary risk reduction prevention approach that should be the real focus of this research or practice-based effort rather than the particular disease outcomes on which it impacts. Even when risk factors or definitive disease emerge, the behavioral focus of secondary and tertiary prevention often is not significantly influenced by the nature of the risk factor of disease but is rather based on the behavioral objective—for example, losing weight, quitting smoking, and so forth.

When it comes to other cross-cutting issues—for example, those that are cross-cutting in the sense of mediating the progression of disease or those involved in adaptation to illness regardless of the particular illness—less categorical thinking has generally been evident. This is probably because these issues are largely being examined by behavioral and social scientists rather than medically trained researchers and theoreticians. The theoretical models that have been posited and examined have thus arisen less from medical model origins.

ORGANIZATION OF VOLUME

Part I of this volume includes chapters that address health risk factors and risk reduction methods that cut across a variety of disease outcomes. Most of these address behavioral risk factors, such as dietary intake, substance abuse, cigarette smoking, sexual risk behavior, physical activity, and sleep. The relationships of these risk behaviors to various diseases is reviewed, and the mediator of behaviors, as in the case of obesity, or the abnormalities that occur in health risk factors, such as in the case of disorders of sleep, are also discussed.

Part II of this volume includes chapters that mediate the relationship between risk behaviors and the development of a variety of diseases, such as in the case of stress, coping, social support, and spirituality. Included in this section are also chapters that address symptom perception and health-care seeking, because these factors are vitally critical to early diagnosis and treatment for many disease outcomes and can significantly affect mortality and morbidity. Finally, a chapter on adherence is also included in this section, because adherence with risk reduction or treatment regimens are major factors affecting disease etiology as well as morbidity and mortality.

Part III of this volume includes three chapters that deal with adaptation to health and disease. Pain is significantly influenced by psychosocial factors even in the absence of underlying biological mechanisms. Separate chapters on family and patient adaptation to illness and disease round out this section, addressing these different aspects of those who are affected by illness.

CONCLUSION

The medical model and much of the organization of federal agencies and nonprofit organizations focus on disease outcomes, even when risk factors are being considered. Yet many of the risk factors and even adaptations to illness are not associated with a single-disease process or disease outcome. Thus, a broader approach to thinking of risk factors, the reduction of risk factors, and even adaptation to illness may be a more appropriate approach for health psychologists who are often not focused on the direct treatment of diseases. This volume attempts to accomplish this.

I

CROSS-CUTTING FACTORS THAT AFFECT HEALTH RISKS

1

BEHAVIORAL ASPECTS OF OBESITY, DIETARY INTAKE, AND CHRONIC DISEASE

DELIA SMITH WEST, JEAN HARVEY-BERINO,
AND JAMES M. RACZYNSKI

Dietary behavior is simple on one level: We are born with the reflexes to eat, and our bodies are built to then manage the nutrients and energy sources that we consume. However, past this simplistic view, dietary behavior and the way in which our food and drink choices affect our risk for diseases are extraordinarily complex, perhaps more complex than any other behavior. This complexity is evident at multiple levels, extending from the physiological level to that involved in food preparation and dietary behavior itself. Our physiology is affected by genetic predispositions, which in turn interact with our food preparation and dietary behaviors and what we consume as calories, fat, and nutrients to influence our risk for a variety of disease outcomes.

A simplified compilation of factors that influence dietary behavior and the impact that food and drink consumption have on chronic disease risk is depicted in Figure 1.1. The physiology of nutrient intake and energy metabolism itself is extraordinarily complex. Foods, fluids, and nutrients are broken down and distributed as needed throughout the body, a process that has multiple regulatory mechanisms to ensure, when functioning properly, an inordinately intricate balance of fluids, sources for energy metabolism, and nutrient and mineral availability within our bodies. Nutrient, fluid, and mineral imbalances can affect physiological mechanisms and body chemistry that then increase risk for particular disease outcomes. Furthermore, energy intake and expenditure determine energy regulation, which is associated with body weight and body composition, which in turn affect disease risk factors. Adding to these complexities at the physiological level are the influences of idiosyncratic sensitivities to certain foods and nutrients, often determined by genetic predispositions, which can affect an individual's susceptibility for certain disease outcomes.

As seen in Figure 1.1, what and how much we choose to consume is determined by a variety of influences. Cultural, social, and psychosocial factors affect learned taste, palatability, and choice preferences. Decisions about dietary intake are also affected by our knowledge, attitudes, and beliefs regarding the meaning of food and health risks or benefits associated with the food. These are determined not only by cultural, social, and psychosocial factors but also by the tremendous volume of information disseminated by both the public and private sectors, information that can be contradictory, inaccurate, or misleading. Consumers are left to sift through this vast amount of dietary information in their decisions about their own personal nutrition objectives. Health care providers are frequently not adequately trained in nutrition and dietary behavior change and therefore can be of limited help in this decision-making process. These decisions are further complicated by challenges in identifying the dietary constituents of food because taste or visual inspection alone cannot reveal the nutrient content. Food availability also affects an individual's consumption and is largely controlled by the food industry. The food industry is, in turn, influenced in its product selection by natural availability, consumer choice, anticipated profits, and regulatory policies and laws. Furthermore, the taste and palatability of foods are affected not only by cultural, social, and psychosocial factors but also by the skill and methods of the food preparer. Finally, what and how much we consume of particular foods and nutrients are influenced by our own personal psychosocial characteristics. Thus, dietary behavior is neither simple nor straightforward.

Adding to these complexities that govern our dietary behavior is the idiosyncratic manner in which our bodies respond to the nutrients and influence our personal risk for a broad variety of disease outcomes. For example, some individuals may be better able to manage sodium than others who are more prone to blood pressure increases. Thus, the path from food consumption to disease is neither simple nor straightforward either.

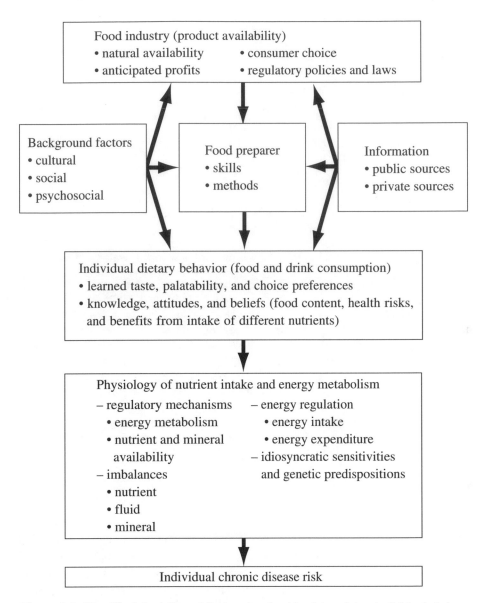

Figure 1.1. Simplified depiction of factors involved in determining individual dietary behavior and chronic disease risk.

PHYSIOLOGY, HEALTH OUTCOMES, AND DIETARY AND NUTRIENT FACTORS

Chronic diseases are the leading cause of death and disability in the United States, accounting for greater morbidity and mortality than acute

TABLE 1.1
Role of Major Dietary Factors in Chronic Disease Outcomes

Health outcome	Dietary factor	Role in disease outcome
Cardiovascular disease	Cholesterol	Total cholesterol, LDL
	Saturated fat	Total cholesterol, LDL, HDL
	Sodium	BP among sodium sensitive
	Alcohol	HDL
	Obesity	Glucose intolerance, BP, dyslipidemia
	Fiber	Total cholesterol, LDL
Hypertension	Obesity	Insulin resistance, hyperinsulinemia, physical changes in kidney, activation sympathetic nervous + reninangiotensin systems
	Alcohol	Excess exacerbates
	Sodium	Excess exacerbates
	Potassium	Peripheral resistance, water and sodium loss, reninangiotensin secretion, adrenergic tone, stimulation sodium–potassium pump
Diabetes (type 2)	Obesity	Insulin sensitivity, glucose uptake
	Caloric intake	Blood glucose levels
	Fat	Dyslipidemia
	Fiber	
Cancer	Obesity	Endometrial, breast, and kidney cancer risk
	Alcohol	Head, neck, liver, colon, rectum, and breast cancer risk
Osteoporosis	Calcium	Acquisition peak bone mass, bone loss in postmenopausal women
	Vitamin D_3	Calcium absorption
	Alcohol	Bone loss
	Phosphorus	Calcium:phosphorus ratio bone loss

infectious diseases and deaths from injury or other traumatic causes. Diet is assuming increasing importance in the prevention and management of a variety of diseases (Institute of Medicine Committee on Dietary Guidelines Implementation, 1991). The most prevalent conditions in which diet plays a prominent role include cardiovascular diseases, diabetes, and cancers. These conditions rank high among the causes of death in the United States (National Center for Health Statistics, 1999). In addition, although not generally life-threatening but nonetheless a source of considerable morbidity, obesity and osteoporosis affect millions of U.S. residents annually and are strongly related to dietary intake. In fact, McGinnis and colleagues estimated that diet and activity patterns were responsible for 14% of the total deaths annually in the United States (McGinnis & Foege, 1993). The dietary constituents that assume a major role in prevention and management of chronic disease are summarized in Table 1.1.

Energy Intake

Total energy intake is derived from the consumption of calories in the form of carbohydrate (4 kcal/gm), protein (4 kcal/gm), fat (9 kcal/gm), and alcohol (7 kcal/gm). Body weight is determined by the balance between the amount of calories ingested and the amount expended. Imbalances in the energy intake versus expenditure equation result in either weight reductions or increases. Thus, although an oversimplification of a complex disorder, energy intake in excess of energy expenditure is centrally involved in the development and maintenance of obesity (Hill, Wyatt, Reed, & Peters, 2003). In fact, the dramatic rise in obesity rates in the United States in recent decades is thought to be a result, at least in part, to the increase in total energy consumed. In 1978, total calorie intake in the United States averaged 1,969 kcal/day, and by 1990 that figure had increased to 2,200 kcal/day (USDA, 1994–1996). This recent increase in total caloric intake primarily reflects increased sugar consumption in the form of soft drinks (Guthrie & Morton, 2000).

Of course, change in body weight is also affected by energy expended. Energy expenditure is divided into three components: resting metabolic rate (RMR), thermic effect of food (TEF), and voluntary activity. Except in extremely active individuals, the resting metabolic rate constitutes the largest portion of the total energy expenditure (TEE). In the resting state, energy is used primarily for mechanical activities necessary to sustain life, such as respiration and circulation. Resting metabolic rate is primarily determined by the amount of an individual's fat-free mass or lean body mass—the more lean body mass, the higher the resting metabolic rate. The amount of lean body mass can vary as a function of gender, age, and muscle development (Johnson, 2000). A small fraction of total energy expenditure is contributed by the process responsible for the digestion and absorption of food, the thermic effect of food. Although the thermic effect of food can vary based on the macronutrient content of a meal, generally it makes up approximately 10% of total energy expenditure (Poehlman & Horton, 1999). The contribution of voluntary activity or physical activity to total energy expenditure is highly variable and can range from as little as 10% in a bed-ridden patient to as much as 50% in an elite athlete (Johnson, 2000). The amount of energy expended in physical or voluntary activity is affected by body size, efficiency of movement, and the fitness level of an individual (Johnson, 2000). Thus, although diet (through total calorie intake) plays a significant role in aberrations in energy balance, it is important not to ignore the components and contribution of energy expenditure.

Obesity is related to increased morbidity and mortality for a number of chronic diseases, including type 2 diabetes, cardiovascular disease (CVD), hypertension, osteoarthritis, and most forms of cancer (Calle, Rodriguez, Walker-Thurmond, & Thun, 2003; Mokdad et al., 2001). Thus, through the development of obesity, excess energy intake is associated with the development of chronic disease. Energy restriction is one of the cornerstones of treatment for obesity. Reducing caloric intake by 500 to 1,000 calories per day has been shown to result in a weight loss of 1 to 2 pounds per week (National Heart, Lung, and Blood Institute's Obesity Education Initiative Expert Panel, 1998). Although fat has twice as many calories per gram as carbohydrate and protein and has been purported to be an independent predictor of obesity (Dreon et al., 1988), restriction of fat calories without total calorie regulation has been shown to be of limited usefulness as an obesity treatment (Harvey-Berino, 1999). Some evidence suggests that a diet that restricts both calories and fat may be of added benefit (Pascale, Wing, Butler, Mullen, & Bononi, 1995) and that fat restriction may be most beneficial for the maintenance of weight loss (Toubro & Astrup, 1997). Unfortunately, regardless of how weight is reduced, the long-term maintenance of weight loss is difficult (Wadden & Foster, 2000).

Calorie restriction is not only a common treatment goal for overweight or obese individuals with a number of chronic diseases but additional research also suggests that in nondiseased animals, calorie restriction can increase longevity (Masoro, 1995) and may prevent the development of some forms of cancer (Kritchevsky, 1997). The impact of energy balance on cancer risk in humans is less clear. Any relationship between dietary energy intake and cancer risk is complicated by the fact that factors related to energy balance, such as rate of childhood growth, age at puberty, consumption of specific dietary constituents, overall body mass index, and level of physical activity may be the key risk factor or factors and not simply total energy intake. Nevertheless, the evidence is convincing that high body mass, itself caused by energy-dense diets, excess energy intake, and lack of physical activity increases the risk of endometrial cancer (Olsen, Trevisan, & Marshall, 1995). Obesity probably also increases the risk of postmenopausal breast cancer (Trentham-Dietz, Newcomb, & Storer, 1997) and has been shown to be positively associated with death from cancers of the breast, uterus, cervix, and ovary among women and with death from prostate cancer among men (Calle et al., 2003). In addition, obesity may increase the risk of death from cancer of the colon and rectum, esophagus, gallbladder, liver, pancreas, and kidney, as well as the risk of death from non-Hodgkins lymphoma and multiple myeloma (Calle et al., 2003; World Cancer Research Fund and American Institute for Cancer Research, 1997).

Fat

Fatty acids are generally classified as saturated, polyunsaturated, and monounsaturated based on their chemical structure. Saturated fatty acids are the most highly saturated with hydrogen and are concentrated in foods of animal origin (e.g., butter, cheese, and fat in meats), although they are also present in some vegetable oils, most notably palm, palm kernel, and coconut. Monounsaturated fatty acids contain only one double bond and, thus, fewer hydrogen atoms. Olive oil, peanut oil, canola oil, peanuts, pecans, almonds, and avocados are all concentrated sources of monounsaturated fats. Finally, polyunsaturated fatty acids are the least saturated with hydrogen and are concentrated in vegetable seeds and the oils they produce. Total fat intake is possibly linked to the development of certain types of cancer (World Cancer Research Fund and American Institute for Cancer Research, 1997) and may be a factor in the development and maintenance of obesity (Dreon et al., 1988). However, clearly the strongest association of fat intake to the development of a chronic disease is the relationship of dietary fat intake and risk of coronary heart disease (CHD).

Cross-population, within-population, clinical, and pathological studies have consistently shown that high serum cholesterol levels increase risk for CHD and are, therefore, associated with the incidence of CHD and CHD mortality. Based on the results of the Coronary Primary Prevention Trial, for every 1% decline in serum cholesterol, a 2% decline in CHD is predicted (Schaefer, 2002). Although examination of total cholesterol levels still constitutes the first screening test for CHD, in the past 30 years, carriers of blood lipids, the lipoproteins, particularly low density lipoproteins (LDL-C) and high density lipoproteins (HDL-C), have come to the forefront as predictors of risk. High LDL-C and low HDL-C levels are associated with increased risk of CHD. Thus, LDL-C has come to be known as the "bad cholesterol" and HDL-C as the "good cholesterol."

Many factors affect blood cholesterol levels, including dietary cholesterol intake; however, high intakes of saturated fat are the *most predictive* of high blood lipids (Hegsted, Ausman, Johnson, & Dallal, 1993). The Seven Countries Study was the first to show that a population's intake of saturated fat was strongly correlated with the serum cholesterol levels of the population (Keys, 1970). Countries with the highest intake of saturated fats (> 15%) have been found to have the highest serum cholesterol levels and the highest CHD mortality. In classic metabolic ward studies, Keys and colleagues (Keys, Anderson, & Grande, 1957) developed equations to predict blood cholesterol responses that accompany changes in saturated fat intake. They found that for every 1% increase in total energy from saturated fat, a 2.7 mg/dl increase in plasma cholesterol is predicted. Thus, although dietary cholesterol can increase total plasma cholesterol and LDL-C levels (Stamler & Shekelle, 1988), its effects are weaker than saturated fat (Esrey, Joseph, & Grover, 1996). Therefore, the American Heart Association and other nationally recognized bodies recommend that healthy diets limit the overall intake of fat and specifically target reductions in saturated fatty acids (Hu & Willett, 2002).

Recently, a debate has ignited regarding the relative benefits of margarine versus butter. This is because consumption of trans-fats, common in foods with hydrogenated vegetable oils such as margarine and processed baked goods and snack foods, also raise LDL-C levels. Trans-fats increase LDL-C more than their nonhydrogenated counterparts but not as much as saturated fats (Feldman, Kris-Etherton, Kritchevsky, & Lichenstein, 1996). U.S. residents consume approximately 3% of their total calories as trans-fats. Currently, there is no clear dose–response relationship between trans-fatty acid intake and CHD risk (Krauss et al., 1996). On the other hand, monounsaturated and omega-3 fatty acids may have a beneficial effect on blood cholesterol levels. Omega-3 fatty acids, primarily found in fish oils, fish oil capsules, and ocean fish, have been shown to lower triglycerides and LDL-C levels (Hu et al., 2002) but only through the use of supplements containing these fish oils. The effect is minor and variable, and unfortunately the long-term benefits of taking supplements are not known. In addition, diets rich in one type of omega-3 fatty acid, alpha linolenic acid (LNA), have been associated with a decreased risk for sudden cardiac death (deLorgeril et al., 1994). Monounsaturated fats, primarily found in olive and peanut oils, have also been shown to lower serum cholesterol, LDL-C, and triglycerides when substituted for saturated fats in the diet (Hu et al., 1997). However, the effect is similar to that for polyunsaturated fats when similarly substituted for saturated fats (Hodson, Skeaff & Chisolm, 2001). In epidemiological studies, people in Mediterranean countries have been found to consume high-fat diets but to have low blood cholesterol levels and low CHD incidence. Among other factors, the main fat source in this population is olive oil that is high in monounsaturated fatty acids. This observation has led to many studies on the benefits of a high-fat/high-monounsaturated fat diet, often called the Mediterranean Diet. A National Cholesterol Education Program Step I diet (30% total fat, 10% saturated fat, 10% monounsaturated fat) and a high monounsaturated fat diet (38% total fat, 10% saturated fat, 18% monounsaturated fat) were equally effective in lowering total cholesterol and LDL-C without changing HDL-C (Ginsberg, 1994). However, although this type of diet has shown beneficial effects, it should be used with caution because of its caloric density. Some clinical trials have shown new atherosclerotic lesions in men who consume higher fat diets (Blankenhorn, Johnson, Mack, el Zein, & Vailas, 1990). Finally, the effectiveness of the Mediterranean Diet may be a result of other factors (e.g., high consumption of fruits and vegetables) than monounsaturated fat intake per se.

Polyunsaturated fat intake (primarily found in foods of vegetable origin) does not impart the same CHD risk as saturated fat or trans-fat. Historically, a higher polyunsaturated to saturated fat ratio was thought to be protective of CHD; however, it is evident that decreasing saturated fats is twice as effective for lowering serum cholesterol levels as increasing polyunsaturated fat intake (Stone, 1990). Although all fatty acids are not created equal, high levels of saturated fats are the most consistent predictors of high blood lipid levels (Hegsted et al., 1993), and therefore most recommendations for a healthy diet remain focused on limiting intake of saturated fats.

Sodium

The greatest health hazard from consuming a diet high in sodium is the risk of hypertension (Stamler, Stamler, & Neaton, 1993). Epidemiological studies of populations support an etiological role for sodium in hypertension development. Primitive societies in which intake is very low (70 mEq/day) have very little hypertension, and blood pressure increases occurring with age that are common in industrialized societies do not occur in these primitive societies (Elliott et al., 1996). Hypertension is prevalent, and stroke is the leading cause of death in countries with very high salt consumption (3450–4600 mg sodium/day). Moreover, therapeutic trials of sodium restriction in hypertensive individuals document modest but significant reductions in blood pressure (Vollmer et al., 2001), although considerable variation in response has been noted. The variability in response to sodium restriction is a result of the fact that only certain segments of the population are salt-sensitive. Salt sensitivity (defined as either a 10 mmHg decrease or greater reduction in blood pressure by salt depletion after salt loading or more than a 5% increase in blood pressure during salt repletion after restriction) is thought to be prevalent in approximately 30 to 50% of hypertensive individuals and 15 to 25% of those who are normotensive (Weinberger, Miller, Luft, Grim, & Fineberg, 1986). Although there is no simple test to determine salt sensitivity, U.S. residents eat more salt than is physiologically required (average intake is approximately 3200 mg sodium/day). Moreover, salt restriction is not physiologically harmful. Thus, dietary recommendations generally suggest a prudent sodium intake not to exceed 6 grams/day (2400 mg/day) for the general population.

Fiber

Dietary fiber is found in soluble and insoluble forms. Soluble fibers include pectins, gums, mucilages, and hemicelluloses. Pectins are found primarily in fruits and vegetables with other forms of soluble fiber found in oat bran, vegetables, and legumes. Insoluble fibers consist primarily of cellulose and hemicelluloses. The major sources of insoluble fibers are fruits with edible skins and seeds and in the bran layer of cereal grains. Consumption of soluble fiber lowers serum cholesterol and LDL-C. An average drop in

LDL-C of 14% for hypercholesterolemic individuals and 10% for normo-cholesterolemic individuals was observed after soluble fiber was added to a low-fat diet (Glore, Van Treeck, Knehans, & Guild, 1994). The American Heart Association recommends that 6 grams of the total 20 to 35 grams of fiber eaten per day should be soluble fiber.

High intakes of soluble fiber (24 to 30 g/day) have also been shown to improve blood glucose response. The relationship between cancer and fiber intake, per se, is not clear; however, there is a clear pattern suggesting diets high in fiber may decrease the risk of pancreatic, colorectal, and breast cancers (World Cancer Research Fund and American Institute for Cancer Research, 1997). U.S. residents currently consume approximately 15 grams of fiber per day, which is well below the recommendation of 20 to 35 grams (Kushi, Myer, & Jacobs, 1999).

Calcium

Because low calcium intakes have been implicated in the development of hypertension (McCarron, 1991), the DASH (Dietary Approaches to Stop Hypertension) diet included healthy amounts of calcium in the form of low-fat dairy products (Appel et al., 1997). Although it is not clear that the success of the DASH diet in lowering blood pressure could be even partly attributed to the emphasis on calcium, it is clear that calcium intake plays a major role in bone health and, thus, ultimately the development of osteoporosis (Kalkwarf, Khoury, & Lanphear, 2003). According to the National Osteoporosis Foundation (National Osteoporosis Foundation, 2002), 44 million U.S. residents are affected by osteoporosis, and 1.5 million fractures associated with osteoporosis occur annually, resulting in more than $17 billion in health care costs each year. Calcium intake from birth to adolescence predicts peak bone mass as an adult (Matkovic et al., 1994); thus, the Food and Nutrition Board of the Institute of Medicine's National Academy of Sciences (1999) recommended that premenopausal women and men consume 1,000 mg/day of calcium and postmenopausal women and men over 51 consume 1200 mg/day to maintain high bone density and mini-mize risk of fractures. The effectiveness of increasing calcium intake dur-ing or after menopause to reduce the incidence of fractures remains controversial; however, evidence suggests that in premenopausal women, bone loss can be significantly reduced with calcium supplementation (McKane et al., 1996). Calcium supplementation has had little effect in early postmenopausal women, but supplementation of 500 mg/day in women with low calcium intakes significantly reduced bone loss in women five years beyond menopause (Reid, Ames, Evans, Gamble, & Sharpe, 1993).

Alcohol

Through its positive influence on HDL-C and triglyceride levels, moderate alcohol consumption (defined as two drinks per day for men and one for women) has been related to the prevention of myocardial infarction and CHD mortality (Steinberg, Pearson, & Kuller, 1991). However, it is estimated that 5 to 7% of hypertension is a result of alcohol consumption, with three drinks per day (3 oz of alcohol) being the threshold for raising blood pressure by approximately 3 mmHg (Krummel, 2000). Alcohol's influence on the development of osteoporosis is less clear. Excessive alcohol intake is thought to be a risk factor for osteoporosis through its toxic effect on osteoblasts; however, social drinking was found to be associated with higher bone density after adjusting for age, sex, body mass index, and estrogen replacement in women (Rapuri, Gallagher, Balhorn, & Ryschon, 2000). Without a doubt, there is convincing evidence that alcohol intake is related to mouth, pharynx, larynx, esophagus, breast, and liver cancer and may be related to colon and rectal cancer (World Cancer Research Fund and American Institute for Cancer Research, 1997). Because of these health risks and the potential addictive problems associated with alcohol consumption, no formal recommendations have been made to consume alcohol to prevent chronic disease.

Dietary Recommendations for a Healthy Diet

At least eight different organizations, mostly federal, have issued dietary guidelines within the past decade. Except for minor differences, they are all very much alike, and when numerical goals are specified, they are surprisingly similar to those established by the Senate Select Committee in 1977. Although the message for each organization seldom contradicts the message from other organizations, each one tends to emphasize a different disease outcome and often targets different dietary nutrients as risk factors. We believe that this multiplicity of recommendations has led to some confusion on the part of the U.S. public. Groups focused on osteoporosis, for instance, may focus on high calcium consumption that, although not contradictory, may be interpreted by the public as contrary to cardiovascular recommendations to limit fat intake from dairy products. Fortunately, the American Cancer Society, the American Dietetic Association, the American Academy of Pediatrics, the National Institutes of Health and the American Heart Association have recently agreed to jointly endorse Unified Dietary Guidelines (Deckelbaum et al., 1999). These guidelines, based on the USDA's Food Guide Pyramid and the recommended daily allowance (RDA) specifications, represent no new recommendations but are, instead, an attempt to

TABLE 1.2
Summary of Major Dietary Recommendations for a Healthy Diet
(Primary Prevention)

Nutrient	Agency	Recommendations
Saturated fat	Unified Dietary Guidelines[a] U.S. Dietary Guidelines, 2000 USDA/DHHS	< 10% calories Choose a diet that is low in saturated fat and cholesterol and moderate in total fat.
Total fat	Unified Dietary Guidelines[a] U.S. Dietary Guidelines, 2000 USDA/DHHS	30% calories Choose a diet that is low in saturated fat and cholesterol and moderate in total fat.
Cholesterol	Unified Dietary Guidelines[a] U.S. Dietary Guidelines, 2000 USDA/DHHS	300 mg/day Choose a diet that is low in saturated fat and cholesterol and moderate in total fat.
Alcohol	U.S. Dietary Guidelines, 2000 USDA/DHHS	If you drink alcoholic beverages, do so in moderation.
Salt	Unified Dietary Guidelines[a] U.S. Dietary Guidelines, 2000 USDA/DHHS	1 teaspoon or 6 grams/day. Choose and prepare foods with less salt.
Fiber	U.S. Dietary Guidelines, 2000 USDA/DHHS	Choose a variety of grains daily, especially whole grains; choose a variety of fruits and vegetables daily.
	IOM–NAS: DRV[b]	25 grams/day.
Calcium	IOM–NAS: DRI[c]	19–50 years: 1000mg/day; 51 years: 1200 mg/day.
Body weight	Unified Dietary Guidelines[a]	Achieve and maintain desirable weight.
	U.S. Dietary Guidelines, 2000 USDA/DHHS	Aim for a healthy weight; be physically active every day.

[a]American Cancer Society, American Heart Association, National Institutes of Health, American Dietetic Association, American Academy of Pediatrics (Deckelbaum et al., 1999).
[b]Institute of Medicine–National Academy of Sciences: Dietary Reference Value.
[c]Institute of Medicine–National Academy of Sciences: Dietary Reference Intake.

minimize confusion among the U.S. population, increase understanding of recommendations, and beneficially affect adherence with dietary recommendations.

The Unified Dietary Guidelines recommend that a healthy diet include no more than 10% of calories as saturated fat, with no more than 30% of total calories from fat of all types. At least 55% of daily calories should be consumed in the form of complex carbohydrates such as fruits, vegetables, and whole grains. Dietary cholesterol should be limited to 300 mg or less per day and salt intake to 6 grams or less per day. Table 1.2 summarizes the major dietary recommendations for the prevention of chronic disease.

The USDA's Food Guide Pyramid translates these nutrient recommendations into servings of foods from five different food groups: dairy, meat, fruits, vegetables, and grains. The range of servings allows for different caloric needs. The graphic depiction of a pyramid emphasizes that the base of our diet should be composed of whole grains, fruits, and vegetables (http://www.nal.usda.gov/fnic/Fpyr/pyramid.html). A high intake of fruits and vegetables has been strongly linked to lower cancer rates (Block, Patterson, & Subar, 1992) and decreased risk of stroke (Joshipura et al., 1999). In addition, individuals consuming vegetarian diets tend to have lower blood pressure than nonvegetarians (Harlan & Harlan, 1995). Moderate intake of milk and dairy products (two to three servings per day) is recommended, with similar suggested intake for meat, poultry, fish, and other protein sources. Finally, fats, sweets, and alcohol are recommended in only limited amounts.

EPIDEMIOLOGY OF OBESITY AND MAJOR NUTRIENT INTAKES: CHANGING TRENDS

Understanding dietary and obesity patterns at a population level not only informs evaluation of the overall state of the public's health but can provide valuable insights that guide efforts to promote healthier dietary behaviors and reduce chronic disease risk.

Obesity

Obesity represents one of the most significant public health problems currently facing the United States. National data indicate that 31% of adults in the United States are obese (body mass index [kg/m^2] ≥ 30) and an additional 34% are overweight (body mass index 25–30; Flegal, Carroll, Ogden, & Johnson, 2002). Of particular concern are the substantial increases in the prevalence of obesity seen in recent years. Rates of obesity have more than doubled in the 40-year period from 1960 to 2000, and all indicators point to a continued rise in prevalence (Flegal et al., 2002). There are some suggestions that this secular trend of increased adiposity can be attributed to decreased physical activity (Lewis et al., 1997), as well as to increased consumption of calorie-dense foods (Kant, Graubard, Schatzkin, & Ballard-Barbash, 1995; Lissner, Heitmann, & Bengtsson, 1997). Although the exact causes of the obesity epidemic may be debated, it is clear that the public health challenge that obesity presents will continue well into the twenty-first century.

Some population groups are disproportionately affected by obesity. Women are significantly more likely to be obese than men. One third (34%) of women are obese compared with 28% of men (Flegal et al., 2002). Furthermore, women appear to be more vulnerable to major weight gain during adulthood (Kuczmarski, 1992; Williamson, Kahn, Remington, &

Anda, 1990). Minority groups also have significantly higher rates of obesity than the general population, with particularly high rates among Mexican Americans, African Americans, and Native Americans. For example, 40% of African Americans and 34% of Mexican Americans meet current obesity criteria (Flegal et al., 2002). Within some Native American tribes, obesity prevalence is as high as 75% of the population (Story, Evans, Fabsitz, Clay, Rock, & Broussard, 1999). In addition, those individuals at greatest risk for obesity are women within these minority populations. The prevalence of obesity is 40% among Mexican American women and 50% among African American women (Flegal et al., 2002), and more than 80% of adult women in some Native American tribes are obese (Story et al., 1999).

Other risk factors for obesity include age and socioeconomic status. The likelihood of being overweight increases with age, with estimates of 15 to 26 pounds gained per decade in adulthood (Lewis et al., 2000). One third (33%) of adults aged 60 to 74 years are obese compared with 26% of adults aged 20 to 29 (Flegal et al., 2002). Obesity is significantly more prevalent among individuals of lower socioeconomic status (Wardle, Waller, & Jarvis, 2002), and the relationship between lower income and increased adiposity may account for the proportionately greater representation of minorities who are obese. However, greater poverty alone does not appear to explain fully the differential rates of obesity within minority populations (Gordon-Larsen, Adair, & Popkin, 2003).

Children are also at increasing risk of obesity (Troiano, Flegal, Kuczmarski, Campbell, & Johnson, 1995), which has some alarming implications for the prevalence of obesity among adults, because a substantial proportion of overweight children become overweight adults (Whitaker, Wright, Pepe, Seidel, & Dietz, 1997). Obesity rates have increased dramatically among youngsters, jumping from 15% to 22% in the period from 1963 to 1991 (Troiano et al., 1995). The transition from preadolescence to adolescence may be a particularly vulnerable developmental phase during which obesity onset is problematic (Dietz, 1994). The explosion of obesity among children has been especially evident among minority children, with rates more than tripling among African American children and adolescents (Troiano et al., 1995). This extraordinary acceleration in early onset obesity has led to calls for more aggressive efforts focused on obesity prevention among children and adolescents (Jackson et al., 2002; Kumanyika, Jeffery, Morabia, Ritenbaugh, & Antipatis, 2002).

Nutrient Intake

Precisely determining the nutrients that people eat is challenging because foods may vary greatly in fat, calorie, and nutrient content depending not only on the specific type of food consumed but also the preparation of the food. For example. the salt content of a particular food may vary substantially depending on how much salt is added during the preparation of the food itself. Even meat can vary in fat content depending on how much fat is trimmed off of the meat during preparation and whether the meat is broiled or fried. Nutrient databases that consider not only the types of foods consumed but also preparation practices have been developed as a means of adding precision to self-report of dietary intake. Food recalls that assess a recent limited time period or questionnaires that estimate the frequency with which certain foods are consumed over a more extended period are commonly recognized methods to assess dietary intake. However, both these methods are influenced by self-report biases; the problem of underreporting food intake by specific groups can skew the interpretation of the diet–disease relationship (Johnson, 2000). In addition, available self-report methods only characterize a limited period, and food consumption may vary across time (Flegal, 1999). Other methods of nutrient assessment involve examining biomarkers for particular nutrients; however, these methods are not readily adaptable to collecting data from large population-based samples and, at least for some biomarkers, reflect only short periods of dietary intake and may be subject to possible bias as a result of dietary changes made specifically for the period of data collection (Willett, 1990). Thus, although assessment measures from large samples may provide sound estimates of energy and nutrient consumption for the overall population, the limitations in our assessment of dietary intake must be recognized. Despite these factors that make it difficult to compare data obtained using different assessment methods and nutrient databases, some good, albeit limited, data on recent consumption levels exist for most nutrients.

Fat

Despite well-publicized recommendations to consume no more than 30% of total calories from fat of all types, typical consumption remains considerably higher than this. The Continuing Survey of Food Intakes by Individuals (CSFII), conducted between 1989 to 1991, suggests that calories consumed in the form of fat fell within the recommended 30% or less range in only about 25% of the U.S. population. About half of the population consumed 30 to 40% of calories as fat, and the remaining quarter of people in the country consumed more than 40% of their calories as fat (Federation of American Societies for Experimental Biology and Life Sciences Research Office, 1995).

Sodium

Fewer than 20% of men and women report using salt on a regular basis at the table (Mattes & Donnelly, 1991). However, most salt in the diet comes from processed food rather than salt added during food preparation. Data from the Third National Health and Nutrition Examination Survey, 1988–1991 (NHANES III) suggest that the median consumption of sodium for most ethnic, gender, and age groups was near or, in most cases, above the recommended level of 2,400 mg (Federation of American Societies for Experimental Biology and Life Sciences Research Office, 1995). However, these data may underestimate true sodium intake because added discretionary salt use was not considered. Mean daily sodium consumption for men across age groups exceeded 4,000 mg (USDA, 1994–1996). Women and older people tended to consume less sodium because there is an association between sodium intake and caloric consumption and men and younger people consume more calories than women and older people, respectively (Subar, Krebs-Smith, Cook, & Kahle, 1998).

Fiber

Results of the most recent Continuing Survey of Food Intake by Individuals (USDA, 1994–1996) similarly reveal that U.S. residents are consuming only about 15 grams of fiber per day (well below the recommendation of 21 to 38 grams per day). NHANES data also suggest that the median intake for adults across age, sex, and ethnic groups ranged from 10 to 20 g of fiber per day, all falling below the current recommended level of 21 to 38 grams (USDA, 1994–1996). Fiber intake was higher in younger (aged 20–59) than older (over 60 years) men, higher in men than women across these two age groups, and highest among Mexican American men. In both age groups, Mexican American men had the highest intake of fiber and African American men had the lowest.

Calcium

Currently, experts consider the United States to be in the midst of a calcium crisis. Calcium intakes are only between 600 and 800 grams per day for women across all age groups, representing an average of less than 80% of the 1989 recommended daily allowance (RDA) for all age groups among women except for those who are less than 12 years of age (USDA, 1994–1996). Only 25% of the adult population consumes the RDA for calcium (USDA, 1994–1996). The Food and Nutrition Board of the Institute of Medicine (Food and Nutrition Board of the Institute of Medicine's National Academy of Sciences, 1998) now recommends that premenopausal women and men consume 1,000 mg/day of calcium and postmenopausal women and men over 51 consume 1200 mg; thus, postmenopausal women consume less than half of the recommended calcium. The high intake of soft drinks (as high as 20% of total calories for adolescent boys) may be substantially responsible for reductions in calcium intake, because soda is increasingly displacing milk in the U.S. diet (Putnam, 2000). This reduction in dairy product intake is of particular concern because U.S. residents get 75% of their calcium from dairy products (Kennedy & Goldberg, 1995).

Alcohol

Currently, alcohol makes up 2% of total caloric intake for U.S. residents.

Fruits and Vegetables

Survey data from the Federation of American Societies for Experimental Biology and Life Sciences Research Office (1995) suggest that a higher percentage of women across all age groups consume the recommended five servings of fruits and vegetables than do men. However, the majority of adults fail to consume adequate fruits and vegetables. Among men, fewer than 20% across all age groups met the five servings per day recommendation. Among women, consumption of the recommended five servings increased across age groups, advancing from only 23% meeting the recommendation among women aged 18 to 39 years to 34% at ages 60 and above. Vegetables are reported to be consumed more often than fruits, particularly among adolescents, men, African Americans, and low-income adults (Federation of American Societies for Experimental Biology and Life Sciences Research Office, 1995). In fact, more than half of individuals, regardless of ethnicity, reported consuming less than one serving of fruit per day in a three-day period, whereas fewer than 13% of individuals across all ethnic groups reported eating less than a single serving of vegetables in the same three-day period (Krebs-Smith, Cook, Subar, Cleveland, & Friday, 1995). African Americans were the most likely to consume less than a serving per day of fruits (61%) and vegetables (12.2%). Whites were the least likely to consume less than a serving per day of fruits (53.7%) and vegetables (8.3%). Half of children and adolescents have less than one serving per day of fruit, and 17% have less than one serving of vegetables daily (Krebs-Smith et al., 1996). Perhaps most alarming are data that indicate that nearly one quarter of the vegetables that children and adolescents eat are French fries (Krebs-Smith et al., 1996). Thus, people of all ages and ethnic groups fall far short of recommended fruit and vegetable intake, with particular deficiencies in fruit consumption.

Summary of Obesity and Nutrient Epidemiological Patterns in the United States

The data on obesity patterns and intake of recommended nutrient levels are not encouraging. Obesity trends are increasing, and nutrient data suggest substantial inadequacies in the dietary intake of most U.S. residents. Despite having various forms of dietary guidance systems in place since the early 1900s, U.S. residents are still not consuming recommended amounts of nutrients or minimum numbers of servings from different food groups. The National Livestock and Meat Board compared what U.S. residents *think* they eat with what they *actually* eat (National Cattlemen's Beef Association, 1994). Although most U.S. residents report that their diets closely reflect the food guide pyramid, in actuality all segments of the population underconsume foods in the vegetable, fruit, grain, and milk group and overconsume fats, oils, and sweets. On average, the meat group was the only food group consumed in recommended amounts. This survey showed that U.S. residents may lack accurate knowledge of serving sizes in addition to not recognizing sources of hidden fats in their diet.

Similar evidence of the misperceptions of the U.S. public when it comes to dietary consumption is revealed in the U.S. Diet and Health Knowledge Survey, 1994–1996, conducted by the U.S. Department of Agriculture (USDA, 1994–1996). In response to questions about calorie and nutrient consumption, the highest proportion of both men and women reported that their diet was "about right" in every category except for fat intake being seen as "too high" among both gender groups. Furthermore, the highest proportion of respondents among both men and women reported that consuming calories and nutrients in line with the dietary guidelines was "very important" to them. Yet the most recent Continuing Survey of Food Intake by Individuals (USDA, 1994–1996) revealed that U.S. residents are consuming more fat (32.8% of calories) and saturated fat (11.3 % of calories) than recommended. In addition, carbohydrate intake was only 51.8% of total calories with fiber intake at 15 grams (well below the recommendation of 25 to 30 grams per day) and calcium intakes between 600 and 800 grams for young women, also well below the recommended levels.

Efforts targeted at improving dietary behavior on an individual level should be emphasized, particularly among individuals who are at elevated risk because of obesity or in cases in which clear evidence exists that certain nutrients convey protective benefits or increase risk for certain disease outcomes. Nonetheless, given the disappointing trends in obesity and low proportions of the U.S. population conforming to nutritional recommendations, we cannot rely solely on individual approaches to create the broad-scale changes that are needed in the United States.

PSYCHOSOCIAL AND BEHAVIORAL FACTORS ASSOCIATED WITH CHANGING DIETARY BEHAVIOR

Dietary behavior change efforts are influenced by a host of factors, including physiological, environmental, psychosocial, and behavioral factors. These dimensions often exert reciprocal determination (Bandura,

1986), such that they interact and influence one another. For example, psychosocial factors can lead an individual to select an environment with particular features and specific environmental features can shape psychosocial functioning and subsequent behaviors. Interventions to promote healthier dietary intake and to reduce obesity risk have tended to focus on isolated aspects of these multifactorial determinants.

Individual Interventions to Change Dietary Behavior

The preponderance of individualized interventions, which provide the dietary behavior intervention to participants either through individual or group sessions, have been grounded explicitly or implicitly in behavioral theories, including social learning theory (Bandura, 1986) and the health belief model (Becker, 1974). These interventions have focused for the most part on either decreasing overall energy consumption as part of weight loss efforts or on altering intake of a specific nutrient or food group (e.g., decreasing sodium intake, increasing fruit and vegetable consumption, increasing fiber, or decreasing fat in the diet). Behavioral models, in general, posit that behavior is initiated and maintained by antecedents that prompt the behavior and consequences that reinforce the behavior. These antecedents and consequences are typically described as mutually interactive or iterative in that they will influence one another. Specific theories focus on different forms of antecedents. Some theories emphasize beliefs and attitudes (e.g., self-efficacy and outcome expectations or perceived risk and susceptibility) to a greater degree, whereas others will stress the impact of environmental factors on behavior (e.g., barriers and facilitators). Similarly, specific theoretical models identify or focus on different consequences of behavior. Despite some differences between the models that drive most research into altering or understanding dietary behavior, some significant similarities emerge. There is a substantial literature on initiating behavior change and comparatively little on maintaining behavior change, although it is widely speculated that different processes may be involved (Rothman, 2000). Not surprisingly, therefore, successful short-term dietary change has been demonstrated more often than successful long-term changes (Kumanyika et al., 2000).

Dietary Change Intervention Outcomes

Dietary change interventions have predominantly focused on weight loss, with a growing body of literature on dietary fat reduction. Strategies typically used in these interventions include self-monitoring of the targeted behavior to provide feedback about the antecedents and consequences of the behavior, modeling of new and appropriate behaviors, and stimulus control to reduce the salience of cues that prompt the old behaviors and to increase cues that enhance the likelihood of the desired new behaviors. Also common in theory-driven intervention packages are strategies to alter attitudes, such as addressing knowledge deficits, altering perceptions or beliefs about the behavior or its outcome, or influencing individuals' self-efficacy for performing the behavior. Strategies to enhance self-efficacy are frequently experiential. Also commonly included are problem-solving methods, relapse-prevention components, and social support strategies.

Outcomes of Obesity Interventions

Obesity interventions typically produce weight losses of 1 to 2 pounds per week (Wadden & Foster, 2000), although the addition of a very low calorie diet ($\leq$ 800 kcal/day) can double weight losses (National Task Force on the Prevention and Treatment of Obesity, 1993) and portion-controlled diets can increase total weight loss by 30% (Jeffery et al., 2000). On average, obesity treatment programs produce an 8% reduction in initial body weight (Foreyt & Goodrick, 1993). Significant health benefits, such as reductions in blood pressure, improvements in lipid profile, and better glycemic control, can be achieved with relatively modest weight losses of 5 to 10% (Wadden, Anderson, & Foster, 1999). The longer an individual remains involved with an intervention program, the greater the weight losses that can be achieved (Perri, Nezu, Patti, & McCann, 1989); therefore, current programs are often 6 to 12 months, with some experts urging that obesity should be considered a chronic medical condition that requires continuous care of some form or another (National Heart, Lung, and Blood Institute's Obesity Education Initiative Expert Panel, 1998). Although initial weight loss is usually quite successful for most individuals, maintenance of weight loss remains a significant challenge (Jeffery et al., 2000). On average, about two thirds of weight loss will be maintained at 52 weeks posttreatment (Foreyt & Goodrick, 1993). Some individuals regain all the weight they have lost, but a small proportion of individuals (35 to 60 %) will sustain their weight losses for an extended period (Wadden & Frey, 1997; Wing & Jeffery, 1999). Individuals successful at maintenance appear to not only maintain a restricted calorie intake but also exercise quite frequently (McGuire, Wing, Klem, Lang, & Hill, 1999).

Different population groups may have greater success in existing weight loss interventions. Men tend to lose more weight than women (Kumanyika, Obarzanek, Stevens, Hebert, & Whelton, 1991), and minority individuals may lose less weight than White individuals (Kumanyika et al., 2002; Wing & Anglin, 1996). Age has been related to weight loss in some studies, but older age has been associated with greater maintenance of weight loss in some studies (McGuire et al., 1999) as well as diminished weight maintenance in others (Ball et al., 1999); thus, the impact of age remains unclear. Children may be the group with the greatest potential to benefit from obesity interventions. Although there has been comparatively little research among children, what little exists is most promising. The work of Epstein and colleagues indicates that obese children (an average of 40% overweight) who participated in a behavioral intervention lost a significant amount of weight during treatment and were able to maintain losses over a 10-year period, with 30% of them no longer obese a decade after treatment ended (Epstein, Valoski, Wing, & McCurley, 1994). Strong family involvement in these programs can enhance the outcomes (Epstein, Valoski, Wing, & McCurley, 1990).

Outcomes of Dietary Fat Interventions

Interventions to reduce dietary fat have been undertaken for a number of health outcomes, including improving lipid profiles, reducing risk of breast cancer, and promoting weight loss. For the most part, these studies have been of short duration and have been able to demonstrate significant reduction in dietary fat intake. For example, the Women's Health Trial dietary intervention achieved a reduction in fat intake from 74 to 34 grams (40 to 27% of total calories) after an 18-month intervention compared with the control group that decreased fat intake by only 7 grams (Kristal et al., 1992). Whether these significant reductions in dietary intake can both be maintained and reduce risk of breast cancer remains to be seen; the Women's Health Initiative is an ongoing 13-year-long clinical trial that has been undertaken to answer this question (Anonymous, 1998). There is some evidence from other studies that the longer the continued contact, the greater the fat reduction that can be achieved (Brunner et al., 1997). In addition, more drastic fat reduction goals may be associated with greater success (Barnard, Akhtar, & Nicholson, 1995).

Interventions guided by the National Cholesterol Education Program (National Cholesterol Education Program, 1994) have also been able to achieve significant reductions in dietary fat intake among adults, as well as significant improvements in plasma lipoproteins (Dengel, Katzel, & Goldberg, 1995; Wood, Stefanick, Williams, & Haskell, 1991). However, greater improvements in lipids occurred when dietary fat restriction was accompanied by weight loss (Dengel et al., 1995) or by exercise (Wood et al., 1991). Interventions to lower total dietary fat intake and saturated fat among children have also been demonstrated to be effective in improving lipids among children with adverse lipid profiles at baseline, with no negative effects on growth and development (DISC Collaborative Research Group, 1995).

Fat restriction as a weight loss strategy rests on the hope that substantial reductions in fat intake will produce a sizable calorie deficit and promote weight loss. In addition, epidemiological observations indicate that consumption of a low-fat diet is associated with lowered risk of obesity. Finally, it has been speculated that an ad libitum diet with fat restrictions might produce greater adherence because dieters might not feel deprived. However, fat restriction (in the absence of calorie restriction) does not appear to be an effective weight loss strategy. Calorie restriction appears to be more effective than fat restriction alone (Harvey-Berino, 1999), and many obesity programs recommend the combination of calorie restriction with specific fat gram goals.

Outcomes of Sodium Reduction Interventions

Sodium restriction has been demonstrated to reduce blood pressure with greater reductions in sodium associated with greater improvements in blood pressure (Cutler, Follmann, & Allender, 1997). It is interesting to note that individuals in interventions that targeted both sodium reduction and weight loss may not be as successful in lowering sodium intake than individuals in interventions that targeted sodium reduction only (Hypertension Prevention Trial Research Group, 1990; Whelton et al., 1998), indicating that there may be some diminution of intervention efficacy with multiple dietary behavior change goals.

Outcomes of Community-Level Fruit and Vegetable Consumption Interventions

Interventions to promote fruit and vegetable consumption have been demonstrated to be effective in producing significant increases in fruit and vegetables, and these changes have been sustained over time. Many of the programs to increase fruit and vegetable intake have been delivered in community settings rather than in the clinical settings typical of weight loss and fat and sodium restriction interventions. In addition, many were funded through the National Cancer Institute initiated 5-A-Day for Better Health Program (Havas et al., 1994). For example, the Maryland Women, Infants and Children (WIC) 5-A-Day Program delivered an intervention to promote vegetable and fruit intake to women presenting for the Special Supplemental Food Program for WIC. Pregnant, breast-feeding, and postpartum women, as well as mothers of infants and young children, receiving WIC services were given a brief nutrition education by peer educators and a series of tailored mailed materials. The intervention produced significant increases in fruit and vegetable intake of about half a serving a day compared with control individuals (Havas et al., 1998). Although the magnitude of the increase was small, the potential for broad public health impact is substantial given the use of peer educators and mail-based interventions.

Worksite-based interventions have also been demonstrated to significantly increase fruit and vegetable consumption, often by increasing the availability of healthy foods and offering theory-based nutrition education on site. Fruit and vegetable intake has been shown to increase by 7 to 19% among participants in the intervention sites (Sorensen et al., 1998, 1999), with significantly greater increases in intervention groups compared with controls. There is some suggestion that programs that incorporate both a work-setting component and a family-based component may produce the greatest impact (Sorensen et al., 1999).

School-based interventions to promote fruit and vegetable intake among children reach similar conclusions. Modest but significant and enduring increases have been achieved among children receiving interventions delivered in classroom settings (Auld, Romaniello, Heimendinger, Hambidge, & Hambidge, 1999; Nader et al., 1999). However, an even more substantial impact on the dietary behavior of children can be achieved when parents are also involved in the intervention (Nader et al., 1996).

Environmental Interventions to Alter Dietary Behavior

The majority of reports of dietary behavior and obesity interventions have targeted the individual, structuring the treatment in group meetings, individual sessions, or other individually administered intervention methods. However, there is strong evidence to support the efficacy of environmental manipulations to promote dietary changes within populations. These may present the most promising avenue for large-scale behavior change and, importantly, for proactive prevention efforts. For example, studies that manipulate the cost and availability of low-fat, low-calorie foods demonstrate that lowering the price and increasing the selection of healthy food choices can result in significant increases in the consumption of these healthier foods (French, Story, & Jeffery, 2001). Similarly, epidemiological studies indicate strong correlations between the amount of shelf space in local grocery stores devoted to low-fat, high-fiber foods and the healthfulness of dietary intake within the local community (Cheadle et al., 1995). In addition, studies of populations in controlled environments such as boarding schools indicate that institutional changes in the purchasing and preparation of foods can produce significant beneficial effects on sodium and dietary fat intake among adolescents (Ellison, Capper, Goldberg, Witschi, & Stare, 1989). Even availability of healthy food choices in the cafeteria has also been shown to favorably impact dietary behavior among adults (Jeffery, French, Raether, & Baxter, 1994). Thus, there are several promising studies of environmental manipulations on dietary behavior. However, the effects within specific cultural or economic subgroups that may be at risk for compromised dietary intake or for obesity have not been well-examined and represent an important arena for further study.

Combined Intervention Approaches

A few intervention approaches have attempted to create changes both within the environment as well as more directly at the individual level. For example, Reynolds, Raczynski, and colleagues (Reynolds et al., 1997) incorporated an intervention to increase fruit and vegetable consumption among 4th-grade students through environmental changes in the cafeteria and in the home by involving parents, in addition to classroom-based, individualized approaches. As another example, in a community-based intervention study in which diet was a focus along with physical activity and tobacco use, Littleton, Cornell, and colleagues (2002) incorporated an intervention that involved both individual food preparation classes along with efforts to change healthy food availability (through advocacy at the local food store and developing a farmers' market). These multilevel approaches at changing the environment through direct advocacy and policy-based approaches in concert with individual-level methods may have synergistic benefits beyond the use of a single-intervention approach and result in greater effectiveness from a population perspective.

CONCLUSION

Dietary behavior, despite appearing relatively straight forward, is complex at a number of different levels. At the physiological level, energy and nutrient regulation interact with genetic and other environmental factors to determine body weight and risk for certain diseases. Dietary preferences, food preparation habits, and dietary behaviors are influenced by cultural, social, and psychosocial factors, as well as by food industry decisions that determine marketing, availability, preparation methods of commercially available food products, and nutrient content of these products. Despite these complexities, it is clear that caloric and nutrient intake are strong risk factors for a variety of disease outcomes and are a contributing factor to sociodemographic group disparities in health outcomes. Although a variety of agencies have presented dietary recommendations for quite some time, these recommendations typically have focused on dietary recommendations linked to particular disease outcomes, leading to some confusion in attempting to reconcile the various recommendations. Fortunately, with recent efforts to present uniform recommendations to the U.S. public, more consistent messages should result. There is hope that this will minimize the public's confusion about dietary recommendations and increase adherence to the recommendations. However, present epidemiological data reveal widespread proliferation in obesity and alarmingly low levels of adherence to recommended dietary intake. These patterns of increasing obesity and suboptimal nutrient intake suggest the need for improved individualized dietary intervention approaches along with broader efforts to enhance dietary behavior. Thus, stronger public health messages to assist in modifying environmental and cultural influences, changes by food industry that alter food availability and marketing, and the development of new regulatory policies and laws that provide a climate supportive of healthy food choices are all avenues worthy of exploration in the critical voyage toward improved dietary behavior, reduced obesity, and enhanced health.

REFERENCES

Anonymous. (1998). Design of the Women's Health Initiative clinical trial and observation study. The Women's Health Initiative Study Group. *Controlled Clinical Trials, 19,* 61–109.

Appel, L. J., Moore, J. A., Obarzanek, E., Vollmer, W. M., Svetkey, L. P., Sacks, F. M., et al. (1997). A clinical trial of the effects of dietary patterns on blood pressure. *New England Journal of Medicine, 336,* 1117–1124.

Auld, G. W., Romaniello, C., Heimendinger, J., Hambidge, C., & Hambidge, M. (1999). Outcomes from a school-based nutrition education program alternating special resource teachers and classroom teachers. *Journal of School Health, 69,* 403–408.

Ball, G. D., Gingras, J. R., Fimrite, A., Villetard, K., Kayman, S., & McCargar, L. J. (1999). Weight relapsers, maintainers, and controls: Metabolic and behavioural differences. *Canadian Journal of Applied Physiology, 24,* 548–558.

Bandura, A. (1986). *Social foundations of thought and action: A social cognitive theory.* Englewood Cliffs, NJ: Prentice-Hall.

Barnard, N. D., Akhtar, A., & Nicholson, A. (1995). Factors that facilitate compliance to a low fat intake. *Archives of Family Medicine, 4,* 153–158.

Becker, M. H. E. (1974). The health belief model and personal health behavior. *Health Education Monograph, 2,* 409–419.

Blankenhorn, D. H., Johnson, R. L., Mack, W. J., el Zein, H. A., & Vailas, L. I. (1990). The influence of diet on the appearance of new lesions in human coronary arteries. *Journal of the American Medical Association, 263,* 1646–1652.

Block, G., Patterson, B., & Subar, A. (1992). Fruit, vegetables and cancer prevention: A review of the epidemiological evidence. *Nutrition and Cancer, 18,* 1–29.

Brunner, E., White, I., Thorogood, M., Bristow, A., Curle, D., & Marmot, M. (1997). Can dietary interventions change diet and cardiovascular risk factors? A meta-analysis of randomized controlled trials. *American Journal of Public Health, 87,* 1415–1422.

Calle, E. E., Rodriguez, C., Walker-Thurmond, K., & Thun, M. J. (2003). Overweight, obesity, and mortality from cancer in a prospectively studied cohort of U.S. adults. *New England Journal of Medicine, 348,* 1625–1638.

Cheadle, A., Psaty, B., Diehr, P., Koepsell, T., Wagner, E., Curry, S., et al. (1995). Evaluating community-based nutrition programs: Comparing grocery store and individual-level survey measures of program impact. *Preventive Medicine, 24,* 71–79.

Cutler, J. A., Follmann, D., & Allender, P. S. (1997). Randomized trials of sodium reduction: An overview. *American Journal of Clinical Nutrition, 65*(2 Suppl.), 643S–651S.

Deckelbaum, R. J., Fisher, E. A., Winston, M., Kumanyika, S., Lauer, R. M., Pi-Sunyer, F. X., et al. (1999). Summary of a scientific conference on preventive nutrition: Pediatrics to geriatrics. *Circulation, 100,* 450–456.

deLorgeril, M., Renaud, S., Mamelle, N., Salen, P., Martin, J. L., Monjaud, I., et al. (1994). Mediterranean alpha-linolenic acid-rich diet in secondary prevention of coronary heart disease. *Lancet, 343,* 1454–1459.

Dengel, J. L., Katzel, L. I., & Goldberg, A. P. (1995). Effect of an American Heart Association diet, with or without weight loss, on lipids in obese middle-aged and older men. *American Journal of Clinical Nutrition, 62,* 715–721.

Dietary Reference Intakes for Calcium, Phosphorus, Magnesium, Vitamin D, and Fluoride. (1999). Washington, DC: Institute of Medicine.

Dietary Reference Intakes for Energy, Carbohydrates, Fiber, Fat, Fatty Acids, Cholesterol, Protein, and Amino Acids (Macronutrients). (2002). Washington, DC: Food and Nutrition Board, Institute of Medicine.

Dietz, W. H. (1994). Critical periods in childhood for the development of obesity. *American Journal of Clinical Nutrition, 59,* 955–959.

DISC Collaborative Research Group. (1995). Efficacy and safety of lowering dietary intake of total fat, saturated fat, and cholesterol in children with elevated LDL-cholesterol: The Dietary Intervention Study in Children (DISC). *Journal of the American Medical Association, 273,* 1429–1435.

Dreon, D. M., Frey-Hewitt, B., Ellsworth, N., Williams, P. T., Terry, R. B., & Wood, P. D. (1988). Dietary fat: Carbohydrate ratio and obesity in middle-aged men. *American Journal of Clinical Nutrition, 47,* 995–1000.

Elliott, P., Stamler, J., Nichols, R., Dyer, A. R., Stamler, R., Kesteloot, H., et al. (1996). INTERSALT revisited: Further analysis of 24 hour sodium excretion and blood pressure within and across populations. INTERSALT Cooperative Research Group. *British Medical Journal, 18,* 1249–1253.

Ellison, R., Capper, A., Goldberg, R., Witschi, J., & Stare, F. (1989). The environmental component: Changing school food service to promote cardiovascular health. *Health Education Quarterly, 16,* 285–297.

Epstein, L. H., Valoski, A., Wing, R. R., & McCurley, J. (1990). Ten-year follow-up of behavioral, family-based treatment for obese children. *Journal of the American Medical Association, 264,* 2519–2523.

Epstein, L. H., Valoski, A., Wing, R. R., & McCurley, J. (1994). Ten-year outcomes of behavioral family-based treatment for childhood obesity. *Health Psychology, 13*(5), 373–383.

Esrey, K. L., Joseph, L., & Grover, S. A. (1996). Relationship between dietary intake and coronary heart disease mortality: Lipid research clinics prevalence follow-up study. *Journal of Clinical Epidemiology, 49*, 211–216.

Federation of American Societies for Experimental Biology, and Life Sciences Research Office. (1995). *Third Report on Nutrition Monitoring in the United States* (Vol. 1–2). Washington, DC: U.S. Government Printing Office.

Feldman, E. B., Kris-Etherton, P. M., Kritchevsky, D., & Lichenstein, A. for the ASCN/AIN Task Force on Trans Fatty Acids of the American Society for Clinical Nutrition and the American Institute of Nutrition. (1996). Position paper on trans fatty acids. *American Journal of Clinical Nutrition, 63*, 663–670.

Flegal, K. M. (1999). Evaluating epidemiologic evidence of the effects of food and nutrient exposures. *American Journal of Clinical Nutrition, 69*(Suppl.), 1339S–1344S.

Flegal, K. M., Carroll, M. D., Ogden, C. L., & Johnson, C. L. (2002). Prevalence and trends in obesity among US adults, 1999–2000. *Journal of the American Medical Association, 288*, 1723–1727.

Food and Nutrition Board of the Institute of Medicine's National Academy of Sciences. (1999). *Dietary reference intakes*. Washington, DC: National Academy Press.

Foreyt, J. P., & Goodrick, G. K. (1993). Evidence for success of behavior modification in weight loss and control. *Annals of Internal Medicine, 119*, 698–701.

French, S. A., Story, M., & Jeffery, R. W. (2001). Environmental influences on eating and physical activity. *Annual Review of Public Health, 22*, 309–335.

Ginsberg, H. N. (1994). Lipoprotein metabolism and its relationship to atherosclerosis. *Medical Clinics of North American, 78*, 1–11.

Glore, S. R., Van Treeck, D., Knehans, A. W., & Guild, M. (1994). Soluble fiber and serum lipids: A literature review. *Journal of the American Dietetic Association, 94*(4), 425–436.

Gordon-Larsen, P., Adair, L. S., & Popkin, B. M. (2003). The relationship of ethnicity, socioeconomic factors, and overweight in U.S. adolescents. *Obesity Research, 11*, 121–129.

Guthrie, J. F., & Morton, J. F. (2000). Food sources of added sweeteners in the diets of Americans. *Journal of the American Dietetic Association, 100*, 43–51.

Harlan, W. R., & Harlan, L. C. (1995). Blood pressure and calcium and magnesium intake. *Hypertension: Pathophysiology, diagnosis, and management* (2nd ed., pp. 1143–1154). New York: Raven Press.

Harvey-Berino, J. (1999). Calorie restriction is more effective for weight loss than dietary fat restriction. *Annals of Behavioral Medicine, 21*, 35–39.

Havas, S., Anliker, J., Damron, D., Langenberg, P., Ballesteros, M., & Feldman, R. (1998). Final results of the Maryland WIC 5-a-Day Promotion Program. *American Journal of Public Health, 88*, 1161–1167.

Havas, S., Heimendinger, J., Reynolds, K., Baranowski, T., Nicklas, T. A., Bishop, D., et al. (1994). 5 A Day for Better Health: A new research initiative. *Journal of the American Dietetic Association, 94*, 32–34.

Hegsted, D. M., Ausman, L. M., Johnson, J. A., & Dallal, G. E. (1993). Dietary fat and serum lipids: An evaluation of the experimental data. *American Journal of Clinical Nutrition, 58*, 245.

Hill, J. O., Wyatt, H. R., Reed, G. W., & Peters, J. C. (2003). Obesity and the environment: Where do we go from here? *Science, 299*, 853–855.

Hodson, L., Skeaff, C. M., & Chisolm, W. A. (2001). The effect of replacing dietary saturated fat with polyunsaturated or monounsaturated fat on plasma lipids in free-living young adults. *European Journal of Clinical Nutrition, 55*, 908–915.

Hu, F. B., Bronner, L., Willett, W. C., Stampfer, M. J., Rexrode, K. M., Albert, C. M., et al. (2002). Fish and omega-3 fatty acid intake and risk of coronary heart disease in women. *Journal of the American Medical Association, 287*, 1815–1821.

Hu, F. B., Stampfer, M. J., Manson, J. E., Rimm, E., Colditz, G. A., Rosner, B. A., et al. (1997). Dietary fat intake and the risk of coronary heart disease in women. *New England Journal of Medicine, 337*, 1491–1499.

Hu, F. B., & Willett, W. C. (2002). Optimal diets for prevention of coronary heart disease. *Journal of the American Medical Association, 288*, 2569–2578.

Hypertension Prevention Trial Research Group. (1990). The Hypertension Prevention Trial: Three-year effects of dietary changes on blood pressure. *Archives of Internal Medicine, 150*, 153–162.

Institute of Medicine Committee on Dietary Guidelines Implementation. (1991). *Improving America's diet and health: From recommendations to action.* Washington, DC: National Academy Press.

Jackson, Y., Dietz, W. H., Sanders, C., Kolbe, L. J., Whyte, J. J., Wechsler, H., et al. (2002). Summary of the 2000 Surgeon General's Listening Session: Toward a national action plan on overweight and obesity. *Obesity Research, 10*, 1299–1305.

Jeffery, R. W., Drewnowski, A., Epstein, L. H., Stunkard, A. J., Wilson, G. T., Wing, R. R., et al. (2000). Long-term maintenance of weight loss: Current status. *Health Psychology, 19*(Suppl.), 5–16.

Jeffery, R. W., French, S. A., Raether, C., & Baxter, J. E. (1994). An environmental intervention to increase fruit and salad purchases in a cafeteria. *Preventive Medicine, 23*, 788–792.

Johnson, R. K. (2000). Energy. In L. K. Mahan & S. Escott-Stump (Eds.), *Food, nutrition and diet therapy* (10th ed., pp. 19–30). Philadelphia: W. B. Saunders.

Joshipura, K. J., Ascherio, A., Manson, J. E., Stampfer, M. J., Rimm, E. B., Speizer, F. E., et al. (1999). Fruit and vegetable intake in relation to risk of ischemic stroke. *Journal of the American Medical Association, 282*, 1233–1239.

Kalkwarf, H. J., Khoury, J. C., & Lanphear, B. P. (2003). Milk intake during childhood and adolescence, adult bone density, and osteoporotic fractures in US women. *American Journal Clinical Nutrition, 77,* 257–265.

Kant, A. K., Graubard, B. I., Schatzkin, A., & Ballard-Barbash, R. (1995). Proportion of energy intake from fat and subsequent weight change in the NHANES I Epidemiologic Follow-up Study. *American Journal of Clinical Nutrition, 61,* 11–17.

Kennedy, E., & Goldberg, J. (1995). *Review of what American children are eating.* Washington, DC: Center for Nutrition Policy and Promotion, USDA.

Keys, A. (1970). Coronary heart disease in seven countries. *Circulation, 41,* 1–4.

Keys, A., Anderson, J. T., & Grande, F. (1957). Prediction of serum cholesterol responses of man to change in fats in the diet. *Lancet, 2,* 959–966.

Krauss, R. M., Deckelbaum, R. J., Ernst, N., Fisher, E., Howard, B. V., Knopp, R. H., et al. (1996). Dietary guidelines for healthy American adults. *Circulation, 94*(7), 1795–1800.

Krebs-Smith, S. M., Cook, A., Subar, A. F., Cleveland, L., & Friday, J. (1995). U.S. adults' fruit and vegetable intakes, 1989 to 1991: A revised baseline for the Healthy People 2000 Objectives. *American Journal of Public Health, 85,* 1623–1629.

Krebs-Smith, S. M., Cook, A., Subar, A. F., Cleveland, L., Friday, J., & Kahle, L. L. (1996). Fruit and vegetable intakes of children and adolescents in the United States. *Archives of Pediatrics and Adolescent Medicine, 150,* 81–86.

Kristal, A. R., White, E., Shattuck, A. L., Curry, S., Anderson, G. L., Fowler, A., et al. (1992). Long-term maintenance of a low-fat diet: Durability of fat-related dietary habits in the Women's Health Trial. *Journal of the American Dietetic Association, 92,* 553–559.

Kritchevsky, D. (1997). Caloric restriction and experimental mammary cacinogenesis. *Breast Cancer Research and Treatment, 46,* 161–173.

Krummel, D. (2000). Nutrition in hypertension. In L. K. Mahan & S. Escott-Stump (Eds.), *Good nutrition and diet therapy* (10th ed., pp. 558–595). Philadelphia: W.B. Saunders.

Kuczmarski, R. J. (1992). Prevalence of overweight and weight gain in the United States. *American Journal of Clinical Nutrition, 55,* 495S–502S.

Kumanyika, S. K., Espeland, M. A., Bahnson, J. L., Bottom, J. B., Charleston, J. B., Folmar, S., et al. (2002). Ethnic comparison of weight loss in the trial of nonpharmacologic interventions in the elderly. *Obesity Research, 10,* 96–106.

Kumanyika, S., Jeffery, R. W., Morabia, A., Ritenbaugh, C., & Antipatis, V. J. (2002). Obesity prevention: The case for action. *International Journal of Obesity, 26,* 425–436.

Kumanyika, S. K., Obarzanek, E., Stevens, V. J., Hebert, P. R., & Whelton, P. K. (1991). Weight-loss experience of black and white participants in NHLBI-sponsored clinical trials. *American Journal of Clinical Nutrition, 53,* 1631S–1638S.

Kumanyika, S. K., Van Horn, L., Bowen, D., Perri, M. G., Rolls, B. J., Czajkowski, S. M., et al. (2000). Maintenance of dietary behavior change. *Health Psychology, 10*(Suppl. 1), 42–56.

Kushi, L. H., Meyer, K. A., & Jacobs, D. R. (1999). Cereals, legumes, and chronic disease risk reduction: Evidence from epidemiologic studies. *American Journal of Clinical Nutrition, 70,* 451s–458s.

Lewis, C. E., Jacobs, D. R., McCreath, H., Keife, C. I., Schreiner, P. J., Smith, D. E., et al. (2000). Weight gain continues in the 1990s: 10-Year trends in weight and overweight from the CARDIA Study. *American Journal of Epidemiology, 151,* 1172–1181.

Lewis, C. E., Smith, D. E., Wallace, D. D., Williams, O. D., Bild, D. E., & Jacobs, D. R. (1997). Seven-year trends in body weight and associations with lifestyle and behavioral characteristics in Black and White young adults: The CARDIA Study. *American Journal of Public Health, 87,* 635–642.

Lissner, L., Heitmann, B. L., & Bengtsson, C. (1997). Low-fat diets may prevent weight gain in sedentary women: Prospective observations from the population study of women in Gothenburg, Sweden. *Obesity Research, 5*(1), 43–48.

Littleton, M. A., Cornell, C. E., Dignan, M., Brownstein, N., Raczynski, J. M., Stalker, V. G., et al. (2002). Lessons learned from the Uniontown Community Health Project. *American Journal of Health Behavior 26,* 34–42.

Masoro, E. J. (1995). Anti-aging action of caloric restriction: Endocrine and metabolic aspects. *Obesity Research, 3,* 241s–247s.

Matkovic, V., Jelic, T., Wardlaw, G. M., Ilich, J. Z., Goel, P. K., Wright, J. K., et al. (1994). Timing of peak bone mass in Caucasian females and its implication for the prevention of osteoporosis. *Journal of Clinical Investigation, 93,* 799–809.

Mattes, R. D., & Donnelly, D. (1991). Relative contributions of dietary sodium sources. *Journal of the American College of Nutrition, 10,* 383–393.

McCarron, D. A. (1991). Epidemiological evidence and clinical trials of dietary calcium's effect on blood pressure. *Contributions to Nephrology, 90,* 2–10.

McGinnis, J. M., & Foege, W. H. (1993). Actual causes of death in the United States. *Journal of the American Medical Association, 270,* 2207–2212.

McGuire, M. T., Wing, R. R., Klem, M. L., Lang, W., & Hill, J. O. (1999). What predicts weight regain in a group of successful weight losers? *Journal of Consulting and Clinical Psychology, 67,* 177–185.

McKane, W. R., Khosla, S., Egan, K. S., Robins, S. P., Burritt, M. F., & Riggs, B. L. (1996). Role of calcium intake in modulating age-related increases in parathyroid function and bone resorption. *Journal of Clinical Endocrinology and Metabolism, 81,* 1699–1703.

Mokdad, A. H., Ford, E. S., Bowman, B. A., Dietz, W. H., Vinicor, F., Bales, V. S., et al. (2001). Prevalence of obesity, diabetes, and obesity-related health risk factors. *Journal of the American Medical Association, 289,* 76–79.

Nader, P. R., Sellers, D. E., Johnson, C. C., Perry, C. L., Stone, E. J., Cook, K. C., et al. (1996). The effect of adult participation in a school-based family intervention to improve children's diet and physical activity: The Child and Adolescent Trial for Cardiovascular Health. *Preventive Medicine, 25,* 455–464.

Nader, P. R., Stone, E. J., Lytle, L. A., Perry, C. L., Osganian, S. K., Kelder, S., et al. (1999). Three-year maintenance of improved diet and physical activity: The CATCH cohort. Child and Adolescent Trial for Cardiovascular Health. *Archives of Pediatrics and Adolescent Medicine, 153,* 695–704.

National Cattlemen's Beef Association. (1994). *Eating in America: A dietary pattern and intake report.* Chicago, IL: Author.

National Center for Health Statistics. (1999). *Deaths: Final data, 1997* (Vol. 47). Washington, DC: Author.

National Cholesterol Education Program. (1994). Second report of the Expert Panel on Detection, Evaluation, and Treatment of High Blood Cholesterol in Adults (Adult Treatment Panel II). *Circulation, 89,* 1333–1445.

National Heart, Lung, and Blood Institute's Obesity Education Initiative Expert Panel. (1998). Clinical guidelines on the identification, evaluation, and treatment of overweight and obesity in adults—The evidence report. *Obesity Research, 6,* 51S–210S.

National Osteoporosis Foundation. (2002). *America's bone health.* Retrieved February 21, 2002, from http://www.nof.org/osteoporosis/stat.htm

National Task Force on the Prevention and Treatment of Obesity. (1993). Very low-calorie diets. *Journal of the American Medical Association, 270,* 967–974.

Olsen, S. H., Trevisan, M., & Marshall, J. R. (1995). Body mass index, weight gain and risk of endometrial cancer. *Nutrition and Cancer, 23,* 141–149.

Pascale, R. W., Wing, R. R., Butler, B. A., Mullen, M., & Bononi, P. (1995). Effects of a behavioral weight loss program stressing calorie restriction versus calorie plus fat restriction in obese individuals with NIDDM or a family history of diabetes. *Diabetes Care, 18,* 1241–1248.

Perri, M. G., Nezu, A. M., Patti, E. T., & McCann, K. L. (1989). Effect of length of treatment on weight loss. *Journal of Consulting and Clinical Psychology, 57,* 450–452.

Poehlman, E. T., & Horton, E. S. (1999). Energy needs: Assessment and requirements in humans. In M. E. Shils, J. A. Olsen, M. Shike, & A. C. Ross (Eds.), *Modern nutrition in health and disease* (pp. 95–104). Baltimore: Williams & Wilkins.

Putnam, J. (2000, January–April). Major trends in U.S. food supply, 1909–1999. *Food Review,* 8–15.

Rapuri, P. B., Gallagher, J. C., Balhorn, K. E., & Ryschon, K. L. (2000). Alcohol intake and bone metabolism in elderly women. *American Journal of Clinical Nutrition, 72,* 1206–1213.

Reid, I. R., Ames, R. W., Evans, M. C., Gamble, G. D., & Sharpe, S. J. (1993). Effect of calcium supplementation on bone loss in postmenopausal women. *New England Journal of Medicine, 328,* 460–464.

Reynolds, K. D., Raczynski, J. M., Binkley, D., Franklin, F. A., Duvall, R. C., DeVane-Hart, K., et al. (1997). Design of "High 5": A school-based cancer education study to promote fruit and vegetable consumption. *Journal of School Health, 12*, 89–94.

Rothman, A. J. (2000). Toward a theory-based analysis of behavioral maintenance. *Health Psychology, 19*(1 Suppl.), 64–69.

Schaefer, E. J. (2002). Lipoproteins, nutrition, and heart disease. *American Journal of Clinical Nutrition, 75*, 191–212.

Sorensen, G., Stoddard, A., Hunt, M. K., Hebert, J. R., Ockene, J. K., Avrunin, J. S., et al. (1998). The effects of a health promotion–health protection intervention on behavior change: The WellWorks Study. *American Journal of Public Health, 88*, 1685–1690.

Sorensen, G., Stoddard, A., Peterson, K., Cohen, N., Hunt, M. K., Stein, E., et al. (1999). Increasing fruit and vegetable consumption through worksites and families in the Treatwell 5-A-Day-Study. *American Journal of Public Health, 89*, 54–60.

Stamler, J., & Shekelle, R. (1988). Dietary cholesterol and human coronary heart disease: The epidemiologic evidence. *Archives of Pathology and Laboratory Medicine, 112*, 1032–1040.

Stamler, J., Stamler, R., & Neaton, J. D. (1993). Blood pressure, systolic and diastolic, and cardiovascular risks. *Archives of Internal Medicine, 153*, 598–615.

Steinberg, D., Pearson, T. A., & Kuller, L. H. (1991). Alcohol and atherosclerosis. *Annals of Internal Medicine, 114*, 967–976.

Stone, N. J. (1990). Diet, lipids and coronary heart disease. *Endocrinology and Metabolism Clinics of North America, 19*, 321–344.

Story, M., Evans, M., Fabsitz, R. R., Clay, T. E., Rock, B. H., & Broussard, B. B. (1999). The epidemic of obesity in American Indian communities and the need for childhood obesity-prevention programs. *American Journal of Clinical Nutrition, 69*, 747S–754S.

Subar, A. F., Krebs-Smith, S. M., Cook, A., & Kahle, L. L. (1998). Dietary sources of nutrients among U.S. adults, 1989–1991. *Journal of the American Dietetic Association, 98*, 537–547.

Toubro, S., & Astrup, A. (1997). Randomized comparison of diets for maintaining obese subjects' weight after major weight loss: Ad lib, low fat, high carbohydrate diet vs fixed energy expenditure. *British Medical Journal, 314*, 29–34.

Trentham-Dietz, A., Newcomb, P. A., & Storer, B. E. (1997). Body size and risk of breast cancer. *American Journal of Epidemiology, 145*, 1011–1019.

Troiano, R. P., Flegal, K. M., Kuczmarski, R. J., Campbell, S. M., & Johnson, C. L. (1995). Overweight prevalence and trends for children and adolescents: The National Health and Nutrition Examination Surveys, 1963–1991. *Archives of Pediatric and Adolescent Medicine, 149*, 1085–1091.

U.S. Department of Agriculture, Agricultural Research Service, Dietary Guidelines Advisory Committee. (2000). *Dietary guidelines for Americans, 2000* (5th ed.). Washington, DC: Author.

Vollmer, W. M., Sacks, F. M., Ard, J., Appel, L. J., Bray, G. A., Simons-Morton, D. G., et al. (2001). Effects of diet and sodium intake on blood pressure: Subgroup analysis of the DASH-sodium trial. *Annals of Internal Medicine, 18*, 1019–1028.

Wadden, T. A., Anderson, D. A., & Foster, G. D. (1999). Two-year changes in lipids and lipoproteins associated with the maintenance of a 5% to 10% reduction in initial weight: Some findings and some questions. *Obesity Research, 7*, 170–178.

Wadden, T. A., & Foster, G. D. (2000). Behavioral treatment of obesity. *Medical Clinics of North America, 84*(2), 441–461.

Wadden, T. A., & Frey, D. L. (1997). A multicenter evaluation of a proprietary weight loss program for the treatment of marked obesity: A five-year follow-up. *Eating Disorders, 22*, 203–212.

Wardle, J., Waller, J., & Jarvis, M. J. (2002). Sex differences in the association of socioeconomic status with obesity. *American Journal of Public Health, 92*, 1299–1304.

Weinberger, M. H., Miller, J. H., Luft, F. C., Grim, C. E., & Fineberg, N. S. (1986). Definitions and characteristics of sodium sensitivity and blood pressure resistance. *Hypertension, 8*(Suppl. II), 127–134.

Whelton, P. K., Appel, L. J., Espeland, M. A., Applegate, W. B., Ettinger, W. H., Kostis, J. B., et al. (1998). Sodium reduction and weight loss in the treatment of hypertension in older persons: A randomized controlled trial of nonpharmacologic interventions in the elderly (TONE). *Journal of the American Medical Association, 279*, 839–846.

Whitaker, R. C., Wright, J. A., Pepe, M. S., Seidel, K. D., & Dietz, W. H. (1997). Predicting obesity in young adulthood from childhood and parental obesity. *New England Journal of Medicine, 337*, 869–873.

Willett, W. (1990). *Nutritional Epidemiology*. New York: Oxford University Press.

Williamson, D. F., Kahn, H. S., Remington, P. L., & Anda, R. F. (1990). The 10-year incidence of overweight and major weight gain in US adults. *Archives of Internal Medicine, 150*, 665–672.

Wing, R. R., & Anglin, K. (1996). Effectiveness of a behavioral weight control program for Blacks and Whites with NIDDM. *Diabetes Care, 19*, 409–413.

Wing, R. R., & Jeffery, R. W. (1999). Benefits of recruiting participants with friends and increasing social support for weight loss and maintenance. *Journal of Consulting and Clinical Psychology, 67*(1), 132–138.

Wood, P. D., Stefanick, M. L., Williams, P. T., & Haskell, W. L. (1991). The effects on plasma lipoproteins of a prudent weight-reducing diet, with or without exercise, in overweight men and women. *New England Journal of Medicine, 325*, 461–466.

World Cancer Research Fund and American Institute for Cancer Research. (1997). *Energy and related factors. Food, nutrition and the prevention of cancer: A global perspective*. Menashev, WI: Banta Books.

2

SUBSTANCE USE DISORDERS

JESSE B. MILBY, JOSEPH E. SCHUMACHER, AND JALIE A. TUCKER

Models of and interventions for substance abuse have evolved throughout the 20th century (Tucker, 1999). After Alcoholics Anonymous (AA) emerged in the mid-1930s following Prohibition (1920–1933), popular and professional conceptions began to shift away from viewing substance abuse as a moral failing that deserved punishment and stigmatization toward viewing it as a disease beyond the volitional control of affected individuals who therefore deserved treatment (Jellinek, 1960). Mutual help groups and professional treatments guided by the 12-step principles of AA are now widespread. Despite the availability of these helping resources, most substance abusers avoid or delay seeking help in the absence of coercion (reviewed by Tucker, 2001). Less than 25% of people with problems seek help from professionals or mutual help groups such as AA or Narcotics Anonymous (NA). The underutilization of services is generally attributed to the continuing stigma of substance abuse and its treatment and to the abstinence-oriented, one-size-fits-all treatment approach offered by dominant 12-step programs.

Manuscript preparation was supported in part by grant no. R01-DA08475 from the National Institute on Drug Abuse and grant nos. R01-AA08972 and K02-AA00209 from the National Institute on Alcohol Abuse and Alcoholism. We thank James Murphy for his help in researching articles on assessment procedures.

Current interventions also are not fully responsive to scientific knowledge about substance abuse. Research has shown that older views of substance abuse as a unitary, progressive disease are incorrect. Rather, substance-related problems are heterogenous and vary along several dimensions, including drug use practices, levels of physical dependence, and the extent to which substance use impairs life/health functioning (Institute of Medicine [IOM], 1990). Each dimension lies along a continuum of severity from none to extreme, and the extent of impairment usually is not uniform across dimensions, both across and within individuals. Change on one dimension can occur without change on the others and can contribute to overall improvement. This variability across dimensions is found across the range of problem severity, including among persons who fulfill clinical diagnostic criteria for a substance use disorder (Grant, Chou, Pickering, & Hasin, 1992). Substance-related problems often are comorbid with other health and behavioral health problems, and they can surface in many settings, including health care, legal, employment, school, and domestic contexts.

The heterogeneity in substance-related problems suggests that interventions should be similarly diverse. The scope, focus, and goals of interventions should correspond to the nature and severity of problems and should be responsive to client preferences (Humphreys & Tucker, 2002; IOM, 1990). Professional interventions, however, continue to be dominated by specialized, intensive treatments that are better suited to helping the minority with substantial functional impairment and physical dependence. Entry into such high-threshold clinical treatments often entails a measure of social, legal, or work-related coercion. These programs are ill-equipped to promote the early detection of emerging problems or to intervene with substance abusers who have more circumscribed problems and for whom clinical treatment is overly costly and sweeping in scope. An exception to this pattern is the universally applied, school-based prevention programs for youths. However, the dominant approach to prevention, the police-led Drug Abuse Resistance Education (DARE) program, is not highly effective (Ennett, Tobler, Ringwalt, & Flewelling, 1994). DARE likely persists in part because of its compatibility with the zero-tolerance drug control policies and laws in the United States.

A major orienting assumption of this chapter is that clinical treatments should be complemented by less intensive, lower threshold interventions offered within and outside of the health care system, thereby forming a more optimal continuum of care that combines clinical and public health approaches to expand the reach and effectiveness of services (Humphreys & Tucker, 2002; IOM, 1990). Epidemiological findings that support the need for this expansion are summarized next. Subsequent sections summarize assessment and intervention approaches for substance use disorders that have an empirical basis of support. Most interventions continue to target substance abusers with more serious problems, but there have been positive developments, particularly in the alcohol field, to offer less intensive services for those with mild to moderate problems and to disseminate them in primary health care and community settings. The chapter concludes with consideration of health care organization and drug policy issues that require attention if an expanded continuum of substance abuse services is to continue to develop and to be integrated into mainstream health care.

EPIDEMIOLOGY OF SUBSTANCE USE AND ABUSE

Population-based survey research has directed attention toward the need to develop an expanded continuum of services and reveals a somewhat different view of substance abuse than the one suggested by clinical research, which tends to reveal less heterogeneity, greater problem severity, and greater chronicity. As summarized next, survey research indicates that (a) substance abuse is among the most prevalent mental disorders; (b) the U.S. substance abuse services system is pluralistic, spans the professional and voluntary sectors, and fails to reach many substance abusers, especially women and those with less severe problems of both genders; and (c) positive change can occur in the absence of clinical treatment.

Substance use, anxiety, and affective disorders are the three most prevalent mental disorders (Howard et al., 1996; Regier et al., 1993). For example, the Epidemiological Catchment Area (ECA) study (Narrow, Regier, Rae, Manderscheid, & Locke, 1993; Regier et al., 1993) of more than 20,000 adults found one-year prevalence rates of 12.6, 9.5, and 9.5% for anxiety, affective, and substance use disorders, respectively, which each exceeded the rates for all other mental disorders assessed. Among substance use disorders, alcohol abuse or dependence is more common than other drug use disorders. The ECA study prevalence rates were 7.4% and 3.1% for any alcohol use and any drug use disorder, respectively. Among illicit drugs, those most commonly misused include marijuana, cocaine, and narcotics, whereas poly-drug abuse, including illicit drug abuse combined with alcohol abuse, has become more common in recent decades (Fischman & Johanson, 1996). Substance use disorders often are comorbid with affective, anxiety, and antisocial personality disorders (Regier et al., 1993) and with medical problems such as accidents and trauma, sexually transmitted diseases (STDs) including but not limited to HIV/AIDS, and liver, heart, gastrointestinal, and neurological damage.

Substance use and abuse varies reliably with age and gender (White & Bates, 1995). Use and abuse are highest in adolescence and early adulthood and then decline with increasing age, with many substance abusers "maturing out" of problem use by mid-life, commonly during their 40s, often without treatment. At all ages, substance use and abuse are more prevalent among males than females. More complex relations have been found with race and ethnicity (Schumacher & Milby, 1999; U.S. Department of Health and Human Services [DHHS], 1997). Some groups (e.g., Caucasians, Hispanics) show higher rates of use and abuse than others (e.g., Asians), but these differences often mask variation within groups and tend to be more pronounced among males than females. For example, Black males under age 45 have a lower prevalence of alcohol abuse and dependence than non-Black males, but those who drink heavily tend to have more alcohol-related problems than non-Black males with similar drinking practices (U.S. DHHS, 1997).

Relatively few substance abusers seek help for their problems, but when they do, their care is diffused across general medical services, mental health–substance abuse specialty programs, human services, and the voluntary support network (Narrow et al., 1993). Women substance abusers tend to be proportionately underrepresented in clinical samples (Schober & Annis, 1996), but relations between utilization patterns and other demographic characteristics (e.g., ethnicity, age) are less well established (Tucker, 2001). Despite their underutilization of substance-focused services, substance abusers and their families tend to be higher than average users of other medical services. Providing substance abuse treatment tends to reduce utilization of medical services, thereby offsetting the cost of substance abuse treatment (Holder, 1998).

Participation in interventions is neither a necessary nor a sufficient condition for problem resolution (reviewed by Tucker, 2003). Some substance abusers achieve stable abstinence without interventions, and others make gradual changes that step down drug use and associated risks, even if enduring abstinence is not attained. In the case of alcohol problems, natural resolutions are more common and include a higher proportion of moderation-drinking outcomes compared to treatment-assisted resolutions, which include a higher proportion of abstinent outcomes (L. C. Sobell, Cunningham, & Sobell, 1996). Finally, whether treated or not, many substance abusers move in and out of periods of abstinence, nonproblem substance use, and substance abuse (Moos, Finney, & Cronkite, 1990; Tucker, 2001, 2003). This variability over time is related to changing environmental circumstances and to individuals' personal and social resources, more so than to the often time-limited effects of substance-focused interventions.

ASSESSMENT AND DIAGNOSIS OF
SUBSTANCE USE DISORDERS

This section summarizes issues and procedures involved in the assessment and diagnosis of substance use disorders for screening and treatment planning purposes. Emphasis is placed on describing the multiple dimensions involved in characterizing substance use disorders (e.g., quantity/frequency of drug use, functional problems related to use) and on the relative utility of different data collection methods (e.g., verbal reports, laboratory tests).

Purpose of Assessment

Identification and assessment of persons with substance-related problems are necessary for selecting appropriate interventions. Assessment will vary according to problem severity, setting (e.g., primary care or specialized drug treatment), available resources (e.g., time, access to laboratory equipment), and purpose of the assessment (e.g., screening, treatment planning, or court evaluation). Assessment is often sequential and overlaps with interventions and follow-up evaluations (Donovan, 1999).

To screen clients for substance-related problems in general medical settings, brief interviews or self-administered questionnaires with high sensitivity, but not necessarily high specificity, are the methods of choice. If the purpose is to establish illegal substance use for judicial–legal purposes, biological tests will be a major data source, but these measures are not particularly useful for treatment planning. If the purpose is to select an intervention and develop behavior change goals, structured interviews will be used to establish a *DSM–IV* diagnosis (American Psychiatric Association, 1994) and characterize substance use practices, contexts surrounding use, associated life–health problems, and level of dependence. In this type of assessment, the interview should build rapport for treatment and discover behavior patterns that lead to craving, use, risky behavior, and relapse. Treatment planning also requires evaluation of motivation for treatment participation and behavior change. The treatment planning interview should adjust to focus on behavior change goals the individual is likely to accept (Miller & Rollnick, 2002).

Role of Self-Reports and Contextual Variables in Assessment

Objective laboratory tests can detect recent alcohol or drug use and are useful for detecting substance abuse (Anton, Litton, & Allen, 1995; Wolff et al., 1999). However, most tests are not highly specific and may be affected by other health problems or environmental exposure (e.g., to smoke containing crack or marijuana residues). The time frame over which such tests reflect alcohol or drug use is fairly short (hours to weeks), depending on the half-life of the drug. Thus, laboratory tests cannot yield temporal pattern information on substance use over lengthy periods, or assess functional relations between substance use and the environment, which are fundamental for implementing effective behavioral interventions. Therefore, verbal reports obtained from substance abusers and verified whenever possible with collateral informants remain the main sources of assessment information (Tucker, Vuchinich, & Murphy, 2001).

An extensive body of research on the accuracy of substance abusers' verbal reports of drug use is available. This research shows reporting accuracy is influenced by the assessment context and measurement characteristics (reviewed by Babor, Brown, & Del Boca, 1990; Tucker et al., 2001). Accuracy can be maximized by (a) minimizing negative consequences for reporting substance use and related problems; (b) providing assurances of confidentiality; (c) collecting reports from individuals whose sobriety has been verified objectively; and (d) using measures that ask about observable events and behaviors and that minimize subjective inferences and "mental averaging."

The role of contextual variables is illustrated in a study that evaluated a brief motivational intervention for pregnant drinkers (Handmaker, Miller, & Manicke, 1999). Levels of drinking reported during an empathic, nonjudgmental interview were more than three times higher than levels reported on a screening questionnaire by such individuals' physicians. These discrepant findings highlight how accuracy is enhanced when verbal reports are collected in a warm, nonjudgmental manner, particularly from subgroups for whom reports of substance use may result in serious repercussions.

Screening and Initial Assessment

Substance abusers surface in many settings other than specialized treatment programs (e.g., emergency rooms, primary care), and screening measures are an essential tool when they do not self-identify. Screening measures are brief and focus on establishing the likely presence and type of substance misuse. When screenings are completed by someone who does not provide treatment, background data and information on personal substance abuse etiology are not useful and unnecessarily lengthen assessment. When individuals present for substance abuse services, the screening phase can be omitted, and the initial assessment can begin with a diagnostic interview aimed at characterizing the nature and severity of problems. This section summarizes screening and initial assessment procedures with adequate psychometric properties (reviewed by Tucker et al., 2001).

Self-Report Screening Measures

Good brief screens for alcohol problems include the Michigan Alcoholism Screening Test (MAST; Selzer, 1971), Alcohol Use Disorders Inventory (AUDIT; Saunders, Aasland, Babor, de la Fuente, & Grant, 1993), and CAGE (Mayfield, McLeod, & Hall, 1974). All take fewer than 10 minutes to administer and can be used in a variety of settings (e.g., primary care, emergency room and work sites) by nonspecialists. The 25-item MAST is more sensitive and reliable than the four-question CAGE, which works well in primary care settings and with older adults (Maisto & McKay, 1995). The AUDIT detects early signs of problem drinking better than the MAST or CAGE and is useful for identifying individuals with mild to moderate problems (Carey & Teitelbaum, 1996). However, because most screening measures were developed for use with treated White males, their utility with females, minorities, and untreated alcohol abusers is less established (Ames, Schmidt, Klee, & Saltz, 1996). The CAGE has been adapted to detect dangerous drinking by pregnant women. Two CAGE derivatives, the TWEAK (Russell, Martier, Sokol, Jacobson, & Jacobson, 1991) and the T-ACE (Sokol, Martier, & Ager, 1989), were normed using Black women in innercity antenatal clinics (Russell, 1994).

Self-report screening measures for drug abuse include the Drug Abuse Screening Test (DAST; Gavin, Ross, & Skinner, 1989) and the Drug Use Screening Inventory (DUSI; Tarter & Kirisci, 1997). The DAST was modeled after the MAST and is highly correlated with *DSM* diagnoses of drug abuse and dependence (Donovan, 1999; L. C. Sobell, Toneatto, & Sobell, 1994). The DUSI assesses alcohol and other drugs of abuse, substance-related functional impairment in nine areas, and can be used with adolescents and adults. Tarter and Kirisci (1997) reported that the DUSI correctly classified 80% of substance abusers and 100% of normal controls.

Biological Tests

Biological tests have utility as screening devices and to monitor drug use during and after treatment, although they tend to lack specificity and typically are sensitive to recent use only (Anton et al., 1995; Wolff et al., 1999). Breath analysis for alcohol use and urine analysis for other drugs of abuse are widely used, inexpensive tests. Saliva tests also are inexpensive, but are less widely used, probably because of the practical impediments involved in collecting samples. Blood tests are more expensive but give precise estimates of blood content and levels of drug metabolites. Hair tests are a developing technology (Hoffman, Wish, Koman, Schneider, Flynn, & Luckey, 1995), but they tend to be overly sensitive to passive smoke exposure and to reflect passive or active drug exposure over variable time periods, depending on the sample. Thus, at this time hair tests can lead to false positives in nonusers and cannot reliably distinguish recent and remote use among drug users.

Commonly used blood tests for alcohol abuse include the liver enzyme gamma-glutamyl transferase (GGT), mean corpuscular volume (MCV), and carbohydrate-deficient transferrin (CDT; Anton et al., 1995; Salaspuro, 1994). GGT is a highly sensitive measure of chronic alcohol abuse but has low specificity among medical populations because several medical conditions can cause elevations (e.g., heart and kidney disease). Increased MCV is associated with recent binge drinking and is a less sensitive but more specific index than GGT. CDT is a highly specific marker of heavy drinking (> 50 g ethanol/day) during the past two weeks. Combining the markers can increase sensitivity, and Anton et al. (1995) recommend a sequential process in which the more sensitive GGT is used for initial screening and is followed by the more specific CDT.

Urinalysis reliably detects most drugs of abuse (Wolff et al., 1999), although detection varies with the half-life of the drug (e.g., one to three days for cocaine, one to three weeks for marijuana). Urinalysis is usually conducted in a two-stage process, beginning with a relatively inexpensive screen (e.g., enzyme immunoassay) and followed by an expensive confirmatory analysis (gas chromatography–mass spectrometry). Accuracy of detection exceeds 95% across most drug classes when this two-stage assessment is used (Cook, Bernstein, Arrington, Andrews, & Marshall, 1995). However, false negatives are a concern because urine samples can be contaminated or diluted (Wolff et al., 1999), and false positives can occur from consuming certain medications and foods (e.g., poppy seeds). Thus, biological indicators are a flawed "gold standard," but they are the best current indicators of drug use.

Diagnosis and Assessment for Intervention Planning and Implementation

Substance abusers who self-identify or who are identified through screenings typically are referred to specialized substance abuse programs for additional assessment and treatment. An exception to this pattern is when additional assessment occurs as part of a brief intervention delivered in the nonspecialized setting where the problem was detected. Good diagnostic and problem-focused assessment procedures available to characterize substance abuse may be found in the following sources, among others (Allen & Columbus, 1995; Donovan, 1999; L.C. Sobell et al., 1994; Tucker et al., 2001). This section highlights the dimensions of problem use that require assessment in service of selecting and implementing interventions and gives examples of measures with good psychometric properties.

Clinical Diagnosis

Classification of substance-related disorders is a vital research area, but findings have not had much impact on practice, and the *DSM* schemes of the American Psychiatric Association remain dominant for reasons other than conceptual or empirical superiority. Current diagnostic criteria of *DSM–IV* (American Psychiatric Association, 1994) are based on the drug dependence syndrome outlined by the World Health Organization (WHO, 1981) and distinguish between abuse and dependence. Abuse entails a pattern of substance use lasting at least 12 months that includes recurrent adverse consequences related to use and functional impairment, without the presence of tolerance, withdrawal, or a pattern of "compulsive" use. Dependence entails three or more of the following: (a) tolerance; (b) withdrawal; (c) substance use in larger amounts or over a longer time than intended; (d) persistent desire or unsuccessful attempts to cut down or control substance use; (e) considerable time spent in obtaining or using the substance, or recovering from the effects of use; (f) curtailing or abandoning important social, occupational, or recreational activities because of substance use; and (g) continuing substance use despite persistent or recurrent physical or psychological problems caused or aggravated by use.

Clinical diagnostic precision can be improved by using a structured interview that can yield a substance-specific *DSM* diagnosis including the Diagnostic Interview Schedule (DIS; Robins, Helzer, Croughan, & Radcliff, 1981) and the Psychiatric Research Interview for Substance and Mental Disorders (PRISM; Hasin et al., 1996). These interviews provide detailed information on lifetime and current substance-related problems and are useful for evaluating possible comorbid psychiatric problems.

The Addiction Severity Index (ASI; McLellan, Luborsky, Woody, & O'Brien, 1980) is the most widely used structured interview specific to assessing substance abuse. It assesses recent and lifetime functioning in seven areas (drug use, alcohol use, psychiatric adjustment, legal problems, social functioning, employment, and medical status) and provides research-based indexes of severity for each area, which can inform treatment selection and planning. An attractive feature of the ASI is its brief follow-up version, which takes 10 to 12 minutes to administer, can be used by telephone to assess treatment outcomes, and can be administered repeatedly by telephone. The initial ASI administration should be conducted in person.

These diagnostic interviews are useful in clinical practice, but they are not useful for evaluating milder substance-related problems or identifying at-risk groups for prevention or early intervention. Most do not assess multiple dimensions of problem use that are central to developing interventions that are problem-specific. Additional dimensions requiring assessment for intervention planning and implementation are described next.

Substance Use Practices

Verbal report measures of alcohol and drug use fall into three categories: (a) quantity/frequency (Q/F) questionnaires that ask respondents to summarize their use over time; (b) retrospective measures that capture temporal patterning of use with different degrees of precision; and (c) prospective self-monitoring of use using diaries, hand-held computers, or telephones. Q/F measures provide quick and reliable estimates of total use but usually underestimate use compared to detailed retrospective or self-monitoring assessments, and they cannot capture variability in use over time, which is basic to conducting a functional analysis. Structured retrospective measures such as the Timeline Followback (TLFB; L. C. Sobell & M. B. Sobell, 1992) interview yield reliable and accurate reports of many dimensions of substance use (e.g., abstinence, light, and heavy drinking days during the past year) that are basic to planning and monitoring interventions. Self-monitoring often yields more complete and accurate reports, especially for fine-grained dimensions of use (e.g., duration of discrete substance use episodes), but compliance may be an issue. Self-monitoring is not highly reactive as long as multiple variables are recorded.

Adverse Consequences of Substance Use

Identifying life–health problems is important, because changes in substance use and life–health functioning often do not coincide. More work has been done on assessing the functional consequences of use in the alcohol than in the drug abuse field (Maisto & McKay, 1995). Psychometrically sound measures of alcohol-related dysfunction (e.g., marital, social, vocational, and legal problems) include the Drinking Problem Index (DPI; Finley, Moos, & Brennan, 1991), the Drinker Inventory of Consequences (DrInC; Miller, Tonigan, & Longabaugh, 1995), and the Drinking Problems Scale (DPS; Cahalan, 1970). Both the ASI and the DUSI assess problems from drug abuse in several areas of functioning.

There are individual differences in duration and amount of alcohol or drug use required to initiate and reinstate dependence symptoms. The Alcohol Dependence Scale (ADS; Skinner & Horn, 1984) is useful for assessing dependence symptoms during the past year

Contexts Surrounding Substance Misuse

Systematic assessment of how environmental features covary with substance use and abuse is an essential part of a functional analysis to plan behavioral interventions (Marlatt & Gordon, 1985). The functional analysis assesses when, where, and with whom drug-seeking usually starts; behaviors that precede drug-seeking and use; topography of drug-taking and associated behaviors, including risky behaviors such as needle-sharing or unprotected sex; and the consequences, both short and long term, of substance use versus maintaining sobriety. Detailed description is obtained for each situation that leads to drug use and guides the formulation of interventions to disrupt behavioral chains of drug-seeking and drug use while reinforcing behaviors that are incompatible with them.

Motives for Substance Use and Behavior Change

Alcohol and drug use expectancies, substance use motives, readiness to change, self-efficacy for change, and cravings or urges are key elements of cognitive–behavioral treatments that often warrant assessment. See Carroll (1999) and Donovan (1999) for reviews. For example, the Stages of Change Readiness and Treatment Eagerness Scale (SOCRATES; Miller & Tonigan, 1996) assigns drinkers to a stage of change based on the transtheoretical model (Prochaska & DiClemente, 1986) and can be used to develop intervention goals that coincide with the client's readiness to change (Miller & Rollnick, 2002). Self-reported expectancies about alcohol and drug effects and measures of self-efficacy to refrain from or reduce substance use in specific situations have been found to predict treatment outcomes (Maisto, Carey, & Bradizza, 1999). Urges to use are important to assess during the behavior change process because they may predict risk of drug use (Tiffany, 1997).

Family History

Alcohol and drug problems tend to run in families. The genetic component of familial patterns appears stronger in males than females, and environmental factors exert considerable influence on both genders. The Family Tree Questionnaire for Assessing Family History of Drinking Problems (Mann, Sobell, Sobell, & Pavin, 1985) is a unique structured measure of a family's substance abuse history across generations. A related issue that requires assessment is emotional and physical abuse related to substance abuse, both currently and in the past.

Comorbidity

Assessment of comorbid conditions is essential for developing effective interventions. Common comorbid conditions include combined alcohol and drug dependence, major depression, and antisocial personality disorder (Grant & Dawson, 1999). Structured interviews such as the DIS (Robbins et al., 1981), objective psychopathology measures such as the Personality Assessment Inventory (PAI; Morey, 1996) and the Millon Clinical Multiaxial Inventory (MCMI–II; Millon, 1992), and brief symptom measures such as the Symptom Checklist–90 (SCL–90; Derogatis, 1977) and the Beck Depression Inventory (BDI; Beck, Ward, Mendelson, Mock, &

Erbaugh, 1961) can be used selectively to evaluate potential comorbidity. Neuropsychological screening or evaluation also may be needed in some cases, especially among long-term alcohol-dependent clients, chronic cocaine abusers, and polydrug abusers (Sobell et al., 1994). Those with significant neuropsychological impairment will likely require interventions not offered in usual substance abuse treatment programs.

HIV/AIDS Risk

Substance abusers, especially those who inject drugs, are at high risk for HIV/AIDS and Hepatitis B and C because of the use of contaminated syringes (Marlatt, 1998). They also are at heightened risk for other STDs stemming from sexual activities associated with drug use. Crack cocaine is commonly traded for sex. Therefore, drug abuse services must be sensitive to clients' increased risk of STDs and offer referrals for testing in a discreet and confidential manner. Also, programs providing services for homeless clients should arrange for tuberculosis (TB) screenings. TB is prevalent among homeless persons, and TB risk may be especially high for those who frequent large public shelters where they share a common sleeping area, breathing each others' exhalations.

Demographic, Cultural, and Political Issues

Certain drug classes, patterns of use, and routes of administration are linked with ethnic, gender, age, and cultural subgroups, and these linkages can change over time, depending on drug availability, price, and broader socioeconomic conditions and political factors. Drugs used by marginalized socioeconomic groups often tend to be stigmatized and punished more than those used by groups with more power. For example, whether intentional or not, the mandatory minimum drug sentencing laws that are part of the U.S. "war on drugs" have disproportionately resulted in the imprisonment of Hispanic and Black males (Marlatt, 1998). Legal penalties for crack cocaine, the cheaper form of cocaine favored by impoverished minorities, are much greater than for powdered cocaine, the more expensive choice of middle- and upper-class White users.

These aspects of drug use and abuse must be considered during the assessment and intervention. Providers must understand the special values and traditions of drug use in subpopulations and the unique vulnerabilities associated with them. Family reaction to, and involvement in, drug problems also may vary.

Gender is another consideration because substance use and abuse are more congruent with male sex roles, and women have long been ostracized for intoxication or substance abuse. Women substance abusers continue to be proportionately underrepresented in treatment samples (Schober & Annis,

1996), and their unique vulnerabilities should routinely be assessed and addressed, including potential difficulties with child rearing, spouse abuse, obstetric and gynecological problems, and depression. Practical barriers to treatment, such as lack of child care, transportation, income, or insurance, may be more influential among women, especially among single mothers who fall below the poverty line. Such women may have precarious housing situations, and the stress and stigma of homelessness can be an overwhelming barrier to treatment entry and participation.

Members of ethnic minorities also have unique treatment impediments, especially if English is not their native language. Treatment centers with multilingual clinical personnel are rare, even in areas of the country where many first-generation immigrants reside.

Summary and Recommendations for Assessment and Diagnosis

Greater emphasis should be placed on screening for substance abuse in nonspecialized health care settings, because persons with problems are common, but their utilization of substance-specific services is not. Selecting, implementing, and monitoring interventions requires the use of assessment procedures that cover the heterogeneous nature of substance use practices and related problems. Many such procedures rely on the verbal reports of substance abusers, which generally are accurate if information is collected from sober individuals in a confidential and empathic manner using sound measurement principles and practices.

INTERVENTIONS FOR ALCOHOL-RELATED PROBLEMS

In a recent review of alcohol-treatment outcome studies, Miller, Andrews, Wilbourne, and Bennett (1998) included a summary table of evidence for the efficacy of specific treatment methods. The table included 41 methods that had a research base of three or more outcome studies and an additional 26 methods that had a base of one or two studies. In descending order of support, the 10 methods that received the best cumulative evidence scores (reflecting data quality and treatment outcomes) were brief intervention, motivational enhancement, social skills training, community reinforcement approach, GABA (gamma-amno-butyric acid) agonist medication, opioid antagonist medication, behavior contracting, client-centered therapy, aversion therapy, and cognitive–behavioral marital therapy.

The obvious conclusion from this review that there is no single effective treatment for alcohol problems, or even a small number of treatment alternatives, was reinforced by the negative findings of Project MATCH (Project MATCH Research Group, 1997), a large multisite clinical trial of alcohol treatment alternatives. Problem drinkers ($N = 1,726$) were randomly assigned to one of three outpatient treatments (12-step facilitation, cognitive–behavioral, or motivational-enhancement therapy) that were similar along nonspecific dimensions, except that the motivational enhancement therapy involved fewer sessions. The study sought to identify pretreatment variables (e.g., client characteristics, psychiatric comorbidity, readiness to change) that enhanced outcomes in each treatment, but few matching variables were identified. All three groups showed reductions in drinking at the one-year follow-up, but the groups did not differ significantly. This result is similar to the common finding in the psychotherapy outcome literature indicating the equivalency of outcomes across different treatment approaches.

Another way to evaluate treatments is to consider both behavioral outcome data and the monetary cost of treatment, which is a key consideration in today's cost-conscious practice environment. In a cost-effectiveness analysis of 33 treatment methods for alcohol problems, Holder (1998) found that modalities with better evidence of effectiveness were not the most expensive ones, whereas modalities with poor evidence of effectiveness were in the higher cost range. Six methods with good evidence of effectiveness (brief motivational counseling, self-control training, stress management, social skills training, community reinforcement approach, marital behavioral therapy) were in the minimal ($0–99) to medium–low ($200–599) cost categories. Methods with no or insufficient evidence of effectiveness (aversion therapy, residential milieu, insight psychotherapy, certain pharmacotherapies) were in the medium–high ($600–999) to high cost ($\geq$ $1,000$) categories.

These findings indicate that there are several effective outpatient interventions for alcohol problems that tend to be relatively briefer, less intensive, and less costly, but that no single approach produces superior outcomes. Treatment manuals are available for the three interventions used in Project MATCH (Kadden et al., 1992; Miller, Zweben, DiClemente, & Rychtarik, 1992; Nowinski, Baker, & Carroll, 1992) and for the Community Reinforcement Approach (Budney & Higgins, 1998; Sisson & Azrin, 1989).

Given these findings, attention has shifted away from developing new psychosocial treatments that are technically different from existing ones toward expanding access to effective, lower cost, and lower threshold services, especially for the underserved majority with mild to moderate problems. Reaching them before their problems become more serious and difficult to change is an important public health goal, because collectively this population segment contributes the bulk of cost and harm as a result of alcohol-related problems (IOM, 1990). As described next, promising developments in service of this agenda include brief interventions and guided self-change approaches, new pharmacotherapies, and new mutual help groups.

Lower Threshold Brief Interventions

Burke, Arkowitz, and Dunn (2002) provided a recent review of research on the efficacy of motivational interviewing (MI; Miller & Rollnick, 2002), the best known brief intervention, and its several adaptations, and M. B. Sobell and L. C. Sobell (1993, 1998) described the related guided self-change approach. These interventions generally seek to empower alcohol and drug abusers with the understanding and information they need to facilitate and manage their own addictive behavior change process when they are motivated to do so. Although there are some differences among the approaches, all are briefer, less intensive, and more accessible than clinical treatments and can be offered in a range of settings by trained nonspecialist providers (Zweben & Fleming, 1999). Typically, brief interventions assess client motivation and resources for change, promote motivation for positive change by exploring the relative merits of substance abuse versus a sober lifestyle, and tailor short and longer term goals accordingly, all in a nonjudgmental, supportive context. Many effective brief interventions also include feedback and advice about behavior change goals and strategies (e.g., see Project MATCH).

Outcome research has shown that, for some clients, especially males with mild to moderate alcohol problems, the brief intervention alone is sufficient to facilitate positive outcomes, including reduced drinking and improved health status (Burke et al., 2002; Larimer et al., 1998; Zweben & Fleming, 1999). In the case of dependent drinkers, brief interventions have been found to increase referrals to specialized care, but they generally are not sufficient to resolve these clients' more serious problems. Although Miller and Rollnick (2002) recently deemphasized the role of feedback and advice in MI (the best known variant among the general class of brief interventions), dismantling studies have not been conducted to identify the essential components of effective brief interventions. What is clear is that the majority of positive studies included information, feedback, and advice for drinking behavior change as part of their intervention (Burke et al., 2002).

Pharmacotherapy

Larimer et al. (1998) reviewed developments in drug treatments for alcohol problems, which are summarized in this section. Antabuse (disulfiram) has been available for decades, but its widespread or coerced use is not justified empirically for most alcohol-dependent clients (Shuckit, 1996). In 1995, naltrexone (ReVia), an opiate antagonist, was approved by the Food and Drug Administration (FDA) for the treatment of drinking problems, based on evidence showing that it increased the time to the first posttreatment drinking episode, decreased the number of posttreatment drinking days, and decreased quantities consumed per drinking day (e.g., O'Malley et al., 1992). Naltrexone thus appears useful early during the posttreatment interval, but it does not improve longer term abstinence rates over psychological counseling alone (O'Malley et al., 1996). Other drugs now under investigation as potential alcohol treatments include (a) acamprosate (calcium acetyl homotaurine), which is approved for use in Europe and appears to reduce the frequency, but not the intensity, of drinking episodes; (b) buspirone (BuSpar), an antianxiety drug that may selectively help alcohol dependent clients with comorbid anxiety disorders; and (c) selective serotonin reuptake inhibitors (SSRIs) for treating alcohol-dependent clients with comorbid depressive disorders. A key question now being researched is whether combining psychosocial and drug therapies enhances outcomes.

Mutual Help Groups

AA and similar abstinence-oriented groups for other drugs of abuse have been a mainstay among helping resources for substance abusers for decades. However, the 12-step principles, spiritual orientation, and abstinence requirement of these groups are not universally appealing. In recent years, several alternative mutual help groups, including Moderation Management, Rational Recovery, Women for Sobriety, and Secular Organization for Sobriety, have arisen to meet the needs of problem drinkers who want a more secular approach to problem resolution, want to entertain the possibility of moderate drinking, or both (Humphreys & Tucker, 2002). None of these approaches, including AA, have been adequately evaluated with respect to drinking outcomes, but they serve an important need in providing an anonymous, low threshold alternative to formal treatment.

Summary and Recommendations for Alcohol-Related Interventions

These recent changes in the alcohol treatment delivery system reflect a growing appreciation for the facts that alcohol problems are common, present in a variety of ways outside of specialized care settings, may resolve readily with minimal interventions in some affected persons, but are a chronic, relapsing disorder in others. A single help-seeking episode may not always be sufficient to produce stable change, but, with easier access to a range of services, individuals will be better able to find the kind of help they need when they need it.

INTERVENTIONS FOR OTHER DRUGS OF ABUSE

In the United States, treatment for drug dependence is offered in more than 11,000 specialized treatment facilities and settings (National Institute on Drug Abuse [NIDA], 1999). Treatment settings include medical hospitals (used primarily for short-term detoxification), private or state-funded residential drug abuse treatment facilities, and community outpatient or day treatment programs. Public providers greatly outnumber private providers and are more accessible to uninsured and indigent consumers, although often such consumers must wait several months for services.

Drug abuse treatment programs in the United States almost exclusively serve individuals with serious and chronic problems. Few engage persons who experiment with or use drugs intermittently. The illegal status of most abused drugs is a significant barrier to engaging at-risk groups in early interventions. Thus, like alcohol treatments, drug abuse treatments do not reach the majority of persons in need, and expanding the range and goals of interventions for drug-related problems, including reducing HIV/AIDS risk, is a priority of NIDA. Despite the accessibility of mutual help groups like NA and Cocaine Anonymous (CA), these groups tend to attract only persons with more severe drug problems.

Like interventions for alcohol problems, drug treatment has evolved from focusing on eliminating drug use to addressing a complex array of associated negative health, social, legal, and psychological problems. Clinical, pharmacological, and mutual help group interventions often are supplemented with family, child care, vocational, mental health, medical, educational, AIDS/HIV, legal, financial, and housing interventions in a comprehensive treatment plan. Multidimensional and multidisciplinary approaches to the presentation of symptoms and causes of drug abuse treat the person holistically and are designed to integrate treatment of all life problems associated with a drug-abusing lifestyle.

Engagement in drug treatment usually results from several internal and external motivating forces. The common belief that a person with a drug problem must "hit bottom" before he or she can benefit from treatment is invalid. Motivational interventions developed for alcohol problems have been generalized to increase motivation for drug abuse treatment engagement and addictive behavior change. External motivators, such as those used by the criminal justice system, child welfare programs, and employment assistance programs, also figure prominently in drug abuse treatment. These systems often offer treatment as an alternative to the severe consequences of imprisonment and loss of child custody or employment. Coercive treatment referrals and negative reinforcement contingencies have been successful in motivating drug abusers to enter and engage treatment. Outcomes among coerced and volunteer clients are similar, although coerced clients often attend more sessions (Stitzer & McCaul, 1987).

Research-Based Drug Treatment Principles and Modalities

NIDA (1999) has recently published a research-based guide to drug addiction treatment. Exhibit 2.1 lists 13 principles of effective treatment from NIDA's guide, which can be readily applied in most treatment models and settings. The principles emphasize the need for a range of interventions, making interventions readily available, not limiting services to detoxification, addressing life problems related to drug abuse, continuously monitoring drug use during interventions, providing aftercare services, and reducing risk of HIV and other STDs.

EXHIBIT 2.1
National Institute on Drug Abuse Principles of Effective Drug
Addiction Treatment

1. No single treatment is appropriate for all individuals.
2. Treatment needs to be readily available.
3. Effective treatment attends to multiple needs of the individual, not just his or her drug use.
4. Treatment needs to be flexible and to provide ongoing assessments of patients needs.
5. Remaining in treatment for an adequate period of time is critical for treatment effectiveness.
6. Individual or group counseling and other behavioral therapies are critical components of effective treatment for addiction.
7. Medications are an important element of treatment for many patients, especially when combined with counseling and other behavioral therapies.
8. Addicted or drug-abusing individuals with coexisting mental disorders should have both disorders treated in an integrated way.
9. Medical detoxification is only the first stage of addiction treatment and by itself does little to change long-term drug use.
10. Treatment does not need to be voluntary to be effective.
11. Possible drug use during treatment must be monitored continuously.
12. Treatment programs should provide assessment for HIV/AIDS, hepatitis B and C, tuberculosis and infectious diseases, and counseling to help patients modify or change behaviors that place themselves or others at risk of infection.
13. Recovery from drug addiction can be a long-term process and frequently requires multiple episodes of treatment.

Note. From *Principles of Drug Addiction Treatment: A Research-Based Guide* (NIH Publication No. 99-4180), 1999, Bethesda, MD: National Institute on Drug Abuse, National Institutes of Health. In the public domain.

Although much misinformation persists about substance abuse treatment and its ineffectiveness, the field has made great strides over the past decade or so. Various substance abuse interventions reduce drug use by 40 to 60% on average (NIDA, 1999). This is comparable to treatment success rates for several chronic disorders, including asthma and hypertension. Intervention modalities summarized have been found effective in controlled outcome studies and are identified in the NIDA drug addiction treatment guide (1999). They generally focus on specific dimensions of abuse or dependence among subgroups of drug abusers and thus are not designed to replace, but rather to supplement, the comprehensive approach to drug abuse treatment described earlier.

Agonist Maintenance Treatment

This outpatient pharmacotherapy for opiate addicts involves synthetic opiate agonist medication, usually methadone, requiring once daily doses, or the longer acting LAAM (levo-alpha-acetylmethoadol), requiring doses once every three days. These agonists alleviate the opiate withdrawal syndrome and block the effects of illicit opiate use. When delivered as part of a program that includes social and vocational rehabilitation and counseling to reduce illegal activities, agonist treatment can reduce illicit opiate use, criminal activities and arrests, and increase employment (Ball & Ross, 1991; Dole, Nyswander, & Warner 1968; Dole et al., 1969). When methadone maintenance treatment is offered without drug counseling and with minimal other services, it is much less effective (McLellan, Arndt, Metzger, Woody, & O'Brien, 1993). Methadone maintenance also reduces the risk and seroprevalence of HIV infection by reducing injection drug use and risky sexual behavior (Metzger, Navaline, & Woody, 1998). Despite its successes, agonist therapy is not effective long-term in maintaining abstinence from illicit opiate use once the therapy has been discontinued (Kleber & Riordan, 1982; Milby, 1988). For this reason, chronic opiate addicts often are maintained on methadone for years.

Individualized Drug Counseling

Counseling focuses on reducing, if not eliminating, illicit drug use and associated problems, including illegal activities, unemployment and underemployment, impaired relationships, and lack of recreational and social activities that do not involve drug use. Use of support groups such as NA and CA is usually encouraged. Client progress toward individualized goals is continually monitored, especially drug use episodes, and the counseling plan and goals are modified as needed. Combining counseling with methadone maintenance treatment reduces opiate use compared to using agonist therapy alone (McLellan et al., 1993). Counseling also facilitates the identification and treatment of drug abusers who have comorbid mental health problems, which improves their outcomes (Woody et al., 1983).

Individual drug counseling was a core component in most of the 55 drug treatment programs investigated in the national Drug Abuse Treatment Outcomes Study (Simpson, Joe, Fletcher, Hubbard, & Anglin, 1999). Although the unique contributions of drug counseling to outcomes were not studied directly, at the one-year follow-up, 23.5% of the cocaine dependent participants ($N = 1,605$) reported weekly cocaine use, compared to 73.1% before treatment. The association between good outcomes and longer treatment durations was especially notable for patients with more serious problems.

Behavior Therapy

Behavioral interventions have long been used in the treatment of substance abuse and have generally shown favorable outcomes (Higgins & Silverman, 1999). Among the behavioral interventions shown to be effective in controlled outcomes studies with drug abusers are several variations of the community reinforcement approach (CRA) and a behavioral drug treatment for adolescents. Higgins and colleagues were instrumental in adapting Hunt and Azrin's (1973) seminal CRA work with alcoholics for use with cocaine and opiate addicts; a manual for their CRA Plus Vouchers program is available (Budney & Higgins, 1998). The intervention targets behaviors contributing to drug use—family interactions, work behaviors, and so forth—that are monitored regularly, along with drug testing. Drug-free urine and other behavior-change goals are reinforced with vouchers that are redeemable for drug-free social and recreational reinforcers. The approach has been found to reduce cocaine use and to help establish and sustain abstinence (Higgins et al., 1994). When used in the context of methadone maintenance treatment, the CRA-voucher intervention has been shown to reduce heroin and cocaine use (Silverman et al., 1996).

Another effective variation of the CRA is the behavioral day treatment program developed by Milby, Schumacher, and colleagues for homeless cocaine-dependent persons. The intervention involves abstinence contingencies for access to drug-free housing and work opportunities and vouchers for recreational items contingent on treatment goal attainment. It has been found to increase abstinence and reduce homelessness (Milby et al., 2000; Milby et al., 1996).

In behavioral therapy for adolescents, family members monitor and reinforce behavior change (Azrin et al., 1994). Praise, access to valued nondrug activities and privileges, and material goods reinforce change. Drug use is monitored regularly with urine tests. The approach has been found to reduce drug and alcohol use, increase abstinence, and improve functioning, including school or employment attendance, family relationships, depression, and reduced out-of-home placement and institutionalization (Azrin et al., 1994, 1996).

Motivational Enhancement Therapy

This brief intervention, described earlier as effective for mild to moderate alcohol problems, has been adapted for use with drug-abusing clients but this adaptation has not been applied and evaluated as extensively as the original intervention for alcohol (Zweben & Fleming, 1999). Budney et al. (1997) found that brief motivational interventions reduced marijuana use in marijuana-dependent clients, and Saunders, Wilkinson, and Phillips (1995) observed short-term improvements among methadone patients who received a brief intervention along with an educational intervention. However, other studies reviewed by Zweben and Fleming (1999) have yielded equivocal or negative results. The approach requires more study with drug abusers.

Relapse Prevention

Developed by Marlatt and Gordon (1985) for use with problem drinkers, relapse prevention (RP) has been adapted for use with cocaine- and other drug-abusing clients. RP has positive posttreatment effects, but effects during treatment are not readily detectable (Carroll et al., 1994). This pattern is not surprising, given that RP focuses on reducing posttreatment relapse risk. RP rejects the loss-of-control notion that any substance use will lead to abuse and systematically analyzes situations, feelings, and cognitions that increase the risk of use, with emphasis placed on distinguishing determinants of lapses and relapses. Developing alternative behaviors and coping responses to the high-risk situations is a key intervention goal. See Marlatt and Gordon (1985) for a detailed discussion of the approach.

Supportive–Expressive Psychotherapy

This manualized, relatively brief therapy has been adapted for use with heroin and cocaine addicts (Luborsky, 1984). It uses supportive therapy techniques to help clients discuss personal experiences and struggles and to identify, process, and change problems with interpersonal relationships. When combined with drug counseling, opiate addicts on methadone maintenance who had comorbid psychopathology showed improved drug-related and functional outcomes compared to those who received drug counseling alone (Woody et al., 1983).

Family Therapy

Multidimensional Family Therapy for Adolescents (MDFT; Diamond & Liddle, 1996; Schmidt, Liddle, & Dakof, 1996) and Multisystematic

Therapy (MST; Henggeler, Schoenwald, Borduin, Rowland, & Cunning-ham, 1998) have demonstrated utility with adolescent drug abusers. Both are comprehensive, intensive outpatient interventions that emphasize family involvement and acquisition of age-appropriate social, school, and other living skills. MST, for example, has been found to reduce drug use during treatment and at six-months posttreatment and to decrease incarcerations and other placements outside of the home (Henggeler, Pickrel, Brondino, & Crouch 1996; Schoenwald, Ward, Henggeler, Pickrel, & Patel, 1996).

Family therapy is a component in the matrix model developed by Ling, Rawson, and colleagues that combines multiple effective interventions in a manualized program that includes family and group therapy, RP, drug and STD education, social support, and mutual help groups. Urine testing is used to monitor drug use and give clients feedback. Controlled studies have shown the approach to be effective in treating cocaine and methamphet-amine dependence (Huber et al., 1997; Rawson et al., 1995).

Harm Reduction: A Conspicuous Gap in U.S. Interventions for Drug Abuse

As this review indicates, an array of relatively effective interventions exists for alcohol and drug abuse. However, treatments do not reach many substance abusers, especially those who do not want to give up drug use but who want to reduce risks associated with it, including HIV infection (Marlatt, 1998). To address the needs of active drug abusers—and in so doing reduce HIV and other STD transmission into the general population—many British Commonwealth and other developed countries have adopted harm-reduction drug policies and interventions (described in MacCoun & Reuter, 2001; Marlatt, 1998). Harm reduction is a public health approach aimed at reducing the harmful consequences of substance use for both the user and the community. All changes that reduce risk of harm associated with substance use are encouraged, even if they fall short of abstinence. Abstinence remains the ultimate goal, but harm-reduction programs recog-nize abstinence may not be attainable for all or may take many attempts to achieve. In the interim, steps can be taken to prevent or minimize substance abuse harm. These may include clean needle exchanges, condom distribution, methadone maintenance, and drug treatment on demand with minimal delays.

Harm-reduction principles and programs depart significantly from U.S. laws, policies, and treatment approaches that variously criminalize drug use and stigmatize users. Harm reduction remains controversial in the United States, despite growing evidence of its effectiveness in reducing HIV risk and seroprevalence rates. In 1997 the National Institutes of Health (NIH) issued a consensus statement documenting the effectiveness of needle exchanges in reducing the spread of HIV/AIDS. A ban continues, however, against the use of federal monies for needle exchanges. Despite significant opposition, including at the federal level, harm reduction programs are gaining a place in American interventions for substance abuse.

CONCLUSION

The U.S. substance abuse services system clearly requires expansion to serve the unmet needs of persons with mild to moderate problems and those with more serious problems who do not enter abstinence-oriented treatments but who wish to reduce the harm associated with substance use (Humphreys & Tucker, 2002). Clinical treatments and mutual help groups will continue to be an important part of an expanded continuum of care, but they should be augmented by a range of interventions that better match the range of consumer needs and preferences and that span community and nonspecialized health care settings.

This expansion will likely involve continued initiatives in the voluntary sector. Mutual help groups that support a broader range of behavior change goals than AA are developing, and the harm-reduction movement, another grassroots initiative, is a growing, though controversial, presence in the United States. Harm-reduction approaches deserve more consideration as a preventive strategy for HIV/AIDS, given that about a third of new HIV infections are associated with substance use, especially injection drug use (NIH, 1997).

Within the health care system, the dissemination of brief interventions in primary care, emergency departments, and other medical settings is central to expanding services for substance abuse (Zweben & Fleming, 1999). As managed care organizations continue to limit utilization of services other than primary care visits (Howard et al., 1996), people with substance abuse and other mental health problems will increasingly present in nonspecialized health care settings. Psychologists are well-suited to provide or supervise integrated behavioral health care in medical settings because of their expertise in behavior change technologies and their comprehensive knowledge of mental health disorders (Miller & Brown, 1997).

Although an expansion of services is desirable, there will be a continuing need for specialized clinical treatments, including inpatient programs, for alcohol- and drug-dependent individuals. In the public sector, treatment slots are limited and often involve long waiting lists, especially in urban areas. Making treatment available "on demand" has been found to increase treatment entry (reviewed by Tucker & Davison, 2000), and this organizational change deserves consideration as a means to increase use of substance abuse services. In the private sector, although many health plans now include a behavioral health benefit, the number and length of reimbursed services (e.g., outpatient therapy sessions) usually are quite limited, and reimbursement levels continue to lag behind coverage for comparable ambulatory medical services (Strum & Wells, 2000). Recent mental health parity legislation has done little to remedy this long-standing and worsening discrepancy in coverage, and the original federal mental health parity legislation, passed in 1996, did not apply to substance abuse services.

As these discrepancies in benefits suggest, there are issues of values, economics, and politics embedded in how U.S. society allocates its health care dollars and configures helping services for health and behavioral health problems. As stated by Strum and Wells (2000), "The past decade has witnessed declining insurance coverage for mental health care, while at the same time, rapid advances have been made in efficacious treatments and clinical practice guidelines for major psychiatric disorders" (p. 254). As discussed earlier in the chapter, this is true for alcohol and drug problems. However, even if the relevant insurance and technology transfer issues were to be remedied, many substance abusers will likely continue to avoid professional services for substance-related problems because of the associated risks and stigma. The risks are especially keen for illegal drug abusers because of the punitive, zero-tolerance stance of the U.S. war on drugs. Whether revisions in federal and state drug laws and policies would be sufficient to shift public opinion about substance abuse in a more compassionate direction is unknown. The harm-reduction movement in Europe and elsewhere suggests that such change is possible. In the absence of such initiatives, the U.S. prison population will almost certainly continue to grow because of drug-related convictions, professional services will continue to be underutilized, and the voluntary helping sector will continue to expand and diversify, because it offers help to substance abusers without undue risk to their civil liberties.

REFERENCES

Allen, J. P., & Columbus, M. (Eds.). (1995). *Assessing alcohol problems: A guide for clinicians and researchers* (Treatment Handbook Series, No. 4). Bethesda, MD: National Institute of Alcohol Abuse and Alcoholism.

American Psychiatric Association. (1994). *Diagnostic and statistical manual of mental disorders* (4th ed.). Washington DC: Author.

Ames, G., Schmidt, C., Klee, L., & Saltz, R. (1996). Combining methods to identify new measures of women's drinking problems Part I: The ethnographic stage. *Addiction, 91*, 829–844.

Anton, R. F., Litton, R. Z., & Allen, J. P. (1995). Biological assessment of alcohol consumption. In J. P. Allen & M. Columbus (Eds.), *Assessing alcohol problems:*

A *guide for clinicians and researchers* (Treatment Handbook Series, No. 4, pp. 31–40). Bethesda, MD: National Institute of Alcohol Abuse and Alcoholism.

Azrin, N. H., Acierno, R., Kogan, E., Donahue, B., Besalel, V., & McMahon, P. T. (1996). Follow-up results of supportive versus behavioral therapy for illicit drug abuse. *Behavioral Research and Therapy, 34,* 41–46.

Azrin, N. H., McMahon, P. T., Donahue, B., Besalel, V., Lapinski, K. J., Kogan, E., et al. (1994). Behavioral therapy for drug abuse: A controlled treatment outcome study. *Behavioral Research and Therapy, 32,* 857–866.

Babor, T. F., Brown, J., & Del Boca, F. K. (1990). Validity of self-reports in applied research on addictive behaviors: Fact or fiction? *Addictive Behaviors, 12,* 5–32.

Ball, J. C., & Ross, A. (1991). *The effectiveness of methadone treatment.* New York: Springer-Verlag.

Beck, A. T., Ward, C. H., Mendelson, M., Mock, J. , & Erbaugh, J. (1961). An inventory for measuring depression. *Archives of General Psychiatry, 4,* 561–571.

Budney, A. J., & Higgins, S. T. (1998). *A community reinforcement plus vouchers approach: Treating cocaine addiction* (NIDA Therapy Manuals for Drug Addiction, Manual 2, NIH Publication No. 98:4309). Rockville, MD: National Institute on Drug Abuse.

Budney, A .J., Kandel, D. B., Cherek, D. R., Martin, B. R., Stephens, R. S., & Roffman, R. (1997). Marijuana use and dependence. *Drug and Alcohol Dependence, 45,* 1–11.

Burke, B. L., Arkowitz, H., & Dunn, C. (2002). The efficacy of motivational interviewing and its adaptations: What we know so far. In W. R Miller & S. Rollnick (Eds.), *Motivational interviewing: Preparing people for change* (2nd ed., pp. 217–250). New York: Guilford Press.

Cahalan, D. (1970). *Problem drinkers: A national survey.* San Francisco: Jossey-Bass.

Carey, K. B., & Teitlbaum, L. M. (1996). Goals and methods of alcohol assessment. *Professional Psychology: Research and Practice, 27,* 460–466.

Carroll, K. M. (1999). Behavioral and cognitive–behavioral treatments. In B. S. McCrady & E. E. Epstein (Eds.), *Addictions: A comprehensive guidebook* (pp. 187–215). New York: Oxford University Press.

Carroll, K., Rounsaville, B., Nich, C., Gordon, L., Wirtz, P., & Gawin, F. (1994). One year follow-up of psychotherapy and pharmacotherapy for cocaine dependence; Delayed emergence of psychotherapy effects. *Archives of General Psychiatry, 51,* 989–997.

Cook, R. F., Bernstein, A. D., Arrington, T. A., Andrews, C. M., & Marshall, G. A. (1995). Methods for assessing drug use prevalence in the workplace: A comparison of self-report, urinalysis, and hair analysis. *International Journal of the Addictions, 30,* 403–426.

Derogatis, L. R. (1977). *SCL–90: Administration, scoring and procedures manual for the revised version.* Baltimore: Clinical Psychometrics Research.

Diamond, G. S., & Liddle, H. A. (1996). Resolving a therapeutic impasse between parents and adolescents in Multi-Dimensional Family Therapy. *Journal of Consulting and Clinical Psychology, 64*, 481–488.

Dole, V. P., Nyswander, M., & Warner, A. (1968). Successful treatment of 750 criminal addicts. *Journal of the American Medical Association, 206*, 2708–2711.

Dole, V. P., Robinson, W., Orraca, J., Towns, E., Searcy, P., & Caine, E. (1969). Methadone treatment of randomly selected criminal addicts. *Journal of the American Medical Association, 280*, 1372–1375.

Donovan, D. M. (1999). Assessment strategies and measures in addictive behaviors. In B. S. McCrady & E. E. Epstein (Eds.), *Addictions: A comprehensive guidebook* (pp. 187–215). New York: Oxford University Press.

Ennett, S. T., Tobler, N. S., Ringwalt, C. L., & Flewelling, R. L. (1994). How effective is drug resistance education? A meta-analysis of Project DARE outcome evaluations. *American Journal Public Health, 84*, 1394–1401.

Finney, J. W., Moos, R. H., & Brennan, P. L. (1991). The Drinking Problem Index: A measure to assess alcohol-related problems among older adults. *Journal of Substance Abuse, 3*, 395–404.

Fischman, M., & Johanson, C. (1996). "Cocaine." In C. Schuster & M. Kuhar (Eds.), *Pharmacological aspects of drug dependence toward an integrated neurobehavior approach* (pp. 159–195). New York: Springer.

Gavin, D. R., Ross, H. E., & Skinner, H. (1989). Diagnostic validity of the Drug Abuse Screening Test in the Assessment of DSM–III drug disorders. *British Journal of Addiction, 84*, 301–307.

Grant, B. F., Chou, S. P., Pickering, R. P., & Hasin, D. S. (1992). Empirical subtypes of DSM–III–R alcohol dependence: United States, 1988. *Drug and Alcohol Dependence, 30*, 755– 784.

Grant, B. F., & Dawson, D. A. (1999). Alcohol and drug use, abuse, and dependence: Classification, prevalence, and comorbidity. In B. S. McCrady & E. E. Epstein (Eds.), *Addictions: A comprehensive guidebook* (pp. 9–29). New York: Oxford University Press.

Handmaker, N. S., Miller, W. R., & Manicke, M. (1999). Findings of a pilot study of motivational interviewing with pregnant drinkers. *Journal of Studies on Alcohol, 60*, 285–287.

Hasin, D. S., Trautman, K. D., Miele, G. M., Samet, S., & Endicott, J. (1996). Psychiatric Research Interview for Substance and Mental Disorders (PRISM): Reliability for substance abusers. *American Journal of Psychiatry, 153*, 1195–1201.

Henggeler, S. W., Pickrel, S. G., Brondino, M .J., & Crouch, J. L. (1996). Eliminating (almost) treatment dropout of substance abusing or dependent delinquents through home-based multidimensional therapy. *American Journal of Psychiatry, 153*, 427–438.

Henggeler, S. W., Schoenwald, S. K., Borduin, C. M., Rowland, M. D., & Cunningham, P. B. (1998). *Multisystemic treatment of antisocial behavior in children and adolescents.* New York: Guilford Press.

Higgins, S. T., Budney, A. J., Bickel, W. K., Foerg, F., Donham, R., & Badger, G. (1994). Incentives improve outcome in outpatient behavioral treatment of cocaine dependence. *Archives of General Psychiatry, 51*, 568–576.

Higgins, S. T., & Silverman, K. (1999). *Motivating behavioral change among illicit-drug abusers: Research on contingency management interventions.* Washington, DC: American Psychological Association.

Hoffman J. A., Wish, E. D., Koman, J. J., Schneider, S. J., Flynn, P. M., & Luckey, J. W. (1995). Self-reported drug use compared with hair analysis and urinalysis. *Problems of drug dependence 1994: Proceedings of the 56th Annual Scientific Meeting of The College on Problems of Drug Dependence* (Vol. II, National Institute of Drug Abuse Research Monograph Series), 327. Rockville, MD: National Institute on Drug Abuse.

Holder, H (1998). The cost offsets of alcoholism treatment. In M. Galanter (Ed.), *Recent developments in alcoholism (Vol. 14): The consequences of alcoholism* (pp. 361–374). New York: Plenum Press.

Howard, K. I., Cornille, T. A., Lyons, J. S., Vessey, J. T., Jueger, R. H., & Saunders, S. M. (1996). Patterns of mental health service utilization. *Archives of General Psychiatry, 53*, 696–703.

Huber, A., Ling, W., Shoptaw, S., Gulati, V., Brethen, P., & Rawson, R. (1997). Integrating treatments for methamphetamine abuse: A psychosocial perspective. *Journal of Addictive Diseases, 16*, 41–50.

Humphreys, K., & Tucker, J. A. (2002). Toward more responsive and effective intervention systems for alcohol-related problems. *Addiction, 97*, 126–132.

Hunt, G. M., & Azrin, N. (1973). A community reinforcement approach to alcoholism. *Behavior Research and Therapy, 11*, 91–104.

Institute of Medicine (IOM). (1990). *Broadening the base of treatment for alcohol problems.* Washington, DC: National Academy Press.

Jellinek, E. M. (1960). *The disease concept of alcoholism.* New Brunswick, NJ: Hill House.

Kadden, R., Carroll, K., Donovan, D., Cooney, N., Monti, P., Abrams, D., et al. (1992). *Cognitive–behavioral coping skills therapy manual: A clinical research guide for therapists treating individuals with alcohol abuse and dependence* (DHHS Publication No. [ADM]92–1895). Rockville, MD: National Institute on Alcohol Abuse and Alcoholism, Department of Health and Human Services.

Kleber, H. D., & Riordan, C. E. (1982). The treatment of narcotic withdrawal: A historical review. *Journal of Clinical Psychiatry, 43*, 30–34.

Larimer, M. E., Marlatt, G. A., Baer, J. S., Quigley, L. A., Blume, A. W., & Hawkins, E. H. (1998). Harm reduction for alcohol problems: Expanding access to and acceptability of prevention and treatment services. In G. A. Marlatt (Ed.), *Harm reduction: Pragmatic strategies for managing high-risk behaviors* (pp. 69–121). New York: Guilford Press.

Luborsky, L. (1984). *Principles of psychoanalytic psychotherapy: A manual for supportive–expressive (SE) treatment.* New York: Basic Books.

MacCoun, R. J., & Reuter, P. (2001). *Drug War heresies: Learning from other vices, times, and places*. Cambridge: Cambridge University Press.

Maisto, S. A., Carey, K. B., & Bradizza, C. M. (1999). Social learning theory. In K. E. Leonard & H. T. Blane (Eds.), *Psychological theories of drinking and alcoholism* (pp. 106–163). New York: Guilford Press.

Maisto, S. A., & McKay, J. R. (1995). Diagnosis. In J. P. Allen & M. Columbus (Eds.), *Assessing alcohol problems: A guide for clinicians and researchers* (Treatment Handbook Series, No. 4, pp. 41–54). Bethesda, MD: National Institute of Alcohol Abuse and Alcoholism.

Mann, R. E., Sobell, L. C., Sobell, M. B., & Pavin, D. (1985). Family tree questionnaire for assessing family history of drinking problems. In D. J. Lettieri, J. E. Nelson, & M. A. Sayers (Eds.), *Alcoholism treatment assessment research instruments* (NIAAA treatment handbook series 2, pp. 162–166). Washington, DC: U.S. Government Printing Office.

Marlatt, G. A. (Ed.). (1998). *Harm reduction: Pragmatic strategies for managing high-risk behaviors* (pp. 69–121). New York: Guilford Press.

Marlatt, G. A., & Gordon, J. R. (Eds.). (1985). *Relapse prevention; Maintenance strategies in the treatment of addictive behaviors*. New York: Guilford Press.

Mayfield, D., McLeod, G., & Hall, P. (1974). The CAGE questionnaire: Validation of a new alcoholism instrument. *American Journal of Psychiatry, 131,* 1121–1123.

McLellan, A. T., Arndt, I., Metzger, D. S., Woody, G. E., & O'Brien, C. P. (1993). The effects of psychosocial services in substance abuse treatment. *Journal of the American Medical Association, 269,* 1953–1959.

McLellan, A. T., Luborsky, L., Woody, G. E., & O'Brien C. P. (1980). An improved diagnostic evaluation instrument for substance abuse patients: The Addiction Severity Index. *Journal of Nervous and Mental Disorders, 168,* 26–33.

Metzger, D. S., Navaline, H., & Woody, G. E. (1998). Drug abuse treatment as AIDS prevention. *Public Health Reports, 113*(Supp. 1), 97–106.

Milby, J. B. (1988). Methadone maintenance to abstinence: How many make it? *Journal of Nervous and Mental Disease, 176,* 409–422.

Milby, J. B., Schumacher, J. E., Raczynski, J. M., Caldwell, E., Engle, M., Michael, M., et al. (1996). Sufficient conditions for effective treatment of substance abusing homeless. *Drug and Alcohol Dependence, 43,* 39–47.

Milby, J. B., Schumacher, J. E., McNamara, C., Wallace, D., Usdan, S., McGill, T., et al. (2000). Initiating abstinence in cocaine abusing dually diagnosed homeless persons. *Drug and Alcohol Dependence, 60,* 55–67.

Miller, W. R., Andrews, N. R., Wilbourne, P., & Bennett, M. E. (1998). A wealth of alternatives: Effective treatment for alcohol problems. In W. R. Miller & N. Heather (Eds.), *Treating addictive behaviors* (2nd ed., pp. 203–216). New York: Plenum Press.

Miller, W. R., & Brown, S. A. (1997). Why psychologists should treat alcohol and drug problems. *American Psychologist, 52,* 1269–1279.

Miller, W. R., & Rollnick, S. (2002). *Motivational interviewing: Preparing people to change addictive behavior* (2nd ed.). New York: Guilford Press.

Miller, W. R., & Tonigan, J. S. (1996). Assessing drinkers' motivation for change: The Stages of Change Readiness and Treatment Eagerness Scale (SOCRATES). *Psychology of Addictive Behaviors, 10,* 81–89.

Miller, W. R., Tonigan, J. S., & Longabaugh, R. (1995). *The Drinker Inventory of Consequences (DrInC): An instrument for assessing adverse consequences of alcohol abuse (test manual)* (NIAAA Project Match Monograph Series, Vol. 4). Rockville, MD: National Institute of Alcohol Abuse and Alcoholism.

Miller, W. R., Zweben, A., DiClemente, C. C., & Rychtarik, R. G. (1992). *Motivational enhancement therapy manual: A clinical research guide for therapists treating individuals with alcohol abuse and dependence* (DHHS Publication No. [ADM]92–1894). Rockville, MD: National Institute on Alcohol Abuse and Alcoholism, Department of Health and Human Services.

Millon, T. (1992). Millon Clinical Multiaxial Inventory: I and II. *Journal of Counseling and Development, 70*(3), 421–426.

Moos, R. H., Finney, J. W., & Cronkite, R. (1990). *Alcoholism treatment: Context, process, and outcome.* New York: Oxford University Press.

Morey, L. C. (1996). *An interpretive guide to the Personality Assessment Inventory (PAI).* Odessa, FL: Psychological Assessment Resources.

Narrow, W. E., Regier, D. A., Rae, D. S., Manderscheid, R. W., & Locke, B. Z. (1993). Use of services by persons with mental and addictive disorders. *Archives of General Psychiatry, 50,* 95–107.

National Institute on Drug Abuse (NIDA). (1999). *Principles of drug addiction treatment: A research-based guide* (National Institutes of Health Publication No. 99–4180). Bethesda, MD: NIDA/NIH.

National Institutes of Health (NIH). (1997). *Interventions to prevent HIV risk behaviors* (NIH Consensus Statement No. 15(2), pp. 1–41). Bethesda, MD: Author.

Nowinski, J., Baker, S., & Carroll, K. (1992). *Twelve step facilitation therapy manual: A clinical research guide for therapists treating individuals with alcohol abuse and dependence* (DHHS Publication No. [ADM]92–1893). Rockville, MD: National Institute on Alcohol Abuse and Alcoholism, Department of Health and Human Services.

O'Malley, S. S., Jaffe, A. J., Chang, G., Rode, S., Schottenfeld, R., Meyer, R., et al. (1992). Naltrexone and coping skills therapy for alcohol dependence: A controlled study. *Archives of General Psychiatry, 49,* 881–887.

O'Malley, S. S., Jaffe, A. J., Chang, G., Rode, S., Schottenfeld, R., Meyer, R., et al. (1996). Six-month follow-up of naltrexone and psychotherapy for alcohol dependence. *Archives of General Psychiatry, 53,* 217–224.

Prochaska, J. O., & DiClemente, C. D. (1986). Toward a comprehensive model of change. In W. R. Miller & N. Heather (Eds.), *Treating addictive behaviors: Processes of change* (pp. 3–27). New York: Plenum Press.

Project MATCH Research Group. (1997). Matching alcoholism treatment to client heterogenity: Project MATCH posttreatment drinking outcomes. *Journal of Studies on Alcohol, 58,* 7–29.

Rawson, R., Shoptaw, S., Obert, J. L., McCann, M., Hasson, A., Marinelli-Cassey, P., et al. (1995). An intensive outpatient approach for cocaine abuse: The Matrix model. *Journal of Substance Abuse Treatment, 12,* 117–127.

Regier, D. A., Narrow, W. E., Rae, D. S., Manderscheid, R. W., Locke, B. Z., & Goodwin, R. K. (1993). The de facto U.S. mental and addictive disorders service system. *Archives of General Psychiatry, 50,* 85–94.

Robins, L. N., Helzer, J. E., Croughan, J., & Ratcliff, K. S. (1981). The NIMH Diagnostic Interview Schedule: Its history, characteristics, and validity. *Archives of General Psychiatry, 38,* 381–389.

Russell, M. (1994). New assessment tools for drinking in pregnancy: T-ACE, TWEAK, and others. *Alcohol Health and Research World, 18,* 55–61.

Russell, M., Martier, S. S., Sokol, R. J., Jacobson, S., & Jacobson, J. (1991). Screening for pregnancy risk drinking: TWEAKING the tests. *Alcoholism: Clinical and Experimental Research, 15,* 638.

Salaspuro, M. (1994). Biological state markers of alcohol abuse. *Alcohol Health and Research World, 18,* 131–135.

Saunders, J. B., Aasland, O. G., Babor, T. F., de la Fuente, J. R., & Grant, M. (1993). Development of the Alcohol Use Disorders Identification Test (AUDIT): WHO collaborative project on early detection of persons with harmful alcohol consumption. *Addiction, 88,* 296–303.

Saunders, B., Wilkinson, C., & Phillips, M. (1995). The impact of a brief motivational intervention with opiate users attending a methadone program. *Addiction, 90,* 415–424.

Schmidt, S. E., Liddle, H. A., & Dakof, G. A. (1996). Effects of multidimensional family therapy: Relationship of changes in parenting practices to symptom reduction in adolescent substance abuse. *Journal of Family Psychology, 10,* 1–116.

Schober, R., & Annis, H. M. (1996). Barriers to help-seeking for change in drinking: A gender-focused review of the literature. *Addictive Behaviors, 21,* 81–92.

Schoenwald, S. K., Ward, D. M, Henggeler, S. W., Pickrel, S. G., & Patel, H. (1996). MSST treatment of substance abusing or dependent adolescent offenders: Costs of reducing incarceration, inpatient, and residential placement. *Journal of Child and Family Studies, 5,* 431–444.

Schumacher, J. E., & Milby, J. B. (1999). Alcohol and Drug Abuse. In J. M. Raczynski & R. J. DiClemente (Eds.), *Handbook of health promotion and disease prevention.* (pp. 207–228). New York: Plenum Press.

Selzer, M. L. (1971). The Michigan Alcoholism Screening Test: The test for a new diagnostic instrument. *American Journal of Psychiatry, 127,* 1653–1658.

Shuckit, M. A. (1996). Recent developments in the pharmacotherapy of alcohol dependence. *Journal of Consulting and Clinical Psychology, 64,* 669–676.

Silverman, K., Higgins, S. T., Brooner, R. K, Montoya, I. D., Cone, E. J., Schuster, C. R., et al. (1996). Sustained abstinence in methadone maintenance patients through voucher-based reinforcement therapy. *Archives of General Psychiatry, 53,* 409–415.

Simpson, D. D., Joe, G. W., Fletcher B. W., Hubbard, R. L., & Anglin, M. D. (1999) A national evaluation of treatment outcomes for cocaine dependence. *Archives of General Psychiatry, 56,* 507–514.

Sisson, R. W., & Azrin, N. H. (1989). The community reinforcement approach. In R. K. Hester & W. R. Miller (Eds.), *Handbook of alcoholism approaches: Effective alternatives* (pp. 242–258). New York: Pergamon Press.

Skinner, H. A., & Horn, J. L. (1984). *Alcohol Dependence Scale (ADS) User's Guide.* Toronto: Addiction Research Foundation.

Sobell, L. C., Cunningham, J. A., & Sobell, M. B. (1996). Recovery from alcohol problems with and without treatment: Prevalence in two population studies. *American Journal of Public Health, 86,* 966–972.

Sobell, L. C., & Sobell, M. B. (1992). Timeline followback: A technique for assessing self-reported alcohol consumption. In R. Litten & J. Allen (Eds.), *Measuring alcohol consumption* (pp. 41–72). Totowa, NJ: Humana Press.

Sobell, M. B., & Sobell, L. C. (1993). *Problem drinkers: Guided self-change treatment.* New York: Guilford Press.

Sobell, M. B., & Sobell, L. C. (1998). Guiding self-change. In W. R. Miller & N. Heather (Eds.), *Treating addictive behaviors* (2nd ed., pp. 189–202). New York: Plenum Press.

Sobell, L. C., Toneatto, T. & Sobell, M. B. (1994). Behavioral assessment and treatment planning for alcohol, tobacco, and other drug problems: Current status with an emphasis on clinical applications. *Behavior Therapy, 25,* 533–580.

Sokol, R. J., Martier, S. S., & Ager, J. W. (1989). The T-ACE questions: Practical prenatal detection of risk drinking. *American Journal of Obstetrics and Gynecology, 160,* 863–870.

Stitzer, M., & McCaul, M. E. (1987). Criminal justice interventions with drug and alcohol abusers. In E. K. Morris & C. J. Braukmann (Eds.), *Behavioral approaches to crime and delinquency: A handbook of application, research and concepts* (pp. 331–361). New York: Plenum Press.

Strum, R., & Wells, K. (2000). Health insurance may be improving—But not for individuals with mental illness. *Health Services Research, 35,* 253–262.

Tarter, R. E., & Kirisci, L. (1997). The Drug Use Screening Inventory for adults: Psychometric structure and discriminative sensitivity. *American Journal of Drug and Alcohol Abuse, 23,* 207–219.

Tiffany, S. (1997). New perspectives on the measurement, manipulation and meaning of drug craving. *Human Psychopharmacology, 12,* 103–113.

Tucker, J. A. (1999). Changing addictive behavior: Historical and contemporary perspectives. In J. A. Tucker, D. M. Donovan, & G. A. Marlatt (Eds.), *Changing addictive behavior: Bridging clinical and public health perspectives* (pp. 3–44). New York: Guilford Press.

Tucker, J. A. (2001). Resolving alcohol and drug problems with and without interventions: Understanding relations between addictive behavior change and the use of services. *Substance Use and Misuse, 36,* 1501–1518.

Tucker, J. A. (2003). Natural resolution of alcohol-related problems. In M. Galanter (Ed.), *Recent developments in alcoholism (Vol. 16): Research on alcoholism treatment* (pp. 77–90). New York: Kluwer Academic/Plenum Press.

Tucker, J. A., & Davison, J. W. (2000). Waiting to see the doctor: The role of time constraints in the utilization of health and behavioral health services. In W. K. Bickel & R. E. Vuchinich (Eds.), *Reframing health behavior change with behavioral economics* (pp. 219–264). Mahwah, NJ: Erlbaum.

Tucker, J. A., Vuchinich, R. E., & Murphy, J. G. (2001). Assessment of substance misuse and related problems. In D. H. Barlow & A. M. Antony (Eds.), *Handbook of assessment, treatment planning, and outcome evaluation: Empirically supported strategies for psychological disorders* (pp. 415–452). New York: Guilford Press.

U.S. Department of Health and Human Services. (1997). *Ninth Special Report to the U.S. Congress on Alcohol and Health* (NIH Publication No. 97-4017). Bethesda, MD: National Institute on Alcohol Abuse and Alcoholism, National Institutes of Health.

White, H. R., & Bates, M. E. (1995). Cessation from cocaine use. *Addiction, 90,* 947–957.

Wolff, K., Farrell, M., Marsden, J., Monteiro, M. G., Ali, R., Welch, S., et al. (1999). A review of biological indicators of illicit drug use, practical considerations and clinical usefulness. *Addiction, 94,* 1279–1298.

Woody, G. E., Luborsky, L., McLellan, A. T., O'Brien, C. P., Beck, A. T., Blaine, J., et al. (1983). Psychotherapy for opiate addicts: Does it help? *Archives of General Psychiatry, 40,* 639–645.

World Health Organization (WHO). (1981). Nomenclature and classification of drugs and alcohol-related problems: A WHO memorandum. *Bulletin WHO, 59,* 225–242.

Zweben, A., & Fleming, M. F. (1999). Brief interventions for alcohol and drug problems. In J. A. Tucker, D. M. Donovan, & G. A. Marlatt (Eds.), *Changing addictive behavior: Bridging clinical and public health perspectives* (pp. 251–282). New York: Guilford Press.

3

CIGARETTE SMOKING

EDWIN B. FISHER, ROSS C. BROWNSON, ANDREW C. HEATH,
DOUGLAS A. LUKE, AND WALTON SUMNER II

The severe health risks of smoking have been widely known since 1950, when Wynder's and others' work identified smoking as a probable cause of lung cancer (Wynder & Graham, 1950; see also Doll & Hill, 1950; Levin, Goldstein, & Gerhardt, 1950; Schreck et al., 1950), subsequently confirmed by the first U.S. Surgeon General's Report on Smoking and Health in 1964 (U.S. PHS, 1964). Latest figures for the United States suggest that approximately 30% of all deaths in the 35- to 69-age group are smoking-related (American Cancer Society, 2003). Accordingly, the prevalence of smoking among adults has declined from 42% in 1965 to 23% in 2001 (CDC, 2003a), and about half of all adults who have smoked in this country have quit (U.S. DHHS, 1989). Nevertheless, with 23% of the adult population continuing to smoke and 17% of high school seniors reporting daily smoking (Johnston, O'Malley, & Bachman, 2003), this widespread, severe public health problem will persist for at least another generation. Problems associated with smoking will increase even more outside the United States, where smoking rates continue to rise and public health

Thanks to Ramaswamy Govindan, MD, for comments on benefits of smoking cessation among cancer patients.

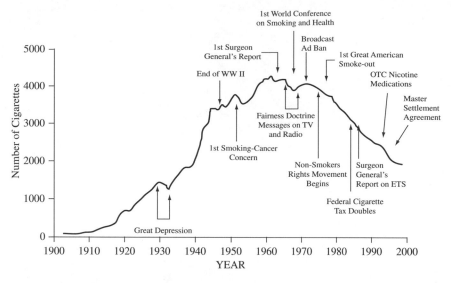

Figure 3.1. Adult per-capita cigarette consumption and major smoking and health events: United States, 1900–2002. From "Tobacco Surveillance in the United States," by G. A. Gianno, Dec. 10, 2003, Paper presented in the session *Where to Find Scientific Data to Support Best Practices in Tobacco Control*, National Conference on Tobacco or Health. Boston, MA. In the public domain.

initiatives are less advanced. A variety of factors both promoted and discouraged smoking in the United States during the 20th century. Cigarettes emerged as the most effective product ever devised to deliver highly addictive nicotine. Cigarette smoking is widely conditioned to cues throughout daily life. The anxiety-reducing and mood-elevating effects of nicotine make smoking especially attractive amid common psychological, social, and economic stressors of daily life. Cigarettes remain among the most heavily marketed consumer products in U.S. society. They are relatively inexpensive and readily available, even to those who are not old enough to purchase them legally. In spite of these diverse and strong factors that encourage smoking, millions have quit. Parallel to the range of factors encouraging smoking, a broad range of public health initiatives discourage smoking, including health information (e.g., Surgeon General's reports), public education and counter-marketing campaigns (e.g., American Legacy Foundation's Truth Campaign), legal and regulatory actions, and a variety of effective smoking-cessation interventions (Figure 3.1).

This chapter takes a broad approach to smoking, covering health effects and epidemiology, the interplay of addiction and biological causes with conditioning and psychological factors, factors related to the initiation of smoking in youth and to its continuance in adulthood, and approaches to preventing smoking and promoting smoking cessation.

EPIDEMIOLOGY OF SMOKING

Decades of research and thousands of epidemiological studies have established cigarette smoking as the "single most important preventable cause of premature death" (U.S. DHHS, 1989). This extensive research has shown that about one of every five American deaths is the result of cigarette smoking (CDC, 2003b). By applying estimates of risks of various health conditions related to smoking and estimates of the prevalence of smoking, health researchers have developed condition-specific estimates of smoking-related mortality. These include an estimated 152,757 cancer deaths per year (including 120,365 deaths from cancers of the lung, trachea, or bronchus), an estimated 181,327 deaths from cardiovascular disease, 90,965 deaths each year from emphysema and other respiratory diseases, and an estimated 3,000 deaths each year from environmental tobacco smoke or "passive smoking" (Brownson, Figgs, & Caisley, 2002). The reports of the U.S. Surgeon General (see http://www.cdc.gov/tobacco/) are excellent sources on the epidemiology of smoking.

Not as widely recognized as the effects of smoking on death rates are its influence even before the emergence of serious disease. A randomized controlled trial of smoking cessation advice found a clinically important decline in sinus complaints in the intervention group (Rose & Hamilton, 1978). In a comparison with quitters, persistent smokers were found to have a 7 to 15% greater increase in outpatient visits over five years, a 30 to 45% greater increase in admissions, and a 75 to 100% greater increase in days in hospital (Wagner, Curry, Grothaus, Saunders, & McBride, 1995).

As analytical epidemiology of the sort just reviewed characterizes risks of disease, descriptive epidemiology characterizes the smoking problem by person (e.g., age, gender, ethnicity), place (e.g., county of residence), and time (e.g., seasonal variation in risk factor patterns). A brief overview of the descriptive epidemiology of smoking in the United States helps to illustrate key issues in smoking control.

Person: High-Risk Groups

In 2001, an estimated 23.4% of adults were current smokers, including 25.5% of men and 21.5% of women (CDC, 2003a). In general, smoking prevalence is higher among poor individuals, reaching 29.8% among U.S. women and 38.7% among men with incomes below the poverty level (CDC,

1999a). Youth of lower socioeconomic status tend to have higher initiation rates (Tyas & Pederson, 1998). However, socioeconomic status interacts with other factors. For example, Michell and Amos (1997) have shown that adolescent females of high social status are more likely to smoke, whereas adolescent males of high social status were less vulnerable.

Smoking trends by educational status are diverging. Since the first Surgeon General's Report on Smoking in 1964, prevalence has declined among more highly educated groups, but it has remained stable among persons with less education (Pierce, Fiore, Novotny, Hatziandreu, & Davis, 1989). Among various racial and ethnic groups, the highest rate of current smoking is among American Indians and Alaskan Natives (36.2%) and the lowest rate is among Asians and Pacific Islanders (16.6%).

Approximately 80% of adults who use tobacco began before age 18 years (U.S. DHHS, 1994). In 2002, 57.2% of high school seniors reported ever trying cigarettes and 26.7% reported smoking in the previous 30 days (Johnston et al., 2003). Use in the previous 30 days among high school seniors is now approximately equal in males (27.4%) and females (25.5%). Prevalence among high school seniors today is highest (32.5%) among White students and lowest (12.1%) among Black students (Johnston et al., 2003).

Place: Geographic Variation

State-specific rates of adult smoking in the United States have shown substantial differences. In 2001, the highest rates of current smoking were shown in Kentucky (30.9%), Oklahoma (28.8%), West Virginia (28.2%), Ohio (27.7%), Indiana (27.5%) Nevada (27.0%), South Carolina (26.2%), and Alaska (26.1%). The lowest rates of current smoking were reported in Utah (13.3%), California (17.2%), Massachusetts (19.7%), Nebraska (20.4%), Oregon (20.5%), Hawaii (20.6%), Connecticut (20.8%) and the District of Columbia (20.8%; CDC, 2003a).

Time: Temporal Trends

As seen in Figure 3.2, the prevalence of cigarette smoking has declined substantially among U.S. adults over the past several decades, from 50.2% in 1965 to 25.5% in 2001 among men, and from 31.9% to 21.5% among women (CDC, 2003a). As seen in Figure 3.3, the 30-day prevalence of tobacco use among high school seniors decreased from the late 1970s to the mid-1980s, when prevalence was approximately 30%. However, during 1991 to 1997, smoking prevalence increased to 36.5%, but has declined again from 1997 through 2002 (Johnston et al., 2003).

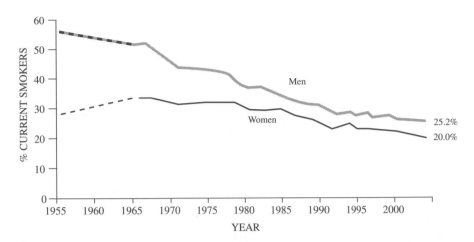

Figure 3.2. Trends in cigarette smoking among adults aged 18 years or older, by sex: United States, 1955–2002. Before 1992, *current smokers* were defined as people who reported having smoked ≥ 100 cigarettes and who currently smoked. Since 1992, *current smokers* were defined as persons who reported having smoked ≥ 100 cigarettes during their lifetimes and who reported now smoking every day or some days. From "Tobacco Surveillance in the United States," by G. A. Gianno, Dec. 10, 2003, Paper presented in the session *Where to Find Scientific Data to Support Best Practices in Tobacco Control*, National Conference on Tobacco or Health. Boston, MA. In the public domain.

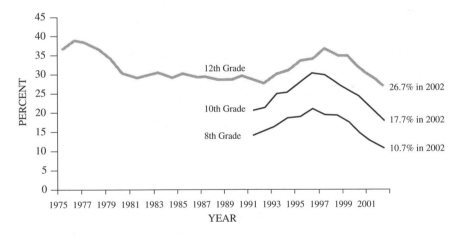

Figure 3.3. Trends in cigarette smoking anytime in the previous 30 days by grade in school: United States, 1975–2002. From *Monitoring the Future Surveys*, Institute for Social Research, University of Michigan, "Tobacco Surveillance in the United States," by G. A. Gianno, Dec. 10, 2003, Paper presented in the session *Where to Find Scientific Data to Support Best Practices in Tobacco Control*, National Conference on Tobacco or Health. Boston, MA. In the public domain.

One final aspect of the epidemiology of smoking should be highlighted. Smoking is a global problem that has increased dramatically worldwide. In response, international efforts to control tobacco are now emerging. For example, the World Health Organization (WHO) has established a Tobacco Free Initiative and has unanimously approved a Framework Convention on Tobacco Control that is "aimed at curbing tobacco-related deaths and disease" (WHO, 2003). This is the first international treaty negotiated under the auspices of WHO.

The convention requires countries to impose restrictions on tobacco advertising, sponsorship, and promotion; establish new labeling and clean indoor air controls; and strengthen legislation to clamp down on tobacco smuggling.

INTERACTIONS AMONG ADDICTION, CONDITIONING, AND GENETICS

At least from Descartes's dualism through much of the 20th century, thinking about human behavior often assumed a dichotomy between soma and psyche, nature and nurture. Frequently the two realms have been thought to be mutually exclusive so that, for example, if a problem includes chemical addiction, then only biological interventions would be useful and behavioral, psychological, or educational efforts would be fruitless.

Over the past 40 years, research in health psychology has articulated not the mutual exclusiveness of psyche and soma but rather their interaction and interdependence. In diseases such as diabetes, we understand that etiology, course, morbidity, and even mortality are strongly associated with behavioral and social forces (Glasgow et al., 1999). Old arguments over whether problems such as schizophrenia are *either* biological *or* psychological have been eclipsed by models integrating (a) biological and psychosocial factors in etiology (e.g., Walker, 2002); (b) familial and social factors in expression, course, and morbidity (e.g., Leff & Vaughn, 1985); (c) utility of family therapy in preventing relapse and rehospitalization (e.g., Falloon et al., 1982); and (d) neuropsychological models of pathognomonic behavior patterns (e.g., Salisbury et al., 1998).

Contemporary understanding of cigarette smoking reflects a similar emphasis on the interaction of psyche and soma. The following sections trace this view in terms of understanding smoking as an addiction and the role of genetics in that addiction and understanding how fundamental psychological factors, reinforcement, and conditioning interact with genetic factors to initiate and maintain that addiction.

Smoking as Addiction

The criteria for addiction to a drug are (a) compulsive pattern of drug use, (b) psychoactive or mood-altering effects involved in the pattern of drug taking, and (c) the drug functioning as a reinforcer that leads to additional drug consumption. As documented in the 1988 Surgeon General's Report, (a) smoking meets all these criteria, (b) nicotine is the drug in tobacco that causes addiction, and (c) the pharmacological and behavioral processes that determine tobacco addiction are similar to those that determine addiction to drugs such as heroin and cocaine (U.S. DHHS, 1988, p. 9). Note that the criteria for addiction are largely behavioral and psychological and that nicotine's functioning as a reinforcer is central to the definition. So smoking is an addiction, but this categorization rests largely on characteristics of smoking behavior and on the central role of reinforcement in addiction.

Nicotine as a Reinforcer

How nicotine maintains smoking behavior has been a topic of much research. The nicotine regulation or titration model (Jarvik, 1977; Kozlowski, Jarvik, & Gritz, 1975) held that smokers regulate their smoking to maintain a level of blood nicotine sufficient to *avoid withdrawal symptoms*. Subsequent research has placed more emphasis on positive and negative reinforcement other than relief of withdrawal symptoms (Pomerleau, Collins, Shiffman, & Pomerleau, 1993). These include mood elevation, anxiety reduction, and arousal from nicotine's stimulant properties (U.S. DHHS, 1988).

Several lines of research implicate reinforcing effects other than relief of withdrawal symptoms. For example, smokers who showed a strong preference for the highest among three concentrations of nicotine nasal spray reported greater positive subjective effects of the nicotine spray than those without a clear preference. They also smoked more in an ad lib smoking session and reported greater dependence. However, they did not report greater relief from withdrawal symptoms (Perkins, Grobe, & Fonte, 1997). In other studies, those who later recall symptoms such as dizziness, heart racing, or nausea in response to their first cigarette are *more* likely to become regular smokers and less likely to quit (Pomerleau et al., 1993; Shiffman, 1989). This is interpreted as showing sensitivity to nicotine as critical to its role as reinforcer. A major review of relapse to smoking (Niaura et al., 1988) also emphasized that the ex-smoker is prone to relapse not to reduce withdrawal symptoms per se but because of the likelihood of reinforcement by nicotine. That relapse is motivated by reinforcement by nicotine does not eliminate the role of negative emotions. Rather, negative affect may be a cue for smoking that may then be reinforced by nicotine's mood elevating or anxiety reducing effects. Relapse prevention should not focus on withdrawal symptoms, but instead include attention to negative affect that may provide powerful cues for nicotine's reinforcing effects.

Adding to the strength of nicotine as a reinforcer of smoking is the speed with which nicotine reaches the central nervous system (Rachlin, 1991): within about seven seconds of inhaling tobacco smoke (Pomerleau & Pomerleau, 1987, p. 117). In contrast, most disincentives for smoking are subtle, insidious, or much delayed, reducing their ability to discourage it. Smoking is an addiction, and powerful reinforcing properties of nicotine are central to that addiction. The next section discusses the evidence for genetic influence in smoking and the apparent pathway of that influence through nicotine's reinforcing effects.

Genetic Influences

Over the past decade, evidence has accumulated that genetic factors influence smoking, accounting for 46 to 84% of the variance in initiation of smoking and 58 to 74% of the variance in persistence (True et al., 1999). Genetic factors appear to affect the tendency to become addicted, given exposure to nicotine. Across different societies and across birth cohorts ranging from the beginning of the 20th century to the present, evidence has been consistent that genetic factors have a major effect on the probability that *exposure* to tobacco will progress to *regular smoking* and on the probability that *regular smoking* will progress to *persistent long-term smoking* (Heath & Madden, 1995). Consistent with the importance of both psyche and soma, expression of genotypes in smoking initiation and nicotine dependence is complex. Multiple environmental and psychological factors that are discussed at length in later sections of this chapter influence the pathways leading from genetic factors to persistent smoking (Heath et al., 1999, 2003; Kendler et al., 1999).

Research has begun to identify pathways through which specific genotypes lead to smoking. For example, a genetically based defect in enzymes necessary for metabolism of nicotine may protect against becoming addicted (Pianezza, Sellers, & Tyndale, 1998). Consistent with the emphasis on nicotine as reinforcer, it is striking that this and other research (Heath et al., 2003; Lerman et al., 1999) is coming to focus on genetic influences on reinforcing and other reactions to nicotine that differentiate (a) those who experiment with cigarettes from those who go on to become regular smokers, and (b) among regular smokers, those who become addicted.

Relationships between smoking and alcohol dependence illustrate the complexity of interactions among genetic and behavioral factors. In one study of both nicotine and alcohol dependence, the heritability of nicotine dependence was 60%, that of alcohol dependence was 55%, and the estimated correlation of these genetic components was +.68 (True et al., 1999). But the link is not just genetic. Smoking reduces reactivity to and increases the ability to tolerate alcohol (Madden, Heath, & Martin, 1997). Thus, smoking may well allow the drinker to drink more before experiencing aversive consequences of alcohol, facilitating patterns of heavy drinking. Heavier drinking may, in turn, lead to dependent drinking. Reciprocally, the ability to drink more may reinforce smoking. These relationships of smoking and alcohol consumption are especially troubling because both are major risk factors for head, neck, and several other cancers and act synergistically on cancer risk.

Conditioning of Smoking

In addition to reinforcement as a way of characterizing the effects of nicotine leading to addiction, a second fundamental principal of psychology that applies to smoking is conditioning. The average, pack-a-day smoker of 20 years has inhaled cigarettes more than one million times (Fisher & Rost, 1986), each inhalation providing an opportunity to increase "the thorough interweaving of the smoking habit in the fabric of daily life" (Pomerleau & Pomerleau, 1987, p. 119). The range of possible conditioning effects surrounding inhaled nicotine addiction is great. The circumstances in which smoking occurs may become discriminative stimuli that signal the occasion for possible reinforcement by smoking and nicotine. Also, through classical conditioning, the circumstances surrounding smoking may evoke conditioned responses that resemble the organismic response to nicotine itself. The complexity of these conditioning effects is increased by the fact that smoking is a sequence of behaviors. Thus, behaviors in the middle of the smoking chain may (a) elicit conditioned responses resembling the pharmacological effects of nicotine, which may (b) reinforce previous behaviors that led to them, (c) be reinforced themselves by the conditioned responses they elicit, and (d) serve as discriminative stimuli for subsequent behaviors, signaling the likelihood of their reinforcement by nicotine. For example, a phone call and the stressful content of the call may each serve as discriminative stimuli, signaling a situation in which the pharmacological effects of nicotine would be especially reinforcing. This may result in reaching for a cigarette, which may then serve as a conditioned stimulus, eliciting conditioned responses that resemble those reinforcing effects of nicotine. These conditioned effects of nicotine may reinforce reaching for the cigarette. All of these may serve as discriminative stimuli for additional steps in the chain and may elicit additional conditioned responses reinforcing earlier steps.

The biological potency and speed with which inhaled nicotine acts also contributes to the strength of conditioning in smoking. Research in classical conditioning has established that stronger unconditioned stimuli, as measured by intensity and amount, lead to more rapid conditioning, stronger conditioned responses, and greater resistance to extinction (Rachlin, 1991). The strong and easily discriminated effects of nicotine (U.S. DHHS, 1988) are predicted, then, to lead to powerful conditioning of cues that accompany them.

The conditioning of smoking is complicated by the varied reinforcing effects of nicotine. Because nicotine may reduce arousal, reduce anxiety, or function as a stimulant, so arousal, anxiety, or lethargy may come to serve both as discriminative stimuli for smoking or, following cessation, as conditioned stimuli for withdrawal symptoms or cravings. For both reasons such moods should elicit urges to smoke, an effect consistent with antecedents of relapse (Shiffman, 1986). In addition, the circumstances that give rise to such emotions or moods, such as time of day, work demands, family conflict, or loneliness may come to signal the occasion for smoking or elicit conditioned withdrawal symptoms.

From the perspective of conditioning, urges are conditioned responses to circumstances that have been associated with nicotine delivery (the presumed unconditioned stimulus). A number of findings illustrate the importance of such conditioning of urges to smoke. Among them, nicotine replacement appears to reduce withdrawal symptoms but not desire to smoke (Henningfield & Nemeth-Coslett, 1988). Desire or cravings are apparently dependent on cues and circumstances associated with previous smoking. Simply providing an alternative source of nicotine does not diminish those conditioned urges. Similarly, smokers report greater withdrawal symptoms if they quit in their natural environment rather than in artificial environments. Presumably the natural environments contain numerous cues associated with earlier smoking (Hatsukami, Hughes, & Pickens, 1985). Also, former smokers manifest physiological reactivity to smoking cues long after they have quit (Abrams, Monti, Carey, Pinto, & Jacobus, 1988).

ENVIRONMENTAL AND PSYCHOLOGICAL INFLUENCES ON THE INITIATION AND MAINTENANCE OF SMOKING

As noted in the section on genetics, multiple environmental and psychological factors link the genetic predisposition to become addicted, given exposure with the phenotype of persistent smoking (Kendler et al., 1999; Heath et al., 1999). This section reviews in detail the extensive research articulating these environmental and psychological factors.

The great majority (> 80%) of smokers try their first cigarette before the age of 18 (U.S. DHHS, 1994). It is not clear how long it takes, nor whether there is much variation in the transition from experimental to regular smoking (e.g., Hirschman, Leventhal, & Glynn, 1984). Teenagers report having difficulty stopping. As barriers to quitting, they report withdrawal symptoms similar to those seen in adults (Biglan & Lichtenstein, 1984) as well as social pressure and urges. Thus, dependence begins early in the smoking career. Indeed, as individuals begin to inhale cigarette smoke, the psychopharmacological properties of nicotine begin contributing to continued smoking (Kozlowski, 1989).

Early initiation of smoking during adolescence enhances the likelihood of adult smoking. In a prospective study, those who reported smoking at least monthly as adolescents were 16 to 20 times more likely to report smoking at least weekly as young adults (Chassin, Presson, Sherman, & Edwards, 1990). Even minimal exposure increases later risk. Those who, as adolescents, reported having smoked one or two cigarettes but none in the previous month were twice as likely to smoke weekly as young adults. Reflecting the influence of genetics noted earlier, psychophysiological sensitivity to initial cigarettes is associated with continued smoking (Heath et al., 2003). Taken together, these results underscore the importance of prevention programs among children and adolescents.

The relationships between early smoking and responses to cigarettes and later smoking also demonstrate a continuity in the psychological and biological forces that support smoking across the lifespan. Accordingly, the following pages show how similar influences apply to both initiation of smoking among youth and maintenance among adults.

Psychological and Behavioral Factors

The 1964 Surgeon General's Report noted a relationship between smoking and what it termed a "tendency to live faster and more intensely" (U.S. PHS, 1964, p. 366). This is reflected in a variety of individual characteristics associated with smoking, including extraversion (e.g., Cherry & Kiernan, 1976; Eysenck, 1980), coffee and alcohol consumption, circadian phase differences (being an "evening type" as opposed to a "morning type"), alcohol consumption, driving accidents, divorce, frequent job changes, low levels of vocational success, and impulsivity (U.S. DHHS, 1989).

That smoking is associated with a tendency "to live faster and more intensely" is also reflected in youth, among whom smoking has been associated with a variety of "problem behaviors" (Jessor, 1987) such as rule-breaking in school, general delinquency, younger age at first intercourse, low levels of child compliance within the family, low levels of responsibility, nonconventionality, impulsivity, rebelliousness, external locus of control, hostility, sensation-seeking, and previous use of alcohol and other substances

(Dielman, Campanelli, Shope, & Butchart, 1987; Lipkus, Barefoot, Williams, & Siegler, 1994; U.S. DHHS, 1989). High school dropouts and seniors not planning to go to college are much more likely to smoke than are those planning for higher education (Johnston et al., 2003; Pirie, Murray, & Luepker, 1988). In contrast, youth who perform well in school or have more mature behavioral skills are less likely to start smoking in the first place (Jessor, 1987).

But smoking is not only related to living fast and intensely. Depression has been linked to smoking in both youth and adults (Anda et al., 1990; Brown, Lewinsohn, Seeley, & Wagner, 1996; Glassman et al., 1990; Patton et al., 1996). The impact of depression extends to difficulty in quitting (Rausch, Nichinson, Lamke, & Matloff, 1990). In the National Health and Nutrition Examination Survey (NHANES), depressed smokers were 40% less likely to quit than nondepressed smokers, even after adjusting for amount smoked, sex, age, and educational attainment (Anda et al., 1990).

The relationship with depression is part of a more general pattern in which smoking is linked to diverse indicators of psychological, social, and economic distress. Teenagers who report high levels of stress are more likely to start smoking (Byrne, Byrne, & Reinhart, 1995) and youth commonly report using smoking to deal with stress (Tyas & Pederson, 1998). Smoking initiation is also associated with low self-esteem and social anxiety (Dielman et al., 1987; Lipkus et al., 1994). Turning to adults, among subgroups defined by gender and marital status, divorced or separated men have the highest prevalence of smoking, at 48.2% (U.S. DHHS, 1988, p. 571). It is interesting to note that divorce, separation, and male sex are also closely linked to suicide and alcoholism (Kaplan & Sadock, 1985). Among a sample of psychiatric outpatients, 52% reported smoking. Prevalence varied with diagnosis: 88% in those with schizophrenia, 49% in patients with major depression (Hughes, Hatsukami, Mitchell, & Dahlgren, 1986). Among male frequenters of a church-sponsored soup kitchen in Charleston, South Carolina, 76% reported smoking cigarettes (McDade & Keil, 1988). These associations with diverse types of distress reflect the facts that the pharmacological characteristics of nicotine and the delivery characteristics of inhaled tobacco smoke make the cigarette well suited as a drug for mitigating diverse psychological reactions to adversity.

In addition to motivational and emotional characteristics, attitudes are also related to development of smoking. Teenagers that do not have a firm commitment against smoking and those with more positive attitudes toward smoking and tobacco products are more likely to start smoking (Jackson, 1998; Pierce, Choi, Gilpin, Farkas, & Merritt, 1996).

Social Environment

Peers and family members have important roles in smoking initiation (Flay et al., 1994). Children of smoking parents are more likely to smoke than children of nonsmoking parents (U.S. DHHS, 1994). Peer smoking influences initial smoking episodes (Friedman, Lichtenstein, & Biglan, 1985), age of smoking initiation (Unger & Chen, 1999), and continuation of smoking among those who already have experimented with cigarettes (Biglan & Lichtenstein, 1984). Although parental influences do not disappear, peer influence on smoking increases during adolescence (Krosnick & Judd, 1982).

The relationship of individual smoking and peer smoking may be bidirectional. A young person's membership in a particular peer group may expose him or her to the example to smoke or to quit. In other cases, a young person may seek membership in a peer group that reflects his or her established intentions about smoking (Chassin, Presson, Sherman, Corty, & Olshavsky, 1984). Complicating matters more, the stimulus of peer smoking may be necessary for other factors to come into play. For example, one study found that anxiety and depression predicted smoking initiation only in the presence of peer smoking (Patton et al., 1998). But individual characteristics may also influence the impact of peer smoking. Seventh-graders who were categorized as "outsiders" because they had few reciprocal friends were affected more by the smoking status of their peers than were those with a large number of reciprocal friends (Aloise-Young, Graham, & Hansen, 1994).

Among four groups that emerged in a study of 7th- and 8th-graders (Mosbach & Leventhal, 1988), "hot-shots" (78% female, popular leaders in academic and extracurricular activities) and "dirts" (63% male, characterized by problem behaviors such as drinking, poor academic performance, and cutting classes) were more likely to smoke than other groups. The "jocks" were also 63% male but low on use of both hard liquor and cigarettes. Depending on group affiliation, different individual characteristics may be related to smoking—problem behaviors for the dirts versus academic and social leadership for the hot-shots.

In addition to parental modeling, smoking is influenced by family climate or family interaction patterns, including indifference, low levels of trust, parental restrictiveness, low levels of parental involvement, low levels of adolescent involvement in family decision making, and, among fathers, harsh criticism, impulsivity and poor ego integration (Brook, Whiteman, Gordon, & Brook, 1983; Hundleby & Mercer, 1987; Mittelmark et al., 1987). In contrast, paternal affection, emotional support, participation in meaningful conversations, and higher expectations for sons were associated with lower likelihood of smoking (Brook et al., 1983). Putting these together, families that provide multiple avenues for identity formation and expression of feelings may obviate the utility of smoking or other problem behaviors as a mode of identity expression (Jessor, 1987).

An interesting extension of social influences on smoking is reflected in sex differences. That women tend to be more attuned to their social surroundings (Acitelli & Antonucci, 1994; Belle, 1987) may also confer a susceptibility to the social surround. Women who live with a smoker are less likely to quit smoking than are men living with a smoker (Gritz, Nielsen, & Brooks, 1996). Cessation efforts may also be compromised by gender stereotypes that discourage women from acting assertively on their own behalf (Blechman, 1981). Women are also more susceptible to societal stereotypes that value a slender figure, and thus are more concerned than men about gaining weight (a common side effect of nicotine cessation) if they quit (Gritz et al., 1996; Secker-Walker et al., 1996).

Sex and distress may interact in women's smoking. Depression, which is related to greater likelihood of smoking and complicates cessation (Glassman et al., 1990), is also more prevalent among women than among men (McGrath, Keita, Strickland, & Russo, 1990). So women are more likely to smoke to reduce negative affect and stress (Gritz et al., 1996; Secker-Walker et al., 1996; Ward, Klesges, Zbikowski, Bliss, & Garvey, 1997).

Tobacco Marketing

Cigarettes are the most heavily marketed consumer product in the United States. (Marketing includes advertising as well as other promotions such as "give-aways" or product placements in movies.) Cigarette advertising and promotional expenditures in the United States in 1997 amounted to $5.66 billion (American Lung Association, 1999). The tobacco industry maintains that advertising is directed to brand preference among current smokers, not to recruiting new smokers. However, only 10% of smokers switch brands each year. If this indeed were the motivation of the tobacco advertising, this would be a modest impact for the most extensive marketing effort in U.S. culture (Davis, 1987).

Advertising and promotional activities influence smoking initiation. Teenagers with greatest exposure to tobacco marketing were subsequently more likely to start smoking and progress to becoming occasional and frequent smokers (Pierce, Choi, Gilpin, Farkas, & Berry, 1998). Similarly, in years when tobacco promotional expenditures are high, rates of smoking initiation among 9th graders are also higher (Redmond, 1999). Finally, cigarette brands that are advertised most frequently in magazines read by teenagers are almost exclusively the brands chosen by first-time 12- to 15-year-old smokers (Pucci & Siegel, 1999).

Cigarette marketing themes reflect psychological perspectives of youth audiences. Among 6th-, 9th-, and 12th-grade students, ratings of oneself corresponded more closely to ratings assigned to models in cigarette advertisements among respondents who were themselves smokers (McCarthy & Gritz, 1987). The Joe Camel campaign of the 1990s reflected the themes of a "cool character" who was independent and quite successful heterosexually. This campaign coincided with sharp increases in Camel's market share, especially among adolescents (Pierce, Gilpin, & Choi, 1999).

Market segmentation is a strategy of tobacco companies to develop advertising and promotional campaigns that will appeal to specific groups within a population. For cigarettes, marketing and advertising are especially segmented according to race, ethnicity, and gender (Davis, 1987). For example, the marketing of Kool cigarettes through association with jazz music is directed toward Black individuals. Kool, along with two other menthol brands, have long held a dominant share of the Black cigarette market (Cummings, Giovino, & Mendicino, 1987). Also, before the 1998 Master Settlement Agreement between the states and the tobacco companies that restricted tobacco marketing aimed at youth, the industry used billboard advertising to target specific markets, including Black Americans (Luke, Esmundo, & Bloom, 2000). Given women's association of smoking with maintaining a slender figure, Virginia Slims offers another example of market segmentation. Ironically, segmentation strategies and the psychosocial characteristics they presume may compete for brand preference. Although 31% of adolescent women smokers said they preferred Virginia Slims in a 1986 study, it was still less popular within this group than the brand associated with a "macho" marketing campaign—Marlboro (Hunter et al., 1986).

During the 1990s, cigarette companies spent hundreds of millions of dollars on "continuity" programs (Sumner & Dillman, 1995). These provide brand-identified merchandise in exchange for proof of purchase labels included with cigarette packs. Philip Morris boasted that 12 million U.S. citizens—approximately 5% of the population—participated in its continuity programs in 1993 to 1994. Furthermore, large prizes such as pool tables encouraged smokers to work together to earn them, likely increasing interpersonal support for continued smoking.

Knowledge of Health Effects of Smoking

Although most Americans recognize that smoking is risky, they seem unaware of the degree to which its dangers dwarf those of other lifestyle-related risk factors. A 1983 Harris survey found that health professionals rated not smoking as the first priority among things Americans can do to protect their health. In contrast, the public rated not smoking as 10th. They rated as more important consuming adequate vitamins and minerals and drinking water of acceptable quality (U.S. DHHS, 1989, pp. 209–210). A 1992 survey by the Gallup Organization for the American Lung Association found that adults still failed to recognize the profundity of smoking's risk. Among automobile accidents, smoking, HIV, homicides, and air pollution, only 22% rated smoking as the leading cause of death (which of course it is). Fifty seven percent gave this ranking to automobile accidents.

The failure to recognize the risk of smoking is even worse among smokers. In the 1992 poll, only 17% of smokers rated smoking as the leading cause of death, in contrast to 26% among nonsmokers. But even if smokers do not fully grasp the importance of quitting smoking, most smokers do recognize that smoking is harmful. One might then wonder why so many persist in smoking. One explanation for the persistence of smoking even with widespread awareness of its riskiness is, of course, its addictive properties. Another contributor to persistence in the face of harm may be a denial of risk among smokers in which personalized acceptance of risk ("Cigarette smoking is dangerous to my health") lags behind general acceptance ("Cigarette smoking is dangerous to health"; Lichtenstein & Bernstein, 1980). Such denial is often seen as a core feature of addiction. Another is that smoking's most feared consequences are delayed many years, relative to the virtual immediacy of its biologically addicting and psychosocial consequences. Relative delay of consequences considerably undermines their influence or decisions.

Economic and Political Barriers to Public Knowledge

Another reason that many smokers discount their risk lies in the lack of forceful government restriction of cigarette marketing. This may lead citizens to infer that smoking must not be as dangerous as antismoking advocates claim (Davis, 1987, p. 725). Internal tobacco company documents released in recent years make clear that they have long suppressed important information: that nicotine is addictive and that the industry's business is selling nicotine delivery; that tobacco and cigarette characteristics are manipulated to deliver higher doses of nicotine more efficiently; that the industry has targeted adolescents. Furthermore, the tobacco industry has been extremely successful at influencing legislative and other political activities through direct campaign contributions (Glantz & Begay, 1994; Luke & Krauss, 2003).

Because they are part of conglomerates with substantial advertising budgets for nontobacco products, tobacco companies' influence in the media extends beyond what their tobacco-related advertising might gain them. Warner (1985) documented efforts of tobacco companies to suppress media coverage of the risks of smoking by threatening loss of advertising revenues from both tobacco and nontobacco products. This influence was also apparent in recent disclosures surrounding the story of Jeffery Wigand, a former tobacco company executive who disclosed tobacco companies' efforts to make cigarettes more addictive and to market them to children and teenagers. CBS network was apparently discouraged by commercial considerations from broadcasting an interview with Wigand.

Why would a highly diversified conglomerate manipulate its nontobacco marketing and economic power to advance the interests of its cigarette division? Part of the answer may be the great profitability of cigarettes in comparison to other product lines. According to the 2002 Annual Report of Altria (2002), the conglomerate that includes Kraft Foods and Philip Morris, tobacco accounted for 59.1% of revenues but 61.7% of income. In contrast, its food businesses account for 37.0% of revenue and 36.3% of income. Even as restrictions on marketing of cigarettes may curtail sales within the United States, the *potential* of sales in Asia and developing nations (35.7% of revenues but only 32.8% of income) motivates determined defense of the tobacco business.

Multiple Determinants and the Persistence of Smoking

The multiplicity of determinants of smoking and the many interactions among them may account for much of the persistence of smoking—a persistence otherwise inexplicable in light of smoking's risks. As summarized in Figure 3.4, the ubiquity of cigarette marketing, the responses conditioned to cigarette advertisements and promotions, and the biological and psychological responses that they trigger are all increased by the profitability of cigarettes. Reciprocally, then, the success in addicting large numbers and keeping them addicted drives the profitability of cigarette marketing.

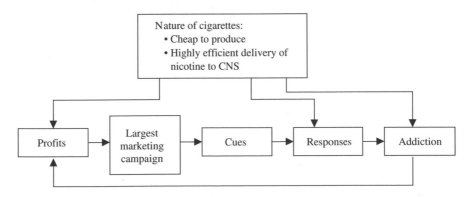

Figure 3.4. Relationships among characteristics of cigarettes, economics of cigarette marketing, and maintenance of addiction to nicotine. CNS = central nervous system.

INTERVENTIONS FOR SMOKING CESSATION: KEY INTERVENTION CHARACTERISTICS

As diverse and powerful as the forces encouraging smoking may be, almost 50% of U.S. adults who have smoked have quit (U.S. DHHS, 1989). The sections that follow describe interventions and programs for smoking cessation. These range widely from brief interventions for individual patients visiting their primary care providers to programs for whole communities to policy initiatives. But first, this section describes key characteristics and features that cut across the various types and settings of smoking cessation interventions.

Key Meta-Analyses

Several meta-analyses of smoking cessation interventions have provided important guidance to the field. These include that of Kottke and colleagues published in 1988 (Kottke, Battista, & DeFriese, 1988) and that of Baillie and colleagues, based on 86 studies and published in 1994 (Baillie, Mattick, Hall, & Webster, 1994). Extensive meta-analyses conducted by the Smoking Cessation Clinical Practice Guideline Panel and Staff of the Agency for Health Care Policy and Research (AHCPR) led to the development of its Clinical Practice Guideline (Fiore et al., 1996). Their implications for psychology and behavioral science are the subject of a review article in the *American Psychologist* (Wetter et al., 1998). These guidelines were revised in June 2000 under the sponsorship of the renamed Agency for Healthcare Research and Quality (AHRQ) and are now referred to in the field and the balance of this chapter as the AHRQ Guidelines (Fiore et al., 2000).

State-of-the-Art: Behavioral Components of Smoking Interventions

A state-of-the-art for smoking cessation that has emerged over 30 years includes the following:

- Setting a target date and specific plan for quitting (Flaxman, 1978);
- Identifying and making specific plans for coping with temptations likely to provoke urges to smoke (Hall, Rugg, Tunstall, & Jones, 1984);
- Recruiting cooperation and encouragement from family or friends (Mermelstein, Cohen, Lichtenstein, Baer, & Kamarck, 1986);
- Continued follow-up and encouragement from professionals (Kottke et al., 1988); and

- Relapse prevention, including guarding against the "abstinence violation effect" of attributing lapses to a fundamental inability to quit (Curry, Marlatt, & Gordon, 1987).

Meta-analysis found an odds ratio of 2.11 for inclusion of behavioral interventions relative to brief medical advice alone (Baillie et al., 1994). The AHRQ Guidelines included testing of a number of behavioral intervention components (Wetter et al., 1998, p. 660). One category was called "general problem solving" (odds ratio relative to no contact = 1.6). This was defined as "training to identify and cope with events or problems that increase the likelihood of smoking, including coping skill training, relapse prevention, and stress management." This category is similar to two components of the state-of-the-art for smoking cessation noted previously: relapse prevention and identifying and making specific plans for coping with temptations likely to provoke urges to smoke.

Importance of Duration and Variety of Treatment

Reviews and meta-analyses conducted over the past several decades have consistently found that the duration of treatment and the variety of treatment components are associated with long-term success (Baillie et al., 1994; Kottke et al., 1988). Regarding variety of interventions, for example, those who receive one brief intervention to promote nonsmoking are 1.48 times more likely to quit than those who receive none. And those who receive two or more types of intervention are also 1.48 times more likely to quit than those who receive only one (Baillie et al., 1994). Table 3.1 summarizes the analyses of type of treatment from the 2000 AHRQ Guidelines (Fiore et al., 2000). As can be seen, the increase in odds ratios is greater going from one to three or four treatment formats than it is going

TABLE 3.1
Summary of Analyses of Type of Treatment and Variety of Treatment from
AHRQ Guidelines

	Odds ratio (95% CI)		Odds ratio (95% CI)
No format	1.0	No format	1.0
Self-help	1.2 (1.02, 1.3)	One format	1.5 (1.2, 1.8)
Telephone counseling	1.2 (1.1, 1.4)	One format	1.5 (1.2, 1.8)
Group counseling	1.3 (1.1, 1.6)	Two formats	1.9 (1.6, 2.2)
Individual counseling	1.7 (1.4, 2.0)	Three or four formats	2.5 (2.1, 3.0)

Note. From *Treating Tobacco Use and Dependence: Clinical Practice Guideline* (p. 63), by M. C. Fiore, W. C. Bailey, S. J. Cohen, S. F. Dorfman, M. G. Goldstein, E. R. Gritz, et al., 2000, Rockville, MD: U.S. Department of Health and Human Services, Public Health Service. In the public domain. CI = confidence interval.

TABLE 3.2

Estimates of Odds Ratios and Abstinence Rates of Smoking Cessation
Interventions According to Total Amount of Contact Time
and Number of Sessions

	Estimated odds ratio (95% CI)	Estimated abstinence rate (95% CI)
Contact time		
0 minutes (reference)	1.0	11.0
1–3 minutes	1.4 (1.1, 1.8)	14.4 (11.3, 17.5)
4–30 minutes	1.9 (1.5, 2.3)	18.8 (15.6, 22.0)
31–90 minutes	3.0 (2.3, 3.8)	26.5 (21.5, 31.4)
91–300 minutes	3.2 (2.3, 4.6)	28.4 (21.3, 35.5)
> 300 minutes	2.8 (2.0, 3.9)	25.5 (19.2, 31.7)
Number of sessions		
0–1 session	1.0	12.4
2–3 sessions	1.4 (1.1, 1.7)	16.3 (13.7, 19.0)
4–8 sessions	1.9 (1.6, 2.2)	20.9 (18.1, 23.6)
> 8 sessions	2.3 (2.1, 3.0)	24.7 (21.0, 28.4)

Note. From *Treating Tobacco Use and Dependence: Clinical Practice Guideline* (pp. 59–60), by
M. C. Fiore, W. C. Bailey, S. J. Cohen, S. F. Dorfman, M. G. Goldstein, E. R. Gritz, et al., 2000, Rockville,
MD: U.S. Department of Health and Human Services, Public Health Service. In the public domain. CI =
confidence interval.

from one type of treatment to another. Thus, success is more related to the
variety of treatments used than to any treatment "magic bullet."

As to duration of treatment, the 2000 AHRQ Guidelines found a
continuum in the effect of each of total contact time or number of sessions.
These are summarized in Table 3.2. In their 1988 review, Kottke and his
colleagues summarized well the literature on variety and duration of
intervention:

> Program development and program delivery will probably be most fruit-
> ful if focused on how the nonsmoking message can be given clearly,
> repeatedly, and consistently through every feasible delivery system; per-
> sonalized advice; printed materials; the mass media; and smoke-free
> medical, work, school, and home environments (p. 2888).

Importance of Support for Cessation

The 2000 AHRQ Guidelines noted the importance to smoking cessation of social support provided as part of and outside of treatment. Within
the broader domain of follow-up and support, social support has also been
shown to be an important predictor of long-term abstinence (e.g.,
Mermelstein et al., 1986). This reflects the profound role of social support
as a predictor of a variety of health outcomes, including mortality (House,

Landis, & Umberson, 1988). As clear as the importance of social support may be, early efforts to use it in smoking cessation were not always successful. For example, a 1986 review of the literature linking social support to success in smoking cessation (Lichtenstein, Glasgow, & Abrams, 1986) noted minimal or no benefits from several interventions intended to generate support for cessation.

Disappointing results of social support interventions have now been superseded by successful programs offered in several settings. For example, addition of a buddy system to individual counseling in a primary care setting increased cessation rates (West, Edwards, & Hajek, 1998). Also, several programs that provide social support through telephone counseling, reviewed later in the chapter, have been successful (Curry, McBride, Grothaus, Louie, & Wagner, 1995; Orleans et al., 1991). Review of the mixed findings in this field (Fisher, 1997) indicated the importance of several factors:

- Supportive interventions that are highly didactic or inflexible are less effective than those that are more flexible and person-centered;
- Teaching skills for gaining support appears less effective than simply providing support; and
- Support functions as a reinforcer; support loses its effects if terminated before ex-smokers no longer need the encouragement or substitute for the psychological effects of nicotine that support may provide (Fisher, 1996).

Support for cessation will tend to coincide with more varied treatments and those of longer duration. The intertwining of these three was well illustrated in a study initiated in the 1970s, the Multiple Risk Factor Intervention Trial (MRFIT). For men at high risk for cardiovascular disease, MRFIT included a range of smoking cessation interventions: (a) professional monitoring every four months; (b) a variety of individual and group-intensive interventions (varying somewhat from one clinical site to another); (c) programs for renewed cessation efforts for those who had relapsed; and (d) frequent activities (e.g., group lectures, promotional events) for MRFIT participants and their family member to promote maintained abstinence (Hughes, Hymowitz, Ockene, Simon, & Vogt, 1981). Six years after randomization (one year after the end of the program), 48.9% of those who smoked at baseline were abstinent in contrast to 28.8% of those who received usual care (Ockene, Hymowitz, Lagus, & Shaten, 1991).

Pharmacological Interventions

Nicotine replacement following cessation reduces withdrawal symptoms, enhances abstinence, and shows a dose-response relationship with cessation (Fisher, Lichtenstein, & Haire-Joshu, 1993; Tonnesen et al., 1988). The 2000 AHRQ Guidelines found an odds ratio relative to placebo of 1.5 (95% confidence interval = 1.3–1.8) for nicotine gum. Relative to placebo, the odds ratio for patches was 1.9 (95% confidence interval = 1.7–2.2), that for nicotine inhaler was 2.5 (95% confidence interval = 1.7–3.6), and that for nicotine nasal spray was 2.7 (95% confidence interval = 1.8–4.1). A separate meta-analysis also found that nasal spray was most effective and that gum and patches were about equal to each other (Silagy, Mant, Fowler, & Lancaster, 2000).

Nicotine replacement can be tailored to replace all of the nicotine a smoker derives daily from cigarettes, estimated at 1 mg per cigarette during ad lib smoking (Benowitz, Zevin, & Jacob, 1998; Dale et al., 1995; Daughton et al., 1999; Silagy et al., 2000), or up to 3 mg per cigarette during restricted smoking. Thus, a pack-a-day smoker consumes about 20 mg per day. Nicotine gum delivers about 50% of its stated dose, so a former pack-a-day smoker would need to use about 10 pieces of 4 mg gum to replace all the nicotine to which he or she was accustomed. Nicotine patches deliver low-peak levels of nicotine, so that a former pack-a-day smoker may feel dissatisfied even on a 21 mg patch. One way to address this is to combine patch with additional nicotine replacement. The 2000 AHRQ Guidelines (Fiore et al., 2000, p. 77) found the combination of patch with either gum or nasal spray significantly more effective than patch alone (odds ratio = 1.9, 95% confidence interval = 1.3–2.6).

In addition to nicotine replacement, bupropion sustained release (SR), marketed as Zyban, has been shown successful in a variety of clinical trials (e.g., Hurt et al., 1997; Jorenby et al., 1999). The 2000 AHRQ Guidelines (Fiore et al., 2000, p. 72) found bupropion SR more effective than placebo (odds ratio = 2.1, 95% confidence interval = 1.5–3.0). Because it is an antidepressant, buproprion might be ideal for depressed smokers, but it has also been found effective for smokers who are not depressed, perhaps because it mimics several of nicotine's effects in the brain.

Other potentially useful drugs include (a) clonidine, an antihypertensive agent with significant side effects and potential for rebound hypertension when discontinued; (b) mecamylamine, another antihypertensive drug; and (c) nortriptyline, a tricyclic antidepressant without the seizure risks of bupropion (Fiore et al., 2000).

The 1988 Surgeon General's Report on smoking as nicotine addiction (U.S. DHHS, 1988) concluded that nicotine replacement is best viewed as an adjunct to counseling or other smoking cessation programs and efforts. A continuing controversy in the literature revolves around whether nicotine replacement alone, with no counseling or patient education, is effective. But this is probably an unproductive debate. The important research questions concern how to provide interventions that can reach large numbers and can maximize the effects of medications for smoking cessation. In fact, the literature is clear that even modest instruction or counseling is better than none. For example, meta-analysis found an odds ratio of 1.91 for those who receive the offer of nicotine gum plus a brief intervention versus those who receive only the offer of nicotine gum (Baillie et al., 1994). The failure of existing nicotine replacement products to displace cigarettes in the marketplace suggests that smokers currently need some formal instruction (Pierce & Gilpin, 2002).

Measurement of Outcomes

Because of the propensity to relapse that is characteristic of addiction, long-term abstinence is important in evaluating interventions. Research is generally considered inconclusive if it does not report abstinence at least 6 months, preferably 12 months, following initiation of cessation interventions.

Self-report is a good indicator of cessation when respondents are not clinically supervised or are unaware of the connection between an intervention and the evaluation survey, such as in random phone surveys conducted to evaluate communitywide interventions. Problems emerge when the evaluation is clearly connected to the intervention, as in smoking cessation interventions conducted in clinical settings. In such cases, it is important to address the possible bias of self-reports of abstinence such as through validation by biochemical tests or interviewers who are blind to respondents' assignments to treatment groups (Glasgow et al., 1993).

PROMOTING SMOKING CESSATION TO LARGE NUMBERS OF SMOKERS

The previous section described key components and characteristics of smoking cessation programs and interventions. The next two sections describe first how these are integrated into programs designed to reach large numbers of smokers and then into interventions that reach individuals or groups in clinical settings.

Self-Help Procedures

A variety of self-help pamphlets, books, videotapes, and Web resources are available commercially and through voluntary agencies, including the

American Lung Association, American Heart Association, and American Cancer Society. Estimates of 12-month abstinence rates range from 8 to 25% (Cohen et al., 1989; Davis, Faust, & Ordentlich, 1984; Sallis et al., 1986). In a meta-analysis of 24 randomized evaluations, Curry (1993) found that self-help methods achieved long-term results comparable to those of intensive interventions. She attributed this to the tendency for success rates of the self-help interventions to increase over time. As opposed to a scheduled group program, self-help materials remain available for the smoker to use again as readiness to quit increases. In another meta-analysis of 41 self-help interventions, the odds ratio of quitting was 1.23 for self-help or brief advice in comparison to no intervention (Lancaster & Stead, 1998).

A commonly misinterpreted statistic is that most ex-smokers have quit "on their own." Just as nature abhors a vacuum, so behavior change as difficult as smoking cessation does not emerge *sui generis*. In reality, although most ex-smokers did not join formal smoking cessation programs, most quit amid a substantial array of health education messages, campaigns to encourage nonsmoking, increased regulation of smoking and increased price of cigarettes, encouragement from health professionals, the help and encouragement of family and friends, and the experience gained from several previous efforts. Documenting and quantifying the influence of such diverse influences on behavior is not easy for traditional research methods in psychology or clinical research (Susser, 1995), but this is an example of an area in which psychology has much to learn from public health population perspectives on behavior change

Telephone Counseling

The telephone is another channel for delivery of brief advice, as well as repeated and more extended counseling and follow-up. The 2000 AHRQ Guidelines (Fiore et al., 2000, p. 62) and an earlier meta-analysis (Lancaster & Stead, 1998) both found evidence for benefits of telephone counseling. In one exemplary program (Hill et al., 1994; Orleans et al., 1991), those who received telephone counseling in addition to a self-help manual and a brochure on social support reported abstinence rates of 27% at 24-month follow-up, compared with 20% for those who received both manuals but no phone counseling. In another study, a dose-response relationship was found between amount of phone counseling added to self-help materials (zero, one, or six contacts) and abstinence at 12-month follow-up (Zhu et al., 1996).

A review (Lichtenstein et al., 1996) found that reactive phone services (those that users have to call) are effective for those who do access them but are not used by many quitters. Proactive services (those that identify and phone smokers without their initiating contact) may be most effective as a supplement to other programs or for smokers who are especially motivated to quit.

Tailoring Interventions

At the border between brief and intensive interventions, a number of studies have evaluated mail or brief phone interventions that are tailored to individual characteristics, such as readiness to change, specific motives for quitting, or reasons for previous relapse. In one study, smokers recruited through a primary care practice first completed a questionnaire. Based on these, a computer-based algorithm then created individualized letters to participants, using a library of text modules addressing specific levels of readiness to change, motives, or other individual factors. Among moderate and light smokers, these individualized mailings yielded higher rates of cessation than standard letters or no treatment (Strecher et al., 1994).

Based on their Transtheoretical Model, which individualizes treatment according to stage of change, Prochaska, Velicer, and their colleagues have evaluated expert systems that generate individualized print information from questionnaire or interview responses (Prochaska, DiClemente, Velicer, & Rossi, 1993). Reviews of the field indicate consistent advantages of tailored manuals and other print materials over nontailored print materials (Skinner, Campbell, Rimer, Curry, & Prochaska, 1999).

Cost Reimbursement

Delivery of even brief or low-cost interventions to large numbers of smokers will, of course, be influenced by their cost and success. This was examined in an ingenious study by Curry and her colleagues (Curry, Grothaus, McAfee, & Pabiniak, 1998) at Group Health Cooperative of Puget Sound. Among participants in smoking cessation services, those who had to pay for some portion of cost achieved higher quit rates than those who received them at no cost. However, offering services at no charge resulted in greater percentage of smokers participating in cessation services. The benefit of increased volume outweighed the difference in effectiveness among participants. As a result, when examined as a percentage not just of participants, but of all smokers in a plan, quit rates were higher in the free condition—2.8% of all smokers—than in the partial or full payment conditions—0.7 to 1.7%.

Dissemination Through Organizations: Workplaces and Communities

In addition to influence by support and encouragement, long-term abstinence of a year or more may be especially tied to the number of smoking friends and relatives in the social network (Cohen et al., 1988; Eisinger, 1971; Graham & Gibson, 1971; Mermelstein et al., 1986). Thus, changing norms for smoking behavior may be especially effective in encouraging maintained cessation.

One place where important social norms may encourage nonsmoking is at work. Reductions in smoking have been reported through workplace programs, aimed either at smoking alone or at multiple cardiovascular risks (Gomel, Oldenburg, Simpson, Chilvers, & Owen, 1997; Gomel, Oldenburg, Simpson, & Owen, 1993). Programs aimed at workplace norms and general support for nonsmoking have reported substantial quit rates, even among smokers who did not join cessation clinics (Fisher et al., 1994). Employees' ratings of management support for such programs and indexes of management support such as instituting smoking policies, were associated with participation, cessation attempts, and ratings of social support for nonsmoking (Cummings, Kelsey, & Nevitt, 1990; Fisher et al., 1988). In addition to smoking cessation programs, workplace restrictions on smoking are associated with quitting among employees as well as decreased exposure to environmental tobacco smoke (Brownson, Hopkins & Wakefield, 2002).

More ambitious than workplace activities are programs to promote nonsmoking across entire communities. Among these, mass media programs achieve modest effects in terms of the percentage of smokers who quit (Flay, 1987) but quite substantial effects, when one considers the numbers of smokers whom they reach. As with smoking cessation in general (Kottke et al., 1988), the more channels of influence supporting cessation, the greater the impact of community programs. Thus, televised programs achieve greater impact when accompanied by printed materials distributed to viewers (Flay, 1987; Warnecke, Langenberg, Wong, Flay, & Cook, 1992) or by group activities that provide local support for cessation (Flay, 1987; Korhonen et al., 1992). Although overall results of the Community Intervention Trial for Smoking Cessation (COMMIT), a large clinical trial of community organizations for smoking cessation, were disappointing, the program did achieve appreciable impact among light and moderate smokers (Lichtenstein et al., 1995). One program that was successful (Fisher et al., 1998) emphasized community participation in program development and was carried out in relatively small city neighborhoods. It may be easier to recruit naturally occurring social support for program goals at the level of the neighborhood, worksite, or small community than at the level of the city or state.

Beyond the community, several comprehensive statewide programs have shown striking benefits. These are reviewed at the end of the chapter.

SMOKING CESSATION IN CLINICAL PRACTICE

Interventions in clinical practice include group programs and intensive counseling. But they also include a few minutes of advice from primary care providers that, as those in the previous section, may reach large numbers of smokers through their routine medical care.

Brief Advice in Primary Care

Brief advice to quit, provision of accompanying cessation materials, presentation of risks individualized by symptoms or family history, and follow-up are effective in promoting cessation through medical settings (Kottke et al., 1988; Ockene, Kristeller, et al., 1991; Rose & Hamilton, 1978; Russell, Wilson, & Taylor, 1979). A meta-analytical review defined "brief advice" as advice delivered in fewer than 20 minutes with the possibility of one follow-up contact (Silagy & Ketteridge, 1998). Smokers receiving such advice were 1.69 times more likely to quit than those receiving usual care. Based on such research, the 2000 AHRQ Guidelines (Fiore et al., 2000, pp. 28–31) emphasized encouraging quitting in primary care through the structure of the "5 As":

> *Ask*: Systematically identify all tobacco users at every visit.
> *Advise*: Strongly urge all tobacco users to quit with advice tailored to their own and family's health histories.
> *Assess*: Determine willingness to make a quit attempt.
> *Assist*: Appropriate to level of readiness, assist the patient in quitting or provide motivational intervention and assurance of availability of future help.
> *Arrange*: Schedule follow-up contact.

Enhancing Interventions in Primary Care

Although brief advice to quit provided by a physician has been found beneficial, the addition of counseling to this advice appears worthwhile. For example, the classic study of physician's advice in the Whitehall Civil Servants' Study (Rose & Hamilton, 1978) included an average of five additional visits to the physician over the following 12 months for support and encouragement. Over the next 10 years, the intervention group reported smoking less than half as many cigarettes as the control group (Rose, Hamilton, Colwell, & Shipley, 1982). When added to or compared with physician's advice alone, a variety of intervention strategies have increased cessation rates, including adding a video on how to quit, counseling by a nurse, follow-up phone calls, referral to self-help materials, referral to group treatment, or giving patients a choice between self-help and group treatment (Hollis, Lichtenstein, Vogt, Stevens, & Biglan, 1993; Whitlock, Vogt, Hollis, & Lichtenstein, 1997).

Intensive Interventions

In 1992, Lichtenstein and Glasgow (1992) noted that the previous decade had seen increased popularity of public health approaches to smoking that sought to disseminate brief, inexpensive interventions to large numbers of people, thereby achieving a greater benefit than intensive interventions delivered to small numbers. They also noted, however, that a growing proportion of heavy smokers found it difficult to quit. This along with research linking smoking to such chronic characteristics as depression suggested a renewed role for intensive interventions addressed to small numbers of high-risk or difficult cases.

Group Smoking Cessation Clinics

These generally incorporate a range of the state-of-the-art behavioral components described earlier. None of these individual tactics is necessary, but their aggregate impact is appreciable (Compas, Haaga, Keefe, Leitenberg, & Williams, 1998). For example, groups that received somewhat different sets of these behavioral procedures did not differ among themselves, but all exceeded the success of a group that received only exercise (Hill, Rigdon, & Johnson, 1993). In another reflection of the importance of behavioral components, a meta-analysis found no advantage for group interventions over individual counseling, provided that individual counseling included comprehensive behavioral procedures similar to the group program (Stead & Lancaster, 1998). Evidence suggests the effectiveness of such programs as they are offered by many hospitals, worksites, and community agencies. For example, an analysis of the American Lung Association's Freedom from Smoking® clinics showed a long-term abstinence rate of 29% (Rosenbaum & O'Shea, 1992), relative to a benchmark of 20% suggested by contemporaneous research (Glasgow & Lichtenstein, 1987).

Programs for Depression and Smoking Cessation

Several studies have evaluated adding components to interventions that are aimed at depression or low mood. Supplementing the combination of a smoking cessation group and nicotine replacement with cognitive–behavior therapy increased success rates among those with history of major depression but not among those with no history of depression (Hall, Muñoz,

& Reus, 1994). Similarly, the addition to self-help materials of a Mood Management Package (relaxation tape, booklet, and chart for monitoring moods and pleasant activities) was especially effective for those with a history of major depressive episodes (Muñoz, Marin, Posner, & Perez-Stable, 1997). Addition to group treatment of cognitive–behavior therapy procedures for alcoholism as well as depression improved outcomes for smokers with histories of alcoholism and depression (Patten, Martin, Myers, Calfas, & Williams, 1998).

Smoking Cessation Among People With Serious and Chronic Diseases

Rates of smoking cessation vary somewhat across serious diseases that are related to smoking. Part of this variation appears attributable to the benefits of quitting. For example, rates of quitting are higher among those recovering from myocardial infarctions (MIs or "heart attacks"), for whom quitting can have a substantial impact on life expectancy, than among those with chronic obstructive pulmonary disease (COPD, emphysema, and bronchitis), for whom quitting may improve quality of life but may not have a substantial impact on disease course (Fisher, Haire-Joshu, Morgan, Rehberg, & Rost, 1990). Gritz, Kristeller, and Burns (1993) provided an extended review of smoking and coexisting disease.

Among patients with cancer related to smoking, 40% of smokers were abstinent two years following surgery for stage I, non–small-cell lung cancer (Gritz, Nisenbaum, Elashoff, & Holmes, 1991). Although one might think that it is too late to quit smoking *after* development of smoking-related cancer, cessation after diagnosis can still enhance survival, reduce risk of additional cancer and other smoking-related diseases, improve response to chemotherapy, and reduce chemotherapy and radiation side effects (Eckhardt, Pulte, Hilsenbeck, Von Hoff, & Eckerdt, 1995; Gritz, 1991).

As with other programs reviewed earlier, the number of intervention channels and strategies appear important also for patients with serious diseases. Among post-MI patients, a combination of print and audiotape information on cessation strategies, counseling by a nurse, nicotine gum, and phone follow-up (weekly for two to three weeks after discharge, then monthly for four months) resulted in 71% abstinence 12 months after discharge, in contrast to 45% in usual care (Taylor, Houston-Miller, Killen, & De-Busk, 1990).

Although smoking cessation among those with diabetes has been the subject of little research, the elevation of risk of cardiovascular disease posed by the combination of smoking and diabetes makes cessation in this group a high priority (Haire-Joshu, Glasgow, & Tibbs, 1999). Yet the prevalence of smoking is not appreciably lower among those with diabetes than among the population at large. Concerns about weight gain complicate smoking cessation in this group. Also, depression is more prevalent among both smokers and those with diabetes, posing additional challenges for smokers who also have diabetes (Haire-Joshu et al., 1999).

Harm Reduction: An Alternative to Cessation

Harm reduction is an emerging theme in tobacco control (Warner, 2002). Harm reduction advocates suggest that replacing cigarettes with safer nicotine products is a logical alternative when smoking cessation is unlikely to succeed (Sumner, 2003). However, harm reduction remains controversial. In addition to unforeseen risks of noncigarette nicotine, a concern is the possibility that some smokers might conclude it is safe to smoke until they develop early stages of disease, after which they can switch to other sources of nicotine, a conclusion that tobacco companies might encourage. In addition, were tobacco companies to develop harm-reduction products, they might expand their markets, encourage transition from harm-reduction products to cigarettes, or confuse issues surrounding regulation of cigarettes.

Synthesizing and Individualizing Intensive Treatment

Based on level of addiction, smoking-related disease or disease risk, comorbidities such as depression and presence–absence of facilitating influences such as social support, intensive interventions may be tailored to specific groups or individuals. Table 3.3 outlines suggested components of such interventions and indications for their use.

Comprehensive Approaches: Advantages, Costs, and Equifinality

A theme of much of this chapter is that the more extended and comprehensive the treatment, the greater will be the likelihood of cessation. This perspective is supported by cost-effectiveness analyses. Although costs increase with more intensive interventions, benefits increase more than enough to make more intensive interventions generally more cost-effective (Warner, 1997). The importance of including variety in treatment, as well as the inclusion of specific behavioral skills, is not limited to smoking cessation. For example, a meta-analysis of 74 programs aimed at a variety of health risks and health promoting behaviors found that the number of different communication channels, as well as patient education and behavioral self-monitoring, were predictive of success (Mullen et al., 1997).

There are no magic bullets in smoking cessation. The variety of intervention elements appears more important than any single component. There is no uniquely good treatment for any particular aspects of smoking cessation. Depending on the individual, nicotine gum, nicotine patch, or bupropion

TABLE 3.3
Indications and Components of Intensive Intervention

Indication	Program component
Addiction (high scores on Fagerstrom tolerance questionnaire (Fagerstrom & Schneider, 1989), "yes" to question whether smoked first cigarette within 30 minutes of waking in the morning, and/or smoke more than 15 cigarettes per day)	Nicotine replacement (gum, patch, inhaler, or nasal spray) or other medication to aid in cessation (e.g., Bupropion or Zyban)
Depression (indicated by commonly used measure, such as Beck Depression Inventory, or by reported use of smoking to cope with low mood and negative affect)	Cognitive–behavior therapy approaches to depression incorporated into treatment; referral for cognitive–behavior therapy (if clinical depression); Bupropion (Zyban) to assist in cessation
Social isolation (e.g., few friends, divorce or widowhood, recent change in living circumstances)	Social support and follow-up by staff via phone or scheduled visits; group treatment; encouragement of development of source(s) of support among friends, fellow workers, etc.
Apparent lack of preparation or skill for coping with circumstances likely to tempt relapse	Self-management training aimed at developing skills for minimizing and/or avoiding temptations
Previous failures, lack of confidence, or concern about relapse	Relapse prevention training addressing "abstinence violation effect"—tendency to attribute "lapse" to fundamental inability to quit
Patients with smoking-related disease or with diseases (e.g., diabetes) or other risk factors (e.g., hypertension) that increase risks of smoking	Tailoring of risk information to address benefits of cessation specific to the patient's clinical status; tailoring of self-management counseling and advice to address disease-specific barriers or concerns (e.g., belief among smokers with diabetes that weight gain is as dangerous as continued smoking)
All	Follow-up by phone or in-person, addressing continued encouragement, self-management of temptations, continued use of medications, relapse prevention, and value of renewed efforts in the face of relapse or return to regular smoking

SR may be effective to ease withdrawal from inhaled nicotine. Similarly, group programs, self-help manuals, or a TV show may teach the key skills for planning a quit and resisting temptations to relapse. Follow-up from professionals, from trained volunteers, or through print or other media may help those who have quit to stay off. In the literature on organizational behavior (Nord & Tucker, 1987), this is termed *equifinality*—in other words, different procedures or programs following different paths to achieve similar ends.

Smoking cessation program components and interventions may be arranged from less to more intensive and costly. Brief interventions are generally more appropriate for those who have not yet made a decision to quit. As noted in the June 2000 update of the AHRQ Guidelines, all smokers who are not ready to quit should be given brief encouragement at every medical encounter. Also, many smokers are able to quit with only the prodding of such brief intervention as the advice of their doctor. Others will need more intensive intervention, especially after they have decided to try to quit and, perhaps, failed with less intensive help in the past. Thus, program components become more intensive and more appropriate for audiences selected according to level of addiction, complicating factors such as depression, or previous failure.

CONCLUSION

Smoking is a paradox. It seems quite a simple behavior, but, as argued throughout this chapter, the influences on smoking range from the brain physiology of nicotine addiction to corporate finance. Corresponding to this breadth of influences on smoking, reductions in the percentage of smokers in the United States have been achieved through a wide range of

> scientific evidence of the relation among disease, tobacco use, and environmental exposure to tobacco; dissemination of this information to the public; surveillance and evaluation of prevention and cessation programs; campaigns by advocates for nonsmokers' rights; restrictions on cigarette advertising; counter advertising; policy changes (i.e., enforcement of minors' access laws, legislation restricting smoking in public places, and increased taxation); improvements in treatment and prevention programs; and an increased understanding of the economic costs of tobacco. (CDC, 1999b, p. 989)

Exemplifying this range of factors promoting nonsmoking, comprehensive statewide programs such as those in California and Massachusetts have seen substantial statewide reductions in smoking (Siegel, 2002). In California, evidence suggests such campaigns have reduced deaths from heart disease

(Fichtenberg & Glantz, 2000). Not relying on magic bullets, these programs embody broad campaigns of public education (including well-financed, creative, and hard-hitting advertisements and billboards countering tobacco marketing), increased taxes on cigarettes, support services for cessation, smoking prevention programs aimed at youth, and multicultural approaches, all coordinated through community-based coalitions. Thus, as reviewed by Siegel (2002), their success rests on their scope as well as on the intensity and aggressiveness of their implementation.

Within research on broad programs to encourage nonsmoking, there is an emerging consensus that tobacco control policies are effective means to prevent youth smoking. In Massachusetts, for example, nonsmoking teenagers living in towns with local tobacco sales restrictions were significantly less likely (odds ratio = .60, $p < .05$) to become smokers than teenagers in towns without such ordinances (Siegel, Biener, & Rigotti, 1999). Nationally, states with the most extensive array of tobacco control policies had significantly lower youth smoking prevalence rates ($r = -.36$, $p = .04$). They also tended to have lower percentages of teenagers who had smoked before age 13 ($r = -.29$, $p = .09$; Luke, Stamatakis, & Brownson, 2000).

As broad approaches to tobacco control grow in the United States, attention needs to turn to the rest of the world. Tobacco has become an international business subject to worldwide economic forces. Accordingly, cooperative efforts to control tobacco need to develop internationally. International initiatives noted earlier in this chapter, including WHO's Tobacco Free Initiative and Framework Convention on Tobacco Control should promote global cooperation on aspects of tobacco control that transcend national boundaries. For example, the Framework Convention on Tobacco Control "requires countries to impose restrictions on tobacco advertising, sponsorship and promotion, establish new labelling and clean indoor air controls and strengthen legislation to clamp down on tobacco smuggling" (WHO, 2003).

As noted at the start of this chapter, the years since the 1964 Surgeon General's Report (U.S. PHS, 1964) have seen a steady decline in smoking, from 42% among persons 18 years of age and older in 1965 to 23% in 2001. Considering that smoking is addictive, that it is relatively cheap and convenient, and that cigarettes are promoted by the most heavily financed marketing campaign in U.S. culture, the changes that have occurred constitute what then surgeon general C. Everett Koop called "a revolution in behavior . . . a major public health success" in his preface to the 25th anniversary Surgeon General's Report issued in 1989 (U.S. DHHS, 1989). As a model for health psychology, research on smoking demonstrates both comprehensive approaches to understanding problems and of doing something about them.

REFERENCES

Abrams, D., Monti, P., Carey, K., Pinto, R., & Jacobus, S. (1988). Reactivity to smoking cues and relapse: Two studies of discriminant validity. *Behavior Research and Therapy, 26,* 225–233.

Acitelli, L. K., & Antonucci, T. C. (1994). Gender differences in the link between marital support and satisfaction in older couples. *Journal of Personality and Social Psychology, 67,* 688–698.

Aloise-Young, P. A., Graham, J. W., & Hansen, W. B. (1994). Peer influence on smoking initiation during early adolescence: A comparison of group members and group outsiders. *Journal of Applied Psychology, 79,* 281–287.

Altria Annual Report. (2002). [No title.] Retrieved February 1, 2004, from www.altria.com/annualreport2002/

American Cancer Society. (2003). *Tobacco control country profiles* (2nd ed.). Atlanta, GA: Author.

American Lung Association. (1999). *Trends in cigarette smoking.* New York: Author.

Anda, R. F., Williamson, D. F., Escobedo, L. G., Mast, E. E., Giovino, G. A., & Remington, P. L. (1990). Depression and the dynamics of smoking. A national perspective. *Journal of the American Medical Association, 264,* 1541–1545.

Baillie, A. J., Mattick, R. P., Hall, W., & Webster, P. (1994). Meta-analytic review of the efficacy of smoking cessation interventions. *Drug and Alcohol Review, 13,* 157–170.

Belle, D. (1987). Gender differences in the social moderators of stress. In R. Barnett, L. Biener, & G. K. Baruch (Eds.), *Gender and stress* (pp. 257–277). New York: Free Press.

Benowitz, N. L., Zevin, S., & Jacob, P. (1998). Suppression of nicotine intake during ad libitum cigarette smoking by high-dose transdermal nicotine. *Journal of Pharmacology and Experimental Therapeutics, 287,* 958–962.

Biglan, A., & Lichtenstein, E. (1984). A behavior–analytic approach to smoking acquisition: Some recent findings. *Journal of Applied Social Psychology, 14,* 207–223.

Blechman, E. A. (1981). Competence, depression and behavior modification with women. In M. Hersen, R. M. Eisler & P. M. Miller (Eds.), *Progress in behavior modification* (Vol. 12, pp. 227–263). New York: Academic Press.

Brook, J. S., Whiteman, M., Gordon, A. S., & Brook, D. W. (1983). Fathers and sons: Their relationship and personality characteristics associated with the son's smoking behavior. *Journal of General Psychology, 142,* 271–281.

Brown, R. A., Lewinsohn, P. M., Seeley, J. R., & Wagner, E. F. (1996). Cigarette smoking, major depression, and other psychiatric disorders among adolescents. *Journal of the American Academy of Child and Adolescent Psychiatry, 35,* 1602–1610.

Brownson, R. C., Figgs, L. W., & Caisley, L. E. (2002). Epidemiology of environmental tobacco smoke exposure. *Oncogene, 21,* 7341–7348.

Brownson, R. C., Hopkins, D. P., & Wakefield, M. A. (2002). Effects of smoking restrictions in the workplace. *Annual Review of Public Health, 23,* 333–348.

Byrne, D. G., Byrne, A. E., & Reinhart, J. I. (1995). Personality, stress and the decision to commence cigarette smoking in adolescence. *Journal of Psychosomatic Research, 39,* 53–62.

Centers for Disease Control. (1999a). Tobacco use—United States, 1900–1999. *Morbidity and Mortality Weekly Reports, 48,* 986–993.

Centers for Disease Control. (1999b). Decline in cigarette consumption following implementation of a comprehensive tobacco prevention and education program—Oregon, 1996–1998. *Morbidity and Mortality Weekly Reports, 48,* 140–143.

Centers for Disease Control. (2003a). Prevalence of current cigarette smoking among adults and changes in prevalence of current and some day smoking—United States, 1996–2001. *Morbidity and Mortality Weekly Reports, 52,* 303–307.

Centers for Disease Control. (2003b). *Targeting tobacco use: The nation's leading cause of death 2003.* Atlanta, GA: Department of Health and Human Services, Centers for Disease Control and Prevention.

Chassin, L., Presson, C. C., Sherman, S. J., Corty, E., & Olshavsky, R. W. (1984). Predicting the onset of cigarette smoking in adolescents: A longitudinal study. *Journal of Applied Social Psychology, 14,* 224–243.

Chassin, L., Presson, C. C., Sherman, S. J., & Edwards, D. A. (1990). The natural history of cigarette smoking. Predicting young-adult smoking outcomes from adolescent smoking patterns. *Health Psychology, 9,* 701–716.

Cherry, N., & Kiernan, K. E. (1976). Personality scores and smoking behaviour. A longitudinal study. *British Journal of Preventive and Social Medicine, 30,* 123–131.

Cohen, S., Lichtenstein, E., Mermelstein, R., Kingsolver, K., Baer, J., & Kamarck, T. (1988). Social support interventions for smoking cessation. In B. H. Gottlieb (Ed.), *Marshalling social support: Formats, processes, and effects* (pp. 211–240). New York: Sage.

Cohen, S., Lichtenstein, E., Prochaska, J., Rossi, J., Gritz, E., Carr, C., et al. (1989). Debunking myths about self-quitting: Evidence from 10 prospective studies of persons who attempt to quit smoking by themselves. *American Psychologist, 44,* 1355–1365.

Compas, B., Haaga, D., Keefe, F., Leitenberg, H., & Williams, D. (1998). Sampling of empirically supported psychological treatments from health psychology: Smoking, chronic pain, cancer, and bulimia nervosa. *Journal of Consulting and Clinical Psychology, 66,* 1–24.

Cummings, K. M., Giovino, G., & Mendicino, A. J. (1987). Cigarette advertising and Black–White differences in cigarette brand preferences. *Public Health Reports, 102,* 698–701.

Cummings, R., Kelsey, J., & Nevitt, M. (1990). Methodological issues: Recurrent health problems: Falls in the elderly. *Annals of Epidemiology, 1,* 49–56.

Curry, S. J. (1993). Self-help interventions for smoking cessation—Review. *Journal of Consulting and Clinical Psychology, 61*(5), 790–803.

Curry, S. J., Grothaus, L. C., McAfee, T., & Pabiniak, C. (1998). Use and cost effectiveness of smoking-cessation services under four insurance plans in a health maintenance organization. *New England Journal of Medicine, 339*, 673–679.

Curry, S., Marlatt, A., & Gordon, J. (1987). Abstinence violation effect: Validation of an attributional construct with smoking cessation. *Journal of Consulting and Clinical Psychology, 55*(2), 145–149.

Curry, S. J., McBride, C., Grothaus, L. C., Louie, D., & Wagner, E. H. (1995). A randomized trial of self-help materials, personalized feedback, and telephone counseling with nonvolunteer smokers. *Journal of Consulting and Clinical Psychology, 63*(6), 1005–1014.

Dale, L. C., Hurt, R. D., Offord, K. P., Lawson, G. M., Croghan, I. T., & Schroeder, D. R. (1995). High-dose nicotine patch therapy. Percentage of replacement and smoking cessation. *Journal of the American Medical Association, 274*, 1353–1358.

Daughton, D. M., Fortmann, S. P., Glover, E. D., Hatsukami, D. K., Heatley, S. A., Lichtenstein, E., et al. (1999). The smoking cessation efficacy of varying doses of nicotine patch delivery systems 4 to 5 years post-quit day. *Preventive Medicine, 28*, 113–118.

Davis, A., Faust, R., & Ordentlich, M. (1984). Self-help smoking cessation and maintenance programs: A comparative study with 12-month follow-up by the American Lung Association. *American Journal of Public Health, 74*, 1212–1217.

Davis, R. (1987). Current trends in cigarette advertising and marketing. *New England Journal of Medicine, 316*, 725–732.

Dielman, T. E., Campanelli, P. C., Shope, J. T., & Butchart, A. T. (1987). Susceptibility to peer pressure, self-esteem, and health locus of control as correlates of adolescent substance abuse. *Health Education Quarterly, 14*, 207–221.

Doll, R., & Hill, A. B. (1950). Smoking and carcinoma of the lung: Preliminary report. *British Medical Journal, 2*, 1225–1236.

Eckhardt, S. G., Pulte, D. E., Hilsenbeck, S., Von Hoff, D., & Eckerdt, J. R. (1995). Response to chemotherapy in smoking and nonsmoking patients with non small cell lung cancer. *Proceedings of the Annual Meeting of the American Society of Clinical Oncology, 14*, 1088.

Eisinger, R. A. (1971). Psychosocial predictors of smoking recidivism. *Journal of Health and Social Behavior, 12*, 355–362.

Eysenck, H. J. (1980). *The causes and effects of smoking.* Beverly Hills, CA: Sage.

Falloon, I. R. H., Boyd, J. L., McGill, C. W., Razani, J., Moss, H. B., & Gilderman, A. (1982). Family management in the prevention of exacerbations of schizophrenia: A controlled study. *New England Journal of Medicine, 306*, 1437–1440.

Fichtenberg, C. M., & Glantz, S. A. (2000). Association of the California Tobacco Control Program with declines in cigarette consumption and mortality from heart disease. *New England Journal of Medicine, 343*, 1772–1777.

Fiore, M., Bailey, W., Cohen, S. J., Dorfman, S. F., Goldstein, M. G., & Gritz, E. R. (1996). *Smoking cessation clinical practice guideline* (P. H. S. Agency for Health Care Policy and Research). Rockville, MD: U.S. Department of Health and Human Services.

Fiore, M. C., Bailey, W. C., Cohen, S. J., Dorfman, S. F., Goldstein, M. G., Gritz, E. R., et al. (2000). *Treating tobacco use and dependence: Clinical practice guideline*. Rockville, MD: U.S. Department of Health and Human Services, Public Health Service.

Fisher, E. B., Jr. (1996). A behavioral–economic perspective on the influence of social support on cigarette smoking. In L. Green & J. H. Kagel (Eds.), *Advances in behavioral economics* (Vol. 3, pp. 207–236). Norwood, NJ: Ablex.

Fisher, E. B., Jr. (1997). Two approaches to social support in smoking cessation: Commodity Model and Nondirective Support. *Addictive Behaviors, 22*, 819–833.

Fisher, E. B., Jr., Bishop, D. B., Levitt-Gilmour, T., Ashenberg, Z., White, T., & Newman, E. (1994). Social support in worksite smoking cessation: Qualitative analysis of the EASE project. *American Journal of Health Promotion, 9*, 39–47, 75.

Fisher, E. B., Jr., Auslander, W. F., Munro, J. F., Arfken, C. L., Brownson, R. C., & Owens, N. W. (1998). Neighbors for a smoke free north side: Evaluation of a community organization approach to promoting smoking cessation among African Americans. *American Journal of Public Health, 88*, 1658–1663.

Fisher, E., Haire-Joshu, D., Morgan, G., Rehberg, H., & Rost, K. (1990). State-of-the-art review: Smoking and smoking cessation. *American Review of Respiratory Disease, 142*, 702–720.

Fisher, E. B., Jr., Levitt-Gilmour, T., Bishop, D. B., Newman, E., Lankester, L., & Tormery, B. (1988). *Impacts on smoking prevalence of organizational and social support in worksite smoking cessation*. Paper presented at the annual meeting of the Society of Behavioral Medicine, Boston.

Fisher, E. B., Jr., Lichtenstein, E., & Haire-Joshu, D. (1993). Multiple determinants of tobacco use and cessation. In C. T. Orleans & J. D. Slade (Eds.), *Nicotine addiction: Principles and management* (pp. 59–88). New York: Oxford University Press.

Fisher, E. B., Jr., & Rost, K. (1986). Smoking cessation: A practical guide for the physician. *Clinics in Chest Medicine, 7*, 551–565.

Flaxman, J. (1978). Quitting smoking now or later: Gradual, abrupt, immediate and delayed quitting. *Behavior Therapy, 9*, 260–270.

Flay, B. (1987). Mass media and smoking cessation: A critical review. *American Journal of Public Health, 77*, 153–160.

Flay, B. R., Hu, F. B., Siddiqui, O., Day, L. E., Hedeker, D., Petraitis, J., et al. (1994). Differential influence of parental smoking and friends' smoking on adolescent initiation and escalation of smoking. *Journal of Health and Social Behavior, 35*, 248–265.

Friedman, L. S., Lichtenstein, E., & Biglan, A. (1985). Smoking onset among teens: An empirical analysis of initial situations. *Addictive Behaviors, 10,* 1–13.

Giovino, G. A. (2003). *Tobacco surveillance in the United States.* Paper presented at the National Conference on Tobacco or Health, Boston.

Glantz, S. A., & Begay, M. E. (1994). Tobacco industry campaign contributions are affecting tobacco control policymaking in California. *Journal of the American Medical Association, 272,* 1176–1182.

Glasgow, R. E., Fisher, E. B., Anderson, B. J., La Greca, A., Marrero, D., Johnson, S. B., et al. (1999). Behavioral science in diabetes: Contributions and opportunities. *Diabetes Care, 22,* 832–843.

Glasgow, R., & Lichtenstein, E. (1987). Long-term effects of behavioral smoking cessation interventions. *Behavior Therapy, 18,* 297–324.

Glasgow, R. E., Mullooly, J. P., Vogt, T. M., Stevens, V. J., Lichtenstein, E., Hollis, J. F., et al. (1993). Biochemical validation of smoking status: Pros, cons, and data from four low-intensity intervention trials. *Addictive Behaviors, 18,* 511–527.

Glassman, A., Helzer, J. E., Covey, L. S., Cotler, L. B., Stetner, F., Tipp, J. E., et al. (1990). Smoking, smoking cessation, and major depression. *Journal of the American Medical Association, 264,* 1546–1549.

Gomel, M. K., Oldenburg, B., Simpson, J. M., Chilvers, M., & Owen, N. (1997). Composite cardiovascular risk outcomes of a work-site intervention trial. *American Journal of Public Health, 87,* 673–676.

Gomel, M., Oldenburg, B., Simpson, J. M., & Owen, N. (1993). Work-site cardiovascular risk reduction: A randomized trial of health risk assessment, education, counseling, and incentives. *American Journal of Public Health, 83,* 1231–1238.

Graham, S., & Gibson, R. W. (1971). Cessation of patterned behavior: Withdrawal from smoking. *Social Science and Medicine, 5,* 319–337.

Gritz, E. (1991). Smoking and smoking cessation in cancer patients. *British Journal of Addiction, 86,* 549–554.

Gritz, E., Kristeller, J., & Burns, D. (1993). Smoking intervention for high-risk groups and patients with medical co-morbidity. In C. Orleans & J. Slade (Eds.), *Nicotine addiction: Principles and management* (pp. 279–309). New York: Oxford University Press.

Gritz, E. R., Nielsen, I. R., & Brooks, L. A. (1996). Smoking cessation and gender: The influence of physiological, psychological, and behavioral factors. *Journal of the American Medical Women's Association, 51,* 35–42.

Gritz, E., Nisenbaum, R., Elashoff, R., & Holmes, E. (1991). Smoking behavior following diagnosis in patients with Stage I non-small cell lung cancer. *Cancer Causes and Control, 2*(2), 105–112.

Haire-Joshu, D., Glasgow, R. E., & Tibbs, T. L. (1999). Smoking and diabetes. *Diabetes Care, 22,* 1887–1898.

Hall, S., Muñoz, R., & Reus, V. (1994). Cognitive–behavioral intervention increases abstinence rates for depressive-history smokers. *Journal of Consulting and Clinical Psychology, 62,* 141–146.

Hall, S. M., Rugg, D., Tunstall, C., & Jones, R. T. (1984). Preventing relapse to cigarette smoking by behavioral skill training. *Journal of Consulting and Clinical Psychology, 52,* 372–382.

Hatsukami, D., Hughes, J., & Pickens, R. (1985). Blood nicotine, smoke exposure and tobacco withdrawal symptoms. *Addiction Behavior, 10,* 413–417.

Heath, A. C., & Madden, P. A. (1995). Genetic influences on smoking behavior. In J. R. Turner, L. R. Cardon, & J. K. Hewitt (Eds.), *Behavior genetic approaches in behavioral medicine* (pp. 37–48). New York: Plenum Press.

Heath, A. C., Madden, P. A. F., Bucholz, K. K., Nelson, E. C., Todorov, A., Price, R. K., et al. (2003). Genetic and environmental risks of dependence on alcohol, tobacco and other drugs. In R. Plomin, I. Craig, J. DeFries, & P. McGuffin (Eds.), *Behavioral genetics in the postgenomic era* (pp. 309–334). Washington, DC: American Psychological Association.

Heath, A. C., Madden, P. A., Grant, J. D., McLaughlin, T. L., Todorov, A. A., & Bucholz, K. K. (1999). Resiliency factors protecting against teenage alcohol use and smoking: Influences of religion, religious involvement and values and ethnicity in the Missouri Adolescent Female Twin Study. *Twin Research, 2,* 145–155.

Henningfield, J., & Nemeth-Coslett, R. (1988). Nicotine dependence-interface between tobacco and tobacco-related disease. *Chest, 98,* 385–395.

Hill, H. A., Schoenbach, V. J., Kleinbaum, D. G., Strecher, V. J., Orleans, C. T., Gebski, V. J., et al. (1994). A longitudinal analysis of predictors of quitting smoking among participants in a self-help intervention trial. *Addictive Behaviors, 19,* 159–173.

Hill, R. D., Rigdon, M., & Johnson, S. (1993). Behavioral smoking cessation treatment for older chronic smokers. *Behavior Therapy, 24,* 321–329.

Hirschman, R. S., Leventhal, H., & Glynn, K. (1984). The development of smoking behavior: Conceptualization and supportive cross-sectional survey data. *Journal of Applied Social Psychology, 14,* 184–206.

Hollis, J., Lichtenstein, E., Vogt, T., Stevens, V., & Biglan, A. (1993). Nurse-assisted counseling for smokers in primary care. *Annals of Internal Medicine, 118*(7), 521–525.

House, J. S., Landis, K. R., & Umberson, D. (1988). Social relationships and health. *Science, 241,* 540–544.

Hughes, G., Hymowitz, N., Ockene, J., Simon, N., & Vogt, T. (1981). The multiple risk factor intervention trial (MRFIT). *Preventive Medicine, 10,* 476–500.

Hughes, J. R., Hatsukami, D. K., Mitchell, J. E., & Dahlgren, L. A. (1986). Prevalence of smoking among psychiatric outpatients. *American Journal of Psychiatry, 143,* 993–997.

Hundleby, J. D., & Mercer, G. W. (1987). Family and friends as social environments and their relationship to young adolescents' use of alcohol, tobacco, and marijuana. *Journal of Marriage and Family, 49,* 151–164.

Hunter, S. M., Croft, J. B., Burke, G. L., Parker, F. C., Webber, L. S., & Berenson, G. S. (1986). Longitudinal patterns of cigarette smoking and smokeless tobacco use in youth: The Bogalusa heart study. *American Journal of Public Health, 76,* 193–195.

Hurt, R. D., Sachs, D. P., Glover, E. D., Offord, K. P., Johnston, J. A., Dale, L. C., et al. (1997). A comparison of sustained-release bupropion and placebo for smoking cessation. *New England Journal of Medicine, 337*(17), 1195–1202.

Jackson, C. (1998). Cognitive susceptibility to smoking and initiation of smoking during childhood: A longitudinal study. *Preventive Medicine, 27,* 129–134.

Jarvik, M. E. (1977). Biological factors underlying the smoking habit. *NIDA Research Monograph, 17,* 122–148.

Jessor, R. (1987). Problem-behavior theory, psychosocial development, and adolescent problem drinking. *British Journal of Addiction, 82,* 331–342.

Johnston, L. D., O'Malley, P. M., & Bachman, J. G. (2003). *Monitoring the future national results on adolescent drug use: Overview of key findings, 2002* (NIH Publication No. 03-5374). Bethesda, MD: National Institute on Drug Abuse.

Jorenby, D. E., Leischow, S. J., Nides, M. A., Rennard, S. I., Johnston, J. A., Hughes, A. R., et al. (1999). A controlled trial of sustained-release bupropion, a nicotine patch, or both for smoking cessation. *New England Journal of Medicine, 340,* 685–691.

Kaplan, H. I., & Sadock, B. J. (Eds.). (1985). *Comprehensive textbook of psychiatry.* Baltimore: Williams & Wilkins.

Kendler, K. S., Neale, M. C., Sullivan, P., Corey, L. A., Gardner, C. O., & Prescott, C. A. (1999). A population-based twin study in women of smoking initiation and nicotine dependence. *Psychological Medicine, 29,* 299–308.

Korhonen, H., Niemensivu, H., Piha, T., Koskela, K., Who, J., Johnson, C., et al. (1992). National TV smoking cessation program and contest in Finland. *Preventive Medicine, 21,* 74–87.

Kottke, T. E., Battista, R. N., & DeFriese, G. H. (1988). Attributes of successful smoking cessation interventions in medical practice: A meta-analysis of 39 controlled trials. *Journal of American Medical Association, 259,* 2882–2889.

Kozlowski, L. T. (1989). Evidence for limits on the acceptability of lowest-tar cigarettes. *American Journal of Public Health, 79,* 198–199.

Kozlowski, L. T., Jarvik, M. E., & Gritz, E. R. (1975). Nicotine regulation and cigarette smoking. *Clinical Pharmacology and Therapeutics, 17,* 93–97.

Krosnick, J. A., & Judd, C. M. (1982). Transitions in social influences at adolescence: Who induces cigarette smoking? *Developmental Psychology, 18,* 359–368.

Lancaster, T., & Stead, L. F. (1998). *Self-help interventions for smoking cessation.* Chichester, England: Cochrane Library.

Leff, J., & Vaughn, C. (1985). *Expressed emotion in families.* New York: Guilford Press.

Lerman, C., Caporaso, N. E., Audrain, J., Main, D. Bowman, E. D., Lockshin, B., et al. (1999). Evidence suggesting the role of specific genetic factors in cigarette smoking. *Health Psychology, 18,* 14–20.

Levin, M. L., Goldstein, H., & Gerhardt, P. R. (1950). Cancer and tobacco smoking: A preliminary report. *Journal of the American Medical Association, 143,* 336–338.

Lichtenstein, E., & Bernstein, D. A. (1980). Cigarette smoking as indirect self-destructive behavior. In N. L. Farberow (Ed.), *The many faces of suicide: Indirect self-destructive behavior* (pp. 243–253). New York: McGraw-Hill.

Lichtenstein, E., & Glasgow, R. (1992). Smoking cessation: What have we learned over the past decade. *Journal of Consulting and Clinical Psychology, 60*(4), 518–527.

Lichtenstein, E., Glasgow, R. E., & Abrams, D. B. (1986). Social support in smoking cessation: In search of effective interventions. *Behavior Therapy, 17,* 607–619.

Lichtenstein, E., Glasgow, R. E., Lando, H. A., Ossip-Klein, D. J., & Boles, S. M. (1996). Telephone counseling for smoking cessation: Rationales and meta-analytic review of evidence. *Health Education Research, 11*(2), 243–257.

Lichtenstein, E., Green, S. B., Lynn, W. R., Corle, D. K., Ockene, J. K., Giffen, C. A., et al. (1995). Community intervention trial for smoking cessation (COMMIT): I. Cohort results from a four-year community intervention. *American Journal of Public Health, 85*(2), 183–192.

Lipkus, I. M., Barefoot, J. C., Williams, R. B., & Siegler, I. C. (1994). Personality measures as predictors of smoking initiation and cessation in the UNC Alumni Heart Study. *Health Psychology, 13,* 149–155.

Luke, D. A., Esmundo, E., & Bloom, Y. (2000). Smoke signs: Patterns of tobacco billboard advertising in a metropolitan region. *Tobacco Control, 9,* 16–23.

Luke, D. A., & Krauss, M. (2003). *Where there's smoke there's money: Tobacco industry campaign contributions and U.S. Congressional voting.* Manuscript under review.

Luke, D. A., Stamatakis, K. A., & Brownson, R. C. (2000). State tobacco control policies and youth smoking behavior in the United States. *American Journal of Preventive Medicine, 19,* 180–187.

Madden, P. A., Heath, A. C., & Martin, N. G. (1997). Smoking and intoxication after alcohol challenge in women and men: Genetic influences. *Alcoholism, Clinical and Experimental Research, 21,* 1732–1741.

McCarthy, W. J., & Gritz, E. R. (1987, Aug.). *Teenagers' responses to cigarette advertising.* Paper presented at the meeting of the American Psychological Association, New York.

McDade, E. A., & Keil, J. E. (1988). *Characterization of a soup kitchen population.* Paper presented at the American Heart Association Conference on Epidemiology, Santa Fe, NM.

McGrath, E., Keita, G. P., Strickland, B. R., & Russo, N. F. (Eds.). (1990). *Women and depression: Risk factors and treatment issues. Final Report of the American Psychological Association's National Task Force on Women and Depression.* Washington DC: American Psychological Association.

Mermelstein, R., Cohen, S., Lichtenstein, E., Baer, J. S., & Kamarck, T. (1986). Social support and smoking cessation and maintenance. *Journal of Consulting and Clinical Psychology, 54,* 447–453.

Michell, L., & Amos, A. (1997). Girls, pecking order and smoking. *Social Science and Medicine, 44,* 1861–1869.

Mittelmark, M. B., Murray, D. M., Luepker, R. V., Pechacek, T. F., Pirie, P. L., & Pallonen, U. W. (1987). Predicting experimentation with cigarettes: The childhood antecedents of smoking study (CASS). *American Journal of Public Health, 77,* 206–208.

Mosbach, P., & Leventhal, H. (1988). Peer group identification and smoking: Implications for intervention. *Journal of Abnormal Psychology, 97,* 238–245.

Mullen, P. D., Simons-Morton, D. G., Ramirez, G., Frankowski, R. F., Green, L. W., & Mains, D. A. (1997). A meta-analysis of trials evaluating patient education and counseling for three groups of preventive health behaviors. *Patient Education and Counseling, 32,* 157–173.

Muñoz, R. F., Marin, B. V., Posner, S. F., & Perez-Stable, E. J. (1997). Mood management mail intervention increases abstinence rates for Spanish-speaking Latino smokers. *American Journal of Community Psychology, 25,* 325–343.

Niaura, R. S., Rohsenow, D. J., Binkoff, J. A., Monti, P. M., Pedraza, M., & Abrams, D. B. (1988). Relevance of cue reactivity to understanding alcohol and smoking relapse. *Journal of Abnormal Psychology, 97,* 133–152.

Nord, W. R., & Tucker, S. (1987). *Implementing routine and radical innovations.* Lexington, MA: D.C. Heath.

Ockene, J., Hymowitz, N., Lagus, J., & Shaten, B. (1991). Comparison of smoking behavior change for SI and UC study groups. *Preventive Medicine, 20,* 564–573.

Ockene, J. K., Kristeller, J., Goldberg, R., Amick, T. L., Pekow, P. S., Hosmer, D., et al. (1991). Increasing the efficacy of physician-delivered smoking interventions: A randomized clinical trial. *Journal of General Internal Medicine, 6,* 1–8.

Orleans, C. T., Schoenbach, V. J., Wagner, E. H., Quade, D., Salmon, M. A., Pearson, D. C., et al. (1991). Self-help quit smoking interventions: Effects of self-help materials, social support instructions, and telephone counseling. *Journal of Consulting and Clinical Psychology, 59,* 439–448.

Patten, C. A., Martin, J. E., Myers, M. G., Calfas, K. J., & Williams, C. D. (1998). Effectiveness of cognitive–behavioral therapy for smokers with histories of alcohol dependence and depression. *Journal of Studies on Alcohol, 59,* 327–335.

Patton, G. C., Carlin, J. B., Coffey, C., Wolfe, R., Hibbert, M., & Bowes, G. (1998). Depression, anxiety, and smoking initiation: A prospective study over 3 years. *American Journal of Public Health, 88,* 1518–1522.

Patton, G. C., Hibbert, M., Rosier, M. J., Carlin, J. B., Caust, J., & Bowes, G. (1996). Is smoking associated with depression and anxiety in teenagers? *American Journal of Public Health, 86,* 225–300.

Perkins, K. A., Grobe, J., & Fonte, C. (1997). Influence of acute smoking exposure on the subsequent reinforcing value of smoking. *Experimental and Clinical Psychopharmacology, 5,* 277–285.

Pianezza, M. L., Sellers, E. M., & Tyndale, R. F. (1998). Nicotine metabolism defect reduces smoking. *Nature, 393,* 750.

Pierce, J. P., Choi, W. S., Gilpin, E. S., Farkas, A. J., & Berry, C. (1998). Tobacco industry promotion of cigarettes and adolescent smoking. *Journal of the American Medical Association, 279,* 511–515.

Pierce, J. P., Choi, W. S., Gilpin, E. A., Farkas, A. J., & Merritt, R. K. (1996). Validation of susceptibility as a predictor of which adolescents take up smoking in the United States. *Health Psychology, 15,* 355–361.

Pierce, J. P., Fiore, M. C., Novotny, T. E., Hatziandreu, E. J., & Davis, R. M. (1989). Trends in cigarette smoking in the United States—Educational differences are increasing. *Journal of the American Medical Association, 261,* 56–60.

Pierce, J. A., & Gilpin, E. A. (2002). Impact of over-the-counter sales on effectiveness of pharmaceutical aids for smoking cessation. *Journal of the American Medical Association, 288,* 1260–1264.

Pierce, J. P., Gilpin, E. A., & Choi, W. S. (1999). Sharing the blame: Smoking experimentation and future smoking-attributable mortality due to Joe Camel and Marlboro advertising and promotions. *Tobacco Control, 8,* 37–44.

Pirie, P. L., Murray, D. M., & Luepker, R. V. (1988). Smoking prevalence in a cohort of adolescents, including absentees, dropouts, and transfers. *American Journal of Public Health, 78,* 176–178.

Pomerleau, O. F., Collins, A. C., Shiffman, S., & Pomerleau, C. S. (1993). Why some people smoke and others do not: New perspectives. *Journal of Consulting and Clinical Psychology, 61,* 723–731.

Pomerleau, O., & Pomerleau, C. (1987). A biobehavioral view of substance abuse and addiction. *Journal of Drug Issues, 17,* 111–131.

Prochaska, J. O., DiClemente, C. C., Velicer, W. F., & Rossi, J. S. (1993). Standardized, individualized, interactive, and personalized self-help programs for smoking cessation. *Health Psychology, 12,* 399–405.

Pucci, L. G., & Siegel, M. (1999). Exposure to brand-specific cigarette advertising in magazines and its impact on youth smoking. *Preventive Medicine, 29,* 313–320.

Rachlin, H. (1991). *Introduction to modern behaviorism* (Vol. 3). San Francisco: Freeman.

Rausch, J. L., Nichinson, B., Lamke, C., & Matloff, J. (1990). Influence of negative affect of smoking cessation treatment outcome: A pilot study. *British Journal of Addiction, 85,* 929–933.

Redmond, W. H. (1999). Effects of sales promotion on smoking among U.S. ninth graders. *Preventive Medicine, 28,* 243–250.

Rose, G., & Hamilton, P. (1978). A randomised controlled trial of the effect on middle-aged men of advice to stop smoking. *Journal of Epidemiology and Community Health, 32,* 275–281.

Rose, G., Hamilton, P. J., Colwell, L., & Shipley, M. J. (1982). A randomised controlled trial of anti-smoking advice: 10 year results. *Journal of Epidemiology and Community Health, 36,* 102–108.

Rosenbaum, P., & O'Shea, R. (1992). Large-scale study of freedom from smoking clinics—Factors in quitting. *Public Health Reports, 107,* 150–155.

Russell, M. A., Wilson, C., & Taylor, G. (1979). Effects of general practitioners' advice against smoking. *British Medical Journal, 188,* 231–235.

Salisbury, D. F., Shenton, M. E., Sherwood, A. R., Fischer, I. A., Yurgelun-Todd, D. A., Tohen, M., et al. (1998). First-episode schizophrenia psychosis differs from first-episode affective psychosis and controls in P300 amplitude over left temporal lobe. *Archives of General Psychiatry, 55,* 173–180.

Sallis, J., Hill, R., Killen, J., Telch, M., Flora, J., Girard, J., et al. (1986). Efficacy of self-help behavior modification materials in smoking cessation. *American Journal of Preventive Medicine, 2,* 342–344.

Schreck, R., Baker, L. A., & Ballad, G. (1950). Tobacco smoking as an etiological factor of cancer. *Cancer Research, 10,* 49–58.

Secker-Walker, R. H., Flynn, B. S., Solomon, L. J., Vacek, P. M., Dorwaldt, A. L., Geller, B. M., et al. (1996). Helping women quit smoking: Baseline observations for a community health education project. *American Journal of Preventive Medicine, 12,* 367–377.

Shiffman, S. (1986). A cluster-analytic classification of smoking relapse episodes. *Addictive Behaviors, 11,* 295–307.

Shiffman, S. (1989). Tobacco "chippers": Individual differences in tobacco dependence. *Psychopharmacology, 97,* 539–547.

Siegel, M. (2002). The effectiveness of state-level tobacco control interventions: A review of program implementation and behavioral outcomes. *Annual Review of Public Health, 23,* 45–71.

Siegel, M., Biener, L., & Rigotti, N. A. (1999). The effect of local tobacco sales laws on adolescent smoking initiation. *Preventive Medicine, 29,* 334–342.

Silagy, C., & Ketteridge, S. (1998). *Physician advice for smoking cessation.* Chichester, England: Cochrane Library.

Silagy, C., Mant, D., Fowler, G., & Lancaster, T. (2000). *Cochrane Database System Review, 3,* CD000146.

Skinner, C. S., Campbell, M. K., Rimer, B. K., Curry, S., & Prochaska, J. O. (1999). How effective is tailored print communication? *Annals of Behavioral Medicine. 21,* 290–298.

Stead, L. F., & Lancaster, T. (1998). *Group programmes for smoking cessation.* Chichester, England: Cochrane Library.

Strecher, V. J., Kreuter, M., Den Boer, D., J., Kobrin, S., Hospers, H. J., & Skinner, C. S. (1994). The effects of computer tailored smoking cessation messages in family practice settings. *Journal of Family Practice, 39,* 262–270.

Sumner, W. (2003). Estimating the health consequences of replacing cigarettes with nicotine inhalers. *Tobacco Control, 12,* 124–132.

Sumner, W., & Dillman, D. G. (1995). A fist full of coupons: Cigarette continuity programmes. *Tobacco Control, 4,* 245–252.

Susser, M. (1995). The tribulation of trials: Intervention in communities. *American Journal of Public Health, 85,* 156–158.

Taylor, C. B., Houston-Miller, N., Killen, J. D., & DeBusk, R. F. (1990). Smoking cessation after acute myocardial infarction: Effects of a nurse-managed intervention. *Annals of Internal Medicine, 113,* 118–123.

Tonnesen, P., Fryd, V., Hansen, M., Helsted, J., Gunnersen, A., Forchammer, H., et al. (1988). Effect of nicotine chewing gum in combination with group counseling on the cessation of smoking. *New England Journal of Medicine, 318*(1), 15–18.

True, W. R., Xian, H., Scherrer, J. F., Madden, P. A., Bucholz, K. K., Heath, A. C., et al. (1999). Common genetic vulnerability for nicotine and alcohol dependence in men. *Archives of General Psychiatry, 56,* 665–661.

Tyas, S. L., & Pederson, L. L. (1998). Psychosocial factors related to adolescent smoking: A critical review of the literature. *Tobacco Control, 7,* 409–420.

Unger, J. B., & Chen, X. (1999). The role of social networks and media receptivity in predicting age of smoking initiation: A proportional hazards model of risk and protective factors. *Addictive Behaviors, 24,* 371–381.

U.S. Department of Health and Human Services (DHHS). (1988). *The health consequences of smoking: Nicotine addiction. A report of the Surgeon General* (DHHS Publication No. (CDC) 88-8406). Rockville, MD: U.S. Department of Health and Human Services, Centers for Disease Control, Center for Health Promotion and Education, Office on Smoking and Health.

U.S. DHHS. (1989). *Reducing the health consequences of smoking—25 years of progress. A report of the Surgeon General* (DHHS publication (CDC) 89-8411). Rockville, MD: U.S. Department of Health and Human Services, Public Health Service, Centers for Disease Control, Center for Chronic Disease Prevention and Health Promotion, Office on Smoking and Health.

U.S. DHHS. (1994). *Preventing tobacco use among young people: A report of the Surgeon General.* Atlanta, GA: U.S. Department of Health and Human Services, Public Health Service, Centers for Disease Control, Center for Chronic Disease Prevention and Health Promotion, Office on Smoking and Health.

U.S. DHHS. (1998). *Tobacco use among U.S. racial/ethnic minority groups.* Atlanta, GA: U.S. Department of Health and Human Services, Public Health Service, Centers for Disease Control, Center for Chronic Disease Prevention and Health Promotion, Office on Smoking and Health.

U.S. Public Health Service (PHS). (1964). *Smoking and health. Report of the Advisory Committee to the Surgeon General of the Public Health Service* (PHS Publication No. 1103). Rockville, MD: U.S. Department of Health, Education, and Welfare, Public Health Service, Center for Disease Control.

Wagner, E. H., Curry, S. J., Grothaus, L., Saunders, K. W., & McBride, C. M. (1995). The impact of smoking and quitting on health care use. *Archives of Internal Medicine, 155,* 1789–1795.

Walker, E. F. (2002). The role of endogenous and exogenous risk factors in the genesis of schizophrenia. In R. J. McMahon & R. D. Peteres (Eds.), *The effects of parental dysfunction on children* (pp. 3–16). New York: Kluwer Academic/ Plenum Press.

Ward, K. D., Klesges, R. C., Zbikowski, S. M., Bliss, R. E., & Garvey, A. J. (1997). Gender differences in the outcome of an unaided smoking cessation attempt. *Addictive Behaviors, 22*, 521–533.

Warnecke, R. B., Langenberg, P., Wong, S. C., Flay, B. R., & Cook, T. D. (1992). The second Chicago televised smoking cessation program: A 24-month follow-up. *American Journal of Public Health, 82*, 835–840.

Warner, K. (1985). Cigarette advertising and media coverge of smoking and health. *New England Journal of Medicine, 312*, 384–388.

Warner, K. E. (1997). Cost effectiveness of smoking-cessation therapies: Interpretation of the evidence and implications for coverage. *Pharmacoeconomics, 11*, 538–549.

Warner, K. E. (2002). Tobacco harm reduction: Promise and perils. *Nicotine and Tobacco Research, 2(Suppl.)*, S61–S71.

West, R., Edwards, M., & Hajek, P. (1998). A randomized controlled trial of a "buddy" system to improve success at giving up smoking in general practice. *Addiction, 93*, 1007–1011.

Wetter, D. W., Fiore, M. C., Gritz, E. R., Lando, H. A., Stitzer, M. L., Hasselblad, V., et al. (1998). The agency for health care policy and research. Smoking cessation clinical practice guideline: Findings and implications for psychologists. *American Psychologist, 53*, 657–669.

Whitlock, E. P., Vogt, T. M., Hollis, J. F., & Lichtenstein, E. (1997). Does gender affect response to a brief clinic-based smoking intervention. *American Journal of Preventive Medicine, 13*, 159–166.

World Health Organization (WHO). (2003). *WHO framework convention on tobacco control, Geneva, Switzerland*. Retrieved February 1, 2004, from www.who.int/ tobacco/en/

Wynder, E. L., & Graham, E. A. (1950). Tobacco smoking as a possible etiologic factor in bronchiogenic carcinoma: A study of 684 proved cases. *Journal of the American Medical Association, 143*, 329–396.

Zhu, S. H., Stretch, V., Balabanis, M., Rosbrook, B., Sadler, G., & Pierce, J. P. (1996). Telephone counseling for smoking cessation: Effects of single-session and multiple-session interventions. *Journal of Consulting and Clinical Psychology, 64*(1), 202–211.

4

THE CONTEXT OF SEXUAL RISK BEHAVIOR

LESLIE F. CLARK, SCOTT D. RHODES, WILLIAM ROGERS,
AND NICOLE LIDDON

Sexual risk behavior takes its toll both in disease and unintended pregnancy. Approximately 12 million new cases of sexually transmitted diseases (STDs) occur each year in the United States (Institute of Medicine and Committee on Prevention and Control of Sexually Transmitted Diseases [IOM], 1997). Each year, almost half of the world's 133 million births are unintended, and more than half of the unintended pregnancies end in abortion (Bongaarts & Westoff, 2000). The rate of unintended pregnancies among adolescents is especially worrisome: Although this rate is declining in the United States, about a million teenagers become pregnant each year, and 95% of these pregnancies are unintended (Centers for Disease Control and Prevention, 2002).

Sexual risk behaviors take a tremendous toll on the nation's resources, both directly through the costs of treating STDs and indirectly through morbidity and reduced social well-being, as well as the economic and societal consequences of unintended births to teenagers and to low-income single parents. The Centers for Disease Control and Prevention (CDC) noted on its Web site in 2002: "Public costs from teenage childbearing totaled $120 billion from 1985–1990; $48 billion could have been saved if each birth had been postponed until the mother was at least 20 years old." Steps to prevent unintended pregnancy and prevent STDs can reap significant economic and social rewards (Orlandi & Dalton, 1998).

Great strides in prevention of STDs have been made both in the laboratory through the development of vaccines to prevent some diseases that can be transmitted sexually, such as hepatitis A and B, and in the clinic and community through behavioral risk reduction efforts, such as the promotion of condom use. However, using a condom may not be a realistic option for the woman who has limited power in a sexual relationship or the adolescent who is striving for peer group acceptance. Psychologists have an extremely important role in documenting psychological processes to identify individuals at risk for STDs and unintended pregnancy, to improve provider–patient interactions, and to develop effective sexual risk reduction interventions.

This chapter focuses on sexual risk, its determinants and consequences, and the current state of prevention research surrounding risky sexual behavior. This chapter is not meant to be an exhaustive summary of knowledge regarding sexual risk and STD infection; rather, it is intended to provide a primer for understanding the impact of STDs in the United States and conventional wisdom concerning risk reduction among women, adolescents, and men who have sex with men.

This chapter begins with a discussion of the medical aspects of STDs, including risk factors for contraction. Next, data on adolescent pregnancy, sexual initiation, and sexual risk in adolescence are reviewed. Third, behavioral interventions to reduce sexual risk for at-risk adolescents, women, and men who have sex with men are discussed. The remainder of the chapter examines the complexities studying the context of sexual risk, including issues of partner perception and relationship intimacy.

THE MEDICAL SIDE OF SEXUAL RISK

STDs are a major health problem in the United States. More than 25 organisms cause infections that are transmitted primarily through sexual contact (IOM, 1997). The number of new STD cases, excluding the human immunodeficiency virus (HIV), in the United States alone is estimated to reach 15 million each year, with a financial burden of more than $17 billion per year (Anonymous, 2000).

Many STDs go unnoticed and untreated because they are often asymptomatic, and an extended lag time may exist between contracting an STD and its repercussions. In addition, the social stigma associated with testing positive for an STD may discourage individuals from seeking counseling, testing, or treatment (IOM, 1997).

HIV, the virus that causes acquired immune deficiency syndrome (AIDS), is perhaps the most widely recognized STD. Evidence suggests a relationship between HIV acquisition and transmission and other STDs (St. Louis, Wasserheit, & Gayle, 1997). Infection with certain STDs increases an individual's susceptibility to HIV by an estimated two to five times, and coinfection with an STD and HIV increases likelihood of HIV transmission from an HIV-infected individual to a previously HIV-uninfected sexual partner (Wasserheit, 1992). Of the 513,486 cases of AIDS reported to the CDC through 1995, more than 62% had died.

Deaths are associated with other STDs as well: cancers related to human papilloma virus (HPV); chronic liver disease and liver cancer associated with hepatitis infection; pelvic inflammatory disease (PID) and ectopic pregnancies; and other complications for pregnant mothers, their unborn fetuses, and neonates. (IOM, 1997).

SEXUALLY TRANSMITTED DISEASE RISK FACTORS IN THE UNITED STATES

The burden of STDs is not equally distributed in the United States. For example, chlamydia is dispersed throughout the country, but in locations with established screening programs the rates are declining. Southern U.S. states continue to have high rates of chlamydia along with a disproportionate amount of gonorrhea and syphilis. High rates of poverty and lack of access to high quality medical care in this region may contribute to the problem (IOM, 1997).

STDs disproportionately affect adolescents and young adults. It is estimated that two thirds of STD infections occur among young people aged 25 years and younger (IOM, 1997). Several factors work to increase the likelihood of infection in sexually active young people. They are more likely to have multiple sex partners in networks of individuals who have high rates of STDs and who tend to have higher rates of unprotected sex (IOM, 1997). Adolescents are also less likely to seek health services and are more likely to encounter barriers to receiving care. Both of these forces prevent them from getting appropriate treatment or adequate prevention information. Biologically, the immature tissue of the cervix makes adolescent females more susceptible to STDs than are adults (IOM, 1997).

Women are more susceptible to contracting STDs than men, and they suffer more severe consequences. STDs are more efficiently transmitted from males to females than from females to males. Once infected, many STDs do not present with symptoms among women and are difficult to diagnose until damage has occurred. The anatomical and physiological differences in male and female reproductive systems account for many of these disparities

(Anonymous, 2000). At the same time, men who have sex with men (MSM) are at greater risk than others for many life-threatening STDs, including HIV infection, hepatitis B infection, and anal cancer compared to heterosexual men (IOM, 1997). Although AIDS incidence has declined among MSM since the beginning of the epidemic, nationally, MSM still represent half of new AIDS cases and three fourths of new male cases. Non–drug-injecting men who have sex with men account for 38% of all AIDS cases and 48% of all men diagnosed with AIDS between July 1996 and June 1997 (National Alliance of State and Territories, 2002). An estimated 42% of all HIV infections between July 1996 and June 1997 were among non–drug-injecting MSM.

Race and ethnicity are also predictors of STD rates. In the United States, Black and Hispanic Americans have much higher STD rates than European Americans. This discrepancy is not a result of the single variable of race–ethnicity. Race is a strong maker for poverty, lower access to health care, limited attempts to receive health care, drug use, and living in communities where STDs are endemic. The risks relevant to contracting, transmitting, or developing complications from an STD can be classified into three categories: biological, social, and behavioral (see Table 4.1).

The study and treatment of STDs in this country is difficult. The U.S. media portrays sexuality as a dominant aspect of life, while society as a whole remains private on issues of sexuality. This impedes educational efforts to target at-risk populations, prohibits health professionals from seeking and obtaining information that could assist them in treating their patients, and limits communication between sex partners and between parents and children (IOM, 1997). A constant pool of infectious yet unsymptomatic individuals serves as a reservoir for disease, making it difficult to control the STD and rid the population of that STD. Furthermore, patients who are tested for STDs may not return for their test results. Thus, partner disclosure, notification, and treatment are of paramount importance to control and prevent STD infections and the subsequent sequelae. Finally, STD reporting regulations are not consistent from state to state, adding to the difficulty of studying and treating STDs.

ADOLESCENCE AND SEXUAL RISK: WHERE WE ARE

In the United States each day, approximately 600 adolescents are infected with syphilis or gonorrhea (Coyle et al., 1996) Three million adolescents contract a sexually transmitted disease each year (IOM, 1997). In 1999, 49.9% of all high school students reported having engaged in sexual activity, and 36% reported sexual activity within the past three months. Black students have the highest rates of sexual initiation: 71% reported

TABLE 4.1
Risks Relevant to Contracting, Transmitting, or Developing Complications From a Sexually Transmitted Disease

Biological	Social	Individual/behavioral
Female (especially adolescents)	Poverty	Early sexual initiation
Current infection with another STD	Inadequate health care	Multiple partners
Asymptomatic infections	Limited access to health care	Intercourse with high-risk partners
Lag from infection to symptoms	Lack of health insurance	High-frequency of intercourse
Uncircumcised males	Commercial sex work	Anal intercourse
Vaginal douching	Homelessness	Uncircumcised males
Sexual practices (i.e., anal intercourse)	Incarceration	Vaginal douching
Hormonal contraceptive use	Migrant workers	Unprotected intercourse (no barrier
IUD use	Drug and alcohol use/abuse	contraceptive used)
Cervical ectopy	Sexual abuse/violence	Intravenous drug use
	Social stigma associated with STDs	Feelings of invulnerability
	Norms preventing discussion of sexuality	Lack of skills in condom negotiation

having initiated sexual intercourse, compared with 54% of Hispanic American students and 45% of European American students. The median age reported for initiation of sexual experience was 16.5 years of age; race–ethnicity-specific ages of sexual initiation are 15.0, 16.2, and 16.7 years of age for Black, Hispanic, and European American students, respectively. The proportion of high school students who reported having had sexual intercourse with four or more partners during their lifetime was 16.2% overall; 34.4% of Black, 16.6% of Hispanic, and 12.4% of European American students, respectively.

For decades, teenage pregnancy and childbearing has remained a significant and prominent social issue. Research suggests that adolescent mothers are more likely to live and raise their children in poverty, and they are more likely to be poorly educated (Ventura & Freedman, 2000). This is especially true for young mothers who have more than one child (Ventura & Freedman, 2000). Teenage mothers also run an increased risk of raising a child alone. From 1960 to 1997, the percentage of all births in the United States that were to unmarried women 15 to 19 years old rose from 15% to 78% (Ventura & Freedman, 2000). Infants born to adolescents are more likely to be born prematurely and at a lower birth weight, which places these infants at a higher risk of morbidity, developmental delays, and mortality (Ventura, Martin, Curtin, Mathews, & Park, 2000).

There has been a general trend over the past 25 years toward reduced adolescent birthrates and pregnancy among industrialized nations (Singh & Darroch, 2000). Most developed countries with available statistics reduced teenage birthrates virtually in half between 1970 and 1995, with the most notable drop occurring in the early 1990s (Singh & Darroch, 2000). Although declining, the U.S. pregnancy rates for 15- to 19-year-old women was 83.6 pregnancies per 1,000 women in 1995.

The trend of decreasing pregnancy rates looks promising. Between 1991 and 1996, the pregnancy rate for U.S. women aged 15 to 19 declined 15%, from 116.5 per 1,000 to 98.7 per 1,000 (Coard, Nitz, & Felice, 2000; Ventura, Mosher, Curtin, Abma, & Henshaw, 2000). Some reasons for the decline include increased condom use, decreasing sexual activity, new methods of birth control including injectables and implants, healthy economic conditions, and a focus on reproductive education (Singh & Darroch, 2000; Ventura et al. 2000).

Some of the most drastic changes have occurred among Black adolescents. The birth rate for Black teenagers that already have one child dropped 28% between 1991 and 1997, a fact likely attributable to an increase in the use of Depo-Provera and Norplant (Ventura et al. 2000). Despite such advances, the pregnancy rates among minority women between the ages of 15 and 19 years remain alarmingly high. The rates for non-Hispanic Black and Hispanic teenagers are roughly double the rate for non-Hispanic White adolescents. Hispanic and Black teenagers are more likely to be sexually active, and if active, more likely to become pregnant. In 1995, 57% of Black and 52% of Hispanic adolescents were sexually active compared with 46% of White teenagers. That same year, about one in three of the sexually active Hispanic and Black teens became pregnant compared to just one in six of sexually active non-Hispanic White adolescents (Ventura et al. 2000). Until 1994, the highest rate of adolescent childbirth belonged to Black Americans, but as of 1997 Hispanic teenagers had the highest birthrate at 97.4 per 1,000. This means that roughly 10% of Hispanic women between the ages of 15 and 19 years had a baby that year, compared to 8% of Black women, 7% of Native American women, and about 4% of White women (Ventura & Freedman, 2000). Differences among these groups can, in part, be attributed to socioeconomic differences.

A current objective of American researchers and policy makers is to continue to lower the number of pregnancies among 15- to 19-year-old women, especially among minority groups (Hacker, Amare, Strunk, & Horst, 2000; Hellerstedt, Smith, Shew, & Resnick, 2000; Franklin & Corcoran, 2000). One emerging challenge is to address sexual issues among those at the bottom of that age range (15- to 17-year-olds) and to extend research and policies to encompass even younger adolescents, whose sexual behaviors are growing riskier but have not been studied systematically (Doswell, 1999). Sexual activity places adolescents at risk for STD infection and unplanned pregnancies. For these reasons, sexual activity in early and middle adolescence is seen as a problem behavior (Brooks-Gunn & Paikoff, 1997).

Adolescent Psychosocial Development

Adolescent sexual activity has been considered one of a group of problem behaviors that also include substance use and delinquency (Jessor, 1982, 1991). However, it is argued that adolescent problem behaviors, including sexual activity, take place in the larger context of normal adolescent experimentation activities that are healthy developmental tasks for the adolescent's identity formulation (Erikson, 1968; Marcia, Waterman, Matteson, Archer, & Orlofsky, 1993). In creating self-identity, the adolescent moves from the parent and family to friends and peer group for affiliation (Erikson, 1966, 1968). The outcome of adolescents' experimentation with different behaviors and values, and their emancipation from childhood parental dependency, is linked to their formulation of an individual identity. The adolescent is making crucial decisions about life at this point (Baumrind & Moselle, 1985).

The criteria for attainment of a mature identity are based on two essential states or activities that Erikson previously identified: crisis–exploration and commitment. Crisis–exploration refers to the period when the adolescent actively examines developmental opportunities and identity issues and questions parentally defined goals and values. The adolescent is beginning to search for personally appropriate options in respect to occupation, goals, values, and beliefs. Commitment pertains to the extent that the individual is personally involved in, and expresses allegiance to, self-chosen aspirations, goals, values, beliefs, and occupation. In applying these concepts to Erikson's adolescent stage of "identity versus role diffusion," Marcia, Waterman, Matteson, Archer, and Orlofsky (1993) suggested four identity statuses: (a) diffusion, (b) foreclosure, (c) moratorium, and (d) identity formulation.

Marcia and colleagues suggest that *identity-diffused–confused* adolescents have not experienced an identity crisis and have not made any personal commitment to a set of beliefs and values (or to a vocation, for example). Identity issues have not been significant, or if they became an issue, they were never explored. *Foreclosed* adolescents have not experienced an identity crisis but have made commitments to goals, values, and beliefs. These commitments emerge from an identification with parents or significant others through socialization, pressures, and "indoctrination" of parents or peers. For example, an adolescent may be committed to peer norms associated with sexual activity, acting on the goals, values, and beliefs of others. *Moratorium* adolescents are in an acute state of crisis and exploration and are actively searching for values to call their own. These adolescents are struggling to define personal identity by experimenting with alternative roles and beliefs. However, they have not made a commitment, or perhaps they have made temporary kinds of commitments. *Identity-achieved* adolescents have progressed through both crisis–exploration and commitment and have resolved identity issues. As a result of this resolution, these adolescents have made a well-defined personal commitment to an occupation, religious beliefs, and a personal value system, and have resolved their attitudes and values concerning sexuality.

From this perspective, sexual activity may play an instrumental role in gaining peer acceptance and respect; in establishing autonomy from parents; in repudiating the norms and values of conventional authority; and in coping with anxiety, frustration, and anticipation of failure (Jessor, 1991). Although "risky behaviors" can be viewed from the perspective of facilitating the process of identity formulation, they can also jeopardize the accomplishment of normal developmental tasks. Such tasks include the fulfillment of expected social roles, the acquisition of essential skills, the achievement of a sense of competence, and the appropriate preparation for transition to young adulthood. Thus, sexual activity may fulfill certain developmental needs but may thwart subsequent developmental transitions.

Determinants of Adolescent Sexual Activity and Pregnancy

A variety of psychosocial determinants have been associated with adolescent sexual risk behavior. Adolescents who (a) have lower intelligence (Halpern, Joyner, Udry, & Suchindran, 2000), (b) experience childhood trauma (Medrano, Desmond, Zule, & Hatch, 1999), (c) are homeless (Clatts & Davis, 1999), (d) use substances (Brook, 1998; Mott, Fondell, Hu, Kowaleski-Jones, & Menaghen, 1996; Rotheram-Borus, Mahler, & Rosario, 1995), or (e) participate in illegal activities (McLaughlin, Reiner, Reams, & Joost, 1999) tend to initiate sex at an earlier age than other adolescents.

Cultural and social factors play a role in sexual onset. Earlier initiation is associated with racial–ethnic minority status (Anonymous, 1998; Coker et al., 1994; Warren et al., 1998), having peers who engage in sexual activity (Mott et al., 1996; Romer et al., 1994), mother's own history of early initiation of sexual activity (Mott et al., 1996), and same-sex orientation (Rosario, Meyer-Bohlburg, Hunter, & Gwadz, 1999; Rotheram-Borus et al., 1995). Sexual initiation is also associated with longer duration of an intimate relationship (Civic, 2000; Rosario et al., 1999). In addition, among high school students, determinants of sexual initiation differ for adolescents who initiate earlier (9th grade) and those who initiate later (11th grade; Chewning & van Koningsveld, 1998).

When studying adolescent sexual behavior, adolescents traditionally have been classified into either having had sex or not having had sex. However, conceptualizing adolescents as "sexually active" or "not sexually active" may obscure understanding adolescent sexual activity by aggregating fundamentally distinct experiences (Miller et al., 1997; Whitaker, Miller, & Clark, 2000). A new approach suggests that a more in-depth categorization of adolescent experience might be more helpful in understanding adolescent sexual risk. According to this new approach, *delayers* are adolescents who have not had sex and do not anticipate having sex within the next year. *Anticipators* are adolescents who have not had sex but anticipate having sex within the next year. Previous research indicates that adolescents' expectations of impending sexual onset are associated with likelihood to initiate sexual activity (Stanton, Li, Black, et al., 1996).

A study of 14- to 16-year-old Black and Latino high school students and their mothers suggested that anticipators were significantly more likely to have engaged in precoital sexual behaviors and to have a potential sex partner (boy- or girlfriend) than were delayers. In addition, compared to delayers, anticipators reported more risk behaviors, more peer modeling of risk behaviors, parents with less effective parenting skills, less involvement in school and church, and a psychological profile of lower self-esteem and control (Miller et al., 1997; Whitaker et al., 2000). This same study showed distinctions among already sexually active adolescents. *Singles* or *steadies* include adolescents who have had sex with only one partner, and *multiples* include adolescents who have had sex with more than one partner. Multiples initiated sex at an earlier age than steadies and were less likely to report condom use (Miller et al., 1997). Prevention specialists advocate targeted interventions based on adolescent factors such as gender, race, age, and setting. Based on the taxonomy we have discussed, interventions should be further tailored to coincide with adolescent sexual experience. The next section discusses intervention research for at-risk adolescents, women, and men who have sex with men.

SEXUAL RISK INTERVENTION RESEARCH

In this section we cover HIV prevention intervention work focusing on prevention among adolescents, women, and men who have sex with men.

Adolescents

Programs differ by their objectives and by intervention setting such as schools, clinics, and community agencies. Some programs are designed to delay sexual onset and increase abstinence or to increase knowledge about STD risk. Still other programs seek to improve skills and norms around condom negotiation and use.

According to the Centers for Disease Control and Prevention, there are currently five curricula that have particularly strong evidence for success in reducing adolescent sexual risk behavior. These interventions are predominantly school-based and include Becoming a Responsible Teen (St. Lawrence, Jefferson, Alleyne, & Brasfield, 1995; St. Lawrence, Brasfield, et al., 1995), Be Proud! Be Responsible! (Jemmott, Jemmott, & Fong, 1998; Jemmott, Jemmott, Fong, & McCaffree, 1999; St. Lawrence, Brasfield, et al., 1995; St. Lawrence, Jefferson, et al., 1995), Get Real About Aids (Main et al., 1994), Reducing the Risk (Kirby, Barth, Leland, & Fetro, 1991), and Focus on Kids (Stanton, Li, Ricardo, et al., 1996). These curricula are theory-based and usually use components of social cognitive theory and the theory of reasoned action–planned behavior.

To illustrate, we describe the program called Reducing the Risk (Kirby et al., 1991). It targets communication skills to prevent pregnancy and STD transmission among adolescents. The theoretical foundation of this 17-session intervention is based on social cognitive theory, social influence theory, and cognitive–behavior theory. To evaluate the intervention, 13 California high schools served as treatment sites. In the nonequivalent control group design, 9th- and 10th-grade health education classes participated in either the intervention curriculum or standard sexuality education (comparison). Eighteen months after the intervention, sexual initiation rates were lower among intervention students than the comparison group students. Among sexually active students, the rate of contraceptive use was higher among intervention than the comparison group students. Parental communication about sex was higher among treatment students as well. The curriculum was originally published in 1989 and has since been promoted as an effective intervention to prevent HIV infection (Kirby, 1999; Kirby et al., 1991).

The role of peers in adolescent interventions requires more study. Because peer-led activity in tobacco, alcohol, and other drug use prevention interventions has been relatively successful, the use of peers in HIV prevention has become increasingly popular. For example, the AIDS Adolescent Prevention Program (AAPP) trains high school peer educators to provide sexual risk reduction activities among middle and high school students (Fairfax, Clark, Wright, Ford, & Shepperd, 1997). The rationale is that the use of peers will change norms and influence behavior, as predicted by social influence research and by peer influence in the AIDS Risk Reduction Model (Catania, Kegeles, & Coates, 1990; Rotheram-Borus et al., 1995). In 1995, this intervention trained 120 peer leaders, who in turned reached 1,587 middle–junior high students and 3,505 senior high students. Although some researchers assert that peer-led, school-based interventions show promise for preventing sexual risk behavior among adolescents, what constitutes effective peer-led intervention in adolescent STD prevention programs is not well defined (Ozer, Weinstein, Maslach, & Siegel, 1997), and a recent study indicates that peer-led intervention can be less effective than classroom-based intervention (Fisher, Fisher, Bryan, & Misovich, 2002).

A new direction in intervention science proposes to prevent sexual risk through more general improvement in life skills (Kirby, 1999). One such lifestyle intervention is the Reach for Health Community Youth Service Learning Program (O'Donnell et al., 1999). The curriculum focuses on sexual activity, substance use, and violence. This intervention used a community service component to help students learn to contribute to their community and understand how classroom activities connect to real-life experiences. The results of a large ($N = 1061$) evaluation of urban school 8th graders indicated that service learning coupled with in-class health instruction had a positive impact on delay of sexual initiation and on abstinence among already sexually active students (O'Donnell et al., 1999). Potential but unexamined mediators of these effects are increased self-esteem, empowerment, out-of-school mentoring, and greater linkages to mainstream social institutions besides schools.

Interventions for Women

Interventions targeting sexual risk reduction among women have been based on the theory of reasoned action (Fishbein, 1990) and social cognitive theory (Bandura, 1994, 1997). According to these theories, consistent condom use is promoted by affecting an individual's motivation, resources, and social supports. Increasing self-efficacy, the belief in one's ability to enact a behavior in a way that will successfully achieve a goal, can help ensure STD prevention.

Project RESPECT was a major intervention study that applied these theories. Men and women visiting STD clinics were provided a multiple-session intervention with skills training to increase condom use and condom-use negotiation. The intervention groups showed statistically significant reductions in STD infections across 3, 6, 9, and 12 months relative to the groups receiving only standard care consisting of didactic messages (Kamb, Dillon, Fishbein, & Willis, 1996; Kamb et al., 1998).

The social cognitive theory also was applied in a San Francisco community-based intervention with 128 Black women 18 to 29 years of age (Wingood & DiClemente, 1996). This curriculum also used the theory of gender and power, which posits that barriers to practicing safer sex arise from larger social issues surrounding male–female power differentials. Economic factors and norms prescribing women's submissive role in society are examples of barriers that may affect a woman's ability to refuse sex or negotiate safer sex with a male partner (Wingood & DiClemente, 1996). Other barriers to condom use include male partner refusal to wear a condom, the negative stigma associated with female-initiated male condom use, and the woman's fear of physical and psychological abuse (Amaro, 1995; Amaro & Gornemann, 1991). In this intervention, the treatment group attended five sessions that emphasized ethnic and gender pride, HIV education, communication skills, negotiation and coping skills, and partner norms. Women randomized to the treatment showed increases in consistent condom use at a three-month follow-up compared to a delayed treatment group and an education-only group.

In an attempt to produce realistic female-controlled alternatives to the male condom, in 1992, the FDA approved a female condom that protects against both unplanned pregnancy and STDs (Cecil, Perry, Seal, & Pinkerton, 1998; Rosenberg, Davidson, Chen, Judson, & Douglas, 1992; Rosenberg & Gollub, 1992). A brief, single-session intervention may increase women's willingness to use the female condom. Evidence comes from a randomized experiment testing a multiple session intervention on sexual health and HIV/AIDS prevention among 334 inner-city housing residents in five national sites (Sikkema et al., 2000). During one session, treatment group participants received instruction on the use of the female condom. Following the instruction, the women were given a package of three female condoms and a bottle of lubricant. The study found a significant but modest increase in female condom use receptivity one week posttest (Sikkema et al., 2000).

It is not altogether clear that female-controlled methods are the answer to the complex circumstances of women's sexual risk. The assumption is that the women who are engaging in unsafe sex actually desire and would use a female-controlled method. In a recent study of minority women, those who rated female-control method as a highly important feature of HIV prevention methods already were more likely to be using a male condom than other women in the study. Women who were more likely to have unprotected sex and who evidenced a higher rate of past STD infection did not tend to rate female control as an important feature of an HIV prevention method. Instead, these women reported the need for a method that was under male partner control and addressed male partner concerns (Murphy, Miller, Moore, & Clark, 2000). For many at-risk women the involvement and support of males may be more effective than female control in reducing sexual risk. In Zambia, an African society in which men heavily influence actions taken within male–female relationships, an approach that counsels couples about condom use has shown remarkable effectiveness (Allen et al., 1992).

Intervention for Men Who Have Sex With Men

Both clinical and behavioral research has begun to explore the utility of postexposure antiretroviral prophylaxis to prevent HIV infection and the identification of predictors of utilization of such medical intervention among MSM (Kalichman, 1998). Vaccination research has expanded to determine factors associated with vaccination of MSM against STDs such as hepatitis (Rhodes, DiClemente, Yee, & Hergenrather, 2000).

Behavioral interventions have been designed and implemented to target those MSM who are identified as being at high risk for HIV infection, including younger men, (Coates, Faigle, & Stall, 1995), ethnic minority men (DiClemente, Lanier, Horan, & Lodico, 1991; Peterson et al., 1996), and substance-using men (Stall, McKusick, Wiley, Coates, & Ostrow, 1986). For example, data from the Multi-Center AIDS Cohort Study, used to project overall risk of infection, lead to the estimate that a 20-year-old male who has sex with other men has a one in five chance of becoming infected before the age of 25 (Coates et al., 1995).

Interventions targeting MSM have evolved from more cognitive–behavioral sex education interventions (Choi et al., 1996; Peterson et al., 1996) to a focus on peer influence models and diffusion of innovation (Rogers, 1983). A case in point is the "Mpowerment" Project, which targets young MSM populations. This intervention is based on the concept that individuals are more likely to adopt new behaviors when favorable evaluations of the new behavior are conveyed to them by individuals whom they perceive as similar to themselves and whom they respect (Kegeles & Hart, 1998; Kegeles, Hays, & Coates, 1997; Kegeles, Hays, Pollack, & Coates, 1999).

UNDERSTANDING SEXUAL BEHAVIOR WITHIN THE CONTEXT OF A SEXUAL RELATIONSHIP

All interventions to promote safer-sex activity face a challenge to the extent that their message is, "Using a condom shows that one cares about a partner." Making this message work requires understanding the relationship context and what the relationship means to the individuals.

Research in behavioral epidemiology has assumed a distinction between a primary sexual relationship and other types of sexual partners. However, these partner labels have different connotations in different contexts. Several labels have been used interchangeably to denote a primary sexual partner, including *primary*, *main*, *regular*, and *steady*. Primary carries a connotation of first among many; main suggests the most frequent sexual partner; steady may refer to consistency of sexual acts across time or some sense of commitment. Researchers assume that certain relationship characteristics, such as having sex exclusively with one partner, may cooccur with the label primary. One such assumption has been supported, in that people report less condom use with primary partners than other partners (Laumann, Gagnon, Michael, & Michaels, 1994). However, none of these categories reveal much about individuals' motivations to use or not to use condoms.

The term *casual sex partner* may be interpreted to mean that the relationship is defined by its sexual function, or that a relationship beyond sexual interaction exists but that the partners do not agree to have sex exclusively with each other. Sex with strangers (often combined with casual partners) has been defined as being sex with a casual date or a pick-up or having paid or been paid for sex. Such classifications have been used as indications of "non-discriminating sex partner recruitment practices," which includes sex with anonymous partners, with someone within 24 hours of meeting, and sex with any partner only once (Seidman, Mosher, & Aral, 1994). Nondiscriminating sex partner recruitment is relevant to STDs because individuals who recruit sex partners indiscriminately in bars and on the street have a higher likelihood of running into an infected partner than do individuals who recruit people they already know through other connections (Aral, Soskoline, Joesoef, & O'Reilly, 1991).

A major problem with this categorization is that it combines sex workers with other sexual partners, even though intercourse with sex workers may represent uniquely high health risks. In addition, these sexual encounters are likely to vary in terms of the objective of the interaction, emotional intimacy, the script of sexual interaction, and other features. In fact, little is known about whether encounters with sex workers share any features with other encounters, including whether or not they are a one-time sexual encounter.

What is needed is an approach that could classify sexual encounters in terms of relationship dimensions such as degree of commitment, functions, exclusivity, and longevity. An example of this approach was taken in a study of 323 Black STD clients interviewed about their sexual partners from the past three months. Reported exclusivity, mutuality, and nonsexual aspects of a relationship were not adequately predicted by the clients' use of partnership labels such as *main* and *casual* (Willis, Mukherjee, Clark, Stephens, & Avery, 1999). Documenting these distinctions can increase our ability to predict risky sexual behavior and provides useful data for the development of interventions to address sexual behavior change.

It is equally important in the arena of sexually transmitted disease to examine the context of multiple sexual partnerships. The issue of multiple or overlapping partners as a sexual risk has been well-documented (Laumann et al., 1994). Research has indicated that Black men are significantly more likely than their White counterparts to have had more than five sexual partners in the past year (Anderson & Dahlberg, 1992; Michael, Gagnon, Laumann, & Kolata, 1994). In an innercity sample, Black men were far more likely than women to report multiple sex partners. Those men who considered themselves single reported 1.9 current sexual partners (single women reported .8). Black men who were married or living with a steady partner reported 3.2 current sexual partners relative to the 1 reported by married or cohabiting White men. It has been argued, somewhat controversially, that Black women may tolerate nonmonogamy among Black men because they acknowledge the relative rarity of "appropriate" Black men who are available for relationships (L. Miller, Burns, & Rothspan, 1995).

STD literature argues for the importance of partner selection research questions in STD prevention. In particular, public health officials advocate more discriminatory partner selection. Understanding how individuals perceive their partners and enact the process of partner recruitment will enable the development of more efficacious communications about partner selection.

Risk Perception and Partner Perception Research

A key component of most models of health behavior, including the health belief model (Becker, 1974; Rosenstock, 1974), protection motivation theory (Rogers, 1975, 1983), the transtheoretical model of change

(Prochaska & DiClemente, 1986; Prochaska, DiClemente, & Norcross, 1992), and the precaution adoption process (Weinstein, 1988; Weinstein & Nicolich, 1993), is the relationship between perceived risk (vulnerability) and the decision to take either risky or preventive action. If ones' perception of risk is high, one will take preventive action. However, people often underestimate their risk or have inaccurate perceptions of risk.

Misperception of sexual risk may be one of the most widely misperceived health risks for sexually active individuals. Contrasted with many other health risks, the risk of STD/HIV is based on actions individuals believe to be under their control, such as wearing a condom and avoiding sexually risky partners (Weinstein, 1988). Also, sexual behavior is unlike other health-related behaviors in that perceived risk is not associated with sexual behavior change. Risk perception predicts protective behavior in general (Weinstein, 1988) and specific health behaviors such as smoking, drinking, exercise, and diet (Harrison, Mullen, & Green, 1992; Janz & Becker, 1984). However, research on HIV finds no relationship between perceived risk and subsequent protective sexual behavior (condom use, number of partners). This is the case among adolescents (Brown, DiClemente, & Reynolds, 1991), gay male populations, and other at-risk individuals (Gerrard, Gibbons, Warner, & Smith, 1993).

It has been suggested that the general model of health risk perception may not apply to the area of sexual risk (Gerrard, Gibbons, Benthin, & Hessling, 1996; Gerrard, Gibbons, & Bushman, 1996; Gerrard et al., 1993; Poppen & Reisen, 1997). Sexual risk perception differs from other perceived health risks in that it is influenced by the changing dynamics of the HIV epidemic, relationship characteristics (communication, duration), and the social nature of perception formation. Assessments of partner-specific risk perceptions may better predict subsequent sexual behavior. Poppen and Riesen (1997) suggested that the conclusion that risk perception and risk-taking behavior are not related may be a result of the exclusion of key social interaction variables (p. 380). The authors also encourage development of multiple-item measures of partner-specific risk perception that includes both ideas about a partner's sexual history as well as emotional reactions to the partner.

Partner Perceptions

Individuals' perception that a potential partner is "safe" plays an important role in forming perceptions of their own sexual risk and actual sexual behavior. In reviewing the sexual practices of heterosexual adolescents, Maticka-Tynedale (1991) concluded that they believed that by selecting safe partners they decreased the risk of AIDS and therefore they did not need to use condoms (see also Hutcherson, 1999). People continue to rely on perceptions of partners as a principal means of assessing a partner's riskiness, and base decisions about condom use on those perceptions (Williams et al., 1992; Woodcock, Stenner, & Ingham, 1992). In fact, individuals may distort their partners' sexual risk behavior rather than adopt protective behavior. For example, people use presumed monogamy and the duration of a partner's past relationships to gauge sexual risk (Malloy, Fisher, Albright, Misovich, & Fisher, 1997). A challenge faced by intervention researchers is how to discourage the use of the partner assessment strategy and encourage consistent condom use with all partners. To do this, we must first understand how individuals decide that a particular partner is safe.

The Partner Safety Beliefs Scale (Clark, Miller, Harrison, Kay, & Moore, 1996) uses items based on well-established predictors of attraction (familiarity, trust, and perceived similarity to oneself) to assess how people judge a partners' HIV safety. High scores on the scale indicate that an individual has confidence in the usefulness of attraction predictors to determine a partner's HIV status. Low scores indicate skepticism about the usefulness of attraction predictors. Perceived familiarity is fostered by perceptions of shared interests, beliefs, goals, social networks, values, and lifestyle (Berscheid, 1988). People may use a sense of familiarity, or how well they feel they know a person, to assess sexual risk. In a study of condom use among sexually active Black and Hispanic male adolescents, confidence in Partner Safety Beliefs was associated with low condom use (Clark et al., 1996).

In subsequent work adding perceived partner risk items to the scale revealed two general factors that reproduced relatively well across a Black male STD sample and a minority (Black and Hispanic American) sample of women attending health clinics. The two factors included (a) perceived partner risk and (b) engendered feelings of familiarity. The first, perceived partner risk, refers to the degree to which an individual suspects a partner may have an STD or HIV because of risky behavior such as excessive flirting, drug use, or promiscuous sexual history. In the study of minority women, citing each factor as reasons for not using condoms was associated with less overall condom use across two years (Clark, Miller, & Liddon, 2004). Although statistically separate, both familiarity and risk refer to a process of overall sexual risk assessment. For this reason, future investigations should consider perceived partner familiarity when predicting condom use.

In a study of Black male STD clinic clients, perceived familiarity of a particular partner predicted lower condom use with that partner (Liddon et al., 2004). However, both partner perceptions and first-time condom use with that partner were associated with relationship characteristics. Men who reported being in steady long-term relationships and who reported a great degree of partner familiarity were more likely to use a condom during initial sexual intercourse. For men who were in nonsteady relationships, high partner familiarity was associated with a lower likelihood of using a condom at initial intercourse with that partner. It may be that individuals who perceive a great deal of familiarity go on to form lasting relationships with that partner. It is also possible, however, that as respondents report on relationships of longer duration or of more intimate contact, their reports of condom use may be less accurate (because of recall bias, for example). These findings suggest that partner perceptions, relationship context, and emotional investment in a partner are important factors in understanding and intervening in sexual risk behaviors.

CONCLUSION

This chapter has discussed the issues surrounding behavioral risks for sexually transmitted disease. For many of these diseases there is not yet a medically known cure, and several have significant health consequences. Interventions within three populations of at-risk individuals—adolescents, women, and men who have sex with men—have been discussed. We have highlighted similarities and differences in approach, settings, and conceptual frameworks used to design, implement, and evaluate these behavior change programs. An understanding of the context in which risky sexual behaviors occurs is critical. This chapter has outlined the developmental transition, the social environment, the various kinds of relationships, and the emotional context of sex. A broader view of sexual risk is needed, incorporating the context of relationships, even in seemingly casual or brief sexual encounters. Psychologists are well-placed to meet the challenges presented by these complex public health problems.

REFERENCES

Allen, S., Tice, J., Van de Perre, P., Serufilira, A., Hudes, E., Nsengumuremyi, F., et al. (1992). Effect of serotesting with counselling on condom use and seroconversion among HIV discordant couples in Africa. *British Medical Journal, 304*(6842), 1605–1609.

Amaro, H. (1995). Love, sex, and power. Considering women's realities in HIV prevention. *American Psychologist, 50*(6), 437–447.

Amaro, H., & Gornemann, I. (1991). Health care utilization for sexually transmitted diseases: Influences of patient and provider characteristics. In J. N. Wasserheit, S. O. Aral, & K. K. Holmes (Eds.), *Research issues in human behavior and sexually transmitted diseases in the AIDS era* (pp. 182–196). Washington, DC: American Society for Microbiology.

Anderson, J. E., & Dahlberg, L. L. (1992). High-risk sexual behavior in the general population. Results from a national survey, 1988–1990. *Sexually Transmitted Disease, 19,* 320–325.

Anonymous. (1998). Prevention of transmission of hepatitis B. *Canadian Medical Association Journal, 159*(1), 71–76.

Anonymous. (2000). *Healthy people 2010.* Washington, DC: U.S. Department of Health and Human Services.

Aral, S. O., Soskoline, V., Joesoef, R. M., & O'Reilly, K. R. (1991). Sex partner recruitment as risk factor STD: Clustering of risky modes. *Sexually Transmitted Diseases, 19,* 320–325.

Bandura, A. (1994). Social cognitive theory and exercise over HIV infection. In R. J. DiClemente & J. L. Peterson (Eds.), *Preventing AIDS: Theories and methods of behavioral intervention* (pp. 25–59). New York: Plenum Press.

Bandura, A. (1997). *Self-efficacy: The exercise of control.* New York: W. H. Freeman.

Baumrind, D., & Moselle, K. A. (1985). A development perspective on adolescent drug abuse. *Alcohol and Substance Abuse in Adolescence, 4*(3–4), 41–67.

Becker, M. H. (1974). The health belief model and personal health behavior. *Health Education, 2,* 324–508.

Berscheid, E. (1988). Interpersonal attraction. In G. Lindzey & E. Aronson (Eds.), *Handbook of social psychology* (3rd ed., Vol. 2, pp. 413–84). New York: Random House.

Bongaarts, J., & Westoff, C. F. (2000). The potential role of contraception in reducing abortion. *Studies in Family Planning, 31*(3), 193–202.

Brook, M. G. (1998). Sexual transmission and prevention of the hepatitis viruses A–E and G. *Sexually transmitted infections, 74*(6), 395–398.

Brooks-Gunn, J., & Paikoff, R. (1997). Sexuality and developmental transitions during adolescence. In J. Schulenberg, J. L. Maggs, & K. Hurrelmann (Eds.), *Health risks and developmental transitions during adolescence* (pp. 190–219). Cambridge: Cambridge University Press.

Brown, L. K., DiClemente, R. J., & Reynolds, L. A. (1991). HIV prevention for adolescents: Utility of the health belief model. *AIDS Education & Prevention, 3*(1), 50–59.

Catania, J. A., Kegeles, S. M., & Coates, T. J. (1990). Towards an understanding of risk behavior: An AIDS risk reduction model (ARRM). *Health Education Quarterly, 17*(1), 53–72.

Cecil, H., Perry, M. J., Seal, D. W., & Pinkerton, S. D. (1998). The female condom: What we have learned thus far. *AIDS and Behavior, 2*(3), 241–256.

Centers for Disease Control and Prevention (CDC). (2002). Teen pregnancy. Retrieved May 31, 2002, from http://www.cdc.gov/nccdphp/teen.htm

Chewning, B., & van Koningsveld, R. (1998). Predicting adolescents' initiation of intercourse and contraceptive use. *Journal of Applied Psychology, 28*(14), 1245–1285.

Choi, K. H., Lew, S., Vittinghoff, E., Catania, J. A., Barrett, D. C., & Coates, T. J. (1996). The efficacy of brief group counseling in HIV risk reduction among homosexual Asian and Pacific Islander men. *AIDS, 10*(3), 319–325.

Civic, D. (2000). College students' reasons for nonuse of condoms within dating relationships. *Journal of Sexual and Marital Therapy, 26*(1), 95–105.

Clark, L. F., Miller, K. S., Harrison, J. S., Kay, K. L., & Moore, J. (1996). The role of attraction in partner assessments and heterosexual risk for HIV. In S. Oskamp & S. Thompson (Eds.), *Understanding and preventing HIV risk behavior: Safer sex and drug use* (pp. 80–99). Thousand Oaks, CA: Sage.

Clark, L. F., Miller, L., & Liddon, N. (2004). *Partner perception and condom use among minority women.* Unpublished manuscript, University of Birmingham, Alabama.

Clatts, M. C., & Davis, W. R. (1999). A demographic and behavioral profile of homeless youth in New York City: Implications for AIDS outreach and prevention. *Medical Anthropology Quarterly, 13*(3), 365–374.

Coard, S. I., Nitz, K., & Felice, M. E. (2000). Repeat pregnancy among adolescents: Sociodemographic, family and health factors. *Adolescence, 35*(137): 193–200.

Coates, T. J., Faigle, M., & Stall, R. D. (1995). *Does HIV prevention work for men who have sex with men?* San Francisco: Center for AIDS Prevention Studies University of California.

Coker, A. L., Richter, D. L., Valois, R. F., McKeown, R. E., Garrison, C. Z., & Vincent, M. L. (1994). Correlates and consequences of early initiation of sexual intercourse. *Journal of School Health, 64*(9), 372–377.

Coyle, K., Kirby, D., Parcel, G., Basen-Engquist, K., Banspach, S., Rugg, D., et al. (1996). Safer choices: A multicomponent school-based HIV/STD and pregnancy prevention program for adolescents. *Journal of School Health, 66*(3), 89–94.

DiClemente, R. J., Lanier, M. M., Horan, P. F., & Lodico, M. (1991). Comparison of AIDS knowledge, attitudes, and behaviors among incarcerated adolescents and a public school sample in San Francisco. *American Journal of Public Health, 81*(5), 628–630.

Doswell, W. M. (1999). Program aims to prevent girls' early sexual behavior. *American Nursing, 31*(6), 23.

Erikson, E. H. (1966). Eight ages of man. *International Journal of Psychiatry, 2*(3), 281–307.

Erikson, E. H. (1968). *Identity: Youth and crisis.* New York: Norton.

Fairfax, J. L., Clark, M. D., Wright, L. S., Ford, D. S., & Shepperd, B. T. (1997). Integrating infrastructure building with peer-focused approaches to HIV prevention education. *Journal of Health Education, 28*(6), S75–S79.

Fishbein, M. (1990). AIDS and behavior change: An analysis based on the theory of reasoned action. *Interamerican Journal of Psychology, 24*, 37–56.

Fisher, J. D., Fisher, W. A., Bryan, A. D., & Misovich, S. J. (2002). Information-motivation-behavioral skills model-based HIV risk behavior change intervention for inner-city high school youth. *Health Psychology, 21*(2), 177–186.

Franklin, C., & Corcoran, J. (2000). Preventing adolescent pregnancy: A review of programs and practices. *Social Work, 45*(1), 40–52.

Gerrard, M., Gibbons, F. X., Benthin, A. C., & Hessling, R. M. (1996). A longitudinal study of the reciprocal nature of risk behaviors and cognition in adolescents: What you do shapes what you think, and vice versa. *Health Psychology, 15*(5), 344–354.

Gerrard, M., Gibbons, F. X., & Bushman, B. J. (1996). Relation between perceived vulnerability to HIV and precautionary sexual behavior. *Psychological Bulletin, 119*(3), 390–409.

Gerrard, M., Gibbons, F. X., Warner, T. D., & Smith, G. E. (1993). Perceived vulnerability to HIV infection and AIDS preventive behavior: A critical review of the evidence. In J. B. Pryor & G. D. Reeder (Eds.), *The social psychology of HIV infection* (pp. 59–84). Hillsdale, NJ: Erlbaum.

Hacker, K. A., Amare, Y., Strunk, N., & Horst, L. (2000). Listening to youth: Adolescent perspectives on teen pregnancy. *Journal of Adolescent Health, 26*(4), 279–288.

Halpern, C. T., Joyner, K., Udry, J. R., & Suchindran, C. (2000). Smart teens don't have sex (or kiss much either). *Journal of Adolescent Health, 26*(3), 213–225.

Harrison, J. A., Mullen, P. D., & Green, L. W. (1992). A meta-analysis of studies of the health belief model with adults. *Health Education Research, 7*, 107–116.

Hellerstedt, W. L., Smith, A. E., Shew, M. L., & Resnick, M. D. (2000). Perceived knowledge and training needs in adolescent pregnancy prevention: Results from a multidisciplinary survey. *Archives of Pediatrics and Adolescent Medicine, 154*(7), 679–684.

Hutcherson, M. K. (1999). Individual, family and relationship predictors of young women's sexual risk perceptions. *Journal of Obstetric, Gynecologic, and Neonatal Nursing, 28*, 60–67.

Institute of Medicine, and Committee on Prevention and Control of Sexually Transmitted Diseases (IOM). (1997). *The hidden epidemic: Confronting sexually transmitted diseases*. Washington, DC: National Academy Press.

Janz, N. K., & Becker, M. H. (1984). The health belief model: A decade later. *Health Education Quarterly, 11*, 1–47.

Jemmott, J. B., Jemmott, L. S., & Fong, G. T. (1992). Reductions in HIV risk-associated sexual behaviors among Black male adolescents: Effects of an AIDS prevention intervention. *American Journal of Public Health, 82*(3), 372–377.

Jemmott, J. B., III, Jemmott, L. S., & Fong, G. T. (1998). Abstinence and safer sex HIV risk-reduction interventions for African American adolescents: A randomized controlled trial. *Journal of the American Medical Association, 279*(19), 1529–1536.

Jemmott, J. B., III, Jemmott, L. S., Fong, G. T., & McCaffree, K. (1999). Reducing HIV risk-associated sexual behavior among African American adolescents: Testing the generality of intervention effects. *American Journal of Community Psychology, 27*(2), 161–187.

Jessor, R. (1982). Problem behavior and developmental transition in adolescence. *Journal of School Health, 52*(5), 295–300.

Jessor, R. (1991). Risk behavior in adolescence: A psychosocial framework for understanding and action. *Journal of Adolescent Health, 12*(8), 597–605.

Kalichman, S. C. (1998). Post-exposure prophylaxis for HIV infection in gay and bisexual men. Implications for the future of HIV prevention. *Health Psychology, 17*(6), 546–550.

Kamb, M. L., Dillon, B. A., Fishbein, M., & Willis, K. L. (1996). Quality assurance of HIV prevention counseling in a multi-center randomized controlled trial. Project RESPECT Study Group. *Public Health Reports, 111*(Suppl. 1), 99–107.

Kamb, M. L., Fishbein, M., Douglas, J. M., Rhodes, F., Rogers, J., Bolan, G., et al. (1998). Efficacy of risk-reduction counseling to prevent human immunodeficiency virus and sexually transmitted diseases: A randomized controlled trial. *Journal of the American Medical Association, 280*(13), 1161–1167.

Kegeles, S. M., & Hart, G. J. (1998). Recent HIV-prevention interventions for gay men: Individual, small-group and community-based studies. *AIDS Education and Prevention, 10*(3 Suppl.), 61–76.

Kegeles, S. M., Hays, R. B., & Coates, T. J. (1997). The Mpowerment Project: A community-level HIV prevention intervention for young gay men. *Lancet, 350*(9090), 1500–1505.

Kegeles, S. M., Hays, R. B., Pollack, L. M., & Coates, T. J. (1999). Mobilizing young gay and bisexual men for HIV prevention: A two-community study. *AIDS, 13*(13), 1753–1762.

Kirby, D. (1999). Reflections on two decades of research on teen sexual behavior and pregnancy. *Journal of School Health, 69*(3), 89–94.

Kirby, D., Barth, R. P., Leland, N., & Fetro, J. V. (1991). Reducing the risk: Impact of a new curriculum on sexual risk-taking. *Family Planning Perspectives, 23*(6), 253–263.

Laumann, E. O., Gagnon, J. H., Michael, R. T., & Michaels, S. (1994). *The social organization of sexuality: Sexual practices in the U.S.* Chicago: University of Chicago Press.

Liddon, N., Clark, L. F., DeLuca, N., Rhodes, S., & Stephens, R. (2004). *Partner perceptions and condom use among African-American male STD clinic clients.* Manuscript submitted for publication, University of Birmingham, Alabama.

Main, D. S., Iverson, D. C., McGloin, J., Banspach, S. W., Collins, J. L., Rugg, D. L., et al. (1994). Preventing HIV infection among adolescents: Evaluation of a school-based education program. *Preventive Medicine, 23*(4), 409–417.

Malloy, T. E., Fisher, W. A., Albright, L., Misovich, S. J., & Fisher, J. D. (1997). Interpersonal perception of the AIDS risk potential of persons of the opposite sex. *Health Psychology, 16*(5), 480–486.

Marcia, J. E., Waterman, A. S., Matteson, D. R., Archer, S. L., & Orlofsky, J. L. (1993). *Ego identity: A handbook for psychosocial research*. New York: Springer.

Maticka-Tynedale, E. (1991). Sexual scripts and AIDS prevention: Variations in adherence to safer sex guidelines by heterosexual adolescents. *Journal of Sex Research, 28,* 45–66.

McLaughlin, C. R., Reiner, S. M., Reams, P. N., & Joost, T. F. (1999). Factors associated with parenting among incarcerated juvenile offenders. *Adolescence, 34*(136), 665–670.

Medrano, M. A., Desmond, D. P., Zule, W. A., & Hatch, J. P. (1999). Histories of childhood trauma and the effects on risky HIV behaviors in a sample of women drug users. *American Journal of Drug and Alcohol Abuse, 25*(4), 593–606.

Michael, R. T., Gagnon, J. H., Laumann, E. O., & Kolata, G. (1994). *Sex in America: A definitive survey*. London: Little, Brown.

Miller, K. S., Clark, L. F., Wendell, D. A., Levin, M. L., Gray-Ray, P., Velez, C. N., et al. (1997). Adolescent heterosexual experience: A new typology. *Journal of Adolescent Health, 20*(3), 179–186.

Miller, L. C., Burns, D., & Rothspan, S. (1995). Negotiating safer sex: The dynamics of African American relationships. In P. J. Kalbfleisch & M. J. Cody (Eds.), *Gender power and communication in human relationships* (pp. 163–188). Hillsdale, NJ: Erlbaum.

Mott, F. L., Fondell, M. M., Hu, P. N., Kowaleski-Jones, L., & Menaghan, E. G. (1996). The determinants of first sex by age 14 in a high-risk adolescent population. *Family Planning Perspectives, 28*(1), 13–18.

Murphy, S. T., Miller, L. C., Moore, J., & Clark, L. F. (2000). Preaching to the choir: Preference for female-controlled methods and HIV/STD risk. *American Journal of Public Health, 90,* 1135–1137.

National Alliance of State and Territories AIDS Districts (NASTAD). (2002, February). *HIV Prevention Bulletin*.

O'Donnell, L., Stueve, A., San Doval, A., Duran, R., Haber, D., Atnafou, R., et al. (1999). The effectiveness of the Reach for Health Community Youth Service learning program in reducing early and unprotected sex among urban middle school students. *American Journal of Public Health, 89*(2), 176–181.

Orlandi, M. A., & Dalton, L. T. (1998). Lifestyle interventions for the young. In S. A. Shumacher, E. B. Schron, J. K. Ockene, & W. L. McBee (Eds.), *The handbook of health behavior change* (pp. 335–356). New York: Springer.

Ozer, E. J., Weinstein, R. S., Maslach, C., & Siegel, D. (1997). Adolescent AIDS prevention in context: The impact of peer educator qualities and classroom environments on intervention efficacy. *American Journal of Community Psychology, 25*(3), 289–323.

Peterson, J. L., Coates, T. J., Catania, J., Hauck, W. W., Acree, M., Daigle, D., et al. (1996). Evaluation of an HIV risk reduction intervention among African-American homosexual and bisexual men. *American Journal of Public Health, 86*(8 Pt. 1), 1129–1136.

Poppen, P. J., & Reisen, C. A. (1997). Perception of risk and sexual self-protective behavior: A methodological critique. *AIDS Education and Prevention, 9*(4), 373–390.

Prochaska, J. O., & DiClemente, C. C. (1986). Toward a comprehensive model of change. In W. Miller & N. Heather (Eds.), *Treating addictive behaviors* (pp. 3–27). New York: Plenum Press.

Prochaska, J. O., DiClemente, C. C., & Norcross, J. C. (1992). In search of how people change: Applications to addictive behaviors. *American Psychologist, 47,* 1102–1114.

Rhodes, S. D., DiClemente, R. J., Yee, L. J., & Hergenrather, K. C. (2000). Hepatitis B vaccination in a high-risk MSM population: The need for vaccine education. *Sexually Transmitted Infections, 76,* 408–409.

Rogers, R. W. (1975). A protection motivation theory of fear appeals and attitudes change. *Journal of Psychology, 91,* 93–114.

Rogers, R. W. (1983). Cognitive and physiological processes in fear appeals and attitudes change: A revised theory of protection motivation. In J. Cacioppo & R. Petty (Eds.), *Social psychophysiology* (pp. 153–176). New York: Guilford Press.

Romer, D., Black, M., Ricardo, I., Feigelman, S., Kaljee, L., Galbraith, J., et al. (1994). Social influences on the sexual behavior of youth at risk for HIV exposure. *American Journal of Public Health, 84*(6), 977–985.

Rosario, M., Meyer-Bahlburg, H. F., Hunter, J., & Gwadz, M. (1999). Sexual risk behaviors of gay, lesbian, and bisexual youths in New York City: Prevalence and correlates. *AIDS Education and Prevention, 11*(6), 476–496.

Rosenberg, M. J., Davidson, A. J., Chen, J. H., Judson, F. N., & Douglas, J. M. (1992). Barrier contraceptives and sexually transmitted diseases in women: A comparison of female-dependent methods and condoms. *American Journal of Public Health, 82*(5), 669–674.

Rosenberg, M. J., & Gollub, E. L. (1992). Commentary: Methods women can use that may prevent sexually transmitted disease, including HIV. *American Journal of Public Health, 82*(11), 1473–1478.

Rosenstock, I. M. (1974). Historical origins of the health belief model. *Health Education Monographs, 2,* 1–8.

Rotheram-Borus, M. J., Mahler, K. A., & Rosario, M. (1995). AIDS prevention with adolescents. *AIDS Education and Prevention, 7*(4), 320–336.

Seidman, S. N., Mosher, W. D., & Aral, S. O. (1994). Predictors of high-risk behavior in unmarried American women: adolescent environment as risk factor. *Journal of Adolescent Health, 15*(2), 126–132.

Sikkema, K. J., Kelly, J. A., Winett, R. A., Solomon, L. J., Cargill, V. A., Roffman, R. A., et al. (2000). Outcomes of a randomized community-level HIV prevention intervention for women living in 18 low-income housing developments. *American Journal of Public Health, 90*(1), 57–63.

Singh, S., & Darroch, J. E. (2000). Adolescent pregnancy and childbearing: Levels and trends in developed countries. *Family Planning Perspectives, 32*(1), 14–23.

St. Lawrence, J. S., Brasfield, T. L., Jefferson, K. W., Alleyne, E., O'Bannon, R. E., III, & Shirley, A. (1995). Cognitive–behavioral intervention to reduce African American adolescents' risk for HIV infection. *Journal of Consulting and Clinical Psychology, 63*(2), 221–237.

St. Lawrence, J. S., Jefferson, K. W., Alleyne, E., & Brasfield, T. L. (1995). Comparison of education versus behavioral skills training interventions in lowering sexual HIV-risk behavior of substance-dependent adolescents. *Journal of Consulting and Clinical Psychology, 63*(1), 154–157.

St. Louis, M. E., Wasserheit, J. N., & Gayle, H. D. (1997). Janus considers the HIV pandemic—Harnessing recent advances to enhance AIDS prevention [editorial]. *American Journal of Public Health, 87*(1), 10–12.

Stall, R., McKusick, L., Wiley, J., Coates, T. J., & Ostrow, D. G. (1986). Alcohol and drug use during sexual activity and compliance with safe sex guidelines for AIDS: The AIDS Behavioral Research Project. *Health Education Quarterly, 13*(4), 359–371.

Stanton, B. F., Li, X., Black, M. M., Ricardo, I., Galbraith, J., Feigelman, S., et al. (1996). Longitudinal stability and predictability of sexual perceptions, intentions, and behaviors among early adolescent African-Americans. *Journal of Adolescent Health, 18*(1), 10–19.

Stanton, B. F., Li, X., Ricardo, I., Galbraith, J., Feigelman, S., & Kaljee, L. (1996). A randomized, controlled effectiveness trial of an AIDS prevention program for low-income African-American youths. *Archives of Pediatric and Adolescent Medicine, 150*(4), 363–372.

Ventura, S. J., & Freedman, M. A. (2000). Teenage childbearing in the U.S., 1960–1997. *American Journal of Preventive Medicine, 19*(1 Suppl.), 18–25.

Ventura, S. J., Martin, J. A., Curtin, S. C., Mathews, T. J., & Park, M. M. (2000). Births: Final data for 1998. *National Statistics Reports, 28*, 1–100.

Ventura, S. J., Mosher, W. D., Curtin, S. C., Abma, J. C., & Henshaw, S. (2000). Trends in pregnancy and pregnancy rates by outcome: Estimates for United States 1976–96. *Vital and Health Statistics, Series 21, Data on Nationality, Marriage and Divorce, 56*, 1–47.

Warren, C. W., Santelli, J. S., Everett, S. A., Kann, L., Collins, J. L., Cassell, C., et al. (1998). Sexual behavior among U.S. high school students, 1990–1995. *Family Planning Perspectives, 30*(4), 170–172, 200.

Wasserheit, J. N. (1992). Epidemiological synergy. Interrelationships between human immunodeficiency virus infection and other sexually transmitted diseases. *Sexually Transmitted Diseases, 19*(2), 61–77.

Weinstein, N. D. (1988). The precaution adoption process. *Health Psychology, 7*(4), 355–386.

Weinstein, N. D., & Nicolich, M. (1993). Correct and incorrect interpretations of correlations between risk perceptions and risk behaviors. *Health Psychology, 12*(3), 235–245.

Whitaker, D. J., Miller, K. S., & Clark, L. F. (2000). The emergence of adolescent activity: Psychosocial profiles of teens at different points in the emergence process. *Family Planning Perspectives, 32,* 111–117.

Williams, S. S., Kimble, D. L., Covell, N. H., Weiss, L. H., Newton, K. J., Fischer, W. A., et al. (1992). College students use implicit personality theory instead of safer sex. *Journal of Applied Social Psychology, 22,* 921–933.

Willis, L. A., Mukherjee, S., Clark, L. F., Stephens, R. M., & Avery, J. (1999, July). *Condom use and willingness to use condoms as predicted by relationship issues among African-American male STD clinic clients.* Paper presented at the International STD Conference, Denver, CO.

Wingood, G. M., & DiClemente, R. J. (1996). HIV sexual risk reduction interventions for women: A review. *American Journal of Preventive Medicine, 12*(3), 209–217.

Woodcock, A. J., Stenner, K., & Ingham, R. (1992). Young people talking about HIV and AIDS: Interpretations of personal risk of infection. *Health Education Research, 7,* 229.

5

PROMOTION OF PHYSICAL ACTIVITY THROUGH THE LIFE SPAN

PATRICIA M. DUBBERT, ABBY C. KING, BESS H. MARCUS, AND JAMES F. SALLIS

Although physical activity and public health remains a relatively new field of study, this chapter reflects substantial progress toward understanding the importance of activity to health and well-being and understanding physical activity behavior. We elected to take a life-span approach, with sections on physical activity in children and adolescents, adults, older adults, and special populations defined by health status rather than age. For each population subgroup, we examine who is active and inactive and how this relates to health risks, measurement issues, and interventions across settings, modalities, and media. Because so many people lead sedentary lives, we emphasize the promotion of healthful physical activity for all individuals—"one of the major public health tasks of our time" (Sallis & Owen, 1999). Where there is information available, we indicate what is known about gender, cultural, and ethnic

This chapter was coauthored by an employee of the United States government as part of official duty and is considered to be in the public domain. Any views expressed herein do not necessarily represent the views of the United States government, and the author's participation in the work is not meant to serve as an official endorsement.

differences in activity and response to interventions. We also touched on environmental and public policy issues that contribute to physical activity participation and change.

We begin with comments about the role of psychologists in exercise assessment and intervention activities. Health psychologists usually work as members of interdisciplinary teams whose membership depends on the population, setting and intervention methods. Patients' medical health care providers must be involved, for example, when working with higher risk populations and in health care settings. As team members, psychologists serve as experts in behavioral theory and models. They can contribute expertise for determining reliability and validity of measures, and assist in determining the acceptability, feasibility, and impact on behavior of activity monitoring methods that are being considered. Health psychologists with expertise in physical activity and exercise have played significant roles in designing and implementing interventions in recent major clinical trials. Health psychologists can serve as the primary interventionists or supervisors of staff who deliver physical activity interventions in some settings. Psychologists with appropriate expertise may also integrate physical activity interventions with more traditional mental health therapies for treatment of mental and physical health problems (Hays, 1999).

PHYSICAL ACTIVITY IN CHILDREN AND ADOLESCENTS

Children are the most physically active segment of the population, and it is inaccurate to refer to most children as "inactive." However, a substantial decline in physical activity has been documented during youth that is partly biological in origin. By the high school years, many young people have adopted a more "adult" lifestyle and have relatively low levels of physical activity. Young people also spend a substantial amount of time in sedentary behaviors, most notably television viewing, that are associated with risk of overweight (Andersen, Crespo, Bartlett, Cheskin, & Pratt, 1998), so sedentary behaviors need to be considered a related behavior with independent health effects.

Epidemiology of Physical Activity and Related Factors in Youth

In addition to the inverse association of physical activity with age, there is consistent evidence that boys are more active than girls from age 4 through high school. The gender difference is larger in studies that use objective rather than self-report measures of physical activity (Sallis, 1993). There are differences in the types of activities chosen, with girls participating more in individual or pair activities and boys choosing more team activities

(Faucette et al., 1995). Boys also report watching more television than girls, and because boys are more physically active, this helps explain the lack of association between television viewing and physical activity for boys (Sallis, Prochaska, & Taylor, 2000). Studies of ethnic differences generally show non-Hispanic White individuals to be more active than Black and Hispanic youth of the same ages. However, the results are not wholly consistent, and few studies adjusted for the effects of socioeconomic status (Sallis et al., 2000). Several studies have demonstrated that Black youth spend much more time watching television than other ethnic groups (Andersen et al., 1998).

The literature on the health effects of physical activity in youth has been reviewed (Biddle, Sallis, & Cavill, 1998; Sallis & Patrick, 1994), and there is evidence for multiple mental health benefits. Numerous randomized controlled trials with healthy adolescents have shown that structured exercise enhances self-esteem and reduces symptoms of anxiety and depression (Calfas & Taylor, 1994). Although the mechanisms of these effects are not known, and few studies have been conducted with clinical samples, the psychological benefits of physical activity for youth appear to be substantial.

The evidence on effects of physical activity in youth on chronic disease risk factors is much weaker than the evidence for adults. However, physical activity can reduce blood pressure among youth with elevated blood pressure and can increase HDL-cholesterol in youth with low levels of HDL cholesterol (Riddoch, 1998). The weak effects seen in most studies may be a result of the generally higher levels of physical activity and healthy levels of risk factors in young people (Riddoch, 1998). There is stronger evidence that physical activity is an important part of obesity treatments for young people (Epstein, Myers, Raynor, & Saelens, 1998). Weight-bearing and strength-enhancing activities clearly promote bone mineral density in young people (Riddoch, 1998), which may reduce lifetime risk of osteoporosis.

Because the health benefits of physical activity are not as well defined as those for adults, physical activity guidelines for youth are based mainly on consensus among experts. A set of guidelines developed by the Health Education Authority of the United Kingdom (Cavill, Biddle, & Sallis, 2001) is generally consistent with recommendations from the National Association for Sport and Physical Education (Corbin & Pangrazi, 1998):

- Primary recommendation: "All young people should participate in physical activity of at least moderate intensity for one hour per day" (p. 3). Brisk walking is an example of a moderate-intensity activity.
- Secondary recommendation: "At least twice a week, some of these activities should help to enhance and maintain muscular strength and flexibility, and bone health" (p. 3). Stretching exercises are an example of activities promoting flexibility.

The 60-minutes-per-day recommendation was adopted based on evidence from objective measures that most young people were meeting an earlier guideline of 30-minutes-per-day, but the prevalence of obesity was continuing to increase (Cavill et al., 2001). The adult vigorous exercise recommendation of three sessions per week of more structured activities was not considered appropriate for youth because of findings that note that few young people engaged in continuous activities (Armstrong & Van Mechelen, 1998).

Existing studies provide limited information on the prevalence of meeting guidelines, because most studies used self-report measures that are known to have poor validity among children. There are large discrepancies between studies using self-report versus objective measures. Based on the Youth Risk Behavior Survey, national prevalence rates for meeting the recommendation of more than 20 minutes of vigorous exercise more than three days per week were 73% for high school males and 57% for females (Centers for Disease Control and Prevention, 1999). However, a study of 375 students in grades 1 through 12 using objective measures (accelerometer) of physical activity indicated only about 3% of high school students met the vigorous exercise guideline. According to objective measures, the prevalence of meeting the 60-minute-per-day guideline for moderate to vigorous physical activity ranged from 100% in grades 1 to 3 to 29% in grades 10 to 12 (Pate et al., 2002). Thus, to establish accurate prevalence rates, additional studies are needed with representative samples using objective measures.

Measurement Issues in Children and Adolescents

Subjective and objective measures of youth physical activity have been evaluated. Each method has strengths and weaknesses, and no ideal measure is available at this time.

Self-Reports and Proxy Reports

Baranowski (Baranowski, 1988) described the complex information-processing demands that prevent children from providing reliable and valid recalls of physical activity. No self-report measure has shown any evidence of validity with children younger than about age 10 years (Sallis & Saelens, 2000). Recalls are also complicated by the variety of activities and rapid changes in children's activity levels. The advantages of self-report are the low cost and the extensive descriptive data that can be collected. The disadvantages are limited reliability and validity.

Of 17 measures reviewed, most had some evidence of validity, but interviewer-administered recalls generally had stronger psychometric characteristics than self-administered recalls (Sallis & Saelens, 2000). The following instruments illustrate that various recall strategies can be used. The Past-Day Physical Activity Recall (PDPAR; Weston, Petosa, & Pate, 1997) is a self-administered survey on which young people report the type and intensity in 30-minute blocks of activities done throughout the day. The Self-Administered Physical Activity Checklist (SAPAC; Sallis, Zakarian, Hovell, & Hofstetter, 1996) requires students to indicate the minutes they spent in each of 21 common activities the previous day. Separate reports are given for before, during, and after school periods, and minutes in sedentary behaviors are also reported. There is some evidence of validity of a one-year recall instrument to assess adolescents' habitual physical activity (Aaron et al., 1995). A two-item survey that assesses days per week adolescents meet the 60-minutes-per-day guideline has shown good evidence of validity, sensitivity, and specificity (Prochaska, Sallis, & Long, 2001).

Most studies have not supported the validity of parent and teacher recall of children's physical activity (Sallis & Saelens, 2000). Adults are not sufficiently aware of children's activity levels to produce accurate reports. However, careful record keeping by both parents and teachers produced a valid estimate of the child's physical activity levels (Manios, Kafatos, & Markakis, 1998).

Direct Observation

Advantages of direct observation by trained observers include high reliability and validity, assessment of most activity characteristics (e.g., intensity and type), and the ability to collect simultaneous information on potential social and environmental influences. Disadvantages include the cost of observers, extensive training and quality control, inability to observe children in all settings, and cost of managing and analyzing data (McKenzie, 2002). McKenzie concluded that interobserver reliability was high for instruments that assessed physical activity in individual children, children in physical education classes, and people in recreational spaces. Several instruments had evidence that their activity categories were related to measures of energy expenditure (McKenzie, 2002).

Electronic Monitors

Although telemetric heart rate monitors and pedometers can be used to assess physical activity in young people, the most widely used monitors are accelerometers. Accelerometers can provide minute-by-minute activity levels (or even more frequent samples) over several weeks, have been repeatedly validated in young people, can produce a variety of summary variables, and create a low participant burden (Welk, 2002). Although initial costs are substantial, monitors can be reused so that it is feasible to apply them in large studies. Because accelerometers are usually worn at the waist and detect trunk motion, an important limitation is their ability to accurately assess some common youth activities such as bicycling, skateboarding, and water activities. Given the large discrepancies in self-reported and objectively monitored physical activity in youth (Pate et al., 2002), there is a strong rationale for applying objective measures whenever possible. Several accelerometers are now on the market and make it possible for the first time to routinely collect objective physical activity data in young people in small and large field studies.

Interventions With Children and Adolescents

Most physical activity intervention studies with young people have been conducted in schools. A 1998 review identified eight published studies in elementary schools, four studies in high schools, and two studies of university students (Stone, McKenzie, Welk, & Booth, 1998). Interventions usually include a classroom component: Some alter physical education, and some have a family component. Goals of health-related physical education programs are to increase physical activity during the physical education class, enhance enjoyment of physical activity so children are motivated to be active outside of school, and improve sports and movement skills.

The largest study was the Child and Adolescent Trial for Cardiovascular Health (CATCH), a multicenter study of 96 schools that evaluated physical activity and nutrition interventions in grades three through five (McKenzie et al., 1996). CATCH was successful in increasing physical activity during physical education class and after school. The Sports Play and Recreation for Kids (SPARK) study evaluated a physical education program and behavioral self-management curriculum for fourth and fifth grade students (Sallis et al., 1997). There were significant effects on physical activity during physical education, physical fitness (Sallis et al., 1997), physical skills (McKenzie, Alcaraz, Sallis, & Faucetter, 1998), and academic achievement (Sallis et al., 1999). Students who participated more in the self-management program increased in physical activity and fitness (Marcoux et al., 1999). The Class of 1989 study was conducted during grades 6 through 12, in conjunction with the Minnesota Heart Health Program (Kelder, Perry, Peters, Lytle, & Klepp, 1995). This seven-year study showed that schools with the multibehavior, self-management curriculum had higher physical activity levels in all years, compared to the control schools. One study was designed to decrease television viewing (Robinson, 1999). The large decreases in television viewing were related to declines in body fat, but physical activity did not increase.

Only two interventions with middle schools have been published. Gortmaker and colleagues (Gortmaker et al., 1999) evaluated a physical activity and nutrition curriculum called Planet Health with components to reduce sedentary behavior. Physical activity was increased and obesity rates were decreased in girls. The Middle School Physical Activity and Nutrition Study (M–SPAN) evaluated environmental and policy interventions to increase physical activity and decrease dietary fat consumed on school campuses (Sallis et al., 2003). The physical education intervention increased physical activity 20% during class time, but the increase was only significant for boys. Attempts to provide more opportunities for physical activity after lunch and after school were not successful, but important barriers to environmental change were identified.

Because family support is often correlated with youth physical activity, and parents control children's access to activity programs and facilities, there is an empirical rationale for family-based physical activity programs (Sallis, 1998). Three studies have evaluated programs for healthy families, and all were unsuccessful in increasing children's physical activity (Sallis, 1998). All of these programs required family attendance at meetings or classes, but regular meeting attendance proved to be a barrier for many families. Improving recruitment and attendance of families and refining the parental behaviors targeted in the programs are the current challenges to researchers in this field.

With obese children, promoting lifestyle physical activity has been more effective than structured exercise, and reinforcing decreases in sedentary behavior is an effective means of increasing physical activity (Epstein et al., 1998). Perhaps these results could be extended by teaching parents of nonobese children to more effectively encourage lifestyle activity and reductions in sedentary behaviors.

Eighty percent of young people's physical activity appears to take place outside of school, and much of this is in organized programs, such as youth sports, dance or other activity classes, and at public recreation centers (Ross, Dotson, Gilbert, & Katz, 1985). Because it is not feasible to provide adequate physical activity in physical education, there is a clear need to explore ways of increasing the physical activity provided by community organizations (Sallis, 1998). Interventions with community programs could target increases in the number of participating youth, amount of physical activity during each session, and number of sessions per week. However, the single published study of a community-based program indicated there are many barriers to integrating youth physical activity programs into communities (Thompson et al., 2003).

A study of adolescents in primary care included a computer-based assessment and planning program, structured counseling by the health care provider, and follow-up by phone or mail (Patrick et al., 2001). The intervention was feasible and had promising effects.

In summary, the school-based physical activity intervention evidence base is well-developed and the results are sufficient for the Guide to

Community Preventive Services (Kahn et al., 2002) to "strongly recommend" health-related school physical education. Thus, the current need is to disseminate evidence-based programs. Educational curriculum approaches also show good results, but the studies are not consistent. Family- and community-based interventions have not been effective, so additional work is needed. Research is just beginning on programs in health-care settings, and no evaluations of mass media or computer-based interventions were located. Youth physical activity intervention guidelines from the Centers for Disease Control and Prevention (CDC, 1997) may be useful for guiding both research and practice.

Gender, Cultural, and Ethnic Differences

As described in an earlier section, there are substantial gender differences, with boys consistently found to be more physically active than girls at all ages (Sallis, 1993). Although several studies indicate that physical activity interventions for youth are more effective for girls than for boys (Gortmaker et al., 1999; Sallis et al., 1999), one study reported the opposite (Sallis et al., 2003). National surveys show that ethnic minority youth are less physically active than non-Hispanic White youth (U.S. Department of Health and Human Services, 1996), but it is not clear whether this can be explained by socioeconomic status. Although many of the youth physical activity interventions have ethnically diverse samples, there is not a large enough evidence base to make conclusions about intervention differences for specific ethnic, racial, and socioeconomic groups. Thus, much more work is needed to promote physical activity in youth, focusing on groups at risk of being relatively inactive. Those risk groups include girls, older adolescents, ethnic minorities, and those from low socioeconomic status backgrounds.

PHYSICAL ACTIVITY IN ADULTS

The physical and psychological benefits of participating in regular physical activity for adults are now clearly established. Physical activity participation affects many aspects of health, including protection against premature mortality, coronary heart disease, hypertension, type II diabetes mellitus, osteoporosis, colon cancer, depression, and anxiety (U.S. Department of Health and Human Services, 1996).

Epidemiology of Physical Activity and Related Factors in Adults

Physical inactivity has been recognized by the American Heart Association (AHA) as an independent risk factor for the development of cardiovascular disease (Fletcher et al., 1992). A recent meta-analysis provided additional evidence that a physically active lifestyle is important to the primary prevention of cardiovascular disease (Williams, 2001). Cardiovascular disease has decreased in recent years as a result in the decline in cigarette use, decreased cholesterol levels, and decreased blood pressure levels (CDC, 1999); however, physical inactivity is one modifiable risk factor for cardiovascular disease (CVD) that has been uninfluenced by public health efforts (CDC, 2001b).

The American College of Sports Medicine (ACSM; American College of Sports Medicine, 1998) and the CDC have developed guidelines to quantify the amount of physical activity required for health benefits. For healthy individuals with no known cardiovascular disease, the current guidelines are that individuals should accumulate at least 30 minutes of moderate-intensity physical activity (i.e., brisk walking) on most, preferably all days of the week (Pate et al., 1995). Unfortunately, knowledge of how to reap the benefits of physical activity and avoid the complications of lifestyles that are too sedentary has lagged far behind the knowledge of why physical activity is important to health. A large proportion of the U.S. adult population does not participate in regular physical activity. Behavioral risk factor surveys during the past decade have consistently found that only 25% of Americans participate in physical activity (CDC, 2001c) at the level recommended by the CDC, the ACSM, the AHA, and the U.S. Surgeon General (U.S. Department of Health and Human Services, 1996).

Measurement Issues in Adults

As with children, a variety of modalities have been used to measure physical activity, fitness, and related behaviors. Self-report measures often used with adults include diaries, logs, recall surveys, retrospective quantitative histories, and global self-reports (Periera, 1997). Direct monitoring (i.e., behavioral observation, accelerometers, heart rate monitors) is more intrusive and expensive but can provide detailed and informative data. Physiological measurement of physical fitness (i.e., cardiorespiratory fitness, muscular fitness, body composition) is often used as a validation standard for other measures. Measures for related psychosocial variables (i.e., self-efficacy for exercise, benefits, barriers, enjoyment of physical activity, environmental factors) with good psychometric properties are available. Measures of physical activity using different methods (e.g., self-report, accelerometer, treadmill fitness) are often only moderately correlated (Montoye, 2000).

Extensive reviews of the various assessment approaches are provided in the Surgeon General's report (U.S. Department of Health and Human Services, 1996) and other publications, including special issues of *Medicine and Science in Sports and Exercise* (Montoye, 2000) and *Research Quarterly in Exercise and Sports* (Wood, 2000). Each of the assessment techniques target particular outcomes and, therefore, has both advantages and disadvantages. Before using a particular measurement technique, it is essential for researchers to first determine the goal of the measurement process (i.e., fitness, level of activity, barriers to activity). This information can be used to determine what is optimal and what is feasible for each situation.

Interventions With Adults

Many studies have evaluated theory-based cognitive and behavioral strategies for increasing participation in physical activity. A recent meta-analysis revealed that cognitive–behavioral individual treatment programs typically produce 10 to 25% increases in physical activity frequency compared to no-treatment controls (Dishman & Buckworth, 1996). Cognitive–behavioral strategies commonly used in these studies included self-monitoring, feedback, reinforcement, behavioral contracting, and incentives. It is difficult to determine which of these strategies are most effective because more than one strategy is typically used in any given study (Dubbert & Stetson, 1999).

At this time, the theoretical models that appear to be the most promising for guiding physical activity interventions are social–cognitive theory (Bandura, 1986), the stages of change model (Prochaska & DiClemente, 1983), and the relapse prevention model (Marlatt & Gordon, 1985). These theoretical models have been used to guide many of the interventions described in this chapter. For example, studies guided by the transtheoretical model have demonstrated that it is useful to match intervention strategies to individuals' stage of motivational readiness for physical activity adoption (Marcus, Rossi, Selby, Niaura, & Abrams, 1992; Marcus et al., 1998).

Face-to-Face Interventions

Face-to-face approaches, sometimes considered the gold-standard of providing interactive feedback to facilitate behavior change, have been found to be effective in promoting physical activity, with participants showing significant increases in fitness and exercise duration (King, Haskell, Taylor, Kraemer, & DeBusk, 1991; King, Haskell, Young, Oka, & Stefanick, 1995). Although efficacious, there are numerous barriers associated with this approach (e.g., work schedules, time, childcare, transportation, cost). Therefore, other delivery channels have been explored.

Telephone-Based Interventions

Another means of providing individualized interventions is through the use of the telephone. Telephone contacts have proven effective for adopting and maintaining physical activity in healthy adults (King et al., 1991; King et al., 1995; Lombard, Lombard, & Winett, 1995) and are cost-effective. Telephone interventions are easy to administer and reduce many of the barriers associated with face-to-face interventions.

Given that physical activity is a behavior that needs to be maintained, delivering a frequent, ongoing "dose" of intervention is important. Findings from Lombard et al. (1995) suggest that telephone contacts for touching base were equally as effective as contacts that are highly structured when people were phoned frequently. In addition, a Scottish campaign integrated a telephone hotline ("fitline") into a television advertisement campaign in an effort to integrate personal contact within a large-scale campaign (Wimbush, MacGregory, & Fraser, 1998). Behavior change was dependent on use of the fitline. Unfortunately, only 16% of those surveyed were aware of the fitline and only 5% of these individuals actually used this line for support. Users of the fitline tended to be of higher socioeconomic status. This suggests a need to develop various forms of follow-up support for mass-media approaches so that a more diverse group can be reached. Tailoring to specific population segments within broad-based community approaches appears to be critically important (Irwin et al., 2003; Marcus et al., 1992).

Print-Based Inventions

A number of studies have used print materials as the primary or sole component of intervention, and these individually tailored, print-based interventions are a low-cost, less time-intensive mechanism for facilitating behavior change. For example, after six months of treatment, individuals who received individualized motivationally tailored print materials that emphasized key social cognitive concepts such as self-efficacy and outcome expectations spent significantly more time exercising per week and were more likely to achieve CDC/ACSM recommended levels of physical activity compared with individuals who received standardized print materials (Marcus et al., 1998). Similar to telephone-based interventions, print-based interventions can potentially be effective for working adults, who, because of work, family, or social demands, may have difficulty attending face-to-face programs.

Counseling in Health Care Settings

Physicians have the potential to counsel a significant proportion of the population about physical activity, but they spend little time doing so (Mann & Putnam, 1985; Mullen & Tabak, 1989; Simons-Morton, Calfas, Oldenburg, & Burton, 1998). Findings from the Provider-Based Assessment and Counseling for Exercise program reveal that even brief interventions that are delivered by physicians who have been trained in both physical activity recommendations for health and that are tailored to patients' level of motivational readiness for change can increase physical activity behavior short-term (Calfas et al., 1996). The efficacy of this approach for enhancing longer term maintenance of physical activity has yet to be established. The recently completed National Heart, Lung, and Blood Institute (NHLBI) randomized, controlled Activity Counseling Trial (ACT) evaluated the two-year efficacy of three primary care-based physical activity interventions of increasingly intensive health educator follow-up in inactive primary care patients, ages 35 to 75 years, recruited from three clinical centers across the United States (Blair et al., 1998; King, Sallis, et al., 1998). All 874 participants received provider advice. The two-year results indicated that women randomized to either of the two health educator follow-up interventions consisting of interactive mailings or mailings plus regular telephone contact had greater increases in fitness. In contrast, no two-year intervention differences were observed among the men. The ACT results suggest that men may not require as much advice and support as women in this type of intervention (Writing Group for the Activity Counseling Trial Research Group, 2001).

Community-Based Strategies

Much of the current knowledge regarding community-based prevention strategies has been gleaned from three U.S. field trials that targeted multiple CVD risk factors (i.e., the Minnesota Heart Health Program; Crow et al., 1986; the Pawtucket Heart Health Program; Carleton, Lasater, Assaf, Felman, & McKinlay, 1995; and the Stanford Five-City Project; Farquhar et al., 1990). Although these mass-media campaigns increased community members' knowledge of the benefits of physical activity, their impact on physical activity behavior was marginal (Young, Haskell, Taylor, & Fortmann, 1996).

In a substudy of the Pawtucket Heart Health Program (Elder et al., 1986), an individual behavior-change model was combined with a public-health approach (Marcus et al., 1992). Stage of motivational readiness was assessed in sedentary adults in the community, and stage-matched self-help manuals were delivered along with a variety of community-based events. Although no comparison group was included, results indicated that 30% of those thinking about changing their behavior at baseline and 60% of occasional exercisers had initiated regular physical activity after the six-week intervention.

Maintenance of Intervention Effects

In general, it appears that although numerous strategies are helpful in increasing physical activity in adults in the short-term, little is known about the process of maintenance (Marcus et al., 2000). Studies have either not followed participants into the maintenance period or have demonstrated that the physical activity habit is short-lived once the intervention is removed. Two notable exceptions are Stanford Summary Vale Health Improvement Project (SSHIP; King et al., 1995) and Project Active (Dunn et al., 1999).

SSHIP, a two-year trial in California, examined preference for structured home-based moderate and vigorous activity versus structured group-based vigorous activity in older middle-aged adults (King et al., 1995). Research participants were randomized to a higher intensity structured group (three days/week of physical activities akin to walking/jogging), a higher intensity telephone supervised home-based program (three days/week), a lower intensity telephone supervised home-based program (five days/week of activities akin to brisk walking), or an assessment-only condition (King et al., 1991). The telephone-supervised home-based programs focusing on either moderate or vigorous intensity activity had significantly greater one-year adherence. At two years, the higher intensity home-based program, which required participants to go out less often to exercise, had higher adherence rates than the lower intensity home-based program.

Project Active was a two-year randomized trial that compared a lifestyle physical activity intervention with a structured exercise program (Dunn et al., 1998, 1999). Both programs included six months of active treatment and 18 months of follow-up. The lifestyle group members met for hourly behaviorally oriented meetings each week that gradually decreased in frequency beginning at six months. The structured group participants were given a six-month membership to a fitness center and met with an exercise trainer working up to five days a week. At six months, both groups were significantly more active than at baseline. At 24 months, both groups still showed significant improvement in energy expenditure and cardiorespiratory fitness from baseline.

Cultural and Ethnic Differences

Lower levels of physical activity participation are associated with lower income, less education, being older, ethnic minority status, and less social support (Dubbert, Carithers, et al., 2002; Trost, Owen, Bauman, Sallis, & Brown, 2002). It is crucial that interventions target these underserved groups, particularly because lower socioeconomic status individuals are less likely to visit a physician for nonurgent health care and receive less advice from their physician on preventive health practices such as physical activity (Billings et al., 1993). Media-based approaches have the potential for reaching underserved populations in a way that is less threatening and costly than talking to a physician. Findings from studies in the literature suggest that it is important to include strategies for increasing community support and to tailor the intervention so that underserved individuals feel the message is relevant to them.

Mass-media campaigns designed to target underserved population segments, such as racial and ethnic minorities, have had mixed results (Gortmaker et al., 1999; Lewis et al., 1993). One successful campaign that targeted low socioeconomic status Black Americans living in targeted residential housing settings demonstrated that community organization, as well as committed and involved community leaders, were important determinants of physical activity behavior change.

PHYSICAL ACTIVITY IN OLDER ADULTS

People over age 65 represent one of the fastest growing population sectors in the United States and other industrialized countries, and they are responsible for the greatest proportion of chronic disease burden and disability on the health care system. Although regular physical activity has been increasingly recognized as an important means for preventing or ameliorating chronic disease morbidity and disability as people age (Buchner & Wagner, 1992), people ages 50 years and older constitute the most sedentary segment of the population (U.S. Department of Health and Human Services, 1996). Thus, efforts to develop interventions to promote increases in regular physical activity among the older adult segment of the population are especially indicated, particularly in light of current evidence demonstrating that even the oldest and frailest groups of elderly individuals can benefit (Fiatarone et al., 1990; Nader et al., 1999).

Epidemiology of Physical Activity and Related Factors in Older Adults

Although a burgeoning literature focusing on the determinants of physical activity currently exists, the majority of the work undertaken in this area to date has focused primarily on adults under the age of 65 (King et al., 1992). When study samples do include older adults, age-specific evaluations of determinants are typically not presented. An additional constraint of the physical activity determinants literature concerns the common use of cross-sectional rather than prospective designs, which prevents a clear understanding of causal relationships among variables and subsequent physical activity levels (King, Stokols, Talen, Brassington, & Killingworth, 2002).

Despite such constraints, a basic understanding of at least some of the factors influencing physical activity levels among older populations is beginning to emerge. These factors can be broadly conceptualized as personal, program-based, or environmental in origin.

Among the personal characteristics that have been examined in the physical activity literature aimed at older adults are sociodemographic variables; health factors; a person's knowledge, attitudes, and beliefs concerning physical activity; and behavioral skills and experiences of relevance to increasing one's physical activity levels (Mills, King, & Stewart, 1998). Those personal factors that appear to be relevant among younger and older adults alike include gender (with women often less active than men), age (with younger seniors often more active than older seniors), smoking status (smokers less physically active than nonsmokers), body weight (more overweight linked with less physical activity), and income and educational achievement (lower levels associated with less activity; Conn, 1998; Elward & Larson, 1992; Rejeski, Brawley, Ettinger, Morgan, & Thompson, 1997; Wister, 1996; Wolinsky, Stump, & Clark, 1995). Among the attitudinal and behavioral variables that appear to be associated with greater levels of physical activity for younger as well as older age groups are one's belief in the value of physical activity for improving health, fitness, and appearance; perceiving fewer barriers to being physically active; having some previous experience with physically active pursuits; and having greater levels of exercise-related self-efficacy (i.e., confidence in one's ability to regularly participate in physical activity). However, as with younger populations, positive physical activity attitudes and beliefs in and of themselves are often insufficient motivators for producing physical activity increases (Mobily, Lemke, Durbe, Wallace, & Leslie, 1987).

Among the program-related factors potentially influencing physical activity participation rates among older adults are physical activity intensity, with moderate intensities preferred over more vigorous intensities; program simplicity and convenience; low monetary costs; and programs that minimize social embarrassment and self-consciousness (King, Oka, et al., 1997; Mills et al., 1998). For at least some subgroups of older adults, programs that contain a social component may also be attractive (King, Rejeski, & Buchner, 1998). However, many of the studies contributing to this knowledge base consist of training studies or studies of samples of currently active individuals. Relatively little is known about program-based preferences among more representative segments of the older population. For example, despite the often-cited conventional wisdom that older adults need and prefer to exercise in a group situation, three population-based community surveys, one population-based worksite survey of middle- and older-aged adults, and a recent national population-based survey of U.S. women ages 40 years and older suggest that a large proportion of both older women and men, irrespective of current physical activity levels, may actually prefer undertaking their physical activity outside of a structured group or class (percentages preferring such "on one's own" formats ranged from 64% to 69%; King & Brassington, 1997; King, Taylor, Haskell, & DeBusk, 1990;

King, Castro, et al., 2000; Lee, 1993). For example, the U.S. Women's Determinants Study results (King, Castro, et al., 2000) indicated that approximately 64% of the 2,900 U.S. women aged 40 years and older who were telephone-interviewed using population-based sampling techniques preferred exercising on one's own with some instruction, as opposed to in a group with an exercise leader, irrespective of ethnicity and current physical activity level.

Environmental factors remain among the least studied, although potentially most far-reaching, avenues for facilitating physical activity participation among older and younger individuals alike. As with younger adults, studies that have evaluated social environmental factors among older adults have found that support from family members, program staff, friends, as well as other exercise participants are significantly positively correlated with physical activity levels (King, Rejeski, et al., 1998). However, the source of social support preferred by the older individual (exercise staff vs. family and friends) may differ depending on exercise program phase (e.g., early adoption of physical activity; maintenance of physical activity; Oka, King, & Young, 1995).

Another potentially important, although currently underused, form of support for older adults is physical activity advice from the person's personal physician (Mills et al., 1998; Simons-Morton et al., 1998). Other environmental factors that have been investigated, albeit less so in older populations, are access to relevant physical activity facilities (Jones & Nies, 1996) and the application of environmental prompts and incentives for physical activity (Young & King, 1995).

Measurement Issues in Older Adults

Despite recent efforts aimed at understanding the physical activity needs of older adults, the optimal physical activity stimulus for securing desirable benefits in health and functioning as people age remains to be fully defined. It is likely, however, that the optimal regimen for older adults will include a combination of endurance, strengthening, and flexibility–balance exercises. A key issue concerns how best to promote regular participation in all of these forms of exercise, both individually and in combination.

With respect to measuring endurance forms of physical activity that constitute the bulk of the physical activity assessment field, several self-report physical activity assessment tools have been developed in recent years that specifically target older populations (Pereira et al., 1997; Washburn, 2000). Such self-report instruments have been developed in response to observations that the lighter forms of physical activity, often engaged in by older adults, are typically underrepresented in many of the most frequently used self-report instruments, which were originally aimed at younger populations, and observations related to potential overreporting of activities among at least some groups of older adults. At least one of the assessment instruments developed specifically for older populations—the Community Health Activities Program for Seniors (CHAMPS) physical activity questionnaire for seniors—has been demonstrated to be sensitive to change in several older adult samples with physical activity interventions ranging from six months to a year (King, Baumann, O'Sullivan, Wilcox, & Castro, 2002; King, Oka, et al. 1997; King, Pruit, et al., 2000; Robinson, 1999; Stewart et al., 1997, 2001).

Interventions With Older Adults

The majority of intervention studies undertaken in the physical activity arena have been targeted at persons under 60 years of age (Dishman & Sallis, 1994; King et al., 1998). A recent review of physical activity interventions targeting older adults concluded that the studies attained reasonable participation rates, which is even more notable given the relatively long follow-up for some of these studies.

Effective interventions to date have generally used behavioral or cognitive–behavioral strategies (e.g., self-monitoring, goal-setting, feedback, stimulus control, support, relapse-prevention training), as opposed to health education or exercise prescriptions alone (Rejeski & Brawley, 1997). The cognitive–behavioral strategies were successfully delivered using a range of formats, including face-to-face contact (Stewart et al., 1997) group instruction (Rejeski & Brawley, 1997), and mediated channels including the telephone (King & Brassington, 1997; King et al., 1995; Stewart et al., 2000). Several investigations of older adults indicate that instruction in behavioral and cognitive strategies to promote physical activity can encourage continued physical activity even following the termination of formal staff-initiated contact (Rejeski & Brawley, 1997).

The few studies that have evaluated fully mediated approaches to physical activity promotion among seniors (e.g., individual instruction using home videotapes; Jette et al., 1999; combinations of human and automated telephone contacts; Dubbert, Cooper, Kirchner, Meydrech, & Bilbrew, 2002; or telephone-linked computer systems; Jarvis, Freidman, Heeren, & Cullinane, 1997; King et al., 2003) have shown encouraging short-term results. Such efforts need to be expanded to include longer evaluation periods and more diverse groups of seniors.

Although use of health provider advice concerning physical activity delivered through primary care settings has demonstrated some success with younger groups of adults, studies aimed specifically at older patients have not always reported consistent results (Goldstein et al., 1999). A year-long trial using nurse counseling for elderly patients in Veterans Affairs Medical

Center primary care clinics achieved good results for adoption and maintenance of walking three to five days a week, along with improved fitness (Dubbert, Cooper, et al., 2002). In light of the substantial amount of disability and health care use occurring among older adults, and their reported interest in receiving physician advice related to physical activity, they remain a prime target for future physical activity intervention efforts delivered through health care settings.

Places of worship and similar community settings may provide potentially useful venues for delivering physical activity messages, particularly to certain subgroups of older adults (e.g., Black Americans; Lasater, Wells, Carleton, & Elder, 1986). Yet such community settings remain understudied (CDC, 2001a).

Low-cost environmental interventions to promote physical activity in the natural setting (e.g., signage prompting use of stairs in public venues) have led to short-term increases in stair use among both women and men (Blamey, Mutrie, & Aitchison, 1995; Brownell, Stunkard, & Albaum, 1980), but these types of interventions have not been evaluated specifically for older adults. Similarly, although the home and local neighborhood environments represent appealing settings to engage in physical activity, especially among older adults, little systematic evaluation of interventions to promote physical activity in these settings has occurred (King, Rejeski, et al., 1998).

PHYSICAL ACTIVITY PROMOTION IN SPECIAL POPULATIONS

With the exception of cardiovascular disease, most population groups defined not by age but by health conditions that affect participation in and response to physical activity have received little attention to date in studies of exercise promotion. These include people with a variety of physical and mental disabilities and many types of chronic illness. For a growing number of such health conditions, evidence is accumulating that appropriate physical activity can provide significant benefits; however, little is known about how to effectively promote safe levels of activity in these higher risk and more challenging populations (Dubbert, 2002).

Epidemiology of Physical Activity in Higher Risk and Disabled Populations

Cardiovascular diseases, including hypertension and coronary disease, are the leading cause of death, disability, and health care expenditures in the United States, and as such received considerable attention in the Surgeon General's Report on Physical Activity and Health (U.S. Department of Health and Human Services, 1996). Health surveys indicate that more than

50 million adult Americans have high blood pressure, and many more have blood pressure levels that are not high enough to warrant the diagnosis of hypertension or drug intervention but that are associated with increased coronary heart disease (CHD) risk. Many of these individuals are also obese. Drug treatment for so many millions is unsatisfactory because of the costs of treatment and the potential adverse impact of medications. Increased physical activity could help many of these individuals to reduce their blood pressure and CHD risk while improving quality of life (Lesniak & Dubbert, 2001).

More than one million Americans survive a myocardial infarction each year, and another 13 million have cardiac disease and symptoms, which can potentially benefit from exercise interventions. Yet only a minority of patients with heart disease currently participate in formal cardiac rehabilitation programs. The benefits of exercise training for these patients include improved fitness and muscular strength and endurance, decreased angina, modest improvements in certain other risk factors including weight, body fat, blood pressure, and lipid profiles, and enhanced well-being (Franklin, 1996).

In comparison to the body of literature examining physical activity and CVD, studies examining the role of physical activity and exercise for most other high-risk and disabled populations are relatively sparse. A growing number of epidemiological studies have examined the association between physical activity and cancer, the second leading cause of premature death in the United States. The Surgeon General's Report (U.S. Department of Health and Human Services, 1996) concluded that, with the exception of colon cancer, the data are inconsistent or too limited to conclude that physical activity is protective against cancers. However, an important priority for future research is to examine the potential benefits of physical activity for various types of cancer survivors.

Rimmer and colleagues (Rimmer, Braddock, & Pitetti, 1996) reviewed the research on physical activity and disability. By somewhat conservative estimates, these authors concluded that more than 50 million Americans can be considered disabled in the sense that they have one or more specific conditions that impair mobility, strength, endurance, or cognitive and motivational capacities. Epidemiological data about physical activity participation for many of these disability groups are lacking, and there have been few controlled studies examining the effects of interventions tailored to the needs and abilities of specific groups (Taylor, Baranowski, & Young, 1998).

Measurement Issues for High-Risk Populations

Patients with CVD and chronic illness and other people who are at greater risk for adverse effects from physical activity or exercise testing require supervision and monitoring by properly trained personnel appropriate to their health conditions. Accurate recall of physical activity may be especially difficult for some of these individuals because of cognitive limitations. For others, existing self-report measures may not be appropriate because they are not designed for those whose activity is limited in intensity or performed differently as, for example, for those people are who are confined to a wheelchair. The possible risks of using an exercise fitness–performance test as a gold standard measure in higher risk individuals (American College of Cardiology/American Heart Association Task Force on Practice Guidelines Committee on Exercise Testing, 1997) must be weighed against the information that can be gained from this kind of assessment to accurately characterize fitness, assess response to exercise stress, and develop an individualized exercise prescription.

Interventions for Disabled and Higher Risk Populations

Most of the data on interventions with higher risk populations come from work with those at risk for or already diagnosed with CVD. Data from several lifestyle modification hypertension trials that included an activity component suggest that interventions including self-monitoring, gradually increasing goals for activity, and counselor support can increase physical activity for two years or more (Elmer et al., 1995). More carefully controlled trials of exercise training have shown that the amount of blood pressure lowering with exercise is less than that of drug therapy, but its beneficial effects on other risk factors make it an attractive intervention to add to total reduction in CHD risk (Lesniak & Dubbert, 2001).

The independent contribution of exercise to improved health and quality of life in cardiac rehabilitation has been difficult to evaluate. A meta-analysis including a number of trials that individually could not demonstrate a significant effect of exercise on death because of heart disease showed that exercise may reduce the risk for fatal myocardial infarctions by 25% (Oldridge, Guyatt, Fischer, & Rimm, 1988). Exercise in cardiac rehabilitation programs is typically initiated in health care or other specialized settings where patients can be closely monitored. Under these conditions, the risk of fatality is low (Franklin, 1996). Although women and elderly patients are less frequently offered the opportunity, studies suggest they respond well and should be encouraged to participate in cardiac rehabilitation programs (Smith, 1996). Many survivors of myocardial infarction are at low risk for subsequent events and can benefit from less costly and more accessible home-based training. A 1998 comprehensive review of studies that included physical activity or fitness measures and followed patients for at least a year (Simons-Morton et al., 1998) concluded that exercise-promotion interventions provided in health care settings successfully increased physical activity for cardiac rehabilitation patients. In this review, approaches including self-monitoring, continuing supervision, and providing equipment were associated with better maintenance of activity and improved fitness over time.

Exercise is not a sufficient intervention for most patients with increased coronary disease risk. Stress management, dietary, and smoking cessation interventions, which are topics addressed in detail in other chapters of this volume, are also important components of the rehabilitation and secondary prevention program for most patients. Health psychologists should appreciate the importance of psychosocial aspects of cardiac rehabilitation. In one study, for example, Blumenthal and others (Blumenthal et al., 1997) observed fewer cardiac events over three years in patients who completed a four-month stress management intervention compared with patients who completed exercise training for the same amount of time.

Most of the work examining the effects of physical activity on individuals who meet diagnostic criteria for psychiatric disorders has been with clinically depressed patients with mild to moderate symptoms. Across studies, aerobic exercise has generally been found to be more effective than no treatment and not different from comparison treatments (usually psychotherapy; Martinsen & Morgan, 1997). However, the dose of physical activity (frequency, duration, intensity, type) needed to produce an antidepressant effect is not yet adequately known. Blumenthal and others have recently reported on a well-controlled study of effects of exercise training for older men and women with major depression (Blumenthal et al., 1999). Patients age 50 and older were randomized to exercise or exercise plus the antidepressant drug sertraline, or sertraline alone. After 16 weeks, all three groups improved and were not significantly different, although the two antidepressant groups improved more rapidly. After 10 months, participants who were exercising were significantly less likely to have relapsed (Babyak et al., 2000).

As with depression, much more research is needed to increase understanding of physical activity and anxiety symptom dose–response relationships (Raglin, 1997). In normal populations, moderate aerobic activity reduces anxiety for several hours. This effect is also observed with higher intensity exercise, but it may be delayed, with the immediate effect being a transient increase in anxiety symptoms. Resistance training does not seem to have these anxiolytic properties, but this conclusion is based on only a small number of studies.

A recently completed Veterans Affairs Cooperative Study of more than 1,000 veterans examined the effects of exercise training alone or in combination with cognitive–behavioral therapy for treatment of Gulf War Veterans Illnesses (GWVI; Donta et al., 2003). GWVI are characterized by unexplained fatigue, pain, and cognitive symptoms resembling chronic fatigue syndrome. Outcomes for fatigue, distress, and mental symptoms suggested only small effects for exercise; improvements for cognitive–behavioral therapy were also modest. Neither treatment affected pain. The small changes observed may have been related to the generally poor adherence; only 7% of patients attended all the prescribed supervised exercise sessions, and 13% did not attend any. This trial was an ambitious attempt to test exercise interventions, but the results illustrate some of the many challenges facing researchers working with physical activity in special populations. The role of exercise programs and physical activity in the treatment of other mental and behavioral disorders has not yet been adequately studied to draw any conclusions (U.S. Department of Health and Human Services, 1996).

Rimmer and colleagues (Rimmer et al., 1996) offered specific suggestions for advancing understanding physical activity and health promotion for disabled populations. First, they encourage obtaining estimates of physical activity on a condition-specific basis. This would assist with the next step of determining the barriers and determinants of physical activity among different subgroups of persons with disabilities. Developing valid and reliable field-based testing instruments to evaluate the fitness levels of persons with disabilities will be necessary to adequately evaluate the impact of interventions. Careful study of disability groups will allow the identification of secondary complications associated with physical inactivity in persons with disabilities. Finally, it will be possible to design and test intervention strategies to promote physical activity in these groups. As the population ages, the number of people with disabilities will increase, creating new opportunities for behavioral scientists to work with other scientists and practitioners with expertise in various disabilities in developing effective intervention strategies (Dubbert, 2002).

ENVIRONMENTAL AND PUBLIC POLICY ISSUES

Ecological models indicate that creating environments supportive of physical activity is critically important, and environmental approaches may complement individual behavior changes strategies by making it easier for people of all ages and abilities to become and stay active (King, Bauman, et al., 2002; Sallis & Owen, 1997, 2002).

Leisure Time Physical Activity

Behavioral scientists have mainly studied recreational environments in relation to physical activity. A small literature was reviewed by Humpel and colleagues (Humpel, Owen, & Leslie, 2002). Access to activity facilities, opportunities for physical activity (such as nearby programs), and aesthetic characteristics of neighborhoods (such as enjoyable scenery) were consistently related to adults' physical activity. There was less evidence that safety concerns were associated with physical activity. For children, time spent outdoors and access to play areas were strongly associated with physical activity (Sallis et al., 2000). On a more ambitious scale, building a walking trail in a rural community was found to promote adoption of physical activity by sedentary adults (Brownson et al., 2000).

Physical Activity as Transportation

In the past few years, physical activity researchers and advocates have begun collaborating with urban planners, architects, and transportation professionals who have been trying to promote walking in communities as a way to reduce pollution from automobiles and improve social cohesion and quality of life. It is clear that the concepts and methods from these fields can be used to enhance environmental and policy research on physical activity (Handy, Boarnet, Ewing, & Kilingworth, 2002; Saelens, Sallis, & Frank, 2003). Although physical activity and health investigators have focused on leisure-time physical activity, urban planners and transportation professionals have been studying walking and cycling to destinations—a completely different subset of physical activities. Almost 20 studies linking aspects of the built environment with walking and cycling for transportation have produced a coherent set of findings (Saelens, Sallis, Black, & Chen, 2003). People walk and cycle more if they live in neighborhoods in which stores or other destinations are nearby (called mixed use); the streets are highly interconnected in a grid pattern so pathways are relatively direct; there are many multifamily housing units; and there are sidewalks. Such traditional neighborhood designs were common in the United States before the 1940s. People walk and cycle less for transportation in communities where residential and commercial uses are separated by large distances; residential streets tend to have long blocks and are poorly connected; and single-family homes on large lots predominate. This approach to building suburban areas has dominated the real estate industry since the 1940s and it is based on the assumption that people will drive everywhere. Based on travel diary data, residents of traditional neighborhoods walk or cycle about 30 minutes more per week than residents of suburban neighborhoods (Saelens et al., 2003). A small study using accelerometers to measure total physical activity found a 60-minute per-week difference between people in traditional and suburban neighborhoods (Saelens et al., 2003). Intervention studies are limited but promising. There are several studies showing that signs prompting stair use (Andersen, Franckowiak, Snyder, Bartlett, & Fontaine,

1998; Brownell et al., 1980) and aesthetic improvements in the stairwells themselves (Boutelle, Jeffery, Murray, & Schmitz, 2001) can motivate a modest increase in stair use at low cost.

Environmental Aspects of Physical Activity: Opportunities and Challenges

Evidence that physical activity is associated with a wide range of environmental characteristics is rapidly accumulating, and transcisplinary research in this area is a high public health priority because environmental factors may contribute greatly to the high population levels of inactivity. As strong environmental and policy correlates of physical activity are identified, a scientific basis for interventions is built. Environmental interventions may overcome some of the limitations of individual behavior change efforts, because environmental changes affect virtually everyone in the environment, and the impact should be relatively permanent. However, there are many obstacles to changing community designs, recreational spaces and programs, and incentives for physical activity. Researchers and practitioners will be challenged in the years ahead to build the database and develop new intervention skills that are needed to create the environments, policies, and programs that will effectively increase physical activity in the whole population.

CONCLUSION

Most people in the United States today are inactive or are insufficiently active and can therefore benefit from interventions that encourage the adoption and maintenance of regular physical activity. A number of studies targeting the promotion and adoption of physical activity have shown that specific behavioral and cognitive–behavioral strategies are efficacious, at least in the short-term. More studies are needed, however, that follow people for longer periods of time so that long-term maintenance of behavior change can be more thoroughly evaluated. Studies are also needed to further understanding of the unique barriers and benefits of exercise for individuals with disabilities and health conditions that affect ability to participate in and the risks associated with physical activity. In addition, continued work on the environmental and public policy level is critical as combined efforts on the macro and micro level will optimize chances for increasing the activity level of the population and access to the mental and physical health benefits of an active lifestyle.

REFERENCES

Aaron, D. J., Kirsika, A. M., Dearwater, S. R., Cauley, J. A., Metz, K. F., & LaPorte, R. E. (1995). Reproducibility and validity of an epidemiologic questionnaire to assess past year physical activity in adolescents. *American Journal of Epidemiology, 142,* 191–201.

American College of Cardiology/American Heart Association Task Force on Practice Guidelines, Committee on Exercise Testing. (1997). ACC/AHA Guidelines for exercise testing: Executive summary. *Circulation, 96*(1), 345–354.

American College of Sports Medicine. (1998). The recommended quantity and quality of exercise for developing and maintaining cardiorespiratory and muscular fitness and flexibility in healthy adults. *Medicine and Science in Sports and Exercise, 30*(6), 975–991.

Andersen, R. E., Crespo, C. J., Bartlett, S. J., Cheskin, L. J., & Pratt, M. (1998). Relationship of physical activity and television watching with body weight and level of fatness among children: Results from the third National Health and Nutrition Examination Survey. *Journal of the American Medical Association, 279,* 938–942.

Andersen, R. E., Franckowiak, S. C., Snyder, J., Bartlett, S. J., & Fontaine, K. R. (1998). Can inexpensive signs encourage the use of stairs? Results from a community intervention. *Annals of Internal Medicine, 129,* 363–369.

Armstrong, N., & Van Mechelen, W. (1998). Are young people fit and active? In S. Biddle, J. F. Sallis, & N. A. Cavill (Eds.), *Young and active? Young people and health enhancing physical activity: Evidence and implications* (pp. 69–97). London: Health Education Authority.

Babyak, M., Blumenthal, J. A., Herman, S., Khatri, P., Doraiswamy, M., Moore, K., et al. (2000). Exercise treatment for major depression: Maintenance of therapeutic benefit at 10 months. *Psychomatic Medicine, 62,* 633–638.

Bandura, A. (1986). *Social foundations of thought and action A social cognitive theory.* Englewood Cliffs, NJ: Prentice-Hall.

Baranowski, T. (1988). Validity and reliability of self report measures of physical activity: An information-processing perspective. *Research Quarterly for Exercise and Sport, 59*(4), 314–327.

Biddle, S., Sallis, J. F., & Cavill, N. A. (1998). *Young and active? Young people and health enhancing physical activity: Evidence and implications.* London: Health Education Authority.

Billings, J., Zeitel, L., Lukomnik, J., Carey, T., Blank, A., & Neman, L. (1993). Impact of socioeconomic status on hospital use in New York City. *Health Affairs (Millwood), 12,* 162–173.

Blair, S. N., Applegate, W. B., Dunn, A. L., Ettinger, W. H., Haskell, W. L., King, A. C., et al. (1998). Activity Counseling Trial (ACT): Rationale, design, and methods. *Medicine and Science in Sports and Exercise, 30*(7), 1097–1106.

Blamey, A., Mutrie, N., & Aitchison, T. (1995). Health promotion by encouraged use of stairs. *British Medical Journal, 311*, 289–290.

Blumenthal, J. A., Babyak, M. A., Moore, K. A., Craighead, W. E., Herman, S., Khatri, P., et al. (1999). Effects of exercise training on older patients with major depression. *Archives of Internal Medicine, 159*, 2349–2356.

Blumenthal, J. A., Jiang, W., Babyak, M. A., Krantz, D. S., Frid, D. J., Coleman, R. E., et al. (1997). Stress management and exercise training in cardiac patients with myocardial ischemia. *Archives of Internal Medicine, 157*, 2213–2223.

Boutelle, K., Jeffery, R. W., Murray, D. M., & Schmitz, K. H. (2001). Using signs, artwork, and music to promote stair use in a public building. *American Journal of Public Health, 91*, 2004–2006.

Brownell, K. D., Stunkard, A. J., & Albaum, J. M. (1980). Evaluation and modification of exercise patterns in the natural environment. *American Journal of Psychiatry, 137*(12), 1540–1545.

Brownson, R. C., Hosemann, R. A., Brown, D. R., Jackson-Thompson, J., King, A. C., Malone, B. R., et al. (2000). Promoting physical activity in rural communities: Walking trail access, use, and effects. *American Journal of Preventive Medicine, 18*, 235–241.

Buchner, D. M., & Wagner, E. H. (1992). Preventing frail health. *Clinics in Geriatric Medicine, 8*, 1–17.

Calfas, K. J., Long, B. J., Sallis, J. F., Wooten, W. J., Pratt, M., & Patrick, K. (1996). A controlled trial of physician counseling to promote the adoption of physical activity. *Preventive Medicine, 25*, 225–233.

Calfas, K. J., & Taylor, W. C. (1994). Effects of physical activity on psychological variables in adolescents. *Pediatric Exercise Science, 6*, 406–423.

Carleton, R. A., Lasater, T. M., Assaf, A. R., Felman, H. A., & McKinlay, S. (1995). The Pawtucket Heart Health Program: Community changes in cardiovascular risk factors and projected disease risk. *American Journal of Public Health, 85*, 777–785.

Cavill, N., Biddle, S., & Sallis, J. F. (2001). Health enhancing physical activity for young people: Statement of the United Kingdom expert consensus conference. *Pediatric Exercise Science, 13*, 12–25.

Centers for Disease Control and Prevention (CDC). (1997). Guidelines for school and community programs to promote lifelong physical activity among young people. *Morbidity and Mortality Weekly Reports, 46*(RR-6), 1–36.

Centers for Disease Control and Prevention (CDC). (1999). Youth risk surveillance—United States, 1999. *Morbidity and Mortality Weekly Reports, 49*(SS-5), 1–95.

Centers for Disease Control and Prevention (CDC). (2001a). Increasing physical activity: A report on recommendations of the Task Force on Community Preventive Services. *Morbidity and Mortality Weekly Reports, 50*(RR-18), 1–14.

Centers for Disease Control and Prevention (CDC). (2001b). Mortality from coronary heart disease and acute myocardial infarction—United States, 1998. *Morbidity and Mortality Weekly Report, 50*(6), 90–93.

Centers for Disease Control and Prevention (CDC). (2001c). Physical activity trends—United States, 1990–1998. *Morbidity and Mortality Weekly Report, 9,* 166–169.

Conn, V. S. (1998). Older adults and exercise Path analysis of self-efficacy related constructs. *Nursing Research, 47*(3), 180–189.

Corbin, C. B., & Pangrazi, R. P. (1998). *Physical activity for children: A statement of guidelines.* Reston, VA: National Association for Sport and Physical Education.

Crow, R., Blackburn, H., Jacobs, D., Hannan, P., Pirie, P., MIttelmark, M., et al. (1986). Population strategies to enhance physical activity: The Minnesota Heart Health Program. *Acta Medica Scandinavica, 771*(Suppl.), 93–112.

Dishman, R. K., & Buckworth, J. (1996). Increasing physical activity: A quantitative synthesis. *Medicine and Science in Sports and Exercise, 28*(6), 706–719.

Dishman, R. K., & Sallis, J. F. (1994). Determinants and interventions for physical activity and exercise. In C. Bouchard, R. J. Shephard, & T. Stephens (Eds.), *Physical activity, fitness, and health* (pp. 214–238). Champaign, IL: Human Kinetics Press.

Donta, S. T., Clauw, D. J., Engel, C. C., Guarino, A. P., Peduzzi, P., Williams, D. A., et al. (2003). Cognitive behavioral therapy and aerobic exercise for Gulf War Veterans' Illnesses. *Journal of the American Medical Association, 289*(11), 1396–1404.

Dubbert, P. M. (2002). Physical activity and exercise: Recent advances and current challenges. *Journal of Consulting and Clinical Psychology, 70*(3), 526–536.

Dubbert, P. M., Carithers, T., Sumner, A. E., Barbour, K. A., Clark, B. L., Hall, J. E., et al. (2002). Obesity, physical inactivity, and risk for cardiovascular disease. *American Journal of the Medical Sciences, 324*(3), 116–126.

Dubbert, P. M., Cooper, K. M., Kirchner, K. A., Meydrech, E. F., & Bilbrew, D. (2002). Effects of nurse counseling on walking for exercise in elderly primary care patients. *Journal of Gerontology: Medical Sciences, 57A*(11), M733–M740.

Dubbert, P. M., & Stetson, B. A. (1999). Cognitive and behavioral approaches to enhancing exercise adherence. In J. Rippe (Ed.), *Lifestyle medicine* (pp. 511–519). Malden, MA: Blackwell Scientific.

Dunn, A. L., Garcia, M. E., Marcus, B. H., Kampert, J. B., Kohl, H. W., III, & Blair, S. N. (1998). Six-month physical activity and fitness changes in Project Active, a randomized trial. *Medicine and Science in Sports and Exercise, 30*(7), 1076–1083.

Dunn, A. L., Marcus, B. H., Kampert, J. B., Garcia, M. E., Kohl, H. W. I., & Blair, S. N. (1999). Comparison of lifestyle and structured interventions to increase physical activity and cardiorespiratory fitness. *Journal of the American Medical Association, 281*(4), 327–334.

Elder, J. P., McGraw, S. A., & Abrams, D. B. Ferriera, A., Lasater, T. M., Longpre, H., et al. (1986). Organizational and community approaches to community-wide prevention of heart disease: The first two years of the Pawtucket Heart Health Program. *Preventive Medicine, 15,* 107–117.

Elmer, P. J., Grimm, R., Jr., Laing, B., Grandits, M., Svendsen, K., Van Heel, N., et al. (1995). Lifestyle intervention: Results of Treatment of Mild Hypertension Study (TOMHS). *Preventive Medicine, 24,* 378–388.

Elward, K., & Larson, E. B. (1992). Benefits of exercise for older adults. *Clinics in Geriatric Medicine, 8*(1), 35–50.

Epstein, L. H., Myers, M. D., Raynor, H. A., & Saelens, B. E. (1998). Treatment of pediatric obesity. *Pediatrics, 101*(Suppl.), 554–570.

Farquhar, J. W., Fortmann, S. P., Flora, J. A., Taylor, C. B., Haskell, W. L., Williams, P. T., et al. (1990). Effects of communitywide education on cardiovascular disease risk factors. *Journal of the American Medical Association, 264*(3), 359–365.

Faucette, N., Sallis, J., McKenzie, T., Alcaraz, J., Kolody, B., & Nugent, P. (1995). Comparison of fourth grade students' out-of-school physical activity levels and choices by gender: Project SPARK. *Journal of Health Education, 26,* S82–S90.

Fiatarone, M. A., Marks, E. C., Ryan, N. D., Meredith, C. N., Lipsitz, L. A., & Evans, W. J. (1990). High-intensity strength training in nonagenarians. *Journal of the American Medical Association, 263*(22), 3029–3034.

Fletcher, G. F., Blair, S. N., Blumenthal, J., Caspersen, C., Chaitman, B., Epstein, S., et al. (1992). AHA Medical/Scientific Statement on Exercise. *Circulation, 86*(1), 340–343.

Franklin, B. A. (1996). Update on secondary prevention of cardiovascular disease and exercise-based cardiac rehabilitation. In A. S. Leon (Ed.), *Physical activity and cardiovascular health* (pp. 151–161). Champaign, IL: Human Kinetics.

Goldstein, M. G., Pinto, B. M., Marcus, B. H., Lynn, H., Jette, A. M., Rakowski, W., et al. (1999). Physician-based physical activity counseling for middle-aged and older adults: A randomized trial. *Annals of Behavioral Medicine, 21*(1), 40–47.

Gortmaker, S. L., Peterson, K., Wiecha, J., Sobol, A. M., Dixit, S., Fox, M. K., et al. (1999). Reducing obesity via a school-based interdisciplinary intervention among youth: Planet Health. *Archives of Pediatrics and Adolescent Medicine, 153,* 409–418.

Handy, S. L., Boarnet, M. G., Ewing, R., & Kilingworth, R. E. (2002). How the built environment affects physical activity. *American Journal of Preventive Medicine, 23*(Suppl. 2), 64–73.

Hays, K. F. (1999). *Working it out.* Washington, DC: American Psychological Association.

Humpel, N., Owen, N., & Leslie, E. (2002). Environmental factors associated with adults' participation in physical activity: A review. *American Journal of Preventive Medicine, 22,* 188–199.

Irwin, M. L., Yasui, Y., Ulrich, C. M., Bowen, D., Rudolph, R. E., Schwartz, R. S., et al. (2003). Effect of exercise on total and intra-abdominal body fat in postmenopausal women. *Journal of the American Medical Association, 289,* 323–330.

Jarvis, K. L., Freidman, R. H., Heeren, T., & Cullinane, P. M. (1997). Older women and physical activity: Using the telephone to walk. *Women's Health Issues, 7*, 24–29.

Jette, A. M., Lachman, M., Giorgetti, M. M., Assmann, S. F., Harris, B. A., Levenson, C., et al. (1999). Exercise—It's never too late: The Strong-for-Life Program. *American Journal of Public Health, 89*(1), 66–72.

Jones, M., & Nies, M. A. (1996). The relationship of perceived benefits of and barriers to reported exercise in older African American women. *Public Health Nursing, 13*(2), 151–158.

Kahn, E. B., Ramsay, L. T., Brownson, R. C., Heath, G. W., Howze, E. H., Powell, K. E., et al. (2002). The effectiveness of interventions to increase physical activity: Review. *American Journal of Preventive Medicine, 22*(Suppl. 4), 73–107.

Kelder, S. H., Perry, C. L., Peters, R. J., Lytle, L. L., & Klepp, K.-I. (1995). Gender differences in the Class of 1989 study: The school component of the Minnesota Heart Health Program. *Journal of School Health, 26*, S36–S44.

King, A. C., Baumann, K., O'Sullivan, P., Wilcox, S., & Castro, C. (2002). Effects of moderate-intensity exercise on physiological, behavioral, and emotional responses to family care-giving: A randomized controlled trial. *Journal of Gerontology: Medical Sciences, 57A*(1), M26–M36.

King, A. C., Blair, S. N., Bild, D. E., Dishman, R. K., Dubbert, P. M., Marcus, B. H., et al. (1992). Determinants of physical activity and interventions in adults. *Medicine and Science in Sports and Exercise, 24*, s221–s236.

King, A. C., & Brassington, G. (1997). Enhancing physical and psychological functioning in older family caregivers: The role of regular physical activity. *Annals of Behavioral Medicine, 29*, 1–11.

King, A. C., Castro, C., Wilcox, S., Eyler, A. A., Sallis, J. F., & Brownson, R. C. (2000). Personal and environmental factors associated with physical inactivity among different racial–ethnic groups of U.S. middle-aged and older-aged women. *Health Psychology, 19*(4), 354–364.

King, A. C., Friedman, R., Marcus, B., Napolitano, M., Castro, C., & Forsyth, L. A. (2003). Increasing regular physical activity via humans or automated technology: The CHAT Trial (abstract). *Annals of Behavioral Medicine*, S111.

King, A. C., Haskell, W. L., Taylor, C. B., Kraemer, H. C., & DeBusk, R. F. (1991). Group- vs. home-based exercise training in healthy older men and women. *Journal of the American Medical Association, 266*, 1535–1542.

King, A. C., Haskell, W. L., Young, D. R., Oka, R. K., & Stefanick, M. L. (1995). Long-term effects of varying intensities and formats of physical activity on participation rates, fitness, and lipoproteins in men and women aged 50 to 65 years. *Circulation, 9*(10), 2596–2604.

King, A. C., Kiernan, M., Oman, R. F., Kraemer, H. C., Hull, M., & Ahn, D. (1997). Can we identify who will adhere to long-term physical activity? Application of signal detection methodology as a potential aid to clinical decision-making. *Health Psychology, 16*, 380–389.

King, A. C., Oka, R., Pruitt, L., Phillips, W., & Haskell, W. L. (1997). Developing optimal exercise regimens for seniors: A clinical trial. *Annals of Behavioral Medicine, 19*(Suppl.), S56.

King, A. C., Pruitt, L. A., Phillips, W., Oka, R., Rodenburg, A., & Haskell, W. L. (2000). Comparative effects of two physical activity programs on measured and perceived physical functioning and other health-related quality of life outcomes in older adults. *Journal of Gerontology: Medical Sciences, 55A*(2), M74–M83.

King, A. C., Rejeski, W. J., & Buchner, D. M. (1998). Physical activity interventions targeting older adults: A critical review and recommendations. *American Journal of Preventive Medicine, 15*, 316–333.

King, A. C., Sallis, J. F., Dunn, A. L., Simons-Morton, D. G., Albright, C. A., Cohen, S., et al. (1998). Overview of the Activity Counseling Trial (ACT) intervention for promoting physical activity in primary health care settings. *Medicine and Science in Sports and Exercise, 30*(7), 1086–1096.

King, A. C., Stokols, D., Talen, E., Brassington, G. S., & Killingworth, R. (2002). Theoretical approaches to the promotion of physical activity: Forging a transdisciplinary paradigm. *American Journal of Preventive Medicine, 23*(2S), 15–25.

King, A. C., Taylor, C. B., Haskell, W. L., & DeBusk, R. F. (1990). Identifying strategies for increasing employee physical activity levels: Findings from the Stanford/Lockheed exercise survey. *Health Education Quarterly, 17*, 269–285.

Lasater, T. M., Wells, B. L., & Carleton, R. A., & Elder, J. P. (1986). The role of churches in disease prevention research studies. *Public Health Reports, 101*, 125–131.

Lee, C. (1993). Factors related to the adoption of exercise among older women. *Journal of Behavioral Medicine, 16*, 323–334.

Lesniak, K. T., & Dubbert, P. M. (2001). Exercise and hypertension. *Current Opinion in Cardiology, 16*, 356–359.

Lewis, C. E., Raczynski, J. M., Heath, G. W., Levinson, R., Hilyer, J. C., & Cutter, G. R. (1993). Promoting physical activity in low-income African-American communities: The PARR project. *Ethnicity and Disease, 3*, 106–118.

Lombard, D. N., Lombard, T. N., & Winett, R. A. (1995). Walking to meet health guidelines: The effect of prompting frequency and prompt structure. *Health Psychology, 14*(2), 164–170.

Manios, Y., Kafatos, A., & Markakis, G. (1998). Physical activity of 6 year old children: Validation of two proxy reports. *Pediatric Exercise Science, 10*, 176–188.

Mann, K. V., & Putnam, R. W. (1985). Physicians' perceptions of their role. I. Cardiovascular risk reduction. *Preventive Medicine, 18*, 54–58.

Marcoux, M. F., Sallis, J. F., McKenzie, T. L., Marshal, S., Armstrong, C. A., & Goggin, K. J. (1999). Process evaluation of a physical activity self-management program for children: SPARK. *Psychology and Health, 14*, 659–677.

Marcus, B. H., Banspach, S. W., Lefebvre, R. C., Rossi, J. S., Carleton, R. A., & Abrams, D. (1992). Using the stages of change model to increase the adoption of physical activity among community participants. *American Journal of Health Promotion, 6,* 424–429.

Marcus, B. H., Bock, B. C., Pinto, B. M., Forsyth, L. H., Roberts, M., & Traficante, R. M. (1998). Efficacy of an individualized, motivationally-tailored physical activity intervention. *Annals of Behavioral Medicine, 20*(3), 174–180.

Marcus, B. H., Dubbert, P. M., Forsyth, L. H., McKenzie, T. L., Stone, E. J., Dunn, A. L., et al. (2000). Physical activity change: Issues in adoption and maintenance. *Health Psychology, 19*(1), 32–41.

Marcus, B. H., Rossi, J. S., Selby, V. C., Niaura, R. S., & Abrams, D. B. (1992). The stages and processes of exercise adoption and maintenance. *Health Psychology, 11,* 386–395.

Marlatt, G. A., & Gordon, J. R. (1985). *Relapse prevention.* New York: Guilford Press.

Martinsen, E. W., & Morgan, W. P. (1997). Antidepressant effects of physical activity. In W. P. Morgan (Ed.), *Physical activity and mental health* (pp. 93–106). Washington, DC: Taylor & Francis.

McKenzie, T. L. (2002). Use of direct observation to assess physical activity. In G. J. Welk (Ed.), *Physical activity assessments for health-related research* (pp. 179–196). Champaign, IL: Human Kinetics.

McKenzie, T. L., Alcaraz, J. E., Sallis, J. F., & Faucetter, F. N. (1998). Effects of a physical education program on children's manipulative skills. *Journal of Teaching in Physical Education, 17,* 327–341.

McKenzie, T. L., Nader, P. R., Strikmiller, P. K., Yang, M., Stone, E., & Perry, C. L. (1996). School physical education: Effects of the Child and Adolescent Trial for Cardiovascular Health. *Preventive Medicine, 25,* 423–431.

Mills, K. M., King, A. C., & Stewart, A. L. (1998). Predictors of physical activity change in older adults (CHAMPS II): Preliminary results. *Gerontologist, 38,* 394.

Mobily, K. E., Lemke, J. H., Durbe, G. A., Wallace, R. B., & Leslie, D. K. (1987). Relationship between exercise attitudes and participation among the rural elderly. *Adapted Physical Education Quarterly, 4,* 36–50.

Montoye, H. J. (2000). Introduction: Evaluation of some measurements of physical activity and energy expenditure. *Medicine and Science in Sports and Exercise, 32*(Suppl.), S439–S441.

Mullen, P., & Tabak, G. R. (1989). Patterns of counseling techniques used by family practice physicians for smoking, weight, exercise, and stress. *Medical Care, 27,* 694–704.

Nader, P. R., Stone, E. J., Lytle, L. A., Perry, C. L., Osganian, S. K., Kelder, S., et al. (1999). Three year maintenance of improved diet and physical activity: The CATCH Cohort. Child and Adolescent Trial for Cardiovascular Health. *Archives for Pediatrics and Adolescent Medicine, 153,* 695–704.

Oka, R. K., King, A. C., & Young, D. R. (1995). Sources of social support as predictors of exercise in women and men ages 50 to 65 years. *Women's Health: Research on Gender, Behavior, and Policy, 1*, 161–175.

Oldridge, N. B., Guyatt, G. H., Fischer, M. E., & Rimm, A. A. (1988). Cardiac rehabilitation after myocardiac infarction: Combined experience of randomized clinical trials. *Journal of the American Medical Association, 260*, 945–950.

Pate, R. R., Freedson, P. S., Sallis, J. F., Taylor, W. C., Sirard, J., Trost, S. G., et al. (2002). Compliance with physical activity guidelines: Prevalence in a population of children and youth. *Annals of Epidemiology, 12*, 303–308.

Pate, R. R., Pratt, M., Blair, S. N., Haskell, W. L., Macera, C. A., Bouchard, C., et al. (1995). Physical activity and public health. A recommendation from the Centers for Disease Control and Prevention and the American College of Sports Medicine. *Journal of the American Medical Association, 273*, 402–407.

Patrick, K., Sallis, J. F., Prochaska, J. J., Lydston, D. D., Calfas, K. J., Zabinski, M. F., et al. (2001). A multicomponent program for nutrition and physical activity change in primary care. *Archives of Pediatrics and Adolescent Medicine, 155*, 940–946.

Pereira, M. A., FitzGerald, S. J., Gregg, E. W., Joswiak, M. L., Ryan, W. J., Suminski, R. R., et al. (1997). A collection of physical activity questionnaires for health-related research. *Medicine and Science in Sports and Exercise, 29*(Suppl.), S1–S205.

Prochaska, J. O., & DiClemente, C. C. (1983). Stages and processes of self-change of smoking: Toward an integrative model of change. *Journal of Consulting and Clinical Psychology, 51*, 390–395.

Prochaska, J. J., Sallis, J. F., & Long, B. (2001). A physical activity screening measure for use with adolescents in primary care. *Archives of Pediatrics and Adolescent Medicine, 155*, 554–559.

Raglin, J. S. (1997). Anxiolytic effects of physical activity. In W. P. Morgan (Ed.), *Physical activity and mental health* (pp. 107–126). Washington, DC: Taylor & Francis.

Rejeski, W. J., & Brawley, L. R. (1997). Shaping active lifestyles in older adults: A group-facilitated behavior change intervention. *Annals of Behavioral Medicine, 19*(Suppl.), S106.

Rejeski, W. J., Brawley, L. R., Ettinger, W. H., Morgan, T., & Thompson, C. (1997). Compliance to exercise therapy in older participants with knee osteoarthritis: Implications for treating disability. *Medicine and Science in Sports and Exercise, 29*, 977–985.

Riddoch, C. (1998). Relationships between physical activity and health in young people. In S. Biddle, J. F. Sallis, & N. A. Cavill (Eds.), *Young and active? Young people and health enhancing physical activity: Evidence and implications* (pp. 17–48). London: Health Education Authority.

Rimmer, J. H., Braddock, D., & Pitetti, K. H. (1996). Research on physical activity and disability: An emerging priority. *Medicine and Science in Sports and Exercise, 28*(8), 1366–1372.

Robinson, T. N. (1999). Reducing children's television viewing to prevent obesity: A randomized clinical trial. *Journal of the American Medical Association, 282,* 1561–1567.

Ross, J. G., Dotson, C. O., Gilbert, G. G., & Katz, S. J. (1985). After physical education: Physical activity outside of school physical education programs. *Journal of Physical Education, Recreation, and Dance, 56*(1), 35–39.

Saelens, B. E., Sallis, J. F., Black, J. B., & Chen, D. (2003). Preliminary evaluation of the Neighborhood Environment Walkability Scale and neighborhood-based differences in physical activity. *American Journal of Public Health, 93,* 1552–1558.

Saelens, B. E., Sallis, J. F., & Frank, L. D. (2003). Environmental correlates of walking and cycling; Findings from the transportation, urban design, and planning literatures. *Annals of Behavioral Medicine, 25,* 80–91.

Sallis, J. F. (1993). Epidemiology of physical activity and fitness in children and adolescents. *Critical Reviews in Food Science and Nutrition, 33,* 403–408.

Sallis, J. (1998). Family and community interventions to promote physical activity in young people. In S. Biddle, J. F. Sallis, & N. A. Cavill (Eds.), *Young and active? Young people and health enhancing physical activity: Evidence and implications* (pp. 150–161). London: Health Education Authority.

Sallis, J. F., Calfas, K. J., Nichols, J. F., Sarkin, J. A., Johnson, M. F., Caparosa, S., et al. (1999). Evaluation of a university course to promote physical activity: Project GRAD. *Research Quarterly for Exercise and Sport, 70,* 1–10.

Sallis, J. F., McKenzie, T. L., Alcaraz, J. E., Kolody, B., Faucette, N., & Hovell, M. F. (1997). The effects of a 2-year physical education program (SPARK) on physical activity and fitness in elementary school students. *American Journal of Public Health, 87,* 1328–1334.

Sallis, J. F., McKenzie, T. L., Conway, T. L., Elder, J. P., Prochaska, J. J., Brown, M., et al. (2003). Environmental interventions for eating and physical activity. *American Journal of Preventive Medicine, 24,* 209–217.

Sallis, J. F., McKenzie, T. L., Kolody, B., Lewis, M., Marshall, S., & Rosengard, P. (1999). Effects of health-related physical education on academic achievement: Project SPARK. *Research Quarterly for Exercise and Sport, 70,* 127–136.

Sallis, J. F., & Owen, N. (1997). Ecological models. In K. Glanz, F. M. Lewis, & B. K. Rimer (Eds.), *Health behavior and health education: Theory, research, and practice* (pp. 403–424). San Francisco: Jossey Bass.

Sallis, J. F., & Owen, N. (1999). *Physical activity & behavioral medicine.* Thousand Oaks, CA: Sage.

Sallis, J. F., & Owen, N. (2002). Ecological models of health behavior. In K. Glanz, B. K. Rimer, & F. M. Lewis (Eds.), *Health behavior and health education: Theory, research, and practice* (3rd ed., pp. 462–484). San Francisco: Jossey-Bass.

Sallis, J. F., & Patrick, K. (1994). Physical activity guidelines for adolescents: Consensus statement. *Pediatric Exercise Science, 6,* 302–314.

Sallis, J. F., Prochaska, J. J., & Taylor, W. C. (2000). A review of correlates of physical activity of children and adolescents. *Medicine and Science in Sports and Exercise, 32*(5), 963–975.

Sallis, J. F., & Saelens, B. E. (2000). Assessment of physical activity by self-report: Status, limitations, and future directions. *Research Quarterly for Exercise and Sport, 71*(2), 1–14.

Sallis, J. F., Zakarian, J. M., Hovell, M. F., & Hofstetter, C. R. (1996). Ethnic, socioeconomic, and sex differences in physical activity among adolescents. *Journal of Clinical Epidemiology, 49,* 125–134.

Simons-Morton, D. G., Calfas, K. J., Oldenburg, B., & Burton, N. W. (1998). Effects of interventions in health care settings on physical activity or cardiorespiratory fitness. *American Journal of Preventive Medicine, 15*(4), 413–430.

Smith, L. K. (1996). Cardiac rehabilitation as secondary prevention: A synopsis of the clinical practice guideline for cardiac rehabilitation. In A. S. Leon (Ed.), *Physical activity and cardiovascular health* (pp. 144–150). Champaign IL: Human Kinetics.

Stewart, A. L., Mills, K. M., King, A. C., Haskell, W. L., Gillis, D., & Ritter, P. L. (2001). CHAMPS physical activity questionnaire for older adults: Outcomes for interventions. *Medicine and Science in Sports and Exercise, 33,* 1126–1141.

Stewart, A. L., Mills, K. M., Sepsis, P. G., King, A. C., McLellan, B., Roitz, K., et al. (1997). Evaluation of CHAMPS, a physical activity promotion program for seniors. *Annals of Behavioral Medicine, 29,* 353–361.

Stewart, A. L., Verboncoeur, C. J., McLellan, B. Y., Gillis, D. E., Rush, S., Mills, K. M., et al. (2000). Physical activity outcomes of CHAMPS II: A physical activity promotion program for older adults. *Journal of Gerontology: Medical Sciences, 56A,* M465–M470.

Stone, E. J., McKenzie, T. L., Welk, G. J., & Booth, M. L. (1998). Effects of physical activity interventions in youth: Review and synthesis. *American Journal of Preventive Medicine, 15,* 298–315.

Taylor, W. C., Baranowski, T., & Young, D. R. (1998). Physical activity interventions in low-income, ethnic minority, and populations with disability. *American Journal of Health Promotion, 15*(4), 334–343.

Thompson, P. D., Buchner, D., Pina, I. L., Balady, G. J., Williams, M. A., Marcus, B. H., et al. (2003). Exercise and physical activity in the prevention and treatment of atherosclerotic cardiovascular disease: A statement from the Council on Clinical Cardiology (Subcommittee on Exercise, Rehabilitation, and Prevention) and the Council on Nutrition, Physical Activity, and Metabolism (Subcommittee on Physical Activity). *Circulation, 107*(24), e9053–e9054.

Trost, S. G., Owen, N., Bauman, A. E., Sallis, J. E., & Brown, W. (2002). Correlates of adults' participation in physical activity: Review and update. *Medicine and Science in Sports and Exercise, 34*(12), 1996–2001.

U.S. Department of Health and Human Services. (1996). *Physical activity and health: A report of the Surgeon General.* Atlanta, GA: U.S. Department of Health and

Human Services, Centers for Disease Control and Prevention, National Center for Chronic Disease Prevention and Health Promotion.

Washburn, R. A. (2000). Assessment of physical activity in older adults. *Research Quarterly for Exercise and Sport, 71*(2), 79–88.

Welk, G. J. (2002). Use of accelerometry-based activity monitors to assess physical activity. In G. J. Welk (Ed.), *Physical activity assessments for health-related research* (pp. 125–141). Champaign, IL: Human Kinetics.

Weston, A. T., Petosa, R., & Pate, R. R. (1997). Validation of an instrument for measurement of physical activity in youth. *Medicine and Science in Sports and Exercise, 29,* 138–143.

Williams, P. (2001). Physical fitness and activity as separate heart disease risk factors: A meta-analysis. *Medicine and Science in Sports and Exercise, 33,* 754–761.

Wimbush, E., MacGregory, A., & Fraser, E. (1998). The effects of a national mass media campaign on walking in Scotland. *Health Promotion International, 13*(1).

Wister, A. V. (1996). The effects of socioeconomic status on exercise and smoking: Age-related differences. *Journal of Aging and Health, 8,* 467–488.

Wolinsky, F. D., Stump, T. E., & Clark, D. O. (1995). Antecedents and consequences of physical activity and exercise among older adults. *Gerontologist, 35*(4), 451–462.

Wood, T. M. (2000). Issues and future directions in assessing physical activity: An introduction to the conference proceedings. *Research Quarterly for Exercise and Sport, 71*(Suppl.), ii.

Writing Group for the Activity Counseling Trial Research Group. (2001). Effects of physical activity counseling in primary care. *Journal of the American Medical Association, 286*(6), 677–687.

Young, D. R., Haskell, W. L., Taylor, C. B., & Fortmann, S. P. (1996). Effect of community health education on physical activity knowledge, attitudes, and behavior: The Stanford Five-City Project. *American Journal of Epidemiology, 144,* 264–274.

Young, D. R., & King, A. C. (1995). Exercise adherence: Determinants of physical activity and applications of health behavior change theories. *Medicine, Exercise, Nutrition, and Health, 4,* 335–348.

6

NORMAL SLEEP
AND SLEEP DISORDERS
IN ADULTS AND CHILDREN

G. VERNON PEGRAM, JOHN McBURNEY, SUSAN M. HARDING,
AND CHRISTOPHER M. MAKRIS

Sleep is a physical state that involves the suspension of voluntary bodily functions and complete or partial suspension of consciousness. It normally occurs as a fundamental part of a natural, cycling pattern of sleep and wakefulness. A more detailed examination of the sleep–wakefulness cycle, using an electroencephalograph (EEG) analysis, reveals that mammalian behavior involves three distinct, readily identifiable behavioral states: wakefulness (W), nonrapid eye movement (NREM) sleep, and rapid eye movement (REM) sleep. If the normal balance among these three behavioral states is altered, a person begins to report the result as symptoms of a sleep disorder. Disruption of the accustomed sleep pattern can result from environmental change, psychological disturbance, pharmacological agents,

We thank James M. Raczynski for his careful editing of the original draft; Jerri Beck for her organization and creativity; Arren Graf for the support and initial editing during the early and later versions of this chapter; and Len Shigley, whose support and suggestions in dealing with references were invaluable.

or physical disease; complaints range from too much wakefulness (insomnia) to too much sleepiness (hypersomnia), thus representing the extremes of the imbalance of the sensitive sleep–wakefulness cycle.

Complaints of problems with sleep are among the most common medical complaints in U.S. society. In fact, approximately 35% of all adults report experiencing insomnia at some time during the previous year (Mellinger, Balter, & Uhlenhuth, 1985). Half of these people consider their problem serious. Add to this number the adults who have obstructive sleep apnea, narcolepsy, and other neurological disorders of excessive somnolence, as well as the many millions with circadian rhythm disorders and parasomnia, and it becomes apparent that at least 40% of all adults experience some type of sleep disorder in their lifetimes (Ohayon et al., 1997).

This chapter provides a brief description of the basic and applied knowledge concerning sleep–wakefulness mechanisms, as well as a review of some of the major sleep disorders and current approaches to treatment and management.

NORMAL SLEEP

Normal sleep occurs in a permissible environment and is defined in terms of behavior and electrographic patterns associated with physiological processes. It is critical to remember that normal sleep is part of a 24-hour cycle of sleep and wakefulness that cannot be appreciated in isolation from the total cycle and is inextricably integrated with the whole process. The body prepares itself for sleep during the day and makes preparations for wakefulness during the night.

The light–dark cycle is a strong regulator of the sleep and wake processes (DeCoursey, 1960; Ralph & Mrosovsky, 1992). Light exposure at morning and evening is the primary tuning force maintaining a balance in the sleep–wake rhythm from day to day under normal conditions. Through the retinohypothalamic tract and the suprachiasmatic nucleus, internal synchrony is maintained among body rhythms, including hormones governing cell division, growth, immune function, metabolism, and temperature cycle (Steiger, 2002).

In addition, our internal body clock is kept tuned to the 24-hour rotation of the earth. For example, cortisol levels rise during sleep, and body temperature begins its rise at the end of sleep to support waking needs (Richardson, Carskadon, Orav, & Dement, 1982). Body temperature declines before bedtime as if to invite us to sleep (Drewes, Nielsen, Arendt-Nielsen, Birket-Smith, & Hansen, 1997). A myriad of such changes in physiological processes support sleep and wake behavior and the transitions between in a complicated but well-orchestrated manner that remains largely unappreciated. When these processes are in harmony, we feel normal. Transitions from wake to sleep or vice versa are easily accommodated at any point during the 24-hour cycle, but being awake at night is not the same as being awake during the day. Likewise, being asleep during the day is not the same as sleeping at night. Each state has its own normal, supportive physiology that is intended to endure for several hours and does not go through transition with equal facility on short notice. By definition, "normal sleep" does not occur in "normal" individuals attempting to sleep during the day. The converse is also true. A mismatch between behavior and physiology is the cardinal feature of all schedule disorders.

NORMAL SLEEP PATTERNS

Normal sleep is described by certain behavioral and electrographic patterns. A normal cycle of sleep occurs in a favorable environmental milieu, involving a comfortable and recumbent position, a suitable temperature, and an absence of skeletal muscle activation or sounds. Sleep onset occurs about the same time each day after certain rituals that prepare for sleep. With these prerequisites, sleep is usually achieved in about 10 minutes and is a pleasant experience. Soothing sounds and stimuli may assist but are not requisite. Sleep is inhibited by pain, stress, anger, and any significant disease or discomforting problem, including temperature excesses and security issues (Drewes et al., 1997; Koulack, Prevost, & DeKoninck, 1985; Okamoto-Mizuno, Mizuno, Michie, Maeda, & Iizuka, 1999).

Changes in electrographic patterns occur during the transition from wake to sleep. With eye closure, alpha waves (8 to 12 Hz) replace beta rhythms (14 Hz and faster) in relaxed wakefulness. At sleep onset, alpha waves are replaced by theta waves (3 to 6 Hz) in association with slow, rolling eye movements, and a decrease in muscle tone is noted. When theta activity predominates in the record, stage I sleep is scored, and sleep onset is said to occur (Rechtschaffen & Kales, 1988). The moment of transition from wake to sleep is probably not a unitary event across all the physiological processes that change at sleep onset (Bonnet & Moore, 1982; Casagrande, DeGennaro, Violani, Braibanti, & Bertini, 1997; Hauri & Olmstead, 1983; Pressman & Fry, 1989; B. Wilhelm, Wilhelm, Lüdtke, Streicher, & Adler, 1998). EEG changes, however, are the easiest to define, because they are unique and the best single objective indicator. Slow-wave sleep or deep sleep is represented by delta EEG activity (0.5 to 3 Hz) (Rechtschaffen & Kales, 1988). These EEG changes represent a major reorganization of cerebral activity at the thalamic level.

Stage 1 sleep is initially perceived as pleasant wakefulness with a subjective anticipation that sleep is near. For this reason, many people fall asleep with the illusion that they are still awake and unaware that they are in the process of losing control of their conscious activity while behind the wheel of a car, in lectures, or in other equally inappropriate situations (Reyner & Horne, 1998).

The progression of normal sleep is predictable in several respects. It is associated with a decrease in movement, eyes closed, and rhythmic breathing that lasts for approximately eight hours. The threshold for responding to sound and other stimuli is elevated. In association with this behavior, a predictable sequence of sleep stages ensues. These changes are defined mainly by EEG patterns. Normal sleep is of two general types, referred to as REM and NREM sleep, as noted earlier. NREM sleep is divided into four stages based on distinctive features in brain wave pattern. In normal sleepers, the initial brief phase or stage 1 sleep is replaced by stages 2, 3, and 4 in a regular sequence. Rapid eye movement sleep replaces NREM sleep after approximately 90 minutes, which is the normal REM latency period (Carskadon & Dement, 1980). Rapid eye movement sleep is associated with vivid mental imagery that we call dreams. The first REM episode is followed by another sequence of NREM stages and then a return to REM sleep again. Rapid eye movement sleep episodes get longer as the night progresses, with an increase in the number of eye movements also occurring in the longer episodes. The intervening NREM sleep, especially in the last half of the night, is mainly limited to stage 2 sleep. Stage 1 is a transient phase of sleep usually occurring at sleep onset, briefly after a body movement, or at the end of a REM sleep episode. Stages 3 and 4 (delta–or slow-wave sleep) are most predominant in the first half of the night only. The normal sleeper changes body position most often in preparation for and after REM sleep episodes. Normal sleep, however, is not associated with leaving the bed or remaining awake and is generally free from disturbance in its sequence of stages. It is most likely to be ended from a REM episode after approximately eight hours of sleep containing from four to five cycles of NREM/REM sleep. Awakening from normal sleep occurs spontaneously and at a predictable time. The person should be refreshed, through sleeping, and desiring to be up and about. The normal sleep quota can be shortened by using an alarm clock or extended by lying in bed or taking naps during the day. A short nap (30 to 60 minutes) about mid-day can be accommodated with no change in the night-time sleep quota. Reducing normal sleep quotas, however, results in an increase in daytime sleepiness based on Multiple Sleep Latency Test (MSLT) scores (Mitler & Miller, 1996). Most people need approximately eight hours of sleep per night, although the amount varies widely (5 to 12 hours) from individual to individual. These lengths of sleep sequences are modified by age, but the pattern established in preadolescence changes only gradually through life. Stages 3 and 4 usually decrease markedly with age, while REM sleep remains fairly constant from ages 6 to 70 (Williams, Karacan, & Hursch, 1974).

NEUROANATOMICAL, NEUROPHYSIOLOGICAL, AND NEUROCHEMICAL SUBSTRATES OF SLEEP

Traditional views regarding sleep have assigned it a primarily passive role, often viewing it as in continuum with coma, and differing from death primarily in its reversibility. However, increasing information regarding the neuroanatomical, neurophysiological, and neurochemical substrates for wakefulness, non-REM, and REM sleep makes it clear that sleep states, as well as states of wakefulness, are dependent on active processes and unique, discrete structures within the central nervous system (Maloney, Mainville, & Jones, 2000; Siegel, 1994; Szymusiak, 1995).

Wakefulness is the result of the effect of ascending excitatory innervation of the forebrain, from brain stem structures, by the ascending reticular activating system. The ascending reticular activating system is composed of two main projection pathways: a dorsal pathway and a ventral pathway. The dorsal pathway projects from the rostral medulla to the intralaminar nuclei of the thalamus and then diffusely to the cerebral cortex via thalamocortical projections. The projections from the rostral medulla include cholinergic, noradrenergic, and dopaminergic neurons. The ventral pathway begins with dopaminergic neurons from the midbrain, which project to the thalamus and subthalamus and, in turn, project to the basal forebrain: the septum, fornix, and anterior commissure region. Lesions along either the dorsal or the ventral pathway, or widespread dysfunction of both cerebral hemispheres, may result in disruption of normal wakefulness (resulting in a state along a continuum from lethargy to stupor to coma). Histaminergic neurons of the tuberoinfundibular nucleus of the posterior hypothalamus play a key role in wakefulness and have important reciprocal interactions with sleep-promoting regions in the anterior hypothalamus. The perifornicial nucleus of the lateral hypothalamus, a region long implicated in the regulation of activity and feeding, may also be responsible for the regulation of the interaction of sleep and wake states through projections of excitatory protein-like neuropeptide hypocretin (orexin) to critical brain regions (Thannickal et al., 2000).

Nonrapid eye movement sleep is generated from multiple locations along the neuraxis as revealed by transection studies in mammals. During NREM sleep, the EEG demonstrates varying degrees of synchronous slowing and the presence of sleep spindles, vertex sharp waves, and K complexes. These findings reflect successive waves of synchronous depolarization and repolarization brought about by reciprocal thalamocortical interaction. The onset of NREM sleep is preceded by various neurochemical and hormonal processes. Many of these processes function and respond to light cues as a part of circadian processes. In the waning hours of light, dopaminergic innervation of the forebrain begins to wane, and the onset of darkness brings increased synthesis of melatonin by the pineal gland. Increased levels of melatonin may facilitate the activation of GABA-ergic neurons in the anterior hypothalamus. The inciting event in the onset of sleep appears to be the release of GABA, the main inhibitory neurotransmitter in the central nervous system, by the anterior hypothalamus. The release of GABA and the withdrawal of both dopaminergic and cholinergic input to the forebrain result in slow-wave sleep. Serotonin levels begin to rise in preparation for sleep onset (Benson, Faull, & Zarcone, 1991). Serotonin may function to modulate sensory input through the thalamus in preparation for sleep onset. Adenosine, which functions both as a neurotransmitter and as a metabolic by-product of energy metabolism, may also play an important role in triggering sleep and in the relationship between fatigue and the need for sleep (Porkka-Heiskanen, Alanko, Kalinchuk, & Stenberg, 2002).

Key EEG features of NREM sleep—such as vertex sharp waves and sleep spindles—appear as a result of complex interactions between both chemically and voltage-gated calcium channels and their projections on the cerebral cortex (McGinty & Szymusiak, 2000). During NREM sleep, cerebral metabolic rates are decreased, and the main role of NREM sleep appears to be rest and reconstitution of neural substrates necessary for conscious wakefulness (Sterman & Bowersox, 1981).

In contrast to NREM sleep, REM sleep is characterized by widespread activation of forebrain structures resulting in high metabolic demands and high levels of energy consumption. REM sleep is a reflection of interaction of discrete localizable structures within the pons and adjacent portions of the mid-brain. The main features of these interactions are well-summarized in the Hobson–McCarley model of REM sleep (Hobson & McCarley, 1977). In this model, neuronal groups in the pons are divided into REM-on and REM-off neurons. REM-off neurons are contained in the anatomically definable nuclear subgroups of the dorsal raphe nucleus and locus coeruleus that secretes serotonin and catecholamines (dopamine and norepinephrine), respectively. High rates of stimulation of either nuclear group results in suppression of the REM state. REM-on cells are contained in the gigantocellular field of the pontine tegmentum and are cholinergic in nature. REM-on cells provide cholinergic projections to the thalamus via the ascending reticular activating system and to the extraocular motor nuclei, as well as providing descending innervation to spinal cord interneurons that inhibit spinal motor neurons (Hobson & McCarley, 1977).

Activation of REM-on neurons results in widespread activation and desynchronization of the cerebral cortex reflected in the desynchronization of EEG and increased cerebral metabolic rate for glucose, intermittent burst of phasic conjugant eye movements, the rapid eye movements for which the stage of sleep derives its name. Descending innervation of glycenergic interneurons that hyperpolarize spinal motor neurons results in flaccid skeletal motor paralysis. The REM-on neurons of the FTG nucleus are, in turn, under executive control of a nucleus reticularis pontis oralis (RPO), a nuclear subgroup of the pedunculi pontine nucleus in the caudal portions of the midbrain. Events that result in activation of the RPO nucleus and triggering of REM phenomena are incompletely understood. It is well-established that under physiological circumstances, REM sleep is only entered after 60 to 120 minutes of NREM sleep. Changes that occur during the later stages of NREM sleep in preparation for the onset of REM may function in a permissive role to allow the release of activity within the RPO nucleus and thereby trigger REM-on cells in the pons. During earlier stages of NREM sleep, high levels of serotonin may serve to suppress release of REM phenomena in much the same way as high levels of dopamine and norepinephrine suppress REM during wakefulness. REM sleep is important for maintenance of cognitive economy and for housekeeping and neural networks that are active during wakefulness (Crick & Mitchison, 1983; Maquet et al., 2000).

Neurochemically, wakefulness is a result of the effects of high levels of acetylcholine (derived from the basal forebrain) in conjunction with norepinephrine, dopamine, and serotonin (derived from the locus coeruleus) and median raphe nucleus transmitted through the thalamus by the ascending reticular activating system to an intact cerebral cortex (Celesia & Jasper, 1966). NREM sleep results from the actions of GABA and adenosine on a metabolically inactive cerebral cortex. REM sleep is the result of high levels of acetylcholine input derived from the FTG region of the pons in the absence of high levels of dopamine and norepinephrine and serotonin. Sleep–wake transition may be a function of reciprocal interactions of the anterior hypothalamus (GABA-ergic, sleep promoting) and the posterior hypothalamus (histaminergic, wakefulness-promoting). These neural mechanisms are subject to modulatory influences of multiple systemic factors including hormones, metabolic by-products, immune and inflammatory substances, and other factors that lie outside the nervous system (Akerstedt et al., 2002; Krnjevic, 1967).

Thus, it is clear that the alternating states of wakefulness, NREM, and REM sleep are actually each unique, active states dependent on specific neural structures, with distinctive neurochemical and neurophysiological properties and characteristics.

PRIMARY SLEEP DISORDERS

The *International Classification of Sleep Disorders* (ICSD; revised) lists 78 different classifications of sleep disorders, with another 11 classifications proposed. The *ICSD* was produced primarily for diagnostic and epidemiological purposes, so that disorders could be indexed. Morbidity and mortality information could also be recorded and retrieved. The more common sleep disorders are discussed in this chapter.

Sleep Apnea

Although insomnia is the most prevalent sleep-related complaint (affecting more than 60 million American adults each year; Ohayon, 2002), sleep apnea is the most common sleep disorder referred for sleep evaluation (Lindberg & Gislason, 2000; Ohayon et al., 1997). Sleep apnea is the temporary absence of breathing (airflow) during sleep for 10 or more seconds in adults. A hypopnea is a reduction in airflow associated with oxygen desaturation or an arousal response. There are three types of sleep apnea: central sleep apnea (characterized by lack of airflow in the absence of ventilatory effort), obstructive sleep apnea (where there is ventilatory effort but no airflow because of upper airway obstruction), and mixed sleep apnea (where there are both central and obstructive components). Mixed sleep apnea is considered a subtype of obstructive sleep apnea (OSA; American Sleep Disorders Association, 1997). OSA is much more common than central sleep apnea. OSA prevalence rate approximates 24% in men and 9% in women who are aged 30 to 60 years (Young et al., 1993).

The number of apnea and hypopnea events per hour of sleep is called the apnea–hypopnea index (AHI) or the respiratory disturbance index (RDI). In adults, the normal RDI is five or fewer events per hour. As the RDI increases, so may the severity of apnea-related symptoms (National Heart, Lung, and Blood Institute Working Group on Sleep Disorders Research—Sleep Apnea, 1995). Sleep apnea may even be life-threatening if not adequately treated (He, Kryger, Zorick, Conway, & Roth, 1988; Partinen & Guilleminault, 1990; Partinen, Jamieson, & Guilleminault, 1988). Therapy may not only improve a patient's quality of life but may also prevent systemic consequences (He et al., 1988; Montserrat, Barbé, & Rodenstein, 2002; Partinen et al., 1988).

When daytime hypersomnolence or insomnia is seen in patients with OSA, patients are diagnosed with OSA syndrome (OSAS), which has a prevalence rate of 2% in women and 4% in men (Young et al., 1993). The risk of developing OSAS increases with age and reaches a maximum between the fifth and seventh decades. Postmenopausal women develop OSAS at a rate similar to that of men of the same age (Guilleminault, Quera-Salva, Partinen, & Jamieson, 1988). Furthermore, sleep complaints are more common and the RDI is significantly higher in Black American compared to White Americans older than 65 years (Ancoli-Israel et al., 1995). Unfortunately, the diagnosis of OSAS is often not made because patients and their physicians are not aware of its symptoms and clinical findings (National Commission on Sleep Disorders Research, 1992).

Consequences of Sleep Apnea

OSAS has numerous consequences (Barbé et al., 1998; Dempsey, 1997; Partinen et al., 1988; Peker, Hedner, Kraiczi, & Loths, 2000; Teran-Santos, Jimenez-Gomez, & Cordero-Guevara, 1999). Patients have disrupted sleep architecture with multiple arousals, resulting in daytime hypersomnolence and evidence of neurobehavioral dysfunction (Kribbs, Getsy, & Dinges, 1992). Irritability, difficulty concentrating, memory impairment, fatigue, and personality changes may occur. Of even greater concern, patients with OSAS have a higher rate of work-related automobile accidents, with one report suggesting a rate of seven times that of the general population (Findley, 1990).

Other systemic consequences of OSAS include hypertension, pulmonary hypertension, cardiac arrhythmias, and increased prevalence of coronary artery disease and stroke. A strong association exists between hypertension and sleep apnea, independent of obesity, age, and sex (Guilleminault, 1987). Furthermore, management of hypertension may be augmented by treating the sleep apnea (Wolk & Somers, 2003). The Sleep Heart Health Study, a large cross-sectional study of more than 6,000 individuals, found that people with OSA had increased multivariable-adjusted relative odds of having self-reported coronary artery disease (Shahar et al., 2001).

Although to date no prospective studies have examined whether therapy of OSAS decreases mortality, He and colleagues reviewed 385 male patients (apnea index > 20 per hour) and found a significant increase in the eight-year cumulative mortality (37% in untreated patients, whereas none of the patients receiving effective therapy died; He et al., 1988).

Pathophysiology of Sleep Apnea

The pathophysiology of OSA is complex because there are many factors influencing upper-airway diameter and muscle tone during sleep. For example, anatomic factors may be the primary factor if the upper airway is small in size; alternatively, neural factors may predominate, contributing to airway narrowing and collapse during sleep.

Signs and Symptoms of Sleep Apnea

Patients with OSA frequently experience loud snoring, which builds to a crescendo, eventually terminating in snorts, gasps, coughing, or witnessed apneic events. This pattern may be repeated hundreds of times nightly. Symptom progression may occur with the use of alcohol or sedatives, in concert with weight gain or while sleeping in the supine body position. The bed partner is also a good source of information. Other associated symptoms include morning headaches, dry mouth, nocturnal diaphoresis, nocturia, confusional arousals, personality changes, cognitive difficulties, decreased libido or impotence, and increased automobile accidents (George & Smiley, 1999).

Risk Factors for Apnea

Risk factors for OSA include obesity, especially if greater than 120% of ideal body weight. Other risk factors include facial skeletal abnormalities, a short thick neck with a circumference of 17 inches or greater in males and 16 inches or greater in females. Physical examination may show nasal obstruction with septal deviation, turbinate hypertrophy, mucosal edema, large tongue with a long, soft palate or uvula, and a small posterior pharynx. Enlarged tonsils may also contribute to upper airway obstruction (Chesson et al., 1997).

Aggravating factors of OSA include alcohol use, especially just before sleep, central nervous system depressant drugs (including benzodiazepines and narcotics), sleep deprivation, allergies, smoking, and sleeping at altitudes greater than 5,000 feet.

Diagnosis and Therapy for Sleep Apnea

The diagnosis of OSA is made with overnight polysomnography evaluating sleep stage, respiratory effort, air flow, arterial oxygen saturation, electrocardiogram, and body position (Chesson et al., 1997). Split-night studies can also be performed, allowing for the diagnosis of OSA during the initial part of the study, followed by a therapeutic trial of nasal continuous positive airway pressure (CPAP) or other treatment modality.

Treatment goals include eliminating sleep fragmentation, apneas, hypopneas, nocturnal oxygen desaturations, and snoring. Therapy should be individualized to the patient. Therapeutic interventions include behavioral therapy and other therapies that alter upper airway tone or anatomy. Behavioral approaches include weight loss with diet or behavioral modification and occasionally bariatric surgery. Avoidance of benzodiazepines and narcotics is important, as is abstinence from alcohol and smoking. Some patients with OSA have apnea only in certain positions—such as in the supine position. For these patients, positional therapy can be quite effective. Medications are not usually effective in OSA therapy. Tricylic antidepressants, including protriptyline, may increase upper airway muscle tone and diminish REM sleep time in cases of mild REM-related OSA syndrome (Clark, Schmidt, Schaal, Boudoulas & Schuller, 1979; Conway, Zorick, Piccone, & Roth, 1982). Oxygen has been used to improve nocturnal oxygen desaturation but does not improve sleep disruption or obstructive sleep apneic events (Gold, Schwartz, Bleecker, & Smith, 1986).

The treatment of choice for OSA is nasal CPAP, which stents the upper airway mechanically (American Sleep Disorders Association Standards of Practice Committee, 1995; Loube et al., 1999). Nasal CPAP machines compress room air and channel it through a nasal interface at a given pressure. The pressure is titrated until obstructive apneas, hypopneas, and snoring are eliminated. Nasal CPAP results in successful treatment in approximately 95% of patients. Patients may complain of mask discomfort, nasal discomfort, air leaks, and skin irritation. Some patients have claustrophobia to the mask and may require behavioral therapy.

Long-term nasal CPAP compliance rates approximates 45% to 70% (Kribbs et al., 1993). Bilevel positive airway pressure is occasionally used and differs from CPAP in that separate pressure settings are used for inspiration and expiration. Using a lower pressure during expiration makes it easier for patients to exhale. This is particularly advantageous for patients with severe pulmonary dysfunction, neuromuscular weakness, or congestive heart failure.

Oral appliances are also used to mechanically stent the upper airway and are most effective in patients with mild OSA. Potential side effects include temporal mandibular joint dysfunction and increased salivation (American Sleep Disorders Association Standards of Practice Committee, 1995).

Surgical techniques have also been developed to alter upper-airway anatomy. Nasal obstruction can be corrected with nasal septoplasty, polypectomy, or turbinate reduction. Soft tissue surgery that alters the posterior airway includes uvulopalatopharyngoplasty (UP3). Postsurgical results of the UP3 procedure show a 55% reduction in the apnea index and a 39% reduction in the RDI (Sher & Goldberg, 2002). Unfortunately, not all patients have a significant therapeutic response, and no predictors have been found for therapeutic response. Adverse effects of surgery include severe pain for at least two weeks, nasal speech, and transient nasal reflux. Other complications may include palatal scarring with retraction (Riley et al., 1997). Finally, region-specific surgeries—including mandibular advancement, linguoplasty and resection, mandibular osteotomy, genioglossus advancement with hyoid myotomy and suspension, and maxillary and mandibular advancement osteotomy—have high success rates in selected patients.

Fortunately, tracheostomy is rarely required with the availability of other treatment modalities. Tracheostomy requires maintenance, and patients may suffer from psychosocial implications of having a tracheostomy.

It is important to follow patients regularly after the initiation of therapy to be sure that symptoms have resolved. Successful treatment may not only improve patients' quality of life but may also decrease morbidity from cardiovascular disease.

Narcolepsy Syndrome

Narcolepsy is a neurological disorder characterized by excessive daytime sleepiness and dysregulation of REM-sleep-related phenomena. Narcolepsy is not a rare disorder but is frequently misdiagnosed and generally undiagnosed. The prevalence of narcolepsy varies widely from a high of 160 per 100,000 in Japan to a low of 0.23 per 100,000 in Israel (2,500-fold difference; Honda, 1979; Hublin, Partinen, Kaprio, Koskenvuo, & Guilleminault, 1994; Lavie & Peled, 1987). The reasons for this wide discrepancy are controversial but may include differences in case definition, case ascertainment, and variability among different racial groups in the genetic predisposition toward narcolepsy. The accepted prevalence rate in the United States varies from 50 to 100 per 100,000 (Silber, Krahn, Olson, & Pankratz, 2002). Age of onset is typically between 15 and 25 years of age, with a second peak occurring between 35 and 45 years of age, primarily in women. Onset in childhood is not uncommon. Delay in diagnosis is typically 14 years from symptom onset (Kryger, Walid, & Manfreda, 2002).

Patients with narcolepsy are severely somnolent and may experience increased somnolence with strong emotions. In addition, they may have sudden brief, irresistible increases in the need to sleep, termed "sleep attacks." However, the sleepiness seen in narcolepsy is not limited to the periods of sleep attacks (Guilleminault, 2000, p. 676).

Of the ancillary features of narcolepsy, cataplexy is the most specific. Cataplexy is characterized by the sudden onset of skeletal motor paralysis typically associated with REM during wakefulness. Clinically, cataplectic attacks are characterized by a sudden loss of postural motor tone without impairment of consciousness. The attacks may be major or minor. In major attacks, patients may completely collapse and fall. With minor attacks, patients may notice head droops, a feeling of weakness in the knees, or a tendency to drop objects they are holding. Cataplexy is often triggered by strong emotion, particularly that associated with laughter or anger. However, the triggers for cataplexy can be idiosyncratic (Stores, 1998).

Hynogogic hallucinations are an additional important ancillary feature of narcolepsy. These are fragmentary dream phenomena extending into drowsy wakefulness as narcoleptics fall asleep or wake up from sleep. They may be confused with visual hallucinations because of depression, schizophrenia, or toxic delirium. Frequently, the content of hypnogogic hallucinations is either sexual or frightening. Among the ancillary features of narcolepsy, hynogogic and hynopopnic hallucinations have been the most strongly associated with negative quality of life (Buzzi & Cirignotta, 2000; Goswami, 1998).

The third ancillary feature of narcolepsy is sleep paralysis. This is the least specific feature for narcolepsy and may occur in an isolated fashion in nonnarcoleptic normal patients. Sleep paralysis is the persistence of REM hypotonia into wakefulness after awakening. Patients with sleep paralysis will describe their minds waking up but their bodies "remaining asleep" and being unable to move. Often, an external stimulus such as a sound or a touch may be required to terminate the sleep paralysis episode. The episodes are not dangerous, but initial episodes can be intensely frightening. Occasionally, sleep paralysis may be so prolonged and so frequent as to present a significant problem.

Recently, REM behavior disorder has been described as an additional feature of narcolepsy. REM behavior disorder is behavioral parasomnia caused by a lack of REM hypotonia during REM sleep. Patients with REM behavior disorder may engage in elaborate parasomnia behaviors that are usually contiguous with dream content. Because of the highly emotionally charged nature of many dreams, this may result in bizarre, agitated behavior that is only comprehensible in the context of the patient's recalled dream content. Patients with REM behavior disorder are at risk for sleep-related injury (Comella, Nardine, Diederich, & Stebbins, 1998; Mahowald, 1999).

Patients with narcolepsy also complain of disrupted nocturnal sleep. Even in narcoleptic patients without symptoms of disrupted nocturnal sleep, sleep architecture is disrupted and is often disorganized.

Pathophysiology of Narcolepsy

The pathophysiology and neurochemistry of narcolepsy has been well-characterized in both humans and in naturally occurring animal models. The principal pathophysiological defect in narcolepsy appears to be an imbalance of cholinergic and aminergic neuronal systems within the central nervous system. In canine narcolepsy models, increased dopamine D2 receptor density has been demonstrated with decreased dopamine release in the amygdala (Bowersox et al., 1987; Nishino et al., 1991). In addition, postmortem autoradiographic studies in human brains also indicate upregulation of D2 receptors (Aldrich, Hollingsworth, & Penney, 1992). An excessive loss of neurons in the ventral amygdala and basal forebrain precedes the onset of signs of narcolepsy in narcoleptic dogs (Siegel et al., 1999). The recent discovery of the mutation responsible for canine narcolepsy has strongly implicated hypothalamic-derived excitatory neuropeptides, hypocretins, in the control of sleep states, motor regulation, and in narcolepsy (Lin et al., 1999). In addition, a mouse knockout mutant has recently been reported in which absence of the gene for the synthesis of the hypocretin precursor peptide results in many features of narcolepsy, including attacks of behavior arrest in which the affected mice enter a REM-like state directly from wakefulness (Chemelli et al., 1999). Hypocretin was absent from the central spinal fluid in seven of nine narcoleptic/cataplexic research participants but present in a narrow range in controls (Nishino, Ripley, Overeem, Lammers, & Mignot, 2000). Postmortem examination of human brains in individuals with narcolepsy–cataplexy has demonstrated highly selective loss of neurons in the lateral hypothalamus, with focal gliosis in the same area (Thannickal et al., 2000). This strongly implies that narcolepsy–cataplexy is a neurodegenerative disorder, with clinical manifestations as a result of the loss of hypocretin–orexin peptide function in brain regions responsible for integration of wakefulness and motor behavior.

The genetics of narcolepsy are complex. Tight linkage to HLA (human leukocyte antigen) loci has been demonstrated (Mignot et al., 2001; Rogers, Meehan, Guilleminault, Grumet, & Mignot, 1997). Initially, strong linkage to HLA DR2 (DR15DQW6DW2) was described. Linkage has more recently been demonstrated to DQB1*060 and DQA1*0102 (John, Wu, & Siegel, 2000; Pelin, Guilleminault, Risch, Grumet, & Mignot, 1998). It is estimated that HLA linkage confers susceptibility to narcolepsy but accounts for no more than 20% of the expression of the condition. Although a strong familial component exists, discordance has been documented in the majority of monozygotic twin pairs. Environmental factors or other genetic loci are felt to be important in the overall pathophysiology and causation of narcolepsy (Mignot et al., 2001). Typically, HLA-linked diseases are autoimmune in nature; however, no immune-related brain injury has been demonstrated in narcolepsy. Narcolepsy may possibly be related to some other alteration of immune function that affects brain function through immune substance modulation of brain activity. It is also possible that narcolepsy is an autoimmune brain disease but that the autoimmune attack is against such a small population of neurons that it cannot yet be demonstrated (Rogers et al., 1997).

Diagnosis and Therapy of Narcolpsy

The diagnosis of narcolepsy is suggested whenever an individual complains of profound daytime somnolence in association with any of the ancillary features of narcolepsy. Frequently, daytime sleepiness will precede the appearance of other ancillary features. Occasionally, diagnostic confusion may arise when ancillary features anticipate the appearance of daytime somnolence or predominate over complaints of sleepiness. This is particularly true of cataplexy, which may be mistaken for epileptic seizures, psychogenic nonepileptic seizures, or syncope. Hypnogogic hallucinations have occasionally been confused with nocturnal hallucinations that are associated with psychotic depression.

The diagnosis of narcolepsy is established by polysomnography and multiple sleep latency tests (MSLT; Mitler & Miller, 1996). A sleep diary should be kept for a week before sleep testing to exclude inadequate sleep as a cause of pathological somnolence. In addition, medication effects must be excluded. In particular, sedative medications that could lead to an overestimate of somnolence or withdrawal from REM-suppressing medications that may lead to REM rebound should be avoided. The positive diagnosis of narcolepsy is made following an overnight polysomnogram that demonstrates disrupted nocturnal sleep but no specific sleep disorder such as OSA sufficient to account for severe daytime sleepiness, followed by an MSLT. In the absence of a clear history of cataplexy, a diagnosis of narcolepsy is made if the MSLT demonstrates a mean sleep latency of fewer than eight minutes with sleep-onset REM in two out of four or five naps. In the presence of a strong history for ancillary features of narcolepsy (i.e., cataplexy), sleep-onset REM during the MSLT is not necessary to establish the diagnosis.

The treatment of narcolepsy is symptom-oriented. The principle symptom of daytime sleepiness is treated with stimulant medications. The mechanism of traditional stimulant medications appears to increase the central nervous system positively for hypocretins. This suggests that modafinil may work through this peptide system. Systemic administration of hypocretin-1 reduces cataplexy and normalizes both sleep and wakefulness in narcoleptic dogs (John et al., 2000).

Cataplexy has been traditionally treated with tricyclic antidepressants, primarily protriptyline, desipramine, or imipramine. More recently, fluoxetine (Prozac) and other SRIs have been demonstrated to have some anticataplectic effect and may be a good initial therapy for cataplexy. Targeted treatment for other features of narcolepsy, including REM behavior disorder and disrupted nocturnal sleep, may involve the judicious use of benzodiazepines such as clonazepam at bedtime.

In addition to the pharmacological management of symptoms in narcolepsy, optimal management includes careful attention to the psychosocial complications of this condition because narcolepsy has profound effects on all aspects of psychosocial function (Guilleminault, 1993). In one study that compared narcolepsy to epilepsy, patients with narcolepsy had more profound effects in the areas of driving, occupational and household accidents, work, recreation, personality, and intrapersonal relationships than a control group of patients with epilepsy. Patient support groups and active advocacy on the part of treating clinicians are essential to optimize patient outcomes in this most difficult of neurological conditions (Broughton, Guberman, & Roberts, 1984; Daniels, King, Smith, & Schneerson, 2001).

Periodic Limb Movement Disorder

Patients with periodic leg movements of sleep (PLMS), also known as nocturnal myoclonus, usually have pronounced jerks in one or both legs. These jerks, or twitches, may be accompanied by flexion at the ankle, knee, and hip. If the jerking is pronounced enough, it will arouse the patient. The leg movements are generally confined to sleep and not seen during wakefulness. The myoclonic jerks usually occur every 20 to 40 seconds and last approximately 1.5 to 4 seconds. Several hundred leg movements may occur during the night, with most occurring during NREM rather than REM sleep.

Complaints of frequent arousals during sleep and aching leg muscles are common. Furthermore, because PLMS may "lighten" sleep and interfere with deep restorative sleep, patients are often chronically fatigued and may exhibit symptoms of depression. Thus, PLMS can be associated with both insomnia and hypersomnia, and an increasing tendency exists to refer to this disorder as periodic movements in sleep (PMS) to distinguish it from myoclonus associated with epilepsy.

Therapy for Periodic Leg Movements of Sleep

The cornerstones for treatment of most cases of PMS are medications that increase dopaminergic activity within the CNS. Initially the drug of choice appeared to be L-dopa (Sinmet, Sinemet CR), but the emergence of treatment-related worsening in symptoms (rebound, augmentation), especially in restless legs syndrome (RLS) associated with PLMS, has dampened initial enthusiasm for this agent (Guilleminault, 1993). Dopa agonists (pramipexole, ropinerole, pergolide) may offer many of the advantages of therapy with L-dopa but with less risk of these complications. Concerns exist regarding drowsiness and sleep attacks with L-dopa agonists, especially pramipexole (Hauser, Gauger, Anderson, & Zesiewicz, 2000). Hypnotic benzodiazepines, especially clonazepam, may be used in selected cases. Antiepileptic drugs, especially gabapentin, carbamazepine, and oxcarbamazepine may also be useful. Analgesics such as tramadol, propoxyphene, codeine, or hydrocodone may be useful in difficult cases. Avoidance of stimulants such as caffeine is helpful. Many medications, principally tricyclic antidepressants, may also aggravate PMS. Iron deficiency, with or without anemia, is also an important cause of PLMS, and assessment of serum ferritin levels is an important component of diagnosis and management of PMS.

Restless Legs Syndrome

Restless legs is a complaint of dysphoria while awake, requiring movement for relief. PLMS frequently coexists with RLS, although the latter may occur independently. Patients often find this syndrome to be so bizarre that they have difficulty describing the problem. Usually, they report feeling as if there is something crawling inside their legs. This sensation appears to occur approximately every hour or two during wakefulness and may be especially troublesome at bedtime. Apparently, moving about or stretching alleviates the symptoms. Thus, to initiate sleep, patients may get out of bed and walk around or take a hot bath before they can go to sleep. As with sleep apnea, the effects of this problem result in a sleep pattern characterized by a marked reduction of delta (or deep) sleep, as well as fragmented sleep and excessive daytime sleepiness.

Current evidence suggests that RLS is genetically transmitted in about one third of the patients (Boghen & Peyronnard, 1976). Moreover, the disorder appears to be transmitted as an autosomal dominant trait (Boghen & Peyronard, 1976; Montagna, Coccagna, & Cirignotta, 1983).

Diagnosis and Therapy of Restless Legs Syndrome

The clinician can establish a relationship between RLS or PLMS and complaints of insomnia by directly inquiring about twitching of the legs while asleep or falling asleep. Input from bed partners is often helpful. To firmly establish a diagnosis of RLS (or PLMS), nocturnal and daytime recordings from the left and right anterior tibialis muscles are necessary. A clue in differentially diagnosing between the two disorders is that patients suffering from RLS exhibit twitching during waking, whereas those suffering from PLMS exhibit twitching exclusively during sleep. Particular emphasis should be placed on learning whether the twitching awakens the patient.

As with PLMS, a variety of pharmacological agents, including anticonvulsants, benzodiazepines, antidepressants, CNS stimulants, opiates, and levodopa have been proposed in the treatment of RLS. In particular, clonazepam (Ohanna, Peled, Rubin, Zomer, & Lavie, 1985; Peled, Rubin, Zomer, & Lavie, 1985), codeine, and propoxyphene have been remarkably effective (Kavey, Hening, & Walters, 1985).

The Parasomnias

The term *parasomnia* refers to a group of acute, episodic, physical phenomena that either occur exclusively during sleep or seem to be exaggerated by sleep (Broughton, 2000, p. 693). The most commonly encountered NREM sleep parasomnias include sleepwalking (somnambulism), sleep terrors, confusional arousal, sleep talking, and bruxism. In most of these disorders, the symptoms usually begin during the first one third of the night. More specifically, partial arousals from delta (or deep) sleep occur, creating the episodes (Kales et al., 1980). Parasomnias are seen more often in relatives of children with these disorders than in relatives of children without the disorder. Finally, although these disorders are not usually associated with psychopathology in children, their occurrence in adults, particularly sleepwalking, sleep terrors, or posttraumatic stress disorder (PTSD) can be associated with psychopathology (Kales, Kales, et al. 1980; Kales et al., 1980).

A parasomnia that has recently received a significant amount of attention is REM sleep behavior disorder (RBD). Also known as loss of REM sleep atonia, this disorder is characterized by a release of skeletal muscle tone during REM sleep. Moreover, a predominance of active behavior is often reported. Typically, the limbs are moved about as if they were being used for the reported dream activity, and the individual may punch or kick as if struggling with an imagined assailant (Doghramji, Connell, & Gaddy, 1987).

Polysomnographic studies have shown the emergence of these behaviors during REM sleep, a stage during which most voluntary muscles normally exhibit atonia. Most patients afflicted with this disorder are middle-aged or elderly, in contrast to most parasomnias, which are more common in children. Although the origin remains unclear, the possibility of a neurological basis is supported by the presence of olivo–ponto–cerebellar degeneration, as well as acute polyradiculitis and delirium tremens in some affected patients (Salva & Guilleminault, 1986). Finally, an animal model of this syndrome has been created by bilateral brain stem lesions in or near the locus coeruleus (Jouvet & Delorme, 1965).

Enuresis during sleep is a common problem that may affect as many as 7,000,000 people. Although not technically classified as a parasomnia, many people refer to it as such because it occurs during sleep. Bed-wetting may occur at any time during the night, but is more common in the first one third of the night, according to Scharf (1986). Children tend to improve about 15% per year until most (95%) outgrow this problem by puberty.

Therapy for the Parasomnias

A combination of behavioral and medical approaches has been successful in speeding the rates of natural resolution of enuresis (Scharf, 1986).

Typically, as with enuresis, children with a parasomnia such as sleep walking and night terrors will tend to grow out of these problems by adolescence. Depending on the type, frequency, and severity, however, pharmacological intervention may be necessary. As in adults, benzodiazepines (especially clonazepam; Klonopin), tricyclics, or anticonvulsants may be helpful. Supportive therapy and family education of the problem are paramount. The disturbing manifestations of REM behavior disorder can be effectively controlled with clonazepam (Schenck, Bundlie, Patterson, & Mahowald, 1987). Furthermore, desipramine has also been reported to benefit selected patients, although it is not well tolerated in the elderly. In addition to pharmacological interventions, it is important to provide the patient with a safe bedroom environment. This can be accomplished by removing furniture with glass and sharp edges, securing doors and windows, and installing padding if necessary (Thorpy & Glovinsky, 1987).

Seizure Activity

Nocturnal seizure activity is relatively rare. Probably fewer than 1% or 2% of patients have shown this problem. The clinician should be alert for disruptions in the polygraphic features of the EEG at night, especially those related to unusual EEG activity resembling spike or spike and wave, which might be associated with an arousal (Broughton, 1984, p. 317). At this point, the patient is usually referred for neurological consultation and recommended treatment. Despite severe hypoxemia and chronic sleep deprivation, abnormal EEG tracings and seizures are rarely seen in sleep apnea patients.

Insomnia

Insomnia is typically defined as the chronic inability to obtain the amount of sleep a person needs for optimal functioning and well-being. This may include difficulty falling asleep, brief awakenings during the night, waking too early, or feeling unrefreshed after a night's sleep. Causes for insomnia can be heterogeneous, including an adjustment sleep disorder that may arise from sudden changes in life (such as moving or bereavement), a psychological disorder (such as depression and anxiety), hypnotic-dependent sleep behavior involving medical disorders (such as thyroid dysfunction), and underlying primary sleep disorders (such as apnea, PLMS, reflux, and pain). Prevalence of insomnia in unselected primary care patients is high, with up to 50% of patients reporting occasional insomnia and 19% reporting chronic insomnia. In those age 65 and older, chronic insomnia is reported by 28%. Insomnia is not a diagnosis, and it is important to recognize that it may occur as a result of other primary sleep conditions such as OSA, periodic limb movements of sleep, or other medical conditions such as gastroesophageal reflux and coronary artery disease (Mellinger et al., 1985; Ohayon et al., 1997).

Although some insomnias are caused by somatic factors, many persistent insomnias seem to be learned habits of poor sleep, with conditioning and internal arousal playing important roles. With conditioned insomnia, the stimuli and rituals surrounding sleep have preceded poor sleep so many times that they themselves can trigger frustration and insomnia. On the other hand, with an internal-arousal insomnia, the patient's desperation to sleep causes increased arousal and an inability to relax, thus leading to insomnia.

Therapy for Insomnia

Treating insomnia requires a careful medical and psychiatric evaluation. Whenever possible, treatment of insomnia should focus on a specific illness or underlying cause. Thus, the treatment plan will vary from person to person and may include psychological support, a change in life patterns, or a change in environment. At other times, it may involve psychotherapy or behavioral therapy. Furthermore, treatment sometimes can be aimed at a specific medical condition that causes pain or discomfort. The following case histories illustrate these points.

Case 1:

> BW was a 68-year-old male with complaints of chronic insomnia. He reported difficulty falling asleep and had frequent nocturnal awakenings. In an attempt to obtain symptomatic relief, he had demonstrated an escalating pattern of sedative hypnotic use. His medical history was positive for severe reflux esophagitis and multiple surgeries to correct a hiatal hernia. The patient had undergone an overnight polysomnogram in 1993 at the age of 60 that revealed frequent PLMS. However, his symptoms persisted despite the treatment of his periodic limb movements. An overnight polysomnogram with dual probe esophageal pH monitoring was performed. This demonstrated a good correlation between the nocturnal awakenings and reflux events. Careful examination of a single reflux event revealed that the abrupt awakening from sleep was triggered by an abrupt drop in esophageal pH at the lower esophageal sphincter followed by a drop in pH at the upper portion of the esophagus consistent with reflux. This occurred despite treatment with standard doses of antireflux agents. Following the diagnosis and more aggressive treatment of acid reflux, the patient's nocturnal awakenings were resolved.

Case 1 illustrates the importance of previously diagnosed medical illness in the differential diagnosis of insomnia. In addition, the high probability of sleep comorbidity is demonstrated.

Case 2:

> A 77-year-old male presented for evaluation of recent onset of difficulty maintaining sleep. He gave a history of nocturia and had occasional vague nocturnal chest discomfort. Past medical history was positive for chronic atrial fibrillation. Overnight polysomnography revealed frequent PLMS associated with microarousals. Following administration of carbidopa/levodopa, PLMS resolved, and fairly frequent central and obstructive apneas became evident. A second overnight polysomnogram was performed for CPAP titration following treatment of PLMS with both short- and long-acting carbidopa/levodopa. This revealed frequent central sleep apneas associated with arousal and runs of ventricular tachycardia with rates of up to 150 beats per minute with ischemic EKG changes. Following the sleep evaluation, a thorough cardiac evaluation resulted in a diagnosis of mild congestive heart failure and ischemic coronary artery disease. Treatment of the congestive heart failure and insertion of a pacemaker have resulted in resolution of the insomnia

Case 2 illustrates the role that cardiovascular conditions may play in causing insomnia. In addition, comorbidity is also demonstrated. In this case, treatment of the PLMS allowed the appearance of central apnea and nocturnal tachycardia with ischemia.

The optimal approach to the complaint of insomnia rests on a careful medical history and physical. Recognizing specific disease processes for which the patient is at high risk can facilitate a successful diagnostic approach. Overnight polysomnography may facilitate the demonstration of specific medical contributors to insomnia and thus permit definitive management of the complaint.

Sleep Disturbances in Fibromyalgia Syndrome

Fibromyalgia syndrome is a chronic disease afflicting 2% of the adult population whose clinical features include diffuse achiness, stiffness, and fatigue, coupled with an examination that demonstrates multiple trigger points in specific areas. (Yunus, Masi, Calabro, Miller, & Feigenbaum, 1981). There is a strong female predominance that represents about 75% of cases (Wolfe & Cathey, 1983). Criteria for the diagnosis of fibromyalgia syndrome include widespread bilateral pain in combination with tenderness of at least 11 of 18 specifically defined tender point sites (Wolfe et al., 1990). Achiness tends to concentrate in the axial locations, such as the lower back, varies in intensity from day to day, and can be exacerbated by other stimuli such as physical exercise, emotional stress, and poor sleep. Fatigue is also a prominent feature and may be a result of a sleep disturbance. Laboratory examination fails to reveal significant abnormalities.

Sleep disturbances are a prominent feature of fibromyalgia syndrome. Subjective complaints include nonrestorative sleep and waking feeling unrefreshed (Moldofsky, Lue, & Smythe, 1983). Patients describe their sleep as being so light that any noise may awaken them, or they may be so restless that they may be conscious of dreaming or thinking during their sleep time. They tend to experience diffuse stiffness, aching, and fatigue even though they have slept eight hours, and on the rare occasion in which they awake feeling rested, they describe little discomfort or fatigue (Moldofsky, Scarisbrick, England, & Smythe, 1975; Schaefer, 1995). Patients also complain of insomnia and early morning awakenings and perceive their sleep as being of poor quality (Drewes et al., 1995). A relationship also seems to exist between poor sleep quality, pain intensity, and attention to pain in patients with fibromyalgia syndrome. Affleck et al. evaluated the sleep of 50 women with fibromyalgia syndrome and found that poor sleepers tended to report significantly more pain than women with high-quality sleep (Affleck, Urrows, Tennen, Higgins, & Abeles, 1996). This study helps to support the hypothesis that nonrestorative sleep may exacerbate pain in fibromyalgia syndrome patients.

Alpha waves (8 to 13 Hz) are associated with relaxed wakefulness (with eyes closed) and intrude on sleep EEG in patients with fibromyalgia syndrome. This alpha EEG anomaly has been implicated in the pathophysiology of fibromyalgia syndrome (McNamara, 1993). Alpha sleep or alpha intrusion may be seen in all stages of NREM sleep, including delta sleep when it is termed alpha-delta (Hauri & Hawkins, 1973). Alpha intrusion is associated with vigilance during sleep and the subjective experience of unrefreshing sleep (Scheuler, Stinshoff, & Kubicki, 1983). Moldofsky et al. altered sleep EEG frequencies using chlorpromazine and L-tryptophan (both of which increase delta sleep) in fibromyalgia syndrome patients and showed that the amount of alpha frequency during sleep correlated with an increase in pain measures (Moldofsky & Lue, 1980). Branco et al. evaluated alpha and delta power in the EEGs of patients with fibromyalgia syndrome and normal controls. Nine of 10 patients with fibromyalgia syndrome exhibited the alpha-delta sleep anomaly that appeared to increase exponentially throughout the night. The alpha-delta anomaly was not observed in any of the control participants. These investigators concluded that alpha intrusion is an intrinsic feature of NREM sleep in patients with fibromyalgia syndrome (Branco, Atalaia, & Paiva, 1994). Taken together, these sleep alterations, sleep EEG findings, and sleep fragmentation may lead to biochemical findings seen in patients with fibromyalgia syndrome.

Therapy of Sleep Disorders in Fibromyalgia

Therapy of fibromyalgia includes behavioral and pharmacological interventions. Behavioral interventions include aerobic exercise, cognitive–behavioral therapies (including relaxation training), reinforcement of healthy behavior patterns, coping skills training, and restructuring of maladaptive behaviors. Other behavioral therapies include biofeedback and hypnotherapy. Pharmacological interventions include tricylic antidepressants such as amitriptyline. Because anxiety and depression amplify pain perception, anxiolytics including alprazolam and selective serotonin reuptake inhibitors have been used. Nonsteroidal antiinflammatory agents such as ibuprofen may also be useful.

All patients should be screened for the presence of primary sleep disorders, including sleep apnea and PLMS, because these disorders are treatable and may improve sleep quality. Sleep hygiene should be discussed with patients to improve their understanding of the need for adequate sleep time and a comfortable and quiet sleep environment. The patient should be instructed on how to have a regular sleep–wake schedule. Lifestyle habits including abstinence from caffeine, alcohol, and physical activity before going to bed should be practiced. Patients should be instructed on relaxation techniques to help with the insomnia associated with fibromyalgia syndrome.

Disorders of the Circadian Rhythm

Sleep disorders of this nature have to do with internal circadian rhythms being properly trained to the 24-hour day; usual bedtime hours must be properly located within the individual's circadian rhythm (Turek, 2000). Many disorders of the sleep–wake schedule arise from mismatches between patients' internal circadian rhythms and society's timetables. As a consequence, patients with these disorders sleep soundly, but not necessarily at the required time.

The primary problem that shift workers encounter is their attempt to restructure their personal circadian clocks by living in a world where all the chemical, physical, and social cues around them are designed for a different orientation (Czeisler & Khalsa, 2000). As a result, mood, well-being, performance, and efficiency are apt to be disrupted by circadian rhythm disarray. Furthermore, factors within the individual such as medical and mental health, as well as those associated with the work place (i.e., the sequence and timing of rotating shifts), contribute to ineffective performance (Turek, 2000). Education seems to be the first step in dealing with the problems of shift work. Particularly important is teaching shift workers what is actually happening to their bodies and how to use sleep hygiene to their advantage (Czeisler & Khalsa, 2000; Turek, 2000). In addition, the application of light at appropriate times can reset the circadian clock. Increasing the light levels under which shift workers work and darkening the sleep quarters have provided significant gains in application, with clear improvement in both the quality of sleep and the productivity during working hours. Furthermore, domestic and social factors play a significant role, and it is essential to protect the shift worker from socially common interruptions of the new daytime sleep patterns and to protect both workers and family members from the social isolation that can develop as a result of shift work (Czeisler & Khalsa, 2000). A certain amount of sleep disturbance is inevitable with shift workers. It is generally much worse for third-shift participants. (Third shift is generally scheduled between 11:00 a.m. to 7:00 a.m. or 12:00 a.m. to 8:00 a.m.) Their feeling of well-being and improved performance can be enhanced by sleeping in a polyphasic manner (i.e., naps) or by taking a short-acting sleeping medication to sleep better during their nonpreferred sleep time.

PEDIATRIC SLEEP DISORDERS

In general, children have few problems with sleep and are recognized as the gold standard for sleep quality. A child is able to fall asleep when tired, sleep soundly despite outside stimuli, and generally awaken refreshed. Unfortunately, not all children sleep soundly throughout the night. It is estimated that approximately one fourth of all children have a sleep disorder that results in difficulties for the child, the parent, or, as is often the case, both. Sleep disorders, such as narcolepsy, circadian rhythm disturbances, and OSA, frequently thought of as adult sleep disorders, may originate in childhood. And, as is true for most disorders that occur in both children and adults, the clinical manifestations can be vastly different. For this reason, the subspeciality of pediatric sleep disorder is beginning to receive the attention it deserves. As always, children are not just little adults.

NORMAL SLEEP IN INFANTS AND CHILDREN

Children's sleep disorders should be described separately, to emphasize that children should not be diagnosed and treated as "little adults."

Birth to 12 Months

Sleep in infancy is considerably different from sleep in later childhood and adulthood. The newborn infant spends more time asleep than awake, sleeping 16 to 17 hours a day. Sleep onset occurs through active sleep (active sleep in infants is similar to REM sleep in adults) and active sleep accounts for more than half of total sleep time (Stern, Parmelee, Akiyama, Schultz, & Wenner, 1969). In the newborn, sleep is randomly distributed throughout the 24-hour day with no consolidation of sleep evident. Over the first six months of life, sleep patterns and circadian rhythms begin to emerge. By three months of age, the infant will have developed a more consistent sleep–wake cycle with diurnal variations noted in sleeping and awakening (Coons & Guilleminault, 1982). By four months of age, most infants will have an early evening period of prolonged wakefulness followed by the longest period of consolidated sleep of the day. By six months of age, total sleep time has decreased from 16 hours per day to approximately 14 hours per day. By one year of age, the child is able to sleep 10 to 11 hours at night and nap for another 2 to 3 hours during the day, for a total sleep time of 12 to 14 hours per day (Sheldon, Spine, & Levy, 1992).

One to Five Years of Age

During the toddler years, a more adult pattern of sleep becomes apparent. Most children between 1 and 3 will take two daytime naps—a short, late-morning nap followed by a longer afternoon nap. By three years of age, most children will take a single, one- to two-hour afternoon nap, and by five years of age most children will have given up naps altogether. The percentage of REM sleep decreases to the adult level of 20% to 25% of sleep by five years of age. Sleep onset through REM sleep, which is common in the infant, is unusual after the age of one, and, if present, is considered pathological. OSA and disorders of initiating and maintaining sleep often present in this age group (Chandler, 1988, p. 110).

Five to 10 Years of Age

Sleep continues to take on a more adult pattern during this time of life. Daytime naps during this period are extremely unusual and, if present, may represent a pathological process. The level of daytime alertness is maximal in the preadolescent, with mean sleep latencies of 15 minutes or longer on the MSLT (Carskadon, Keenan, & Dement, 1987).

Adolescence

At 10 years of age, total sleep time is approximately 9 to 10 hours, and sleep time is consistent from night to night. During the teenage years, adolescents' total sleep needs remain at approximately 9 to 10 hours per night; however, external forces often result in significantly less total sleep time. Adolescents are faced with increasing demands from school, work, and social activities that result in later bedtimes and less total sleep time. This is particularly true on weeknights, when rise time is fixed by the school schedule. On weekends, adolescents will often sleep three to four hours longer to make up the sleep debt that has accumulated through the week. These sleep patterns frequently persist into young adulthood.

SLEEP-RELATED BREATHING DISORDERS

A sleep-related breathing disorder occurs when increased resistance to airflow results in a disturbance in sleep and alterations in daytime performance, and is referred to as OSAS.

Obstructive Sleep Apnea

In 1892, Osler noted that "chronic enlargement of the tonsillar tissues is an affectation of great importance, and it may influence in an extraordinary way the mental and bodily development of children" (pp. 335–339). Guilleminault and colleagues, in 1976, published a series of studies of eight children aged 5 to 14 with OSA. The children in this series had daytime sleepiness, school difficulties, enlarged tonsils, and abnormal sleep studies consistent with the diagnosis of OSA. Although the exact incidence of pediatric OSA is unknown, it is thought to affect 2% to 4% of all children. Children with habitual snoring associated with alterations in daytime function, indicating a sleep-related breathing disorder, constitute 10% to 12% of the population (Ali, Pitson, & Stradling, 1995; Owen, Canter, & Robinson, 1996).

OSA in children varies significantly from that in adults. Adults will have numerous, often prolonged, obstructive events in which frequent desaturations, arousals, and disrupted sleep architecture occurs. In contrast, children frequently have prolonged hypopneas associated with an increase in P_{CO_2} and a decrease in P_{O_2}. Arousals are much less common, and sleep architecture is generally maintained (Marcus, Lutz, Carroll, & Bamford, 1998). The most common complaint of parents regarding their child's sleep is habitual snoring. However, not all children with OSA are noted to snore. Parents may report respiratory pauses, grunting, snorting, or gasping breathing patterns. In an effort to maintain a patent airway, children occasionally will sleep in unusual postures, such as sitting in a chair or lying prone with the neck hyperextended. Children with OSAS are more likely to have nightmares, night terrors, bruxism, sleep walking, and nocturnal enuresis. Correcting the respiratory abnormalities often results in improvement of the parasomnia. While awake, breathing is generally normal, although mouth breathing is not unusual. Unlike adults with OSA, in which excessive daytime somnolence is a consistent finding, daytime sleepiness is present only in approximately 50% of children with OSAS. Declining school performance, hyperactivity, aggressive behavior, and attention deficit disorder have all been associated with OSA in children (Marcus, 1997a). If left untreated, OSAS may result in significant alterations in pulmonary artery pressure and right heart failure. Any child who presents with heart failure, particularly if the failure is on the right side, should be assessed for OSAS.

The pathogenesis of OSA is not completely understood in adults or in children. Many children with snoring will have an increase in upper airway resistance that results in arousals and alterations in sleep but that does not result in a detectable change in airflow at the nose and mouth (Guilleminault, Stoohs, Clerk, Cetel, & Maistros, 1993). Therefore, a gradient of increasing resistance to airflow ranging from no significant resistance (as in the majority of children) to mildly increased resistance (primary snoring or upper-airway resistance) to markedly increased resistance (obstructive apnea) exists. Increases in airflow resistance can occur in a variety of circumstances. The narrowing of the upper airway secondary to adenotonsillar hypertrophy is the primary condition leading to OSAS in childhood. However, the degree of the enlargement of the tonsils and adenoids is not proportional to the degree of OSA. It is possible for children with large tonsils and adenoids to have restful sleep with no daytime symptoms whatsoever. Conversely, children with only mild to moderate adenotonsillar hypertrophy may have quite severe OSA. Therefore, other less well-understood factors also play a role in the development of sleep-related breathing disorders in childhood.

A number of medical syndromes and conditions exist in which narrowing of the upper airway and OSA occur. These include, but are not limited to, neuromuscular disorders, Down's syndrome, Beckwith–Wiedemann syndrome, Crouzon syndrome, Pierre Robin sequence, Treacher Collins syndrome, sickle cell anemia, and Prader–Willi syndrome. In addition, children with cerebral palsy often have poor control of the muscles of the upper airway, both awake and asleep, and are more prone to OSA (Shintani et al., 1998). Physical findings in children with OSA are often nonspecific. Most adults with OSA are obese, whereas children with OSAS can be of normal weight, may have growth failure, or be obese. On HEENT (head, eyes, ears, nose, throat) exam adenoidal facies, mouth breathing, enlarged tonsils, allergic shiners, or evidence of mid-face hypoplasia or retro/micrognathia may be present (American Thoracic Society, 1996).

Diagnosis of obstructive sleep apnea usually requires a nocturnal polysomnographical study. Because of the differences already noted between adult OSA and childhood OSA, it is important that these studies be obtained in a sleep laboratory that is accustomed to dealing with children. Parents should be encouraged to stay with the child during the study; daytime studies should be avoided; and children should not be given sedatives to induce sleep. It is important that either transcutaneous CO_2 or end-tidal CO_2 is monitored throughout the study because children may have prolonged periods of hypoventilation and elevated P_{CO_2}.

The majority of children with OSAS will respond to surgical intervention, with the procedure of choice being an adenotonsillectomy (Wiet, Bower, Seibert, & Griebel, 1997). In a small percentage of patients, adenotonsillectomy will not result in satisfactory results, and they may require continuous positive (CPAP) airway pressure or bilevel positive airway pressure (BiPAP; Marcus, 1997b). The use of a nasal positive pressure device in a child can be quite challenging, but with a high level of commitment by the family and staff successful therapy is possible in most children (Waters, Everett, Bruderer, & Sullivan, 1995). As children grow and changes in airway structure occur rather abruptly, nocturnal polysonmographic (NPSG) studies should be repeated every 6 to 12 months.

Questions remain concerning whether children with OSA are likely to become adults with OSA. OSA does run in families, and children who were once "cured" by adenotonsillectomy may develop OSA later in adolescence or adulthood.

Central Apnea

Central apnea can occur in children with a wide variety of disorders. Congenital central hypoventilation syndrome (CCHS), formerly known as Ondine's curse, is a disorder associated with hypoventilation secondary to an abnormality of central chemoreceptors (Guilleminault & Robinson, 1998). Children with CCHS present within the first few days of life with periods of apnea and cyanosis. Frequently, these children require prolonged (often lifelong) mechanical ventilation. Initially, mechanical ventilation is delivered through a tracheostomy tube, but, as the child grows older, other options for ventilation, such as diaphragmatic pacing and noninvasive mask ventilation, become available.

Riley–Day syndrome (familial dysautonomia) is an autosomal–recessive disorder that is seen most commonly in children of Ashkenazi Jewish descent (Axelrod, Nachitagal, & Dancis, 1974). These children have decreased central chemoreceptor response to hypercapnia and hypoxia and associated central apnea. In addition, they have cyclical vomiting, temperature instability, frequent dehydration, and are noted to cry without tears.

Neuromuscular disorders such as Duchenne's muscular dystrophy and congenital muscular dystrophy are often associated with nocturnal hypoventilation. Alterations in nocturnal respiratory patterns in children with neuromuscular disorders include central hypoventilation and OSAS. Decreases in nocturnal ventilation during sleep occur long before alterations in awake breathing patterns are identifiable (Hukins & Hillman, 2000), and correcting the nocturnal respiratory abnormalities with noninvasive positive pressure ventilation can correct blood gas abnormalities and improve the level of daytime functioning (Hill, 1993).

THE SLEEPLESS CHILD

The causes and treatments of the sleepless child are usually different from those in an adult. Differences also usually exist between infant, toddler, older child, and adolescent.

Childhood Sleeplessness

Sleeplessness in childhood differs dramatically from adult insomnia. In general, the child is able to obtain an adequate amount of sleep (sleep quantity is normal), but the timing of the child's sleep or nocturnal arousals result in sleep deprivation in the parent. Often, the clinician is faced with an alert, energetic, approximately three-year-old child who is brought to clinic by a tired, irritable parent.

The most important aspect of the evaluation of a child who presents with insomnia is to obtain a detailed history. Important aspects of the history include evening routine for the child and the family, the time at which the child is normally placed in bed, where the child is placed in bed, and the rituals associated with bedtime. Sleep latency and factors that appear to interfere with sleep onset, nocturnal sleep patterns including the number of awakenings, length of awakenings, and arise time should be documented. A description of the quality of sleep and the presence of snoring, movements, or unusual behaviors should be noted. Daytime naps (number, timing, and length of naps), difficulties arising, daytime behavior, degree of alertness, and level of daytime sleepiness should also be recorded. Other important aspects of the history include caffeine intake, current medications, developmental milestones, and family history of sleep disorders. A two-week sleep diary documenting sleep onset, nocturnal arousals, wake-up time, and naps is invaluable in the assessment of the child's sleep problems. The differential diagnosis of sleeplessness in childhood includes sleep onset association disorder, limit setting disorder, excessive nocturnal fluid intake, phase disorders, parasomnias, and sleep-related breathing disorders (Owens-Stively et al., 1997).

Sleep Onset Association Disorder

Sleep onset association disorder is a fairly common problem occurring in infants and children younger than five years of age. In this disorder, the child is able to initiate sleep without difficulty. However, the parent is an active participant in the process of "putting" the child to sleep. When the child awakens during the night, which is a normal process, he or she is unable to return to sleep without the help of the parent. Instead of experiencing a brief arousal and then falling back to sleep, the child becomes fully aroused, cries, and wakes the parent. Once present, the parent is able to recreate the "bedtime environment," and the child falls asleep quickly. Because children, like adults, awaken briefly several times a night, this process repeats itself throughout the night. Practices that can result in the development of sleep onset association disorder include placing the child in bed with a bottle or pacifier, rocking or patting the child, or having the child fall asleep in the parent's arms. Treatment for sleep onset disorder is relatively straightforward, requiring stabling new behavioral patterns in which sleep onset occurs under conditions that do not require the parents' presence. The child can be held until sleepy, but once the child appears sleepy, he or she should be placed in bed and allowed to fall asleep alone and without a bottle or pacifier. Once the child learns to make the transition from wakefulness to sleep without the presence of the parent, the problems with nocturnal awakenings will resolve (Blum & Carey, 1996; Edwards & Christophersen, 1994; Ferber, 1985).

Limit-Setting Disorder

Limit-setting disorder is most commonly seen in toddlers and younger school-age children and is characterized by the child being unable or unwilling to go to sleep at bedtime. Once asleep, the child will sleep through the night without difficulty. Battles between the child and parent become a nightly occurrence. The child will leave his or her bedroom with complaints such as hunger, thirst, stomachache, headache, fears of monsters, or the need to go to the bathroom. The more frequent the request or complaint by the child, the more distraught the parent often becomes. Eventually parents commonly either lose their temper or give in to the child's wishes to delay bedtime. This cycle usually repeats itself each night, reinforcing the behavior. The diagnosis is usually made by history alone. It is important that other sleep disorders, such as circadian rhythm disorders, are identified and treated. Limit-setting disorder may also be associated with deeper family conflicts and poor parenting skills, and an evaluation by a psychologist or psychiatrist is often warranted (Ferber, 1985). Keys to treating this disorder include firm, consistent application of bedtime rules. Helping the parents to develop a set of bedtime rules that must be adhered to by both parents and the child can be quite helpful. Positive reinforcement using a reward system has been shown to be effective in some cases (Friman et al., 1999).

Nocturnal Eating (or Drinking) Syndrome

Nocturnal eating syndrome is seen in infants and toddlers who awaken several times a night and feed. Nocturnal hunger becomes a conditioned response that is reinforced by the nightly feeds. Children can take as much as 32 ounces of liquid during the night when fed, causing additional disruption of sleep secondary to the discomfort of large nocturnal meals and numerous wet diapers. Sleep for the child and the parents becomes fragmented and of poor quality. Nocturnal eating or drinking syndrome is treated by gradually reducing the frequency and volume of feeds over a three- to four-week period. Once the volume of each feed is down to 1 to 2 ounces, the bottle can be taken away usually without difficulty (Ferber, 1985). If nocturnal awakenings persist, it is likely that the child has sleep-onset association disorder and should be treated as outlined earlier.

Excessive Daytime Sleepiness

Excessive daytime sleepiness (EDS) in children is often overlooked by parents, teachers, and health care workers. Children with EDS are often labeled as being lazy or as having a behavioral or attention deficit disorder (Guilleminault & Pelayo, 1998; Wise, 1998). Identifying EDS in children can be difficult, as children may not appear somnolent but rather be seen as inattentive or hyperactive. Too often children are referred only once their sleepiness is profound and they are falling asleep in class and are experiencing academic failure. Most often, the etiology of the daytime sleepiness is the result of poor quality or decreased quantity of nocturnal sleep. Therefore, careful evaluation of the child for sleep-related breathing disorder, circadian rhythm disorder, periodic limb movements, or poor sleep hygiene should be carried out. The evaluation begins with a detailed history regarding the child's sleep and sleep patterns, a physical examination, and most important, a two-week sleep diary. If it appears that the child has EDS with what appears to be an adequate night of sleep, then work-up for disorders of excessive somnolence should be initiated. A nocturnal polysomnography study is required to eliminate other correctable sleep disorders such as a sleep-related respiratory problems or periodic limb movements. If the nocturnal polysomnogram (NPSG) study does not document a correctable abnormality, the child should be evaluated by MSLT designed to objectively quantify the degree of daytime sleepiness and determine if there is an abnormality in the control of REM sleep (Carskadon & Dement, 1982; Kotagal &

Goulding, 1996). Treatment should follow those discussed earlier for specific sleep disorders and should be individualized to the patient.

Narcolepsy

As noted earlier, narcolepsy is a disorder characterized by excessive daytime sleepiness, often associated with cataplexy, sleep paralysis, or hypnagogic hallucinations. Narcolepsy is a life-long and, at times, debilitating disorder. Although narcolepsy is most commonly diagnosed in young adults, symptoms often have been present for several years, or even decades, before the diagnosis is made. Most patients with narcolepsy report symptoms dating back to the teenage years. The most common presenting symptom of narcolepsy is excessive daytime sleepiness, although there have been reports of prepubertal children presenting with cataplexy alone (Guilleminault & Pelayo, 1998; Wise, 1998). An NPSG is obtained to ensure the child had an adequate night's sleep and that other sleep disorders are not present. Following the NPSG, an MSLT is carried out to quantify the degree of daytime sleepiness and to determine if an abnormality in REM sleep is present. The diagnosis of narcolepsy in children is made if on the MSLT there is a shortened mean sleep latency (mean sleep onset during five naps of less than seven minutes) with two or more sleep-onset REM naps recorded (Carskadon & Dement, 1982). A urinary drug screen should be obtained at the time of the MSLT to be certain that drug use or abuse is not a contributing factor. Often in younger children with daytime sleepiness, initial evaluation may not be diagnostic of narcolepsy. However, over time these children may develop a more classic picture of narcolepsy with cataplexy and sleep-onset REM on daytime nap studies.

Treatment of narcolepsy in children is similar to that of adults. Narcoleptics also have a higher incidence of other sleep disorders, such as OSA and periodic limb movements, and addressing these issues is an important aspect of therapy. Maintaining good sleep hygiene practices and offering scheduled naps either at school or after school can be quite beneficial. If these strategies alone are not successful, then stimulant therapy will be required using methylphenidate and dextroamphetamine (Basset, Chetrit, Caslander, & Billiard, 1996; Kotagal, 1996; Kotagal & Goulding, 1996).

The genetics of narcolepsy are not well understood at this time. Human leukocyte antigen (HLA) DRB1*0602 is found in 85% to 95% of White individuals, 90% to 95% of Black individuals, and 100% of Japanese individuals with narcolepsy but in less than 30% of the general population. Recent findings implicate abnormalities in the hypocretin (orexin) receptor 2 as being the underlying causative factor in narcolepsy (Chemelli et al., 1999; Mignot, Hayduk, Black, Grumet, & Guilleminault, 1997). These findings may lead to better therapies and possibly eventually a cure for narcolepsy.

Idiopathic Hypersomnia

Idiopathic hypersomnia is characterized by excessive daytime sleepiness without evidence of cataplexy or sleep-onset REM episodes. This disorder is much less common than narcolepsy but, like narcolepsy, frequently develops during the second decade of life. These children generally have normal sleep architecture with a prolonged nocturnal sleep period and daytime sleepiness. On the MSLT, mean sleep latencies of less than five minutes are seen; however, sleep-onset stage REM sleep is not present during daytime naps. Unlike narcoleptics, in which a short nap is often refreshing, these children remain tired and feel nonrefreshed following a daytime nap. Idiopathic hypersomnia is a diagnosis of exclusion and is only made once other disorders have been ruled out. Similar to narcolepsy, the treatment for idiopathic hypersomnia includes improving the quality of nocturnal sleep by improving sleep hygiene and maintaining a structured sleep–wake cycle. If daytime symptoms persist, stimulant therapy is recommended (Bessetti & Alrich, 1997; "Randomized Trial," 2000).

Kleine–Levin Syndrome

Kleine–Levin syndrome occurs most commonly in males about the time of puberty. It is characterized by episodic periods of hypersomnia and binge eating. The episodes of hypersomnia last from a few days to several weeks, with sleep time averaging 18 to 20 hours per day. Behavioral changes associated with the hypersomnia include binge eating, aggressive behavior, and sexual inhibition. In between episodes of hypersomnia, the child returns to a normal state of both mental and physical health. The prognosis is generally good as the episodes of hypersomnia gradually become less severe and less frequent. To date, no therapies have been found to prevent occurrence of the attacks. With episodes of hypersomnia, stimulant therapy can be used, although the success with these agents has been limited.

CIRCADIAN RHYTHM ABNORMALITIES

Once the monophasic sleep–wake cycle in children is in place (i.e., one sleep period in 24 hours), a number of factors can interfere with this process. These circadian factors are described next.

Delayed Sleep Phase Syndrome

Delayed sleep phase syndrome is a disorder that occurs in children of all ages. This disorder is characterized by a shift of the sleep–wake cycle to a much later hour. Once sleep onset occurs, sleep is unremarkable. When these children are allowed to sleep in and awaken on their own, they generally feel well-rested and are able to function normally. This schedule, however, makes it difficult for the parent and child if they have morning commitments such as work or school. Delayed sleep phase syndrome is quite common in the adolescent population when academic pressures, extracurricular school activities, work, and interpersonal relationships take up more and more of the adolescent's time. Bedtime becomes later and school start time is earlier as the child advances through high school. In the United States, by the 10th grade, more than 50% of students are sleeping less than seven hours per night on school nights. Recovery from the week's accumulated sleep debt occurs on weekends, with the adolescent sleeping in until the late morning or early afternoon (Carskadon, Wolfson, Acebo, Tzischinsky, & Seifer, 1998; Wolfson & Carskadon, 1998). Treatment for delayed sleep phase syndrome is best carried out by maintaining a strict sleep–wake schedule. Arise time should be fixed within one hour of the weekday rise time each and every day. Early morning light therapy, either with natural sunlight or with a light box, can be quite helpful in advancing the sleep phase back to a more desired time. One of the major obstacles in the treatment of delayed sleep phase disorder is the removal of secondary gains the child receives by maintaining a delayed sleep phase. Examples of secondary gains could include time alone, extra time for television, telephone, and the Internet. If a child continues to show reluctance to correct his or her behavior, then formal counseling should be recommended.

Irregular Sleep–Wake Cycle

Irregular sleep–wake cycle occurs predominantly in children with developmental delays or neurological deficits. A child with an irregular sleep–wake cycle will sleep for short one- to two-hour intervals dispersed throughout a 24-hour cycle but will usually obtain a normal amount of sleep for his or her age. This type of sleep pattern can be disruptive to the family if the child spends much of the nighttime awake. A two-week sleep diary can be helpful in identifying this disorder. In examining the child's daytime activities, it often is evident that the child spends much of the day in a nonstimulating environment, taking frequent naps. Limited studies examining behavioral treatment in which the child is kept from napping during the day and maintained on a rigid nocturnal sleep schedule have shown promising results. A few small, noncontrolled trials of melatonin in children with irregular sleep schedules and developmental delays have documented limited success (Jan & O'Donnell, 1996; Palm, Blennow, & Wetterberg, 1997). However, at this time the routine use of melatonin in the pediatric population cannot be recommended.

Childhood Parasomnias

Parasomnias are episodic events that occur during sleep or sleep onset and are associated with activation of the central nervous system and frequently with skeletal muscle activity. Parasomnias are classified according to the sleep–wake state during which they most commonly occur (Mahowald & Schenck, 1993).

Disorders of Arousal

Disorders of arousal result when there is incomplete or partial arousal from sleep. These disorders include sleep walking (somnambulance), confusional arousals, and night terrors. Each of these disorders occurs as an arousal out of slow-wave sleep, which generally occurs in the first third of the night. The child appears confused or disoriented, has minimal response to outside stimulation, and will often exhibit automatic behavior. The events are relatively brief, generally lasting less than 10 minutes, and are not recalled by the child the following morning. Disorders of arousal are most commonly seen in childhood and, in fact, are often considered by parents and care takers as being normal in children. Diagnosis of partial arousals is usually made by history alone, although at times it is difficult to distinguish disorders of arousals from nocturnal seizures or REM behavior disorders (Mahowald, 1999). Nocturnal polysomnographic studies with expanded EEG montage can be helpful in differentiating between disorders of arousal and a seizure disorder. Once the diagnosis of a disorder of arousal is made, the family can be reassured as to the benign nature of these disorders. The natural history of this disorder is that the events become less frequent and less severe as the child grows older. If the child experiences somnambulism, then safety measures need to be addressed. As with all sleep disorders, sleep deprivation should be avoided, and good sleep hygiene practices should become second nature. During the episodes, the child should be gently directed back to the bedroom, but efforts to arouse the child should be avoided, because this may exacerbate the episode. In severe cases in which the child is in danger of hurting him- or herself or when episodes recur several times per night, drug therapy may be warranted. A benzodiazepine such as clonazepam is the drug of choice when pharmacological intervention is required (Schenck & Mahowald, 1996).

Sleep–Wake Transition Disorders

These disorders are characterized by motor activity that occurs in the transition from wakefulness to sleep, from sleep to wakefulness, or during sleep stage changes. These disorders occur at some time in almost all children.

The motor activities can be excessive and result in undesirable side effects such as disruption of sleep or injury.

Sleep starts or hypnic myoclonia are brief myoclonic jerks that occur during the transition from wakefulness to sleep. These events are generally benign and do not result in significant interruption in sleep quality. Rarely, however, they can be quite severe and result in sleep-onset insomnia. Sleep starts need to be differentiated from periodic limb movements that can have a larger impact on sleep quality.

Somniloquy (sleep talking) is a common, benign disorder that occurs during sleep–wake or sleep stage transitions. Sleep talking is more common during periods of stress, after sleep deprivation, or in response to an arousal. Other than maintaining good sleep hygiene practices, no specific therapy is recommended or required for sleep talking.

Stereotypical movements that most often occur at sleep onset characterize rhythmic movement disorders. Head banging (*jactatio capitis nocturna*) or body rocking are the most common rhythmic movement disorders seen in children (Klackenberg, 1971). With body rocking, the child will position him- or herself on knees and elbows and rhythmically rock his body back and forth. With head banging, the child violently throws the head from the anterior to posterior position in a repetitive fashion, often banging his or her head on the wall or side of the crib. The rhythmic movement disorders are most commonly seen in the first two to three years of life, occurring in greater than 50% of infants less than one year of age. The episodes decrease with age, but on occasion can persist into adolescence or adulthood. Injury is uncommon, although soft tissue injury to the face or scalp may occur. The disorder does not require treatment except in extreme circumstances. Rhythmic movement disorders are more likely to persist and to result in injury in children with neurological deficits.

Sleep Disorders Associated With Psychiatric Disorders

Psychiatric problems and insomnias can present together and, in fact, often potentiate each other. In general, disturbed sleep serves as a diagnostic sign in patients with depression because it is so common. More specifically, sleep and depression are characterized by long sleep latencies, many awakenings during the night, early morning awakenings, low delta sleep, and shortened REM latencies, as well as a significant amount of REM sleep early in the night (Kupfer, Reynolds, Grochocinski, Ulrich, & McEachran, 1986). Any sleep disturbance associated with depression should initially be addressed by treating the underlying affective disorder. Patients with psychiatric disorders that are characterized by anxiety and agitation, in addition to those exhibiting avoidance behavior, generally have difficulty falling asleep, experience frequent and long awakenings from sleep, have a decreased amount of delta sleep, and demonstrate relatively long REM latencies (Uhde, 2000).

Another condition that can cause sleep disruptions is mitral valve prolapse (MVP) with dysautonomia. More specifically, this condition can create a significant amount of anxiety, including sleep panic attacks and difficulty maintaining sleep. Effective treatment has been demonstrated with a variety of medications, including beta blockers such as atenolol and also clonazepam at bedtime. Modifications in diet, including the reduction of caffeine and refined sugars, plus increasing exercise and fluid replacement have been shown to be important components in the control of the symptoms of MVP. The neurological and psychiatric disorders are presented in much more detail elsewhere (Frederickson, 1988).

CONCLUSION

Sleep disorders can range from temporary and annoying to life-long and life-threatening. Accurate diagnosis and treatment of certain sleep disorders can dramatically alter not only a patient's quality of life but his or her actual physical well-being as well. This adds to the urgency of the need for greater knowledge in this field.

Adequate normal sleep should leave the individual rested, both physically and mentally, and prepared to meet the challenges of the new day. When sleep is insufficient in quality or quantity, a person is often not up to those challenges. In some cases, patients are unaware that a sleep disorder is the root of the problem. The initial complaint may be excessive daytime sleepiness or leg cramps or an inability to remain asleep. Only a thorough medical examination, often followed by evaluation in a sleep clinic, can distinguish the symptom from the problem. Traditionally, sleep disorders have been underreported by patients or have been seen as mere symptoms of other physical conditions. Physicians can now use certain guidelines for determining the possibility of a sleep disorder and deciding when to refer the patient to a sleep specialist.

Patients who complain of excessive daytime sleepiness are often getting insufficient sleep at night. Among the causes for this are sleep apnea, circadian rhythm disruption, use of certain medications or alcohol, narcolepsy or idiopathic hypersomnia, periodic limb movements or restless legs, nocturnal reflux, chronic pain, and parasomnias. Some neurological disorders, cardiovascular diseases, respiratory diseases, or asthma can also interfere with restful sleep and result in excessive daytime sleepiness.

Any patient complaining of chronic insomnia may be losing sleep for one of a number of reasons. Because the need for good-quality sleep is so important, any prolonged loss of restful sleep should be cause for a medical evaluation, followed by sleep analysis as needed. Sleep itself, its basic mechanisms, and sleep disorders are now being studied in greater depth and are being more fully understood than ever before. Armed with the advances in diagnosing and treating a wide range of sleep disorders, clinicians will be able to offer choices and improved quality of life to their patients for whom a "good night" is more than a closing line.

REFERENCES

Affleck, G., Urrows, S., Tennen, H., Higgins, P., & Abeles, M. (1996). Sequential daily relations of sleep, pain intensity, and attention to pain among women with fibromyalgia. *Pain, 68,* 363–368.

Akerstedt, T., Billiard, M., Bonnet, M., Ficca, G., Garma, L., Mariotti, M., et al. (2002). Awakening from sleep. *Sleep Medicine Review, 6*(4), 267–286.

Aldrich, M. S., Hollingsworth, Z., & Penney, J. B. (1992). Dopamine-receptor autoradiography of human narcoleptic brain. *Neurology, 42,* 410–415.

Ali, N. J., Pitson, D., & Stradling, J. R. (1995). Natural history of snoring and related behavior problems between the ages of 4 and 7 years. *Archives of Diseases in Childhood, 71,* 74–76.

American Sleep Disorders Association. (1997). Daniel J. Buysse, Chair ASDA, Sonology Committee. The International Classification of Sleep Disorders, Revised. *Diagnostic and coding manual* (pp. 52–61). Rochester, MN: American Sleep Disorders Association.

American Sleep Disorders Association Standards of Practice Committee. (1995). Practice parameters for the treatment of snoring and obstructive sleep apnea with oral appliances. *Sleep, 18,* 511–513.

American Thoracic Society. (1996). Standards and indications for cardiopulmonary sleep studies in children. *American Journal of Respiratory and Critical Care Medicine, 153,* 866–878.

Ancoli-Israel, S., Klauber, M. R., Stepnowsky, C., Estline, E., Chinn, A., & Fell, R. (1995). Sleep–disordered breathing in African-American elderly. *American Journal of Respiratory and Critical Care Medicine, 152,* 1946–1949.

Axelrod, F. B., Nachitagal, R., & Dancis, J. (1974). Familial dysautonomia: Diagnosis, pathogenesis and management. *Advances in Pediatrics, 21,* 75–96.

Barbé, F., Pericas, J., Muñoz, A., Findley, L., Anto, J.M., & Agusti, A. G. (1998). Automobile accidents in patients with sleep apnea syndrome—An epidemiological and mechanistic study. *American Journal of Respiratory and Critical Care Medicine, 158,* 18–22.

Basset, A., Chetrit, M., Caslander, B., & Billiard, M. (1996). Use of modafinil in the treatment of narcolepsy: A long-term follow-up study. *Neurophysiologie Clinique, 26,* 60–66.

Benson, K. L., Faull, K. F., & Zarcone, V. P. (1991). Evidence for the role of serotonin in the regulation of slow wave sleep in schizophrenia. *Sleep, 14*(2), 133–139.

Bessetti, C., & Alrich, M. S. (1997). Idiopathic hypersomnia. A series of 42 patients. *Brain, 120*, 1423–1435.

Blum, N. J., & Carey, W. B. (1996). Sleep problems among infants and young children. *Pediatrics in Review, 17*, 87–92.

Boghen, D., & Peyronnard, J. M. (1976). Myoclonus in familial restless legs syndrome. *Archives of Neurology, 33*, 368–370.

Bonnet, M. H., & Moore, S. E. (1982). The threshold of sleep: Perception of sleep as a function of time asleep and auditory threshold. *Sleep, 5*, 267–276.

Bowersox, S. S., Kilduff, T. S., Faull, K. F., Zeller-DeAmicus, L., Dement, W. C., & Ciaranello, R. D. (1987). Brain dopamine receptor levels elevated in canine narcolepsy. *Brain Research, 402*, 44–48.

Branco, J., Atalaia, A., & Paiva, T. (1994). Sleep cycles and alpha-delta sleep in fibromyalgia syndrome. *Journal of Rheumatology, 21*, 1113–1117.

Broughton, R. (1984). Epilepsy and sleep: A synopsis and prospectus. In R. Degen & E. Niedermeyer (Eds.), *Epilepsy, sleep, and sleep deprivation* (pp. 317–356). Amsterdam, Netherlands: Elsevier.

Broughton, R. J. (2000). NREM arousal parasomnias. In M. H. Kryger, T. Roth, & W. C. Dement (Eds.), *Principles and practices of sleep medicine* (3rd ed., pp. 693–706). Philadelphia: W.B. Saunders.

Broughton, R. J., Guberman, A., & Roberts, J. (1984). Comparison of the psychosocial effects of epilepsy and narcolepsy/cataplexy: A controlled study. *Epilepsia, 25*, 423–433.

Buzzi, G., & Cirignotta, F. (2000). Isolated sleep paralysis: A web survey. *Sleep Research Online, 3*, 61–66.

Carskadon, M. A, & Dement, W. C. (1980). Distribution of REM sleep on a 90 minute sleep-wake schedule. *Sleep, 2*, 309–317.

Carskadon, M. A., & Dement, W. C. (1982). The Multiple Sleep Latency Test: What does it measure? *Sleep, 5*, S67–S72.

Carskadon, M. A., & Dement, W. C. (1987). Sleepiness in the normal adolescent. In C. Guilleminault (Ed.), *Sleep and its disorders in children* (pp. 53–65). New York: Raven Press.

Carskadon, M. A., Wolfson, A. R., Acebo, C., Tzischinsky, O., & Seifer, R. (1998). Adolescent sleep patterns, circadian timing and sleepiness at a transition to early school days. *Sleep, 21*, 871–881.

Casagrande, M., DeGennaro, L., Violani, C., Braibanti, P., & Bertini, M. (1997). A finger-tapping task and a reaction time task as behavioral measures of the transition from wakefulness to sleep: Which task interferes less with the sleep onset process. *Sleep, 20*, 301–312.

Celesia, G. G., & Jasper, H. H. (1966). Acetylcholine released from cerebral cortex in relation to state of activation. *Neurology, 16*, 1053–1066.

Chandler, S. H. (1988). In M. Anch, C. Browman, & M. Miller (Eds.). *Sleep: A scientific perspective* (p. 110). Englewood Cliffs, NJ: Prentice-Hall.

Chemelli, R. M., Willie, J. T., Sinton, C. M., Elmquist, J. K., & Scammell, T. (1999). Narcolepsy in orexin knockout mice: Molecular genetics of sleep regulation. *Cell, 98,* 437–451.

Chesson, A. L., Jr., Ferber, R. A., Fry, J. M., Grigg-Damberger, M., Hartse, K. M., Hurwitz, T. D., et al. (1997). The indications for polysomnography and related procedures. American Sleep Disorders Association Review. *Sleep, 20,* 423–487.

Clark, R. W., Schmidt, H. S., Schaal, S. F., Boudoulas H., & Schuller, D. E. (1979). Sleep apnea: Treatment with protriptyline. *Neurology, 29,* 1287–1292.

Comella, C. L., Nardine, T. M., Diederich, N. J., & Stebbins, G. T. (1998). Sleep-related violence, injury, and REM sleep behavior disorder in Parkinson's disease. *Neurology, 51,* 526–529.

Conway, W. A., Zorick, F., Piccione, P., & Roth, T. (1982). Protriptyline in the treatment of sleep apnoea. *Thorax, 37,* 49–53.

Coons, S., & Guilleminault, C. (1982). Development of sleep-wake patterns and non-rapid eye movement sleep stages during the first six months of life in normal infants. *Pediatrics, 69,* 793–798.

Crick, F., & Mitchison, G. (1983). The function of dream sleep. *Nature, 304,* 111.

Czeisler, C. A., & Khalsa, S. B. (2000). The human circadian timing system and sleep-wake regulation. *Principles and practices of sleep medicine* (pp. 353–375). Philadelphia: W.B. Saunders.

Daniels, E., King, M. A., Smith, I. E., & Schneerson, J. M. (2001). Health-rated quality of life in narcolepsy. *Journal of Sleep Research, 10,* 75–81.

DeCoursey, P. J. (1960). Daily light sensitivity rhythm in a rodent. *Science, 131,* 33–35.

Dempsey, J. A. (1997). Sleep apnea causes daytime hypertension (editorial). *Journal of Clinical Investigation, 99,* 1–2.

Doghramji, K., Connell, T. A., & Gaddy, J. R. (1987). Loss of REM sleep atonia: Three case reports. *Sleep Research, 16,* 327.

Drewes, A. M., Nielsen, K. D., Taagholt, S. J., Bjerregard, K., Svendsen, L., & Gade, J. (1995). Sleep intensity in fibromyalgia: Focus on the microstructure of the sleep process. *British Journal of Rheumatology, 34,* 629–635.

Drewes, A. M., Nielsen, K. D., Arendt-Nielsen, L., Birket-Smith, L., & Hansen, L. M. (1997). The effect of cutaneous and deep pain on the electroencephalogram during sleep—An experimental study. *Sleep, 20,* 632–640.

Edwards, K. J., & Christophersen, E. R. (1994). Treating common sleep problems in children. *Journal of Developmental and Behavioral Pediatrics, 15,* 207–213.

Ferber, R. (1985). *Solve your child's sleep problems.* New York: Fireside Books.

Findley, L. J. (1990). Automobile driving in sleep apnea. *Progress in Clinical Biology Research, 57,* 337–343.

Frederickson, L. (1988). *Confronting mitral valve prolapse syndrome.* San Marcos, CA: Avant Books.

Friman, P. C., Hoff, K. E., Schnoes, C., Freeman, K. A., Woods, D. W. & Blum, N. (1999). The bedtime pass: An approach to bedtime crying and leaving the room. *Archives of Pediatric and Adolescent Medicine, 153*, 1027–1029.

George, C. F., & Smiley, A. (1999). Sleep apnea and automobile crashes. *Sleep, 22*, 790–795.

Gold, A. R., Schwartz, A. R., Bleecker, E. R., & Smith, P. L. (1986). The effects of chronic nocturnal oxygen administration upon sleep apnea. *American Review of Respiratory Disease, 134*, 925–929.

Goswami, M. (1998). The influence of clinical symptoms on quality of life in patients with narcolepsy. *Neurology, 50*, S31–S36.

Guilleminault, C. (1987). Obstructive sleep apnea: A review. *Psychiatric Clinics of North America, 10*, 607–621.

Guilleminault, C. (1993). Dopaminergic treatment of restless legs and rebound. *Neurology, 43*, 445.

Guilleminault, C. (2000). Narcolepsy. In M. H. Kryger, T. Roth, & W. C. Dement (Eds.), *Principles and practices of sleep medicine* (3rd ed., pp. 676–686). Philadelphia: W.B. Saunders.

Guilleminault, C., Eldridge, F. L., Simmons, F. B., & Dement, W. C. (1976). Sleep apnea in eight children. *Pediatrics, 58*, 23–30.

Guilleminault, C., & Pelayo, R. (1998). Narcolepsy in prepubertal children. *Annals of Neurology, 43*, 135–142.

Guilleminault, C., Quera-Salva, M. A., Partinen, M., & Jamieson, A. (1988). Women and the obstructive sleep apnea syndrome. *Chest, 93*, 1199–1205.

Guilleminault, C., & Robinson, A. (1998). Central sleep apnea. *Otolaryngologic Clinics of North America, 31*, 1049–1065.

Guilleminault, C., Stoohs, R., Clerk, A., Cetel, M., & Maistros, P. (1993). A cause of excessive daytime sleepiness. The upper airway resistance syndrome. *Chest, 104*, 781–787.

Hauri, P., & Hawkins, D. (1973). Alpha-delta sleep. *Electroencephalography and Clinical Neurophysiology, 34*, 233–237.

Hauri, P., & Olmstead, E. (1983). What is the moment of sleep onset for insomniacs? *Sleep, 6*, 10–15.

Hauser, R. A., Gauger, L., Anderson, W. M., & Zesiewicz, T. A. (2000). Pramipexole-induced somnolence and episodes of daytime sleep. *Movement Disorder, 15*, 658–663.

He, J., Kryger, M. H., Zorick, F. J., Conway, W., & Roth, T. (1988). Mortality and apnea index in obstructive sleep apnea. *Chest, 94*, 9–14.

Hill, N. S. (1993). Non-invasive ventilation. Does it work, for whom, and how? *American Review of Respiratory Disease, 147*, 1050–1055.

Hobson, J. A., & McCarley, R. W. (1977). The brain as a dream state generator: An activation-synthesis hypothesis of the dream process. *American Journal of Psychiatry, 134*, 1335–1348.

Honda, Y. (1979). Census of narcolepsy, cataplexy and sleep life among teen-agers in Fujisawa City. *Sleep Research, 8,* 11.

Hublin, C., Partinen, M., Kaprio, J., Koskenvuo, M., & Guilleminault, C. (1994). Epidemiology of narcolepsy. *Sleep, 17,* S7–S12.

Hukins, C. A., & Hillman, D. R. (2000). Daytime predicters of sleep hypoventilation in Duchenne muscular dystrophy. *American Journal of Respiratory and Critical Care Medicine, 161,* 166–170.

International Classification of Sleep Disorders (Rev.). (2000). Chicago: Academy of Sleep Medicine.

Jan, J. E., & O'Donnell, M. E. (1996). Use of melatonin in the treatment of pediatric sleep disorders. *Journal of Pineal Research, 21,* 193–199.

John, J., Wu, M. F., & Siegel, J. M. (2000). Systemic administration of hypocretin-1 reduces cataplexy and normalizes sleep and waking durations in narcoleptic dogs. *Sleep Research Online, 3,* 23–28.

Jouvet, M., & Delorme, J. F. (1965). Locus caeruleus et sommeil paradoxal. *Comptes Rendus des Seances de la Société de Biologie et de ses Filiales, 159,* 895–899.

Kales, A., Soldatos, C. R., Caldwell, A. B., Kales, J. D., Humphrey, F. J. II, Charney, D. S., et al. (1980). Somnabulism. Clinical characteristics and personality patterns. *Archives of General Psychiatry, 37,* 1406–1410.

Kales, J. D., Kales, A., Soldatos, C. R., Caldwell, A. B., Kales, J. D., Humphrey, F. J. II, et al. (1980). Night terrors: Clinical characteristics and personality patterns. *Archives of General Psychiatry, 37,* 1413–1417.

Kavey, N., Hening, W., & Walters, A. (1985). Treatment of restless legs and periodic movements in sleep with opioids [abstract]. *Sleep Research, 14,* 177.

Klackenberg, G. (1971). Rhythmic movements in infancy and early childhood. A prospective longitudinal study of children. Data on psychic health and development up to 8 years of age. *Acta Pediatrica Scandinavica* (Suppl. 224), 74–83.

Kotagal, S. (1996). Narcolepsy in children. *Seminars in Pediatric Neurology, 3,* 36–43.

Kotagal, S., & Goulding, P. M. (1996). The laboratory assessment of daytime sleepiness in childhood. *Journal of Clinical Neurophysiology, 13,* 208–218.

Koulack, D., Prevost, F., & DeKoninck, J. (1985). Sleep, dreaming, and adaptation to a stressful intellectual activity. *Sleep, 8,* 244–253.

Kribbs, N. B., Getsy, J. E., & Dinges, D. F. (1992). Investigation and management of daytime sleepiness in sleep apnea. In N. A. Saunders & C. E. Sullivan (Eds.), *Sleep and breathing* (2nd ed., pp. 575–604). New York: Marcel Dekker.

Kribbs, N. B., Pack, A. I., Kline, L. R., Smith, P. L., Schwartz, A. R., Schubert, N. M., et al. (1993). Objective measurements of patterns of nasal CPAP use by patients with obstructive sleep apnea. *American Review of Respiratory Disease, 147,* 887–895.

Krnjevic, K. (1967). Chemical transmission and cortical arousal. *Anesthesiology, 28,* 100–105.

Kryger, M. H., Walid, R., & Manfreda, J. (2002). Diagnoses received by narcolepsy patients in the year prior to diagnosis by a sleep specialist. *Sleep, 25,* 36–41.

Kupfer, D. J., Reynolds, C. F. III, Grochocinski, V. J., Ulrich, R. F., & McEachran, A. (1986). Aspects of short REM latency in affective states: A revisit. *Psychiatry Research, 17,* 49–59.

Lavie, P., & Peled, R. (1987). Narcolepsy is a rare disease in Israel. *Sleep, 10,* 608–609.

Lin, L., Faraco, J., Li, R., Kadotani, H., Rogers, W., Lin, X., et al. (1999). The sleep disorder canine narcolepsy is caused by a mutation in the *Hypocretin (Orexin) receptor 2* gene. *Cell, 98,* 365–376.

Lindberg, E., & Gislason, T. (2000). Epidemiology of sleep-related obstructive breathing. *Sleep Medicine Reviews, 4*(5), 411–433.

Loube, D. I., Gay, P. C., Strohl, K. P., Pack, A. I., White, D. P., & Collop, N. A. (1999). Indications for positive pressure treatment of adult obstructive sleep apnea patients: A consensus statement. *Chest, 115,* 863–866.

Mahowald, M. W. (1999). REM sleep behavior disorder. In S. Gilman (Ed.), *Neurobase.* San Diego, CA: Arbor.

Mahowald, M. W., & Schenck, C. H. (1993). Parasomnia purgatory: The epileptic/non-epileptic parasomnia interface. In J. A. Rowan & J. Gates (Eds.), *Non-epileptic seizures* (pp. 123–139). Boston: Butterworth-Heinemann.

Maloney, K. J., Mainville, L., & Jones, B. E. (2000). c-Fos expression in GABAergic, serotonergic and other neurons of the pontomedullary reticular formation and raphe after paradoxical sleep deprivation and recovery. *Journal of Neuroscience, 20,* 4669–4679.

Maquet, P., Laureys, S., Peigneux, P., Fuchs, S., Petiau, C., Phillips, et al. (2000). Experience-dependent changes in cerebral activation during human REM sleep. *Nature Neuroscience, 3,* 831–836.

Marcus, C. L. (1997a). Clinical and pathophysiological aspects of obstructive sleep apnea in children. *Pediatric Pulmonology Supplement, 16,* 123–124.

Marcus, C. L. (1997b). Management of obstructive sleep apnea in childhood. *Current Opinion in Pulmonary Medicine, 3,* 464–469.

Marcus, C. L., Lutz, J., Carroll, J. L., & Bamford, O. (1998). Arousal and ventilatory responses during sleep in children with obstructive sleep apnea. *Journal of Applied Physiology, 84,* 1926–1936.

McGinty, D., & Szymusiak, R. (2000). The sleep–wake switch: A neuronal alarm clock. *Nature Medicine, 6,* 510–511.

McNamara, M. E. (1993). Alpha sleep: A mini review and update. *Clinical Electroencephalography, 24,* 192–193.

Mellinger, G. D., Balter, M. B., & Uhlenhuth, E. H. (1985). Insomnia and its treatment. Prevalence and correlates. *Archives of General Psychiatry, 42,* 225–232.

Mignot, E., Hayduk, R., Black, J., Grumet, F. C., & Guilleminault, C. (1997). HLA DQBI*0602 is associated with cataplexy in 509 narcoleptic patients. *Sleep, 20,* 1012–1020.

Mignot, E., Lin, L., Rogers, W., Honda, Y., Qui, X., Lin, X., et al. (2001). Complex HLA-DR and -DQ interactions confer risk of narcolepsy-cataplexy in three ethnic groups. *American Journal of Human Genetics, 68,* 686–699.

Mitler, M. M., & Miller, J. C. (1996). Methods of testing for sleepiness. *Behavioral Medicine, 21,* 171–183.

Moldofsky, H., & Lue, F. A. (1980). The relationship of alpha delta EEG frequencies to pain and mood in "fibrositis" patients with chlorpromazine and L-tryptophan. *Electroencephalography and Clinical Neurophysiology, 50,* 71–80.

Moldofsky, H., Lue, F. A., & Smythe, H. (1983). Alpha EEG sleep and morning symptoms of rheumatoid arthritis. *Journal of Rheumatology, 10,* 373–379.

Moldofsky, H., Scarisbrick, P., England, R., & Smythe, H. (1975). Musculoskeletal symptoms and non-REM sleep disturbance in patients with "fibrositis syndrome" and healthy subjects. *Psychosomatic Medicine, 37,* 341–351.

Montagna, P., Coccagna, G., & Cirignotta, F. (1983). Familial restless legs syndrome: Long-term follow-up. In C. Guilleminault & E. Lugaresi (Eds.), *Sleep/wake disorders: Natural history, epidemiology and long-term evolution* (pp. 231–236). New York: Raven Press.

Montserrat, J. M., Barbé, F., & Rodenstein, D. O. (2002). Should all sleep apnoea patients be treated? *Sleep Medicine Reviews, 6*(1), 7–14.

National Commission on Sleep Disorders Research. (1992). *Wake up America: A national sleep alert—Report of the National Commission on Sleep Disorders Research* (Department of Health and Human Services Publication No. 92). Washington, DC: U.S. Government Printing Office.

National Heart, Lung, and Blood Institute Working Group on Sleep Disorders Research Sleep Apnea—National Institutes of Health. (1995). *Is your patient at risk?* (NIH Publication No. 95-3803). Washington, DC: U.S. Government Printing Office.

Nishino, S., Arrigoni, J., Valtier, D., Miller, J. D., Guilleminault, C., Dement, W. C., et al. (1991). Dopamine D2 mechanisms in canine narcolepsy. *Journal of Neuroscience, 11,* 2666–2671.

Nishino, S., Ripley, B., Overeem, S., Lammers, G. J., & Mignot, E. (2000). Hypocretin (orexin) deficiency in human narcolepsy. *Lancet, 355,* 39–40.

Ohanna, N., Peled, R., Rubin, A. H., Zomer, J., & Lavie, P. (1985). Periodic leg movements in sleep: Effect of clonazepam treatment. *Neurology, 35,* 408–411.

Ohayon, M. M. (2002). Epidemiology of insomnia: What we know and what we still need to learn. *Sleep Medicine Reviews, 6*(2), 97–111.

Ohayon, M. M., Guilleminault, C., Paiva, T., Priest, R. G., Rapoport, D. M., Sagales, T., et al. (1997). An international study of sleep disorders in the general population: Methodological aspects of the use of the Sleep-EVAL system. *Sleep, 20,* 1086–1092.

Okamoto-Mizuno, K., Mizuno, K., Michie, S., Maeda, A., & Iizuka, S. (1999). Effects of humid heat exposure on human sleep stages and body temperature. *Sleep, 22,* 767–773.

Osler W. (1892). Chronic tonsillitis. In *Principles and practices of medicine* (pp. 335–339). New York: Appleton.

Owen, G. O., Canter, R. J., & Robinson, A. (1996). Snoring, apnoea and ENT symptoms in the paediatric community. *Clinical Otolaryngology and Allied Sciences, 21,* 130–134.

Owens-Stively, J., Frank, N., Smith, A., Hagino, O., Spirito, A., Arrigan, M., et al. (1997). Child temperament, parenting, discipline style, and daytime behavior in childhood sleep disorders. *Journal of Developmental and Behavioral Pediatrics, 18*(5), 314–321.

Palm, L., Blennow, G., & Wetterberg, L. (1997). Long-term melatonin treatment in blind children and young adults with circadian sleep-wake disturbances. *Developmental Medicine and Child Neurology, 39,* 319–325.

Partinen, M., & Guilleminault, C. (1990). Daytime sleepiness and vascular morbidity at seven-year follow-up in obstructive sleep apnea patients. *Chest, 97,* 27–32.

Partinen, M., Jamieson, A., & Guilleminault, C. (1988). Long-term outcome for obstructive sleep apnea syndrome patients. *Chest, 94,* 1200–1204.

Peker, Y., Hedner, J., Kraiczi, H., & Loths, S. (2000). Respiratory disturbance index: An independent predictor of mortality in coronary artery disease. *American Journal of Respiratory and Critical Care Medicine, 162,* 81–86.

Peled, R., & Lavie, P. (1987). Double-blind evaluation of clonazepam on periodic leg movements in sleep. *Journal of Neurology, Neurosurgery, and Psychiatry, 50*(12), 1679–1681.

Pelin, Z., Guilleminault, C., Risch, N., Grumet, F. C., & Mignot, E. (1998). HLA-DQB1*0602 homozygosity increases relative risk for narcolepsy but not disease severity in two ethnic groups. US Modafinil in Narcolepsy Multicenter Study Group. *Tissue Antigens, 51,* 96–100.

Porkka-Heiskanen, T., Alanko, L., Kalinchuk, A., & Stenberg, D. (2002). Adenosine and sleep. *Sleep Medicine Reviews, 6,* 321–332.

Pressman, M. R., & Fry, J. M. (1989). Relationship of autonomic nervous system activity to daytime sleepiness and prior sleep. *Sleep, 12,* 239–245.

Ralph, M. R., & Mrosovsky, N. (1992). Behavioral inhibition of circadian responses to light. *Journal of Biolological Rhythms, 7,* 353–359.

Randomized trial of modafinil as a treatment for the excessive daytime somnolence of narcolepsy. (2000). US Modafinil in Narcolepsy Multicenter Study Group. *Neurology, 14,* 1166–1175.

Rechtschaffen, A., & Kales, A. (1988). *A manual of standardized terminology, techniques, and scoring system for sleep stages of human subjects* (NIH Publication No. 204). Washington, DC: U.S. Government Printing Office.

Reyner, L. A., & Horne, J. A. (1998). Evaluation "in-car" countermeasures to sleepiness: Cold air and radio. *Sleep, 21,* 46–50.

Richardson, G. S., Carskadon, M. A., & Orav, E. J., & Dement, W. C. (1982). Circadian variation of sleep tendency in elderly and young adult subjects. *Sleep, 5,* S82–S94.

Riley, R. W., Powell, N. B., Guilleminault, C., Pelayo, R., Troell, R. J., & Li, K. K. (1997). Obstructive sleep apnea surgery: Risk management and complications. *Otolaryngology—Head and Neck Surgery, 117,* 648–652.

Rogers, A. E., Meehan, J., Guilleminault, C., Grumet, F. C., & Mignot, E. (1997). HLA DR15 (DR2) and DQB1*0602 typing studies in 188 narcoleptic patients with cataplexy. *Neurology, 48,* 1550–1556.

Salva, M. A., & Guilleminault, C. (1986). Olivo-ponto-cerebellar degeneration, abnormal sleep, and REM sleep without atonia. *Neurology, 36,* 576–577.

Schaefer, K. M. (1995). Sleep disturbances and fatigue in women with fibromyalgia and chronic fatigue syndrome. *Journal of Obstetric Gynecology and Neonatal Nursing, 24,* 229–233.

Scharf, M. (1986). *Waking up dry: How to end bedwetting forever.* Cincinnati, OH: Writers Digest Books.

Schenck, C. H., Bundlie, S. R., Patterson, A. L. & Mahowald, M. W. (1987). Rapid eye movement sleep behavior disorder: A treatable parasomnia affecting older adults. *Journal of the American Medical Association, 257,* 1786–1789.

Schenck, C. H., & Mahowald, M. W. (1996). Long-term, nightly benzodiazepine treatment for injurious parasomnias and other disorders of disrupted nocturnal sleep in 170 adults. *American Journal of Medicine, 100,* 333–337.

Scheuler, W., Stinshoff, D., & Kubicki, S. (1983). The alpha sleep pattern: Different from other sleep patterns and effects of hypnotics. *Neuropsychobiology, 10,* 183–189.

Shahar, E., Whitney, C. W., Redline, S., Lee, E. P., Newman, A. B., Javier Neito, F., et al. (2001). Sleep-disordered breathing and cardiovascular disease. *American Journal of Respiratory and Critical Care Medicine, 163,* 19–25.

Sheldon, S. H., Spine, J. P., & Levy, H. B. (1992). *Pediatric sleep medicine.* New York: W.B. Saunders.

Sher, A. E., & Goldberg, A. M. (2002). Upper airway surgery for obstructive sleep apnea. *Lung Biology in Health and Disease.* New York: Marcel Dekker.

Shintani, T., Asakura, K., Ishi, K., Yoshida, M., Kataura, A., & Ogasawara, H. (1998). Obstructive sleep apnea in children with cerebral palsy. *Nippon Jibi-inkoka Gakkai Kaiho, 101,* 266–271.

Siegel, J. M. (1994). Brainstem mechanisms generating REM sleep. In M. H. Kryger, T. Roth, & W. C. Dement (Eds). *Principles and practice of sleep medicine* (pp. 125–144). Philadelphia: Saunders.

Siegel, J. M., Nienhuis, R., Gulyani, S., Ouyang, S., Wu, M. F., Mignot, E., et al. (1999). Neuronal degeneration in canine narcolepsy. *Journal of Neuroscience, 19,* 248–257.

Silber, M. H., Krahn, L. E., Olson, E. J., & Pankratz, V. S. (2002). The epidemiology of narcolepsy in Olmsted County, Minnesota: A population-based study. *Sleep*, *25*, 197–202.

Steiger, A. (2002). Sleep and the hypothalamo-pituitary adrenocortical system. *Sleep Medicine Review*, *6*, 125–138.

Sterman, M. B., & Bowersox, S. S. (1981). Sensorimotor electroencephalogram rhythmic activity: A functional gate mechanism. *Sleep*, *4*, 408–422.

Stern, E., Parmelee, A. H., Akiyama, Y., Schultz, M. A., & Wenner, W. H. (1969). Sleep style characteristics in infants. *Pediatrics*, *43*, 65–70.

Stores, G. (1998). Sleep paralysis and hallucinosis. *Behavioural Neurology*, *11*, 109–112.

Szymusiak, R. (1995). Magnocellular nuclei of the basal forebrain: Substrates of sleep and arousal regulation. *Sleep*, *18*, 478–500.

Teran-Santos, J., Jimenez-Gomez, A., & Cordero-Guevara, J. (1999). The association between sleep apnea and the risk of traffic accidents. Cooperative Group Burgos-Santander. *New England Journal of Medicine*, *340*, 847–851.

Thannickal, T. C., Moore, R. Y., Nienhuis, R., Ramanathan, L., Gulyani, S., Aldrich, M., et al. (2000). Reduced number of hypocretin neurons in human narcolepsy. *Neuron*, *27*, 469–474.

Thorpy, M. J., & Glovinsky, P. B. (1987). Parasonmias. *Psychiatric Clinics of North America*, *10*, 623–639.

Turek, F. W. (2000). Introduction to chronobiology: Sleep and the circadian clock. In *Principles and practices of sleep medicine* (pp. 319–320). New York: W.B. Saunders.

Uhde, T. W. (2000). Anxiety disorders. In *Principles and practice of sleep medicine* (3rd ed., pp. 1123–1139). New York: W.B. Saunders.

Waters, K. A., Everett, F. M., Bruderer, J. W., & Sullivan, C. E. (1995). Obstructive sleep apnea: The use of nasal CPAP in 80 children. *American Journal of Respiratory and Critical Care Medicine*, *152*, 780–785.

Wiet, G. J., Bower, C., Seibert, R., & Griebel, M. (1997). Surgical correction of obstructive sleep apnea in the complicated pediatric patient documented by polysommography. *International Journal of Pediatric Otorhinolaryngology*, *41*, 133–143.

Wilhelm, B., Wilhelm, H., Lüdtke, H., Streicher, P., & Adler, M. (1998). Pupillographic assessment of sleepiness in sleep-deprived healthy subjects. *Sleep*, *21*, 258–265.

Williams, R. L., Karacan, I., & Hursch, C. J. (1974). *Electroencephalography (EEG) of human sleep: Clinical applications*. New York: John Wiley.

Wise, M. S. (1998). Childhood narcolepsy. *Neurology*, *50*, S37–S42.

Wolfe, F., & Cathey, M. A. (1984). Prevalence of primary and secondary fibrositis. *Journal of Rheumatology*, *10*, 965–968.

Wolfe, F., Smythe, H. A., Yunus, M. B., Bennett, R. M., Bombardier, C., Goldenberg, D. L., et al. (1990). The American College of Rheumatology 1990 Criteria for the Classification of Fibromyalgia. Report of the Multi-Center Criteria Committee. *Arthritis and Rheumatism, 33,* 160–172.

Wolfson, A. R., & Carskadon, M. A. (1998). Sleep schedules and daytime functioning in adolescents. *Child Development, 69,* 875–887.

Wolk, R., & Somers, V. K. (2003). Cardiovascular consequences of obstructive sleep apnea. *Clinical Chest Medicine, 24,* 195–205.

Young, T., Palta, M., Dempsey, J., Skatrud, J., Weber, S., & Badr, S. (1993). The occurrence of sleep-disordered breathing among middle-aged adults. *New England Journal of Medicine, 328,* 1230–1235.

Yunus, M., Masi, A. T., Calabro, J. J., Miller, K. A., & Feigenbaum, S. L. (1981). Primary fibromyalgia (fibrositis): Clinical study of 50 patients with matched normal controls. *Seminars in Arthritis and Rheumatism, 11,* 151–172.

II

MEDIATORS OF RISK

7

STRESS, COPING, AND SOCIAL SUPPORT IN HEALTH AND BEHAVIOR

PAMELA DAVIS MARTIN AND PHILLIP J. BRANTLEY

In this chapter we review the vast areas of stress, coping, and social support and include a discussion of the theoretical foundations and developmental history of these concepts. We also provide a discussion of the individual factors associated with the experience of stress as well as use of coping strategies or social support resources. Finally, we discuss the association between stress, coping, social support, and health outcomes.

DEFINITION OF STRESS

The diversity of opinion surrounding the definition of *stress* has created disagreements among stress researchers, preventing stress from becoming a universally accepted construct. In particular, it has been argued that the concept of stress is too broad and ambiguous to adequately define. Despite such criticisms, investigators have attempted to define the nature of stress, primarily described in terms of stimulus, response, or interactional theories.

Stimulus Theories

Cannon's (1939) seminal work on homeostasis was the first to identify stress as a stimulus, comprising any event that prepares the organism for the "fight or flight" response. This approach highlights the objective nature of stress and applies the term *stressor* to the specific internal, external, psychological, and biological events that produce the stress response. Elliott and Eisdorfer (1982) emphasized the stimulus properties of stressors (e.g., frequency, intensity, and duration) in their classification system consisting of (a) acute, time-limited (e.g., surgery); (b) stressor sequences (e.g., divorce); (c) chronic, intermittent (e.g., sexual difficulty); and (d) chronic (e.g., job stress). Although stimulus definitions of the stress response may provide a useful taxonomy, the prevalent view among stress researchers emphasizes the importance of individual differences in stress appraisal.

Response Theories

In contrast to the stimulus approach, other theorists have defined stress as the response an organism makes to changes in its environment. Selye (1974) defined stress as the "nonspecific response of the body to any demand" (p. 27). In a similar vein, Everly (1989) described stress as a "physiological response that serves as a mechanism of mediation, linking any given stressor to its target-organ effect or arousal" (p. 7).

The primary physiological representation of the stress response involves the sympatho–adrenomedullary (SAM) and hypothalamo–pituitary–adrenocortical (HPA) systems. When an organism prepares to cope with a stressful stimulus, the flight or fight response is active through electrochemical changes in the brainstem, which mobilize the SAM axis to release catecholamines (e.g., epinephrine and norepinephrine) via the adrenal medulla (Jemmott & Locke, 1984). Selye (1982) described this increased metabolic activity to mobilize stress resources as a *catatoxic* response, whereas if no coping resources are available, a *syntoxic* response would occur. During the syntoxic response, passive tolerance behaviors (e.g., hypervigilance and withdrawal) activate the HPA pathways, resulting in cortisol and corticosteroid release.

These neuroendocrine changes correspond with the biobehavioral stress response (alarm, resistance, exhaustion) described by Selye (1936) as the general adaptation syndrome (GAS). During the alarm phase, the sympathetic nervous and HPA systems are stimulated. Hyperarousal of these systems occur during the resistance phase, as the body's homeostatic mechanisms attempt to compensate for the physiological effects of the stressor.

Finally, if the organism is unsuccessful in coping with the stressor, exhaustion occurs. Both psychological and physiological symptoms of exhaustion may be manifested, with illness and eventual death occurring with sustained application of the stressor (Selye, 1982).

Although the hormones of the SAM and HPA have received the most attention, additional hormones have also been established as producing physiological reactions to stress. Stress responses have been associated with elevated levels of growth hormone and prolactin in the pituitary gland, as well as with increased secretions of the natural opiates beta-endorphin and enkephalin (Baum & Grunberg, 1995). All of these hormones have been implicated as important components of immune functioning.

Interactional Theories

Both the stimulus and response theories have been criticized for their lack of attention to individual differences. Stemming from these critiques, interactional descriptions of the stress response emerged, focusing on the relationship between individual and environmental variables in mediating the stress response.

In the transactional model, stress is the "particular relationship between the person and environment that is appraised by the person as taxing or exceeding his or her resources and endangering his or her well-being" (Lazarus & Folkman, 1984, p. 19). This view of stress emphasizes the cognitive variables that mediate a person's response to his or her environment. The perception of the event or situation, and the individual's efforts to manage the stress situation, are defined in terms of two interacting processes: appraisal and coping (Lazarus & Folkman, 1984). Appraisal refers to the cognitive process that connotes meaning to the stressful situation for the individual. Specifically, situations are appraised in terms of their expected or potential outcomes (i.e. positive, negative, or neutral). Thus, appraisals can be influenced by a variety of factors, including learning history, personality, and the availability of internal or external resources. Coping, which is discussed in more detail later, usually refers to a variety of methods implemented by the individual in an effort to manage stressful situations. An individual's ability to use coping strategies can alter biological functioning and thus affect health outcomes via a variety of mechanisms, such as influencing neuroendocrine stress responses, contributing to changes in health or risk behaviors or altering the individual's cognitive or behavioral response to illness (Holroyd & Lazarus, 1982). The transactional model thus suggests that an individual's response to stress is an interaction between their appraisal of the situation and coping resources.

MEASUREMENT OF STRESS

With no uniform definition of stress, psychometricians have encountered difficulty reaching a consensus about appropriate stress measurements. The primary types of stress that have been examined in the literature include life events (e.g., major stressors, divorce), chronic stress (e.g., long-term stressors, poverty) and daily hassles (e.g., minor life events such as being late for work). Laboratory-simulated stressors and physiological measures of stress responding have been used as objective measures of stress. However, the most commonly used measures of stress continue to be subjective, self-report questionnaires.

Traditionally, researchers have used laboratory methods such as noxious physical stimuli (e.g., electric shock) or frustrating psychological tasks (e.g., mental arithmetic) to assess the physiological effects (e.g., heart rate) of stress. However, these procedures have often been plagued with methodological and ethical concerns and criticized for their limited generalizability because they can only simulate naturally occurring stress (Brantley & Jones, 1993). Blood and urinary assays are often used to assess corticosteroid and catecholamine levels, which may improve the validity of stress assessment when used in conjunction with other stress measures (Brantley, Dietz, McKnight, Jones, & Tulley, 1988). However, the use of biochemical measures alone is not recommended, because they are susceptible to several confounding events outside the realm of stress (e.g., caffeine ingestion, exercise).

Life-events research stemmed from the stimulus view of stress. Holmes and Rahe (1967) set the standard for life-events scales with the Social Readjustment Rating Scale (SRRS). The SRRS, a 43-item self-report questionnaire, assesses major life events and estimates the amount of readjustment in life change units (LCUs).In addition, development of the Life Experiences Survey (LES; Sarason, Johnson, & Siegel, 1978) contributed to the growth of stress assessment. This 57-item scale yields positive, negative, and total stress scores by assessing an individual's perception of an items' desirability and degree of impact on a 7-point Likert-type scale.

Opinions regarding the LCU measures have been mixed. In a review of LCU measures, face validity, simplicity, generalizability, and predictive validity with regard to psychiatric or physical illnesses were noted as positive characteristics of these instruments (Horowitz, Schaefer, Hiroto, Wilner, & Levin, 1977). Nevertheless, critics have voiced concern over the psychometric properties of LCU scales and the possibility of compromised recall because of the temporal remoteness between event occurrence and scale administration. As expected, the subjective nature of life-event instruments has fueled disputes regarding stress assessment. Brown (1989) cited the possibility of response biases creating, exaggerating, or attenuating associations between stress and relevant outcome variables. The temporal remoteness of assessments has also been examined, and studies suggest that the low to moderate reliability of life-event scales is compromised when research participants are asked to recall events for longer than one year (Dohrenwend, Dohrenwend, Dodson, & Shrout, 1984). Life-events measures have also been criticized for not assessing an individual's perception of the degree of stress experienced or measuring positive life events. However, the development of the LES (Sarason et al., 1978) and the Uplifts Scale (Kanner, Coyne, Schaefer, & Lazarus, 1981) addressed both of these concerns. Despite these earlier criticisms, life-events measures continue to be among the most widely used psychological tools for stress measurement and are still judged to be useful for practitioners and researchers (Scully, Tosi, & Banning, 2000).

Important distinctions about the nature of stressful life events have emerged from life-events research. Traditionally, stress research has focused on major life events. However, evidence suggests that minor stressors may influence health outcomes more than major stressors (Brantley & Jones, 1989). This observation emphasizes the need to distinguish between major life events and minor life events, termed *daily stressors* or *hassles*.

Kanner et al. (1981) first directed attention to minor stressors with the Hassles Scale. This 117-item questionnaire measures severity and frequency of minor stressors over the previous month on a 3-point Likert-type scale. Similarly, Kanner and colleagues (1981) developed the Uplifts Scale, an index of desirable minor life events, as a measure of the often-ignored concept of positive stress. Extending the focus on minor stressors, Brantley, Waggoner, Jones, and Rappaport (1987) developed the Daily Stress Inventory (DSI). Minimizing the problem of temporal remoteness, this 58-item questionnaire measures the frequency and impact of minor stressors likely to occur on a daily basis. The Weekly Stress Inventory (WSI; Brantley, Jones, Boudreaux, & Catz, 1997) was designed to conduct assessments over longer intervals (i.e., several weeks or months). The WSI has demonstrated good concurrent validity with the DSI. In a recent longitudinal study, psychological assessments across a six-month period provided a stable indicator of minor stress in a sample of adults recruited from primary care medical clinics (Scarinci, Ames, & Brantley, 1999). Dissatisfaction with event-specific measures led to the construction of the Perceived Stress Scale (PSS; Cohen, Kamarck, & Mermelstein, 1983), a measure of appraisal of global life stress. Although the developers have reported adequate reliability and validity and better predictive power than life-events scores, some researchers have indicated that the PSS contains confounds with outcome measures that are greater than those associated with minor life-event scales (Lazarus, DeLongis, Folkman, & Gruen, 1985).

INDIVIDUAL DIFFERENCES IN THE STRESS RESPONSE

A number of demographic variables have been studied in regard to life events; however, extant research has not identified direct and consistent relationships between these variables and stress outcomes. Lower socioeconomic status has been associated with higher rates of stressful events (Scarinci et al., 1999) as well as cardiovascular disease (Steptoe et al., 2002). Various explanations for this finding have been posited, including the interceding effects of discrimination, and differences in coping mechanisms or social support resources (see Gallo & Matthews, 2003, for review). However, additional research is needed to evaluate the proposed explanatory models. Similarly, investigations of gender differences in stress outcomes have focused primarily on sex role and personality distinctions but have not typically delineated these variables apart from the lower levels of income, educational, and occupational status also experienced by women (see Gore & Colton, 1991, for a review). Finally, with regard to age differences, although researchers have noted that elderly individuals may experience more stressors because of increased incidence of chronic illness and major life events, it is still unclear how these stressors may differentially affect outcomes in this population (see Strack & Feifel, 1996, for a review).

STRESS AND HEALTH

Researchers and clinicians have used a variety of measures to assess the impact of stress on psychiatric and medical populations. Research has indicated that the effect of minor stressors on the progression of physical and psychological illness may be greater than the influence of major stressors (Brantley & Jones, 1993). However, critics maintain that minor life-events scales contain measures of physical symptoms and psychological distress, thereby confounding studies that investigate the relationship between minor life events and health.

Psychological factors, including life stress and coping, are believed to affect health primarily through direct physiological mechanisms or the alteration of health-related behaviors. In a review of the literature, Brantley and Garrett (1993) summarized the proposed models of stress and illness, which included (a) changes in physiological functioning, (b) increased high risk behavior, (c) decreased resistance to disease, (d) neurological hypersensitivity, or (e) inadequate coping. Investigations examining the specific relationship between stress and illness have consistently reported correlations between psychological distress and symptom presentation of both acute and chronic illness, with the most consistent evidence found for infectious diseases, cancer, cardiovascular disease, and chronic conditions such as diabetes, asthma, and gastrointestinal disorders.

Associations between stress and changes in immune functioning have been consistently found in the literature. Glaser, Kiecolt-Glaser, and colleagues have found high periods of psychological stress to be associated with greater incidences of infectious diseases (Glaser et al., 1987); the development, duration, and frequency of herpesvirus episodes (Kiecolt-Glaser & Glaser, 1988); higher antibody titers to latent herpesviruses (Glaser, Kiecolt-Glaser, Speicher, & Holliday, 1985); and significantly lower levels of natural killer (NK) cell activity (Kiecolt-Glaser et al., 1984). In addition, Cobb and Steptoe (1996) found that those who reported a higher rate of stressful life events were at greater risk for upper-respiratory infections.

Several sources have cited evidence supporting a link between stress and cancer. In particular, the stress of being diagnosed with cancer has been associated with the subsequent development of depression and linked to reductions in natural killer cell and other immune system activities (Linn, Linn, & Jensen, 1982; Shekelle et al., 1981). In addition, major life events have also been directly associated with increased incidence of certain cancers and a depression of T-cell and natural killer cell activity by the immune system (Bartrop, Luckhurst, Lazarus, Kiloh, & Penny, 1997; Pettingale & Hussein, 1994).

The evidence linking stress to cardiovascular disease has been indirect. The most consistent associations have been found among stress, personality, and behavioral variables, such as hostility and Type A behavior pattern, and intermediary factors, such as severity of underlying coronary disease (Kop, 1997). Psychological stress has been identified as a potential trigger for acute coronary events (Kop, 1997) and an exacerbating factor in various coronary symptoms, (Rozanski et al., 1988). A recent longitudinal study found that minor rather than major life events were more important in the development of cardiovascular disesase risk, especially when associated with Type A personality features (Twisk, Snel, Kemper, & van Mechelen, 1999). In summary, although the role of stress in the pathogenesis of cardiovascular disease may be indirect, consistent evidence has linked certain psychosocial factors affected by stress and the manifestation of cardiovascular disease risk (see Kop, 1997, for a review).

Chronic illness has been cited as the most prevalent of all the major life stressors. Diabetes mellitus is a chronic endocrine disease constituting the fourth leading cause of death due because of disease in the United States (Mokdad et al., 2003). Stress has been shown to alter metabolic activity in diabetics (Goetsch, 1989) and trigger release of growth hormone, causing insulin resistance and pancreatic hormone stimulation (Surwit, Ross, & Feinglos, 1991).

Investigation of the relation between weight and stress is an emerging area of research. Several studies have noted the psychosocial influences of stressful life events on weight gain. In particular, increased levels of chronic stress, such as caring for an Alzheimer patient or being a firefighter, are associated with weight gain (Gerace & George, 1996; Vitaliano, Russo, Scanlan, & Greeno, 1996). Abnormal neuroendocrine stress responses have been proposed and stressful life events have been inversely correlated with serum prolactin and urinary cortisol levels in women (Ferreira et al., 1995). Obese individuals have demonstrated a stress-induced pattern of abnormal glucose and insulin responses (Seematter et al., 2000) and increased vascular reactions such as elevated diastolic pressure and peripheral resistance (Davis, Twamley, Hamilton, & Swan, 1999). These findings in particular are of interest given the epidemic rise in obesity.

Although there is substantial support for the physiological effects of stress, research on the effects of stress on health behavior is limited. It has been suggested that stress hinders the performance of global health behaviors (Wiebe & McCallum, 1986), suppresses the performance of positive health behaviors such as exercise and proper nutrition (Lindquist, Beilin, & Knuiman, 1997; Stetson, Rahn, Dubbert, Wilner, & Mercury, 1997), and increases the frequency of maladaptive health behaviors such as excessive eating, smoking, and alcohol consumption. Although there is limited information regarding the mechanisms leading to poor health behaviors, it has been proposed that stress affects a variety of factors, including social functioning and mental health, which may then influence the willingness or capabilities of the individual to engage in health-promoting behaviors (Hellerstedt & Jeffery, 1997). During times of stress, performance of health behaviors may become a source of stress (Stetson et al., 1997) or it is possible that stress may lead to a priority shift regarding health behavior and other matters may take precedence (Griffin, Friend, Eitel, & Lobel, 1993).

STRESS MANAGEMENT

Stress management programs are designed to decrease the negative impact of stress on the individual by improving knowledge, skills, and behaviors. When developing a stress management program, clinicians must be aware of client characteristics such as personality variables, lifestyle, motivation level, coping skills, and level of distress to achieve an optimal therapeutic effect (Brantley & Thomason, 1995). Although a myriad of psychotherapeutic approaches have been offered across stress management programs, they all focus on the common goals of decreasing the negative impact of stress and improving coping skills. For example, cognitive restructuring techniques are used as a means to alter an individual's perception of stressors or his or her ability to cope with stress, and relaxation techniques are used as a means of reducing physiological arousal.

Physiological arousal is a common symptom of stress response and is associated with a variety of somatic and psychiatric disorders. Relaxation techniques are a well-established treatment for hyperarousal and muscular tension. Progressive relaxation training (PRT), teaching patients to tense and relax various isolated muscles, has been a widely accepted treatment strategy with broad clinical utility. Biofeedback training adds an element of medical technology to relaxation principles. Through techniques such as electromyography (EMG) training, individuals presumably learn to decrease muscle tension and autonomic reactivity. Meditative procedures such as yoga and transcendental meditation represent the oldest relaxation techniques. Use of meditation procedures in clinical settings is limited, but research has suggested that there may be beneficial effects (Carlson, Speca, Patel, & Goodey, 2003).

Stress can lead to maladaptive behavioral patterns, and many stress management programs focus on developing and maintaining appropriate health behaviors to deter the negative effects of stress. Stress-related disorders have been associated with sedentary behavior (Brownell, 1982), and physical activity has been found to have stress-buffering effects (Carmack, Boudreaux, Amaral-Melendez, Brantley, & de Moor, 1999). In addition, because excessive eating, tobacco use, and alcohol abuse are often a maladaptive attempt to cope with stressful situations, stress management skills are usually incorporated into health behavior management programs (e.g., smoking cessation, cardiac rehabilitation; see chap. 3, this volume).

General behavioral strategies aimed at the effect management of activities of daily living are also commonly used in stress management programs. Time management skills, focusing on establishing priorities, maintaining leisure and enjoyable activities, and scheduling time effectively, are especially useful strategies for managing stress overload. In addition, teaching assertive behaviors, effective communication skills, and conflict management may minimize stress by curtailing interpersonal discord or providing individuals with a sense of control.

Finally, stress management programs frequently address maladaptive cognitions related to stress. Beck (1984) proposed that cognitive structuring and appraisal of stressful situations prepare organisms for action and result in behavioral inclinations and affective expression. During times of intense stress, distorted cognitions can lead to maladaptive behaviors and emotions. Cognitive applications in stress management programs attempt to disrupt the aberrant cycle of cognition, behavior, and affect.

Overall, stress management techniques have been shown to be effective in a variety of chronic illnesses. Findings with HIV, diabetic, cancer, and asthma patients have demonstrated that stress management programs can decrease psychological distress, improve coping skills, and improve some physiological measures of illness (Antoni et al., 2001; Henry, Wilson, Bruce, Chisholm, & Rawling, 1997; Hockemeyer & Smyth, 2002; Lutgendorf, Antoni, & Ironson, 1997). The application of stress management techniques to a variety of illnesses and the inexpensive nature of these programs continues to make them the cornerstone of behavioral medicine interventions.

FUTURE DIRECTIONS IN STRESS RESEARCH

Although the field of stress research continues to be marked by disagreement over the nature and assessment of the stress concept, interest in stress and stress-mediated outcomes is abundant. Thoits (1995) reviewed the state of stress research and highlighted several directions for future investigations. For example, additional elucidation of the relationship between stress and physical health outcomes is needed, with specific attention paid to the exacerbating or attenuating effects of negative and positive stress. In terms of chronic stress, issues related to chronic employment stress have been most consistently studied, and examination of other types of chronic stress (e.g., marital, parental, financial) is lacking. In a similar vein, inquiry is needed into the carryover effects of stressors experienced in different environments or contexts, such as how employment stress may affect marital stress. Investigations clarifying the relationships between the sequence of stressful life events and both physical and psychological consequences is desired. In addition, the identification of associations between physical and mental health effects is recommended via the assessment of multiple outcomes. Additional exploration of the potential impact of socioeconomic status and racism as stressors in various populations (e.g., women, Black Americans, elderly individuals) would also be beneficial. Certainly the ease of implementation and the cost-effectiveness of stress management interventions suggest that additional development and evaluation of behavioral treatment programs should be explored to expand the number of medical patients who have access to these interventions. Finally, emerging interest in the physiological mechanisms underlying stress-related outcomes has stemmed from recent studies correlating stress with memory impairment (Sapolsky, 1996), development of cardiovascular disease risk factors (Steptoe et al., 2002), measurements of body mass index, waist–hip ratio and body fat distribution (Bell, Summerson, Spangler, & Konen, 1998; Mariemi et al., 2002) and a pattern of behavioral and physiological responding termed *civilization syndrome* (Bjorntorp, Holm, & Rosmond, 2000).

COPING

Coping has been viewed as both a mediator and moderator of the relationship between the experience of stress and subsequent negative outcomes such as illness. Individuals are often diverse in their response to the same situation, and the same individual may vary responses to similar stressors over time. As a consequence, inquiry into how and why people respond differently to stress has become the focus of much research in the past three decades.

Definition of Coping

Analogous to the problem of defining stress is the difficulty in establishing agreement regarding the definition of coping. The concept of coping is often described in general terms and can incorporate several areas of functioning: behavioral, cognitive, affective, and physiological. Coping has been commonly described in terms of specific cognitions and behaviors (Lazarus & Folkman, 1984) or more generally as any response to stress (Silver & Wortman, 1980). More recently, researchers have expanded the concept of coping to include "proactive coping," which focuses on the actions taken to prevent exposure to stressors or the experience of stress (Aspinwall, 1997). The vague and wide variation of the definition of coping has made it difficult to compare data and thus hindered the integration and application of research findings to advance the understanding of this construct.

There is a general consensus that coping is a process that involves an individual's appraisal and management of stressful situations. The most commonly used definition of coping, developed by Lazarus and Folkman (1984), states that coping is the "constantly changing cognitive and behavioral efforts to manage specific external and/or internal demands that are appraised as taxing or exceeding the resources of the person" (p. 141). In other words, the degree of stress is determined by an individual's perception of a situation, whereas the actual coping process consists of the thoughts or actions used to handle the stressful situation. The stress buffering effect of coping appears to be associated with several processes, including the removal of a stressor or associated demands, minimization of the stress response, augmentation of available coping resources or modification of stress appraisal. Research exploring the ways in which people cope has become an important and rapidly expanding subfield of stress research.

The concept of coping grew out of attempts to explain the variation in stress responses. Several areas of psychology have contributed to the concept of coping, including animal experimentation, ego psychology, and cognitive psychology. The three principal coping models derived from psychoanalytic, personality and cognitive-transactional theories, are reviewed.

Coping Models

The earliest models of coping, based on ego psychology concepts, emphasized the role of defense mechanisms and conscious or unconscious processes used to deal with stressors (Haan, 1977). Researchers also focused on the development of classification systems to categorize coping styles based on the degree of maturity or level of psychological adjustment (Valliant, 1977). Research within this theoretical framework has been criticized for extremely small sample sizes, poor interrater reliability, and lack of consideration for the nature of stressful circumstances (Folkman, 1992).

Psychoanalytical theory also contributed to the proliferation of research into individual preferences for coping styles. Dispositional or trait theorists place emphasis on the relatively stable personality characteristics that influence behavior in a wide range of situations, particularly the choice of coping responses. A variety of questionnaires have been used to assess various traits believed to be associated with coping responses. These assessments typically measure the traits on a continuum such as repression–sensitization (Byrne, 1961) or monitoring–blunting (Miller, 1987). The unidimensional nature of dispositional theories has been criticized for underestimating the complexity of the coping process (Lazarus, 1993).

By the late 1970s, the focus of coping shifted to an emphasis on the actions of the individual, including covert cognitions as well as overt behaviors. The contextual or process models are primarily represented by the cognitive model of coping proposed by Lazarus and Folkman (1984). This model describes a dynamic process of shifting cognitions and behaviors used to manage stressful internal or external environmental demands. This process is determined by an individual's perception of an event, including the primary appraisal of personal significance of a situation and the secondary appraisal of the options for coping with the situation. The process is dynamic because of the interaction and feedback between the individual and the environment that affects appraisals directly through coping efforts or indirectly through changes in the environmental situation (Folkman, 1992). The two most commonly identified dimensions of coping associated with this model are problem-focused coping, directed toward managing the problem or situation, and emotion-focused coping, directed toward managing emotion. Some of the criticisms of the process model include lack of assessment of contextual influences, as well as the stable interaction between the individual and the environment (Lazarus, 1993).

Measurement of Coping

As the various coping definitions and conceptualizations would suggest, coping has been assessed as a disposition, trait, style, or an event-specific factor. Several methods, including questionnaires, interviews, and observational techniques, have been used to assess coping. The developments in coping assessment have paralleled the changes in theoretical models. For example, earlier coping measurement emphasized trait measures, such as ego strength, whereas more recent instruments have focused on coping behaviors used in response to specific events.

Although there are a variety of coping measures available (see Schwarzer & Schwarzer, 1996, for a review), the most widely used measure is the Ways of Coping Questionnaire (Folkman & Lazarus, 1988). This measure consists of a large pool of items that describe a broad range of cognitive and behavioral coping responses. Respondents rate on a 4-point Likert-type scale the use of various coping strategies during a particular stressful situation. The analysis of items yields a score on eight dimensions and distinguishes between problem- and emotion-focused coping techniques. A variety of specialized questionnaires based on these instruments have been developed to assess specific illness populations.

The multidimensional aspect of coping is evidenced by the multiple coping measures available and the plethora of coping classifications that have been proposed. For example, the extensively used Ways of Coping Questionnaire has been subjected to multiple factor analyses and has produced from two to eight factors, with each analysis yielding slightly different factor labels (e.g., McCrae, 1984; Scheier, Weintraub, & Carver, 1986). In particular, the two earliest identified coping dimensions, problem-focused and emotion-focused coping, have continued to attract a majority of research attention, perhaps because of their simplicity. Other simplified broad coping categories that have been proposed include vigilant versus avoidant (Roth & Cohen, 1986) and engagement versus disengagement (Tobin, Holroyd, Reynolds, & Wigal, 1989). However, these simplified models have been criticized as being unable to capture the complexity of the coping processes. In an effort to reflect the intricate nature of the coping process, more detailed systems have been proposed that further subdivide the problem- and emotion-focused categories (e.g., Houston, 1991). Although detailed subgrouping may be necessary to understand the complex nature of coping, there is no current consensus regarding the most appropriate set of classifications or number of coping mechanisms. Although this line of research provides a window through which to examine coping strategies used to manage stressors, it does not address the issue of coping efficacy.

The effectiveness of a coping strategy is most commonly assessed according to the nature of the outcome, such as physical or psychological illness. A positive outcome is usually equated with an efficacious strategy. Outcome variables should be independent of the coping variable, theoretically relevant to the coping variable, and proximate to the coping variable to minimize the effects of extraneous factors that could dilute the interpretation of proposed associations (Folkman, 1992). Physiological outcomes have also been suggested as an appropriate method to detect whether a coping strategy is effective, because biochemical measures (e.g., corticosteriod levels) can change during the coping and adaptation process (Steptoe, 1991). However, reliance on one system or measure can be misleading because the coping process can be associated with differential physiological effects in several systems. There are numerous contradictory findings in regard to the evaluation of efficacy of coping strategies. For example, denial has been linked to both positive and negative outcomes (e.g., Lazarus & Folkman, 1991). The literature has not reached a consensus regarding what coping strategies are most efficacious in regard to minimizing the effects of stress on physical and mental health outcomes. Based on the numerous contradictory findings, it appears likely that no one particular type of coping strategy will be identified as universally effective.

The assessment of coping has been criticized in a number of areas. In a review of coping assessment, Schwarzer and Schwarzer (1996) noted that problems exist globally in the stability, generality, and dimensionality of coping assessment. More specifically, as the variety of definitions would suggest, there has been a lack of conceptual clarity associated with the measurement of coping. Items are not clearly stated, which allows subjective interpretation and increases the likelihood of confusion, error, and ambiguity. In addition, one coping behavior may serve multiple coping functions. Thus, the overlap between coping behavior classification and function has resulted in many of the scales attempting to reconcile issues of multicollinerity (Schwarzer & Schwarzer, 1996). A majority of studies in the coping literature reflect use of measures that assess the type and frequency of coping techniques and fail to collect data on coping efficacy. Therefore, although quantitative methods have broadened our understanding of coping, the weaknesses referenced are likely contributors to the inconsistent or contradictory findings that limit the description or explanation of the coping construct.

Individual Differences in Coping

Numerous factors such as situational, personality, and cultural variables can influence the coping process. The exploration of individual differences has been an important area of study; however, findings have often been mixed or inconsistent. Lazarus (1993), in a review of coping theory and research, attempted to summarize some of the general findings of the coping literature. For instance, individuals tend to use coping strategies representative of both emotion- and problem-focused categories in most stressful situations (Folkman & Lazarus, 1980). In addition, some coping strategies are used consistently across situations (e.g., positive reappraisal) whereas others are not (e.g., social support) (Folkman, Lazarus, Gruen, & DeLongis, 1986). In summary, the choice of coping strategies and the resulting outcomes may vary widely between individuals and situations.

Research has consistently demonstrated that individuals use different forms of coping depending on the nature of the stressor. For example, McCrae (1984) classified stressors into three categories (loss, threat, and challenge) and found that participants consistently used different coping strategies depending on the type of stressor experienced. Faith, fatalism, and wishful thinking were used when faced with a threatening situation; emotional expression, faith, and fatalism when faced with a loss situation; and rational action, perseverance, positive thinking, intellectual denial, restraint, self-adaptation, drawing strength from adversity, and humor when faced with a challenging situation. In a follow-up study, individuals were most likely to use "mature" coping strategies when dealing with challenges and least likely to use these strategies when dealing with losses (McCrae & Costa, 1986).

Research findings also consistently report that appraisal influences choice of coping strategy. For example, the more severe a stressor is appraised, the greater the number of responses used (McCrae, 1984). In addition, individuals who perceive the stressor as controllable are more likely to use problem-focused strategies, whereas uncontrollable situations are met with emotion-focused or avoidance strategies (Thoits, 1991).

Although much research has examined only the choice of strategies used, a large body of research exists in regard to the efficacy of coping strategies. In particular, some researchers have found that the nature of the stressor determines the effectiveness of the strategies. The most common finding in the literature is related to the differential effects of problem- or emotion-focused coping in regard to controllability of the stressful situation. In general, when dealing with a controllable stress, active or problem-focused strategies are most often associated with positive outcomes, whereas in uncontrollable situations, emotion-focused strategies are associated with positive outcomes. Time may play a role in determining which type of coping strategy will be most effective. For example, avoidant strategies may be beneficial when dealing with short-term or uncontrollable stressors but over time become less effective (Suls & Fletcher, 1985).

Differences in personal attributes have also been examined to determine the effectiveness or choice of coping strategy. Individuals with higher levels of personal control are more likely to have fewer negative outcomes in regard to physical or psychological distress when exposed to stress (Turner & Roszell, 1994). Higher levels of self-esteem and optimism have also been associated with the use of problem-focused strategies and positive outcomes (e.g., Thoits, 1995).

There are a limited number of studies examining the relationship between demographic variables and coping strategies. In regard to gender, a few differences are occasionally found in the coping literature. Men are more likely to use a problem-solving response to stressors, whereas women are more likely to be expressive in their response style and seek social support (Thoits, 1995). In addition, women have also been noted to use more avoidant strategies (McCrae, 1989). However, men and women do differentially demonstrate problem-solving responses in certain environmental situations (Thoits, 1991). For example, men are more likely to demonstrate problem solving in work situations whereas women are more likely to demonstrate these types of responses in family situations (e.g., Folkman & Lazarus, 1980). Thoits (1995) has posited that this may reflect the differing level of control felt in these situations. There are contradictory findings regarding differences in coping related to age, and no clear conclusions have been reached regarding the role of aging in adjustment to stress (see Strack & Feifel, 1996, for reviews). There has been some evidence to suggest that older individuals are less likely to use behavioral strategies (Folkman, Lazarus, Pimley, & Novacek, 1987). Therefore, there is currently a need to expand exploration of the role of demographic variables.

Coping and Health

Numerous studies have examined the association between coping strategies and illness. In more recent studies, active behavioral coping strategies have generally been found to be associated with more positive outcomes in a variety of illness populations, whereas avoidant coping strategies are more likely to be associated with negative outcomes (e.g., Mulder, Antoni, Duivenvoorden, & Kauffmann, 1995). There is some evidence to suggest that individuals who are ill are less flexible in their overall coping or problem-solving abilities (Schwartz, Peng, Lester, Daltroy, & Goldberger, 1998). In addition, strategies reflecting active coping strategies have been associated with better compliance when dealing with controllable illness stressors, whereas emotion-focused strategies have been associated with compliance when assessing uncontrollable illness stressors (Christensen, Benotsch, Wiebe, & Lawton, 1995). In an ambitious undertaking, Penley and colleagues completed a meta-analytical review of the relationship between coping and health (Penley, Tomaka, & Wiebe, 2002). In general they noted that problem-focused coping strategies were associated with positive health outcomes. However, they did note differences between physical and psychological outcomes and characteristics of the stressors.

A large body of literature has focused on the effects of coping on psychological distress or mental health issues. In regard to depression, emotion-focused or avoidance-based coping styles have been associated with higher levels of distress and poorer psychological outcomes (e.g., Cronkite, Moos, Twohey, Cohen, & Swindle, 1998; Sherbourne, Hays, & Wells, 1995), whereas problem-directed strategies have been associated with less psychological symptomatology (e.g., Aldwin & Revenson, 1987). Coping patterns have also been associated with anxiety disorders. For example, patients with panic disorder were more likely to use avoidant coping strategies than patients with other anxiety disorders (Vollrath & Angst, 1993). The results of the meta-analytical review were consistent with the previous literature and found, for example, that strategies such as confrontive, distancing, self-control, accepting responsibility, escape–avoidance, and wishful thinking were usually associated with negative psychological outcomes (Penley et al., 2002). Despite the vast amount of research in this area, the question of which coping strategies are associated with psychological adjustment still has not been definitively answered, which is likely because of the need to account for moderating variables such as the type of outcome variable and type of stressor.

Coping strategies have also been noted to have positive and negative impacts on health behaviors. In problem drinkers, active and cognitive coping styles have been associated with decreases in long-term alcohol consumption and dysphoria, whereas individuals with avoidant coping styles were more likely to report mood disturbance (Moos, Finney, & Cronkite, 1990). In smokers, problem solving and cognitive restructuring coping strategies have been associated with quitting (Carey, Kalra, Carey, Halperin, & Richards, 1993). In addition, avoidant coping styles in response to stress have been associated with decreased food intake, whereas use of social support has been associated with increased snacking behaviors (Ogden & Mtandabari, 1997).

Future Directions in Coping Research

Despite the limitations found in the coping literature, interest in coping processes continues to grow. Thoits (1995) reviewed the coping literature and found several areas that need additional evaluation. First, more research is needed to determine the contexts in which coping strategies are most effective. Second, coping research efforts should be expanded in regard to individual differences such as gender, race, age, and socioeconomic status. Third, efforts to examine the relations between coping strategies and constructs such as self-esteem and locus of control should be continued. As expected, numerous researchers have noted the need to refine coping terminology and classification systems, as well as assessment methods, to improve the evaluation of the complexities of the coping process (e.g., Compas, Connor, Osowiecki, & Welch, 1997). Emphasis also needs to be placed on elucidating the role of individual factors in the development of effective coping strategies, as well as identifying and understanding the mechanisms or processes involved in mediating or moderating the impact of stress (Aldwin & Brustom, 1997; Zeidner & Saklofske, 1996).In addition, some researchers indicate that there is need to increase efforts to understand the nature of coping strategies that are not commonly assessed, such as effortful versus involuntary processes (Compas et al., 1997). Finally, the results of a meta-analysis of the coping literature noted that research on the association between coping and physical health outcomes needs to be further expanded and that future studies need to take into account the moderating effects of type of health outcome and situational characteristics (Penley et al., 2002).

SOCIAL SUPPORT

Although there is no single definition of social support on which all sources agree, the term usually refers to a wide range of social networks and the resources they provide for the individual or group in question. Similar to the constructs of stress and coping, researchers have argued that the term *social support* is too complex to be captured by a single definition and have tried to subdivide social support into meaningful categories or components. House and Kahn (1985) have divided social support into three major categories appropriate for measurement: social networks, social relationships, and specific social supports. Social relationships define the existence, quantity, and types of relationships currently available to the individual or group under study. Social networks are those proposed in formal network theory and include assessments of network size, density, and homogeneity. The last category, social support, refers to the actual resources (e.g., emotional support, information) provided by others.

Similarly, Cohen and his colleagues (Cohen & Wills, 1985) have proposed that social support measures be divided into structural and functional support measures. Structural support measures are designed to determine the existence of social ties and the connections between those ties (e.g. marital status, number of relations who know one another), whereas functional support measures assess what these relationships provide (e.g., money, affection). However, despite the classification system used, the inclusion of tangible (e.g., monetary support, physical assistance) and intangible components (e.g., praise, advice) in the conceptualization of social support appears to be a common element.

Whether investigators use functional measures of social support or tangible measures, it appears more useful to assess recipient *perceptions* of support as opposed to more objective indexes of social support. This is based on the consistent finding of stronger agreement between an individual's perception of their social resources and indexes of their health (Antonucci & Israel, 1986; Wellington & Kessler, 1986). It is also important to distinguish whether people's appraisal of their social resources represents what they perceive they have actually *received* from others (behavioral social support) or whether their appraisal indicates their view of the support *available* to them (cognitive social support). Distinguishing between these types of appraisals is important, because outcomes based on these differing perceptions are often not highly correlated (Sarason, Sarason, & Pierce, 1990; Schwarzer & Leppin, 1991).

Models of Social Support

An individual's perception of attachment to social networks may take shape early in his or her life. These attachment behaviors are then carried over into adulthood so that the individual perceives others as sources of mutual support. Lakey and Dickinson (1994), in their examination of first-year college students, found that participants' perceptions of support from newly acquired college friends closely matched ratings of previous family support.

One theory proposed to explain the health benefits of social support states that social support exerts a direct positive effect, regardless of life circumstances. This model postulates that having large social networks provides individuals with high levels of social reinforcement and identifiable roles within their community (Cohen & Wills, 1985). This generalized support provides a sense of stability and predictability, which then promotes feelings of well-being and self-worth. Health benefits are realized either by improved neuroendocrine functioning, making an individual less susceptible to disease (Davis & Swan, 1999), or by the reduction of high-risk health behaviors or the promotion of healthy behaviors (Brantley & Ames, 2001).

A direct-effects model has also been hypothesized to account for the adverse effects of low levels of social support (Baumeister & Leary, 1995). This model proposes that the need for human attachment, including social support, is fundamental and innate. When this basic evolutionary need goes unmet, physical and psychological distress results. Primate studies are used as evidence by these authors to support the negative outcomes (e.g., inability to mate, shorter life expectancy) associated with poor social networks. This theory is also supported in reviews of population studies (e.g., Berkman,

1995), suggesting a strong association exists between social isolation and mortality from all causes.

Another predominate model used to account for the positive effects of social support is the buffer hypothesis (Cohen & Wills, 1985). This model postulates that social support is a protective factor that shields or buffers an individual from the negative effects of stressful life events. Buffering is assumed to occur at two points in the stress-disorder chain. First, social support may attenuate a person's appraisal of a stressful event by providing assurance that resources are available to deal with the challenge at hand. Second, the presence or assistance of others may lessen the impact of the stress experience on the individual by reducing or eliminating physiological stress responses, attenuating affective reactions, or reducing maladaptive responses. The buffer model predicts that the association between stress and negative health outcomes is minimized under conditions of optimal social support. It also suggests that the effect of support is greater for individuals at higher levels of stress. Support has been found for both the buffering model and the direct effects model and appears to be somewhat dependent on the methodology used in the particular studies (Wills & Fegan, 2001).

A variant of the buffer model is the matching hypothesis (Cohen & McCay, 1984). It states that stressors present specific coping demands that can only be buffered by support meeting those demands. Supports must match both the conditions and the individuals involved to be effective. For example, an individual in need of money for food will gain little from compliments designed to enhance self-esteem. Support without regard to the needs at hand may not be helpful, and, in fact, incompatible support may actually lead to heightened distress. Despite the apparent logic of this theory, attempts to demonstrate matching have met with mixed success (Hobfoll & Vaux, 1993; Martin, Davis, Baron, Suls, & Blanchard, 1994).

Measurement of Social Support

Dozens of questionnaires have been developed to measure social support, and several authors have reviewed these measures at length (e.g., Heitzmann & Kaplan, 1988; Sarason & Sarason, 1994). The measurement of social support, like stress and coping, is marked by a diversity of instruments representing the multitude of conceptualizations of the construct. The fact that it can be measured so many ways makes interpretation of findings difficult across studies (King, 1997). One review reported that 19 social support questionnaires have published reliability data, and 13 offer some type of validity data (Heitzmann & Kaplan, 1988). Sarason and Sarason (1994) divided social support questionnaires into three major classifications: those assessing social networks, appraisal of support received, and perceived availability of support.

Network Measures

These provide an estimate of individuals' attachments within social groups. They typically assess network characteristics including structural and interactional properties (e.g., size, density), qualitative indicators (e.g., relationship quality ratings), and reciprocity of relationships (i.e., how one-sided relationships are). The Social Network List (SNL; Stokes, 1983) is an example of a network measure. It asks respondents to list as many as 20 people involved in their lives. Respondents then indicate which of the named are relatives and with whom they feel they could confide or turn to for assistance in a time of need. Scoring provides network estimates of size, density, and numbers of friends and relatives.

Network measures possess face validity and have been used extensively in population studies of social support and health concerns (King, 1997). Experience has taught that assessing more than 5 to 10 members of an individual's social network provides little additional useful information (Stokes, 1983). Research using network measures also suggests there is a point of diminishing returns in terms of the desirable number of social confidants. In short, the demands associated with maintaining large networks may not be offset by what one receives in return (Stokes & Wilson, 1984). Finally, although they have provided promising leads for research, network measures do not appear to be sensitive of the association of social support and health indexes (House & Kahn, 1985).

Received Support

Based on the notion that quality of social support is more important than quantity (i.e., network size), these measures assess perceptions of actual support received by individuals. An example of a received support measure is the Inventory of Social Supportive Behaviors (ISSB) developed by Barrera, Sandler, and Ramsey (1981). This questionnaire contains 40 behaviorally oriented items that allow respondents to rate how frequently other people performed specific activities for the respondent (e.g., loaning money, giving physical affection) during the previous month.

Perceived Available Support

These brief interviews and questionnaires estimate perceived external resources. The Interpersonal Support Evaluation List (ISEL; Cohen, Mermelstein, Karmack, & Hoberman, 1985) is a measure of perceived available support. This questionnaire allows respondents to indicate their agreement on a 4-point scale with 40 statements concerning their social resources. There is also a 48-item student version of the questionnaire. Along with a total score, there are four subscales that classify types of perceived available support. These are labeled tangible, belonging, self-esteem, and appraisal.

Measuring perceived versus received support may be more appropriate at different points in time (Schwarzer & Leppin, 1991). For example, it may be more appropriate to evaluate perceived support under normal circumstances, such as times when people do not need to heavily rely on others. This would give an index of their general sense of being cared for and loved by others. Received social support may be more relevant once the need for support occurs, and the amount and types of support actually received would be of greater interest in this situation. Discrepancies between ratings of received and perceived support may result from many sources, such as the failure of significant others to respond in the appropriate manner or misjudgments about the availability of support. Thus, methodological decisions regarding the number and timing of assessments may dictate what measures are most appropriate for use.

Social Support and Health

Scientists have long noted the association between social ties and health. One of the first empirical investigations of social support conducted by Durkeim (1951) reported higher rates of suicide in less "socially integrated" individuals. Two influential review papers by Cassel (1976) and Cobb (1976) summarized human and animal studies examining social environment and health, and are credited with sparking the interdisciplinary study of the area now referred to as social support research. The conclusions of these authors emphasized the buffering effects of social support during times of increased stress. Cassel (1976) believed that efforts to improve health would be more beneficial if they were targeted at improving social supports as opposed to reducing stressful events. However, most of the studies reviewed by Cassell and Cobb relied on self-report and cross-sectional data, and critics have since minimized the importance of social networks and raised questions about causal priorities between social support and health indexes (e.g., LaRocco, House, & French, 1980). The basis of this criticism is the argument that investigators were not able to distinguish whether satisfying social relationships enhance health or healthy individuals simply report more satisfying social relationships.

Later epidemiological studies used long-term prospective designs, allowing for a more precise examination of the potential health benefits of social support (e.g., Orth-Gomer & Johnson, 1987; Schoenbach, Kaplan, Fredman, & Kleinbaum, 1986). Findings of these studies suggests social networks were significant predictors of age-adjusted mortality rates even after controlling for baseline health status and high-risk health behaviors such as smoking. In addition, the mediating role of social support was found to be stronger in men than women and in urban as opposed to rural populations. These studies as well as subsequent research suggest that there are more beneficial health effects associated with marriage for males than for females. Women, on the other hand, appear to benefit more from same-sex relationships with friends and family than do men. Hibbard and Pope (1992) found that women who report positive social relationships at their work sites had lower mortality rates than nonemployed women. In fact, they found nonemployed women to have an 80% greater risk of death during the study period than employed women who reported low levels of social support in their work sites. Regardless of gender, elderly individuals tend to suffer social isolation for a variety of reasons and may be at particular risk for adverse health outcomes (Revicki & Mitchell, 1990).

Schoenbach et al. (1986) examined the role of social support among Black Americans. Their results indicated that the relationship between social networks and health was stronger among White as opposed to Black males, whereas among women the association was less clear. Black women had higher relative risk ratios than White women, but the risk ratios for Black women reported by Schoenbach and colleagues were lower than the risk ratios reported for White women in the other community studies.

The importance of social support to the onset of disease is less well-established. Many studies examining social networks and disease onset have focused on the incidence of coronary heart disease (CHD). For example, Orth-Gomer and colleagues studied 736 men who were free of heart disease at the onset of a six-year study. They found that measures of the men's social network predicted onset of CHD, despite controlling for a variety of coronary risk factors (Orth-Gomer, Rosengren, & Wilhelmsen, 1993).

A stronger case has been made for the impact of social support on the course and progression of existing illnesses. A large literature suggests that social support is linked to successful management of a variety of illnesses, including CHD (King, 1997), diabetes (Gary-Sevilla et al., 1995), cancer (Helgeson & Cohen, 1996), HIV disease (Green & Kocsis, 1996), and obesity (Wing & Jeffrey, 1999).

Future Directions in Social Support Research

One area in need of additional study is the examination of the relative effects of social support and other psychosocial variables in accounting for the positive effects of social support on health outcomes (Sarason, Pierce, & Sarason, 1994). For example, it may be that certain intermediary variables, such as personality traits (e.g., introversion–extroversion), affect both illness and social support. Cohen and Williamson (1991) reported in their review of stress and infectious disease that both social support and social skill were negatively correlated with illness. One mechanism may be that people with poor social skills also lack other coping skills and as a result poorly manage their health in a manner similar to the way they manage other people. Another possible explanation is that people with good social skills are better able to communicate their needs to others and are therefore more likely to receive the amount and type of support they need to adjust to illness or engage in health behaviors.

Additional study is also needed to acquire a better understanding of how individuals' perceptions of social support are formed. Basic research into human memory indicates that judgments of others are often based more on subjective, trait-based impressions than on objective data derived from past interactions (Hastie & Park, 1986). It follows logically that earlier judgments of others would, in turn, affect our perceptions of their support. Another area in need of additional study is investigation into the relationship of social support to other qualities of human relationships. For example, is it possible that perceived social support is simply another term for relationship satisfaction (Lakey & Drew, 1997)?

Another open area of investigation is the analysis of environmental variables that may be affecting the social support–illness relationship. For instance, social support appears to have a greater positive impact on stressors of short duration than those of longer, chronic duration (Schwarzer & Leppin, 1991). Explanations for this finding may be that over time the support network may simply burnout from extended effort. For example, there is often the expectation by support providers that efforts to comfort will be rewarded by improvement in that individual's condition. When significant improvement fails to occur, supportive individuals may feel inadequate, or even rejected. This may, in turn, lead to reactions of criticism and hostility rather than support. Therefore, longitudinal studies measuring perceived social support over time are needed to isolate those environmental factors influencing the social support–illness relationship.

Provider characteristics is another area that has been given little attention thus far. For example, support providers may have their own difficulties coping with stressful situations, and may, as a result, provide little support to the individual directly affected by the stressor. For instance, certain family members may not handle the diagnosis of cancer in a loved one well. They may instead withdraw emotionally or even blame the loved one for contracting the disease (Dunkel-Schetter & Bennett, 1990). Similarly, Schwarzer and Weiner (1991) reported an association between the coping behaviors of the recipient and the likelihood of continued support by providers. Individuals who engaged in active coping during times of stress were more likely to receive social support than those who used less adaptive coping strategies.

CONCLUSION

As a result of extensive psychosocial and medical research efforts, the study of stress has evolved into an important scientific subdiscipline, augmented by a collateral interest in the mediating and moderating effects of coping and social support. Comparable problems with definition and assessment are noted with each of these constructs, and there is a paucity of available information regarding the effects of age, gender, ethnicity, and cultural factors. Despite these limitations, our expanded knowledge about the nature of stress, coping, and social support has resulted in positive outcomes and promising avenues of future inquiry. The effects of stress, coping, and social support on psychological and physical health have been studied in a wide variety of populations and continue to provide new insight into the relationships between these variables and quality of life. Public awareness of the scientific findings of new sources of stress and their subsequent health effects has been heightened in recent years by media attention. Clinical application of knowledge about the effects of stress and the buffering effects of coping and social support resources have made stress management programs a universally accepted form of health intervention, thus improving the lives of many individuals.

REFERENCES

Aldwin, C. M., & Brustom, J. (1997). Theories of coping with chronic stress: Illustrations from the health psychology and aging literatures. In B. H. Gottlieb (Ed.), *Coping with chronic stress* (pp. 75–103). New York: Plenum Press.

Aldwin, C. M., & Revenson, T. A. (1987). Does coping help? A reexamination of the relationship between coping and mental health. *Journal of Personality and Social Psychology, 53*(2), 337–348.

Antoni, M. H., Lehman, J. M., Kilbourn, K. M., Boyers, A. E., Culver, J. L., Alferi S. M., et al. (2001). Cognitive–behavioral stress management intervention decreases prevalence of depression and enhances benefit finding among women under treatment for early-stage breast cancer. *Health Psychology, 20*, 458–459.

Antonucci, T. C., & Israel, B. A. (1986). Veridicality of social support: A comparison of principal and network member responses. *Journal of Consulting and Clinical Psychology, 54*, 432–437.

Aspinwall, L. G. (1997). Where planning meets coping: Proactive coping and the detection and management of potential stressors. In S. L. Freidman & E. K. Scholnick (Eds.), *The developmental psychology of planning; Why, how and when do we plan?* (pp. 285–320). Mahwah, NJ: Erlbaum.

Barrera, M., Sandler, I. N., & Ramsey, T. B. (1981). Preliminary development of a scale of social support: Studies on college students. *American Journal of Community Psychology*, 9(4), 435–447.

Bartrop, R. W., Luckhurst, E., Lazarus, L., Kiloh, L. G., & Penny, R. (1997). Depressed lymphocyte function after bereavement. *Lancet, 1*, 834–836.

Baum, A., & Grunberg, N. (1995). Measurement of stress hormones. In S. Cohen, R. C. Kessler, & L. U. Gordon (Eds.), *Measuring stress: A guide for health and social scientists* (pp. 175–192). New York: Oxford University Press.

Baumeister, R. F., & Leary, M. R. (1995). The need to belong: Desire for interpersonal attachments as a fundamental human motivation. *Psychological Bulletin, 117*(3), 497–529.

Beck, A. (1984). Cognitive approaches to stress. In R. Woolfolk & P. Lehrer (Eds.), *Principles and practice of stress management* (pp. 255–305). New York: Guilford Press.

Bell, R. A., Summerson, J. H., Spangler, J. G., & Konen, J. C. (1998). Body fat, fat distribution, and psychosocial factors among patients with Type 2 diabetes mellitus. *Behavioral Medicine, 24*(3), 138–143.

Berkman, L. F. (1995). The role of social relations in health promotion. *Psychosomatic Medicine, 57*, 245–254.

Bjorntorp, P., Holm, G., & Rosmond, R. (2000). Metabolic diseases: The hypothalamic arousal syndrome. In D. I. Mostofsky & D. H. Barlow (Eds.), *The management of stress and anxiety in medical settings* (pp. 282–289). Needham Heights, MA: Allyn & Bacon.

Brantley, P. J., & Ames, S.C. (2001). Psychobiology of health and disease. In H. E. Adams & P. B. Sutker (Eds.), *Comprehensive handbook of psychopathology* (3rd ed., pp. 777–795). New York: Plenum Press.

Brantley, P. J., Dietz, L. S., McKnight, G. T., Jones, G. N., & Tulley, R. (1988). Convergence between the daily stress inventory and endocrine measures of stress. *Journal of Consulting and Clinical Psychology, 56*, 549–551.

Brantley, P. J., & Garrett, V. D. (1993). Psychobiological approaches to health and disease. In R. Sutker & H. Adams (Eds.), *Comprehensive handbook of psychopathology* (pp. 647–670). New York: Plenum Press.

Brantley, P. J., & Jones, G. N. (1989). *Daily stress inventory: Professional manual*. Odessa, FL: Psychological Assessment Resources.

Brantley, P. J., & Jones, G. N. (1993). Daily stress and stress-related disorders. *Annals of Behavioral Medicine, 15*(1), 17–25.

Brantley P. J., Jones G. N., Boudreax, E., & Catz S. L. (1997). The Weekly Stress Inventory. In C. P. Zalaquett (Ed.), *Evaluating stress: A book of resources* (pp. 405–420). Lanham, MD: Scarecrow Press.

Brantley, P. J., & Thomason, B. T. (1995). Stress and stress management. In A. J. Goreczny (Ed.), *Handbook of health and rehabilitation psychology* (pp. 275–289). New York: Plenum Press.

Brantley, P. J., Waggoner, C. D., Jones, G. N., & Rappaport, N. (1987). A daily stress inventory: Development, reliability, and validity. *Journal of Behavioral Medicine, 10,* 61–73.

Brown, G. W. (1989). Life events and measurement. In G. W. Brown & T. O. Harris (Eds.), *Life events and illness* (pp. 3–45). New York: Guilford Press.

Brownell, K. (1982). Obesity: Understanding and treating a serious, prevalent and refractory disorder. *Journal of Consulting and Clinical Psychology, 50,* 820–840.

Byrne, D. (1961). The repression-sensitization scale: Rationale, reliability, and validity. *Journal of Personality, 29,* 334–349.

Cannon, W. B. (1939). *The wisdom of the body* (2nd ed.). New York: Norton.

Carey, M. P., Kalra, D. L., Carey, K. B., Halperin, S., & Richards, C. S. (1993). Stress and unaided smoking cessation: A prospective study. *Journal of Consulting and Clinical Psychology, 61*(5), 831–838.

Carlson, L. E., Speca, M., Patel, K. D., & Goodey, E. (2003). Mindfulness-based stress reduction in relation to quality of life, mood, symptoms of stress and immune parameters in breast and prostrate cancer outpatients. *Psychosomatic Medicine, 65,* 571–581.

Carmack, C. L., Boudreaux, E., Amaral-Melendez, M., Brantley, P. J., & de Moor, C. A. (1999). Aerobic fitness and leisure physical activity as moderators of the stress–illness relation. *Annals of Behavioral Medicine, 21*(3), 251–257.

Cassel, J. (1976). The contribution of the social environment to host resistance. *American Journal of Epidemiology, 104,* 107–123.

Christensen, A. J., Benotsch, E. G., Wiebe, J. S., & Lawton, W. J. (1995). Coping with treatment-related stress: Effects on patient adherence in hemodialysis. *Journal of Consulting and Clinical Psychology, 63,* 454–459.

Cobb, J. M., & Steptoe, A. (1996). Psychosocial stress and susceptibility to upper respiratory tract illness in an adult population sample. *Psychosomatic Medicine, 58*(5), 404–412.

Cobb, S. (1976). Social support as a moderator of life stress. *Psychosomatic Medicine, 38,* 300–314.

Cohen, S., Kamarck, T., & Mermelstein, R. (1983). A global measure of perceived stress. *Journal of Health and Social Behavior, 24,* 385–396.

Cohen, S., & McKay, G. (1984). Social support, stress and the buffering hypothesis: A theoretical analysis. In A. Baum, S. E. Taylor, & J. E. Singer (Eds.), *Handbook of psychology and health* (pp. 254–276). Hillsdale, NJ: Erlbaum.

Cohen, S., Mermelstein, R., Karmack, T., & Hoberman, H. B. (1985). Measuring the functional components of social support. In I. G. Sarason & B. Sarason (Eds.), *Social support: Theory, research and applications* (pp. 73–94). The Hague, the Netherlands: Martinus Nijhoff.

Cohen, S., & Williamson, G. M. (1991). Stress and infectious disease in humans. *Psychological Bulletin, 109,* 5–24.

Cohen, S., & Wills, T. A. (1985). Stress, social support and the buffering hypothesis. *Psychological Bulletin, 98,* 310–357.

Compas, B. E., Connor, J., Osowiecki, D., & Welch, A. (1997). Effortful and involuntary responses to stress: Implications for coping with chronic stress. In B. H. Gottlieb (Ed.), *Coping with chronic stress* (pp. 105–130). New York: Plenum Press.

Cronkite, R. C., Moos, R. H., Twohey, J., Cohen, C., & Swindle, R., Jr. (1998). Life circumstances and personal resources as predictors of the ten-year course of depression. *American Journal of Community Psychology, 26*(2), 255–280.

Davis, M. C., & Swan, P. D. (1999). Association of negative and positive social ties with fibrinogen levels in young women. *Health Psychology, 18*(2), 131–139.

Davis, M. C., Twamley, E. W., Hamilton, N. A., & Swan, P. D. (1999). Body fat distribution and hemodynamic stress responses in premenopausal obese women: A preliminary study. *Health Psychology, 18,* 625–633.

Dohrenwend, B. S., Dohrenwend, B. P., Dodson, M., & Shrout, R. E. (1984). Symptoms, hassles, social supports, and life events: Problem of confounded measures. *Journal of Abnormal Psychology, 93,* 222–230.

Dunkel-Schetter, C., & Bennett, T. L. (1990). Differentiating the cognitive and behavioral aspects of social support. In B. R. Sarason, I. G. Sarason, & G. R. Pierce (Eds.), *Social support: An interactional view* (pp. 267–296). New York: Wiley.

Durkheim, E. (1951). *Suicide* (J. A. Spalding & C. Simpson, Trans.). Glencoe, IL: Free Press. (Original work published 1897)

Elliott, G. R., & Eisdorfer, C. (1982). *Stress and health.* New York: Springer.

Everly, G. S. (1989). *A clinical guide to the treatment of the human stress response.* New York: Plenum Press.

Ferreira, M. F., Sobrinho, L. G., Pires, J. S., Silva, M. E. S., Santos, M. A., & Sousa, M. F. (1995). Endocrine and psychological evaluation of women with recent weight gain. *Psychoneuroendocrinology, 20,* 53–63.

Folkman, S. (1992). Making the case of coping. In B. C. Carpenter (Ed.), *Personal coping: Theory, research and application* (pp. 31–46). Westport, CT: Praeger.

Folkman, S., & Lazarus, R. S. (1980). An analysis of coping in a middle-aged community sample. *Journal of Health and Social Behavior, 21,* 219–239.

Folkman, S., & Lazarus, R. S. (1988). *Manual for the Ways of Coping Questionnaire.* Palo Alto, CA: Consulting Psychologists Press.

Folkman, S., Lazarus, R. S., Gruen, R. J., & DeLongis, A. (1986). Appraisal, coping, health status, and psychological symptoms. *Journal of Personality and Social Psychology, 50*(3), 571–579.

Folkman, S., Lazarus, R. S., Pimley, S., & Novacek, J. (1987). Age differences in stress and coping processes. *Psychology and Aging, 2,* 171–184.

Gallo, L. C., & Matthews, K. A. (2003). Understanding the association between socioeconomic status and physical health: Do negative emotions play a role? *Psychological Bulletin, 129,* 10–51.

Gary-Seville, M. E., Nava, L. E., Malacara, J. M., Huerta, R., de Leon, J. D., Mena, A., et al. (1995). Adherence to treatment and social support in patients with non-insulin-dependent diabetes mellitus. *Journal of Diabetes and Its Complications, 9,* 81–86.

Gerace, T. A., & George, V. A. (1996). Predictors of weight increases over 7 years in firefighters and paramedics. *Preventive Medicine, 25,* 593–600.

Glaser, R. Kiecolt-Glaser, J. K., Speicher, C. E., & Holliday, J. E. (1985). Stress, loneliness, and changes in herpes virus latency. *Journal of Behavioral Medicine, 8,* 249–260.

Glaser, R., Kiecolt-Glaser, J. K., Speicher, C. E., & Holliday, J. E. (1985). Stress, loneliness, and changes in herpes virus latency. *Journal of Behavioral Medicine, 8,* 249–260.

Glaser, R., Rice, J., Sheridan J., Fertel, R., Sout, J., Speicher, C. E., et al. (1987). Stress-related immune suppression: Health implications. *Brain, Behavior, and Immunity, 1,* 7–20.

Goetsch, V. L. (1989). Stress and blood glucose in diabetes mellitus: A review and methodological commentary. *Annals of Behavioral Medicine, 11,* 102–107.

Gore, S., & Colten, M. E. (1991). Gender, stress and distress: Social–relational influences. In J. Eckenrode (Ed.), *The social context of coping* (pp. 139–163). New York: Plenum Press.

Green, J., & Kocsis, A. (1996). Social support and well-being in HIV disease. In G. L. Cooper (Ed.), *Handbook of stress, medicine, and health* (pp. 291–306). Boca Raton, FL: CRC Press.

Griffin, K. W., Friend, R., Eitel, P., & Lobel, M. (1993). Effects of environmental demands, stress, and mood on health practices. *Journal of Behavioral Medicine, 16,* 643–661.

Haan, N. (1977). *Coping and defending: Processes of self-environmental organization.* New York: Academic Press.

Hastie, R., & Park, B. (1986). The relationship between memory and judgement depends on whether the judgement task is memory-based or on-line. *Psychological Review, 93,* 258–268.

Hellerstedt, W. L., & Jeffery, R. W. (1997). The association of job strain and health behaviors in men and women. *International Journal of Epidemiology, 26,* 575–583.

Heitzmann, C. A., & Kaplan, R. M. (1988). Assessment of methods for measuring social support. *Health Psychology, 7,* 75–109.

Helgeson, V. S., & Cohen, S. (1996). Social support and adjustment to cancer: Reconciling descriptive, correlational, and intervention research. *Health Psychology, 15*(2), 135–148.

Henry, J. L., Wilson, P. H., Bruce, D. G., Chisholm, D. J., & Rawling, P. J. (1997). Cognitive–behavioural stress management for patients with non-insulin dependent diabetes mellitus. *Psychology, Health and Medicine, 2,* 109–118.

Hibbard, J. H., & Pope, C. R. (1992). Women's employment, social support, and mortality. *Women and Health, 18*(1), 119–133.

Hobfoll S. E., & Vaux, A. (1993). Social support: Social resources and social context. In L. Goldberger & S. Breznitz (Eds.), *Handbook of stress: Theoretical and clinical aspects* (2nd ed., pp. 685–705). New York: Free Press.

Hockemeyer, J., & Smyth, J. (2002). Evaluating the feasibility and efficacy of a self-administered manual-based stress management intervention for individuals with asthma: Results from a controlled study. *Behavioral Medicine, 27*, 161–173.

Holmes, T. H., & Rahe, R. H. (1967). The social readjustment rating scale. *Journal of Psychosomatic Research, 11*, 213–218.

Holroyd, K. A., & Lazarus, R. S. (1982). Stress, coping and somatic adaptation. In L. Goldberger & S. Breznitz (Eds.), *Handbook of stress: Theoretical and clinical aspects* (pp. 21–35). New York: Free Press.

Horowitz, M., Schaefer, C., Hiroto, D., Wilner, N., & Levin, B. (1977). Life event questionnaires for measuring presumptive stress. *Psychosomatic Medicine, 39*, 413–430.

House, J. S., & Kahn, R. L. (1985). Measures and concepts of social support. In S. Cohen & S. L. Syme (Eds.), *Social support and health* (pp. 83–108). Orlando, FL: Academic Press.

Houston, B. K. (1991). Stress and coping. In C. R. Snyder & C. E. Ford (Eds.), *Coping with negative life events: Clinical and social psychological perspectives* (pp. 373–399). New York: Plenum Press.

Jemmott, J. B., & Locke, S. E. (1984). Psychosocial factors, immunologic mediation, and human susceptibility to infectious diseases: How much do we know? *Psychological Bulletin, 95*, 78–108.

Kanner, A. D., Coyne, J. C., Schaefer, C., & Lazarus, R. S. (1981). Comparison of two modes of measurement: Daily hassles and uplifts versus major life events. *Journal of Behavioral Medicine, 4*, 1–39.

Kiecolt-Glaser, J. K., Garner, W., Speicher, C., Penn, G. M., Holliday, J. E., & Glaser, R. (1984). Psychosocial modifiers of immunocompetence in medical students. *Psychosomatic Medicine, 46*, 7–14.

Kiecolt-Glaser, J. K., & Glaser, R. (1988). Behavioral influences on immune function: Evidence for the interplay between stress and health. In T. M. Field, P. M. McCabe, & N. Schneiderman (Eds.), *Stress and coping across development* (pp. 189–205). Hillsdale, NJ: Erlbaum.

King, K. B. (1997). Psychological and social aspects of cardiovascular disease. *Annals of Behavioral Medicine, 19*(3), 264–270.

Kop, W. J. (1997). Acute and chronic psychological risk factors for coronary syndromes: Moderating the effects of coronary artery disease severity. *Journal of Psychosomatic Research, 43*(2), 167–181.

Lakey, B., & Dickinson, L. G. (1994). Antecedents of perceived social support. *Cognitive Therapy and Research, 18*, 39–53.

Lakey B., & Drew, J. B. (1997). A social–cognitive perspective on social support. In G. R. Pierce, B. Lakey, I. G. Sarason, & B. R. Sarason (Eds.), *Sourcebook of social support and personality* (pp. 107–140). New York: Plenum Press.

LaRocco, J. M., House, J. S., & French, J. R., Jr. (1980). Social support, occupational stress, and health. *Journal of Health and Social Behavior, 21*(3), 202–218.

Lazarus, R. S. (1993). Coping theory and research: Past, present and future. *Psychosomatic Medicine, 55,* 234–247.

Lazarus, R. S., DeLongis, A., Folkman, S., & Gruen, R. (1985). Stress and adaptational outcomes: The problem of confounded measures. *American Psychologist, 40,* 770–779.

Lazarus, R. S., & Folkman, S. (1984). *Stress, appraisal, and coping.* New York: Springer.

Lazarus, R. S., & Folkman, S. (1991). The concept of coping. In A. Monat & R. S. Lazarus (Eds.), *Stress and coping: An anthology* (pp. 189–206). New York: Colombia University Press.

Lindquist, T. L., Beilin, L. J., & Knuiman, M. W. (1997). Influence of lifestyle, coping, and job stress on blood pressure in men and women. *Hypertension, 29,* 1–7.

Linn, B. S., Linn, M. W., & Jensen, J. (1982). Degree of depression and immune responsiveness. *Psychosomatic Medicine, 44,* 128–129.

Lutgendorf, S. K., Antoni, M. H., & Ironson, G. (1997). Cognitive–behavioral stress management decreases dysphoric mood and herpes simplex virus-type 2 antibody titers in symptomatic HIV-seropositive gay men. *Journal of Consulting and Clinical Psychology, 65,* 31–43.

Mariemi, J., Kronholm, E., Aunola, S., Toikka, T., Mattlar, C. E., Koskenvuo, M., et al. (2002). Visceral fat and psychosocial stress in identical twins discordant for obesity. *Journal of Internal Medicine, 251,* 35–43.

Martin, R., Davis, G. M., Baron, R. S., Suls, J., & Blanchard E. B. (1994). Specificity in social support: Perceptions of helpful and unhelpful provider behaviors among irritable bowl syndrome, headache, and cancer patients. *Health Psychology, 13,* 432–439.

McCrae, R. R. (1984). Situational determinants of coping responses: Loss, threat, and challenge. *Journal of Personality and Social Psychology, 46*(4), 919–928.

McCrae, R. R. (1989). Age differences and changes in the use of coping mechanisms. *Journal of Gerontology, 44,* 161–169.

McCrae, R. R., & Costa, P. T., Jr. (1986). Personality, coping and effectiveness in an adult sample. *Journal of Personality, 54,* 385–405.

Miller, S. M. (1987). Monitoring and blunting: Validation of a questionnaire to assess styles of information-seeking under threat. *Journal of Personality and Social Psychology, 52,* 345–353.

Mokdad, A. H., Ford, E. S., Bowman, B. A., Dietz, W. H., Vinicor, F., Bales, V. S., et al. (2003). Prevalence of obesity, diabetes and obesity related health risk factors, 2001. *Journal of the American Medical Association, 289,* 76–79.

Moos, R. H., Finney, J. W., & Cronkite, R. C. (1990). *Alcoholism treatment: Context, process, and outcome.* New York: Oxford University Press.

Mulder, C. L., Antoni, M. H., Duivenvoorden, H. J., & Kauffmann, R. H. (1995). Active confrontational coping predicts decreased clinical progression over a one-year period in HIV infected homosexual men. *Journal of Psychosomatic Research, 39*(8), 957–965.

Ogden, J., & Mtandabari, T. (1997). Examination stress and changes in mood and health related behaviors. *Psychology and Health, 12,* 289–299.

Orth-Gomer, K., & Johnson, J. V. (1987). Social network interaction and mortality: A six year follow-up study of a random sample of the Swedish population. *Journal of Chronic Disease, 40,* 949–957.

Orth-Gomer, K., Rosengren, A., & Wilhelmsen, L. (1993). Lack of social support and incidence of coronary heart disease in middle-aged Swedish men. *Psychosomatic Medicine, 55*(1), 37–43.

Penley, J. A., Tomaka, J., & Wiebe, J. S. (2002). The associations of coping to physical and psychological health outcomes: A meta-analytic review. *Journal of Behavioral Medicine, 25,* 551–603.

Pettingale, K. W., & Hussein, M. (1994). Changes in immune status following conjugal bereavement. *Journal of the American Medical Association, 10,* 145–150.

Revicki, D. A., & Mitchell, J. P. (1990). Strain, social support, and mental health in rural elderly individuals. *Journal of Gerontology, 45*(6), S267–S274.

Roth, S., & Cohen, L. J. (1986). Approach, avoidance, and coping with stress. *American Psychologist, 41*(7), 813–819.

Rozanski, A., Bairey, C. N., Krantz, D. S., Freidman, J., Resser, K. J., Morell, M., et al. (1988). Mental stress and the induction of silent myocardial ischemia in patients with coronary artery disease. *New England Journal of Medicine, 318,* 1005–1012.

Sapolsky, R. M. (1996). Why stress is bad for your brain. *Science, 273,* 749–750.

Sarason, B. R., & Sarason, I. G. (1994). Assessment of social support. In S. A. Shumaker & S. M. Czajkowski (Eds.), *Social support and cardiovascular disease* (pp. 41–63). New York: Plenum Press.

Sarason, B. R., Sarason, I. G., & Pierce, G. R. (1990). Traditional views of social support and their impact on assessment. In B. R. Sarason, I. G. Sarason, & G. R. Pierce (Eds.), *Social support: An interactional view* (pp. 9–25). New York: Wiley.

Sarason, I. G., Johnson, J. H., & Siegel, J. M. (1978). Assessing the impact of life changes: Development of the life experiences survey. *Journal of Consulting and Clinical Psychology, 46,* 348–349.

Sarason, I. G., Pierce, G., & Sarason, B. R. (1994). General and specific perceptions of social support. In W. Avison & I. Gotlib (Eds.), *Stress and mental health: Contemporary issues and prospects for the future* (pp. 151–177). New York: Plenum Press.

Scarinci, I. C., Ames, S. C., & Brantley P. J. (1999). Chronic minor stressors and major life events experienced by low-income patients attending primary care clinics: A longitudinal examination. *Journal of Behavioral Medicine, 22,* 143–156.

Scheier, M. F., Weintraub, J. K., & Carver, C. S. (1986). Coping with stress: Divergent strategies of optimists and pessimists. *Journal of Personality and Social Psychology, 51*(6), 1257–1264.

Schoenbach, V. J., Kaplan, B. H., Fredman, L., & Kleinbaum, D. G. (1986). Social ties and mortality in Evans County, Georgia. *American Journal of Epidemiology, 123*(4), 577–591.

Schwartz, C. E., Peng, C. K., Lester, N., Daltroy, L. H., & Goldberger, A. L. (1998). Self-reported coping behavior in health and disease: Assessment with a card sort game. *Behavioral Medicine, 24*(1), 41–44.

Schwarzer, R., & Leppin, A. (1991). Social support and health: A theoretical and empirical overview. *Journal of Social and Personal Relationships, 8,* 99–127.

Schwarzer, R., & Weiner, B. (1991). Stigma controllability and coping as predictors of emotions and social support. *Journal of Social and Personal relationships, 8,* 133–140.

Schwarzer, R., & Schwarzer, C. (1996). A critical survey of coping instruments. In M. Zeidner & N. S. Endler (Eds.), *Handbook of coping: Theory, research, and applications* (pp. 107–132). New York: John Wiley & Sons.

Scully, J., Tosi, H., & Banning, K. (2000). Life events checklists: Revisiting the social readjustment rating scale after 30 years. *Educational and Psychological Measurement, 60,* 864–876.

Seematter, G., Guenat, E., Schneiter, P., Cayeux, C., Jequier, E., & Trappy, L. (2000). Effects of mental stress on insulin-mediated glucose metabolism and energy expenditure in lean and obese women. *American Journal of Physiology, Endocrinology and Metabolism, 279,* 799–805.

Selye, H. (1936). A syndrome produced by diverse nocuous agents. *Nature, 138,* 32.

Selye, H. (1974). *Stress without distress.* Philadelphia: Lippincott.

Selye, H. (1982). History and present status of the stress concept. In L. Goldberger & S. Breznitz (Eds.), *Handbook of stress: Theoretical and clinical aspects* (pp. 7–20). New York: Free Press.

Shekelle, R. B., Raynor, W. J., Ostfeld, A. M., Garron, D. C., Bieliauskas, L. A., Liu, S. C., et al. (1981). Psychological depression and 17-year risk of death from cancer. *Psychosomatic Medicine, 43,* 117–125.

Sherbourne, C., Hays, R. D., & Wells, K. B. (1995). Personal and psychological risk factors for physical and mental health outcomes and course of depression among depressed patients. *Journal of Consulting and Clinical Psychology, 63*(3), 345–355.

Silver, R. L., & Wortman, C. B. (1980). Coping with undesirable life events. In J. Garber & M. E. P. Seligman (Eds.), *Human helplessness* (pp. 272–375). New York: Academic Press.

Steptoe, A. (1991). Psychological coping, individual differences and physiological stress responses. In C. L. Cooper & R. Payne (Eds.), *Personality and stress: Differences in the stress process* (pp. 205–233). New York: John Wiley & Sons.

Steptoe, A., Feldman, P. J., Kunz, S., Owen, N., Willemsen, G., & Marmot, M. (2002). Stress responsivity and socioeconomic status: A mechanism for increased cardiovascular risk? *European Heart Journal, 23,* 1757–1763.

Stetson, B. A., Rahn, J. M., Dubbert, P. M., Wilner, B. I., & Mercury, M. G. (1997). Prospective evaluation of the effects of stress on exercise adherence in community-residing women. *Health Psychology, 16,* 515–520.

Stokes, J. P. (1983). Predicting satisfaction with social support from social network structure. *American Journal of Community Psychology, 11,* 141–152.

Stokes, J. P., & Wilson, D. G. (1984). The inventory of socially supportive behaviors: Dimensionality, prediction, and gender differences. *American Journal of Community Psychology, 12,* 53–60.

Strack, S., & Feifel, H. (1996). Age differences, coping, and the adult life span. In M. Zeidner & N. S. Endler (Eds.), *Handbook of coping: Theory, research, and applications* (pp. 485–501). New York: John Wiley & Sons.

Suls, J., & Fletcher, B. (1985). The relative efficacy of avoidant and nonavoidant coping strategies: A meta-analysis. *Health Psychology, 4*(3), 249–288.

Surwit, R. S., Ross, S. L., & Feinglos, M. N. (1991). Stress, behavior, and glucose control in diabetes mellitus. In P. M. McCabe & N. Schneiderman (Eds.), *Stress, coping, and disease* (pp. 97–117). Hillsdale, NJ: Erlbaum.

Thoits, P. A. (1991). Gender differences in coping with emotional distress. In J. Eckenrode (Ed.), *The social context of coping* (pp. 107–138). New York: Plenum Press.

Thoits, P. A. (1995). Stress, coping, and social support processes: Where are we? What next? *Journal of Health and Social Behavior* [extra issue], 53–79.

Tobin, D. L., Holroyd, K. A., Reynolds, R. B., & Wigal, J. K. (1989). The hierarchical factor structure of the Coping Strategies Inventory. *Cognitive Therapy and Research, 13,* 343–351.

Turner, R. J., & Roszell, P. (1994). Psychological resources and the stress process. In W. R. Avison & I. H. Gotlib (Eds.), *Stress and mental health: Contemporary issues and the prospects for the future* (pp. 179–210). New York: Plenum Press.

Twisk, J., Snel, J., Kemper, H., & van Mechelen, W. (1999). Changes in daily hassles and life events and the relationship with coronary heart disease risk factors: A 2-year longitudinal study in 27–29 year old males and females. *Journal of Psychosomatic Research, 46,* 229–240.

Valliant, G. E. (1977). *Adaptation to life.* Boston: Little, Brown.

Vitaliano, P. P., Russo, J., Scanlan, J. M., & Greeno, C. G. (1996). Weight changes in caregivers of Alzheimer's care recipients: Psychobehavioral predictors. *Psychology and Aging, 11,* 155–163.

Vollrath, M., & Angst, J. (1993). Coping and illness behavior among young adults with panic. *Journal of Nervous and Mental Disease, 181*(5), 303–308.

Wellington, E., & Kessler, R. C. (1986). Perceived support, received support, and adjustment to stressful life events. *Journal of Health and Social Behavior, 27,* 78–89.

Wiebe, D. J., & McCallum, D. M. (1986). Health practices and hardiness as mediators in the stress–illness relationship. *Health Psychology, 5*, 425–438.

Wills, T. A., & Fegan, M. F. (2001). Social networks and social support. In A. Baum, T. A. Revenson, & J. E. Singer (Eds.), *Handbook of health psychology* (pp. 209–234). Mahwah, NJ: Erlbaum.

Wing, R. R., & Jeffrey, R. W. (1999). Benefit of recruiting participants with friends and increasing social support for weight loss and weight maintenance. *Journal of Consulting and Clinical Psychology, 67*, 132–138.

Zeidner, M., & Saklofske, D. (1996). Adaptive and maladaptive coping. In M. Zeidner & N. S. Endler (Eds.), *Handbook of coping: Theory, research, and applications* (pp. 505–531). New York: John Wiley & Sons.

8

SPIRITUALITY, RELIGION, AND HEALTH: A SCIENTIFIC PERSPECTIVE

CARL E. THORESEN AND ALEX H. S. HARRIS

When, if at all, should religious and spiritual (RS)[1] concerns be considered by health psychologists in their professional and scholarly roles? This question remains exciting for some and disconcerting for others. Several issues are involved. Some health psychologists, and other health-related professionals, either dismiss out-of-hand the possibility that RS factors could influence health or they remain unconvinced by the evidence that any such relationship exists, particularly for any relationship that would lead to the consideration of RS factors in professional practice (e.g., Sloan, Bagiella, & Powell, 1999). On the other hand, some proponents of considering RS factors in research and in practice contend that enough empirical evidence now exists to take seriously the strong possibility that RS-oriented beliefs and behaviors are related to improved outcomes, as evidenced by less disease and better health (e.g., McCullough, Hoyt, Larson, Koenig, & Thoresen, 2000). From a somewhat different perspective, some view

---

[1] We use the abbreviation "RS" throughout the chapter to signify "Religious and/or Spiritual" to save space. Spirituality and religion are often used interchangeably yet actually represent somewhat distinct if not independent constructs for many persons. We discuss the topic more fully later in this chapter.

RS factors primarily as a multicultural–diversity issue to be examined, much in the same sense that other ethnic and cultural factors that have been associated with health processes and outcomes (American Psychological Association, 2002; Worthington, Kurusu, McCollough, & Sandage, 1996).

We are mindful that the RS–health connection has also achieved the status of a hot topic. Books and articles on this issue are proliferating at an accelerating rate, some focused on theory and research (e.g., Pargament, 1997), some on applied or clinical issues (e.g., Miller, 1999), but most directed to the general public, such as Chopra's (2000) *How to Know God,* Peck's perennial bestseller (1976/1993) *The Road Less Travelled,* and Moore's (1994) *Care of the Soul.* At a minimum, health psychologists and other professionals need to be informed about this growing area of public and professional interest and concern. In the same way that health psychologists are now called on to be knowledgeable about complementary and alternative medical programs and processes, they also need to develop a well-informed rationale for whatever perspective is taken about the role of RS factors in disease, health, and quality of life (Miller & Thoresen, 2003; Thoresen, 1999).

This chapter familiarizes readers with some theoretical perspectives and empirical evidence concerning the possible roles of RS factors in health and illness. We believe that a healthy skepticism is in order, one that remains open to the possibility that RS-related beliefs and behaviors may indeed be important to address, yet one that raises questions and requires rigorous empirical evidence based on well-controlled studies (Smith, 2001). We introduce the harsh critic to conceptual perspectives and suggestive data that create a more tempered doubt. We also introduce the uncritical advocate (some might say "cheerleader") to evidence and concerns that will encourage more modest claims and tentative conclusions (Thoresen & Harris, 2002).

To facilitate a more informed perspective, we address the following questions: Does RS involvement influence health? Is there empirical evidence of sufficient quality to justify an answer to this question? What possible mechanisms might explain or account for a relationship if one exists? How should health psychologists respond to this information in terms of controlled research, clinical practice, and professional training? The focus of this chapter is primarily on more theoretical and conceptual issues, examining the nature of relevant empirical evidence, and exploring strategies to improve the quality of research in this area. The more practice-oriented reader interested in integrating RS-oriented interventions or sensitivity into clinical practice is referred to Miller (1999) and Richards and Bergin (1997, 2000) for useful presentations of several specific clinical issues and strategies. In addition, for a broader discussion of psychology and religion issues, see Baumeister's (2002) special issue on the topic.

After a brief discussion of core concepts and definitions, we discuss a recent meta-analysis on the relationship between RS factors and all-cause mortality and also describe a few interesting and well-conducted research studies on the RS-health relationship. We also review some of the conclusions of a recent Office of Behavioral and Social Science Research/National Institutes of Health (OBSSR/NIH) panel that examined the evidence linking RS and health (Miller & Thoresen, 2003).

RELIGION AND SPIRITUALITY: IDENTICAL OR DISTINCT CONCEPTS?

Although rigorous epidemiological research in this area has been fairly recent, concern with the meaning of the terms *religion* and *spirituality* has a long if not controversial history (Pargament, 1997). The following basic questions seem at issue: Are religion (or religiousness) and spirituality the same? If not, in what ways do they differ? Should spirituality be subsumed within a religious framework, or is religion one of the manifestations or features of spirituality? Pargament (1999) made it clear that researchers and theorists in this area typically disagree on definitions of religion and spirituality, perhaps in the way that psychologists often disagree on what is the best way to view and assess personality or abnormality.

Broadly speaking, the term *religion* is often viewed as societal phenomena, involving social institutions with rules, rituals, covenants, and formal procedures. By contrast, a growing number view spirituality in terms of the individual's personal experience, often seen as connected to religion but not necessarily associated with any organized religion (Fuller, 2001; Miller & Thoresen, 1999; Roof, 1999). Religiousness, however, is often used to convey the individual's personal experience as part of an organized religion, a view advocated by William James (1902). In a sense, religiousness is synonymous with spirituality. For example, in several Northern European countries, religiousness is often used in ways that spirituality is increasingly used in the United States as a personal experience outside of being involved in formal religion (Gallup & Jones, 2001; Walsh, 1998).

The Oxford English Dictionary offers 10 pages of reference material on the concept of spirituality (Simpson & Weiner, 1991). Two related themes dominate. First, spirituality is concerned with life's most animating or vital principles or qualities (the term *spiritus* in Latin means "the breath," that which is most vital to life). Second, spirituality involves the more immaterial features of life, as distinct from the body or other more tangible and material things. Third, the spiritual involves seeking what is perceived as sacred in life, including an experiential striving to connect in some way with God or a higher power or ultimate reality in a transcending sense.

What is perceived as sacred can vary widely, including differing conceptions of God or another ultimate power, of what is transcendent, and about
different people, places, activities, and features of life deemed sacred or
divine. In many ways what connects religion and spirituality is their shared
concern with the sacred, especially with the need to foster spiritual practices
in living (Thoresen, Oman, & Harris, in press).

Some contend that religion is the more inclusive concept, with spirituality as religion's major focus: "Religion is a search for significance in ways
related to the sacred" (Pargament, 1999, p. 11). Others imply that spirituality
may be a more inclusive term than religion or religiousness (Roof, 1999).
We suspect that these constructs represent two overlapping circles (Venn
diagrams) with spirituality sharing with religion some overlapping areas and
with each having distinct, nonoverlapping areas (Miller & Thoresen, 2003).
We also believe that if spirituality is to mean something more than any
personal idiosyncratic belief or experience, it concerns seeking what is sacred
and transcendent in life. Put somewhat differently, spiritual striving has to
do with trying to get beyond one's own often highly self-absorbed ego (Walsh,
1998). A more extended discussion of the many cultural, psychological, and
theological issues surrounding the definition and conceptualization of these
terms is well beyond the scope of this chapter (see Emmons & Crumpler,
1999; Miller & Delaney, in press).

Miller and Thoresen (2003) recommended one way to conceptualize
spirituality and religiousness that seems to fit with existing methodological
and assessment approaches in the behavioral sciences. They offered the
following key assumptions about spirituality and religiousness as well as
religion:

- These concepts represent primarily functional or process-
  oriented phenomena, not fixed structural characteristics. That
  is, spiritual factors are concerned with the changing nature of
  what the person does, thinks, feels, and subjectively experiences
  within particular social cultural settings or contexts. In that
  sense, as with the term *health*, *spirituality* and *religiousness* are
  more action verbs than static nouns.
- Both religion and spirituality are multidimensional, existing in
  multidimensional space, and both are observable and have latent (i.e., not currently observable) features, much like the
  concepts of personality, health, and love. Just as personality is
  more than behavior, health is more than blood pressure, and
  love is more than sexual arousal, spirituality is more than personal experiences and religiousness more than attending church
  services. One does not, for example, just have some spirituality
  or none at all. Rather, all people have some configuration of

spirituality, just as all people have some pattern of personality or health.

- Both concepts in their entirety cannot be adequately assessed only by questionnaires of a single or a few items nor with only one mode of assessment, such as written surveys. Unlike fixed traits or unchanging characteristics of individuals, most spiritual and religious factors change with time and circumstances. Therefore multiple assessments are much more needed than brief single-occasion assessments.

It is possible to conceptualize religion and spirituality as having four major dimensions: (a) overt behaviors; (b) beliefs; (c) motivations, goals, and values; and (d) subjective experiences. Each is probably related to the other but appear distinct enough to assess separately. One of the major shortcomings in most research has been the failure to disaggregate the multiple dimensions of spirituality and religiousness (e.g., Powell, Shahabi, & Thoresen, 2003). That is, theory and assessment has been limited to a macro level and simple assessments (e.g., frequency of religious service attendance) rather than examining dimensions at a more micro specific level (e.g., specific beliefs and behaviors related to attending services; Seybold & Hill, 2001).

WHAT IS KNOWN REGARDING THE RELIGIOUS AND SPIRITUAL FACTOR–HEALTH CONNECTION?

In this section, we provide a general overview of the extensive literature on RS factor–health relationships. We summarize the conclusions of a recent National Institutes of Health (NIH) panel that examined the evidence that specific RS factor–health relationships exist. We discuss a recent meta-analysis on the relationship between RS factors and all-cause mortality, and comment on a few well-conducted state-of-the-art research studies on the relationships between attending religious services and mortality.

Religious and Spiritual Factors and Mortality, Morbidity, and Functional Disability

Associations between religious involvement, broadly defined, and various health outcomes have been reported (McCullough et al., 2000). The vast majority of the research has been cross-sectional and correlational in nature. Furthermore, research conducted to date has focused on religion or religiousness, not spirituality seen as independent of any religious affiliation. Such studies are much needed.

Those who are more religiously involved, compared to those not involved, have been found to have lower rates of coronary disease, emphysema, cirrhosis, and suicide (e.g., Comstock & Partridge, 1972); lower blood pressure (Larson, Koenig, & Kaplan, 1989); lower rates of myocardial infarction (Madalie, Kahn, & Neufeld, 1973); improved physical functioning, medical regime compliance, self-esteem, and lower anxiety and health-related worries one year after surgery in heart transplant patients (e.g., Harris et al., 1995); reduced levels of pain in cancer patients (Yates, Chalmer, & St. James, 1981); better perceived health and less medical service use (Frankel & Hewitt, 1994); decreased functional disability in the nursing home dwelling for elderly individuals (e.g., Idler & Kasl, 1997); and reduced all-cause mortality (McCullough et al., 2000). Hundreds of studies have reported positive relationships of RS and physical as well as mental health (e.g. Koenig, 1998; Levin, 1994). A major question, however, is whether these associations represent valid evidence that RS factors in some way cause or influence health status, either health processes or health outcomes (Oman & Thoresen, 2002).

Religious Involvement and All-Cause Mortality

To help shed light on this question, McCullough et al. (2000) examined 29 independent published studies, with a total sample of 125,826 adults. A total of 15 control variables (possible covariates that could account for differences in mortality) were used, ranging from sociodemographic factors to specific health behaviors. Higher frequency of religious attendance was found, independent of other plausible or established predictors, such as nonsmoking or exercise, to predict less risk of mortality People not attending services had 29% more risk of death (odds ration [OR] = 1.29, confidence interval [CI] = 1.20, 1.39) or an effect size of 0.10 compared to people attending services at least weekly or more. This difference accounted for about seven years difference in life expectancy. Other factors, as expected, also significantly predicted fewer deaths, such as being married, having good social support, having positive perceptions of overall health, and being female. Public measures of RS involvement, such as attending services, predicted mortality. However, measures of private religiousness, such as reading scripture or perceived comfort from religious beliefs, were not predictive.

Note that the effect of religious attendance was not readily explained by higher levels of social support, which itself was also a significant independent predictor of less mortality. Oman, Thoresen, and McMahon (1999) found that among older adults, those volunteering to serve others in need (for many a spiritual practice) also with higher levels of social support combined to have an additive effect, predicting more than 60% fewer deaths compared to those not volunteering and not having higher social support.

Keep in mind that all measures used in these studies were brief, often consisting of only one or a few questionnaire item(s), and can be criticized as not assessing adequately the constructs involved. For example, using one questionnaire item about how often one attends religious services does not capture the breadth of experiences involved in attending services. Some may be health-enhancing, some unrelated to health status, and some could even be health-endangering. When averaged together, we remain ignorant of those who may benefit a great deal from a spiritual practice and those who may be harmed from a health perspective (Thoresen et al., in press). Note also that few psychological variables were used in these studies, nor, with rare exception, have more specific measures of contextual and cultural factors been assessed (Chatters, 2000).

A Few Well-Controlled Epidemiological Studies

Earlier work in this area may not have sufficiently acknowledged the need to control for competing explanations that could account for health outcomes. For example, cigarette smoking is clearly related to morbidity and mortality. Failure to adequately control for smoking in any health-related study involving RS factors understandingly raises questions. Recently, the focus has been on using state-of-the-art epidemiological research designs, often with large samples, to see if RS factors predict health status, especially mortality.

These four studies do not demonstrate that RS factors cause or produce less mortality or better health, that is because these data remain correlational, even if they have been gathered prospectively (Ellison & Levin, 1998). They suggest that, on average, religious service attendance is indeed associated with less mortality from all causes. But unexplained is which persons may, in terms of health, benefit more or less, nor what mechanisms account for any benefit gained.

The study by Hummer, Rogers, Nam, and Ellison (1999) deserves additional comment. First, the study used the largest national sample (> 21,000) yet examined and explored the influence of more than 15 covariates. Second, seven cause-of-death variables were also studied besides all-cause mortality (e.g., circulatory or infectious mortality). Third, the results showed somewhat of a dose–response effect in terms of all-cause mortality. Compared to those attending more than once a week, nonattenders had 50 percent more deaths, occasional attenders (once a month or so) 24 percent more deaths, and weekly attenders 21 percent more deaths. Fourth, different disease categories revealed different outcomes. For example, religious attendance significantly predicted less respiratory and residual (other) related deaths in the full model (all covariates used). That is, compared to those attending more than once weekly, nonattenders had twice as many respiratory deaths (RR = 2.11, p < .05) and had almost 2½ times (RR = 2.42, p < .05) more deaths from residual causes. However, the association between religious service attendance and circulatory diseases (the largest single disease type) showed only marginal significance (p < .10) in the full model (RR = 1.32), as did deaths from infectious diseases (RR = 2.92). If the influence of the control variables, such as sociodemographics, social support, health status, and health behaviors, had not been explored, the relationship of religious attendance and mortality would have been greatly exaggerated (e.g., for all cause mortality RR = 1.87 instead of 1.50). In this study high religious attendance proved to be more predictive of mortality than moderate or light smoking (but not heavy smoking), age, or ethnic group (Black vs. White), and slightly less predictive of mortality than male gender.

Musick, House, and Williams (in press) demonstrated the need to disaggregate broad, complex dimensions such as "religious involvement." These investigators explored various combinations of covariates to see which best clarify possible RS factors and mortality relationships. They found that once health behaviors (e.g., smoking, exercise) were entered in the analysis, religious attendance no longer predicted mortality. However, when they entered private religiousness into the model (e.g., watching religious television, reading scripture) as a separate factor not combined with other spiritual factors, attendance was again a significant predictor of mortality. Such findings revealed the urgent need to assess more specific factors instead of only using broad RS concepts. One can readily speculate, given the way constructs have been measured, that some of the RS and health relationships may actually turn out to be much stronger than current evidence suggests. As already noted, possible negative or harmful relationships may also become clearer, especially if more psychological factors are used to permit study of possible individual-by-RS interactions effects (e.g., narcissistic characteristics interacting with religious attendance and mortality).

Finally, the issue of possible pathways or mechanisms by which RS factors might influence health status was raised by Strawbridge, Cohen, Shema, and Kaplan (1997). In the only major RS and health study to date using repeated measures (four occasions over 28 years), they found evidence that those frequently attending services were much more likely to alter their negative health behaviors than those never attending services. The differences in making changes ranged from about 40% to 90% for such behaviors as stopping smoking; starting to exercise regularly; and improving social, community, and family contacts. Unfortunately, RS factors were not assessed repeatedly.

Strawbridge et. al., (2001) presented more recent evidence in this ongoing study. Adjusting for age and gender, high attenders who were depressed were less likely to remain depressed ($RR = 2.31$, $p < .01$) than depressed–nonattenders. In addition, they found dramatic gender differences, possibly explaining why high-attending men showed no differences in mortality compared to nonattending men. Women were found to be more likely to change health behaviors than men. For example, high-attending women stopped heavy alcohol drinking more often ($RR = 4.67$) and were no longer depressed ($RR = 3.56$) compared to women who never or seldom attended services. Men, by contrast, were much less likely to improve their health behaviors significantly. Evidence for health behaviors possibly mediating RS factors (such as high frequency of service attendance) with mortality is provided by these data. That is, the association of religious attendance with reduced mortality may be explained, at least in part, by changes in risky health behaviors, such as abusing alcohol and smoking (attendance → health behaviors → mortality). Evidence in this study could be interpreted as demonstrating that RS involvement has no influence on mortality for men, only for women. However such interpolation would move beyond the limits of this study that only used frequencies of attending religious services assessed on only one occasion in 1964 to represent RS factors over 28 years.

This study suggests that men who reported frequent attendance of religious services in 1964 did not differ significantly from nonattending men in 1964 with all-cause mortality over 28 years. However, no information on these men about other RS-related behaviors, beliefs, motivations, values, and experiences is available. Also, little is known about the high-attending women from this study other than their attendance of religious services. Is the observed relationship with reduced mortality for these women adequately explained by their changes in risky health behaviors, such as reduced smoking or depression? Was the magnitude of change in these risky behaviors predictive of reduced mortality? These questions deserve study in helping clarify how an RS factor such as attendance alters health outcomes.

Need for Mediational Studies

Studies that probe how specific social, psychological, and contextual factors may mediate the observed RS and health relationship are greatly needed. Although results of recent studies cited earlier suggest that religious attendance independently predicted all-cause mortality (McCullough et al., 2000), they did not suggest how religious attendance could explain reductions in mortality. This relationship seems neither direct nor straightforward. One of the problems with a "unique variance" approach (i.e., seeking independent added value for any predictor) often used in longitudinal studies is that it may not adequately describe relationships among factors often related to each other (e.g., religious attendance may be related to perceived social or emotional support). A useful step-by-step strategy to examine the evidence of possible mediating factors has been offered by Baron and Kenny (1986) and is further discussed by George, Ellison, and Larson (2002) in terms of RS research. Tix and Frazier (1998) offer a rare example of exploring possible mediators on life satisfaction in how Protestant and Catholic women and others cope with the aftermath of surgery.

Which Comes First? The Temporal Sequence Issue

An issue that emerges when state-of-the-art studies are considered is in what order do variables influence or relate to the health outcome? Often, the sequence of events that eventually may influence health remains unclear. One variable might even occur initially before another factor but then take place concurrently with still other factors. Clarifying the sequence of variables can improve our understanding the role(s) of possible causes and how they function over time.

T. Miller, Smith, Turner, Guijarro, and Hallet (1996) offered a useful example of ways to reduce confusion and a caveat about relying on popular cross-lag panel and structural equation models (SEM). Many predictor and outcome variables are themselves variable, as the name implies, rather than constant or highly stable factors. If an RS predictor fluctuates, such as a specific RS behavior, cognition, or experience, then correlational research designs assessing RS factors on only one occasion over several years can create invalid, if not misleading, evidence. Miller et al. (1996) demonstrated the problem of unstable temporal order of predictors in studying what leads to marijuana use in teenagers. He found that cross-lag panel analysis and structural equation models provided results indicating that self-use preceded marijuana use by friends. However, use of either log linear or discrete time series analysis revealed a more complicated sequence. First-time marijuana use was found to occur before use by friends, but the pattern of self- and friend use occurring concurrently best predicted continued marijuana use.

Cross-lag correlation, path analysis, and SEMs have been shown to be suspect for trying to tease out temporal or causal relationships from even longitudinal data, to say nothing of the heightened difficulties with cross-sectional studies. The work of Rogosa (e.g., Rogosa, 1980, 1987, 1988) has described the advantages and use of a growth-curve approach to modeling change over time, especially for understanding individual differences in growth-curve patterns. These methods are available and may greatly improve understanding of the influence of variables of individual health-related pathways.

Experimental Religious and Spiritual Studies With Health Outcomes

Unfortunately, relatively few experimentally designed studies of RS factors and health exist. Worthington et al. (1996) reviewed almost 150 RS and health-related studies, including those examining mental health. Roughly, only 7% involved experimental designs. Such studies have primarily been conducted in the areas of meditation and prayer, mostly intercessory prayer in which one or more people pray for the recovery of someone suffering, for example, from a serious chronic disease. Such studies, especially meditation studies have, however, often been conducted within a secular framework (e.g., Kabat-Zinn et al., 1998). Seeman, Dubin, and Seeman (2003) have carefully reviewed these studies in terms of their impact on neurophysiological outcomes (also see Miller, 1999).

Alexander, Langer, Newman, and Chandler (1989) conducted one of the few studies to date that compared transcendental mediation (TM), mindfulness meditation (MF), and relaxation training. In addition, an assessment control condition was used. Participants were assessed in terms of short-term mortality rates and reversing age-related declines in physical health. After 36 months, the TM group was found most improved on measures of cognitive and behavioral flexibility, mental health, and systolic blood pressure, followed by the MF group, the relaxation group, and the assessment control group, respectively. After three years, the survival rate for the TM group was 100% compared to 87.5% for the MF group, 65% for the relaxation group, and 62.5% for the assessment control group.

Other controlled intervention studies using an RS factor as an intervention or adjunct to treatment have been conducted. For example, Propst et al. (1992) found cognitive–behavioral therapy using religious imagery to be somewhat more effective with religious clients than a nonreligious version, although the benefit was not maintained at follow-up. Byrd (1988) and Sicher, Targ, Moore, and Smith (1998) have reported double-blind studies on the effect of intercessory prayer on mortality and other health outcomes. Among patients recovering from acute myocardial infarction, for example, Byrd found that patients in the prayer condition did substantially better than control patients on a number of health-related outcome categories at the experimentwide $p < .05$ level, including requiring 7% fewer antibiotics at discharge ($p < .005$) and 6% less need for intubation ($p < .002$) than among the comparison group. In addition, they had 6% fewer pulmonary edema ($p < .03$), 6% less congestive heart failure ($p < .03$), and 5% less cardiopulmonary arrest ($p < .02$), although these differences failed to reach statistical significance at the experimentwide $p < .05$ level.

In a rigorously conducted replication of the Byrd study published in the *Archives of Internal Medicine*, Harris, Gowda, et al. (1999) found that a

prayed-for group of coronary intensive care unit (CCU) patients had better
CCU overall course scores (index of several major procedures and outcomes,
including reinfarction and death) than the usual care group, but length and
number of hospital stays were not significantly affected. Researchers in this
study controlled for response expectancy effects (Kirsch & Lynn, 1999) by
obtaining permission from their institutional review board (IRB) not to
inform anyone that patients may be prayed for. Thus, attending physicians,
nurses, and patients remained uninformed about the study. Results such as
these do not shed light on how prayer works, only that it may have objectively
measurable and clinically important effects on health outcomes. For a review
of other spiritually or religiously oriented health interventions, see Harris,
Thoresen, McCullough, and Larson (1999).

Religious and Spiritual Factors and Mental Health

Religious and spiritual involvement or experiences appear associated
with a variety of desirable as well as undesirable mental health outcomes
(e.g., Bergin, 1983; Exline, Yali, & Sanderson, 2000; Gartner, Larson, &
Allen, 1991; Levin, Markides, & Ray, 1996; McCullough, Larson, & Worthington, 1998; Pargament, Smith, Koenig, & Perez, 1998; Worthington et al.,
1996). Certain indicators or forms of RS involvement, such as greater
frequency of church attendance, have been related to greater subjective
well-being and life and marital satisfaction, as well as less depressive symptoms, suicide, delinquency, and substance abuse (McCullough et al., 1998).
Others researchers have found certain RS factors, such as the presence of
religious strain (Exline et al., 2000), difficulty forgiving God (Exline, Yali,
& Lobel, 1999), and "negative" religious coping styles (Pargament et al.,
1998) related to undesirable mental health variables, such as greater stress,
depression, and suicidality.

Worthington et al. (1996) mentioned that the relationships observed
between RS variables and health variables depend greatly on which multidimensional constructs are used to measure outcomes as well as RS factors.
Consistent with this view, Gartner et al. (1991) observed that most studies
linking religious commitment to psychopathology used paper-and-pencil
personality tests in an attempt to measure theoretical constructs, whereas
research linking RS factors to positive mental health have focused on
behavioral events that could be reliably observed and measured. Of the 30
studies on the RS–mental health relationship reviewed by Worthington
et al. (1996), some found RS involvement associated with desirable mental
health variables (e.g., Ellison, 1991) and some found no association with
undesirable variables (e.g., Masters, Bergin, Reynolds, & Sullivan, 1991).
Two studies found certain forms of religious involvement or experience
positively related to undesirable mental health variables, such as shame

(Richards, Smith, & Davis, 1989) or negatively associated with desirable variables, such as well-being (Galanter, 1986). In a review of 139 research studies published in the *American Journal of Psychiatry* and *Archives of General Psychiatry* between 1978 through 1989, Larson et al. (1992) generally found a positive relationship between religious commitment and mental health.

An important literature exists examining the role of RS in recovery from drug and alcohol abuse. Miller and Bennett (1998) reviewed the scientific evidence that various assertions regarding relationships between specific RS factors and variables related to addiction and substance abuse could be supported. The following assertions were found to be strongly supported by the evidence—that is, with multiple studies with appropriate research designs, RS involvement predicts less use and problems related to substance use (e.g., Hardesty & Kirby, 1995), involvement in Alcoholics Anonymous predicts better outcome after outpatient treatment (e.g., Williams, Stout, & Erickson, 1986), significant denominational differences exist with respect to substance abuse (e.g., Francis, 1994), and meditation-based treatments reduce alcohol use and problems (e.g., Alexander, 1994). Other assertions were supported by "reasonable" or "some" evidence. The interested reader is also referred to Booth and Martin (1998).

The current state of empirical research in the area of RS and mental health, although clearly suggestive, remains modest. Broad or at times ambiguous measures of religiosity, such as religious involvement, have provided correlational results promising enough to warrant additional investigation. However, more investigation into possible underlying mechanisms is needed from well-controlled longitudinal studies. Many studies have suffered from several research problems, especially participant selection and sampling problems (George et al., 2002). Issues of inadequate measurement are a particular concern, because using only questionnaires to assess mental health may not provide data that are valid (Shedler, Mayman, & Mavis, 1993).

Recent studies have begun to address some of these issues by using better sampling strategies, controlling for relevant covariates, and using prospective instead of cross-sectional designs (e.g., Levin et al., 1996). Some studies have begun to look more closely at the role of specific contextual factors, such as the extent to which community residents adhere to a single religion or a small number of faiths (e.g., Ellison, Bartkowski, & Anderson, 1999; Ellison, Burr, & McCall, 1997). These studies generally have found favorable associations between religious involvement and well-being for specific populations while controlling for relevant covariates. More studies are needed to clarify what type of religious involvement is associated with what mental health variable for whom under specific conditions. Again, the need to move beyond exclusive use of questionnaires on one occasion is imperative.

Besides being associated with mental health and illness, RS factors may also be important in the treatment process or therapeutic relationship. Substantial differences have emerged in religious values between clients and health care providers, and these differences could influence treatment outcomes, especially for highly religious clients (Chatters, 2000; Worthington et al., 1996). As already noted, some evidence suggests that when secular interventions, such as cognitive–behavioral therapy (CBT), are adapted to include specific RS concepts, effectiveness may be increased for religious clients (e.g., Propst et al., 1992). Given the large number of religiously active people in the United States, this approach to treatment deserves particular attention.

The fairly extensive RS and mental health literature, given its many limitations, leads us to believe that RS involvement may have positive, negative, or negligible influence on mental health status. Outcomes probably depend on the extent and form of the RS involvement and several specific person and contextual factors (Chatters, 2000). As mentioned earlier, the current wave of theoretical and empirical attention devoted to establishing the salutary effects of RS involvement may have been an understandable reaction to the long-standing pathologizing of religious involvement and spiritual experience by many scientists generally and psychologists and psychiatrists in particular (e.g., Ellis, 1971; Freud, 1961). A more balanced view and research agenda will clarify the health implications of various forms of RS involvement and how moderating or mediating factors associated with person and context factors may influence health (Lukoff, Lu, & Turner, 1992). Note also that the *Multicultural Guidelines* recently published by American Psychological Association recognizes religious and spiritual beliefs and practices as a multicultural issue deserving consideration in professional training, service, and research (American Psychological Association, 2002).

STATE OF THE SCIENTIFIC EVIDENCE: THE OFFICE OF BEHAVIORAL AND SOCIAL SCIENCES RESEARCH IN THE NATIONAL INSTITUTES OF HEALTH PANEL

In 1999, the Office of Behavioral and Social Sciences Research in the National Institutes of Health (OBSSR/NIH) created an expert panel of behavioral scientists to conduct a rigorous and dispassionate review of the empirical literature on RS and health. Next we offer a summary of some major findings, focused primarily on physical health (see George, Ellison, & Larson, 2002, for mental health review). Some comments are offered on possible psychosocial mediators, neurobiological findings, measurement, and contextual factors. We strongly encourage reading articles from this panel

(George et al., 2002; Hill & Pargament, 2003; Miller & Thoresen, 2003; Powell, Shahabi, & Thoresen, 2003; Seeman et al., 2003).

Physical Health Report

A system was used for evaluating and rating individual studies using A for excellent to C for serious methodological problems (Powell et al., 2003). In addition, the rated strength of the evidence (rated from persuasive to insufficient or no evidence) was used to describe relationships between different RS dimensions (e.g., public religiousness, depth of religiousness, or private religiousness) and specific health outcomes (e.g., all-cause mortality, cardiovascular morbidity, physical disability). Each study was judged on the adequacy of how RS was conceptualized and assessed, the quality of the research design (e.g., how many and what kind of "control" variables or covariates, cross-sectional or prospective), and the appropriateness of statistical methods. Attention was given separately to whether the data supported an RS factor as an independent variable. The following summary captures the highlights of this report:

- Persuasive evidence exists of a positive and independent relationship between attending religious services weekly or more often and less all-cause mortality in general population samples. However some studies also provide evidence not supporting this relationship.
- Insufficient evidence exists of any RS relationship and cancer mortality.
- Some evidence exists of a positive RS relationship for cardiovascular mortality.
- Persuasive evidence exists of a positive relationship for attending religious services and other types of mortality (other than cardiovascular disease or cancer).
- Some evidence exists not supporting an RS relationship with cardiovascular or cancer morbidity.
- Reasonable evidence exists of a positive RS relationship with combined cardiovascular morbidity and mortality.
- Persuasive evidence exits that RS factors are not associated with combined cancer morbidity and mortality.
- Some evidence exists of a positive relationship between attendance at religious services and disability as well as for RS factors and recovery from acute illness.

Powell et al. (2003) called for research to clarify why frequent attenders at religious services experience lower mortality rates, especially noting the almost complete lack of study of psychological variables that seem highly promising for providing insights into this major finding. They also cited a need to clarify and begin studies of those people who are highly spiritual but not involved in any organized religion, because growing numbers identify themselves as spiritual but not religious (e.g., Fuller, 2001; Roof, 1999). The unexamined area of positive emotions and behaviors was noted, because they may explain part of the RS and health relationship. Cited, for example, were recent studies (e.g., Musick, Herzog, & House, 1999) demonstrating that volunteering to help others, often called "selfless service" in religious contexts, has been shown in well-controlled epidemiological studies to predict less all-cause mortality. In one study, volunteering was found to independently predict mortality more strongly than receiving social support or moderate levels of smoking and exercise (Oman et al., 1999).

Possible Psychosocial Mediators

George et al. (2002) found that despite the well-accepted notion that psychosocial factors, such as social ties and social interaction, play an important role in any RS effect on health, the evidence for this was essentially weak and inconsistent. In assessing 10 hypotheses, only two were judged to be persuasive in terms of the evidence: Health practices do mediate a small proportion of the relationship of attending services and mortality; and social ties failed to show evidence that they mediate a small proportion of attending services and mortality. Most areas could not be evaluated because of insufficient evidence.

In addition, minimal evidence was found that religious attendance mediated reduced depression and that religious affiliation–denomination mediated overall health status. The authors called for more studies of psychological factors, such as perceived coherence in one's life and various personality factors. Especially recommended were studies that assess RS and other variables repeatedly over time, especially to clarify the temporal order of mediating and moderating variables, currently lacking in the literature.

Neurobiological Pathways

Seeman et al. (2003) commented on the promising but small number of well-controlled studies on RS and physiological processes related to health. Some studies have looked at RS and blood pressure or immune functioning, but almost all have used some form of meditation–relaxation as the RS factor under study. These studies have examined effects on brain activity, immune competence, neuroendocrine levels (e.g., cortisol), and cardiovascular reactivity. Most studies have used special populations and limited RS factors, most of which are associated with Eastern religious traditions, such as TM. Suggestive evidence implicates meditation practices with changes in cardiovascular, neuroendocrine, and immune functioning. RS factors may play an important role in reducing a person's allostatic load—that is, the burden on the body's major regulatory systems and organs to adjust for imbalances (e.g., overload of sympathetic or immune systems) caused by demands and stressors (McEwen, 1998).

Contextual Factors

Although largely ignored until recently, except for religious affiliation and denomination factors, little is known from controlled empirical studies about specific contexts and their relationship to health and RS. Chatters (2000) suggested reasons why contextual factors have been neglected: stereotyping, a historical focus, and lack of developmentally sensitive perspectives. Contextual factors, such as family, are very influential over time, although this may not be obvious to outsiders nor detected in studies that assess RS with one or a few questionnaire items. Almost all contextual factors used have been reductionistic. Examples include viewing Asian Americans or Hispanics as if they were homogeneous groups or viewing church organizations or settings as if they were interchangeable (American Psychological Association, 2002).

RESEARCH ISSUES AND RECOMMENDATIONS

Several conceptual, methodological, and analytical issues are relevant to improving of RS factor and health research. We briefly discuss a few issues and possible next steps in research in the next sections.

How Might Religious and Spiritual Factors Work to Influence Health?

Different models have tried to explain the relationship between RS and health outcomes. None has adequately accounted for the complexities involved. Powell et al. (2003) offered several possible pathways that RS variables could eventually influence health status. Overall, 10 major constructs were identified, all of which could indirectly alter health-related processes. These include:

- *Context*: Background and situational factors, such as demographics, social background, psychological makeup bearing on genetics;
- *Social environment*: Influences both spiritual and religious factors and person variables, including family, social network, culture, stressors, among others;

- *Person variables*: Broad range of current health-related behaviors, cognitions, and emotional functioning, including positive as well as negative person variables;
- *Neural and neuroendocrine mediators*: Linked to person variables, they include a variety of neural and endocrine functioning, such as sympathetic adrenal medullary pathway and HPA axis (e.g., cortisol);
- *Target organs*: Influenced by neural–neuroendocrine processes reacting with pathogens to produce symptoms. Includes, for example, cardiovascular and immune functioning;
- *Symptoms*: Includes specific symptoms (e.g., pain, arrhythmias, cholesterol/lipids);
- *Chronic illness*: Persistent patterns, including symptoms that may not be readily observable, leading to chronic illness–disease, such as congestive heart failure, infectious diseases, addictive disorders;
- *Healing*: Changes in symptoms and degree of illness–disease may be experienced, sometimes occurring even in the presence of diminishing or unchanged health status;
- *Health*: The model's end state broadly defined to include physical, social, and psychological states and processes, such as perceived meaning and purpose in life, hope, sense of coherence, and self-management–mastery skills.

Clearly, from this kind of broad perspective a variety of processes are involved, far beyond the one-directional, univariate framework often used. Oman and Thoresen (2002) and others (Levin, 1994) have cautioned against reductionistic frameworks that ask, in effect, "Does religion cause health?" as if either construct was simple and straightforward (e.g., a person is either religious or not religious or people are either healthy or sick). Many processes are at work in a variety of settings when it comes to health and well-being, as well as disease. The same is true of spirituality, religion, and religiousness (Miller & Thoresen, 2003; Pargament, 1997). One could also argue, given the multiple processes that may be involved, that health status, especially changes in health, could also influence certain spiritual and religious factors, such as experiencing a greater closeness or relationship with God or higher power, increasing daily spiritual experiences, or spending more time serving those in need. Such changes in turn could alter particular health-related processes. Keefe and colleagues touched on this complexity, for example, in finding that greater daily spiritual experiences best predicted pain level the following day and indirectly influenced self-efficacy to manage pain that in turn predicted longer term pain (Keefe et al., 2001).

Unfortunately, almost all empirical studies to date have not been designed to test conceptual models or theory but rather to empirically establish that a nontrivial relationship exists between an RS factor and some health outcome, often morbidity or mortality. An important next step is for researchers to describe specific models and possible mechanisms hypothesized to occur and to design studies capable of providing support or disconfirmatory evidence about models and mechanisms. Such models should also consider how health-related concepts are used.

In a much-publicized study, Oxman, Freeman, and Manheimer (1995) found lack of participation in social or community groups and absence of perceived strength and comfort from religion to predict markedly higher mortality in patients who underwent elective heart surgery. The tempting conclusion is that strength and comfort from religion and participation in groups reduces mortality. Although this conclusion seems supported by the data, it may be premature. In the Oxman et al. (1995) study, it is possible that people who gained strength and comfort from their religion were also those who experienced strength and comfort from a variety of sources, such as friendships, community, and marriage. It is also possible that the capacity to experience life as comforting and strengthening predicts mortality independent of the source. Reporting strength and comfort from one's religion may have been a proxy for optimism or another dispositional or personality factor that was independent of religion in any integral fashion. With clearer pictures of how RS is conceptualized, and improved strategies to clarify relationships between variables, coupled with experimental designs, understanding of the processes linking possible RS factors with health will become clearer and, one hopes, will lead to implications for improved assessment and practice.

Ryff and Singer (1998) offered an intriguing model of health to consider that goes well beyond the biomedical perspective. They argued that health is far more than the lack of disease and suggested several positive psychological concepts, such as meaning and purpose and perceived self-mastery. Use of an expanded conception of health could help bring to bear the personal strengths and resiliences of persons that often remain ignored but could greatly clarify why some benefit more or less from health care practices and from spiritual and religious factors related to health and disease.

The Cheerleading Problem

Indiscriminate advocacy can be as detrimental to the development of knowledge as rigid, closed-minded skepticism. Much recent research has focused on the health benefits of RS involvement rather than on potential or actual health liabilities of such involvement. The focus on the positive influences of RS involvement may be the understandable reaction to the traditional view in psychology and psychiatry that pathologizes religion (e.g., Ellis, 1971). Note that until the *Diagnostic and Statistical Manual of Mental Disorders* was last revised (*DSM–IV;* American Psychiatric Association, 1994), RS-related issues were seen as indicative of pathology rather than normal adjustment problems. Unfortunately, research designs or instrumentation that gives RS factors every chance to succeed and little if any chance to fail risk being dismissed as religious advocacy in scientific clothing. Not only must research in this area be rigorously designed and conducted and use appropriate analytical tools, but energy must be put into examining the undesirable consequences of specific forms of RS involvement.

Recently the highly critical commentary of some, such as Sloan and colleagues (e.g., Sloan et al., 1999), warning of the grave dangers if medical and psychological health practitioners use RS factors, has provided a useful antidote to overstated beneficial claims. Yet repeating excessive criticisms with little or no well-controlled empirical evidence to support them becomes just another form of advocacy, what could be called "negative cheerleading" (Sloan & Bagiella, 2002).

Intuitively there seems to be more appeal that RS involvement may have either beneficial or detrimental impact on health, depending on a host of relevant factors. Some impressive research in this area has begun to document healthy and unhealthy forms of RS involvement (e.g., Exline et al., 1999, 2000; Pargament et al., 1998). Rather than asking if the behaviors, beliefs, and experiences that constitute a person's spiritual or religious involvement are only associated with better health, it is more useful and scientifically sound to ask which facets of RS involvement, given particular person and context factors, are associated with undesirable health outcomes (e.g., Exline et al., 2000; Richards & Bergin, 1997). Booth (1992) offered, for example, case material on the health effects of religious extremism and fanaticism as well as religious addictions and dependencies. Pargament (1997) discussed the downside of negative religious coping and those struggling with their religious beliefs or spiritual experiences.

Linking Conceptualization and Measurement

Religion and spirituality are complex, multidimensional constructs. In designing studies and relevant measurement tools, it is important to specify which aspect of the construct is being measured as well as a theoretical rationale for doing so. Ellison and Levin (1998) made a useful theoretical distinction between the functional and behavioral aspects of religious involvement. They argued that identification and measurement of the possible functional roles of religion, such as providing an existential or meaning framework, coping strategies, or support for health behaviors, will pay dividends in terms of understanding the mechanisms through which health is influenced. Most, but not all, empirical studies have focused on behavioral aspects of religious involvement, such as church attendance, and have ignored the functions religious involvement or spiritual experiences may or may not serve.

For example, Pargament and colleagues (e.g., Pargament, Ensing, Falgout, & Olsen, 1990; Pargament et al., 1998) have focused on religious coping, as distinct from other religious or spiritual behaviors, and have identified different types of religious coping as well as the desirable and undesirable health correlates of each. This approach is grounded in the idea that one function of religion is to help people cope with life stressors. These researchers constructed definitions that distinguish between religious and nonreligious coping. In this way, the theoretical proposition that religion serves a coping function can be tested. Once different forms of religious coping have been characterized and assessed, more precise and useful statements can be made regarding the health consequences of particular religious coping behaviors in particular situations by people with certain characteristics.

Assessment of specific features of a particular domain (either religion or spirituality) with instruments validated for the target population will yield more useful results than only using a more general factor, such as frequency of religious service attendance (Hill & Pargament, 2003; Miller & Thoresen, 1999). Furthermore, we need to operationalize concepts in ways that challenge conceptual models and have at least the potential of data-embarrassing hypotheses (i.e., providing disconfirming evidence). Thoresen and Eagleston (1985) offered some examples of controlled studies designed to challenge a theoretical explanation presumably supported by empirical findings from other studies. We also need to heed the notion that not all spiritual or religious experiences and processes can be adequately assessed and understood by current scientific methods or concepts. In that sense we may have problems similar to those faced by theoretical physics and cosmology in trying to understand and explain how the universe works.

CONCLUSION

Conclusions about the emerging area of RS and health as well as concerns need to be highly tentative and stated more in the spirit of reasoned conjectures based on mostly suggestive evidence. These following conjectures and concerns strike us as justified at this point in time. We have recognized elsewhere the difficulties in dealing with the topic of spirituality, religiousness, and health from a more dispassionate and detached yet sensitive perspective (Oman & Thoresen, 2002; Thoresen, 1999; Thoresen &

Harris, 2002; Thoresen, Harris, & Oman, 2001). Some may find our conjectures overly conservative and cautious, others may see them as overly optimistic. We hope our comments will appear reasonable and justified, encouraging some to take up the question of RS and health and study it empirically.

- With the large number of Americans who currently profess a belief in God or a higher power (96%), attend religious services regularly (42%), consider their religious–spiritual beliefs as very important in their lives (67%), associate frequent religious involvement with greater happiness (47%), and express the need for spiritual growth (82%), RS factors clearly deserve consideration by health care professionals in research, training, and in conventional as well as alternative–complementary health care practice (Gallup, 1995; Myers, 2000).
- RS factors are significantly associated with some physical, mental, and overall health factors, but the lack of adequate controls and designs in many studies has seriously limited understanding of how these relationships work.
- Evidence linking frequent attendance at religious services to reduced all-cause mortality, and to a lesser extent of cardiovascular diseases, is persuasive, but our understanding of this relationship remains unclear. However, evidence linking religious attendance and other RS factors to cancer has not been demonstrated.
- Evidence linking RS factors to mental health and other health and disease problems remains suggestive at best. Confusion about such relationships may be a result of failure to use adequate control variables known to influence mental health and other health problems and as a result of the lack of studies exploring possible mediating and moderating variables, such as person variables.
- Missing in almost all major studies has been the careful study of person and psychological factors (distinct from social support or social ties), specific contextual or environmental factors, and physiological processes that could clarify pathways linking RS to health outcomes. In addition, RS factors represent a multicultural issue and merits consideration as a significant feature of a person's lifestyle that can influence health positively or negatively, especially when health is viewed as a multidimensional construct that extends far beyond a biomedical or biological framework.
- The need to use a much greater variety of research designs and assessment strategies, combining more qualitative with more

quantitative methods, seems imperative. Problems, questions, and issues need to dictate the use of particular designs and methods.

- Evidence is generally lacking that RS-related factors, such as providing help to others (selfless service or altruistic behavior), forgiveness, and meditation, provide preventive and remedial health benefits, but it is highly suggestive and deserves careful study.
- Recently the topic of spiritual modeling has emerged based primarily on Bandura's social cognitive theory (Bandura, 2003; Oman & Thoresen, 2003). This area of observational learning and the related vicarious processes seem especially promising as a way to understand how many spiritual and religious beliefs and practices are acquired and maintained. Conceivably some of the most positive as well as the most negative effects of RS factors on health could be better understood by careful study of who is serving as influential spiritual models and what are the consequences of such modeling in terms of overall health and well-being effects.
- The notion that some RS factors could lead in time to less disease and illness and greater subjective well-being and quality of life is theoretically plausible and deserves to be studied from a broad perspective that spans the social, behavioral, and medical sciences in collaboration of those in the humanities.

Perhaps the 21st century will provide the needed impetus to health psychologists and other professionals to reconsider their perspectives on the role of RS factors in health and well-being along with disease, illness, and disabilities. Few psychologists have received any professional training on this topic. Yet it remains a major concern for many, if not most, of those we serve as well as those whom we study. As with some issues of church and state, reproductive health, and morality and character, matters of the spirit are issues that often elicit strong reactions charged with emotional energy. We believe, however, that the time has come to address this topic with rigor and with respect. Significant improvements in health care effectiveness, quality of life, and well-being could emerge if we do so with the patience and perseverance required.

REFERENCES

Alexander, C. N. (1994). Treating and preventing alcohol, nicotine and drug abuse through transcendental meditation: A review and meta-analysis. *Alcoholism Treatment Quarterly, 11,* 13–87.

Alexander, C. N., Langer, E. J., Newman, R. I., & Chandler, H. M. (1989). Transcendental meditation, mindfulness and longevity: An experimental study with the elderly. *Journal of Personality and Social Psychology, 57*, 950–964.

American Psychiatric Association. (1994). *Diagnostic and statistical manual of mental disorders* (4th ed.). Washington, DC: Author.

American Psychological Association. (2002). *Guidelines on multicultural education, training, research, practice, and organizational change for psychologists.* Washington, DC: Author.

Bandura, A. (2003). On the psychological mechanisms of spiritual modeling. *International Journal for the Psychology of Religion, 13*, 167–173.

Baron, R. M., & Kenny, D. A. (1986). The moderator–mediator variable distinction in social psychological research: Conceptual, strategic, and statistical considerations. *Journal of Personality and Social Psychology, 51*, 1173–1182.

Baumeister, R. F. (2002). Religion and psychology: Introduction to the special issue. *Psychological Inquiry, 13*, 165–247.

Bergin, A. E. (1983). Religiosity and mental health: A critical reevaluation and meta-analysis. *Professional Psychology: Research and Practice, 14*, 170–184.

Booth, L. (1992). *When God becomes a drug: Breaking the chains of religious addiction and abuse.* Los Angles: Tarcher.

Booth, J., & Martin, J. E., (1998). Spiritual and religious factors in substance use, dependence, and recovery. In H. Koenig (Ed.), *Handbook of religion and mental health* (pp. 175–202). San Diego, CA: Academic Press.

Byrd, R. B. (1988). Positive therapeutic effects of intercessory prayer in a coronary care unit population. *Southern Medical Journal, 81*, 826–829.

Chatters, L. M. (2000). Religion and health: Public health research and practice. *Annual Review of Public Health, 21*, 335–367.

Chopra, D. (2000). *How to know God; The soul's journey into the mystery of mysteries.* New York: Random House.

Comstock, G. W., & Partridge, K. B. (1972). Church attendance and health. *Journal of Chronic Diseases, 25*, 665–672.

Ellis, A. (1971). *The case against religion: A psychotherapists view.* New York: Institute for Rational Living.

Ellison, C. G. (1991). Religious involvement and subjective well-being. *Journal of Health and Social Behavior, 32*, 80–99.

Ellison, C. G., Bartkowski, J. P., & Anderson, K. L. (1999). Are there religious variations in domestic violence? *Journal of Family Issues, 20*, 87–113.

Ellison, C. G., Burr, J. A., & McCall, P. L. (1997). Religious homogeneity and metropolitan suicide rates. *Social Forces, 76*, 273–299.

Ellison, C. G., & Levin, J. S. (1998). The religion–health connection: Evidence, theory, and future directions. Special Issue: Public health and health education in faith communities. *Health Education and Behavior, 25*, 700–720.

Emmons, R. A., & Crumpler, C. A. (1999). Religion and spirituality? The roles of santification and the concept of God. *International Journal for the Psychology of Religion, 9*, 17–24.

Exline, J. J., Yali, A. M., & Lobel, M. (1999). When God disappoints: Difficulty forgiving God and its role in negative emotion. *Journal of Health Psychology, 4*, 365–380.

Exline, J. J., Yali, A. M., & Sanderson, W. C. (2000). Guilt, discord, and alienation: The role of religious strain in depression and suicidality. *Journal of Clinical Psychology, 4*(3), 365–379.

Francis, L. J. (1994). Denominational identity, church attendance and drinking behaviour among adults in England. *Journal of Alcohol and Drug Education, 39*, 27–33.

Frankel, B. G., & Hewitt, W. E. (1994). Religion and well-being among Canadian university students: The role of faith groups on campus. *Journal for the Scientific Study of Religion, 33*, 62–73.

Freud, S. (1961). *The future of an illusion* (J. Strackey, Trans.). New York: Norton.

Fuller, R. C (2001). *Spiritual but not religious.* New York: Oxford University Press.

Galanter, M. (1986). "Moonies" get married: A psychiatric follow-up study of a charismatic religious sect. *American Journal of Psychiatry, 143*, 1245–1249.

Gallup, G. (1995) *The Gallup Poll: Public opinion 1995.* Wilmington, DE: Scholarly Resources.

Gallup, G., Jr., & Jones, T. (2001). *The next American spirituality: Finding God in the twenty-first century.* Colorado Springs, CO: Cook.

Gartner, J., Larson, D. B., & Allen, G. D. (1991). Religious commitment and mental health: A review of the empirical literature. Special Issue: Spirituality: Perspectives in theory and research. *Journal of Psychology and Theology, 19*, 6–25.

George, L. K., Ellison C. G., & Larson D. (2002). Explaining the relationship between religious involvement and health. *Psychological Inquiry, 13*, 190–200.

Hardesty, P. H., & Kirby, K. M. (1995). Relation between family religiousness and drug use within adolescent peer groups. *Journal of Social Behavior and Personality, 10*, 421–430.

Harris, A. H. S., Thoresen, C. E., McCullough, M. E., & Larson, D. B. (1999). Spiritually and religiously-oriented health interventions. *Journal of Health Psychology, 4*, 413–434.

Harris, R. C., Dew, M. A., Lee, A., Amaya, M., Buches, L., D., R., & Coleman, G. (1995). The role of religion in heart-transplant recipients' long-term health and well-being. *Journal of Religion and Health, 34*, 17–32.

Harris, W. S., Gowda, M., Kolb, J. W., Strychacz, C. P., Vacek, J. L., Jones, P. G., et al. (1999). A randomized, controlled trial of the effects of remote, intercessory prayer on outcomes in patients admitted to the coronary care unit. *Archives of Internal Medicine, 159*, 2273–2278.

Hill, P. C., & Pargament, K. I. (2003). Advances in the conceptualization and measurement of religion and spirituality: Implications for physical and mental health research. *American Psychologist, 58,* 64–74.

Hummer, R. A., Rogers, R. G., Nam, C. B., & Ellison, C. G. (1999). Religious involvement and U.S. adult morality. *Demography, 36,* 272–285.

Idler, E. L., & Kasl, S. V. (1997). Religion among disabled and nondisabled persons II: Attendance at religious services as a predictor of the course of disability. *Journals of Gerontology: Series B: Psychological Sciences and Social Sciences, 52,* S306–S316.

James, W. (1902). *Varieties of religious experience.* New York: Random House.

Kabat-Zinn, J., Wheeler, E., Light, T., Skillings, A., Scharf, M. J., Cropley, T. G., et al. (1998). Influence of a minfulness meditation-based stress reduction intervention on rates of skin clearing in patients with moderate to servere psoriasis undergoing phototherapy (UVB) and photochemotherapy (PUVA). *Psychosomatic Medicine, 60,* 625–632.

Keefe, F. J., Affleck, G., Lefebvre, J., Underwood, L., Caldwell, D. S., Drew, J., et al. (2001). Living with rheumatoid arthritis: The role of daily spirituality and daily religious and spiritual coping. *Journal of Pain, 2, 101–110.*

Kirsch, I., & Lynn, S. J. (1999). Automaticity in clinical psychology. *American Psychologist, 54,* 504–515.

Koenig, H. G. (Ed.). (1998). *Handbook of religion and mental health.* San Diego, CA: Academic Press.

Larson, D. B., Koenig, H. G., & Kaplan, B. H. (1989). The impact of religion on men's blood pressure. *Journal of Religion and Health, 28,* 265–278.

Larson, D. B., Sherrill, K. A., Lyons, J. S., Craigie, F. C., Thielman, S. B., Greenwood, M. A., et al. (1992). Associations between dimensions of religious commitment and mental health reported in the American Journal of Psychiatry and Archives of General Psychiatry: 1978–1989. *American Journal of Psychiatry, 149,* 557–559.

Levin, J. S. (1994). Religion and health: Is there an association, is it valid, and is it causal? *Social Science and Medicine, 38,* 1475–1482.

Levin, J. S., Markides, K. S., & Ray, L. A. (1996). Religious attendance and psychological well-being in Mexican Americans: A panel analysis of three-generations data. *Gerontologist, 36,* 454–463.

Lukoff, D., Lu, F., & Turner, R. (1992). Toward a more culturally sensitive *DSM–IV:* Psychoreligious and psychospiritual problems. *Journal of Nervous and Mental Disease, 180,* 673–682.

Madalie, J. H., Kahn, H. A., & Neufeld, H. N. (1973). Five-year myocardial infarction incidence: II. Association of single variables to age and birthplace. *Journal of Chronic Disease, 26,* 329–349.

Masters, K. S., Bergin, A. E., Reynolds, E. M., & Sullivan, C. E. (1991). Religious life-styles and mental health: A follow-up study. *Counseling and Values, 3,* 211–224.

McCullough, M. E., Hoyt, W. T., Larson, D. B., Koenig, H. G., & Thoresen, C. (2000). Religious involvement and mortality: A meta-analytic review. *Health Psychology, 19,* 211–222.

McCullough, M. E., Larson, D. B., & Worthington, E. L. (1998). Mental Health. In D. B. Larson, J. P. Swyers, & M. E. McCullough (Eds.), *Scientific research on spirituality and health: A consensus report* (pp. 55–67). Rockville, MD: National Institute for Healthcare Research.

McEwen, B. S. (1998). Protective and damaging effects of stress mediators. *New England Journal of Medicine, 338,* 171–179.

Miller, T. Q., Smith, T. W., Turner, C. W., Guijarro, M. L., & Hallet, A. J. (1996). Meta-analytic review of research on hostility and physical health. *Psychological Bulletin, 119,* 322–348.

Miller, W. R. (Ed.). (1999). *Integrating spirituality into treatment.* Washington, DC: American Psychological Association.

Miller, W. R., & Bennett, M. E. (1998). Addictions: Alcohol/drug problems. In D. B. Larson, J. P. Swyers, & M. E. McCullough (Eds.), *Scientific research on spirituality and health: A consensus report* (pp. 69–82). Rockville, MD: National Institute for Healthcare Research.

Miller, W. R., & Delaney, H. D. (Eds.). (in press). *Judeo–Christian perspectives on psychology: Human nature, motivation, and change.* Washington, DC: American Psychological Association.

Miller, W. R., & Thoresen, C. E. (1999). Spirituality and health. In W. Miller (Ed.), *Integrating spirituality into treatment* (pp. 3–18). Washington, DC: American Psychological Association.

Miller, W. R., & Thoresen, C. E. (2003). Spirituality, religion, and health: An emerging research field. *American Psychologist, 58,* 24–35.

Moore, T. (1994). *Care of the soul; A Guide for cultivating depth and sacredness in everyday life.* New York: Harper.

Musick, M. A., Herzog, A. R., & House, J. S. (1999). Volunteering and mortality among older adults: Findings from a national sample. *Journals of Gerontology: Series B: Psychological Sciences and Social Sciences, 54,* S173–S180.

Musick, M. A., House, J. S., & Williams, D. R. (in press). Attendance at religious services and mortality in a national sample. *Journal of Health and Social Behavior.*

Myers, D. (2000). The funds, the friends, and the faith of happy people. *American Psychologist, 55,* 56–67.

Oman, D., & Thoresen, C. E. (2002). Does religion cause health?: Differing interpretations and diverse meanings. *Journal of Health Psychology, 7,* 365–380.

Oman, D., & Thoresen, C. E. (2003). Spiritual modeling: The key to spiritual and religious growth? *International Journal for the Psychology of Religion, 13,* 149–166

Oman, D., Thoresen, C. E., & McMahon, K. (1999). Volunteerism and mortality. *Journal of Health Psychology, 4,* 301–316.

Oxman, T. E., Freeman, D. H., & Manheimer, E. D. (1995). Lack of social participation or religious strength and comfort as risk factors for death after cardiac surgery in the elderly. *Psychosomatic Medicine, 57*, 5–15.

Pargament, K. I. (1997). *The psychology of religion and coping: Theory, research, and practice*. New York: Guilford Press.

Pargament, K. I. (1999). Psychology of religion and spirituality. *International Journal for the Psychology of Religion, 9*, 3–16.

Pargament, K. I., Ensing, D. S., Falgout, K., & Olsen, H. (1990). God help me: I. Religious coping efforts as predictors of the outcomes to significant negative life events. *American Journal of Community Psychology, 18*, 793–824.

Pargament, K. I., Smith, B. W., Koenig, H. G., & Perez, L. (1998). Patterns of positive and negative religious coping with major life stressors. *Journal for the Scientific Study of Religion, 37*, 710–724.

Peck, M. S. (1993). *The road less traveled*. New York: Simon & Schuster. (Original work published 1976)

Powell, L. H., Shahabi, L., & Thoresen, C. E. (2003). Religion and spirituality: Linkages to physical health. *American Psychologist, 58*, 36–52.

Propst, L. R., Ostrom, R., Watkins, P., & Terri, D. (1992). Comparative efficacy of religious and non-religious cognitive–behavioral therapy for the treatment of clinical depression in religious individuals. *Journal of Consulting and Clinical Psychology, 60*, 94–103.

Richards, P. S., & Bergin, A. E. (1997). *A spiritual strategy for counseling and psychotherapy*. Washington, DC: American Psychological Association.

Richards P. S., & Bergin, A. E. (Eds.). (2000). *Handbook of psychotherapy and religious diversity*. Washington, DC: American Psychological Association.

Richards, P. S., Smith, S. A., & Davis, L. F., (1989). Healthy and unhealthy forms of religiousness manifested by psychotherapy clients: An empirical investigation. *Journal of Research in Personality, 23*, 506–524.

Rogosa, D. (1980). A critique of cross-lagged correlation. *Psychological Bulletin, 88*, 245–258.

Rogosa, D. (1987). Casual models do not support scientific conclusions: A comment in support of Freedman. *Journal of Educational Statistics, 12*(2), 185–195.

Rogosa, D.(1988). Myths about longitudinal research. In K. W. Schaie & R. T. Campbell (Eds.), *Methodological issues in aging research* (pp. 171–209). New York: Springer.

Roof, W. (1999). *The spiritual marketplace: Baby boomers and the remaking of American religion*. Princeton, NJ: Princeton University Press.

Ryff, C. D., & Singer, B. (1998). The contours of positive human health. *Psychological Inquiry, 9*, 1–28.

Seeman, T. E., Dubin, L. F., & Seeman, M. (2003). Religiosity/spirituality and health: A critical review of the evidence for biological pathways. *American Psychologist, 58*, 53–63.

Seybold, K. S., & Hill, P. C. (2001). The role of religion and spirituality in mental and physical health. *Current Directions in Psychological Science, 10*(1), 21–24.

Shedler, J., Mayman, M., & Manis, M. (1993). The illusion of mental health. *American Psychologist, 48*, 1117–1131.

Sicher, F., Targ, E., Moore, D., & Smith, H. (1998). A randomized double-blind study of the effect of distant healing in an advanced AIDS population. *Western Journal of Medicine, 169*, 356–363.

Simpson, J., & Weiner, E. (1991). *Oxford English Dictionary*. Oxford: Oxford University Press.

Sloan, R. P., & Bagiella, E. (2002). Claims about religious involvement and health outcomes. *Annals of Behavioral Medicine 24*, 14–21.

Sloan, R. P., Bagiella, E., & Powell, T. (1999). Religion, spirituality, and medicine. *Lancet, 353*, 664–667.

Smith, T. W. (2001). Religion and spirituality in the science and practice of health psychology: Openness, skepticism, and the agnosticism of methodology. In T. G. Plante & A. C. Sherman, (Eds.), *Faith and health: Psychological perspectives* (pp. 355–381). New York: Guilford Press.

Strawbridge, W. J., Cohen, R. D., Shema, S. J., & Kaplan, G. A. (1997). Frequent attendance at religious services and mortality over 28 years. *American Journal of Public Health, 87*, 957–961.

Strawbridge, W. J., Shema, S. J., Cohen, R. D., & Kaplan, G. A. (2001). Religious attendance increases survival by improving and maintaining good health behaviors, mental health, and social relationships. *Annals of Behavioral Medicine, 23*, 68–74.

Thoresen, C. E. (1999). Spirituality and health: Is there a relationship? *Journal of Health Psychology, 4*, 291–300.

Thoresen, C. E., & Eagleston, J. R. (1985). Counseling for health. *Counseling Psychologist, 13*, 15–87.

Thoresen, C. E., & Harris, A. H. S. (2002). Spirituality and health: What's the evidence and what's needed? *Annals of Behavioral Medicine, 24*, 3–13.

Thoresen, C. E., Harris, A. H. S., & Oman, D. (2001). Spirituality, religion, and health: Evidence, issues, and concerns. In T. G. Plante & A. C. Sherman (Eds.), *Faith and health: Psychological perspectives* (pp. 15–52). New York: Guilford Press.

Thoresen, C. E., Oman, D., & Harris, A. H. S. (in press). Religious practices and their effects on health: Judeo–Christian and scientific perspectives. In W. R. Miller & H. D. Delaney (Eds.), *Judeo–Christian perspectives on psychology: Human nature, motivation, and change*. Washington, DC: American Psychological Association.

Tix, A. P., & Frazier, P. A. (1998). The use of religious coping during stressful life events: Main effects, moderation and mediation. *Journal of Consulting and Clinical Psychology, 66*, 411–422.

Walsh, R. (1998). *Essential spirituality*. New York: Wiley.

Williams, J. M., Stout, J. K., & Erickson, L. (1986). Comparison of the importance of Alcoholics Anonymous and outpatient counseling to maintenance of sobriety among alcohol abusers. *Psychological Reports, 58,* 803–806

Worthington, E. L., Jr., Kurusu, T. A., McCollough, M. E., & Sandage, S. J. (1996). Empirical research on religion and psychotherapeutic processes and outcomes: A 10-year review and research prospectus. *Psychological Bulletin, 119,* 448–487.

Yates, J. W., Chalmer, B. J., & St. James, P. (1981). Religion in patients with advanced cancer. *Medical and Pediatric Oncology, 9,* 121–128.

9

SYMPTOM PERCEPTION AND HEALTH CARE-SEEKING BEHAVIOR

RENÉ MARTIN AND HOWARD LEVENTHAL

In 1999, the *New York Times* reported an abrupt and dramatic increase in people seeking medical attention for heartburn (Brody, 1999). On initial analysis, this behavioral pattern appeared to be straightforward. Someone's daily activities were disrupted by the discomfort of heartburn, so she requested medical treatment and advice. In other words, symptoms elicited self-referral behavior. In fact, the title of this chapter implies such a relationship. However, the *Times* also noted that most of these care-seekers already were being treated by gastroenterologists for chronic heartburn. It appeared that the self-referral epidemic was not prompted by heartburn or changes in heartburn symptoms per se. Instead, the exodus followed the publication of a *New England Journal of Medicine* paper reporting that chronic heartburn was associated with a dramatic increase in the risk of esophageal cancer (Lagergren, Bergström, Lindgren, & Nyrén, 1999).

The public response to the publication of Lagergren et al.'s (1999) study reflects the complexities that characterize the association between

Preparation of this chapter was supported by American Heart Association/Iowa Affiliate Beginning Grant-in-Aid 98-06373X and NINR grant NR04886.

symptom perception and health care-seeking behavior. Specifically, heart-burn was a familiar, ongoing symptom for many of these patients. Their care-seeking behaviors were not triggered by heartburn but by changes in how they understood heartburn and in their affective responses to heartburn episodes. This example illustrates how the time between symptom awareness and care seeking is not an empty interval. Indeed, an examination of reported activities from symptom onset to entry into the health care delivery system led Safer, Tharps, Jackson, and Leventhal (1979) to divide the self-referral period into three segments. The first, an appraisal period, is defined by activities directed at determining whether the symptoms were indicative of illness. The second period, labeled illness delay, encompasses attempts to determine whether the illness warranted medical attention. The third and final period involves the time that passes between the judgment that medical intervention was necessary and actual contact with health care providers (e.g., waiting for an appointment, making transportation arrangements). This chapter will review how cognitive representations, affective processes, and contextual variables influence the first two stages described by Safer et al. In addition, we will discuss factors likely to generate appropriate versus inappropriate use of health care resources.

THE IMPERFECT ASSOCIATION BETWEEN SYMPTOMS AND HEALTH CARE-SEEKING BEHAVIOR

The fact that symptoms contribute to health care seeking is unquestionable. Several studies have shown that almost all patients who enter the health care system present with symptom complaints (Berkanovic, Telesky, & Reeder, 1981; Cameron, Leventhal, & Leventhal, 1993; Costa & McCrae, 1980; E. A. Leventhal, Hansell, Diefenbach, Leventhal, & Glass, 1996; Stoller, 1997). However, as illustrated by the heartburn example, movement from symptom perception to seeking health care is affected by a host of processes in the intervening periods of appraisal and illness delay.

People, even those who apparently are healthy, routinely experience all sorts of physical symptoms (Bishop, 1984; Kutner & Gordon, 1961; Pennebaker, 1982; Safer et al., 1979). For example, samples of healthy adult and undergraduate research participants reported that they commonly experienced a wide variety of somatic complaints (Leventhal & Diefenbach, 1991; Martin et al., 1999). Symptoms range from minor to catastrophic in both the level of discomfort produced and the disruption of daily activities. To further complicate matters, seemingly mild symptoms sometimes are a harbinger of serious disease, whereas disruptive symptoms are not always markers of serious pathology. Thus, the layperson continually is confronted with the task of discerning trivial symptoms from those that are potentially dangerous.

Symptom perception does not always lead to self-referral behavior. For example, A. Scambler and colleagues (A. Scambler, Scambler, & Craig, 1981) estimated that fewer than half of symptomatic individuals seek health care. Similarly, among a sample of adults who recorded daily symptoms for 28 days, medical consultation was sought for only 30% of reported symptoms (Sorofman, Tripp-Reimer, Lauer, & Martin, 1990). Thus, care-seekers may represent only the tip of the "illness iceberg" (G. Scambler & Scambler, 1985). Laypeople often choose to manage symptoms on their own, without professional intervention (Hannay & Maddox, 1976; Ingham & Miller, 1979; Schober & Lacroix, 1991; White, Williams, & Greenberg, 1961). Self-treatment undoubtedly is appropriate for many symptoms. However, medical screening of a large British sample revealed that most (57%) had never consulted health care providers regarding serious symptoms for which self-referral would have been appropriate (Ingham & Miller, 1979).

Laypeople often delay in seeking medical care, even when symptoms are potentially life threatening. Myocardial infarction (MI), or heart attack, victims provide an excellent example. Self-referral delay in the context of an evolving MI is an obstacle to effective treatment and is associated with mortality and morbidity (Gunnar, Bourdillon, & Dixon, 1990; National Heart Attack Alert Program Coordinating Committee, 1994). However, even though most laypeople can accurately identify common symptoms of a heart attack, such as chest pain (Goff et al., 1998), 22% of MI victims delay longer than six hours before seeking urgently needed medical attention (Goff, Nichaman, Ramsey, Meyer, & Labarthe, 1995). The complex relationship between symptom perception and self-referral behavior was illustrated in a study by Johnson and King (1995); these researchers found that heart attack victims were significantly more likely to delay in seeking medical care when the actual symptoms experienced were inconsistent with their beliefs and expectations about how a heart attack "should" unfold.

Finally, people sometimes seek health care unnecessarily. Physicians report that most patients seek medical intervention for minor complaints, which presumably could have been managed at home (National Center for Health Statistics, 1980). In addition, practitioners often are unable to identify any tangible cause for patients' presenting symptoms (Backett, Heady, & Evans, 1954; Barsky, 1981). In at least some of these cases, the patients may be somatizing (Fink, 1996; Shorter, 1995; Speckens, Van Hemert, Bolk, Rooijmans, & Hengeveld, 1996)—that is, they may manifest psychological distress as physical symptoms. Inappropriate use of health care services is expensive in terms of effort and resources. In addition, patients who enter the health care system unnecessarily risk exposing themselves to the iatrogenic consequences of medical treatment (Peters, Stanley, Rose, & Salmon, 1998).

WHAT IS A SYMPTOM?

Multiple pathways exist for the generation of the somatic sensations that initiate the symptom perception process. For example, fever, shivering, and fatigue are produced by the chemical response of the immune system (cytokines) that signal the hypothalamus (Hart, 1988). Difficulties in executing thoracic movements and feeling a need for air create the symptoms of breathlessness that accompany pulmonary diseases (Harver & Mahler, 1998). Information regarding tactile contact, position, temperature, and pain travels from the periphery to the spinal cord and ascends to the thalamus via either the dorsal column-lemniscal or anterolateral systems (Guyton, 1991). Sensory inputs such as these provide the raw data of symptom perception. Not all somatic sensations represent symptoms, of course. For example, it is possible to feel one's weight being supported by a chair; yet this somatic sensation is not a symptom. Symptom perception requires additional information processing and interpretation by the cerebral cortex.

In operationalizing the symptom construct, it is important to differentiate among symptoms and related concepts. Health care providers generally distinguish between *disease* and *illness*, for example. Disease is the consequence of disruptions or abnormalities of the body's normal function, whereas illness is the individual's subjective experience of that dysfunction (Barondess, 1979; Jennings, 1986; Lau, 1997; Watson & Pennebaker, 1991). A parallel distinction can be made between *symptoms* and *signs*. A sign is an objective index of pathology, such as an elevated blood pressure or temperature reading or erythema (redness) at the site of an injury. In contrast, symptom experience is, by definition, private. The term *symptom* captures several important events. Simply stated, a symptom is the perception of a disruptive physical or psychological state that is perceived to reflect disease or dysfunction. Thus, although sensory perceptions may initiate a symptom experience, these perceptions are elaborated on by a wide range of cognitive, affective, and behavioral processes (Harver & Mahler, 1998; H. Leventhal & Leventhal, 1993). Each aspect of the symptom experience is discussed in greater detail later in the chapter.

Symptoms are experienced as disruptive (Cameron et al., 1993). Symptoms are problematic, not in their own right but because they interfere with daily life. A headache impairs concentration, a tender knee impedes the ability to climb stairs, and a mysterious lump provokes insomnia and fears of developing cancer. A physical sensation that produces no emotional or tangible problems is unlikely to be perceived as a symptom.

Symptoms are perceived to be indicative of disease, disorder, or dysfunction. As described previously, symptoms represent a central component of the illness experience and self-referral behavior. When asked to define the concept of *health*, diverse groups ranging from children to health care providers report that being healthy includes the absence of symptoms (B. Baumann, 1961; Laffrey, 1986; Natapoff, 1978). Similarly, most laypeople mentioned the presence of symptoms when asked to operationalize the meaning of *sickness* (Lau, 1997; Lau, Bernard, & Hartmann, 1989) or to define the meaning of *health* (Borawski, Kinney, & Kahana, 1996; Idler, Hudson, & Leventhal, 1999). Patients consistently report symptoms for disorders that are known to be asymptomatic, such as hypertension (L. Baumann & Leventhal, 1985; Meyer, Leventhal, & Gutmann, 1985). This suggests that it is difficult to comprehend a disease state unless it is accompanied by salient symptoms.

Although the prototypical symptom is a physical complaint, symptoms also can be psychological in nature. Consistent with this perspective, Lau and associates found that lay descriptions of symptoms emphasize physical maladies but also sometimes incorporate psychological phenomena (Lau, 1997; Lau et al., 1989). For example, symptoms of depression include anhedonia and feelings of worthlessness. As with physical symptoms, psychological symptoms are of concern because they disrupt normal daily function.

Symptom perception involves both bottom-up and top-down processes (Brownlee, Leventhal, & Leventhal, 2000). As described previously, somatic sensations provide the raw data, or bottom-up component, for the symptom-perception process. Thus, symptoms generally are grounded in a reality of somatic sensation. According to Pennebaker's (1982) competition-of-cues model, attentional processes are an important determinant of whether somatic sensations are noticed or overlooked in any given context. In the laboratory, research participants who are instructed to focus on internal sensations (e.g., one's breathing) report more symptoms than those who are externally focused (Fillingim & Fine, 1986; Padgett & Hill, 1989; Pennebaker & Lightner, 1980; Watson & Pennebaker, 1991). A similar pattern is observed in naturalistic settings. Symptom complaints are more common in dull or boring occupational and residential environments (Moos & Van Dort, 1977; National Center for Health Statistics, 1980; Wan, 1976). Once a somatic sensation has been noticed, the meaning assigned to that sensation will influence the subjective experience of symptoms. In addition, baseline mood and affective responses shape symptom perception. These elements represent top-down processes and will be the focus of additional attention later in this chapter.

Symptoms elicit cognitive, affective, and behavioral responses. Because symptoms are perceived as disruptive warning flags, the symptomatic individual attempts to correct or at least improve the situation. Behavioral responses to symptoms vary widely and include simply tolerating the symptom, self-management through home remedies, seeking social support, and consulting health care providers. Efforts to understand the meaning and implications of a symptom and concurrent affective reactions also represent important intrapersonal responses. H. Leventhal and colleagues characterize the response to symptoms as a self-regulatory process, directed toward the restoration of equilibrium (Cameron et al., 1993; H. Leventhal, 1970; H. Leventhal & Diefenbach, 1991; H. Leventhal, Meyer, & Nerenz, 1980).

Finally, although our emphasis is on lay symptom perception and response, symptoms are important from the perspective of health care providers. Practitioners, whether physicians, nurses, psychologists, or other allied health professionals, understand the language of symptoms. Symptoms provide a basis for communication between patients and professional care providers. Presenting symptoms suggest avenues of inquiry for health care providers and figure prominently in professional recommendations regarding diagnostic procedures and treatment (E. Leventhal et al., 1996).

THEORETICAL PERSPECTIVES ON HEALTH CARE-SEEKING BEHAVIOR

We have seen that although patients visiting a health care provider typically present with symptom complaints, the experience of symptoms does not necessarily prompt self-referral behavior. How, then, does the layperson go about determining whether a particular symptom warrants professional attention? Consistent with Heider's (1958) conceptualization of the naive scientist, ordinary people function as lay diagnosticians in interpreting symptoms and selecting coping procedures. Just as any physician systematically evaluates a patient's condition, the layperson is aware, albeit informally, of the quality, onset, and duration of his or her own symptoms. The symptoms are compared to those previously experienced by either the self or known others. Patterns of covariation are assessed; that is, the potential contributory or even causal role of environmental factors is evaluated. Thus, the sufferer formulates a lay diagnosis (e.g., "I think I'm catching a cold" or "This lump could be a cancerous growth"). Whereas a physician might consult with colleagues regarding a challenging case, the layperson may confer with family members and friends for information, comparison, and social support. Responses to palliative efforts and temporal changes are observed, testing the veracity of the lay diagnosis. If needed, the diagnosis is revised. Ultimately, health care-seeking behavior will occur if self-referral is consistent with the person's understanding of the symptom experience. We will use the common sense model (CSM) of health and illness behavior, developed by H. Leventhal and colleagues (H. Leventhal, 1970; H. Leventhal & Diefenbach, 1991; H. Leventhal et al., 1980), to organize our discussion of factors known to influence the processes of self-diagnosis and symptom management. However, before proceeding, we briefly will review three precursors of the CSM: the health belief model and the theories of reasoned action and planned behavior.

The Health Belief Model

Developed in the tradition of economic utility approaches, the health belief model (HBM; Becker, 1974; Becker & Maiman, 1975; Hochbaum, 1958; Rosenstock, 1974) posits that health care-seeking behavior is determined by beliefs regarding the nature and severity of the health threat and perceptions of personal vulnerability. In addition, self-referral behavior occurs only if medical consultation is viewed as likely to be effective and if the perceived benefits of a health care visit (e.g., pain relief, resolution of infection, reassurance) outweigh the perceived costs (e.g., inconvenience, monetary expense, side effects, anxiety). Although effective in characterizing preventive health behaviors among well-educated, White populations (J. C. Anderson & Bartkus, 1973; Gochman, 1972; Wolinsky, 1978), the generalizability of the HBM to minority populations is limited. In addition, the HBM is a poor predictor of behavioral responses to acute health threats. The model also ignores affective reactions and does not attempt to conceptualize the mechanisms involved in elaborating on or converting somatic sensations to symptoms or feelings of vulnerability. These limitations aside, the HBM is the closest precursor to the CSM. In early studies based on the model (e.g., Hochbaum, 1958), vulnerability beliefs were operationalized in ways similar to that used in the CSM (i.e., as perceptual cues). In addition, both approaches treated symptoms and health messages as triggers that activated these beliefs.

The Theories of Reasoned Action and Planned Behavior

The theory of reasoned action (TRA; Fishbein & Ajzen, 1974) extended the HBM to incorporate the contributions of intentions and perceived norms. According to the TRA, health care seeking will occur if attitudes toward the action are positive and if the action is viewed as consistent with norms or expectations for appropriate behavior. The model also posits that the intention to seek medical intervention mediates the associations between attitudes, subjective norms, and actual self-referral behavior. The theory of planned behavior (TPB; Ajzen, 1991; Ajzen & Fishbein, 1972, 1980; Hecker & Ajzen, 1983) added the concept of self-efficacy to the equation, suggesting that perceptions of competency and control also were important in predicting health behaviors. The TRA and TPB provided a general framework for examining care-seeking behaviors and drew attention to the importance of perceived norms. However, these models failed to incorporate specific perceptions or beliefs about illness threats and also ignored the role of affective processes in decision making and behavior. H. Leventhal's CSM drew its focus on perceived norms from the TRA and TPB models.

The Common Sense Model of Health and Illness Behavior

The CSM of health and illness behavior views symptom perception and health care seeking as a self-regulatory problem-solving process (Brownlee et al., 2000; H. Leventhal, 1970; H. Leventhal & Diefenbach, 1991; H. Leventhal et al., 1980). The underlying assumption of the model is that illness cognition mirrors the basic processes that comprise cognition in general. In other words, people think and reason about health and illness much as they process information in any other domain. The CSM proposes that health behaviors, including medical self-referral, are a function of naive theories of health threats. These theories consist of representations or beliefs about the threat and action plans or procedures for coping with the threat. There is broad agreement that cognitive representations of illness incorporate five elements (described in detail later in the chapter), each characterized by abstract and experiential dimensions. The CSM further assumes that the cognitive and affective systems make independent and potentially interactive contributions to behavior. Finally, the CSM posits that contextual factors, such as personality and sociocultural roles, exert their behavioral effects by shaping both representations and action plans or procedures. The CSM is unique in its attention to the specific content of illness representations, the abstract and experiential mechanisms underlying the representations, procedures making up these theories, and the contribution of the social context to them.

COGNITIVE REPRESENTATIONS OF ILLNESS

Multiple approaches have been taken to identify the content of illness representations (see Scharloo & Kaptein, 1997, for a review), including open-ended interviews, multidimensional scaling, and factor analyses. As introduced previously, five types of information are integrated in the organizational structure of naive theories or cognitive representations of illness, and both concrete and abstract mechanisms contribute to each component (L. Baumann, Cameron, Zimmerman, & Leventhal, 1989; Lau, 1997; Meyer et al., 1985; Skelton & Croyle, 1991). First, symptoms are labeled or identified. A burning sensation beneath the sternum might be labeled as "heartburn" or "angina," for example. The somatic burning sensation is a tangible experience, whereas the word *heartburn* is an abstract, symbolic representation. Bishop and associates have suggested that labels are formulated through a process of matching symptoms to disease prototypes or beliefs about how a particular disorder typically is manifested (Bishop, 1991; Bishop, Briede, Cavazos, Grotzinger, & McMahon, 1987; Bishop & Converse, 1986).

Cognitive representations of illness also include beliefs regarding the likely temporal course of symptoms and illness. This includes expectations about the probable duration of symptoms and their fluctuations. For example, one might expect an episode of heartburn to resolve rapidly after imbibing antacids. Alternatively, an asthmatic individual might expect periodic flares of coughing and wheezing, interspersed with relatively asymptomatic periods. Deviations from the expected temporal course are likely to be perceived as worrisome and may prompt symptom reevaluation and relabeling.

Symptom causal attributions and perceived consequences represent the third and fourth components of naive theories of illness. For example, the layperson might conclude that the heartburn episode was a consequence of eating a spicy meal and the asthma attack might be attributed to exposure to ragweed pollen. Perceived consequences include both short- and long-term probable outcomes. Returning to our example, the heartburn sufferer might expect the short-term consequences to be a sleepless night, whereas the long-term consequences might involve the development of esophageal cancer. As we will see, beliefs about etiology and consequences have important implications for illness-coping procedures, including self-referral behavior.

Finally, cognitive representations of illness include expectations about symptom control and cure. Our heartburn sufferer might expect antacids to relieve an acute episode, the drug Prilosec to provide ongoing symptom amelioration, and the surgical repair of a hiatal hernia to provide a complete cure. Treatment expectations in Western industrialized nations often approximate the biomedical model of the health care delivery system (Peters et al., 1998). However, beliefs regarding symptom control are strongly influenced by culture. For example, in southeast Asia, rubbing oiled skin with the edge of a coin is expected by some to relieve fever (Pachter, 1994).

MALADAPTIVE HEALTH CARE-SEEKING BEHAVIOR

Ideally, laypeople and professional care providers will agree about which symptoms are serious and likely to benefit from medical treatment. Thus, care will be sought promptly for serious symptoms, whereas minor disorders will be managed without professional intervention. However, disparities sometimes emerge between the lay and professional perspectives. Laypeople sometimes mislabel or misattribute symptoms that a health care provider would judge to be significant and in need of professional attention. For example, a life-threatening scenario is likely to develop if the sufferer mistakes anginal discomfort for heartburn. Unrealistic temporal expectations also may contribute to delays in seeking treatment, such as mistakenly assuming that a lingering cough and sinus pressure following a bout with the flu will resolve harmlessly with the passage of time. Alternatively, care may be sought unnecessarily if the layperson expects the symptoms to resolve more quickly than is realistic (e.g., assuming that the nasal congestion of a cold should vanish in 24 hours). Laypeople and health care providers also may differ in their expectations regarding symptom consequences. A new pain might mean cancer or some other serious threat to the layperson but simply strained muscles to the health care provider, generating an unnecessary health care visit.

Our characterization of maladaptive self-referral behavior is not intended to imply that the traditional health care delivery system is the only correct or appropriate perspective for the management of symptoms and illness. Instead, by highlighting sources of deviation between the lay and medical models, we hope to illustrate the "psycho-logic" of lay health and illness behaviors. Lay illness behaviors only appear to be confusing or irrational if the content of their illness representations is unknown. For example, one of the author's sons suffered pneumonia at the age of six. On the way home from the pediatrician's office, he tearfully apologized for not brushing his teeth more carefully and promised meticulous oral hygiene in the future. On the surface, his comments and coping plans made no sense at all in the context of pneumonia. However, his intentions were logical with regard to his cognitive representation of his illness. Careful questioning revealed that he understood that "germs in the mouth" caused tooth decay. He had extrapolated that those same pathogens could be inhaled, causing his pneumonia. Thus, responses to illness make sense, given the layperson's grasp of the symptoms and their consequences. Some research has explored how disparities between lay and medical illness models can compromise treatment compliance (e.g., M. Cohen, Tripp-Reimer, Smith, Sorofman, & Lively, 1994). However, little data speak to how mismatches between lay and medical models might influence self-referral behavior.

QUALITATIVE DIFFERENCES BETWEEN CARE-SEEKERS AND CONTROL INDIVIDUALS

Cameron et al. (1993) provided an excellent example of how symptom representations determine heath care-seeking behavior. Participants in a large sample of community-dwelling adults were paired on the basis of age, sex, and medical ratings of health status. Care-seekers were interviewed before seeing their health care provider. In addition, care-seekers' matched controls also were contacted and interviewed. In both cases, interviews addressed symptoms, mood, and illness representations.

Cameron et al.'s (1993) results indicated that symptoms were necessary but insufficient determinants of self-referral behavior. That is, all care-seekers reported symptoms, but not all participants with new symptoms sought medical care. Several characteristics differentiated care-seekers from their non–care-seeking matched controls who reported symptoms. Overall, care-seekers described more detailed cognitive representations of their symptoms. In particular, they tended to label their symptoms as manifestations of some particular disease. Compared to symptomatic matched controls, care-seekers perceived their symptoms to be more serious. Care-seekers also reported greater pain and disruption in their activities of daily living. In addition, care-seekers had given greater thought to symptom consequences before scheduling a clinic appointment. Finally, care-seekers reported more active coping efforts than symptomatic matched controls, and care-seekers tended to appraise their coping efforts as unsuccessful. Among the qualitative differences that distinguished care-seekers from matched controls, perceived seriousness emerged as the best predictor of self-referral behavior. Janz and Becker (1984) similarly found that health care-seeking behavior was motivated by the perception of serious symptoms. Subsequent research by E. Leventhal and Crouch (1997) found that self-referral was especially likely to occur when self-care was perceived as ineffective or if sufferers were unable to identify a plausible symptom label.

THE RECIPROCAL ASSOCIATION BETWEEN SYMPTOMS AND REPRESENTATIONS

Intuitively, it appears obvious that the perception of symptoms leads to cognitive analysis and the integration of information within illness representational frameworks. Although correct, this characterization is incomplete. The association between symptoms and representations is reciprocal. According to the symmetry hypothesis, people label symptoms, and symptom labels generate the expectation that certain relevant symptoms will be present. For example, a layperson might seek a physician's advice for symptoms of fatigue, failing to notice or monitor additional expected symptoms (e.g., scratchy throat and tender lymph nodes) until *after* receiving the diagnosis of mononucleosis. L. Baumann et al. (1989) found support for the symmetry hypothesis in the laboratory. Participants who were given bogus feedback regarding an elevated blood pressure reading then reported symptoms (e.g., headache, face flushing) consistent with those commonly reported by hypertensives.

DECISION RULES IN LAY SYMPTOM EVALUATION

We are cognitive misers and motivated tacticians in evaluating episodes of symptoms and illness, just as we are in processing information in any other domain (Fiske & Taylor, 1991). That is, we conserve cognitive energy and resources whenever possible, and information processing is influenced by current goals and needs. Empirical studies have revealed certain decision rules or heuristics that increase the speed and efficiency of symptom evaluation. For example, health threats tend to be viewed as serious if they are perceived to be rare, whereas more common ailments are considered to be relatively minor (the *prevalence rule*; Ditto & Jemmott, 1989). When symptoms covary with challenging environmental events, the symptoms sometimes are attributed to stress rather than illness (the *stress–illness rule*). Ambiguous symptoms are particularly likely to be attributed to stress, especially when the stressor onset was recent (Cameron, Leventhal, & Leventhal, 1995). However, sustained stressors often are believed to cause illness, and nonambiguous symptoms (e.g., hemmorhage) prompt care-seeking, regardless of background stressors. Finally, symptoms with a mild, gradual onset tend to be attributed to normal consequences of the aging process rather than to illness (the *age–illness rule*; Prohaska, Keller, Leventhal, & Leventhal, 1987).

The evaluation of an ambiguous symptom is an effortful process, which some people may try to avoid entirely. For example, elderly individuals sometimes adopt the general perspective that their physical and cognitive energies are limited. Therefore, the responsibility for symptom evaluation and decision-making is delegated to health care providers in an effort to conserve one's limited resources (the *conservation rule*; E. Leventhal & Crouch, 1997; E. Leventhal, Leventhal, Schaefer, & Easterling, 1993). Like most heuristics, the prevalence, stress–illness, age–illness, and conservation rules are used because they are adaptive and usually lead to the formulation of appropriate lay diagnoses. However, under certain circumstances, these decision rules may generate maladaptive health care-seeking behavior.

COGNITIVE REPRESENTATIONS AND "IF–THEN" RULES

Cognitive representations of illness have clear implications for illness-coping behaviors, including self-referral. The associations among illness representations and procedural responses can best be characterized by Anderson's (1987, 1993) "if–then" rules. Behavioral responses (the "then" component) are directed toward salient goals shaped by the illness representation (the "if" component). Behavioral procedures essentially test the hypothesis implicit in the cognitive representation. For example, *if* I have heartburn, *then* I will take an antacid. *If* the substernal discomfort unexpectedly persists despite self-medication, *then* I may reevaluate my assessment of the situation. *If* I decide, instead, that I probably am having a heart attack, *then* I will dial 911. The "if–then" conceptualization illustrates the limitations of broad taxonomies of coping behaviors (e.g., categorizing coping as emotion- or problem-focused), such as those developed by Lazarus and Folkman (1984) and Carver, Scheier, and Weintraub (1989). Although these broad approaches can apply to almost any situation, they miss crucially interesting characteristics of specific situations. Telephoning emergency services and taking an antacid in response to chest pain both are examples of problem-focused coping with vastly different consequences, depending on the biological processes underlying the pain.

Omnibus coping taxonomies not only fail to provide insight into which individual will undertake a particular problem-focused strategy and why, they also ignore the expectations linked to specific coping procedures and the effects of these expectations on postaction appraisals. Expectations regarding identity, timeline, cause, consequences, and control—the five domains involved in the representation of illness—are explicit or implicit for each procedure selected to regulate symptoms and illness (i.e., the perceived and conceived identity of the problem). These expectations reflect perceptions and beliefs regarding the illness and how the procedure is expected to interact with it. Take our case of heartburn as an example. If it is identified as an acute problem, caused by and temporally following an especially spicy dinner, two tablespoons of an antacid could be seen as an appropriate self-treatment. The expectation that one has identified the appropriate treatment is based on the perceived cause of the heartburn, and the perception that the liquid will contact and soothe the painful area (cause of action and expected control) and do so on contact within moments (timeline for control). The long-term consequences of the heartburn and antacid are believed to be nil. If the heartburn does not respond to treatment (i.e., returns and persists for days), its identity may shift to ulceration, cancer, and so forth, which would identify other procedures for management, perhaps including the use of medical care. Once again each procedure would have an associated set of expectations based on the representation of both the illness and the procedure, as well as their interaction. Generic concepts such as problem-focused coping ignore the details that are integral to the self-regulation process.

THE INFLUENCE OF AFFECT ON SYMPTOM PERCEPTION AND HEALTH CARE-SEEKING BEHAVIOR

As previously observed, H. Leventhal's CSM posits that affective processes exert independent effects on health and illness behaviors. The conceptualization of affect and cognition as parallel processes has a rich history in both philosophy and psychology (Hilgard, 1980; McGuire, 1969). Whereas cognitive representations of illness direct the selection and evaluation of coping procedures, the emotional response to an illness episode will elicit behaviors directed at modulating distress. It is important to note that the cognitive and affective responses to symptoms may be compatible or incompatible. That is, affective processes may independently facilitate or inhibit health care-seeking behavior. For example, a man who is having difficulty urinating might avoid a prostate exam if he is afraid of the discomfort and embarrassment associated with the procedure, if he feels anxious and threatened at the prospect of learning that he might have cancer, or if he is more fearful of the treatment for prostate cancer (surgery) and its consequences (e.g., incontinence, loss of sexual function) than of the cancer itself. On the other hand, if he comprehends the potential seriousness of prostatic cancer (e.g., he has seen a friend suffer the pain from bone metastases from disseminated prostatic disease) and appreciates the benefits of early detection and treatment, his fear of the disease may facilitate seeking a medical consultation. Affective responses can exert multiple, bottom-up effects on the symptom-perception process. Pain and distress can prompt specific coping behaviors, including avoidance, and they can affect the representation of the problem. Fear may stimulate a catastrophic interpretation of a symptom. For example, fear might convince a heartburn sufferer that the symptoms are caused by cancer rather than what was consumed for dinner (Brownlee et al., 2000). Research on emotion, symptom perception, and self-referral behavior has emphasized two areas: fear and negative affect.

Fear

The fear-drive model and empirical studies of the effects of fear communications provided an early foundation for understanding the effects of emotion on symptom perception and self-referral behavior. The fear-drive model (Dollard & Miller, 1950; Miller, 1951) assumed that fearful emotions were classically conditioned to environmental cues. The aversive experience of fear was thought to motivate behaviors directed at fear reduction. Effective responses subsequently were reinforced and learned through operant or instrumental conditioning processes. Empirical studies of the effects of fear communications revealed that two components were important in motivating health behavior (H. Leventhal, Singer, & Jones, 1965; H. Leventhal, Watts, & Pagano, 1967). First, the message had to elicit feelings of fear and personal vulnerability. Second, the fear message had to be accompanied by an action plan incorporating tangible instructions for how to effectively address the threat. Thus, both affective and cognitive processes were necessary if a message was to stimulate health behavior.

Negative Affect

Negative affect (NA) or neuroticism is positively correlated with symptom reports, with correlations ranging in magnitude from .20 to .50 (Costa & McCrae, 1980, 1985, 1987; Pennebaker, 1982; Watson & Pennebaker, 1989). However, some studies show that NA is not a strong predictor of objective indexes of health (Costa & McCrae, 1987; Watson & Pennebaker, 1989). This suggests that NA should be treated as a nuisance variable in any study searching for a relationship between stress and illness in cross-sectional data via self-reports of symptoms and illness (Davison & Pennebaker, 1996; Watson & Pennebaker, 1991). The expectation is that high NA individuals with symptom complaints will not necessarily be in poor health. Instead, according to the symptom perception hypothesis, negatively affective people either may complain about normal physical sensations or they may exaggerate the seriousness of veridical health problems (Watson & Pennebaker, 1989, 1991).

Watson and Pennebaker (1991) proposed that the competition-of-cues model (Pennebaker, 1982) might explain the positive association between NA and symptom complaints. High NA people tend to focus on internal sensations (Watson & Clark, 1984; Watson, Clark, & Carey, 1988), and as discussed previously, symptom reports increase in the laboratory when research participants are internally focused. Consistent with this line of reasoning, negatively affective people tend to be vigilant in monitoring the environment for threats (Cloninger, 1987; Gray, 1982, 1985; Pennebaker, 1989; Tellegen, 1985), interpreting ambiguous stimuli as threatening (Watson & Clark, 1984). These tendencies may cause minor symptoms to be labeled as troublesome or serious (Barsky & Klerman, 1983; Costa & McCrae, 1985; Watson & Pennebaker, 1991).

Recent findings suggest more complex associations among NA, symptom perception, and self-referral behavior. Diefenbach, Leventhal, Leventhal, and Patrick-Miller (1996) administered a variety of inoculations to a sample of adults and monitored complaints of local signs (e.g., redness at injection site) and systemic symptoms (e.g., vague flu-like complaints). The overall results were inconsistent with Watson and Pennebaker's (1989, 1991) symptom-perception hypothesis. Depressive affect was associated with systemic complaints in cross-sectional analyses. However, NA was unrelated to longitudinal systemic symptoms and to local signs in both cross-sectional and longitudinal analyses. Participants generally were fairly accurate in their symptom reports, regardless of level of NA. Smith, Wallston, and Dwyer (1995) similarly found, among a sample of arthritis patients, that disease severity was a better predictor of discomfort and impairment complaints than was NA.

Observing that most research linking NA to symptom complaints used cross-sectional designs, E. Leventhal et al. (1996) undertook a longitudinal study of two large samples of elder adults. The results elucidated the distinction between state and trait NA. Trait NA was found to be a poor predictor of symptom complaints over time. However, state negative mood was positively associated with symptom complaints six months later, even after controlling for baseline symptoms. Although few longitudinal studies have investigated the NA–symptom link, S. Cohen et al. (1995) found that NA was a prospective predictor of nasal congestion and sneezing. Aneshensel, Frerichs, and Huba (1984) also found that depression (a component of NA) predicted physical illness longitudinally. In addition, several studies have emerged suggesting that anxiety (another dimension of NA) may increase susceptibility to heart disease (see review by Kubzansky, Kawachi, Weiss, & Sparrow, 1998). In interpreting their findings, E. Leventhal et al. speculated that state NA might diminish immune resistance and increase vulnerability to disease, leading to symptom complaints.

Taken together, recent findings suggest that the effects of trait NA are strongest for vague symptoms, measured in cross-sectional designs (Diefenbach et al., 1996; E. Leventhal et al., 1996). It is possible that trait NA may be associated with cross-sectional symptom complaints because high NA persons may remember negative events, such as aversive symptoms, especially well (Diefenbach et al., 1996). Alternatively, trait NA primarily may influence the intensity of symptom complaints, rather than the absolute number of symptoms reported (Diefenbach et al., 1996). At this point, it appears unlikely that the association among NA and symptom complaints simply reflects the tendency for neurotic individuals to complain indiscriminately. Future research should carefully evaluate whether state NA might play a causal role in the development of disease.

Contextual Effects

The common-sense theoretical perspective emphasizes cognitive and affective mechanisms in health and illness behavior. However, the social context exerts important effects on symptom perception and self-referral as well. The basic cognitive and affective processes are likely to be constant across various social environments. Contextual factors, such as the lay referral network, culture, and social and self-identity, act as moderating variables.

That is, contextual variables are important because they enhance or inhibit the salience of representational components and affective responses.

THE LAY REFERRAL NETWORK

Laypeople often choose not to evaluate and respond to symptoms of illness by themselves. Instead, they turn to members of the lay referral network, including family members, friends, and acquaintances (Friedson, 1961). The lay network provides opportunities for support, information gathering, and social comparison. Suls, Martin, and Leventhal (1997) described three scenarios in which social comparisons shape symptom perception and health care-seeking behavior. First, someone suffering a symptom might share that experience with others in an effort to understand the symptom's meaning. Suls et al. (1997) found that most lay symptom consultations focused on labeling the symptom, determining its etiology, and obtaining procedural advice for symptom management. Cameron et al. (1993) also found that lay consultation served an important communicative function that reduced feelings of isolation in the face of threat.

Second, the presence of others who are (or have been) ill with demonstrable disorders influences personal symptom perception. For example, exposure to someone suffering from a contagious disease (e.g., chicken pox, strep throat) increases self-monitoring for similar symptoms and the likelihood that any new symptoms that appear will be attributed to the contagious exposure. Family medical history sensitizes people to the appearance and meaning of relevant symptoms. Lay people are more likely to seek medical treatment if a family member has suffered a similar problem in the past (Turk, Litt, Salovey, & Walker, 1985).

Third, episodes of mass psychogenic illness demonstrate that ill others influence our symptom perceptions and representations, even when the illnesses in question are not medically validated (Colligan, Pennebaker, & Murphy, 1982). For example, Kerckhoff and Back (1968) reported an episode in which a busy industrial plant was forced to close because a large group of employees reported symptoms of nausea and fever. Although plant workers attributed their symptoms to insect bites, the Centers for Disease Control and Prevention was unable to document any environmental or medical evidence of disease. Ultimately, the symptoms were attributed to anxiety or stress. Normally, the ambiguous symptoms reported by workers bitten by the "June Bug" would have gone unnoticed or been dismissed as trivial. However, the stressful factory environment and exposure to others with similar symptom complaints combined to generate an episode of hysterical contagion.

It is clear, as Zola (1973) pointed out long ago, that lay networks can perform multiple functions. For example, as members of a network, we may engage in social sanctioning of those others perceived to be in need of medical attention; in other words, we nag until the symptomatic loved one seeks medical care. Other evidence also suggests that lay consultants often encourage care seeking (Cameron et al., 1993; Oberlander, Pless, & Dougherty, 1993; Sanders, 1982). We also are sensitive to the effects our symptoms have on others around us. If we are "socially responsible," we are especially likely to self-refer for medical care when our symptoms disrupt family and work relationships (Apple, 1960; Zola, 1973). However, just as friends and family members sometimes offer unhelpful social support (Dakof & Taylor, 1990; Martin, Davis, Baron, Suls, & Blanchard, 1994; Rook, 1984), the lay referral network may discourage care seeking. Others are especially likely to inhibit care seeking if they distrust or dislike the health care delivery system (Suls & Goodkin, 1994). A number of researchers have observed that strong social networks are associated with delays in seeking medical intervention (Berkanovic et al., 1981; Granovetter, 1978; Liu & Duff, 1972). The reason for this counterintuitive finding is not clear. It is possible that sufferers surrounded by supportive others experience less subjective ambiguity and anxiety about their state of well-being. Alternatively, a large active support network may encourage the individual to remain active and involved, despite symptoms. Finally, lay consultation is a time-consuming processing. However astute the lay consultants might be, the very act of discussing the presence and potential meanings of symptoms requires time and delays entry into the health care delivery system (Suls et al., 1997).

In summary, the evidence indicates that lay referral networks are important moderators of decisions and delay in seeking health care. Support providers may either encourage or discourage care seeking, depending on the circumstances. It is clear, however, that networks do not simply act on the symptomatic or ill individual; individuals experiencing symptoms and physical or emotional dysfunction actively seek advice and support. And the needs of the symptomatic or ill person will affect the type of advice sought and the persons from whom it is sought. The individual's common-sense model of his or her illness is one such moderator. If I assume my gastric distress is caused by tainted food, I will select a comparison from another who has eaten the same or similar meals at the same places: My hypothesis will be confirmed if he or she also is experiencing heartburn. On the other hand, if I am frightened because I believe that my gastric distress is caused by esophageal cancer, I may seek out and share my concerns with that person I believe most likely to be reassuring (Leventhal, Hudson, & Robitaille, 1997). Just as common-sense models influence personal health and illness behavior, they determine how and whom we select for information and assistance. They also affect how we respond to others when they are ill. If we believe that diseases such as cancer and AIDS are infectious and have serious and uncontrollable consequences, we may be reluctant to shake hands with or be near someone who is afflicted. Indeed, if we believe these diseases are infectious and asymptomatic in their most virulent stages, we may be threatened by and motivated to avoid individuals perceived as carriers—for example, in the case of AIDS, gay men. Our reactions and recommendations will be determined by our cognitive representation of the other's symptoms and our affective response to his or her state of illness.

Culture as a Moderating Variable

Culture is an important contextual determinant of symptom perception and interpretation. Somatization—that is, expressing distress via physical symptoms—appears to be more common in nonindustrialized cultures; within Western cultures, manifestations of stress as physical symptoms is more common among groups with low socioeconomic status, low education, and rural locales (Kleinman & Kleinman, 1985; Leff, 1977; Mezzich & Raab, 1980; Watson & Pennebaker, 1991; Westermeyer, 1985).

Culture-specific beliefs shape the content of cognitive representations of illness (Brownlee et al., 2000; Lau, 1997; Pachter, 1994; Weller, 1984) and have implications for coping strategies. For example, culture-specific beliefs regarding hypertension have been found to influence medical treatment compliance among Black Americans (Heurtin-Roberts & Reisin, 1992). Less is known about the impact of culturally determined beliefs on self-referral behaviors per se. An early study by Clark (1959) found that Mexican American migrant farm workers often did not seek medical attention for symptoms that a health care provider would consider to be serious. The rationale was that these symptoms were common in the migrant worker environment. Consistent with the prevalence rule (Ditto & Jemmott, 1989), the fact that the symptoms were ordinary made them seem less serious.

Although it may be reasonable to assume that basic cognitive and affective processes determine symptom perception across cultures, cross-cultural research on illness representation is limited (Lau, 1997). The almost exclusive use of Western, industrialized populations means that contagion and physiological malfunctions have been overemphasized in illness representation research. Weller (1984) stressed the importance of evaluating the variability and relative influence of different dimensions of illness representations across a wide variety of cultural settings.

Stereotypes and Social Identity

Just as we hold stereotypes or beliefs about the characteristics common to ethnic or occupational groups, we also share stereotypes about the victims of different diseases. These stereotypes then influence the processes of symptom labeling and attribution. Martin, Gordon, and Lounsbury (1998) explored the impact of gender-related stereotypes regarding heart disease on the interpretation of cardiac-related symptoms. In samples of undergraduates, community-dwelling adults, and physicians, they found that cardiac symptoms were discounted or minimized, not for women in general but specifically for female victims who reported concurrent life stressors. Martin et al.'s results speak not only to beliefs about heart disease risk but also to broader beliefs about women, emotional distress, and somatization. Recent follow-up studies suggest a similar attributional pattern when women report symptoms of gallbladder disease and melanoma in the context of stressful events (Martin & Lemos, 2002); results also indicated that health care-seeking behavior was perceived as more important for males suffering symptoms of heart disease, gallbladder disease, and melanoma than for females reporting identical symptoms. At first glance, the stereotype that women are prone to somatization appears plausible because several studies have demonstrated that women report more physical symptoms than do men (Nathanson, 1975, 1977; Pennebaker, 1982; Verbrugge, 1989). However, these findings must be interpreted with caution because they are limited to healthy populations; gender differences in symptom complaints disappear when objective indexes for disease are present (Gijsbers van Wijk & Kolk, 1997). Healthy women may notice more symptoms than do men, perhaps as a function of internal versus external attentional focus; however, symptom reports in women do not appear to translate into self-referral false alarms (Gijsbers van Wijk & Kolk, 1997).

The working self-concept (Markus & Nurius, 1986) exerts a top-down effect on the processes of symptom perception and health care-seeking behavior (Brownlee et al., 2000); in other words, salient aspects of self-identity will influence cognitive and affective responses to symptoms. Levine and Reicher (1996) found that young adults interpreted symptoms of illness and injury differently, depending on whether gender identity or identity as a future physical education teacher was highly accessible. This suggests different environments tap various aspects of the self-concept, with implications for health and illness behavior.

CONCLUSION

To return to our opening example of heartburn sufferers, cognitive, affective, and contextual factors played an important role in the wave of self-referral behavior that followed the publication of Lagergren et al.'s (1999) results linking heartburn and esophageal cancer. Whereas heartburn previously had represented a source of discomfort, sufferers now realized that the reflux of gastric acid into the esophagus also could produce lasting damage. Media reports included the information that esophageal cancer almost always is fatal. Bouts of heartburn that once had seemed merely annoying now became acutely frightening. Finally, exposure to newspaper and television reports provided a powerful source of social influence regarding the appropriate response to heartburn. It is likely that heartburn became a topic of conversation and social comparison among affected individuals. Thus, chronic heartburn sufferers were interpreting familiar symptoms in a new social context. Many subsequently sought medical attention not because of changes in symptomatology but because their cognitive representations and affective responses related to heartburn had changed. Heartburn and esophageal cancer were the symptom and disease of 1999, repeating the pattern in which symptomatic individuals, health care providers, purveyors of medicinals, and advocacy groups together construct the disease of the year, decade, or century (Shorter, 1995). With good fortune, the construction matches biological science and medical treatment. All too often, there is a mismatch (e.g., with chronic fatigue syndrome and many of psychiatric disorders) and the hope that it will be resolved with new science and better treatments.

REFERENCES

Ajzen, I. (1991). The theory of planned behavior. *Organizational Behavior and Human Decision Processes, 50,* 179–211.

Ajzen, I., & Fishbein, M. (1972). Attitudes and normative beliefs as factors influencing behavioral intentions. *Journal of Personality and Social Psychology, 21,* 1–9.

Ajzen, I., & Fishbein, M. (1980). *Understanding attitudes and predicting social behavior.* Englewood Cliffs, NJ: Prentice-Hall.

Anderson, J. C., & Bartkus, D. (1973). Choice of medical care: A behavioral model of health and illness behavior. *Journal of Health and Social Behavior, 14,* 348–362.

Anderson, J. R. (1987). *The architecture of cognition.* Cambridge, MA: Harvard University Press.

Anderson, J. R. (1993). *The adaptive character of thought.* Hillsdale, NJ: Erlbaum.

Aneshensel, C. S., Frerichs, R. R., & Huba G. J. (1984). Depression and physical illness: A multiwave, nonrecursive causal model. *Journal of Health and Social Behavior, 25,* 350–371.

Apple, D. (1960). How laymen define illness. *Journal of Health and Social Behavior, 13,* 219–228.

Backett, E. M., Heady, J. A., & Evans, J. C. (1954). Studies of a general practice. II. The doctor's job in an urban area. *British Medical Journal, 1,* 109–123.

Barondess, J. A. (1979). Disease and illness: A crucial distinction. *American Journal of Medicine, 66,* 375–376.

Barsky, A. (1981). Hidden reasons some patients visit doctors. *Annals of Internal Medicine, 94,* 492–297.

Barsky, A. J., & Klerman, G. L. (1983). Overview: Hypochondriasis, bodily complaints, and somatic symptoms. *Psychosomatic Medicine, 50,* 510–519.

Baumann, B. (1961). Diversities in conceptions of health and physical fitness. *Journal of Health and Human Behavior, 2,* 39–46.

Baumann, L. J., Cameron, L. D., Zimmerman, R. S., & Leventhal, H. (1989). Illness representations and matching labels with symptoms. *Health Psychology, 8,* 449–469.

Baumann, L. J., & Leventhal, H. (1985). "I can tell when my blood pressure is up, can't I?" *Health Psychology, 4,* 203–218.

Becker, M. H. (1974). *The health belief model and personal health behavior.* Thorofare, NJ: Charles B. Slack.

Becker, M. H., & Maiman, L. A. (1975). Sociomedical determinants of compliance with health and medical care recommendations. *Medical Care, 13,* 10–24.

Berkanovic, E., Telesky, C., & Reeder, S. (1981). Structural and social psychological factors in the decision to seek medical care for symptoms. *Medical Care, 19,* 693–709.

Bishop, G. D. (1984). Gender, role, and illness behavior in a military population. *Health Psychology, 3,* 519–534.

Bishop, G. D. (1991). Understanding the understanding of illness: Lay disease representations. In J. A. Skelton & R. T. Croyle (Eds.), *Mental representations in health and illness* (pp. 32–59). New York: Springer-Verlag.

Bishop, G. D., Briede, C., Cavazos, L., Grotzinger, R., & McMahon, S. (1987). Processing illness information: The role of disease prototypes. *Basic and Applied Social Psychology, 8,* 21–43.

Bishop, G. D., & Converse, S. A. (1986). Illness representations: A prototype approach. *Health Psychology, 5,* 95–114.

Borawski, E., Kinney, J., & Kahana, E. (1996). The meaning of older adults health appraisals: Congruence with health status and determinant of mortality. *Journal of Gerontology: Social Sciences, 51B,* S157–S170.

Brody, J. E. (1999, April 27). Chronic heartburn, an ominous warning. *New York Times,* p. D6.

Brownlee, S., Leventhal, E. A., & Leventhal, H. (2000). Regulation, self-regulation, and regulation of the self in maintaining physical health. In M. Boekartz, P. R. Pintrich, & M. Zeidner (Eds.), *Handbook of self-regulation* (pp. 369–416). San Diego, CA: Academic Press.

Cameron, L., Leventhal, E. A., & Leventhal, H. (1993). Symptom representation and affect as determinants of care seeking in a community-dwelling, adult sample population. *Health Psychology, 12,* 171–179.

Cameron, L., Leventhal, E. A., & Leventhal, H. (1995). Seeking medical care in response to symptoms and life stress. *Psychosomatic Medicine, 57*, 37–47.

Carver, C. S., Scheier, M. F., & Weintraub, J. K. (1989). Assessing coping strategies: A theoretically based approach. *Journal of Personality and Social Psychology, 56*, 267–283.

Clark, M. (1959). *Health in the Mexican-American culture*. Berkeley: University of California Press.

Cloninger, C. R. (1987). Neurogenetic adaptive mechanism in alcoholism. *Science, 236*, 410–416.

Cohen, M. Z., Tripp-Reimer, T., Smith, C., Sorofman, B., & Lively, S. (1994). Explanatory models of diabetes: Patient practitioner variation. *Social Science and Medicine, 38*, 59–66.

Cohen, S., Doyle, W. J., Skoner, D. P., Fireman, P., Gwaltny, J. M., & Newsom, J. T. (1995). State and trait negative affect as predictors of objective and subjective symptoms of respiratory viral infections. *Journal of Personality and Social Psychology, 68*, 159–169.

Colligan, M., Pennebaker, J. W., & Murphy, L. (Eds.). (1982). *Mass psychogenic illness: A social psychological perspective*. Hillsdale, NJ: Erlbaum.

Costa, P. T., Jr., & McCrae, R. R. (1980). Somatic complaints in males as a function of age and neuroticism: A longitudinal analysis. *Journal of Behavioral Medicine, 3*, 245–257.

Costa, P. T., Jr., & McCrae, R. R. (1985). Hypochondriasis, neuroticism, and aging: When are somatic complaints unfounded? *American Psychologist, 40*, 19–28.

Costa, P. T., Jr., & McCrae, R. R. (1987). Neuroticism, somatic complaints, and disease: Is the bark worse than the bite? *Journal of Personality, 55*, 299–316.

Dakof, G. A., & Taylor, S. E. (1990). Victims' perceptions of social support: What is helpful from whom? *Journal of Personality and Social Psychology, 58*, 80–89.

Davison, K. P., & Pennebaker, J. W. (1996). Social psychosomatics. In E. T. Higgins & A. W. Kruglanski (Eds.), *Social psychology: Handbook of basic principles* (pp. 102–130). New York: Guilford Press.

Diefenbach, M. A., Leventhal, E. A., Leventhal, H., & Patrick-Miller, L. (1996). Negative affect relates to cross-sectional but not longitudinal symptom reporting: Data from elderly adults. *Health Psychology, 15*, 282–288.

Ditto, P. H., & Jemmott, J. B., III. (1989). From rarity to evaluative extremity: Effects of prevalence information on evaluations of positive and negative characteristics. *Journal of Personality and Social Psychology, 57*, 16–26.

Dollard, J., & Miller, N. E. (1950). *Personality and psychotherapy*. New York: McGraw Hill.

Fillingim, R. B., & Fine, M. A. (1986). The effects of internal versus external information processing on symptom perception in an exercise setting. *Health Psychology, 5*, 115–123.

Fink, P. (1996). Somatization—Beyond symptom count. *Journal of Psychosomatic Research, 40*, 7–10.

Fishbein, M., & Ajzen, I. (1974). Attitudes towards objects as predictors of single and multiple behavioral criteria. *Psychological Review, 81*, 59–74.

Fiske, S. T., & Taylor, S. E. (1991). *Social cognition.* New York: McGraw-Hill.

Friedson, E. (1961). *Patients' views of medical practice.* New York: Russell Sage.

Gijsbers van Wijk, C. M., & Kolk, A. M. (1997). Sex differences in physical symptoms: The contribution of symptom perception theory. *Social Science and Medicine, 45*, 231–246.

Gochman, D. (1972). Development of health beliefs. *Psychological Reports, 31*, 259–266.

Goff, D. C., Nichaman, M. Z., Ramsey, D. J., Meyer, P. S., & Labarthe, D. R. (1995). A population-based assessment of the use and effectiveness of thrombolytic therapy: The Corpus Christi Heart Project. *Annals of Epidemiology, 5*, 171–178.

Goff, D. C., Sellers, D. E., McGovern, P. G., Meischke, H., Goldberg, R. J., Bittner, V., et al. (1998). Knowledge of heart attack symptoms in a population survey in the United States. *Archives of Internal Medicine, 158*, 2329–2338.

Granovetter, M. S. (1978). The strength of weak ties. *American Journal of Sociology, 31*, 1360–1369.

Gray, J. A. (1982). *The neuropsychology of anxiety: An enquiry into the functions of the septo-hippocampal system.* New York: Oxford University Press.

Gray, J. A. (1985). Issues in the neuropsychology of anxiety. In A. H. Tuma & J. D. Maser (Eds.), *Anxiety and the anxiety disorders* (pp. 5–25). Hillsdale, NJ: Erlbaum.

Gunnar R. M., Bourdillon, P. D., & Dixon, D. W. (1990). ACC/AHA guidelines for the early management of patients with acute myocardial infarction: A report of the American College of Cardiology/American Heart Association Task Force on Assessment of Diagnostic and Therapeutic Cardiovascular Procedures. *Circulation, 82*, 664–707.

Guyton, A. C. (1991). *Textbook of medical physiology.* Philadelphia: W. B. Saunders.

Hannay, D. R., & Maddox, E. J. (1976). Symptom prevalence and referral behavior in Glasgow. *Social Science and Medicine, 10*, 185–189.

Hart, B. L. (1988). Biological basis of the behavior of sick animals. *Neuroscience and Biobehavioral Reviews, 12*, 123–137.

Harver, A., & Mahler, D. A. (1998). Sensation, symptom and illness. In D. A. Mahler (Ed.), *Dyspnea* (pp. 1–34). New York: Marcel Dekker.

Hecker, B. L., & Ajzen, I. (1983). Improving the prediction of health behavior: An approach based on the theory of reasoned action. *Academic Psychology Bulletin, 5*, 11–19.

Heider, F. (1958). *The psychology of interpersonal relations.* New York: Wiley.

Heurtin-Roberts, S., & Reisin, E. (1992). The relation of culturally influenced lay models of hypertension to compliance with treatment. *American Journal of Hypertension, 5*, 787–792.

Hilgard, E. (1980). The trilogy of mind: Cognition, affection, and conation. *Journal of the History of the Behavioral Sciences, 16,* 107–117.

Hochbaum, G. (1958). *Public participation in medical screening programs* (DHEW Publication No. 572, Public Health Service). Washington, DC: U.S. Government Printing Office.

Idler, E. L., Hudson, S. V., & Leventhal, H. (1999). The meanings of self-ratings of health: A qualitative and quantitative approach. *Research on Aging, 21,* 458–476.

Ingham, I., & Miller, P. (1979). Symptom prevalence and severity in a general practice. *Journal of Epidemiology and Community Health, 33,* 191–198.

Janz, N., & Becker, M. (1984). The health belief model: A decade later. *Health Education Quarterly, 2,* 1–47.

Jennings, D. (1986). The confusion between disease and illness in clinical medicine. *Canadian Medical Association Journal, 135,* 865–870.

Johnson, J. A., & King, K. B. (1995). Influence of expectations about symptoms on delay in seeking treatment during a myocardial infarction. *American Journal of Critical Care, 4,* 29–35.

Kerckhoff A. C., & Back, K. W. (1968). *The June Bug: A study of hysterical contagion.* New York: Appleton-Century-Crofts.

Kleinman, A., & Kleinman, J. (1985). Somatization: The interconnections in Chinese society among culture, depressive experiences, and the meanings of pain. In A. Kleinman & B. Good (Eds.), *Culture and depression: Studies in the anthropology and cross cultural psychiatry of affect and disorder* (pp. 429–490). Berkeley: University of California Press.

Kubzansky, L. D., Kawachi, I., Weiss, S. T., & Sparrow, D. (1998). Anxiety and coronary heart disease: A synthesis of epidemiological, psychological, and experimental evidence. *Annals of Behavioral Medicine, 20,* 47–58.

Kutner, B., & Gordon, G. (1961). Seeking care for cancer. *Journal of Health and Human Behavior, 2,* 171–178.

Laffrey, S. C. (1986). Development of a health conception scale. *Research in Nursing and Health, 9,* 107–113.

Lagergren, J., Bergström, R., Lindgren, A., & Nyrén, O. (1999). Symptomatic gastroesophageal reflux as a risk factor for esophageal adenocarcinoma. *New England Journal of Medicine, 340,* 825–831.

Lau, R. R. (1997). Cognitive representations of health and illness. In D. S. Gochman (Ed.), *Handbook of health behavior research I: Personal and social determinants* (pp. 51–69). New York: Plenum Press.

Lau, R. R., Bernard, T. M., & Hartmann, K. A. (1989). Further explorations of common-sense representations of common illnesses. *Health Psychology, 8,* 195–219.

Lazarus, R. S., & Folkman, S. (1984). *Stress, appraisal, and coping.* New York: Springer.

Leff, J. (1977). The cross-cultural study of emotions. *Culture, Medicine, and Psychiatry, 1*, 317, 350.

Leventhal, E. A., & Crouch, M. (1997). Are there differences in perceptions of illness across the lifespan? In K. J. Petrie & J. A. Weinman (Eds.), *Perceptions of health and illness: Current research and applications* (pp. 77–102). London: Harwood Academic Press.

Leventhal, E. A., Hansell, S., Diefenbach, M., Leventhal, H., & Glass, D. C. (1996). Negative affect and self-report of physical symptoms: Two longitudinal studies of older adults. *Health Psychology, 15*, 192–199.

Leventhal, E. A., Leventhal, H., Schaefer, P., & Easterling, D. (1993). Conservation of energy, uncertainty reduction and swift utilization of medical care among the elderly. *Journal of Gerontology: Psychological Sciences, 48*, 78–86.

Leventhal, H. (1970). Findings and theory in the study of fear communications. In L. Berkowitz (Ed.), *Advances in experimental social psychology* (Vol. 5, pp. 119–186). San Diego, CA: Academic Press.

Leventhal, H., & Diefenbach, M. (1991). The active side of illness cognition. In J. A. Skelton & R. T. Croyle (Eds.), *Mental representation in health and illness* (pp. 247–272). New York: Springer-Verlag.

Leventhal, H., Hudson, S., & Robitaille, C. (1997). Social comparison and health: A process model. In B. Buunk & F. X. Gibbons (Eds.), *Health, coping and well being: Perspectives from social comparison theory* (pp. 411–432). Hillsdale, NJ: Erlbaum.

Leventhal, H., & Leventhal, E. A. (1993). Affect, cognition and symptom reporting. In C. R. Chapman & K. M. Foley (Eds.), *Current and emerging issues in cancer pain: Research and practice* (pp. 153–173). New York: Raven Press.

Leventhal, H., Meyer, D., & Nerenz, D. (1980). The common sense representation of illness danger. In S. Rachman (Ed.), *Contributions to medical psychology* (Vol. 2, pp. 7–30). New York: Pergamon Press.

Leventhal, H., Singer, R., & Jones, S. (1965). Effects of fear and specificity of recommendations upon attitudes and behavior. *Journal of Personality and Social Psychology, 2*, 20–29.

Leventhal, H., Watts, J. C., & Pagano, F. (1967). Effects of fear and instructions on how to cope with danger. *Journal of Personality and Social Psychology, 6*, 313–321.

Levine, R. M., & Reicher, S. D. (1996). Making sense of symptoms: Self-categorization and the meaning of illness and injury. *British Journal of Social Psychology, 35*, 245–256.

Liu, W. T., & Duff, R. W. (1972). The strength in weak ties. *Public Opinion Quarterly, 42*, 361–367.

Markus, H. R., & Nurius, P. (1986). Possible selves. *American Psychologist, 41*, 954–969.

Martin, R., Davis, G. M., Baron, R. S., Suls, J., & Blanchard, E. B. (1994). Specificity in social support: Perceptions of helpful and unhelpful provider behaviors among irritable bowel syndrome, headache, and cancer patients. *Health Psychology, 13,* 432–439.

Martin, R., Gordon, E. E. I., & Lounsbury, P. (1998). Gender disparities in the interpretation of cardiac-related symptoms: The contribution of common sense models of illness. *Health Psychology, 17,* 346–357.

Martin, R., & Lemos, K. (2002). From heart attacks to melanoma: Do common sense models of somatization influence symptom interpretation for female victims? *Health Psychology, 21,* 25–32.

Martin, R., Wan, C. K., David, J. P., Wegner, E. L., Olson, B. D., & Watson, D. (1999). Style of anger expression: Relation to expressivity, personality, and health. *Personality and Social Psychology Bulletin, 25,* 1196–1207.

Meyer, D., Leventhal, H., & Gutmann, M. (1985). Common-sense models of illness: The example of hypertension. *Health Psychology, 4,* 115–135.

Mezzich, J., & Raab, E. (1980). Depressive symptomatology across the Americas. *Archives of General Psychiatry, 37,* 818–823.

McGuire, W. J. (1969). The nature of attitudes and attitude change. In G. Lindsey & E. Aronson (Eds.), *The handbook of social psychology* (2nd ed., Vol. 3, pp. 136–314). Reading, MA: Addison-Wesley.

Miller, N. E. (1951). Learnable drives and rewards. In S. S. Stevens (Ed.), *Handbook of experimental psychology* (pp. 435–472). New York: Wiley.

Moos, R., & Van Dort, B. (1977). Physical and emotional symptoms and campus health center utilization. *Social Psychiatry, 12,* 107–115.

Natapoff, J. N. (1978). Children's views of health: A developmental study. *American Journal of Public Health, 68,* 995–999.

Nathanson, C. A. (1975). Illness and the feminine role: A theoretical review. *Social Science and Medicine, 9,* 57–62.

Nathanson, C. A. (1977). Sex, illness and medical care: A review of data, theory, and method. *Social Science & Medicine, 11,* 13–26.

National Center for Health Statistics. (1980). *Geographic patterns in the risk of dying and associated factors ages 35–74 years* (Series 3, No. 18). Washington, DC: U.S. Government Printing Office.

National Heart Attack Alert Program Coordinating Committee, 60 Minutes to Treatment Working Group. (1994). Emergency department: Rapid identification and treatment of patients with acute myocardial infarction. *Annals of Emergency Medicine, 23,* 311–329.

Oberlander, T. F., Pless, I. B., & Dougherty, G. E. (1993). Advice seeking and appropriate use of a pediatric emergency department. *American Journal of Developmental Care, 147,* 863–867.

Pachter, L. M. (1994). Culture and clinical care: Folk illness beliefs and behaviors and their implications for health care delivery. *Journal of the American Medical Association, 271,* 690–694.

Padgett, V. R., & Hill, A. K. (1989). Maximizing athletic performance in endurance events: A comparison of coping strategies. *Journal of Applied Social Psychology, 19,* 331–340.

Pennebaker, J. W. (1982). *The psychology of physical symptoms.* New York: Springer-Verlag.

Pennebaker, J. W. (1989). Confession, inhibition, and disease. In L. Berkowitz (Ed.), *Advances in experimental social psychology* (Vol. 22, pp. 211–244). Orlando, FL: Academic Press.

Pennebaker, J. W., & Lightner, J. M. (1980). Competition of internal and external information in an exercise setting. *Journal of Personality and Social Psychology, 39,* 165–174.

Peters, S., Stanley, I., Rose, M., & Salmon, P. (1998). Patients with medically unexplained symptoms: Sources of patients' authority and implications for demands on medical care. *Social Science and Medicine, 46,* 559–565.

Prohaska, T. R., Keller, M. L., Leventhal, E. A., & Leventhal, H. (1987). Impact of symptoms and aging attribution on emotions and coping. *Health Psychology, 6,* 495–514.

Rook, K. S. (1984). The negative side of social interaction: Impact on psychological well-being. *Journal of Personality and Social Psychology, 46,* 1097–1108.

Rosenstock, I. M. (1974). The health belief model and preventive health behavior. *Health Education Monographs, 2,* 354–386.

Safer, M., Tharps, D., Jackson, T., & Leventhal, H. (1979). Determinants of three stages of delay in seeking care at a medical clinic. *Medical Care, 17,* 11–29.

Sanders, G. S. (1982). Social comparison and perceptions of health and illness. In G. S. Sanders & J. Suls (Eds.), *Social psychology of health and illness* (pp. 129–157). Hillsdale, NJ: Erlbaum.

Scambler, A., Scambler, G., & Craig, D. (1981). Kinship and friendship networks and women's demand for primary care. *Journal of the Royal College of General Practitioners, 26,* 746–750.

Scambler, G., & Scambler, A. (1985). The illness iceberg and aspects of consulting behavior. In R. Fitzpatrick & J. Hinton (Eds.), *The experience of illness* (pp. 32–50). London: Tavistock.

Scharloo, M., & Kaptein, A. (1997). Measurement of illness perceptions in patients with chronic somatic illness: A review. In K. J. Petrie & J. A. Weinman (Eds.), *Perceptions of health and illness: Current research and applications* (pp. 103–154). London: Harwood Academic Press.

Schober, R., & Lacroix, J. M. (1991). Lay illness models in the enlightenment and the 20th century: Some historical lessons. In J. A. Skelton & R. T. Croyle (Eds.), *Mental representations in health and illness* (pp. 10–31). New York: Springer-Verlag.

Shorter, E. (1995). Sucker-punched again! Physicians meet the disease-of-the-month syndrome. *Journal of Psychosomatic Research, 39,* 115–118.

Skelton, J. A, & Croyle, R. T. (1991). Mental representation, health, and illness: An introduction. In J. A. Skelton & R. T. Croyle (Eds.), *Mental representations in health and illness* (pp. 1–9). New York: Springer-Verlag.

Smith, C. A., Wallston, K. A., & Dwyer, K. A. (1995). On babies and bathwater: Disease impact and negative affectivity in the self-reports of persons with rheumatoid arthritis. *Heath Psychology, 14,* 64–73.

Sorofman, B., Tripp-Reimer, T., Lauer, G. M., & Martin, M. E. (1990). Symptom self-care. *Holistic Nursing Practice, 4,* 45–55.

Speckens, A. E. M., Van Hemert, A. M., Bolk, J. H., Rooijmans, H. G. M., & Hengeveld, M. W. (1996). Unexplained physical symptoms: Outcome, utilization of medical care and associated factors. *Psychological Medicine, 26,* 745–752.

Stoller, E. P. (1997). Medical self care: Lay management of symptoms by elderly people. In M. G. Ory & G. DeFries (Eds.), *Self-care in later life: Research, program, and policy issues* (pp. 24–61). New York: Springer.

Suls, J., & Goodkin, F. (1994). Medical gossip and rumor: Their role in the lay referral system. In R. F. Goodman & A. Ben-Zeev (Eds.), *Good gossip* (pp. 169–179). Lawrence: University Press of Kansas.

Suls, J., Martin, R., & Leventhal, H. (1997). Social comparison, lay referral, and the decision to seek medical care. In B. P. Buunk & F. X. Gibbons (Eds.), *Health, coping, and well-being: Perspectives from social comparison theory* (pp. 195–226). Mahwah, NJ: Erlbaum.

Tellegen, A. (1985). Structures of mood and personality and their relevance to assessing anxiety, with an emphasis on self-report. In H. H. Tuma & J. D. Maser (Eds.), *Anxiety and the anxiety disorders* (pp. 681–706). Hillsdale, NJ: Erlbaum.

Turk, D. C., Litt, M. D., Salovey, P., & Walker, J. (1985). Seeking urgent pediatric treatment: Factors contributing to frequency, delay, and appropriateness. *Health Psychology, 4,* 43–59.

Verbrugge, L. M. (1989). The twain meet: Empirical explanations of sex differences in health and mortality. *Journal of Health and Social Behavior, 30,* 282–304.

Wan, T. (1976). Predicting self-assessed health status: A multivariate approach. *Health Services Research, 11,* 464–477.

Watson, D., & Clark, L. A. (1984). Negative affectivity: The disposition to experience aversive emotional states. *Psychological Bulletin, 96,* 465–490.

Watson, D., Clark, L. A., & Carey, G. (1988). Positive and negative affectivity and their relation to anxiety and depressive disorders. *Journal of Abnormal Psychology, 97,* 346–353.

Watson, D., & Pennebaker, J. W. (1989). Health complaints, stress, and disease: Exploring the central role of negative affectivity. *Psychological Review, 96,* 234–254.

Watson, D., & Pennebaker, J. W. (1991). Situational, dispositional, and genetic bases of symptom reporting. In J. A. Skelton & R. T. Croyle (Eds.), *Mental representations in health and illness* (pp. 60–84). New York: Springer-Verlag.

Weller, S. S. (1984). Cross cultural concepts of illness: Variables and validation. *American Anthropologist, 86,* 341–351.

Westermeyer, J. (1985). Psychiatric diagnosis across cultural boundaries. *American Journal of Psychiatry, 142,* 798–805.

White, K. L., Williams, T. F., & Greenberg, B. G. (1961). The ecology of medical care. *New England Journal of Medicine, 265,* 885–892.

Wolinsky, F. D. (1978). Assessing the effects of predisposing, enabling, and illness-morbidity characteristics on health service utilization. *Journal of Health and Social Behavior, 19,* 384–396.

Zola, I. (1973). Pathways to the doctor: From person to patient. *Social Science and Medicine, 7,* 577–689.

10

MEDICAL REGIMEN ADHERENCE: CONCEPTS, ASSESSMENT, AND INTERVENTIONS

SUZANNE BENNETT JOHNSON AND DAWN NEWMAN CARLSON

After treatment for congestive heart failure and diabetes mellitus, Emma Jones was discharged home with a list of instructions and prescriptions. That evening, she reached into her bag of medications and looked at the bottles. "I don't know what to do with all of these pills. The directions are confusing. What does PO bid mean?" (72-old-female)

Sixteen months ago, Bobby was diagnosed with type 1 diabetes. Recently he was admitted to the hospital, for the third time for diabetic ketoacidosis. Bobby has a history of poor self-care. He rarely monitors his blood glucose, he takes his insulin injections at different times from day to day, and he has poor dietary habits. His parents believe that it is Bobby's responsibility to manage his own diabetes. (12-year-old boy)

Poor patient adherence to medical recommendations has been dubbed the "$100 Billion Problem" (Mistry & Sorrentino, 1999). Literature reviews suggest that a third of patients fail to follow medical prescriptions for acute illnesses; rates of poor adherence to chronic disease management prescriptions are even higher (DiMatteo, 1994; Rand, 1993; Rapoff, 1999). With the increasing prevalence of chronic disease, poor regimen adherence is becoming a major health care problem. Chronic diseases currently account for 70% of deaths in the United States (Centers for Disease Control and Prevention, 1999); most of these diseases place complex daily disease management demands on the patient, often for the rest of the patient's life.

This chapter supported in part by National Institutes of Health Grants RO1-HD13820 and R01-HL69736 and National Institutes of Health Training Grant T32-HD07524.

Adherence to medical regimens is a behavioral and not a medical phenomenon. Hence, strategies to assess adherence and interventions to improve a patient's daily disease management are not components of the usual medical armamentarium (Johnson, 1993). However, the role of patient behavior, in addition to medical prescriptions, is receiving increasing attention. The objective of this chapter is to provide an overview of (a) the prevalence and cost of medical regimen adherence problems in pediatric and adult populations; (b) issues relevant to definition and terminology; (c) the extent of inadvertent noncompliance; (d) the extent of professional noncompliance; (e) strategies to assess medical regimen adherence; (f) adherence-related theoretical models; (g) barriers to regimen adherence; and (h) interventions to improve adherence. Given the large number of issues and the limited space, each will be addressed briefly, with more detailed references provided. The chapter ends with a discussion of the important expertise the health psychologist can bring to the care of medical patients.

PREVALENCE AND COST OF POOR PATIENT ADHERENCE TO MEDICAL REGIMENS

Varying degrees of medical regimen adherence have been documented depending on the method of assessment, the criteria used for defining acceptable adherence, the regimen prescribed, and the setting in which adherence was assessed (Rapoff, 1999; Rapoff & Barnard, 1991; Sherbourne, Hays, Ordway, DiMatteo, & Kravitz, 1992). Adherence to chronic disease management regimens appears to be more problematic than adherence to acute regimens (Cameron & Gregor, 1987). It is estimated that a third of patients fail to adhere to short-term treatment plans (e.g., completing an antibiotic course; DiMatteo, 1994), whereas 50% of patients mismanage longer term treatment regimens (e.g., medication and glucose testing recommendations for diabetes care; Eklerling & Kors, 1984; Fennerty, 1978; Jette, 1982; O'Brien, 1980; Rapoff, 1999; Rapoff & Barnard, 1991; Sackett & Snow, 1979; Turk & Meichenbaum, 1991). When the health condition is asymptomatic (e.g., hypertension), approximately 70% of patients fail to adhere to recommended treatment (Sherbourne et al., 1992). Similarly, more than 75% of patients neglect or are unable to follow recommended lifestyle changes such as exercising or following dietary suggestions (Epstein & Cluss, 1982).

The impact of poor medical regimen adherence has been exacerbated by the increasing prevalence of chronic disease in the U.S. population. More than 90 million Americans live with chronic illnesses such as diabetes, cancer, HIV/AIDS, and cardiovascular disease (Centers for Disease Control and Prevention, 2004); these diseases account for 70% of annual U.S.

mortality (Centers for Disease Control and Prevention, 1999). Chronic diseases are not limited to adult populations. Children with chronic illnesses now make up a larger proportion of pediatric practices. Approximately 30% of U.S. children live with at least one chronic condition; 10% have a serious condition resulting in significant distress or limitations in childhood activities (Newacheck, 1994).

Inadequate adherence to medical regimens has been linked to more than 125,000 deaths annually, as well as innumerable unnecessary clinic appointments, additional diagnostic tests, emergency room visits, hospitalizations, and nursing home admissions. The estimated annual cost to treat medical ailments associated with poor medical regimen adherence is $13 billion to $15 billion (Berg, Dischler, Wagner, Raia, & Palmer-Shevlin, 1993; DiMatteo, 1994; Mistry & Sorrentino, 1999; Rapoff, 1999), placing a huge financial strain on the nation's health care system.

COMPLIANCE, ADHERENCE, OR SELF-MANAGEMENT

For many years, *compliance* was the term used to describe a patient's medical regimen behaviors. However, some have argued that compliance connotes a sense of passive patient acceptance of provider recommendations. *Adherence* is preferred terminology, because it suggests that the patient plays an active role in accepting the provider's recommendations. More than 15 years ago, Glasgow, Wilson, and McCaul (1985) argued that both *adherence* and *compliance* are problematic constructs, because provider recommendations are often so vague and nonspecific that judgments cannot be readily made as to whether or not the patient is "adherent." Glasgow et al. (1985) suggested a new terminology, *self-care behaviors*, to describe what patients do every day to manage their own diseases. *Self-care* or *self-management* is now accepted terminology, although *compliance* and *adherence* are terms that continue to be widely used.

Inadvertent Noncompliance

Although we often think of noncompliance as willful disregard of provider prescriptions, patients are often inadvertently noncompliant. Through patient–provider miscommunication, failure to recall information accurately, or knowledge and skill deficits, a patient may believe that he or she is carefully following a treatment prescription when, in fact, the patient is behaving in ways that are contrary to provider recommendations. Investigators and clinicians need to be aware that patient and provider reports of provider prescriptions are often inconsistent. Similarly, patients may appear to be conscientious, taking their medication at the correct time each day and carrying out other aspects of their medical regimens at specified intervals. However, closer inspection of their actual behavior may reveal numerous technical errors, potentially leading to incorrect medication administration or inadvertent noncompliance with other treatment tasks.

Haynes (1979), probably the most cited author on the subject, defined compliance as "the extent to which a person's behavior (in terms of taking medications, following diets, or executing lifestyle changes) coincides with medical advice" (pp. 2–3). Historically, health care providers have focused almost exclusively on the patient's behavior, ignoring the poor quality of medical or health advice. Instructions to patients are frequently so vague as to be minimally useful. Although drug types and doses may be specified, other aspects of the treatment regimen are often described in general, nonspecific terms (e.g., "get some exercise" or "avoid high-fat foods"). Such suggestions are too general to serve as a standard against which the patient's behavior can be compared.

Patients often leave the clinical encounter without a clear understanding of what disease management behaviors are required. For example, Page, Verstraete, Robb, and Etzwiler (1981) compared recommendations given by health care providers in a childhood diabetes clinic with patients' and parents' recall of those recommendations. Providers gave an average of seven recommendations per patient. Patients (and parents of younger children) recalled an average of only two recommendations. Furthermore, 40% of the "recommendations" patients and parents recalled were not even made by the provider. Similar findings were reported by Falvo and Tippy (1988), who examined patient recall in a family practice clinic; only 50% of instructions given by the physician were recalled by the patients. Cline et al. (1999) assessed elderly heart failure patients' knowledge of prescribed medication; 45% of the patients failed to recall the name of the medication prescribed, 50% were unable to state the prescribed dose, and 64% were unable to recall when the medication was to be taken. These studies clearly highlight the extent of patient–provider miscommunication even in cases where both patients and providers are well-meaning and motivated. Obviously, if a patient or parent does not have a clear understanding of the recommended treatment, adherence to the treatment is not possible. In such cases, the patient may be inadvertently noncompliant because the patient or parent fails to understand or recall the regimen prescriptions.

Other types of knowledge or technical skill deficits may lead to inadvertent noncompliance. Careful observation of patient disease management behaviors often uncovers problems with technique or dosing previously unknown to the patient or provider. For example, insulin-injection and glucose testing errors have been documented in both children and adults with diabetes (Johnson, 1992; Perwien, Johnson, Dymtrow, & Silverstein, 2000). Careful observation of parents giving factor replacement therapy to their hemophiliac sons uncovered numerous administration errors despite years of experience (Sergis-Deavenport & Varni, 1983). Winkelstein et al.'s (2000) study of asthmatic children documented deficient metered-dose inhaler (MDI) technique in 93% of the children (these children's parents were unaware of their children's deficits). Larson, Hahn, and Ekholm (1994) reported more than 75% of adult asthmatic patients, who had previously received training in the nine-step MDI process, made at least one technical error. In all of these examples, patients or parents believed that they were following a recommended treatment protocol, but because of technical skill deficits, they were inadvertently noncompliant.

Professional Noncompliance

In the previous section, we highlighted some of the primary reasons motivated patients are often inadvertently noncompliant with their medical regimens: inadequately communicated or vague medical advice; patient failure to acquire, recall, or retain the specifics of the treatment regimen; and patient knowledge or technical skills deficits that prevent successful adherence with a specific treatment task. However, it is important to recognize that many providers are themselves misinformed and skill-deficient. Although there is often an implicit assumption that health care providers adhere to recommended treatment guidelines, the evidence on professional noncompliance is markedly reminiscent of the literature on patient noncompliance (see Miechenbaum & Turk, 1987; Myers & Midence, 1998, for reviews). The term *professional noncompliance* was coined by Ley (1981), who ascertained that 51% to 100% of patients did not receive appropriate medication or treatment advice (Myers & Midence, 1998). Numerous studies have demonstrated that physicians often fail to give patients an appropriate treatment prescription; some make unjustified changes in patients' medication protocols (Schleifer et al., 1991), others fail to adhere to recommended medication guidelines (Cohen, Berner, & Dubach, 1985), and still others prescribe incorrect medication regimens (Rao, Mookerjee, Obasanjo, & Chaisson, 2000). Professional noncompliance extends beyond medication prescriptions and includes noncompliance with health care procedures and practices (Frolkis, Zyzanski, Schwartz, & Suhan, 1998; Levin & Ornstein, 1990) as well as preventative guidelines (Costanza, Stoddard, Zapka, Gaw, & Barth, 1992; Nilasena & Lincoln, 1995). It is not surprising that professional noncompliance has been linked to higher disease relapse rates (Peeters, Koren, Jacubovicz, & Zipursky, 1988) and increased patient hospitalizations (Haldeman, Croft, Giles, & Rashidee, 1999). A recent report by the Institute of Medicine (Kohn, Corrigan, & Donaldson, 1999) highlighted the extent and seriousness of medical errors made by knowledgeable professionals. The report estimated that between 44,000 and 98,000 Americans admitted to hospitals die each year as a result of professional medical errors, making medical errors the eighth leading cause of death in the United States.

Issues surrounding the appropriateness of provider recommendations and prescriptions are important and challenging. Patient adherence will make a difference only in cases where the treatment prescribed is effective; even perfect compliance with an inadequate or inappropriate treatment recommendation will not result in improved health status, and in some cases, could result in harm.

ASSESSING PATIENT ADHERENCE

There are a variety of patient adherence assessment strategies from which to choose. The approach selected should be based on conceptual issues as well as the reliability and validity of the method. Available reliability data should demonstrate that the method measures the adherence behavior of interest in a consistent fashion. Relevant validity studies should suggest that the method is sensitive to differences between patients in levels of adherence behaviors as well as any behavior change within a patient. In most cases, it is helpful to select methods that are nonreactive—in other words, the process of measuring adherence does not induce change in patient adherence behaviors.

CONCEPTUAL ISSUES

Many of the conceptual issues important to adherence assessment have been discussed in the previous section on inadvertent noncompliance. To assess whether a patient is adherent with a particular disease management prescription, there must be a clear provider recommendation to which the patient's behavior can be compared. Also, the patient must understand the recommendation, must be able to recall (or readily access) the recommendation, and must have the necessary knowledge and technical skills to carry out the recommendation. These issues are not trivial but have not been given sufficient attention in the literature or in clinical practice.

Researchers and clinicians often view compliance or noncompliance as a traitlike characteristic of the patient. Patients are described as "noncompliant," suggesting some personality characteristic that permeates the patient's approach to disease management. We now know that adherence behaviors are often complex; patients may be adherent with one component of a treatment regimen but not another. In fact, when multiple regimen behaviors are required, correlations between adherence rates across the regimen behaviors are often quite low (Byron, 1998; Meichenbaum & Turk,

1987). In type 1 diabetes, for example, there are at least six different components of the treatment regimen (insulin administration, exercise, types of foods consumed, amount of calories consumed, frequency of food consumption and glucose testing, and concentrated sweet consumption) that are all unrelated to each other (see Johnson, 1992, for a review). Variance in adherence across different components of a complex treatment regimen has been documented for many diseases and conditions including hypertension (Kravitz et al., 1993), cystic fibrosis (Passero, Remor, & Salomon, 1981), epilepsy (Hazsard, Hutchinson, & Krawiecki, 1990), diabetes (Orme & Binik, 1989), and orthodontics (Gross, Samson, Sanders, & Smith, 1988), suggesting that single indicator assessments of adherence will prove inadequate in many, if not most, situations. For most complex disease management regimens, assessing one disease management behavior will tell us little or nothing about the patient's other disease management behaviors. As desirable as it may be to assess adherence with a brief questionnaire or interview, the behavioral complexity inherent in many disease management prescriptions will severely limit the utility of such an approach in both clinical and research contexts.

Finally, for many diseases, health outcomes and adherence behaviors are, unfortunately, treated as if they are one and the same. Patients who are in poor health are presumed to be noncompliant and those in good health are presumed to have followed the doctor's prescriptions conscientiously. This approach presumes a perfect correspondence between patient behavior and health outcomes. In fact, health status is a product of a variety of factors in addition to patient behavior, including the appropriateness and effectiveness of the treatment prescribed. As mention previously, perfect adherence with an ineffective treatment regimen will have no positive effect on health status (and in some cases, it can result in harm). The link between patient adherence behaviors and health status is often quite complex; we do many patients a disservice by treating them as one and the same (Johnson, 1994).

ADHERENCE ASSESSMENT METHODS

Common methods of assessing adherence include health status indicators, provider ratings, biological assays, behavioral observations, permanent products, electronic monitors, and patient report.

Health Status Indicators

For many diseases, indicators of health status offer a poor substitute for a more direct assessment of adherence behaviors. For example, the literature has failed to document a 1:1 correspondence between diabetes regimen adherence and glycemic control (see Johnson, 1992, for a review). Yet, providers continue to use glycosylated hemoglobin levels, an index of glycemic control over the preceding two to four months, as their primary adherence assessment strategy (Clarke, Snyder, & Nowacek, 1985). Patients in good glycemic control are presumed to be adherent; those in poor glycemic control are assumed to be noncompliant. Unfortunately, such an approach may subtly encourage the provider to blame the patient whenever the patient's health status is less than satisfactory. As well, using health status indicators to measure adherence provides no information about what the patient is or is not doing relevant to the multiple components of diabetes care. Elevated glycosylated hemoglobin levels indicate that something is wrong, but they do not provide specific information about what is wrong with either the provider's prescriptions or the patient's disease management behaviors.

These issues are not limited to diabetes. Many diseases, including hypertension (Taylor, Sackett, Johnson, Gibson, & Roberts, 1978), HIV (Miller & Hays, 2000), cystic fibrosis (Sanders, Gravestock, Wanstall, & Dunne, 1991; Quittner, Espelage, Levers-Landis, & Drotar, 2000), asthma (Eney & Goldstein, 1976; Weinstein & Faust, 1997), and coronary artery disease (Colquhoun, 2000; Rand, 1993), have failed to document a strong 1:1 link between patient adherence behaviors and health status. For most diseases, the relationship between patient adherence behaviors and health status is complex; patient adherence behaviors are one of many potential determinants of health status. As a consequence, for most diseases, health status indicators provide a poor, and sometimes misleading, substitute for more direct adherence assessment strategies.

Provider Ratings

Provider ratings of patient adherence are often unreliable (Bender, Milgrom, & Rand, 1997; Finney, Hook, Friman, Rapoff, & Christopherson, 1993; Gudas, Koocher, & Wyplj, 1991; Johnson, 1992; Matusi, 1997; Mushlin & Appel, 1977) and suffer from the same conceptual and methodological problems as health status indicators. Research suggests that the specificity of provider estimates (the proportion of patients estimated to be adherent who end up being adherent) is generally high, whereas sensitivity (the proportion of patients estimated to be nonadherent who end up being nonadherent) is quite low (Finney et al., 1993; Gilbert, Evans, Haynes, & Tugwell, 1980). This inaccuracy has been attributed to clinical judgement bias and insensitivity toward the patient's associated behavioral and psychosocial issues. Because the provider is usually aware of the patient's current health status, this knowledge is likely to influence provider ratings of patient adherence (Rapoff, 1999; Rudd, 1993). As a result, provider ratings of patient adherence are rarely made independent of the patient's current health status. This is an example of the confounding of constructs that occurs when a health status measure is used as a substitute for a behavioral measure. Also, provider ratings are typically global in nature; the patient is rated as adherent or nonadherent based on a traitlike conceptualization of compliance. As mentioned previously, there is now convincing evidence that for many diseases, adherence is a multivariate construct; multiple behaviors are involved that are not highly related to one another (Johnson, 1992; Rapoff, 1999; Rudd, 1993). Global ratings of patient adherence can never accurately capture this complexity of adherence.

Biological Assays

Biological assays are sometimes used to assess whether a particular medication has been taken. Either the medication or a metabolite of it is assessed directly or markers, biologically inert substances that are coupled with the active medication, are used. Unfortunately, assays of this type have proved to be of limited utility (see Rudd, 1993, for a review). Assays or markers are available for only a limited number of medications and provide a crude indicator of whether medication was taken. They are usually poor indicators of the consistency or timing of medication taking.

Behavioral Observations

Behavioral observations offer an assessment strategy that is highly specific and particularly useful for reliably detecting knowledge or technical skill deficits that may be undermining a patient's ability to adhere to a recommended treatment regimen. As described previously, careful observation of patient disease management behaviors often uncovers problems and difficulties that can be easily corrected through reinstruction and practice (see Johnson, 1992; Larson et al., 1994; Rapoff, 1999, for reviews). Observational methods have also been successfully used to assess a wide range of adherence behaviors in a variety of contexts, including the home (Epstein et al., 1981; Lowe & Lutzer, 1979; Steel, 1994), therapeutic summer camps for chronically ill children (Hanson & Pichert, 1986; Lorenz, Christensen, & Pichert, 1985; Reynolds, Johnson, & Silverstein, 1990), and hospitals and clinics (Gilbert & Varni, 1988; Van Beerendonk, Mesters, Mudde, & Tan, 1998; Wing, Koeske, New, Lamparski, & Becker, 1986). However, observational methods are usually labor-intensive, requiring observer training to ensure reliable behavioral coding. Issues of measurement reactivity also need to be considered. In some cases, if the patient knows that disease management behaviors are being observed by members of the family or others, the patient may change the behaviors selected for observation. The patient may become more adherent than usual. Or the patient may seek ways to deceive the observer by making observation exceedingly difficult or by appearing more adherent than is actually the case.

Permanent Products

Permanent products, such as pill counts, pharmacy refills, or counting glucose test strips, are also used as an adherence assessment procedure. If a behavior is associated with a quantifiable product, the product can be counted as an indirect measure of the adherence behavior (Johnson, 1992).

Counting the number of pills remaining in a bottle of prescribed medication is probably the most well-known use of a permanent product and has been commonly used in ambulatory drug trials. Such an approach presents a number of logistical problems, including the patient's failure to return the pill vial for counting. Even in cases where the vial is returned, patients may engage in a variety of behaviors that could contribute to the invalidation of pill counts. These include intentionally disposing of medication via "pill dumping," sharing the medication, taking prescribed pills from a different medication dispenser, and taking the correct number of pills at the wrong time (Rudd et al., 1989). If the patient is aware of the purpose of the pill count, the patient may be even more likely to engage in duplicitous behavior. Also, pill counting is a crude estimate of overall medication consumption and provides no information about timing of medication use.

Prescription refills may be more accurate than pill counts because of potentially lower social desirability demand characteristics. However, the accuracy of prescription refills will be undermined in cases where patients fill prescriptions in different pharmacies. Also, patients may horde, share, or resell pills; simply refilling a prescription does not guarantee that the medication was taken as prescribed (Rudd, 1993).

Although permanent products have limitations when used alone and tend to overestimate use (Pullar, Kumar, Tindall, & Feely, 1989; Rudd et al., 1989), they may serve to corroborate adherence data obtained from other sources.

Electronic Monitors

Some of the most exciting developments in adherence measurement have been in the area of microelectronic monitors (Cramer, 1995). Advances in microprocessor technology have permitted access to objective data relevant to a variety of disease management behaviors. The monitors store data over an extended period of time, and for most devices, data can be directly downloaded for analysis. Devices have been developed to monitor medication adherence behaviors such as opening pill bottles (Bender et al., 1997; Miller & Hays, 2000), discharging oral and inhaled medications (Bender et al., 1997; Matsui et al., 1992; Quittner et al., 2000), and blood glucose monitoring (Wilson & Endres, 1986; Wysocki, Green, & Huxtable, 1989).

The Medication Event Monitor System (MEMS) is a microprocessor placed inside the cap of a pill vial; it records the time and date each time the bottle is opened, for up to 18 months (Mistry & Sorrentino, 1999; Rapoff, 1999). This device has been used to assess adherence across multiple chronic disease populations (da Costa, Rapoff, Lemanek, & Goldstein, 1997; Kruse, 1991; Lau, Matsi, Greenberg, & Koren, 1998; McKenney, Munroe, & Wright, 1992; Rand, 1993).

Quittner and colleagues (2000) used several electronic monitoring devices to assess adherence among children with cystic fibrosis. Patients were provided with the Doser-CT (Medalogic Corporation), a device that attaches to a metered-dose inhaler and records the date and frequency of activation across a 24-hour period for up to 45 days. Electronic devices were also used to assess airway clearance. For children receiving chest physiotherapy (CPT), their parents wore wrist actigraphs that recorded the date and duration of the parent's rhythmic movement. For those patients who wore a ThAIRapy vest, the vest had a built-in monitoring device for recording the date, time, and duration of its activation for up to a one-year duration.

In asthma patients, two electronic devices have been examined: the Nebulizer Chronolog (or the updated version known as the Medilog) and the Doser. The Nebulizer Chronolog attaches to the MDI and records each use of the MDI and stores up to 2000 events. The Doser, a less expensive device, is an electronic cap that records daily uses of the inhaler; however, it does not record the time of use (Bender et al., 1997; Quittner et al., 2000; Rapoff, 1999; Rudd, 1993).

For patients with diabetes, self-monitoring of blood glucose in the home environment became available approximately 20 years ago and revolutionized how the disease was managed. Before that time, patients were forced to rely on urine glucose test results, an extremely crude index of actual blood glucose levels. Currently, electronic meters are widely available for monitoring blood glucose levels. Most of these meters store the date, time, and test results for two- to four-month periods (Goldstein et al., 1995). Daily home blood glucose monitoring, using any of a number of available electronic meters, is now considered standard care for all patients with type 1 diabetes and for all type 2 patients who take insulin or sulfonylureas (American Diabetes Association, 2000).

Electronic measures of adherence have demonstrated a unique set of strengths—for example, precise recordings of time and date of treatment, establishing medication patterns over long periods of time, and providing data on over- and underdosing and dosage delays. However, the devices have their limitations. Currently, there are only a few specific behaviors for which electronic monitors have been developed. As with pill counts, the electronic monitor must be returned for the data acquired to be downloaded. Even when the data are downloaded, the validity of the data obtained cannot be guaranteed. A MEMS cap can be opened or a Doser activated with no actual ingestion of the medication. Patient dumping of medications has been documented (Rudd et al., 1989). In addition, electronic monitors are often expensive and prone to technical problems, which can result in the loss of data (Bender et al., 1997; Quittner et al., 2000; Rapoff, 1999; Rudd, 1993).

Patient Report

Patient self-reports concerning regimen adherence are often viewed with suspicion; what patients say they do may bear little resemblance to actual behavior because patients may be markedly influenced by what they believe the doctor wants to hear. However, there is a general consensus that patient reports of noncompliance are more valid than reports of compliance (Cramer, 1991; Epstein & Cluss, 1982; Quittner et al., 2000).

In addition, there is increasing evidence that good-quality adherence data can be obtained when a nonjudgmental approach is taken and patients are asked to report about specific behaviors over a recent time frame. One approach is to ask patients to rate their adherence for each component of a complex medical regimen over a recent time interval using a questionnaire or structured interview format. Examples of this approach include Quittner's Treatment Adherence Questionnaire developed for children with cystic fibrosis (Quittner et al., 2000), Hanson's Self-Care Adherence Inventory used with patients who have type 1 diabetes (Hanson et al., 1996), and Klinnert's Family Asthma Management Scale (Klinnert, McQuaid, & Gavin, 1997).

Others have successfully used written diaries to measure adherence (Glasgow, McCaul, & Schafer, 1987), although obtaining good compliance with such a time-consuming request can be problematic (Johnson, 1993), and the concordance of written records and electronic data has not always been good. For example, Gonder-Fredrick, Julian, Cox, Clarke, and Cater, (1988) found that only 43% of diaries maintained by adults with diabetes matched electronic records from glucose meters.

Some of the richest adherence data have been obtained using 24-hour recall interviews. Johnson and her colleagues used this approach to assess the multiple components of the daily diabetes management regimen and in a series of studies demonstrated both the reliability and validity of this technique (see Johnson, 1993, 1995, for reviews). Multiple interviews are recommended to ensure a representative sample of patient adherence behaviors. Because memory errors can and do occur with all recall strategies, where possible, both the patient and a significant other should be interviewed about the patient's behavior. What the patient may "forget," the significant other may remember. Special consideration should be given when interviewing young children about behaviors involving time (e.g., time of medication administration or meals). However, it appears that with brief practice, children as young as 6 years can provide reliable adherence data about all aspects of their daily care. The method has been used with a number of other chronically ill populations, including cystic fibrosis (Quittner et al., 2000), breast cancer (Buzzard, 1996), and hemodialysis (Sharma, 1988). Advantages of the approach include the level of detail that can be obtained about the multiple components of a complex medical regimen. Also, the interviews can be conducted by telephone, and little is demanded from the patient other than the time (approximately 20 minutes) to conduct each interview. However, trained interviewers are required, and when multiple interviews with multiple informants are conducted, the process becomes labor-intensive.

THEORIES OF MEDICAL REGIMEN ADHERENCE

Several theories have been developed to explain health behavior. The health belief model is perhaps the oldest and most widely used (Strecher & Rosenstock, 1997). The model proposes that adherence is a product of five variables: (a) perceived susceptibility (the extent to which the patient believes he or she is at-risk); (b) perceived severity (the extent to which the patient believes that the consequences of noncompliance are serious); (c) perceived benefits (the extent to which the patient believes he or she will benefit from a particular health behavior); (d) perceived barriers (the costs of adhering to a medical regimen); and (e) cues to action (internal or external triggers that prompt health behavior).

Bandura's (1997) self-efficacy theory posits that health behavior is a product of perceived self-efficacy (the belief in one's ability to carry out a certain action) and outcome expectancies (the anticipated consequences of a particular health behavior). Perceived self-efficacy is, in turn, influenced by a number of variables, including past history, experience observed in others, verbal persuasion by others, and the patient's physical and emotional state.

The theory of reasoned action/planned behavior has also enjoyed widespread appeal, including application to health behavior (Ajzen, 1991). In this theory, health behavior is a product of behavioral intentions (the perceived likelihood a patient will perform a behavior) and perceived behavioral control (whether the patient believes he or she can perform the behavior and the expected consequences of performing the behavior). Behavioral intentions are, in turn, a product of several factors, including attitudes toward the behavior, subjective norms (whether significant persons in the patient's life approve or disapprove of the behavior and whether the patient is motivated to meet these significant others' expectations), and perceived behavioral control.

Finally, Prochaska's transtheoretical model of change has been specifically applied to health behavior (Prochaska, Redding, & Evers, 1997). Patients are presumed to progress through five stages of change: (a) precontemplation (the patient does not intend to change in the foreseeable future); (b) contemplation (the patient intends to change in the next six months); (c) preparation (the patient intends to change in the immediate future); (d) action (the patient engages in a behavior change); and (e) maintenance (the patient attempts to maintain a behavior change and avoid relapse).

It is beyond the scope of this chapter to review the relative merits of these theories of adherence; they share a number of commonalities as well as some notable differences. The reader is referred to Rapoff's (1999) and Horne and Weinman's (1998) excellent and more detailed discussions.

BARRIERS TO MEDICAL REGIMEN ADHERENCE

What barriers seem to interfere with patients' medical regimen adherence? In previous sections of this chapter, we addressed the significant impact poor patient–provider communication, patient failure to accurately recall provider recommendations, and patient knowledge and skill deficits can have on a patient's ability to adhere to a medical regimen. In addition, we discussed the role of professional noncompliance as a critical barrier to positive health outcomes, even in patients who successfully comply with their medical regimen.

Throughout the literature, a variety of other factors have been identified as potential barriers to medical regimen adherence. These include disease duration (e.g., longer duration is associated with poorer adherence; Brownbridge & Fileding, 1994), regimen complexity (e.g., greater regimen complexity is associated with poorer adherence; Bamberger et al., 2000; Haysford & Ross, 1988), social support (e.g., social isolation is associated with poorer adherence; Friedland & Williams, 1999; Roberts, 2000; Sherbourne et al., 1992), treatment side effects (e.g., more negative side effects are associated with poorer adherence; Leickly et al., 1998; Miller & Hays, 2000), comorbid disorders (e.g., comorbid disorders are associated with poorer adherence; Besch, 1995; Carney et al., 1995), patient beliefs about the treatment regimen (e.g., strong concerns about potential adverse effects of a medication is associated with poorer adherence; Horne & Weinman, 1999), patient age (e.g., adolescents are more likely to be nonadherent than younger children; Johnson et al., 1992; Johnson, Williams, & Marshall, 1999), and treatment costs (e.g., more expensive regimens are associated with poorer adherence; Spilker, 1991).

However, reviews of this extensive literature suggest great inconsistency in findings; what may be deemed as a barrier for adherence with one disease management regimen may not affect another (Bryon, 1998; Morris & Schultz, 1992). For example, adolescence is generally viewed as a time of increased noncompliance. This finding has been reported for both patients with diabetes (Hauser et al., 1990; Johnson, Freund, Hanson, & Malone, 1990; Johnson et al., 1992; Kovacs, Goldston, Obrosky, & Iyengar, 1992) and cystic fibrosis (Geiss, Hobbs, Hammersley-Maercklew, Kraner, & Henley, 1992; Gudas et al., 1991). Yet, studies of pediatric cancer patients suggest that children, rather than adolescents, had the highest rate of nonadherence (Manne, Jacobson, Garfinkle, Gerstein, & Redd, 1993; Phipps & DeCuir-Whalley, 1990).

Although a great number of barriers to medical regimen adherence have been identified, few consistencies have been found across diseases and patient populations. With a few exceptions, barriers to adherence may be highly disease- and population-specific, and in some cases, individual-specific, demanding a careful assessment at the individual patient level.

INTERVENTIONS TO IMPROVE ADHERENCE

When patients have been provided information, trained in skills to solicit information during routine medical visits, and are encouraged to take responsibility for making decisions about their medical care, studies suggest that patients increase their adherence to their treatment regimens while simultaneously becoming active players in their medical care (Greenfield, Kaplan, & Ware, 1985).

Strategies geared toward improving adherence are often classified as educational, behavioral, and organizational (Dunbar, Marshall, & Hovell, 1979). However, an approach that combines strategies is often most effective (Thatcher-Shope, 1981; also see Myers & Midence, 1998, and Rapoff, 1999, for reviews). Educational strategies include verbal and written instructions designed to educate the patient about the treatment regimen, possible side effects, and importance and benefits of consistent adherence. A combination of written and oral information, as well as use of audiovisual information, has proved useful (Mullen, Green, & Persinger, 1985). In some cases, the provider needs to reassure the patient and address the patient's underlying fears before the patient is able to focus on or remember the clinician's recommendations (Mellins, Evans, Clark, Zimmerman, & Wiseman, 2000).

Overall, studies of educational interventions have found that information and skills are necessary, but not sufficient, for improved adherence (Morris & Schulz, 1992). Patient education effects may be short-lived and need to be combined with other intervention strategies to ensure long-lasting effects (Rapoff & Barnard, 1991).

Numerous studies have documented the benefits of behavioral strategies, such as setting goals, contracting, assessing the patient's readiness for self-care, breaking tasks into small, manageable steps, self-monitoring, enlisting social support, checking patient commitment to key tasks, use of cues, reminders, and adherence incentives (Baum & Creer, 1986; Matsui, 1997; Rapoff, 1999; Rapoff & Barnard, 1991; Von Korff, Gruman, Schaefer, Curry, & Wagner, 1997). For example, Park, Morrell, and Frieske (1991) used medication organizers (seven-day organizer with compartments for different times) to improve medication adherence in older adults. An external reminding device, such as a beeping wristwatch, was used successfully to improved medication adherence in hypertensive patients (Park, Shifren, Morrell, & Watkins, 1997). A more comprehensive behavioral program was initiated by Litzelman and colleagues (1993) with diabetic patients. The intervention included patient education about foot care, a self-care contract with the patients, and monthly reminders via telephone and postcard. Health care providers were given practice guidelines and informational flow sheets on foot-related risk factors, and reminder stickers were attached to patients' medical records. Those patients receiving the intervention were less likely to have serious foot lesions, more likely to report appropriate foot-care self-monitoring behaviors at home, more likely to have foot examinations during office visits, and more likely to receive foot-care education from health care providers. This intervention is notable because it successfully addressed both patient and professional compliance, with important positive health outcomes.

Organizational strategies to improve patient and professional adherence include increasing access to health care services, providing continuity of care, reducing the complexity of regimens, increasing provider supervision, and training providers in current practice guidelines (Becker, 1985; Rapoff, 1999; Rapoff & Barnard, 1991; Von Korff et al., 1997). For example, recent studies have shown that when low-income children lack continuing primary care for their asthma, increased levels of morbidity result (Billings et al., 1993; Halfon & Newachek, 1993). Evans et al. (1997) addressed this problem by training providers in current guidelines for asthma care, which increased their ability to identify children with asthma (improved asthma detection) and led to improved continuing care (children with asthma were seen more frequently and consistently).

In summary, there is a large literature documenting the success of intervention programs designed to improve patient adherence (Cramer & Spilker, 1991; Devine, 1996; Devine & Pearcy, 1996; Dunbar-Jacob, Dwyer, & Dunning, 1991; Dusseldorp, van Elderen, Maes, Meulman, & Kraaij, 1999; Mullen, Laville, Biddle, & Lorig, 1987; Mullen, Mains, & Velez, 1992; Mullen et al., 1985; Myers & Midence, 1998; Rapoff, 1999; Roter et al., 1998). Interventions are more likely to succeed if education and skill-training instruction are combined with behavioral strategies in an organizational structure that attends to professional behavior as well as patient behavior.

CONCLUSION

Health psychologists are uniquely trained to address medical regimen adherence issues. They have expertise in behavioral assessment and interventions that can be readily applied to the multiple demands faced by patients prescribed complex treatment regimens, as well as their providers and health care organizations. In many cases, health psychologists will develop disease-specific assessment and intervention strategies using basic principles of behavioral assessment and treatment. In other cases, they will apply procedures and strategies developed by others (often health psychologists) to the needs of a particular medical population(s) or health care organization. Because they are health psychologists, they understand the biology underlying the diseases they treat, while bringing to bear their psychological expertise in the assessment and treatment of these patients. They can offer conceptual clarity to the treatment team, emphasizing the important role of both patient and provider behavior, as well as the assessment of health outcomes and organizational structure, to the successful management of the medical patient. They serve as leaders in the scientific study of patient and provider behavior, medical regimen adherence assessment methods, intervention strategies, and work to clarify the often complex relationships between provider behavior, the health care environment, patient daily disease management behaviors, and health outcomes.

REFERENCES

Ajzen, I. (1991). The theory of planned behavior. *Organizational Behavior and Human Decision Processes, 50,* 179–211.

American Diabetes Association. (2000). Position statement: Tests of glycemia in diabetes. *Diabetes Care, 23*(Suppl. 1), S80–S82.

Bamberger, J. D., Unick, J., Klein, P., Fraser, M., Chesney, M., & Katz, M. H. (2000). Helping the urban poor stay with antiretroviral HIV drug therapy. *American Journal of Public Health, 90,* 699–701.

Bandura, A. (1997). *Self-efficacy: The exercise of control.* New York: Freeman.

Baum, D., & Creer, T. L. (1986). Medication compliance in children with asthma. *Journal of Asthma, 82,* 79–84.

Becker, M. H. (1985). Patient adherence to prescribed therapies. *Medical Care, 23,* 539–555.

Bender, B., Milgrom, H., & Rand, C. (1997). Nonadherence in asthmatic patients: Is there a solution to the problem? *Annals of Allergy and Asthma Immunology, 79,* 177–185.

Berg, J. S., Dischler, J., Wagner, D. J., Raia, J., & Palmer-Shevlin, N. (1993). Medication compliance: A health care problem. *Annals of Pharmacotherapy, 27*(Suppl.), 2–21.

Besch, C. L. (1995). Compliance in clinical trials. *AIDS, 9,* 1–10.

Billings, J., Zeitel, L., Lukomnik, J., Carey, T. S., Blank, A. E., & Newman, L. (1993). Impact of socioeconomic status on hospital use in New York City. *Health Affairs, 12,* 162–173.

Bryon, M. (1998). Adherence to treatment in children. In L. Myers & K. Midence (Eds.), *Adherence to treatment in medical conditions* (pp. 161–190). Newark, NJ: Gordon & Breach.

Brownbridge, G., & Fielding, D. M. (1994). Psychosocial adjustment and adherence to dialysis treatment regimens. *Pediatric Nephrology, 8,* 744–749.

Buzzard, I. M. (1996). Monitoring dietary change in a low-fat diet intervention study: Advantages of using 24-hour dietary recalls versus food records. *Journal of the American Dietetic Association, 96,* 574–579.

Cameron, K., & Gregor, F. (1987). Chronic illness and compliance. *Journal of Advanced Nursing, 12,* 671–676.

Carney, R. M., Saunders, R. D., Freeland, K. E., Stein, P., Rich, M. W., & Jaffe, A. S. (1995). Association of depression with reduced heart rate variability in coronary artery disease. *American Journal of Cardiology, 76,* 562–566.

Centers for Disease Control and Prevention. (1999). *Chronic diseases and their risk factors: The nation's leading cause of death.* Retrieved January 27, 2004, from http://www.cdc.gov/nccdphp/statbook/pdf/cdrf1999.pdf

Centers for Disease Control and Prevention. (2004). *Chronic disease prevention.* Retrieved January 27, 2004, from http://www.cdc.gov/nccdphp/

Clarke W., Snyder A., & Nowacek G. (1985). Outpatient pediatric diabetes-I. Current practices. *Journal of Chronic Diseases, 38,* 85–90.

Cline, C. M., Bjorck-Linne, A. K., Israelsson, B. Y., Willenheimer, R. B., & Erhardt, L. R. (1999). Non-compliance and knowledge of prescribed medication in elderly patients with heart failure. *European Journal of Heart Failure, 2,* 145–149.

Cohen, D., Berner, U., & Dubach, U.C. (1985). Physician compliance in the management of hypertensive patients. *Journal of Hypertension, 3*(Suppl. 3), S73–S76.

Colquhoun, D. (2000). Issues in managing hyperlipidaemia. *Family Physician, 29,* 215–219.

Costanza, M. E., Stoddard, A. M., Zapka, J. G., Gaw, V. P., & Barth, R. (1992). Physician compliance with mammography guidelines: Barriers and enhancers. *Journal of the American Board of Family Practice 5,* 143–152.

Cramer, J. A. (1991). Overview of methods to measure and enhance patient compliance. In J. Cramer & B. Spilker (Eds.), *Patient compliance in medical practice and clinical trials* (pp. 3–10). New York: Raven Press.

Cramer, J. A. (1995). Microelectronic systems for monitoring and enhancing patient compliance with medication regimens. *Drugs, 49,* 321–327.

Cramer, J. A., & Spilker, B. (Eds.) (1991). *Patient compliance in medical practice and clinical trials.* New York: Raven Press.

da Costa, I. G., Rapoff, M. A., Lemanek, K., & Goldstein, G. L. (1997). Improving adherence to mediation regimens for children with asthma and its effect on clinical outcome. *Journal of Applied Behavioral Analysis, 30,* 687–691.

Devine, E. C. (1996). Meta-analysis of the effects of psychoeducational care in adults with asthma. *Research in Nursing and Health, 19,* 367–376.

Devine, E. C., & Pearcy, J. (1996). Meta-analysis of the effects of psychoeducational care in adults with chronic obstructive pulmonary disease. *Patient Education and Counseling, 29,* 167–178.

DiMatteo, M. R., (1994). Enhancing patient adherence to medical recommendations. *Journal of the American Medical Association, 271,* 79–80.

Dunbar, J. M., Marshall, G. D., & Hovell, M. F. (1979). Behavioral strategies for improving compliance. In R. B. Haynes, D. W. Taylor, & D. L. Sackett (Eds.), *Compliance in health care* (pp. 174–190). Baltimore: Johns Hopkins University Press.

Dunbar-Jacob, J., Dwyer, K., & Dunning, E.J. (1991). Compliance with antihypertensive regime: A review of the research in the 1980's. *Annals of Behavioral Medicine, 13,* 31–39.

Dusseldorp, E., van Elderen, T., Maes, S., Meulman, J. & Kraaij, V. (1999). A meta-analysis of psychoeducational programs for coronary heart disease patients. *Health Psychology, 18,* 506–519.

Eklerling, L., & Kors, M. B. (1984). Research on compliance with diabetic regimens: Application to practice. *Journal of the American Dietetic Association, 84,* 805–809.

Eney, R. D., & Goldstein, E. D. (1976). Compliance of chronic asthmatics with oral administration of theophylline as measured by serum and salivary levels. *Pediatrics, 57,* 513–517.

Epstein, L., Beck, S., Figueroa, J., Farkas, G., Kazdin, A., Daneman, D., et al. (1981). The effects of targeting improvements in urine glucose on metabolic control in children with insulin dependent diabetes. *Journal of Applied Behavior Analysis, 14*, 365–375 .

Epstein, L., & Cluss, P. (1982). A behavioral medicine perspective on adherence to long-term medical regimens. *Journal of Consulting and Clinical Psychology, 50*, 950–971.

Evans, D. E., Mellins, R., Lobach, K., Ramos-Bonoan, C., Pinkett-Heller, M., Wiesemann, S., et al. (1997). Improving care for minority children with asthma: Professional education in public health clinics. *Pediatrics, 99*, 157–164.

Falvo, D., & Tippy, P. (1988). Communicating information to patients: Patient satisfaction and adherence as associated with resident skill. *Journal of Family Practice, 26*, 643–647.

Fennerty, F. A. (1978). The problem of noncompliance. *Medical Times, 106*, 71–75.

Finney, J. W., Hook, R. J., Friman, P. C., Rapoff, M. A., & Christopherson, E. R. (1993). The overestimates of adherence to pediatric medical regimens. *Child Health Care, 22*, 297–304.

Friedland, G. H., & Williams, A. (1999). Attaining higher goals in HIV treatment: The central importance of adherence. *AIDS, 13*(Suppl. 1), S61–S72.

Frolkis, J. P., Zyzanski, S. J., Schwartz, J. M., & Suhan, P. S. (1998). Physician noncompliance with the 1993 National Cholesterol Education Program (NCEP–ATPII) guidelines. *Circulation, 98*, 851–855.

Geiss, S. K., Hobbs, S. A., Hammersley-Maercklein, G., Kramer, J. C., & Henley, M. (1992). Psychosocial factors related to perceived compliance with cystic fibrosis treatment. *Journal of Clinical Psychology, 48*, 99–103.

Gilbert, A., & Varni, J. W. (1988). Behavioral treatment for improving adherence to factor replacement therapy by children with hemophilia. *Journal of Compliance in Health Care, 3*, 67–76.

Gilbert, J. R., Evans, E. E., Haynes, R. B., & Tugwell P. (1980). Predicting compliance with a regimen of digoxin therapy in family practice. *Canadian Medical Association Journal, 123*, 119–123.

Glasgow, R., McCaul, D., & Schafer, L. (1987). Self-care behaviors and glycemic control in type 1 children. *Journal of Chronic Diseases, 40*, 399–412.

Glasgow, R., Wilson, W., & McCaul, D. (1985). Regimen adherence: A problematic construct for diabetes research. *Diabetes Care, 8*, 300–301.

Goldstein, D., Little, R., Lorenz, R., Malone, J., Nathan, D., & Peterson, C. (1995). Technical review: Tests of glycemia in diabetes. *Diabetes Care, 18*, 896–909.

Gonder-Fredrick, L. A., Julian, D. M., Cox, D. J., Clarke, W. L., & Cater, W. R. (1988). Self-measurement of blood glucose accuracy of self-reported data and adherence to recommended regimens. *Diabetes Care, 2*, 579–585.

Greenfield, S., Kaplan, S., & Ware, J. E., Jr. (1985). Expanding patient involvement in care: Effects on patient outcomes. *Annals of Internal Medicine, 102*, 520–528.

Gross, A., Samson, G., Sanders, S., & Smith, C. (1988). Patient noncompliance: Are children consistent? *American Journal of Orthodontics and Dentofacial Orthopedics, 93*, 518–519.

Gudas, L. J., Koocher, G. P., & Wyplj, D. (1991). Perceptions of medical compliance in children and adolescents with cystic fibrosis. *Developmental and Behavioral Pediatrics, 12*, 236–247.

Haldeman, G. A., Croft, J. B., Giles, W. H., & Rashidee, A. (1999). Hospitalization of patients with heart failure: National hospital discharge survey, 1985 to 1995. *American Heart Journal, 137*, 352–360.

Halfon, N., & Newachek, P. W. (1993). Childhood asthma and poverty: Differential impacts and utilization of health services. *Pediatrics, 91*, 56–61.

Hanson, C., DeGuire, M., Schinkel, A., Kolterman, O., Goodman, J., & Buckingham, B. (1996). Self-care behaviors in insulin-dependent diabetes: Evaluative tools and their associations to glycemic control. *Journal of Pediatric Psychology, 21*, 467–482.

Hanson, S., & Pichert, J. (1986). Perceived stress and diabetes control in adolescents. *Health Psychology, 5*, 439–452.

Hauser, S. Y., Jacobson, A. M., Lavori, P., Wolfsdorf, J. I., Herskowitz, R. D., Milley, J. E., et al. (1990). Adherence among children and adolescents with insulin-dependent diabetes mellitus over a four-year longitudinal follow-up: II. Immediate and long-term linkages with the family milieu. *Journal of Pediatric Psychology, 15*, 527–542.

Haynes, R. (1979). Introduction. In R. Haynes, D. Taylor, & D. Sackett (Eds.), *Compliance in health care* (pp. 2–3). Baltimore: Johns Hopkins University Press.

Haysford, J. R., & Ross, C. K. (1988). Medical compliance in juvenile rheumatoid arthritis: Problems and perspectives. *Arthritis Care and Research, 1*, 190–197.

Hazsard, A., Hutchinson, S. J., & Krawiecki, N. (1990). Factors related to adherence to medication regimens in pediatric seizure patients. *Journal of Pediatric Psychology, 15*, 543–555.

Horne, R., & Weinman, J. (1999). Patients' beliefs about prescribed medicines and their role in adherence to treatment in chronic physical illness. *Journal of Psychosomatic Research, 6*, 555–567.

Horne, R., & Weinman, J. (1998). Predicting treatment adherence: An overview of theoretical models. In L. Myers & K. Midence (Eds.), *Adherence to treatment in medical conditions* (pp. 25–50). New Delhi, India: Harwood Academic.

Jette, A. M. (1982). Improving patient co-operation with arthritis treatment regimens. *Arthritis and Rheumatism, 25*, 447–453.

Johnson, M. J., Williams, M., & Marshall, E. S. (1999). Adherent and nonadherent medication-taking in elderly hypertensive patients. *Clinical Nursing Research, 8*, 318–335.

Johnson, S. B. (1992). Methodological issues in diabetes research: Measuring adherence. *Diabetes Care, 15*, 1658–1672.

Johnson, S. B. (1993). Chronic diseases in childhood: Assessing compliance with complex medical regimes. In M. A. Krasnegor, L. Epstein, S. B. Johnson, & S. J. Yaffe (Eds.), *Developmental aspects of health compliance behavior* (pp. 15–184). Hillsdale, NJ: Erlbaum.

Johnson, S. B. (1994). Health behavior and health status: Concepts, methods and applications. *Journal of Pediatric Psychology, 9,* 129–141.

Johnson, S. B. (1995). Managing insulin-dependent diabetes mellitus in adolescence: A developmental perspective. In J. Wallander & L. Siegel (Eds.), *Adolescent health problems: A behavioral perspective* (pp. 265–288). New York: Guilford Press.

Johnson, S. B., Freund, A., Hansen, C. A., & Malone, J. (1990). Adherence health status relationships in childhood diabetes. *Health Psychology, 6,* 606–631.

Johnson, S. B., Kelly, M., Henretta, J. C., Cunningham, W. R., Tomer, A., & Silverstein, J. H. (1992). A longitudinal analysis of adherence and health status in childhood diabetes. *Journal of Pediatric Psychology, 17,* 537–553.

Klinnert, M., McQuaid, E., & Gavin, L. (1997). Assessing the family asthma management system. *Journal of Asthma, 34,* 77–88.

Kohn, L., Corrigan, J., Donaldson, M. (Eds.). (1999). *To err is human: Building a safer health system.* Washington, DC: National Academy Press.

Kovacs, M., Goldston, D., Obrosky, S. D., & Iyengar, S. (1992). Prevalence of predictors of pervasive noncompliance with medical treatment among youths with insulin-dependent diabetes mellitus. *Journal of the American Academy of Child and Adolescent Psychiatry, 31,* 1112–1119.

Kravitz, R. L., Hays, R. D., Sherbourne, C. D., DiMatteo, M. R., Rogers, W. H., Ordway, L., et al. (1993). Recall of recommendations and adherence to advice among patients with chronic medical conditions. *Archives of Internal Medicine, 153,* 1869–1878.

Kruse, W. H. (1991). Compliance with treatment of hyperlipoproteinemia in medical practice and clinical trials. In J. A. Cramer & B. Spilker (Eds.), *Patient compliance in clinical practice and medical trials* (pp. 175–176). New York: Raven Press.

Larson, J. S., Hahn, M., & Ekholm, B. (1994). Evaluation of conventional press and breath MDI technique in 501 patients. *Journal of Asthma, 31,* 193–199.

Lau, R. C., Matsi, D., Greenberg, M., & Koren, G. (1998). Electronic measurement of compliance with mercaptopurine in pediatric patients with acute lymphoblastic leukemia. *Medical and Pediatric Oncology, 30,* 85–90.

Leickly, F. E., Wade, S. L., Crain, E., Kruszon-Moran, D., Wright, E. C., et al. (1998). Self-reported adherence, management behavior, and barriers to care after an emergency department visit by inner city children with asthma. *Pediatrics, 8,* 101–106.

Levin, S. J., & Ornstein, S. M. (1990). Management of hypercholesterolemia in a family practice setting. *Journal of Family Practice, 31,* 613–617.

Ley, P. (1981). Professional noncompliance: A neglected problem. *British Journal of Clinical Psychology, 20,* 151–154.

Litzelman, D. K., Slemenda, C. W., Langefeld, C. D., Hays, L. M., Welch, M. A., Bild, D. E., et al. (1993). Reduction of lower extremity clinical abnormalities in patients with non–insulin-dependent diabetes mellitus. A randomized, controlled trial. *Annals of Internal Medicine, 119,* 36–41.

Lorenz, R., Christensen, N., & Pichert, J. (1985). Diet-related knowledge, skill, and adherence among children with insulin-dependent diabetes mellitus. *Pediatrics, 75,* 872–876.

Lowe, K., & Lutzker, J. (1979). Increasing compliance to a medical regimen with a juvenile diabetic. *Behavior Therapy, 10,* 57–64.

Manne, S. L., Jacobsen, P. B., Gorfinkle, K., Gerstein, F., & Redd, W. H. (1993). Treatment adherence difficulties among children with cancer: The role of parenting style. *Journal of Pediatric Psychology, 18,* 47–62.

Matusi, D. M. (1997). Drug compliance in pediatrics. *Pediatric Clinics of North America, 44,* 1–14.

Matsui, D., Hermann, C., Braudo, M., Ito, S., Olivieri, N., & Koren, G. (1992). Clinical use of the medication event monitoring system: A new window into pediatric compliance. *Clinical Pharmacology and Therapeutics, 52,* 102–103.

McKenney, J. M., Munroe, W. P., & Wright, J. T. (1992). Impact of an electronic medication aid on long-term blood pressure control. *Journal of Clinical Pharmacology, 32,* 277–283.

Meichenbaum, D., & Turk, D. C. (1987). *Facilitating treatment adherence: A practitioner's guidebook.* New York: Plenum Press.

Mellins, R. B., Evans, D., Clark, N., Zimmerman, B., & Wiesemann, S. (2000). Developing and communicating a long-term treatment plan for asthma. *American Family Physician, 61,* 2419–2428.

Miller L. G., & Hays, R. D. (2000). Adherence to combination therapy: Synthesis of the literature and clinical implications. *AIDS Reader, 10,* 177–185.

Mistry, S. K., & Sorrentino, A. P. (1999). Patient nonadherence: The $100 billion problem. *American Druggist, 216,* 56–62.

Morris, L. S., & Schultz, R. M. (1992). Patient compliance—An overview. *Journal of Clinical Pharmacy and Therapeutics, 17,* 283–295.

Mullen, P. D., Green , L. W., & Persinger, G. S. (1985). Clinical trials of patient education for chronic conditions: A comparative meta-analysis of intervention types. *Preventative Medicine, 14,* 753–781.

Mullen, P. D., Laville, E. A., Biddle, A. K., & Lorig, K. (1987). Efficacy of psycho-educational interventions on pain, depression, and disability in people with arthritis: A meta-analysis. *Journal of Rheumatology, 14,* 33–39.

Mullen, P. D., Mains, D. A., & Velez, R. (1992). A meta-analysis of controlled trials of cardiac patient education. *Patient Education and Counseling, 19,* 143–162.

Mushlin, A. I., & Appel, F. A. (1977). Diagnosing potential noncompliance: Physician's ability in a behavioral dimension of medical care. *Archives of Internal Medicine, 137,* 318–321.

Myers, L., & Midence, K. (Eds.). (1998). *Adherence to treatment in medical conditions.* Newark, NJ: Gordon & Breach.

Newacheck, P. (1994). Poverty and childhood chronic illness. *Archives of Pediatric and Adolescent Medicine, 148,* 1143–1149.

Nilasena, D. S., & Lincoln, M. J. (1995). A computer-generated reminder system improves physician compliance with diabetes preventive care guidelines. *Social Science and Medicine, 15,* 57–61.

O'Brien, M. E. (1980). Hemodyalysis regimen compliance and social environment. *Nursing Research, 29,* 250–255.

Orme, C. M., & Binik, Y. M. (1989). Consistency of adherence across regimen demands. *Health-Psychology, 8,* 27–43.

Page, P., Verstraete, D. G., Robb, J. R., & Etzwiler, D. D. (1981). Patient recall of self-care recommendations in diabetes. *Diabetes Care, 4,* 96–98.

Park, D. C., Morrell, R. W., & Frieske, D. (1991). Cognitive factors and the use of over-the-counter medication organizers by arthritis patients. *Human Factors, 33,* 57–67.

Park, D. C., Shifren, K., Morrell, R. W., & Watkins, K. (1997, Nov.). *The use of cognitive interventions to improve medication adherence in African-Americans with hypertension.* Paper presented at the Gerontological Society of America, Philadelphia.

Passero, M. A., Remor, B., & Salomon, J. (1981). Patient–reported compliance with cystic fibrosis therapy. *Clinical Pediatrics, 20,* 264–268.

Peeters, M., Koren, G., Jacubovicz, D., & Zipursky, A. (1988). Physician compliance and relapse rates of acute lymphoblastic leukemia in children. *Clinical Pharmacology and Therapeutics, 43,* 228–232.

Perwien, A., Johnson, S. B., Dymtrow, D., & Silverstein, J. (2000). Blood glucose monitoring skills in children with type 1 diabetes. *Clinical Pediatrics, 39,* 351–357.

Phipps, S., & DeCuir-Whalley, S. (1990). Adherence issues in pediatric bone marrow transplantation. *Journal of Pediatric Psychology, 15,* 459–475.

Prochaska, J., Redding, C., & Evers, K. (1997). The transtheoretical model and stages of change. In K. Glanz, F., Lewis, & B. Rimer (Eds.), *Health behavior and health education: Theory, research, and practice* (2nd ed., pp. 60–84). San Francisco: Jossey-Bass.

Pullar, T., Kumar, S., Tindall, H., & Feely, M. (1989). Time to stop counting tablets? *Clinical Pharmacology Therapeutics, 46,* 163–168.

Quittner, A. L., Espelage, D. L., Levers-Landis, C., & Drotar, D. (2000). Measuring adherence to multiple treatments in childhood chronic illness: Considering multiple methods and sources of information. *Journal of Clinical Psychology in Medical Settings, 7,* 41–54.

Rand, C. S. (1993). Measuring adherence with therapy for chronic diseases: Implications for the treatment of heterozygous familial hypercholesterolemia. *American Journal of Cardiology, 72,* 68D–74D.

Rao, S. N., Mookerjee, A. L., Obasanjo, O. O., & Chaisson, R. E. (2000). Errors in the treatment of tuberculosis in Baltimore. *Chest, 117,* 734–737.

Rapoff, M. A. (1999). *Adherence to pediatric medical regimens*. New York: Kluwer Academic/Plenum Press.

Rapoff, M. A., & Barnard, M. U. (1991). Compliance with pediatric medical regimens. In J. Cramer & B. Spilker (Eds.), *Patient compliance in medical practice and clinical trials* (pp. 73–98). New York: Raven Press.

Reynolds, L., Johnson, S. B., & Silverstein, J. (1990). Assessing daily diabetes management by 24-hour recall interview: The validity of children's reports. *Journal of Pediatric Psychology, 15*, 493–509.

Roberts, K. J. (2000). Barriers to and facilitators of HIV-positive patients' adherence to antiretroviral treatment regimens. *AIDS Patient Care and STDS, 14*, 155–168.

Roter, D. L., Hall, J. A., Merisca, R., Nordstrom, B., Cretin, D., & Svarstad, B. (1998). Effectiveness of interventions to improve patient compliance: A meta-analysis. *Medical Care, 36*, 1138–1161.

Rudd, P. (1993). The measurement of compliance: Medication taking. In M. A. Krasnegor, L. Epstein, S. B. Johnson, & S. J. Yaffe (Eds.), *Developmental aspects of health compliance behavior* (pp. 185–213). Hillsdale, NJ: Erlbaum.

Rudd, P., Byyny, R. L., Zachary, V., Lo Verde, M. E., Titus, C., Mitchell, W. D., et al. (1989). The natural history of medication compliance in a drug trial: Limitations of pill counts. *Clinical Pharmacological Therapy, 46*, 169–176.

Sackett, D. L., & Snow, J. C. (1979). The magnitude of compliance and noncompliance. In R. B. Haynes, D. W. Taylor, & D. L. Sackett (Eds.), *Compliance in health care* (pp. 11–22). Baltimore: Johns Hopkins University Press.

Sanders, M. R., Gravestock, F. M., Wanstall, K., & Dunne, M. (1991). The relationship between children's treatment-related behavior problems, age and clinical status in cystic fibrosis. *Journal of Pediatric Child Health, 27*, 290–294.

Schleifer, S. J., Bhardwaj, S., Lebovits, A., Tanaka, J. S., Messe, M., & Strain, J. J. (1991). Predictors of physician nonadherence to chemotherapy regimens. *Cancer, 67*, 945–951.

Sergis-Deavenport, E., & Varni, J. W. (1983). Behavioral assessment and management of adherence to factor replacement therapy in hemophilia. *Journal of Pediatric Psychology, 8*, 367–377.

Sharma, M. (1988). Validation of 24-hour dietary recall: A study in hemodialysis patients. *Journal of Renal Nutrition, 8*, 199–202.

Sherbourne, C. D., Hays, R. D., Ordway, L., DiMatteo, M. R., & Kravitz, R. L. (1992). Antecedents of adherence to medical recommendations: Results from the medical outcomes study. *Journal of Behavioral Medicine, 15*, 447–469.

Spilker, B. (1991). Methods of assessing and improving patient compliance in clinical trials. In J. A. Cramer & B. Spilker (Eds.), *Patient compliance in clinical practice and medical trials* (pp. 37–56). New York: Raven Press.

Steel, L. G. (1994). Identifying technique errors. Self-monitoring of blood glucose in the home setting. *Journal of Gerontological Nursing, 20*, 9–12.

Strecher, V., & Rosenstock, I. (1997). The health belief model. In K. Glanz, F. Lewis, & B. Rimer (Eds.), *Health behavior and health education: Theory, research, and practice* (2nd ed., pp. 41–59). San Francisco: Jossey-Bass.

Taylor, D. W., Sackett, D. L., Johnson, A. L., Gibson, E. S., & Roberts, R. S. (1978). Compliance with antihypertensive drug therapy. *Annals of the New York Academy of Science, 304,* 390–403.

Thatcher-Shope, J. (1981). Medication compliance. *Pediatric Clinics of North America, 28,* 5–21.

Turk, D. C., & Meichenbaum, D. (1991). Adherence to self-care regimens: The patient's perspective. In J. Sweet, R. Rozensky, & S. Tovian (Eds.), *Handbook of clinical psychology in medical settings* (pp. 249–268). New York: Plenum Press.

Van Beerendonk, I., Mesters, I, Mudde, A. N., & Tan, T. D. (1998). Assessment of the inhalation technique in outpatients with asthma or chronic pulmonary disease using a metered-dose inhaler or dry powder device. *Journal of Asthma, 35,* 273–279.

Von Korff, M., Gruman, J., Schaefer, J., Curry, S. J., & Wagner, E. H. (1997). Collaborative management of chronic illness. *Annals of Internal Medicine, 127,* 1097–1102.

Weinstein, A. G., & Faust, D. (1997). Maintaining theophylline compliance/ adherence in severely asthmatic children. *Annals of Allergy Asthma and Immunology, 79,* 311–318.

Wilson, D., & Endres, R. (1986). Compliance with blood glucose monitoring in children with type 1 diabetes mellitus. *Journal of Pediatrics, 108,* 1022–1024.

Wing, R. R., Koeske, R., New, A., Lamparski, D., & Becker, D. (1986). Behavioral skills in self-monitoring of blood glucose. Relationship to accuracy. *Diabetes Care, 9,* 330–333.

Winkelstein, M. L., Huss, K., Butz, A., Eggleston, P., Vargas, P., & Rand, C. (2000). Factors associated with medication self-administration in children with asthma. *Clinical Pediatrics, 39,* 337–345.

Wysocki, T., Green, L., & Huxtable, K. (1989). Blood glucose monitoring by diabetic adolescents: Compliance and metabolic control. *Health Psychology, 8,* 267–284.

III

ADAPTATION TO HEALTH
AND DISEASE

11

THE BIOPSYCHOSOCIAL PERSPECTIVE OF PAIN

ROBERT J. GATCHEL AND ANN MATT MADDREY

Pain is a pervasive medical problem in the United States: In approximately 10% of visits to physicians, patients give pain as the reason for the visit (Woodwell, 2000); it affects more than 50 million Americans; and it costs more than $70 billion annually in health care costs and lost productivity (Gatchel & Mayer, 2000). The pervasiveness of pain has resulted in it now being considered a fifth vital sign (added to pulse, blood pressure, core temperature, and respiration). In this chapter, the biopsychosocial perspective of pain will be reviewed. As will become apparent, this perspective has proven to be the most heuristic one to embrace when considering issues of pain etiology, assessment, and treatment. Before presenting this perspective and a discussion of the many issues related to pain, we will provide a brief historical overview of the evolution of the biopsychosocial perspective of pain.

This chapter was supported in part by Grant nos. 3R01-MH46452, 2K02-MH01107, and 2R01-DE10713 from the National Institutes of Health.

HISTORICAL OVERVIEW

As previously reviewed (Gatchel, 1999, in press), the history of attempts to understand the etiology and treatment of pain parallels the historical changes that have occurred in medicine in general. Starting during the Renaissance period, with the great revolution in scientific knowledge in the areas of anatomy, biology, physiology, and physics, a *biomedical reductionism* approach developed. This approach argued that concepts such as the mind or soul were not needed to explain physical functioning or behavior. This new "mechanistic" approach to the study of human anatomy and physiology began to foster a dualistic viewpoint that the body and mind functions separately and independently. Before the Renaissance period, physicians had approached the understanding of mind–body interactions in a more holistic way. These physicians also served the multiple roles of philosopher, teacher, priest, and healer. The one historical figure who is often viewed as popularizing and solidifying this dualistic viewpoint was the 17th-century French philosopher René Descartes (1596–1650). Descartes postulated that the mind or soul was a completely separate entity parallel to, and incapable of, affecting physical matter or somatic possesses in any significant or direct way. This novel and revolutionary biomedical reductionism philosophy of medicine then became viewed as the only acceptable basis for explaining diseases through understanding mechanical laws and physiological processes and principles.

Although this reductionistic approach to medicine played a valuable role in bringing medicine out of the Dark Ages and stimulated significant discoveries and maturation of the field as a science, it subsequently had a stifling effect on the field during the 19th and 20th centuries when clinical research began to appear that emphasized the importance of taking into account mind (or psychological) factors for a more thorough understanding of a physical disorder. A discussion of the emergence of this *biopsychosocial* approach will be presented later in this chapter.

Early Theories of Pain

Descartes initially conceptualized pain as a specific type of activity in the sensory nervous system. He viewed the pain system as a "straight-through" channel from the skin directly to the brain. In his analogy, a pain system was imagined to be like the bell-ringing mechanism in a church: If someone pulls the rope at the bottom of the tower, the bell rings at the top. Thus, he proposed that a flame applied to the hand sends particles in the hand into activity and that motion is transmitted up the arm and neck into the head, where it activates something like an alarm system. The person feels the pain and responds to it. This purely deductive theory of pain physiology, even though it lacked any empirical evidence, influenced the study and management of pain for the next few centuries.

Subsequently, a much more formal model of this pain process was proposed by von Frey in 1894, called the *specificity theory of pain*. This theory proposed that sensory receptors were responsible for the transmission of specific sensations, such as pain, touch, warmth, and pressure, and that the various receptors had different structures that made them differentially sensitive to various types of stimulation. Therefore, pain was perceived as having a specific central, as well as peripheral, set of mechanisms—similar to those that operate for other bodily senses.

At about this same point in time, Goldschneider proposed an alternative model, which he called the *pattern theory of pain*. Goldschneider conceptualized pain sensations as being the result of transmission of nerve impulse *patterns* that were produced and coded at the peripheral stimulation site and that the differences in the patterning and quantity of peripheral nerve fiber discharges produced differences in the quality of sensation. He assumed that the experience of pain was the result of the central nervous system's coding of nerve impulse patterns and not simply the result of a specific connection between pain receptors and pain sites.

Although these two theories were initially accepted by the scientific community, there was insufficient evidence accumulated over time to totally explain pain, even though there was some level of support for each (Gatchel & Weisberg, 2000). Moreover, various empirical findings could not be accounted for by either of these two theories. Again, this strict mechanistic, biomedical reductionist approach to medicine began to subside somewhat because of the advent of important work implicating the role of psychosocial factors in medical disorders. Indeed, Bonica (1953) had pointed out the various shortcomings of both of these earlier two purely mechanistic models of pain.

The Gate-Control Theory of Pain

The first major theory of pain, which emphasized the close interaction between psychosocial and physiological processes affecting pain, was that of Melzack and Wall (1965). They introduced the *gate-control theory of pain*, which accounted for many diverse factors involved in pain perception. Its primary contribution to the scientific community was the introduction of the importance of central nervous system *and* psychosocial variables in the pain perception process. It highlighted the potentially significant role of psychosocial factors in the perception of pain (Melzack, 1993). Although the physiological processes involved in the gate-control model were initially challenged and suggestions were made that the model was incomplete (e.g., Nathan, 1976; Schmidt, 1972), additional research accumulated that prompted some revision and reformulation of the original model (Wall, 1989). Nevertheless, the gate control model of pain has proven quite resilient in the face of recent scientific data and theoretical challenges, to the point that it still provides the most heuristic perspective of the wide range of pain phenomena encountered in medical settings today. Of course, like most scientific models, a more refined model will mostly likely evolve over time as the understanding of pain neurophysiology, neurotransmission, and opioid receptors increases.

The Neuromatrix Model of Pain

Melzack (1999) has extended the gate-control theory of pain and integrated it with models of stress. This neuromatrix theory makes a number of assumptions about pain, primarily that pain is a major stressor that obstructs homeostatic mechanisms.

This neuromatrix theory of pain integrates a great deal of physiological and psychological evidence. Although the various components of the theory, as well as the theory itself, still requires a great deal of systematic investigation, it offers another promising way of conceptualizing pain and should stimulate a great deal of future clinical research. Turk and Monarch (2002) have recently summarized the major elements of this model.

The Biopsychosocial Perspective of Pain

The biopsychosocial model of pain, which is now accepted as the most heuristic approach to the understanding and treatment of pain disorders, views physical disorders such as pain as a result of a complex and dynamic interaction among physiological, psychological, and social factors, which perpetuate and may worsen the clinical presentation. Each individual experiences pain uniquely. The range of psychological, social, and economic factors can interact with physical pathology to modulate patients' reports of symptoms and subsequent disability. The development of this biopsychosocial approach has grown rapidly during the past decade, and a great deal of scientific knowledge has been produced in this short period of time concerning the best care of individuals with complex pain problems, as well as pain prevention and coping techniques.

As Turk and Monarch (2002) have discussed in their comprehensive review of the biopsychosocial perspective on chronic pain, individuals differ significantly in how frequently they report physical symptoms, in their tendency to visit physicians when experiencing identical symptoms, and in their responses to the same treatments. Quite frequently, the nature of patients' responses to treatment has little to do with their objective physical conditions. For example, White, Williams, and Greenberg (1961) earlier noted that less than one third of all individuals with clinically significant symptoms consult a physician. On the other hand, from 30% to 50% of patients who seek treatment in primary care do not have specific diagnosable disorders (Dworkin & Massoth, 1994). Turk and Monarch (2002) go on to make the distinction between *disease* and *illness* in better understanding chronic pain. The term *disease* is generally used to define "an objective biological event" that involves the disruption of specific body structures or organ systems caused by anatomical, pathological, or physiological changes. *Illness*, in contrast, is generally defined as a "subjective experience or self-attribution" that a disease is present. An illness will yield physical discomfort, behavioral limitations, and psychosocial distress. Thus, illness references how sick individuals and members of their families live with, and respond to, symptoms and disability. This distinction between disease and illness is analogous to the distinction made between *pain* and *nociception*. Nociception involves the stimulation of nerves that convey information about tissue damage to the brain. Pain, on the other hand, is a more subjective perception that is the result of the transduction, transmission, and modulation of sensory input. This input may be filtered through individuals' genetic composition, earlier learning histories, current physiological status, and sociocultural influences. Pain, therefore, cannot be comprehensively assessed without a full understanding of the person who is exposed to the nociception. The biopsychosocial model focuses on *illness*, which is the result of the complex interaction of biological, psychological, and social factors. With this perspective, diversity in pain or illness expression (including its severity, duration, and psychosocial consequences) can be expected. The interrelationships among biological changes, psychological status, and the sociocultural context all need to be taken into account in fully understanding pain, patients' perception, and their response to illness. A model or treatment approach that focuses on only one of these core sets of factors will be incomplete. Indeed, the treatment efficacy of a biopsychosocial approach to pain has consistently demonstrated the heuristic value of this model (Turk & Monarch, 2002).

ACUTE VERSUS CHRONIC PAIN

Pain is usually broadly categorized as *acute*, *chronic*, or *recurrent*, depending on its time course. This broad classification of pain duration is often used to better understand the biopsychosocial aspects that may be important when conducting assessment and treatment. For example, many times chronic pain is a result of unresolved acute pain episodes, resulting in accumulative biopsychosocial effects such as prolonged physical deconditioning, anxiety, and stress. This type of time categorization information, obviously, can be extremely helpful in directing specific treatment approaches to the type of pain that is being evaluated.

Acute pain is usually indicative of tissue damage and is characterized by momentary intense noxious sensations (i.e., nociception). It serves an important biological signal of potential tissue–physical harm. Some anxiety may initially be precipitated, but prolonged physical and emotional distress usually is not. Indeed, anxiety, if mild, can be quite adaptive in that it stimulates behaviors needed for recovery, such as the seeking of medical attention, rest, and removal from the potentially harmful situation. As the nociception decreases, acute pain usually subsides.

Chronic pain is traditionally defined as pain that lasts six months or longer, well past the normal healing period one would expect for its protective biological function. Arthritis, back injuries, and cancer can produce chronic pain syndromes and, as the pain persists, it is often accompanied by emotional distress such as depression, anger, and frustration. Such pain can also often significantly interfere with activities of daily living. There is much more health utilization in an attempt to find some relief from the pain symptoms, and the pain has a tendency to become a preoccupation of an individual's everyday living.

Intense, *episodic* pain, reoccurring for more than three months, is often referred to as *recurrent pain*. Recurrent pain episodes are usually brief (as are acute pain episodes); however, the reoccurring nature of this type of pain makes it similar to chronic pain in that it is distressing to patients. Such episodes may develop without a well-defined cause, and then may begin to generate an array of emotional reactions, such as anxiety, stress, and depression–helplessness. Often, pain medication is used to control the intensity of the recurrent pain, but it is not usually helpful in reducing the frequency of the episodes that a person experiences. It should also be noted that patients often find it difficult to distinguish between chronic and recurrent pain. Patients will often present with "chronic-like" symptoms from prolong episodes of, say, headache or back pain. These do not always fit the description of chronic pain but are usually persistent and can be as disabling. It should be kept in mind that all pain, be it acute, chronic, or recurrent, may often be accompanied by emotional distress. A health care professional will need to understand the different factors, such as physiological, sociocultural, environmental, and pathophysiological (i.e., a comprehensive biopsychosocial evaluation) associated with all three types of pain to treat and predict response to treatment of these patients.

THE BIOPSYCHOSOCIAL APPROACH TO PAIN
ASSESSMENT AND MANAGEMENT

The biopsychosocial approach to pain assessment and management appropriately conceptualizes pain as a complex and dynamic interaction among physiological, psychological, and social factors that often results in, or at least maintains, pain. It cannot be broken down into distinct, independent psychosocial or physical components. Each individual also experiences pain uniquely. The complexity of pain is especially evident when it persists over time, as a range of psychological, social, and economic factors can interact with physical pathology to modulate a patient's report of pain and subsequent disability. The model uses physiological, biological, cognitive, affective, behavioral, and social factors, as well as their interplay, when explaining a patient's report of pain.

There is now a revolution in developing a more comprehensive, biopsychosocial understanding of pain. Besides the greater appreciation of psychosocial factors that contribute to the pain process, there is a growing understanding of how endocrine modulation of pain mechanisms occur. Also, research on pain mechanisms and pathways has greatly expanded in scope during the past few years, including the use of a wide array of techniques such as anatomical, electrophysiological, genetic, molecular biological, and pharmacological approaches. Technical advances have also improved methods for identifying brain regions involved during various neurological and psychiatric conditions. This synergy across disciplines will, one hopes, lead to the most effective methods to manage pain, because it will help us understand how the nervous system senses, interprets, and responds to pain (Gatchel & Turk, 1999).

Gatchel (in press) and Turk and Monarch (2002) have provided a more comprehensive review of the biopsychosocial perspective on chronic pain. Earlier, Turk and Flor (1999) had also indicated that, within a biopsychosocial context, pain problems need to be "viewed longitudinally as ongoing, multifactorial processes in which there is a dynamic and reciprocal interplay among biological, psychological, and social cultural factors that shapes the experience in responses of patients" (p. 20). Thus, to comprehensively assess pain, one must be certain to account for such potential interactions before prescribing the best treatment regimen, individualized for a particular patient with pain.

General Assessment Issues

There are three broad categories of measures—physical, psychological, and socioeconomic—that have been used to assess patients. However, these three major measurement categories (or biopsychosocial referents) may not always display high concordance with one another when measuring a construct such as pain. It has long been noted in the psychology literature, for example, that self-report, overt behavior, and physiological indexes of a construct such as pain or stress sometime show low correlations among one another (e.g., Gatchel, 2000). Therefore, if one uses a self-report measure as a primary index of a construct such as pain and compares it to the overt behavioral or physiological index of the same construct, direct overlap cannot automatically be expected. Moreover, two different self-report indexes or physiological indexes of the same construct may not be as highly correlated as one would desire. What has plagued the evaluation arena in general has been the lack of agreement on particular measures and the wide variation of measures used to document a construct such as pain, as well as changes in how this construct has been conceptualized over time. Therefore, the literature is replete with many different measurement techniques and tests of pain. However, the literature is beginning to demonstrate which measures appear to be the most reliable and valid (Gatchel, 2001). The reader is referred to a number of recent works that provide comprehensive reviews of "good measurements" of pain (e.g., Gatchel, 2001; Gatchel & Weisberg, 2000; Turk & Melzack, 2001).

It should also be pointed out that there are two important assumption traps that pain-management professionals need to avoid when considering the best assessment measure to use. First of all, one cannot automatically assume, on an a priori basis, that one assessment measure will necessarily be more valid or reliable than another. In general, the more objectively quantified the measure is, the more likely it can be empirically established as a valid and reliable referent or marker. The second assumption trap is that a physical measure will always be more objective than self-report psychosocial measures. However, no matter what the level of accuracy or sophistication of a mechanical device used in collecting physiological measures, it is always the case that human interpretation often must be used in the understanding of the resulting findings. In addition, it must be remembered that a patient's performance during a physical assessment protocol can be greatly influenced by fear of pain or injury, motivation, instructional set, and so forth (Gatchel, 2001).

Specific Pain Assessment Techniques

The common denominator of all assessment methods are the qualities of validity, reliability (reproducibility), and predictive value (e.g., Anderson, Pope, Frymoyer, & Snook, 1991). However, there often remain frequent misunderstandings over the appropriate use of assessments based on the generalizability of the scientific reports of validity to the circumstances in which the health care professional is using the assessment method. Such ambiguities can be minimized by examining the match between the clinical context in which a test is evaluated and the patient to whom it is applied in the clinical setting. Basically, it is answering the question of test validity by addressing "valid for what?" issue. Assessment methods may be valid for measuring specific biological–physiological states but have no validity in predicting, for example, impairment, disability, or activities of daily living. Moreover, the results of the test may or may not be valid for informing or clarifying treatment planning.

Of course, it must be kept in mind that, when embracing a comprehensive biopsychosocial assessment model, it is important to consider each successive measure in context with the other measures to be integrated. This will lead to the most comprehensive assessment of a patient, which will then significantly contribute to the development of the most effective treatment regimen for dealing with the pain problem. A step-wise approach to assessment is recommended (Gatchel, 2000), which proceeds from global indexes of biopsychosocial concomitants of pain to more detailed evaluations of specific diagnoses. Likewise, a stepped-care framework for managing pain is also advocated (Gatchel, in press). It should be kept in mind that no one type of assessment measure can usually "capture" all the important characteristics when considering a patient's report of pain. Rather, integrating a number of assessment tools is needed.

It should be kept in mind that pain is a cardinal symptom of disease. However, pain sometimes does not fit neatly into an evaluative–curative model of medical care. Nevertheless, evaluation of pain should include a medical history, physical examination, and appropriate medical tests. Indeed, several important organizations in the United States have developed new standards for the evaluation of pain. The Joint Commission on Accreditation of Healthcare Organizations (JCAHO) requires that pain severity be documented using a pain scale. In addition, patients' own words to describe their pain, pain location, duration, aggravating and alleviating factors, present pain management regimen and effectiveness, the effects of pain, their pain goals, and a physical examination are all to be documented on initial assessment (www.jcaho.org/standards/pm.html).

The Commission for the Accreditation of Rehabilitation Facilities (CARF) has also developed new guidelines for the assessment of patients with pain or candidates for rehabilitation programs. This requires not only a medical evaluation but evaluation of patient functioning, physical assessment, psychosocial assessment, social and vocational assessments, and spirituality referral when indicated. It requires that the participants in the assessment include the patient, physician, and a psychologist. Additional assessments may be made by a physical therapist, occupational therapist, vocational specialist, and a biofeedback therapist. Assessment criteria for entry into a pain management rehabilitation program must be matched to predicted outcomes, frequency of service, intensity of service, and duration of service. Pediatric patients must have their family included as a part of the assessment team.

Pain Management Techniques

Pain, especially when it becomes chronic in nature, often cannot be "cured" but rather only managed. This is also true for other chronic medical conditions such as hypertension, diabetes, asthma, and so forth. Moreover, currently, a major trend in the pain management literature is a movement away from the homogeneity of pain patients myth and toward attempts to match treatment to specific assessment outcomes of patients (e.g., Turk & Gatchel, 1999; Turk & Monarch, 2002; Turk & Okifuji, 2001). Because groups of patients may differ in psychosocial and behavioral characteristics, even when the medical diagnosis is identical, such patient differences and treatment matching is important to consider. Traditionally, patients with the same medical diagnosis or set of symptoms were "lumped" together (e.g., chronic back pain, fibromyalgia, neuropathic pain) and then treated in the same way, as though "one size fits all." However, it has been shown that there are differential responses of pain patients with the same diagnosis to the same treatment. As a consequence, it is important that treatment should be individually tailored for each patient based on the careful biopsychosocial assessment of that particular patient. It is often the case that two chronic low back pains patients, for example, will require slightly different treatment programs because of differences in their physical, psychosocial, or socioeconomic presentations. Turk and Okifuji (2001) have provided a comprehensive review of the importance of this treatment-matching process, and literature to support the greater clinical efficacy of such a matching approach strategy. Indeed, taking the approach of delineating homogeneous *subgroups* among patients with pain will provide an extremely important basis for the development of more specific, optimal treatment regimens for these different subgroups of patients.

Gatchel (1991, 1996) has conceptualized how acute pain can progress into a chronic pain situation. This progression from acute to chronic pain is characterized as a three-stage model (Figure 11.1). In Stage 1 of this model, referred to as the *acute phase*, normal emotional reactions (such as fear, anxiety and worry) develop subsequent to the patient's perception of pain. As noted earlier, this is a natural emotional reaction that often serves a protective function by prompting the individual to heed the pain signal and, if necessary, seek out medical attention for it. However, if the perception of pain exists beyond a two- to four-month period (which is usually considered a normal healing time for most pain syndromes), the pain begins to develop into a more chronic condition, leading into Stage 2 of the model.

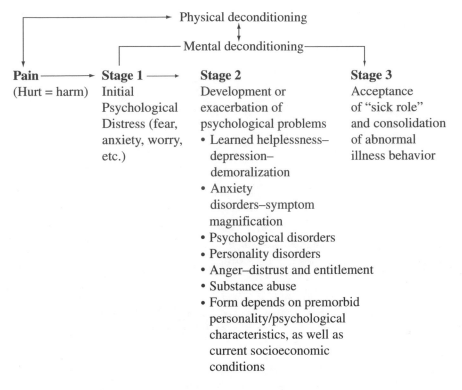

Figure 11.1. Progression of the mental deconditioning process and its interaction with physical deconditioning.

During this second stage, physiological and behavioral problems are often exacerbated. Learned helplessness, anger, distress, and somatization are typical symptoms of patients in this stage. Often, the extent of these symptoms usually depends on the individual's preexisting personality–psychosocial structure, in addition to socioeconomic and environmental conditions. The model proposes a *diathesis–stress* perspective, in which the stress of coping with pain can lead to exacerbation of the individual's underlying psychological characteristics. Finally, the progression to complex interactions of physical, psychological, and social processes characterize Stage 3, which represents the chronic phase of the model. As a result of the chronic nature of the pain experience and the stress that it creates, the patient's life begins to revolve around the pain and the behaviors that maintain it. The patient begins to adopt a "sick role" in which any excuse from social and occupational responsibilities become routine. As a consequence, the patient now becomes accustomed to the avoidance of responsibility, and other reinforcers serve to maintain such maladaptive behavior.

A CONCEPTUAL MODEL OF HOW ACUTE PAIN DEVELOPS INTO CHRONIC PAIN

Superimposed on these three stages is what is referred to as the "physical deconditioning syndrome," originally emphasized by Mayer and Gatchel (1988). This refers to a significant decrease in physical capacity (such as strength, mobility, and endurance) resulting from disuse and the resultant atrophy of the injured area. There is usually a two-way pathway between the physical deconditioning and the three stages described earlier. For example, physical deconditioning can feed back and negatively affect the emotional well-being and self-esteem of individuals. This can lead to additional negative psychosocial sequelae. Conversely, negative emotional reactions such as depression can feed back to physical functioning (e.g., by decreasing the motivation to get involved in work or recreational activities, and thereby contributing to physical deconditioning).

DISTINCTIONS AMONG PRIMARY, SECONDARY, AND TERTIARY PAIN MANAGEMENT

Distinctions among primary, secondary, and tertiary pain management care, highlighted earlier in the clinical research by Mayer (1995) and subsequently reviewed by Gatchel (1996), are helpful because they suggest that the type of biopsychosocial treatment required for each is substantially different. In discussing back pain rehabilitation, for example, the term *primary care* is usually applied to acute cases of pain of limited severity. Basic symptom-control methods are used in relieving pain during the normal early healing period. Frequently, some basic psychological reassurance that the acute pain episode is temporary and will soon be resolved is quite effective. *Secondary care* represents reactivation treatment administered to those patients who do not improve simply through the normal healing process. It is administered during the transition from acute (primary) care to the eventual return to work. Such treatment has been designed to promote return to productivity before advanced physical deconditioning and significant psychosocial barriers to returning to work occur. At this phase, more active psychosocial intervention may need to be administered to those patients who do not appear to be progressing. Finally, *tertiary care* requires an interdisciplinary and intensive treatment approach. It is intended for those patients suffering the effects of physical deconditioning and chronic disability. In general, it differs from secondary care in regard to the intensity of rehabilitation services required, including psychosocial and disability management. The critical elements of interdisciplinary care, such as functional restoration, involve the following:

- Formal, repeated quantification of physical deficits to guide, individualize, and monitor physical training progress;
- Psychosocial and socioeconomic assessment to guide, individualize, and monitor disability behavior-oriented interventions and outcomes;
- Multimodal disability management program using cognitive–behavioral approaches;
- Psychopharmacological interventions for detoxification and psychological management;
- Interdisciplinary, medically directed team approach with formal staffing, frequent team conferences, and low staff-to-patient ratios; and
- Ongoing outcome assessment using standardized objective criteria.

Such interdisciplinary biopsychosocial treatment programs have been shown to be extremely efficacious, as well as cost-effective, in successfully managing chronic pain patients, relative to less intensive, single-modality treatment programs (e.g., Deschner & Polatin, 2000; Mayer & Polatin, 2000).

In terms of primary and secondary care, the clinician must be aware of many psychosocial factors that can contribute to an acute pain episode becoming subacute and then chronic. A patient may progress through a number of stages (reviewed previously) as his or her pain and disability becomes more chronic. These may create significant barriers to recovery if they are not effectively dealt with. These barriers to recovery include the psychosocial variables discussed earlier, as well as functional, legal, and work-related issues that can greatly interfere with the patient's return to full functioning and a productive lifestyle. It is important that members of the health care team be knowledgeable about all psychosocial issues while the patient is in treatment. This knowledge allows staff members not only to understand and serve the patient better but also to be more effective in problem-solving if the patient's physical progress is slow or nonexistent.

As a treatment approach, a Step Care Framework (Von Korff, 1999) that is similar to the primary, secondary, and tertiary pain management distinctions described earlier is advocated. *Step 1* is the lowest intensity of intervention, which consists of addressing a patient's fear–avoidance belief about pain through education, information, and advice about the importance of returning to activities of daily living as soon as possible. *Step 2* refers to the need for increasing intensity of intervention and is reserved for patients who may continue to report pain six to eight weeks following the onset of an episode and who demonstrate persistent limitations in activities of daily living. Finally, *Step 3* is for those patients who fail to improve with either Step 1 or Step 2 interventions. These patients are the ones who continue to experience significant disability and are at risk for becoming permanently disabled. Intervention at this step may be much more costly and complex than Step 1 and 2 interventions. It is at this step where more complex biopsychosocial issues need to be addressed, using an intensive interdisciplinary treatment approach.

CHRONIC PAIN MANAGEMENT

As earlier noted, when pain becomes chronic, a more intensive tertiary care or interdisciplinary treatment approach is required because of the significant effects of physical deconditioning and chronic disability. This approach will be reviewed in more detail, because it requires the most coordinated type of care and is used with the most costly pain problems. The critical elements of this interdisciplinary approach were highlighted earlier. There have been a number of reviews that have documented the clinical efficacy of such interdisciplinary treatment of chronic pain patients (e.g., Deschner & Polatin, 2000; Gatchel & Turk, 1999; Wright & Gatchel, 2002). Such interdisciplinary programs are needed for chronic pain patients who have complex needs and requirements. Although they represent a small minority of pain patients, a significant number of patients, nevertheless, fail to benefit from the combination of spontaneous healing and short-term, symptom-focused treatment. They also become financial burdens on their insurance carriers as well as the health care system in general. They often fail to experience significant pain relief after repeated and extended contacts with several different physicians and other health care providers. Psychosocial distress, physical deconditioning, secondary gains and losses, and medication issues often complicate their presentation. Therefore, this stage of treatment is much more complex and demanding of health care professionals. As such, the strengths of multiple disciplines working together to address complex issues confronting chronic pain patients is greatly needed. The overall therapeutic focus should be toward independence and autonomy, while acknowledging when certain physical limitations cannot be overcome. The commission on Accreditation of Rehabilitation Facilities (CARF) requires that a certified pain management team include at least a physician, specialized nurse, a physical therapist, and a clinical psychologist or psychiatrist. However, often an occupational therapist is required because return-to-work and vocational retraining issues become important in managing chronic patient patients.

Finally, one variant of chronic pain management program—functional restoration—has been extensively reviewed by Mayer and Polatin (2000). The clinical effectiveness of functional restoration has been well-documented. The interdisciplinary treatment team consists of the following:

- The physician serves as a medical director of the treatment plan and must have a firm background in providing medical rehabilitation for these types of pain disorders frequently encountered. Formal training may vary from anesthesiology, orthopaedic surgery, psychiatry, or occupational medicine to internal medicine. The physician needs to assume a direct role in the medical management of patients' pain by providing the medical history to the treatment team and by taking direct responsibility for medication management for any other medical interventions. Often, other team members and outside consultants may be involved in the medical treatment of patients, but it is physicians' responsibility to coordinate these medical contributions to the patients' care.
- Although not all programs use nursing services, any pain management program that provides anesthesiology services involving injections, nerve blocks, and other medical procedures will require a nurse. Nurses assist physicians, follow-up procedures, and interact with patients in the role of case managers, as well as providing patient education. Nurses may be viewed as physician-extenders and educators who have a strong impact on patients.
- Although physicians and nurses play a major role in managing the physical status of patients, psychologists play the leading role in the day-to-day maintenance of the psychosocial aspects and status of patients' care. Significant psychosocial barriers to positive outcomes of the treatment may develop as patients progress from acute through subacute to the chronic stage of a pain syndrome (as reviewed earlier in this chapter). Psychologists are responsible for performing a full psychosocial evaluation, which includes identification of psychosocial barriers and the assessment of patients' psychological strengths and weaknesses. A cognitive–behavioral treatment approach can then be used to address important psychosocial issues such as pain-related depression, anxiety, fear, as well as psychopathology. A cognitive–behavioral treatment approach has been found to be the most appropriate modality with patients in a team program such as this.
- Physical therapists interact daily with patients regarding any physical progression issues toward recovery. Effective communication with other team members is crucial so that patients' fear of exercise will not interfere with their reconditioning effort. Physical therapists also help to educate patients by addressing the physiological bases of pain and teaching ways of reducing

the severity of pain episodes through the use of appropriate body mechanics and pacing.

- Occupational therapists are involved in both physical and vocational aspects of patients' treatment. The great majority of patients participating in an interdisciplinary program are likely not to be working because of their pain. Often, they have become pessimistic about the prospect of returning to work. Occupational therapists address these vocational issues and the physical determinants on underlying disability. These therapists also play an important educational role in teaching patients techniques for managing pain on the job in ways that do not jeopardize their employment status. Finally, occupational therapists can play an important role as case managers in contacting employers to obtain job descriptions and other information, as well as vocational retraining if necessary.

- Constant, effective communication among all treatment personnel is required during which patient progress can be discussed and evaluated. This is important so patients hear the same treatment philosophy and message from each of the treatment team members. Indeed, many times patients are in conflict about their own future treatment and may seek out any conflict between team members and use it to compromise treatment goals.

- A formal interdisciplinary treatment team meeting should occur at least once a week to review patient progress and to make any modifications in the treatment plan for each patient. Individually tailoring treatment for patients is essential.

- Evaluating and monitoring treatment outcomes in a systematic fashion is essential for not only treatment outcomes evaluations but also for quality assurance purposes for the treatment team.

SPECIAL TOPICS AND POPULATIONS

In this section, some important mediating factors that may affect the pain perception process are discussed. Most significantly, the potential impact of cultural, as well as sex and gender, are highlighted.

Cultural Factors and Pain

There can be no doubt that cultural and social factors significantly influence the perception of pain (Baum, Gatchel, & Krantz, 1997). For example, a classic study by Tursky and Sternbach (1967) demonstrated significant differences and reactions to electric shock among ethnic groups. Although overly stereotypical in nature, results revealed that "Yankees" (Protestants of British descent) displayed a "matter of fact" orientation toward pain and assumed that it was a common experience. In contrast, Irish participants tended to inhibit their pain expressions and suffering; Italians demonstrated immediacy to pain experience and emotionally exaggerated their pain, demanding fast relief. Jewish participants also emotionally exaggerated their pain and had great concerns about the meaning and any future implications of the pain. As this same time, Christopherson (1966) also demonstrated that there are significant differences in the magnitude of pain responding to identical pain stimulation as a function of the cultural background of an individual, although these specific cultural differences may not be as prevalent today.

These differences in attitudes and responses to pain appear to be learned. For example, investigations of dental fears in children have found that a child's family attitudes and feelings toward the dental treatment procedure are important in determining the child's own anxiety about dental treatment (e.g., Milgrom, Mand, King, & Weinstein, 1995). In one such study, it was found that children with anxious mothers displayed significantly more emotional negative behavior during a tooth extraction than do children of mothers with low anxiety (Weisenberg, 1977). Negative expectations about pain, which can also be culturally learned, can affect pain. For example, chronic pain patients reported more negative self-statements and social thoughts, and reported more severe pain, than other types of pain, suggesting that these negative thoughts intensify or prolong pain (Gil, Williams, Keefe, & Beckham, 1990).

Of course, such examples do not imply that all pain is learned and culturally determined. The major point is that our pain perceptions and responses often have a significant psychology-learning component (which can be affected by cultural factors) that directly and significantly contribute to the experiences of pain. Again, this indicates how psychosocial factors can play a direct role in the pain experience. How one acts to pain sensation is as important an issue as the specific physiological mechanisms involved in transmitting and generating pain experiences.

The Role of Sex and Gender in Pain

Until quite recently, both clinicians and researchers have basically ignored potential differences in how males and females report a variety of symptoms associated with common health problems, such as self-reported pain. An important question that remains and requires a great deal of additional research is whether these differences are a result of sex factors (i.e., physiological differences between the sexes) or gender factors (i.e., differences in role learning between the genders). According to Miaskowski (1999), there can be no doubt that men and women respond quite differently to both painful stimuli and pain medication. On the basis of a comprehensive review of the literature, Miaskowski found the following:

- Experimental pain studies with humans have suggested that gender differences are present in pain thresholds and levels of tolerance, with females generally reporting lower pain thresholds and less tolerance to painful stimuli.
- Results from acute pain studies have indicated that males and females tend to express themselves quite differently when describing their sensations of pain associated with a specific clinical problem.
- A number of chronic pain problems appear to a have specific gender distribution. For example, there is a higher prevalence of temporomandibular disorders and fibromyalgia in females relative to males.
- Several studies have suggested that females reported either better analgesic effects or a more prolonged duration of analgesia using certain opioid analgesics.
- Results from several studies also suggested that there appears to be a gender bias in how health care professionals respond to male and female reports of acute in chronic pain. For example, male professionals respond more sympathetically to female patients than to male patients.

Such results clearly indicate that clinicians need to be aware of gender differences when caring for patients with pain. However, additional research is needed to delineate the mechanisms that underlie these gender and sex differences. Such delineation, one hopes, will provide better insight into the use of different assessment and treatment techniques for males and females.

CONCLUSION

As Walco and Harkins (1999) have noted, important lifespan developmental processes are often overlooked in the assessment and treatment of pain. Fortunately, there is a currently greater attempt to develop specific pain assessment and management techniques for infants and children, as well as for elderly individuals. However, little attention has been paid to the key characteristics of pain that may change over the course of the lifespan to require such separate approaches. For example, Walco and Harkins (1999) have pointed out that there is currently little known about key aspects of childhood history that may subsequently affect pain syndromes in adults or about significant events early in life that may have an impact on pain in elderly individuals. Developmental research is needed to answer these important questions.

Again, as discussed in the earlier sections on the role of sex, gender, and cultural factors in pain that must be taken into account by clinicians in the assessment treatment process, and this also holds true for developmental factors. Fortunately, a number of comprehensive reviews of pain assessment–treatment approaches to children (McGrath & Hiller, 2002) and for elderly individuals (Pawlick & Middaugh, 2002) have been provided. This should help in individualizing treatment for pain patients. Again, as was earlier discussed, a major trend in the pain assessment–management literature is a movement away from the homogeneity myth and toward attempts to match treatment to specific assessment outcomes of patients. Assessment–treatment approaches need to be individually tailored for each patient based on the careful biopsychosocial assessment of that particular patient, while taking into account cultural, gender/sex, and developmental age differences.

REFERENCES

Anderson, G. B. J., Pope, M. H., Frymoyer, J. W., & Snook, S. H. (1991). Occupational low back pain: Assessment, treatment, and prevention. In M. H. Pope, G. B. J. Anderson, J. W. Frymoyer, & D. B. Chaffin (Eds.), *Epidemiology and cost* (pp. 91–132). St. Louis, MO: Mosby Year Book.

Baum, A., Gatchel, R. J., & Krantz, D. (1997). *An introduction to health psychology* (3rd ed.). New York: McGraw-Hill.

Bonica, J. J. (1953). *The management of pain*. Philadelphia: Lea & Febiger.

Christopherson, V. (1966). *Socio-cultural correlates of pain* (Final Report of Project #1390, Vocational Rehabilitation Administration). Washington, DC: U.S. Department of Health, Educational and Welfare.

Deschner, M., & Polatin, P. B. (2000). Interdisciplinary programs: Chronic pain management. In T. G. Mayer, R. J. Gatchel, & P. B. Polatin (Eds.), *Occupational musculoskeletal disorders: Function, outcomes and evidence* (pp. 629–638). Philadelphia: Lippincott, Williams & Wilkins.

Dworkin, S. F., & Massoth, D. L. (1994). Temporomandibular disorders and chronic pain: Disease or illness? *Journal of Prosthetic Dentistry, 72*(1), 29–38.

Gatchel, R. J. (1991). Early development of physical and mental conditioning in painful spinal disorders. In J. G. Mayer, V. Mooney, & R. J. Gatchel (Eds.), *Contemporary conservative care for painful spinal disorders* (pp. 278–289). Philadelphia: Lea & Febiger.

Gatchel, R. J. (1996). Psychological disorders and chronic pain: Cause and effect relationships. In R. J. Gatchel & D. C. Turk (Eds.), *Psychological approaches to pain management: A practitioner's handbook* (pp. 33–52). New York: Guilford Press.

Gatchel, R. J. (1999). Perspectives on pain: A historical overview. In R. J. Gatchel & D. C. Turk (Eds.), *Psychosocial factors in pain: Critical perspectives* (pp. 3–17). New York: Guilford Press.

Gatchel, R. J. (2000). How practitioners should evaluate personality to help manage patients with chronic pain. In R. J. Gatchel & J. N. Weisberg (Eds.), *Personality characteristics of patients with pain* (pp. 241–258). Washington, DC: American Psychological Association.

Gatchel, R. J. (2001). *Compendium of outcome instruments for assessment and researchers spinal disorders*. La Grange, IL: North American Spine Society.

Gatchel, R. J. (in press). The influence of personality characteristics on pain patients: Implications for causality in pain. In G. Young, A. Kane, & K. Nicholson (Eds.), *Causality: Psychological knowledge and evidence in court*. Washington, DC: American Psychological Association.

Gatchel, R. J., & Mayer, T. G. (2000). Occupational musculoskeletal disorders: Introduction and overview of the problem. In T. G. Mayer, R. J. Gatchel, & P. B. Polatin (Eds.), *Occupational musculoskeletal disorders: Function, outcomes, and evidence* (pp. 3–8). Philadelphia: Lippincott, Williams & Wilkins.

Gatchel, R. J., & Turk, D. C. (1999). Interdisciplinary treatment of chronic pain patients. In R. J. Gatchel & D. C. Turk (Eds.), *Psychosocial factors in pain: Critical perspectives* (pp. 435–444). New York: Guilford Press.

Gatchel, R. J., & Weisberg, J. N. (2000). *Personality characteristics of patients with pain*. Washington, DC: American Psychological Association.

Gil, K. M., Williams, D. A., Keefe, F. J., & Beckham, J. C. (1990). The relationship of negative thoughts to pain and psychological distress. *Behavior Therapy, 21*, 349–362

Mayer, T. G., & Gatchel, R. J. (1988). *Functional restoration for spinal disorders: The sports medicine approach*. Philadelphia: Lea & Febiger.

Mayer, T. G. (1995). Spine rehabilitation: Secondary and tertiary nonoperative care. *Spine, 20*, 2060–2066.

Mayer, T. G., & Polatin, P. B. (2000). Tertiary nonoperative interdisciplinary programs: The functional restoration variant of the outpatient chronic pain management program. In T. G. Mayer, R. J. Gatchel, & P. B. Polatin (Eds.) *Occupational musculoskeletal disorders: Function, outcomes, and evidence* (pp. 639–650). Philadelphia: Lippincott, Williams & Wilkins.

McGrath, P., & Hiller, L. (2002). A practical cognitive behavioral approach for treating children's pain. In D. C. Turk & R. J. Gatchel (Eds.), *Psychological approaches to pain management* (2nd ed., pp. 534–552). New York: Guilford Press.

Melzack, R. (1993). Pain: Past, present and future. *Canadian Journal of Experimental Psychology, 47*(4), 615–629.

Melzack, R. (1999). Pain and stress: A new perspective. In R. J. Gatchel & D. C. Turk (Eds.), *Psychosocial factors in pain: Critical perspectives* (pp. 89–106). New York: Guilford Press.

Melzack, R., & Wall, P. D. (1965). Pain mechanisms: A new theory. *Science, 50*, 971–979.

Miaskowsi, C. (1999). The role of sex and gender in pain perception and responses to treatment. In R. J. Gatchel & D. C. Turk (Eds.), *Psychosocial factors in pain: Critical perspectives* (pp. 401–411). New York: Guilford Press.

Milgrom, P., Mand, L., King, B., & Weinstein P. (1995). Origins of childhood dental fear. *Behavior Research and Therapy, 33*, 313–319.

Nathan, P. W. (1976). The gate control theory of pain: A critical review. *Brain, 99*, 123–158.

Pawlick, K., & Middaugh, S. (2002). Persistent pain in the older patient. In D. C. Turk & R. J. Gatchel (Eds.), *Psychological approaches to pain management* (2nd ed., pp. 553–572). New York: Guilford Press.

Schmidt, R. F. (1972). The gate control theory of pain: An unlikely hypothesis. In R. Jansen, W. D. Keidel, A. Herz, C. Streichele, J. P. Payne, & R. A. P. Burt (Eds.), *Pain: Basic principles, pharmacology, therapy* (pp. 57–71). Stuttgart, Germany: Thieme.

Turk, C. D., & Flor, H. (1999). Chronic pain: A biopsychosocial perspective. In R. J. Gatchel & D. C. Turk (Eds.), *Psychosocial factors in pain: Critical perspectives* (pp. 18–34). New York: Guilford Press.

Turk, D. C., & Gatchel, R. J. (1999). Psychosocial factors in pain: Revolution and evolution. In R. J. Gatchel & D. C. Turk (Eds.), *Psychosocial factors in pain: Critical perspectives* (pp. 481–493). New York: Guilford Press.

Turk, D. C., & Melzack, R. (2001). *Handbook of pain assessment* (2nd ed.). New York: Guilford Press.

Turk, D. C., & Monarch, E. S. (2002). Biopsychosocial perspective on chronic pain. In D. C. Turk & R. J. Gatchel (Eds.), *Psychological approaches to pain management* (2nd ed., pp. 3–29). New York: Guilford Press.

Turk, D. C., & Okifuji, A. (2001). Matching treatment to assessment of patients with chronic pain. In D. C. Turk & R. Melzack (Eds.), *Handbook of pain assessment* (2nd ed., pp. 400–416). New York: Guilford Press.

Tursky, B., & Sternbach, R. A. (1967). Further physiological correlates of ethnic differences in responses to shock. *Psychophysiology, 4*, 67–74.

Von Korff, M. (1999). Pain management in primary care: An individualized stepped-care approach. In R. J. Gatchel & D. C. Turk (Eds.), *Psychosocial factors in pain: Critical perspectives* (pp. 360–373). New York: Guilford Press.

Walco, G. A., & Harkins, W. (1999). Lifespan developmental approaches to pain. In R. J. Gatchel & D. C. Turk (Eds.), *Psychological factors in pain: Outreach perspectives* (pp. 107–117). New York: Guilford Press.

Wall, P. D. (1989). The dorsal horn. In P. D. Wall & R. Melzack (Eds.), *Textbook of pain* (2nd ed., pp. 102–111). New York: Churchill Livingstone.

Weisenberg, M. (1977). Cultural and racial reactions to pain. In M. Weisenberg (Ed.), *The control of pain* (pp. 91–112). New York: Psychological Dimensions.

White, K. L., Williams, F., & Greenberg, B. G. (1961). The etiology of medical care. *New England Journal of Medicine, 265*, 885–886.

Woodwell, D. A. (2000). *National Ambulatory Medical Survey: 1998 summary advanced data from Vital and Health Statistics No. 315.* Hyattsville, MD: National Center for Health Statistics.

Wright, A. R., & Gatchel, R. J. (2002). Occupational musculoskeletal pain and disability. In D. C. Turk & R. J. Gatchel (Eds.), *Psychological approaches to pain management: A practitioner's handbook* (2nd ed., pp. 349–364). New York: Guilford Press.

12

FAMILY ADAPTATION IN ILLNESS, DISEASE, AND DISABILITY

TIMOTHY R. ELLIOTT AND RICHARD M. SHEWCHUK

Families are in a unique situation with regard to health and health-related problems, and the various roles family members assume may change over time. For example, parents and extended family members model behaviors for younger members that potentially promote or compromise their health. Families also react in ways to the health problems of a member that can foster or impede recovery. At some point in time, each member of the family will assume a patient role and require the assistance of some health care delivery system. In addition, family members often assume the role of caregiver for an ill or disabled member, and this role is increasingly common in American society. Families also differ in terms of their composition and

This chapter was supported by grants from the National Institute on Disability and Rehabilitation Research, Office of Special Education and Rehabilitative Services, U. S. Department of Education (Grant nos. H133B30025, H133N5009, and #H133B980016A), and from the National Center for Injury Prevention and Control and the Disabilities Prevention Program, National Center for Environmental Health (Grant no. R49/CCR412718-01), and by Grant no. #R49/CCR403641, U.S. DHHS, Centers for Disease Control and Prevention, National Center for Injury Prevention and Control to the University of Alabama at Birmingham. Its contents are solely the responsibility of the authors and do not necessarily represent the official views of the funding agencies. The authors are grateful to J. Scott Richards and Monica Kurylo for their helpful critique of an earlier version of this chapter.

boundaries; families from different ethnic backgrounds vary in the degree to which they include nonblood kin ("fictive kin") and members from older and extended generations in their immediate family circle. In all of these roles and in all of these situations, family members act in ways that directly or indirectly augment or aggravate the health of other members. These dynamics are thus ripe for scholarly understanding and clinical attention.

The past decade has witnessed a greater appreciation and understanding of the family (and its various forms) and its impact on personal health. Before this era, there was considerable confusion—if not outright disagreement—on the role of the family in the development, maintenance, remediation, and rehabilitation of health problems. Two edited books that appeared during this time frame (Akamatsu, Stephens, Hobfoll, & Crowther, 1992; Turk & Kerns, 1985) probably represent the best available statements on the field of family health psychology. These scholarly works approached the topic from different perspectives, and to a certain degree, these differences reflect some of the problems this emerging field has experienced.

The Turk and Kerns book (1985), although acknowledging the role of interpersonal dynamics, was couched in a behavioral tradition and capitalized on emerging interest in family issues from the perspective of behavioral medicine. The Akamatsu et al. book (1992) was more eclectic, taking into consideration perspectives on family health offered by social, developmental, and family psychology. To a great extent, contributors to this book were sensitive to trends in health psychology that recognized the role of the family in personal health. These books notwithstanding, the empirical literature remains largely fragmented and patiently waits for some attempt at scholarly integration.

Converging evidence will not wait for this integration; our knowledge base clearly documents that many family issues are involved in personal health, and these issues fall within the purview of professional psychology. Moreover, we are learning that the involvement of the family may be crucial to the success of interventions designed for the health of any one family member. Failure to take the family into account may disrupt routine prescriptions for health and recovery. Unfortunately, the lack of scholarly integration and the subsequent lack of concise and logical directions for meaningful interventions limit the contributions professional psychology can have in influencing public and health policy for families and in developing cost-effective, efficacious health service delivery programs.

In this chapter, we review the different scholarly perspectives that have guided the psychological study and treatment of issues in family health to date. We consider the various contributions of these perspectives and emphasize empirical advances that have enriched the literature. We consider limitations that are common to these different views and note some contemporary contributions that illustrate the potential inherent in bridging these perspectives and addressing these limitations. We conclude with a comment about implications for research, practice, and policy formation.

DIFFERING PERSPECTIVES AND CONVERGING EVIDENCE

Psychologists affiliated with social, clinical, and developmental psychology have scholarly investment in the study of the family. These different strands have their respective intellectual legacies that guide theoretical and clinical assumptions about family behavior. The rapid growth in health psychology and the accompanying rise in psychology as a health care profession have forced researchers and clinicians to evaluate the role of the family in health matters with a greater penchant for scholarly cross-fertilization. Health psychology has been instrumental in this enterprise because by definition it draws on all the major systems in psychology. In reviewing family behavior in health, it is instructive to survey the relevant schools of psychological thought in the study of families and accompanying contributions.

THE SOCIAL PSYCHOLOGY OF THE FAMILY
AND PERSONAL HEALTH

The social psychological perspective readily embraces the study of people in the context of interpersonal relations and group dynamics and considers the personal and social–cognitive processes that influence interpersonal behavior. Social psychologists are traditionally attuned to the application and refinement of theoretical explanations of family behavior. Social psychologists have rigorously examined the myriad facets of social support that might buffer or mediate the impact of stress on family member health (Pierce, Sarason, & Sarason, 1996). Others have advanced the study of family relationships from the perspective of social exchange theories (e.g., equity: Walster, Berschied, & Walster, 1973; interdependence: Kelley, 1979). Social–cognitive models have enriched the study of coping processes (Lazarus & Folkman, 1984) and attributional activity (S. Thompson, 1991) among family members facing health-related problems.

There is considerable evidence that social support plays an instrumental role in family adaptation to health problems. For example, higher levels of available social support and more social contact have been associated with the well-being of family caregivers of persons with severe physical disability (Schulz, Tompkins, Wood, & Decker, 1987) and less depression among those care-giving for stroke patients (S. Thompson, Bundek, & Sobolew-Shubin, 1990). Lower levels of family support are associated with a greater mortality rate over a five-year period among hemodialysis patients (Christiansen, Wiebe, Smith, & Turner, 1994). Patients with chronic health problems seem to find practical assistance from spouses and other family members to be especially supportive (Dakof & Taylor, 1990).

Unfortunately, the social support concept is of limited utility in understanding family dynamics in health and illness. It is difficult, for example, to determine exactly who provides social support and the circumstances that determine its supportive function (Suls, 1982). Family members are not always "supportive" and spousal partners in fact can be a source of considerable stress (Coyne & DeLongis, 1986). Subsequent research on the heels of these observations has revealed several mechanisms that affect the provision and receipt of social support in the family.

The availability of emotional support is directly associated with caregiver depression and anxiety experienced by family members throughout the first year in the caregiver role (Shewchuk, Richards, & Elliott, 1998). Mothers who have more personal resources (e.g., self-esteem, mastery), more intimacy from personal relationships, and lower discomfort in seeking support report more support over a year of caregiving for a child with chronic illness (Hobfoll & Lerman, 1989). For many mothers who provide care to a child with a disability or chronic disease, available social support seems to wane over time (Quittner, Glueckauf, & Jackson, 1990). The erosion of support from family members may be attributed, in part, to patient emotional distress, which can burden and alienate family members (Bolger, Foster, Vinokur, & Ng, 1996) and induce anger expressions (Lane & Hobfoll, 1992).

Other studies argue that family member adjustment may be better understood in the context of other social–psychological processes. Family interaction patterns have stronger associations with cardiac patients' reports of health behavior than social support variables (Franks, Campbell, & Shields, 1992). Marital quality and satisfaction may be directly related to patient adjustment following the onset of disease and disability (Coyne & Smith, 1991; Thompson et al., 1990). Relationships between family caregivers and care recipients that have been more communal before disease onset are associated with fewer symptoms of depression among these partners in the caregiving process (Williamson & Schulz, 1995).

Social–cognitive processes that guide interpersonal behaviors also aid family members considerably when a loved one incurs a debilitating condition. For example, family caregivers who find a sense of meaning in their role also report less distress than those who do not (Thompson, 1991). Family members engage in reality-negotiation strategies when a member incurs a sudden-onset disability from a traumatic event, and their expressions of hope and optimism are often mistaken by professional staff as manifestations of denial (Elliott & Kurylo, 2000). Higher levels of hope are uniquely associated with improved caregiver adjustment, and this effect seems to be most pronounced under conditions of high stress specific to the condition (Horton & Wallander, 2001).

Social–cognitive processes are also implicated in the ways in which family members cope with health problems. Caregiver ability to cope in an instrumental, problem-focused manner may be a better predictor of their adjustment than perceived social support (Chwalisz, 1996). Caregivers and care recipients who rely on palliative, emotion-focused coping strategies seem to have more distress than those who use more problem-focused strategies (Pakenham, 1998). The convenient dichotomy of problem- and emotion-focused coping is attractive for research and clinical use. Yet couples adjusting to the health problems of a partner may use more complex coping strategies that focus on the relationship itself or that compliment the coping efforts of the partner (Coyne & Smith, 1994; Lyons, Mickelson, Sullivan, & Coyne, 1998; Wright & Aquilino, 1998).

Social psychological research has done much to advance understanding of individual and group mechanisms in families that augment or complicate personal health. In many respects, social psychologists normalize human behavior and have less bias toward the detection of pathology. The social psychological perspective has been instrumental in recognizing personal assets and healthy behaviors, which, in turn, foster a more optimal view of individual and social resources among people in general. This tradition has been less concerned with the clinical aspects of professional practice, however; therefore, at times it is difficult to ascertain the clinical implications of this research.

THE FAMILY SYSTEMS TRADITION

In contrast to the academic approach of social psychology, family systems theories evolved from a strong clinical heritage shared by practitioners in psychiatry, social work, counseling, and psychology. These clinic-based models often eschewed the rather linear enterprise of formal data collection in favor of intuitive, complex descriptions of family interaction patterns grounded in clinical observations and professional opinion. Recognizing the interdependence of the various members of a family system, these theorists were among the first to observe the role of an "identified patient" in a family and the reciprocal link between illness behaviors and family interactions.

In a highly influential work, Minuchin and colleagues argued that family interaction patterns are directly related to the development and exacerbation of psychosomatic illnesses in children, and these patterns can be rigid, overly protective, and enmeshed (Minuchin et al., 1975). This model was used to understand symptom presentation among children with a variety of chronic conditions (e.g., diabetes, asthma, etc.) and to guide strategic family interventions. This landmark work has received careful scrutiny, and critics now acknowledge the lack of empirical evidence for this perspective (Coyne & Anderson, 1989).

Recent and well-controlled observational research indicates that families with an asthmatic child ("asthmatic" families) disagree less than "nonasthmatic" families, and asthmatic families may be more likely to recruit their children's input into dyadic discussions (Northey, Griffin, & Krainz, 1998). However, these behaviors were unrelated to marital quality, contrary to the motivational premise in the Minuchin model, which then raises doubts about reasons for these interactions. Such communicative patterns could be useful in long-term coping, monitoring, and managing a chronic condition (Northey, et al., 1998).

Although the psychosomatic model seems an inadequate explanation of family behavior, it has stimulated a greater appreciation of family member interactions that might affect adjustment following illness and disability. There is compelling evidence linking the reactions of one spouse to the adjustment of the other following the onset of a health problem. Spouses may engage in a type of coping behavior intended to buffer their partners from stress that might in fact exacerbate their partners' health problem (e.g., protective buffering, overprotectiveness), and both may have to cope with the others' emotional needs (Coyne & Smith, 1991). Protective buffering has been associated with greater distress and marital dissatisfaction among wives of men recuperating from myocardial infarction (Coyne & Smith, 1991; Suls, Green, Rose, Lounsburg, & Gordon, 1997). In addition, patient attempts to buffer the spouse from concerns about the condition are associated with greater patient distress (Suls et al., 1997).

Patients who feel overprotected by their family caregiver are more depressed than those who do not; interestingly, overprotectiveness corresponded with caregivers' negative attitudes toward the patient in one study (Thompson & Sobolew-Shubin, 1993). Overprotectiveness may not be a maladaptive behavior per se, but the feelings and attitudes—such as hostility toward the affected family member—may be directly related to patient distress (Fiske, Coyne, & Smith, 1991). Spousal criticism, in particular, has been predictive of greater patient distress and maladaptive coping behaviors (Manne & Zautra, 1989), with patient health-compromising behaviors (Franks, et al., 1992), and with increased primary care use of cardiac patients (Fiscella, Franks, & Shields, 1997).

Although the psychosomatic model proposed by Minuchin speculated that family interaction patterns could be related to immunological alterations in an ill child, the lack of operational definitions and testable hypotheses have rendered this model unusable for examining psychophysiological reactions in family members. Nevertheless, work by Kiecolt-Glaser and colleagues has demonstrated that poor marital quality may be related to greater depression and depressed immune function among women (Kiecolt-Glaser et al., 1987). Spouses who perceive their partner as dominant have greater blood pressure reactivity during marital interactions, suggesting cardiovascular reactivity is sensitive to spousal interactions (Brown, Smith, & Benjamin, 1998). Elaborate research designs reveal that, over time, the health of a family caregiver may be compromised by disruptions in cardiovascular and immune functioning (see Vitaliano, 1997).

The family systems tradition anticipated the study of reciprocal dynamics and developmental processes among family members with regard to personal health. However, the lack of precise operational definitions and of testable and verifiable hypotheses has circumscribed the utility of these models. Perhaps more than other schools of thought, this heritage has often focused heavily on the study of unhealthy—if not pathological—families. This negative bias also limits the usefulness of these models, particularly in understanding and working with well-adjusted families that face health problems. Finally, although this tradition offers many implications for professional practice, actual clinical practice is considered the purview of highly skilled, specialized, expert providers in intense therapeutic encounters that may not be particularly cost-effective or efficacious for most health care service delivery systems.

THE BEHAVIORAL PERSPECTIVE: LEARNED RESPONSES, COGNITIONS, AND ABILITIES

As professional psychology adapted to the demands and challenges of the medical setting, many practitioners applied learning theories to the study and treatment of client problems. Many of these approaches used operant models of behavior that prevailed in academic psychology at the time interest in health psychology was developing. Cognitive–behavioral models that incorporated social learning principles (Bandura, 1978) have proved particularly useful in understanding family adjustment.

In his conceptualization of chronic illness behavior, Fordyce (1976) posited that well-intentioned efforts by a spouse to allay the pain and suffering expressed by a partner would inadvertently reinforce "disabled" behavior and reward the patient for emitting these behaviors. Other tangible reinforcers for this behavior could include a reprieve from household tasks and familial obligations and avoidance of mundane, unpleasant chores. Resumption of health behaviors would indicate ability to engage in these tasks and risk a decline in attention and favors from the caring spouse.

This line of reasoning generated inquiry into the possible negative effects of spouse reactions to patient displays of chronic pain and distress.

Initial observational studies found that spouses were generally responsive to patient expressions of pain, and these reactions were associated with greater marital satisfaction (Block, 1981). Spouses of chronic pain patients were found to be more solicitous than spouses of persons without pain (Romano et al., 1992). Field research revealed that spouses' recorded diary accounts of supportive responses were negatively associated with patient activity levels, and conversely, their punishing reactions were associated with greater patient activity (Flor, Kerns, & Turk, 1987).

Other studies suggest that families may experience a lack of positive reinforcement (or opportunities for such) following the onset of a chronic health problem. Quittner and colleagues have found that maternal caregivers of children with chronic disease have fewer leisure activities, because they are preoccupied with caregiving tasks (Quittner, Opipari, Regoli, Jacobsen, & Eigen, 1992). Time spent in recreation might mediate the relationship between role strain of parents and their distress (Quittner et al., 1998). Couples who have a member with a severe physical disability spend less time in leisure pursuits than other couples (Urey & Henggeler, 1987). This dearth of meaningful, rewarding leisure time may deny family members the opportunity to experience positive reinforcement and positive moods associated with these activities.

There are other discernible behavioral patterns associated with more optimal outcomes. Parents of children known to be compliant with treatment regimens for phenylketonuria were found to have more effective written and verbal problem-solving skills than parents of children with poor compliance (Fehrenbach & Peterson, 1989). Parents can also model effective coping skills for their ill children, who, in turn, may use similar strategies with beneficial results (Kliewer & Lewis, 1995).

A strict emphasis on operant principles does not accommodate the role of cognitions learned in ongoing interactions with the environment, and many researchers have relied on cognitive–behavioral models to understand the different beliefs, interpretations, and skills that affect family reactions to health problems. Although there are many different models that take into account beliefs and cognitions, a promising line of research has been guided by a cognitive–behavioral model of social problem-solving abilities (D'Zurilla & Nezu, 1999). This is an appealing model because it features a logical framework with testable hypotheses, a supportive literature base, a psychometrically sound measure, and clear directions for interventions (D'Zurilla & Nezu, 1999). Maternal caregivers who have a greater sense of confidence in their problem-solving ability report higher levels of adjustment than those who lack this confidence (Noojin & Wallander, 1997). Family caregivers who lack skills in emotional regulation and who harbor pessimism about their ability to solve problems and handle stress report increasing levels of distress and ill health over the first year of caregiving (Elliott, Shewchuk, & Richards, 2001).

Elliott, Shewchuk, and Richards (1999) found caregiver problem-solving abilities were associated with patient psychological adjustment and physical health. Caregiver tendencies to carelessly and impulsively solve problems were significantly predictive of patient's lower acceptance of disability at discharge from a rehabilitation hospital. When a group of these patients were evaluated a year later for the occurrence of a decubitus ulcer (i.e., a pressure sore), a predictive model including caregiver impulsive and careless styles correctly classified 87.88% of those with and without ulcers. Although the exact mechanisms for this relationship remain unclear, it seems that care recipients were sensitive to their caregivers' penchant for problem solving and sensed that the caregiver may not, at times, "care less" about taking the prerequisite time and energy to assist in self-care regimens necessary for preventing secondary complications.

Several cognitive–behavioral theorists have tried to adopt ideas from the family systems models (e.g., Turk, Kerns, & Rosenberg, 1992). This synthesis has yet to be realized to any noticeable degree in research and practice. The behavioral agenda has generated a rich empirical study of family behavior and has often provided clear and logical directions for clinical interventions that can be used by a variety of health professionals, including those with more generalized (and less specialized) skills.

Contributions From Child and Developmental Psychology

For many years, child and developmental psychologists studied family reactions to ill health and disability with the relatively straightforward notion that the mere presence of a chronic condition or disability was sufficient stress to cause disruptions in family functioning (Harper, 1991). In support of this premise, descriptive research found that siblings of a child with a disability have a greater risk for behavioral and emotional problems (Breslau & Prabucki, 1987). Other descriptive work suggests that many couples experience considerable strain following the onset of severe disability in a spouse. For example, the divorce rate among persons with spinal cord injuries exceeds the national average (DeVivo, Hawkins, Richards, & Go, 1995); the likelihood of remarriage remains low throughout the lifespan for both men and women who acquire spinal cord injuries (DeVivo & Richards, 1996). At first glance, these data seem to indicate that a severe health problem adversely disrupts family life.

Over the ensuing years, psychologists in this arena developed a greater appreciation of the many factors that can mediate reactions to the health problems of a family. Child and pediatric psychologists have contributed greatly to the appreciation of the family context. Some of the popular research models in this literature offer a large conceptual framework that can encompass many variables from different theoretical perspectives, and these models do not necessarily proffer potentially falsifiable hypotheses based on their own internal logic. Nevertheless, these integrative models have played a pivotal role in advancing a biopsychosocial agenda in the study of families and health (Harper, 1991).

These frameworks are often described as disability–stress–coping models, and they were designed to explain why some children fare better in chronic illness than others. Wallander and colleagues (Wallander & Varni, 1989; Wallander, Varni, Babani, Banis, & Wilcox, 1989) proposed that a child's adjustment is determined by characteristics of the condition and by the risk and resistance factors unique to the family and its members. These factors can include individual difference and environmental variables such as family member adjustment, social support, coping styles, appraisal processes, and family cohesion and competence. Thompson and colleagues offer a similar model that emphasizes the transactional nature of stress and coping and the role of maternal adjustment in caring for a child (Thompson, Gil, Burbach, Keith, & Kinney, 1993).

Child adjustment is associated with maternal adjustment (Wallander, Varni, Babani, Banis, & Wilcox, 1988), but maternal adjustment is influenced more by stress, family support, and personal resources than the severity of the child's condition or the functional abilities of the child (Wallander, Pitt, & Mellins, 1990; Wallander & Varni, 1989; Wallander, Varni, Babani, & DeHaan, 1989; Wallander et al., 1989). Behavioral problems and health complaints of adolescents with chronic disease are more likely in families who are lower in family competence (Kell, Kliewer, Erickson, & Ohene-Frempong, 1998). Parental support and coping behavior are positively associated with a child's compliance with self-care regimens (Chaney & Peterson, 1989; Hanson, Henggeler, & Burghen, 1987).

Several longitudinal studies indicate that family coping behaviors are vital to adjustment over time. Spouses' use of avoidance coping was predictive of poorer parental adjustment one year later among parents of children with juvenile rheumatoid disease (Timko, Stovel, & Moos, 1992). In a parallel study, parental risk and resistance factors—including fathers' drinking problems, parental strain, and social activities—were predictive of child adjustment four years later (Timko, Baumgartner, Moos, & Miller, 1993). Families that have effective problem-solving abilities in their interpersonal interactions exhibit less distress, and these benefits can be observed three years later (Rivara et al., 1996). Family coping behavior soon after the onset of brain injury may be a major determinant of patient behavioral outcomes in the first year of injury (Kinsella, Ong, Murtagh, Prior, & Sawyer, 1999).

The work in pediatric psychology has advanced to the extent that the role of family members is routinely acknowledged as a major focus of psychological intervention (Kazak, Segal-Andrews, & Johnson, 1995). Moreover, many pediatric psychologists are well aware of the impact different social, educational, and medical agencies have on the well-being of parents and children coping with a health problem, and they advocate for the need to intervene with these systems on behalf of the family (Kazak et al., 1995).

Shared Problems

These different strands of inquiry clearly indicate that personal health is intricately entwined with the reactions and behaviors of other family members. These perspectives vary with respect to their explanations for the motivation and effects of family behaviors and in their dictates for interventions with families. But these models are also similar in that they share common problems that have not been resolved in current research. In particular, research to date has yet to fully address issues of minority status and ethnic backgrounds, gender differences in family roles, and use of measurement devices and methodological designs sensitive to the dynamic interplay and evolution of family life (Drotar, 1997; Kazak, 1997).

Issues of Ethnicity and Culture

Research in family health psychology is beginning to address issues facing individuals of minority status and other ethnic backgrounds. The very constitution of family in minority ethnic groups can differ from the majority in American society. For many European American families, the close family consists of mother, father, and children; in many minority families, the close family can also include grandparents, aunts, and uncles (Alpert, 1990; Basic Behavioral Science Task Force, 1996). Black families often include members not related by blood or marriage but by shared values, norms, and beliefs (Belgrave, Davis, & Vajada, 1994). Studies indicate that caregivers in Black families can be close or distant relatives or fictive kin and that the quality of care does not vary with the closeness of blood relationship (Lawton, Rajagopal, Brody, & Kleban, 1992; White-Means & Thorton, 1990). The extended family structure and the collectivist spirit characteristic of many minority families suggests that these families might be able to cope better with a disabling condition of a family member than can White American families.

Research comparing Black and White American families, in fact, indicates that Black families may cope better with the challenge imposed by a disability than White American families. Pickett, Vraniak, Cook, and

Bertram (1993) found that Black parents of children with disabilities had higher feelings of self-worth and lower levels of depression than White American parents with disabled children. Caregiving for Alzheimer's dementia patients has been associated with less depression and higher life satisfaction in Black caregivers than in White American caregivers (Haley et al., 1995). The diminished negative impact of caregiving in Black families appears to be related to a view of caregiving as an expected family function (Haley et al., 1996) and an ongoing regard for ill family members independent of their cognitive and behavioral abilities (Dilworth-Anderson & Marshall, 1996). Caution is warranted in extrapolating from this research, however, as other longitudinal data suggest that Black caregivers experience similar complications with ill health as White caregivers, despite observed differences between the two groups on self-report measures of depression and life satisfaction (Roth, Haley, Owen, Clay, & Goode, 2001).

The limited amount of research on the relationship between minority status and martial status after a disabling injury is mixed. DeVivo and Fine (1985) reported that Black minority status was significantly associated with a higher divorce rate among persons with spinal cord injuries. In a more recent study, Black and Latino individuals with spinal cord injuries display higher, but not significantly different, divorce rates than White Americans (DeVivo et al., 1995).

Issues of Gender

Women usually assume caregiver roles for ill family members, and research has subsequently focused on mothers, wives, and daughters in these roles (Moen, Robison, & Dempster-McClain, 1995). Women in caregiving roles report more distress than husbands and sons in similar roles, but these differences could be attributed to the willingness of women to report distress (Gallagher-Thompson, Coon, Rivera, Powers, & Zeiss, 1998) and the different appraisal processes between men and women (Burman & Margolin, 1992).

Women and men may differ in their willingness to resume roles after incurring a severe health problem. Husbands were found to increase household activity after a wife experienced a myocardial infarction; nevertheless, these wives still assumed as many household duties as the husbands (Rose, Suls, Green, Lounsburg, & Gordon, 1996). It is tenuous to believe, however, that these men were shirking responsibility; it is possible that the homemaker role was important to the wives in this study and that they were unwilling to relinquish these activities.

The emotional needs of men and women may also vary considerably after the onset of chronic illness. Although fathers and mothers of children with spinal bifida reported less parental satisfaction than those in a comparison group, the mothers of these children—and not the fathers—reported higher levels of social isolation and lower levels of perceived parental competence (Holmbeck et al., 1997). These mothers were also more likely to rely on avoidant coping behaviors, implying a possible association between palliative coping behaviors, lower competence, and distress. In other research, women with lupus who engaged in more physically intimate behavior with their partners had greater relationship satisfaction but those who avoided intimacy or who were more likely to initiate contact had more distress (Druley, Stephens, & Coyne, 1997). Intimacy may be a salient correlate of psychosocial adjustment for women regardless of their role in the family system.

With a few notable exceptions (e.g., Timko et al., 1993), fathers have been neglected in this literature (Kazak, 1997). Yet, fathers may play a crucial role in the adjustment of a family member with a health problem. In one of the more sophisticated studies to date, Chaney, Mullins, Frank, and Peterson (1997) found that child adjustment over a year was directly related to increases in fathers' distress and not the mothers' distress. A decline in fathers' adjustment was inversely related to mothers' adjustment. This study illustrates the transactional and systemic nature of adjustment and coping among men and women in family roles.

Issues of Measurement and Meaning

Most measures of family functioning have varied across studies, depending on the theoretical perspectives and research questions under investigation. There are a few omnibus measures of family functioning that feature respectable psychometric qualities, and these appear often in the literature (e.g., the Family Environment Scale: Moos & Moos, 1986; the Family Crises Oriented Personal Evaluation Scales: Olson et al., 1985; the Family Adaptability and Cohesion Scales: Olson et al., 1985). These are excellent measures of coping, distress, adaptability, and cohesion, and they appear to be sensitive to changes in family dynamics.

However, psychometric measures—whether based in theoretical frameworks or empirical bootstrapping—ultimately serve the clinical and theoretical interests of the investigators and are often insensitive to the ways family adjust and find meaning in their circumstances. In response to illness and disability, many family members experience a greater sense of closeness, a greater emphasis on family and personal relationships, and positive changes in shared family values, personal growth, and meaning (Elliott & Mullins, 2004). Researchers invested in pathological models of behavior usually ignore aspects of positive adjustment. This bias then misrepresents the personal experience of many family members and perpetuates a pessimistic—if not overly simplistic—portrayal of family life following illness and disability. A more informed approach would help us distinguish families who are at risk for difficulties from those who may have the resources for positive growth.

Moreover, we do not know, and we do not routinely solicit, family member opinions and experiences—in their own words—for use in research and practice (Shewchuk & Elliott, 2000). Before we can thoroughly understand the mechanisms within the "black box" that connect psychological variables with outcomes, and then develop strategic and meaningful interventions that affect these mechanisms, we must recognize family members as experts on the "realities of their daily lives" (Mechanic, 1998, p. 284). Qualitative research designs may prove vital in this enterprise (Fiese & Bickham, 1998).

Several qualitative techniques can be used to procure information for use in tailoring intervention programs. For example, essays by participants of a caregiver support group were analyzed to detect themes faced by caregivers of persons with brain injuries (Chwalisz & Stark-Wroblewski, 1996). Others have used structured focus groups with participants representative of the population under consideration to identify problems and their possible solutions (Elliott & Shewchuk, 2002). This information was then used to develop a Q-sort technique to identify problems new caregivers were experiencing and to provide these caregivers with problem-solving training specific to the problems they identified (Elliott & Shewchuk, 2000). Others have used more intensive, structured interview systems to understand the unique problems of patients and their family members (Long, Glueckauf, & Rasmussen, 1998).

It is intriguing that these studies (Chwalisz & Stark-Wroblewski, 1996; Elliott & Shewchuk, 2002; Long et al., 1998) found that family members were most concerned with issues about interpersonal relationships, quality of life, emotional commitments, accessible health care, and educational–training opportunities for the care provider and care recipient. Interventions that address the specific needs of families and their members, as they perceive them, may be more likely to succeed (Burman & Margolin, 1992).

Bridges to the Future: Integrative Research

The different approaches to the study of family adaptation to health and disability often offer contradictory avenues for intervention. The lack of a cohesive, overarching model is, in part, to blame for this problem, but it is unlikely that this need will be remedied in the near future. Traditional academic paradigms expect researchers to focus on the development and advancement of isolated, individual research programs, which ultimately do little to bridge the gaps that currently exist in research and practice. Moreover, the press to develop new theoretical explanations may not necessarily rectify the problems in this area.

Thoughtful essays on the needs and problems facing families and their health have emphasized the need to view families as competent, yet dynamic, entities that are influenced by an array of societal systems (Aneshensel, Pearlin, Mullan, Zarit, & Whitlatch, 1995; Kazak, 1997). Furthermore, Drotar (1997) has urged researchers to use complex, multilevel modeling techniques that can accommodate multiple characteristics and measures over time to detect intraindividual trajectories of change in field and intervention research.

Several studies have demonstrated how linear modeling techniques can be incorporated to analyze growth-curve trajectories in adjustment to chronic illness and disability. Clay, Wood, Frank, Hagglund, and Johnson (1995), in a study of children with juvenile rheumatoid arthritis (JRA), found that mothers' state anger and fathers' distress were associated with growth trajectories in children's behavioral problems. Parental ratings of cohesion were also predictive of these growth-factor scores. In a more detailed and elegant application of these techniques, Frank et al. (1998) demonstrated how personal and familial characteristics are more predictive of adjustment over time than disease characteristics in a study of children with JRA or insulin-dependent diabetes, and a comparison group. Hierarchical linear modeling was also used by Shewchuk et al. (1998) to illustrate the dynamic changes that can occur over the first year of the caregiver career.

These rather sophisticated tools may be particularly helpful in identifying individuals and families who may be at risk for experiencing problems and developing secondary complications following the onset of a chronic health problem. The Elliott et al. (2001) study, for example, was instrumental in identifying cognitive–behavioral characteristics of caregivers who gradually developed problems with depression, anxiety, and ill health over the initial year of caregiving. Such predictive ability could permit psychologists to identify and monitor families at risk, and provide appropriate support and assistance as needed.

CONCLUSION

To determine appropriate interventions for families, it may be necessary to conduct a careful analysis of the contributions professional psychology can offer families in traditional and emerging roles. Critiques of the intervention research in family health psychology indicate that psychoeducational strategies are consistently more effective than other modalities, presumably because these approaches address the specific needs of family members and often actively involve family members (Burman & Margolin, 1992; Campbell & Patterson, 1995). Others maintain that family therapies are still better for working with families that have a member who presents symptoms sensitive to family distress and interaction patterns (e.g., asthma, diabetes; Campbell & Patterson, 1995). Interventions that include spouses as part of patient treatment, without any clear goals specific for the spouse, do not seem to be particularly effective (e.g., J. Moore & Chaney, 1985). However, programs that educate the spouse about a health condition and skills in self-care and coping and that instill a greater understanding of the patient experience are more promising (e.g., L. Moore, 1989).

It is vital to consider the multiple systems that directly impinge not only on the delivery of needed services to families but also on the availability and access to health care in contemporary society. The number of chronic health problems has escalated in U.S. society, and health care programs have limited services to individuals with these conditions, thus compelling many family members to assume caregiver roles (Hoffman, Rice, & Sung, 1996). The role of the family caregiver has intensified with dramatic cutbacks in health care services, and the emergence of managed care as the predominant health care paradigm has had many adverse effects on families with a member who has a chronic disease or disability (Council on Scientific Affairs, 1993). With these changes in health care allocation—and with increases in the incidence of chronic disease and disability—more individuals will be compelled to assume the role of primary caregiver for a family member who incurs chronic disease or disability. Chronic health conditions and the management of symptoms associated with them account for approximately 68% of all health care expenditures in American health care systems, and this may represent the greatest single challenge facing modern health care (Frank, 1997). It is highly probable that families will incur even more responsibility for care as the population ages and financial resources necessary for health care are further strained.

Professional psychologists in the contemporary health care environment are concerned with matters above and beyond the provision of services to the individual client (Elliott & Shewchuk, in Johnstone et al., 1995). Psychology is a stakeholder at the highest levels of any health care service delivery system, and it should have a voice in resource allocation and in the reasonable dispersion of funds that support research and service endeavors germane to national and community health care priorities. It is incumbent on professional psychology to consider novel and strategic ways to promote, facilitate, and deliver ecologically valid interventions for families and to advocate on behalf of families in health and public policy.

Unfortunately, family interventions to date have not demonstrated the sort of clinical efficacy and cost-effectiveness that would engender interest among most policy makers (Thoits, 1995). Effective and policy-relevant interventions will address the problems experienced by families and help them become more active and expert in their own self-management and to operate competently as formal extensions of health care systems (Wagner, Austin, & Von Korff, 1996). Patients and families who live daily with chronic disease and disability probably have more influence on their health than any single professional health care provider; therefore, these individuals should receive the requisite training and ongoing support commensurate with their responsibilities and activities for self-care (Lengnick-Hall, 1995). This will necessitate a collaborative rather than an authoritarian or paternalistic partnership with families that includes their opinions about needs and solutions in research projects and service delivery programs (Israel, Schulz, Parker, & Becker, 1998; Lengnick-Hall, 1995). It may also require more community-based, in-home intervention programs than typically offered by most professional psychologists (Campbell & Patterson, 1995). Counseling delivered via long-distance technologies (e.g., interactive Internet video, speaker phone) appear to be equally effective as face-to-face counseling in reducing problems experienced by families and preadolescents with epilepsy; and family members may prefer these home-based modalities over the traditional office visit (Glueckauf et al., 2002).

Current health care delivery systems have limited use for high-cost service providers who account for a significant amount of health care expenditures; their utility in long-term and home-based prevention and health maintenance programs may have a lower payoff for families than behaviorally based intervention programs (Zarit & Pearlin, 1993, p. 314). Unfortunately, policy makers often view behavioral interventions—as typically described and prescribed by psychologists—"as prohibitively labor intensive, because they equate it with one-to-one counseling by highly trained and expensive staff" (Leviton, 1996, p. 47). It is possible that delivery of interventions best suited for families will be provided by low-cost personnel who are able to conduct routine evaluations and provide guidance for self-management (Wagner et al., 1996).

Psychologists can have immense impact in developing, evaluating, and delivering interventions to families that address the practical, everyday needs of families who have a member with a chronic health problem. In some cases, theory-based interventions can be effectively delivered in community settings by low-cost personnel (e.g., problem-solving training for family caregivers via telephone sessions with a nurse; Grant, Elliott, Weaver, Bartolucci, & Giger, 2002). Program evaluation research and predictive models that take into account unique patient–family subgroups will help identify individuals who require more intensive therapeutic interventions from skilled staff and who are most likely to benefit from these high-cost services (Shewchuk & Elliott, 2000).

REFERENCES

Akamatsu, T. J., Stephens, M. A. P., Hobfoll, S. E., & Crowther, J. H. (1992). *Family health psychology*. Washington, DC: Taylor & Francis.

Alpert, S. M., (1990). Caregiving as a cultural system: Conceptions of filial obligation and parental dependency in urban America. *American Anthropologist, 92,* 319–331.

Aneshensel, C. S., Pearlin, L. I., Mullan, J. T., Zarit, S. H., & Whitlatch, C. J. (1995). *Profiles in caregiving: The unexpected career*. San Diego, CA: Academic Press.

Bandura, A. (1978). The self system in reciprocal determinism. *American Psychologist, 33,* 344–358.

Basic Behavioral Science Task Force. (1996). Basic behavioral science research for mental health: Sociocultural and environmental processes. *American Psychology, 51,* 772–731.

Belgrave, F. Z., Davis, A., & Vajada, J. (1994). An examination of social support source, type, and satisfaction among African American and Caucasians with disabilities. *Journal of Social Behavior and Personality, 9*(5), 307–320.

Block, A. R. (1981). An investigation of the response of the spouse to chronic pain behavior. *Psychosomatic Medicine, 43,* 415–422.

Bolger, N., Foster, M., Vinokur, A. D., & Ng, R. (1996). Close relationships and adjustment to a life crises: The case of breast cancer. *Journal of Personality and Social Psychology, 70,* 295–309.

Breslau, N., & Prabucki, K. (1987). Siblings of disabled children: Effects of chronic stress in the family. *Archives of General Psychiatry, 44,* 1040–1046.

Brown, P. C., Smith, T. W., & Benjamin, L. S. (1998). Perceptions of spouse dominance predict blood pressure reactivity during marital interactions. *Annals of Behavioral Medicine, 20,* 286–293.

Burman, B., & Margolin, G. (1992). Analysis of the association between marital relationships and health problems: An interactional perspective. *Psychological Bulletin, 112,* 39–63.

Campbell, T. L., & Patterson, J. M. (1995). The effectiveness of family interventions in the treatment of physical illness. *Journal of Marital and Family Therapy, 21,* 545–583.

Chaney, J., Mullins, L. L., Frank, R. G., & Peterson, L. (1997). Transactional patterns of child, mother, and father adjustment in insulin-dependent diabetes mellitus: A prospective study. *Journal of Pediatric Psychology, 22,* 229–244.

Chaney, J., & Peterson, L. (1989). Family variables and disease management in juvenile rheumatoid arthritis. *Journal of Pediatric Psychology, 14,* 389–403.

Christiansen, A. J., Wiebe, J., Smith, T., & Turner, C. (1994). Predictors of survival among hemodialysis patients: Effects of perceived family support. *Health Psychology, 13,* 521–525.

Chwalisz, K. (1996). The perceived stress model of caregiver burden: Evidence from the spouses of persons with brain injuries. *Rehabilitation Psychology*, *41*, 91–114.

Chwalisz, K., & Stark-Wroblewski, K. (1996). The subjective experiences of spouse caregivers of persons with brain injuries: A qualitative analysis. *Applied Neuropsychology*, *3*, 28–40.

Clay, D., Wood, P. K., Frank, R. G., Hagglund, K., & Johnson, J. (1995). Examining systematic differences in adaptation to chronic illness: A growth modeling approach. *Rehabilitation Psychology*, *40*, 61–70.

Council on Scientific Affairs, American Medical Association. (1993). Physicians and family caregivers; A model for partnership. *Journal of the American Medical Association*, *269*, 1282–1284.

Coyne, J. C., & DeLongis. A. (1986). Going beyond social support: The role of social relationships in adaptation. *Journal of Consulting and Clinical Psychology*, *54*, 454–460.

Coyne, J. C., & Anderson, B. J. (1989). The "psychosomatic family" reconsidered II: Recalling a defective model and looking ahead. *Journal of Marital and Family Therapy*, *15*, 139–148.

Coyne, J. C., & Smith, D. A. (1994). Couples coping with a myocardial infarction: Contextual perspective on patient self-efficacy. *Journal of Family Psychology*, *8*, 43–54.

Coyne, J. C., & Smith, D. A. (1991). Couples coping with a myocardial infarction: A contextual perspective on wives' distress. *Journal of Personality and Social Psychology*, *61*, 404–412.

Dakof, G. A., & Taylor, S. E. (1990). Victim's perceptions of social support: What is helpful for whom? *Journal of Personality and Social Psychology*, *58*, 80–89.

DeVivo, M. J., & Fine, R. (1985). Spinal cord injury: Its short-term impact on marital status. *Archives of Physical Medicine and Rehabilitation*, *66*, 501–504.

DeVivo, M. J., Hawkins, L. N., Richards, J. S., & Go, B. K. (1995). Outcomes of post-spinal cord injury marriages. *Archives of Physical Medicine and Rehabilitation*, *76*, 128–136.

DeVivo, M. J., & Richards, J. S. (1996). Marriage rates of persons with spinal cord injury. *Rehabilitation Psychology*, *41*, 321–339.

Dilworth-Anderson, P., & Marshall, S. (1996). Social support in its cultural context. In G. R. Pierce, B. R. Sarason, & I. G. Sarason (Eds.), *Handbook of social support and the family* (pp. 67–79). New York: Plenum Press.

Drotar, D. (1997). Relating parent and family functioning to the psychological adjustment of children with chronic health conditions: What have we learned? What do we need to know? *Journal of Pediatric Psychology*, *22*, 149–165.

Druley, J. A., Stephens, M. A. P., & Coyne, J. (1997). Emotional and physical intimacy in coping with lupus: Women's dilemmas of disclosure and approach. *Health Psychology*, *16*, 506–514.

D'Zurilla, T. J., & Nezu, A. (1999). *Problem-solving therapy: A social competence approach to clinical intervention.* New York: Springer.

Elliott, T., & Kurylo, M. (2000). Hope over disability: Lessons from one young woman's triumph. In C. R. Snyder (Ed.), *The handbook of hope: Theory, measures, and applications* (pp. 373–386). New York: Academic Press.

Elliott, T., & Mullins, L. L. (2004). Counseling families and children with disabilities. In D. Atkinson & G. Hackett (Eds.), *Counseling diverse populations* (3rd ed., pp. 151–170). New York: McGraw-Hill.

Elliott, T., & Shewchuk, R. (2000). Problem solving therapy for family caregivers of persons with severe physical disabilities. In C. Radnitz (Ed.), *Cognitive–behavioral interventions for persons with disabilities* (pp. 309–327). New York: Jason Aronson.

Elliott, T., & Shewchuk, R. (2002). Using the nominal group technique to identify the problems experienced by persons who live with severe physical disability. *Journal of Clinical Psychology in Medical Settings, 9,* 65–76.

Elliott, T., Shewchuk, R., & Richards, J. S. (1999). Caregiver social problem-solving abilities and family member adjustment to recent-onset physical disability. *Rehabilitation Psychology, 44,* 104–123.

Elliott, T., Shewchuk, R., & Richards, J. S. (2001). Family caregiver social problem solving abilities and adjustment during the initial year of the caregiver role. *Journal of Counseling Psychology, 48,* 223–232.

Fehrenbach, A. M., & Peterson, L. (1989). Parental problem-solving skills, stress, and dietary compliance in phenylketonuria. *Journal of Consulting and Clinical Psychology, 57,* 237–241.

Fiese, B. H., & Bickham, N. L. (1998). Qualitative inquiry: An overview for pediatric psychology. *Journal of Pediatric Psychology, 23,* 79–86.

Fiscella, K., Franks, P., & Shields, C. G. (1997). Perceived family criticism and primary care utilization: Psychosocial and biomedical pathways. *Family Process, 36,* 25–41.

Fiske, V., Coyne, J., & Smith, D. A. (1991). Couples coping with myocardial infarction: An empirical reconsideration of the role of overprotectiveness. *Journal of Family Psychology, 5,* 4–20.

Flor, H., Kerns, R. D., & Turk, D. (1987). The role of spouse reinforcement, perceived pain, and activity levels of chronic pain patients. *Journal of Psychosomatic Research, 31,* 251–259.

Fordyce, W. E. (1976). *Behavioral methods in chronic pain and illness.* St. Louis, MO: Mosby.

Frank, R. G. (1997). Lessons from the great battle: Health care reform 1992–1994. *Archives of Physical Medicine and Rehabilitation, 78,* 120–124.

Frank, R. G., Thayer, J., Hagglund, K., Veith, A., Schopp, L., Beck, N., et al. (1998). Trajectories of adaptation in pediatric chronic illness: The importance of the individual. *Journal of Consulting and Clinical Psychology, 66,* 521–532.

Franks, P., Campbell, T. L., & Shields, C. G. (1992). Social relationships and health: The relative roles of family functioning and social support. *Social Science and Medicine, 34,* 779–788.

Gallagher-Thompson, D., Coon, D. W., Rivera, P., Powers, D., & Zeiss, A. (1998). Family caregiving: Stress, coping and intervention. In M. Hersen & V. B. Van Hasselt (Eds.), *Handbook of clinical geropsychology* (pp. 469–493). New York: Plenum Press.

Glueckauf, R. L., Fritz, S., Ecklund-Johnson, E., Liss, H., Dages, P., & Carney, P. (2002). Videoconferencing-based family counseling for rural teenagers with epilepsy: Phase 1 findings. *Rehabilitation Psychology, 47,* 49–72.

Grant, J., Elliott, T., Weaver, M. Bartolucci, A., & Giger, J. (2002). A telephone intervention with family caregivers of stroke survivors after hospital discharge. *Stroke, 33,* 2060–2065.

Haley, W. E., Waff, D., Coleton, M., Ford, G., West, C., Collins, R., et al. (1996). Appraisal, coping, and social support as mediators of well-being in Black and White family caregivers of patients with Alzheimer's disease. *Journal of Consulting and Clinical Psychology, 64,* 121–129.

Haley, W. E., West, C. A. C., Wadley, V. G., Ford, G. F., White, F. A., Barrett, J. J., et al. (1995). Psychological, social, and health impact of caregiving: A comparison of Black and White dementia family caregivers and non-caregivers. *Psychology and Aging, 10,* 540–552.

Hanson, C. L., Henggeler, S. W., & Burghen, G. A. (1987). Social competence and parental support as mediators of the link between stress and metabolic control in adolescents with insulin-dependent diabetes mellitus. *Journal of Consulting and Clinical Psychology, 55,* 529–533.

Harper, D. C. (1991). Paradigms for investigating rehabilitation and adaptation to childhood disability and chronic illness. *Journal of Pediatric Psychology, 16,* 533–542.

Hobfoll, S. E., & Lerman, M. (1989). Predicting receipt of social support: A longitudinal study of parents' reactions to their child's illness. *Health Psychology, 8,* 61–77.

Hoffman, C., Rice, D., & Sung, H. (1996). Persons with chronic conditions: Their prevalence and costs. *Journal of the American Medical Association, 276,* 1473–1479.

Holmbeck, G. N., Gorey-Ferguson, L., Hudson, T., Seefeldt, T., Shapera, W., Turner, T., et al. (1997). Maternal, paternal, and marital functioning in families of preadolescents with spina bifida. *Journal of Pediatric Psychology, 22,* 167–181.

Horton, T., & Wallander, J. L. (2001). Hope and social support as resilience factors against psychological distress of mothers who care for children with chronic physical conditions. *Rehabilitation Psychology, 46,* 382–399.

Israel, B. A., Schulz, A. J., Parker, E. A., & Becker, A. B. (1998). Review of community-based research: Assessing partnership approaches to improve public health. *Annual Review of Public Health, 19,* 173–202.

Johnstone, B., Frank, R. G., Belar, C., Berk, S., Bieliaukas, L. A., Bigler, E. D., et al. (1995). Psychology in health care: Future directions. *Professional Psychology: Research and Practice, 26,* 341–365.

Kazak, A. E. (1997). A contextual family/systems approach to pediatric psychology: Introduction to the special issue. *Journal of Pediatric Psychology, 22,* 141–148.

Kazak, A. E., Segal-Andrews, A. M., & Johnson, K. (1995). Pediatric psychology research and practice: A family/systems approach. In M. C. Roberts (Ed.), *Handbook of pediatric psychology* (pp. 84–104). New York: Guilford Press.

Kell, R. S., Kliewer, W., Erickson, M. T., & Ohene-Frempong, K. (1998). Psychological adjustment of adolescents with sickle cell disease: Relations with demographic, medical and family competence variables. *Journal of Pediatric Psychology, 23,* 301–312.

Kelley, H. H. (1979). *Personal relationships: Their structure and processes.* Hillsdale, NJ: Erlbaum.

Kiecolt-Glaser, J. K., Fisher, L., Ogrocki, P., Stout, J. C., Speicher, C. E., & Glaser, R. (1987). Marital quality, marital disruption, and immune function. *Psychosomatic Medicine, 49,* 13–34.

Kinsella, G., Ong, B., Murtagh, D., Prior, M., & Sawyer, M. (1999). The role of the family for behavioral outcome in children and adolescents following traumatic brain injury. *Journal of Consulting and Clinical Psychology, 67,* 116–123.

Kliewer, W., & Lewis, H. (1995). Family influences on coping processes in children and adolescents with sickle cell disease. *Journal of Pediatric Psychology, 20,* 511–525.

Lane, C., & Hobfoll, S. E. (1992). How loss affects anger and alienates potential supporters. *Journal of Consulting and Clinical Psychology, 60,* 935–942.

Lawton, M. P., Rajgopal, D., Brody, E., & Kleban, M. H. (1992). The dynamics of caregiving for a demented elder among Black and White families. *Journal of Gerontology, 47,* S156–S164.

Lazarus, R., & Folkman, S. (1984). *Stress, appraisal, and coping.* New York: Springer.

Lengnick-Hall, C. A. (1995). The patient as the pivot point for quality in health care delivery. *Hospital and Health Services Administration, 40,* 25–39.

Leviton, L. C. (1996). Integrating psychology and public health: Challenges and opportunities. *American Psychologist, 51,* 42–51.

Long, M. P., Glueckauf, R. L., & Rasmussen, J. (1998). Developing family counseling interventions for adults with episodic neurological disabilities: Presenting problems, persons involved, and problem severity. *Rehabilitation Psychology, 43,* 101–117.

Lyons, R. E., Mickelson, K. D., Sullivan, M. J., & Coyne, J. (1998). Coping as a communal process. *Journal of Social and Personal Relationships, 15,* 579–605.

Manne, S. L., & Zautra, A. J. (1989). Spouse criticism and support: Their association with coping and psychological adjustment among women with rheumatoid arthritis. *Journal of Personality and Social Psychology, 56,* 608–617.

Mechanic, D. (1998). Public trust and initiatives for new health care partnerships. *Milbank Quarterly, 76,* 281–302.

Minuchin, S., Baker, L., Rosman, B., Liebman, R., Milman, L., & Todd, T. (1975). A conceptual model of psychosomatic illness in children. *Archives of General Psychiatry, 32*, 1031–1038.

Moen, P., Robison, J., & Dempster-McClain, D. (1995). Caregiving and women's well-being: A life course approach. *Journal of Health and Social Behavior, 36*, 259–273.

Moore, J. E., & Chaney, E. F. (1985). Outpatient group treatment of chronic pain: Effects of spouse involvement. *Journal of Consulting and Clinical Psychology, 53*, 326–339.

Moore, L. I. (1989). *Behavioral changes in male spinal cord injured following two types of psychosocial rehabilitation experience.* Unpublished doctoral dissertation, St. Louis University, MO.

Moos, R. H., & Moos, B. S. (1986). *Family environment scale.* Palo Alto, CA: Consulting Psychologists Press.

Noojin, A. B., & Wallander, J. L. (1997). Perceived problem-solving ability, stress, and coping in mothers of children with physical disabilities: Potential cognitive influences on adjustment. *International Journal of Behavioral Medicine, 4*, 415–432.

Northey, S., Griffin, W. A., & Krainz, S. (1998). A partial test of the psychosomatic family model: Marital interaction patterns in asthma and non-asthma families. *Journal of Family Psychology, 12*, 220–235.

Olson, D. H., McCubbin, H. I., Barnes, H., Larsen, A., Muxen, M., & Wilson, M. (1985). *Family inventories—Revised.* St. Paul: University of Minnesota Press.

Pakenham, K. I. (1998). Couple coping and adjustment to multiple sclerosis in care receiver–carrier dyads. *Family Relations, 47*, 269–277.

Pickett, S. A., Vraniak, D. A., Cook, J. A., & Bertram, J. (1993). Strength in adversity: Blacks bear burden better than Whites. *Professional Psychology: Research and Practice, 24*, 460–467.

Pierce, G. R., Sarason, B. R., & Sarason, I. G. (1996). *Handbook of social support and the family.* New York: Plenum Press.

Quittner, A. L., Espelage, D., Opipari, L., Carter, B., Eid, N., & Eigen, H. (1998). Role strain in couples with and without a child with a chronic illness: Associations with marital satisfaction, intimacy, and daily mood. *Health Psychology, 59*, 1266–1278.

Quittner, A. L., Glueckauf, R., & Jackson, D. (1990). Chronic parenting stress: Moderating versus mediating effects of social support. *Journal of Personality and Social Psychology, 59*, 1266–1278.

Quittner, A. L., Opipari, L., Regoli, M., Jacobsen, J., & Eigen, H. (1992). The impact of caregiving and role strain on family life: Comparisons between mothers of children with cystic fibrosis and matched controls. *Rehabilitation Psychology, 37*, 275–290.

Rivara, J., Jaffe, K., Polissar, N., Fay, G., Liao, S., & Martin, K. (1996). Predictors of family functioning and change 3 years after traumatic brain injury in children. *Archives of Physical Medicine and Rehabilitation, 77*, 754–764.

Romano, J. M., Turner, J. A., Friedman, L. S., Bukcroft, R. A., Jensen, M. P., Hops, H., et al. (1992). Sequential analysis of chronic pain behaviors and spouse responses. *Journal of Consulting and Clinical Psychology, 60,* 777–782.

Rose, G. L., Suls, J., Green, P. J., Lounsburg, P., & Gordon, E. (1996). Comparison of adjustment, activity, and tangible social support in men and women patients and their spouses during the six months of post-myocardial infarction. *Annals of Behavioral Medicine, 18,* 264–272.

Roth, D. L., Haley, W., Owen, J., Clay, O., & Goode, K. (2001). Latent growth models of the longitudinal effects of dementia caregiving: A comparison of African American and White family caregivers. *Psychology and Aging, 16,* 427–436.

Schulz, R., Tompkins, C., Wood, D., & Decker, S. (1987). The social psychology of caregiving: Physical and psychological costs of providing support to the disabled. *Journal of Applied Social Psychology, 17,* 401–428.

Shewchuk, R., & Elliott, T. (2000). Family caregiving in chronic disease and disability: Implications for rehabilitation psychology. In R. G. Frank & T. Elliott (Eds.), *Handbook of rehabilitation psychology* (pp. 553–563). Washington, DC: American Psychological Association.

Shewchuk, R., Richards, J. S., & Elliott, T. (1998). Dynamic processes in health outcomes among caregivers of patients with spinal cord injuries. *Health Psychology, 17,* 125–129.

Suls, J. (1982). Social support, interpersonal relations, and health: Benefits and liabilities. In G. S. Sanders & J. Suls (Eds.), *Social psychology of health and illness* (pp. 255–277). Hillsdale, NJ: Erlbaum.

Suls, J., Green, P., Rose, G., Lounsburg, P., & Gordon, E. (1997). Hiding worries from one's spouse: Associations between coping via protective buffering and distress in male post–myocardial infarction patients and their wives. *Journal of Behavioral Medicine, 20,* 333–349.

Thoits, P. A. (1995). Stress, coping, and social support processes: Where are we? What next? *Journal of Health and Social Behavior* (Suppl.), 53–79.

Thompson, R. J., Gil, K., Burbach, D., Keith, B., & Kinney, T. (1993). Role of child and maternal processes in the psychological adjustment of children with sickle cell disease. *Journal of Consulting and Clinical Psychology, 61,* 468–474.

Thompson, S. C. (1991). The search for meaning following a stroke. *Basic and Applied Social Psychology, 12,* 81–96.

Thompson, S. C., Bundek, N., & Sobolew-Shubin, A. (1990). The caregivers of stroke patients: An investigation of factors associated with depression. *Journal of Applied Social Psychology, 20,* 115–129.

Thompson, S. C., & Sobolew-Shubin, A. (1993). Overprotective relationships: A nonsupportive side of social networks. *Basic and Applied Social Psychology, 14,* 363–383.

Timko, C., Baumgartner, M., Moos, R. H., & Miller, J. J. (1993). Parental risk and resistance factors among children with juvenile rheumatoid disease: A four-year predictive study. *Journal of Behavioral Medicine, 16,* 571–588.

Timko, C., Stovel, K. W., & Moos, R. H. (1992). Functioning among mothers and fathers of children with juvenile rheumatic disease: A longitudinal study. *Journal of Pediatric Psychology, 17,* 705–724.

Turk, D. C., & Kerns, R. D. (1985). *Health, illness, and families.* New York: John Wiley & Sons.

Turk, D. C., Kerns, R. D., & Rosenberg, R. (1992). Effects of marital interaction on chronic pain and disability: Examining the down side of social support. *Rehabilitation Psychology, 37,* 259–274.

Urey, J. R., & Henggeler, S. W. (1987). Marital adjustment following spinal cord injury. *Archives of Physical Medicine and Rehabilitation, 68,* 69–74.

Vitaliano, P. P. (Ed.). (1997). Physiological and physical concomitants of caregiving: Introduction to the special issue. *Annals of Behavioral Medicine, 19*(2).

Wagner, E. H., Austin, B. T., & Von Korff, M. (1996). Organizing care for patients with chronic illness. *Milbank Quarterly, 74,* 511–544.

Wallander, J. L., Pitt, L. C., & Mellins, C. A. (1990). Child functional independence and maternal psychosocial stress as risk factors threatening adaptation in mothers of physically or sensorially handicapped children. *Journal of Consulting and Clinical Psychology, 58,* 818–824.

Wallander, J. L., & Varni, J. (1989). Social support and adjustment in chronically ill and handicapped children. *American Journal of Community Psychology, 17,* 185–201.

Wallander, J. L., Varni, J., Babani, L., Banis, H., & Wilcox, K. (1988). Children with chronic physical disorders: Maternal reports of their psychological adjustment. *Journal of Pediatric Psychology, 13,* 197–212.

Wallander, J. L., Varni, J., Babani, L., Banis, H., & Wilcox, K. (1989). Family resources as resistance factors for psychological maladjustment in chronically ill and handicapped children. *Journal of Pediatric Psychology, 14,* 157–173.

Wallander, J. L., Varni, J., Babani, L., & DeHaan, C. (1989). The social environment and the adaptation of mothers of physically handicapped children. *Journal of Pediatric Psychology, 14,* 371–387.

Walster, E., Berscheid, E., & Walster, G. W. (1973). New directions in equity research. *Journal of Personality and Social Psychology, 25,* 151–176.

White-Means, S., & Thornton, M. (1990). Ethnic differences in the production of informal home health care. *Gerontologist, 30,* 758–768.

Williamson, G. M., & Schulz, R. (1995). Caring for a family member with cancer: Past communal behavior and affective reactions. *Journal of Applied Social Psychology, 25,* 93–116.

Wright, D. L., & Aquilino, W. S. (1998). Influence of emotional support exchange in marriage on caregiving wives' burden and marital satisfaction. *Family Relations, 47,* 195–204.

Zarit, S. H., & Pearlin, L. I. (1993). Family caregiving: Integrating informal and formal systems for care. In S. H. Zarit, L. I. Pearlin, & K. W. Schaie (Eds.), *Caregiving systems: Informal and formal helpers* (pp. 303–316). Hillsdale, NJ: Erlbaum.

13

PATIENT ADAPTATION TO CHRONIC ILLNESS

KATHARINE E. STEWART, DANA ROSS, AND SHANNON HARTLEY

Continued advances in medical and pharmaceutical technologies have dramatically affected not only the incidence and prevalence of many types of illness but also increased life expectancies, especially among individuals in developed nations. As a result of these advances, some illnesses (e.g., HIV disease) that were previously characterized by rapid progression now have typical courses that span decades. In addition, increasing life expectancies have been associated with increasing prevalence of age-associated chronic conditions, such as osteoarthritis and cardiovascular disease. These changes have resulted in an increasing emphasis on the ways in which medical and behavioral sciences may improve quality of life and adaptation to chronic illness.

However, the process of adaptation to chronic illness is remarkably complex, both affecting and affected by multiple domains of the individual's experience. Research on adaptation to chronic illness is characterized by multiple theoretical models, numerous approaches to assessment of individual adaptation, and the ongoing need for methodologies that can adequately characterize the complex, longitudinal processes involved.

DOMAINS OF ADAPTATION TO CHRONIC ILLNESS

Adaptation can be conceptualized as existing across four interdependent domains: biological, social, emotional, and behavioral. Exhibit 13.1 lists the major concerns associated with each domain. The biological domain includes the biological consequences of the illness or disability, the age of the person affected, and the presence of secondary mental disorder such as depression or anxiety. This domain also includes physical functionality, which may be easily measured in terms of specific tasks, as well as more subjective experiences, such as level of pain.

EXHIBIT 13.1.
Domains of Patient Adaptation to Chronic Illness

Biological
   Direct effects of the illness or disability: fatigue, pain, nausea, fever, etc.
   Management of medication side effects
   Functionality and autonomy
   Adjustment to disease progression
   Depression secondary to the illness or disability
   Age of person affected

Social
   Management of isolation (self- and other-initiated)
   Management of stigma
   Relationships with health care personnel
   Preservation and redefinition of relationships with family and friends
   Reordering time in terms of schedule adjustments
   Cultural perspectives

Emotional
   Self-image issues
   Financial issues
   Relationships with health care personnel
   Impact on family members as a group and as individuals
   Preservation and redefinition of relationships with family and friends
   Redefinition of normalcy
   Finding personal meaning in illness/disability experience
   Reassessment of values
   Spirituality issues
   Medication side effect issues

Behavioral
   Prevention of health crises (symptom monitoring)
   Health maintenance
   Management of health crises
   Adherence to regimen

Social domain adaptation covers a broad range of social issues, such as handling relationships with medical personnel and redefining relationships with family and friends. It is this domain that addresses patients' needs to develop skills in setting priorities, adjusting schedules to allow for changes brought about by the chronic illness, and making maximum use of good days. The social domain also addresses a paradoxical situation related to the stigma of chronic illness: Chronic illness is an intensely personal experience that may be a source of public curiosity, outcry, and debate (e.g., chronic obstructive pulmonary disease [COPD], HIV disease). Moreover, each of the social adaptation issues must be examined in light of differing cultural expectations.

The emotional domain includes issues of self-identity for the people suffering from a chronic illness, the impact of the chronic illness on the family as a whole as well as on its individual members, and the need to redefine normalcy. Self-identity encompasses body image and sexuality issues as well as issues of roles played in interpersonal interactions. Also, there may be ambivalent feelings toward medications that help relieve the symptoms of the illness but cause unpleasant side effects. Another important item in this domain is the reassessment of values. Some of the values-related issues are (a) quality versus sanctity of life; (b) individual versus group benefit; and (c) dependence versus autonomy (Dean, 1990). Related to values assessment is the need to feel useful, which for some people is quite strong and is related to issues of self-identity. This domain is greatly affected by cultural perspectives.

Behavioral domain adaptation concerns issues of health maintenance; adherence to medication and care regimens; and preventing, preparing for, and managing health crises that are bound to occur. The patient's cultural identification plays an important role in this domain. For example, using both conventional medicine and culturally traditional healers may be common among some groups, although the use of traditional healers may not be disclosed to physicians or other health care personnel.

The four domains are interconnected; one domain cannot be affected without reverberations in another domain. In addition, a bidirectional relationship exists among the domains. For example, adherence to regimen, from the behavior domain, can affect the management of stigma, from the social domain, because individuals may adhere to treatment in an effort to reduce visible signs or symptoms. Others may manage stigma by avoiding medication-taking in public places or in the workplace. It is important to keep in mind the interconnectedness of the domains; failure to do so may result in an incomplete, and, therefore, inadequate perception of the person's adaptation to chronic illness.

These domains, and their interconnectedness, have been further developed in several theoretical models of the adaptation process. In this chapter, we review several of the prominent models of patients' adaptation to chronic illnesses, examine the ways in which these models may enhance the understanding of interventions to improve adaptation, and review the major instruments used by both researchers and clinicians to assess adaptation.

Characteristics of an Ideal Model

Although each model reviewed has particular strengths and weaknesses, it is useful to consider what characteristics are particularly important for such theoretical models to include. An ideal model of adaptation must address several important issues if it is to contribute to understanding, assessment, prediction, and intervention of adaptive processes in clinical populations.

First, the model must address the reciprocal influences of biological, psychological, social, and behavioral patient variables and the disease process. That is, the model must account for the ways in which these individual and social variables affect and are affected by disease stage, disease progression, or disability severity. Second, the model should be sufficiently broad to be applicable to a range of chronic illnesses and disabilities. Third, the model should address the influence of gender, ethnicity, cultural identification, and life stage on the adaptive process. Fourth, the usefulness of the model will be restricted if it is not prospectively predictive of patient adaptation level or if appropriate interventions cannot be derived from application of the model to clinical cases.

These criteria describe characteristics of what we believe to be an ideal model of patient adaptation. Next, we discuss several models of patient adaptation in the context of this ideal. Each model has particular strengths that warrant additional evaluation and application.

The Engel Biopsychosocial Model

The biopsychosocial model emphasizes the importance of biological, psychological, and social factors as having a combined influence on health and illness. The biopsychosocial model was proposed by Engel (1977) as a comprehensive alternative method of assessing illness in contrast to the biomedical model, which maintains that illness can be solely defined by biological malfunctions.

Important to the construction of this model was the influence of general systems theory (von Bertalanffy, 1976). This theory argues that nature is divided into separate units, each with its own distinct qualities, organized within a hierarchy, making each a component of a higher unit. Illness can best be understood through the comprehension of the larger system of which it is a part; subsequently, the impact of physical illness or disability may be estimated only by also considering the coping resources and social support system of the patient. Although behavioral aspects are not explicitly outlined, the model indicates that behavior is an important component of health outcomes via mediating mechanisms.

Engel's model outlines three routes by which a psychosocial factor can affect a health outcome: direct, indirect, and moderating. Direct effects are those that cause a predictable change in the relationship with the health outcome. For example, a patient's religious beliefs may preclude her from receiving some medical interventions for diabetes. This psychosocial factor has a direct effect on her health, regardless of the status of her illness. Indirect effects can be defined through mediational processes. For example, a patient's depressive symptoms may decrease his motivation to comply with a prescribed exercise regimen, ultimately leading to a heart attack precipitated by high cholesterol and low physical activity levels. Finally, moderating effects alter the causal relationship between a psychosocial factor and a particular health outcome. As an example, lack of social supports can advance HIV disease (Ingram, Jones, Fass, Neidig, & Song, 1999; Swindells et al., 1999).

The main theme of the model is the reciprocal influence of biological, psychological, and social influences on the disease process. The model guides the clinician in evaluating all aspects of patient functioning, including gender, ethnic, and cultural influences. The biopsychosocial model is adaptable and allows flexible application to individual patient issues. It has been successfully applied to a wide variety of conditions, including chronic pain (Stroud, Thorn, Jensen, & Boothby, 2000), diabetes (Peyrot, McMurry, & Kruger, 1999), renal disease (White & Grenyer, 1999), prostate cancer (Kunkel, Bakker, Myers, Oyesanmi, & Gomella, 2000) and cardiac disease (Buselli & Stuart, 1999).

The model may not, however, offer great predictive utility regarding a patient's level of adaptation. The model is better used for understanding the process and maintenance of chronic illness and may therefore guide interventions specifically addressed to patient needs.

The Lazarus and Folkman Model

A cognitive–phenomenological theory of stress developed by Lazarus and Folkman (1984) addressed adaptation to chronic illness through its focus on adaptation to stressors. Stressors are mediated by two factors. The first factor is appraisal (primary appraisal), which involves the individual's personal estimation of the significance of the stressor and an estimation of the individual's resources to handle it. Primary appraisal is influenced by factors related to the background and personality of the individual, such as gender, culture, or ethnic identity; therefore, it is characterized by stability across situations (Folkman, Lazarus, Gruen, & DeLongis, 1986).

The second factor is coping (secondary appraisal), which is composed of the thoughts and behaviors used to manage the stressor. Secondary appraisal is largely influenced by physical and social environment and may be thought of as context-specific. Primary appraisal leads to secondary appraisal through the individual's estimation of her or his ability to change the stressor or to utilize resources to manage the stressor. Adaptation then involves applying the form of coping that is deemed most appropriate by the individual to the particular stressor.

In this model, there are two types of coping: problem-focused, which emphasizes the external, environmental aspects of the stress situation; and emotion-focused, which emphasizes the internal, affective aspects of the stress situation. Emotion-focused coping reflects the acceptance of the illness by the individual, with no intent of active alteration of the circumstances imposed by the illness. Lazarus and Folkman (1984) proposed that problem-focused coping, with its emphasis on appraisal of illness as a situation capable of being altered by the individual, would be related to better functioning and adjustment. This model suggests that the result of coping may be a change in the individual's self-identity or other cognitive schema.

The Lazarus and Folkman model addresses the reciprocal influences of disease process variables and the biological, social, behavioral, and psychological variables by conceptualizing the primary and secondary appraisal process as an iterative loop, in constant revision as variables change. This ecological model has been used to describe adaptation processes for a wide variety of chronic illness groups, including cardiovascular and gastroenterological disorders, diabetes, and chronic pain (Bombardier, D'Amico, & Jordan, 1990; Felton & Revenson, 1984).

The predictive validity of the model needs additional work; the theory originally hypothesized that emotion-focused coping strategies were related to less successful adaptation and problem-focused coping strategies were related to more successful adaptation. Subsequent research indicates that this is not the case (cf., White, Richter, & Fry, 1992; see also Bombardier et al., 1990). The addition of a variable reflecting self-efficacy in management of the disease and its effects may increase the predictive nature of this model, which is well-suited for describing the process of adaptation across a number of domains and populations.

Roy's Adaptation Model

Roy's adaptation model (1984) describes the individual's constant interaction with her or his environment in terms of focal, contextual, or residual environmental stimuli. Focal stimuli are the type and duration of the illness (e.g., insulin-dependent diabetes first diagnosed in an individual 15 years earlier). Focal stimuli include most factors in the biological domain. Contextual stimuli are factors that directly affect the focal stimuli; they include demographic characteristics (e.g., sex, race, social status, patient education level), ability to tolerate stress as a result of life changes, health promotion activities (including self-initiated regimens), and health-related hardiness (i.e., a personality construct encompassing attitudes toward challenge, commitment, and control). Emotional, social, and behavioral domain issues would all be subsumed in the contextual category in Roy's model. Residual stimuli are unknown factors that may influence either focal or contextual stimuli and may not be readily apparent to the clinician during patient presentation; in fact, patients may be unaware of them. Again, these residual stimuli may include items from the emotional, social, and even behavioral domains.

In Roy's model, a semistructured phase model, the individual is an adaptive system making perceptions about the impact of the illness and then responding either adaptively or ineffectively within four modes: physiological, self-concept, role function, and interdependence. However, the model does not explicitly address the critical characteristic of interdependence among the focal, contextual, and residual variables.

Pollock's Adaptation of Roy's Model

Pollock (1986) elaborated on Roy's (1984) adaptation model to clarify concepts and relationships for chronic illness. Pollock's framework was developed to integrate the specific variables of chronicity (including type and duration of illness), stress, adaptive behavior, and hardiness as the characteristics of adaptation. The model addresses adaptation in terms of levels, which were defined as the effectiveness of the individual's behavior in physiological and psychosocial domains.

This model proposed that physiological and psychosocial functioning are related and that a higher level of adaptation is associated with increased effectiveness of the individual's behavior in promoting her or his physiological and psychosocial integrity. Pollock's modification of Roy's model addresses the reciprocal influences of patient variables, the disease process, and social variables. For example, the contextual stimuli may examine the reciprocal effects of gender roles and cultural identity on disease processes.

Although not specifically addressed, contextual stimuli could also account for the effects of lifespan and developmental issues such as with the different issues raised by complex adherence demands on a teenager versus on a retirement-aged adult.

This ecological model has been used to examine adaptation to several different chronic illnesses, including diabetes, multiple sclerosis, hypertension, and rheumatoid arthritis. However, its predictive capability may be questioned, given evidence of the lack of association of physiological and psychosocial functioning in some diagnostic groups (Pollock, 1986, 1990). These findings may be related to the absence within the model of two significant variables: patient perception of the illness in terms of limitations imposed by disability and meaning ascribed by the patient to the illness. Pollock's model may be best suited for discriminating psychosocial characteristics of diagnostic groups to aid in the design of illness-specific interventions.

The Livneh and Antonak Model

Livneh and Antonak (1997), in their comprehensive review of adaptation to chronic illness and disability, propose a conceptual framework of adaptation based on their review of the literature, which, they believe, reveals a lack of support for phase models. Phase models, which propose that adaptation takes place in a universal and linear fashion, are distinct from ecological models, which describe distinct psychosocial reactions and interactions with illness or disability. Although a subset of these reactions may be conceptualized on a continuum from maladaptive to adaptive, these ecological models do not propose an orderly sequence that is universally experienced by people with chronic conditions.

Working from earlier models, Livneh and Antonak proposed that variables associated with, or antecedent to, chronic illness and disability can be organized into four main classes of antecedent variables: (a) disability-related (e.g., type of condition, body areas affected, lethality); (b) sociodemographic (e.g., gender, age, ethnicity, socioecononomic status); (c) individual difference or personality (e.g., coping strategies, locus of control, personal meaning of the condition, health-related beliefs); and (d) social and environmental (e.g., social support network characteristics, economic support, social stigma of the condition). The extent of positive adaptation and the swiftness of adaptive response are characterized as significantly influenced by the interactions within these classes.

Livneh and Antonak also distinguished between the adaptation process and an individual's adaptation status, noting that the process of adaptation is fluid and dynamic, whereas status (i.e., adaptation vs. maladaptation) is best conceptualized as the final outcome of interest in the model. Adaptation process is based on the distinct reactions described in adaptation literature:

anxiety, depression, and acceptance–adjustment. Individuals may experience movement among these various reactions depending on the influences of the four classes of antecedent variables listed earlier.

This ecological model is extremely comprehensive and can be used to hypothesize underlying causes of differences in adaptation between individuals with the same condition and similarities of adjustment across different illnesses or disabilities. In addition, the model allows clinicians to prospectively predict adaptation based on an assessment of the four classes of antecedent variables (Livneh & Antonak, 1990). Interventions based on the model may address modification of functioning within the four classes of antecedent variables or may be focused on treatment of psychological or emotional states in the more maladaptive range of adjustment.

EVALUATING INTERVENTIONS IN THE CONTEXT OF EXISTING MODELS

Each of these models provides a mechanism by which individuals' adaptation to various illnesses may be conceptualized, assessed, and improved. Even though interest in intervention efforts aimed at increasing patient adaptation to chronic illness is growing, the literature provides examples of few theoretically based interventions. However, many successful interventions fit within the frameworks of these models. The examples described next illustrate the applicability of theory in guiding intervention design and emphasize the need for increasing use of theoretically based intervention research.

Cardiovascular Disorder

In a project investigating the effect of psychosocial and educational programs on the physical and psychosocial improvement of patients who had survived a myocardial infarction, Oldenberg, Perkins, and Andrews (1985) found that addition of an affective component to the standard education was associated with maintenance at one year of improved measures of psychological adaptation, including reduced anxiety and improved lifestyle. The Oldenberg study does not address the direct effects of psychosocial factors on health outcome as hypothesized by the biopsychosocial model. However, indirect effects are examined through the use of heart disease education and relaxation training; moderating effects of the counseling session component focused on anxieties and fears as part of the intervention strategy. When examining the study in the context of the Folkman and Lazarus appraisal model, it is clear that intervention sessions including strategies to handle anxiety and fears of the post–heart-attack patients involved the iterative process of primary and secondary appraisals, leading to the outcome of reduced psychological symptomatology.

When examined in terms of Roy's adaptation model, the focal stimuli are the experience and survival of a heart attack. The contextual stimuli include the demographics of the patients (all male, within a specified age range), health promotion activities (the educational component of the intervention), and health-related hardiness (addressed within the affective component). The residual stimuli are, of course, unknown. In terms of Pollock's modification of Roy's model, the Oldenberg study does not address levels of adaptation, except in terms of the relative outcomes of the intervention and control groups. However, the study does address the reciprocal nature of patient, disease, and social variables.

Finally, the Oldenburg study does not make Livneh and Antonak's distinction between adaptation process and adaptation status; however, three of the four main classes of variables are well-accounted for. Disability-related variables are addressed in participant selection of post–myocardial-infarction patients. Sociodemographic variables are addressed in terms of the gender and age range of study participants. The study addresses social and environmental variables by including education regarding heart disease and its treatment, coronary risk factors, and sexual functioning. Individual differences and personality are not addressed in the Oldenberg study, except through the addition of the affective component, which was limited to expression of individual anxiety and fears within a group context. Nevertheless, the group receiving the affective component maintained psychological functioning at follow-up and the other groups did not.

Cancer

In a study of psychosocial functioning of clients with cancer, Gordon and colleagues (1980) compared an education-only group with a group that received a multidimensional program including education, emotional support and guidance, and referral of services to other health care facilities. The Gordon study did not examine direct psychosocial effects on health outcomes, as suggested by the biopsychosocial model. However, indirect effects included in the intervention were a cancer education component and relaxation training. Components of the study that may be described as moderating effects include counseling and support sessions and service referral to related health care facilities.

Lazarus and Folkman's model of adaptation can be applied to the Gordon study by conceptualizing primary appraisal as the original baseline psychosocial functioning, which is altered through secondary appraisal throughout the course of the intervention. Both problem-focused and emotion-focused coping were emphasized in the intervention. The first coping type was addressed in terms of the referral services to other facilities as well as by including relaxation training. The enhanced intervention included a counseling component during which clients expressed feelings and were offered support addressing the emotion-focused component of the Lazarus and Folkman model.

In terms of Roy's adaptation model, the study addressed focal stimuli by limiting the research to cancer patients. Contextual stimuli were addressed in part through participant selection criteria of similar sociodemographic and medical characteristics. Moreover, contextual stimuli were addressed by including relaxation techniques and encouraging patients to take more control over their environments. Residual stimuli were not hypothesized.

Considering the Gordon study in terms of Pollock's model, adaptation levels were accounted for by assessment of degree of functioning along 13 life domains, including affect, body image, family and social issues, and health locus of control. The findings of the intervention appear to support Pollock's hypothesis that psychosocial and physiological functioning are related; clients receiving the enhanced intervention not only experienced a more rapid decline in affective symptoms, they also returned to work earlier and demonstrated more life activity.

The four main classes of antecedent variables of Livneh's model are easily applied to the study. The disability-related variable was addressed through the use of the cancer education component as well as through the use of referral to other health care facilities. Sociodemographic variables were found to be not significantly related to health outcomes measured by the study. Individual differences were addressed by the counseling and support sessions, as well as by the health care referral service. Finally, social and environmental variables were included in the cancer education component, the counseling and support sessions, and the health care referral services.

Summary and Implications for Intervention Programs

These are but two examples of the ways in which intervention studies do and do not address the constructs posited by the major theoretical models of patient adaptation. Each model provides a theoretical base from which to examine patient adjustment within interventions, which then provides for interpretation of outcomes related to those interventions. These studies, as well as meta-analyses of intervention program results (Astin, Beckner, Soeken, Hochberg, & Berman, 2002; Rossy et al., 1999), confirm the importance of addressing patient adaptation through a variety of interventions. Indeed, Rossy et al. (1999) and Astin et al. (2002) found that non-pharmacological treatment is a critical and highly effective aspect of treatment that can dramatically improve overall treatment success rates, particularly for patients with chronic conditions. Specific intervention strategies that have demonstrated the most success include patient education, relaxation training (including progressive muscle relaxation and visualization), communication and problem-solving skills training, and thought-restructuring techniques.

However, other types of programs beyond these individual-level interventions should be considered as well. Each model of patient adaptation describes not only intrapersonal but also interpersonal, social, and cultural influences on outcomes. Thus, interventions that address these types of influences may serve as important aspects of comprehensive programs to enhance patient adaptation. These may include family-level educational and treatment programs, social support groups for similar patients, and community interventions to enhance community members' understanding of a particular condition or disease.

The models described suggest that, to be most effective, intervention approaches must be carefully selected in the context of multiple cognitive, personality, social, and cultural variables. Throughout the duration of treatment, these issues may affect patients' willingness to engage in therapy and the extent to which interventions can succeed. For example, patients' social systems may be more or less supportive of the idea that psychological issues have an impact on health, and this will affect the extent to which patients are willing to acknowledge the role that these issues play in adaptation to their illness. Attitudes about psychotherapy or behavioral treatment, often a function of patients' social or cultural systems, will also influence the extent to which patients or their family members will engage in and adhere to these treatments, whether as part of clinical research or treatment programs. Comprehensive assessment of the types of variables described in these models may give behavioral scientists and clinicians important guidance in identifying the issues that will affect patients' engagement in and response to treatment.

Both research and patient care activities that are focused on improving patient adaptation may benefit from using the theoretical models described earlier as a framework, because the models provide a clear rationale for including certain components and constructs and hypothesize specific outcomes. However, reliance on a theoretical model for the development of interventions must be accompanied by careful selection of adequate measures appropriate to the patient population and variables of interest.

MEASURES OF ADAPTATION TO CHRONIC ILLNESS

The current literature provides both disease-specific and general measures for assessment of patient adaptation. A comprehensive assessment of patient adaptation may benefit from a combination of both approaches.

However, for the purposes of this chapter, we focus on the instruments that provide for general assessment of adaptation, to maximize understanding of the importance of the four major domains of adaptation—biological, social, emotional, and behavioral—within the instruments. There are four major instruments commonly used to assess adaptation to general medical and psychiatric illnesses. These are the General Health Questionnaire (60-item version), the Millon Behavioral Health Inventory, the Sickness Impact Profile, and the Psychological Adjustment to Illness Scale, each discussed in turn next.

The General Health Questionnaire

The General Health Questionnaire (60-item version; GHQ–60; Goldberg, 1972) is a self-report questionnaire designed to screen for poor adaptation and psychological symptomatology within general medical populations. Items concern typical functioning and assessment of new symptoms, with questions such as "Been able to enjoy your normal day-to-day activities?" and "Felt constantly under strain?" Responses compare recent with most usual state, indicating whether the behaviors or symptoms have occurred within a range of "Less than usual" to "Much more than usual." The respondent's score indicates global general health.

This unidimensional instrument is reported to have adequate sensitivity, specificity, and reliability and is reported to avoid eliciting undue social desirability response (Burvill & Knuiman, 1983; Parkes, 1980). Moreover, the GHQ–60 has been translated into at least 16 languages and has been used to assess adaptation for a wide variety of chronic illnesses, including rheumatoid arthritis, cancer, cerebral palsy, epilepsy, gastroenteritis, hypertension, chronic obstructive pulmonary disease, heart disease, and chronic pain.

The Millon Behavioral Health Inventory

The Millon Behavioral Health Inventory (MBHI; Millon, Green, & Meagher, 1979) is composed of 150 true–false statements organized into four domains: coping styles, psychogenic attitudes, psychosomatic complaints, and prognostic index. The MBHI was designed with three goals in mind. First, the instrument allows psychologists to make a psychological characterization of general medicine patients. Second, it allows for investigation of the relationship of disease course and patient emotional needs, coping styles, and motivation. Third, from the information gained in achieving the second goal, interventions may be designed to address specific patient needs.

Reliability and construct validity are reported to be adequate. However, factor analysis results have not supported the instrument's domain structure. There is no information regarding potential response bias. The multidimensional MBHI has been used as the basis for modification of patient-specific interventions for chronic pain patients and for patients with cancer, kidney disease, coronary surgery, and digestive disorders.

The Sickness Impact Profile

The Sickness Impact Profile (SIP; Bergner, Bobbit, Carter, & Gilson, 1981) was developed as a measure of health status outcome as a means of evaluating health care services. This 136-item instrument is composed of 12 subscales: ambulation, mobility, body care and movement, social interaction, alertness behavior, emotional behavior, communication, sleep and rest, eating, work, home management, recreation and pastimes. A Spanish version of the SIP has been developed (Gilson et al., 1980). Test–retest reliability values are reported to be adequate, as is construct validity. The SIP may be susceptible to response bias, and it may be less accurate in positive changes relative to negative changes in the patient's adaptation. The SIP has been used to study adaptation in patients with rheumatoid arthritis, cancer, chronic pain, diabetes mellitus, heart disease, multiple sclerosis, and hyperthyroidism.

The Psychosocial Adjustment to Illness Scale

The Psychosocial Adjustment to Illness Scale (PAIS; Derogatis, 1986) is a multidimensional scale designed to assess psychosocial adjustment to medical illness and its corresponding effects. The 46-item instrument consists of seven subscales: health care orientation, vocational environment, domestic environment, sexual relationships, extended family relationships, social environment, and psychological distress. The subscales of the PAIS are reported to have adequate construct validity. Test–retest reliability has not been reported, and there is no information regarding response bias. The PAIS has shown discriminative and predictive validity in patients with chronic illnesses and disorders such as rheumatoid arthritis, cancer, hypertension, kidney disease, heart disease, and gastroenteritis.

Implications of General Assessment Instruments

Recent discussion in the field has focused on the fact that paper-and-pencil assessments of coping or adaptation may not be adequate, given the inherent problems with retrospective memory and introspection required for assessment completion in addition to problems in applying general "checklist" assessments to specific medical conditions (Coyne & Racioppo, 2000). Clinicians may wish to use a general assessment instrument as a guide to patient adjustment issues, but should be sure to consider a general psychiatric assessment, disease-specific assessments, and interviews with family or significant others to gain a comprehensive understanding of patient functioning. Assessment of patient adjustment to chronic illness must balance the need for standardized measures with the need for individualized approaches, particularly when assessments are used for both clinical and scientific application.

CONCLUSION

A patient's adaptation to a chronic illness or disability is a complex, long-term process that is influenced by a remarkable number of forces, both internal and external. Because of the remarkable variability both among individuals and among disease processes (e.g., COPD, renal disease, multiple sclerosis, HIV disease), a generalist approach to adaptation requires comprehensive theories and assessment approaches. We have attempted to review several models that we believe offer important perspectives on the adaptation process, as well as general assessment instruments that can facilitate measurement of individual adaptation.

However, it is important to note that several challenges remain if we are to improve our understanding of the individual adaptation process. First, behavioral scientists and clinicians will be best served by designing and implementing model-based interventions so that the existing models can be tested, evaluated, and modified. Second, assessment strategies must include both general and disease-specific instruments, and such instruments must be validated on populations that accurately represent the populations affected by a given illness. Third, research must recognize and address the challenges of adequately characterizing adaptation as both an outcome and a process. As suggested by Sommerfield and McCrae (2000), both longitudinal, within-subjects designs and cross-sectional, between-subjects designs are needed if we are to fully understand the process of adaptation and factors that influence patient outcomes.

REFERENCES

Astin, J. A., Beckner, W., Soeken, K., Hochberg, M. C., & Berman, B. (2002). Psychological interventions for rheumatoid arthritis: A meta-analysis of randomized controlled trials. *Arthritis and Rheumatism, 47*(3), 291–302.

Bergner, M., Bobbit, R. A., Carter, W. B., & Gilson, B. S. (1981). The Sickness Impact Profile: Development and final revision of a health status measure. *Medical Care, 19,* 787–805.

Bombardier, C. H., D'Amico, C. D., & Jordan, J. S. (1990). The relationship of appraisal and coping to chronic illness adjustment. *Behavior Research and Therapy, 28*(4), 297–304.

Burvill, P. W., & Knuiman, M. W. (1983). Which version of the General Health Questionnaire should be used in community studies? *Australian and New Zealand Journal of Psychiatry, 17*, 237–242.

Buselli, E. F., & Stuart, E. M. (1999). Influence of psychosocial factors and biopsychosocial interventions on outcomes after myocardial infarction. *Journal of Cardiovascular Nursing, 13*(3), 60–72.

Coyne, J. C., & Racioppo, M. W. (2000). Never the twain shall meet? Closing the gap between coping research and clinical intervention research. *American Psychologist, 55*(6), 655–664.

Dean, H. E., (1990). Political and ethical implications of using quality of life as an outcome measure. *Seminars in Oncology Nursing, 6*, 303–308.

Derogatis, L. R. (1986). The Psychosocial Adjustment to Illness Scale. *Journal of Psychosomatic Research, 30*, 77–91.

Engel, G. L. (1977). The need for a new medical model: a challenge for biomedicine. *Science, 196*(4286), 129–136.

Felton, B. J., & Revenson, T. A. (1984). Coping with chronic illness: A study of illness controllability and the influence of coping strategies on psychological adjustment. *Journal of Consulting and Clinical Psychology, 52*, 343–353.

Folkman, S., Lazarus, R. S., Gruen, R. J., & DeLongis, A. (1986). Appraisal, coping, health status, and psychological symptoms. *Journal of Personality and Social Psychology, 50*(3), 571–579.

Gilson, B. S., Erickson, D., Chavez, C. T., Bobbitt, R. A., Bergner, M., & Carter, W. B. (1980). A Chicano version of the Sickness Impact Profile (SIP). *Culture, Medicine, and Psychiatry, 4*, 137–150.

Goldberg, D. P. (1972). *The detection of psychiatric illness by questionnaire.* London: Oxford University Press.

Gordon, W. A., Freidenbergs, I., Diller, L., Hibbard, M., Wolf, C., & Levine, L. (1980). The efficacy of psychosocial intervention with cancer patients. *Journal of Consulting and Clinical Psychology, 48*, 743–759.

Ingram, K. M., Jones, D. A., Fass, R. J., Neidig, J. L., & Song, Y. S. (1999). Social support and unsupportive social interactions: Their association with depression among people living with HIV. *AIDS Care, 11*(3), 313–329.

Kunkel, E. J., Bakker, J. R, Myers, R. E., Oyesanmi, O., & Gomella, L. G. (2000). Biopsychosocial aspects of prostate cancer. *Psychosomatics, 41*(2), 85–94.

Lazarus, R. S., & Folkman, S. (1984). *Stress appraisal and coping.* New York: Springer.

Livneh, H., & Antonak, R. F. (1990). Reactions to disability: An empirical investigation of their nature and structure. *Journal of Applied Rehabilitation Counseling, 21*(4), 13–21.

Livneh, H., & Antonak, R. F. (1997). *Psychosocial adaptation to chronic illness and disability.* Gaithersburg, MD: Aspen.

Millon, T., Green, C. J., & Meagher, R. B., Jr. (1979). The MBHI: A new inventory for the psychodiagnostician in medical settings. *Professional Psychology, 10,* 529–539.

Oldenberg, B., Perkins, R. J., & Andrews, G. (1985). Controlled trials of psychological intervention in myocardial infarction. *Journal of Consulting and Clinical Psychology, 53,* 852–859.

Parkes, K. R. (1980). Social desirability, defensiveness, and self-report psychiatric inventory scores. *Psychological Medicine, 10*(4), 735–742.

Peyrot, M., McMurry, J. F., & Kruger, D. F. (1999). A biopsychosocial model of glycemic control in diabetes: Stress, coping, and regimen adherence. *Journal of Health and Social Behavior, 40*(2), 141–158.

Pollock, S. E. (1986). Human responses to chronic illness: Physiologic and psychosocial adaptation. *Nursing Research, 35*(2), 90–95.

Pollock, S. E. (1993). Adaptation to chronic illness: A program of research for testing nursing theory. *Nursing Science Quarterly, 6*(2), 86–92.

Pollock, S. E., Christian, B. J., & Sands, D. (1990). Responses to chronic illness: Analysis of psychological and physiological adaptation. *Nursing Research, 39*(5), 300–304.

Rossy, L. A., Buckelew, S. P., Dorr, N., Hagglund, K. J., Thayer, J. F., McIntosh, M. J., et al. (1999). A meta-analysis of fibromyalgia treatment interventions. *Annals of Behavioral Medicine, 21*(2), 180–191.

Roy, S. C. (1984). *Introduction to nursing: An adaptation model* (2nd ed.). Englewood Cliffs, NJ: Prentice-Hall.

Sommerfield, M. R., & McCrae, R. R. (2000). Stress and coping research: Methodological challenges, theoretical advances, and clinical applications. *American Psychologist, 55*(6), 620–625.

Stroud, M. W., Thorn, B. E., Jensen, M. P., & Boothby, J. L. (2000). The relation between pain beliefs, negative thoughts, and psychosocial functioning in chronic pain patients. *Pain, 84*(2–3), 347–352.

Swindells, S., Mohr, J., Justis, J. C., Berman, S., Squier, C., Wagener, M. M., et al. (1999). Quality of life in patients with human immunodeficiency virus infection: impact of social support, coping style and hopelessness. *International Journal of STD and AIDS, 10*(6), 383–391.

von Bertalanffy, L. (1976). Health research: the systems approach. In H. Werley, A. Zuzich, M. Zajowski, & A. D. Zagornik (Eds.), *Health research: The systems approach* (pp. 5–13). New York: Springer.

White, N. E., Richter, J. M., & Fry, C. (1992). Coping, social support, and adaptation to chronic illness. *Western Journal of Nursing Research, 14*(2), 211–224.

White, Y., & Grenyer, B. F. (1999). The biopsychosocial impact of end-stage renal disease: The experience of dialysis patients and their partners. *Journal of Advanced Nursing, 30*(6), 1312–1320.

AUTHOR INDEX

Numbers in italics refer to listings in reference sections.

Armstrong, C. A., 176
Armstrong, N., 150, 171
Arndt, I., 61, 70
Arrigan, M., 227
Arrigoni, J., 226
Arrington, T. A., 50, 67
Asakura, K., 228
Ascherio, A., 36
Ashenberg, Z., 111
Aspinwall, L. G., 243, 257
Assaf, A. R., 158, 172
Assmann, S. F., 174
Astin, J. A., 415, 419
Astrup, A., 14, 40
Atalaia, A., 204, 221
Atnafou, R., 143
Audrain, J., 114
Auld, G. W., 31, 33
Aunola, S., 263
Auslander, W. F., 111
Ausman, L. M., 15, 36
Austin, B. T., 395, 403
Avery, J., 135, 146
Avrunin, J. S., 40
Axelrod, F. B., 210, 220
Azrin, N. H., 56, 62, 63, 67, 69, 73

Babani, L., 388, 403
Babor, T. F., 48, 49, 67, 72
Babyak, M. A., 167, 171, 172
Bachman, J. G., 75, 114
Back, K. W., 315, 323
Backett, E. M., 301, 319
Badger, G., 69
Badr, S., 230
Baer, J. S., 69, 92, 109, 115
Bagiella, E., 269, 288, 297
Bahnson, J. L., 37
Bailey, W. C., 93, 94, 110, 111
Baillie, A. J., 92, 93, 97, 108
Bairey, C. N., 264
Baker, L. A., 75, 118, 401
Baker, S., 56, 71
Bakker, J. R., 409, 420
Balabanis, M., 120
Balady, G. J.
Bales, V. S., 38, 263
Balhorn, K. E., 19, 39
Ball, G. D., 28, 33
Ball, J. C., 61, 67

Ballad, G., 75, 118
Ballard-Barbash, R., 21, 37
Ballesteros, M., 36
Balter, M. B., 184, 225
Bamberger, J. D., 342, 346
Bamford, O., 208, 225
Bandura, A., 26, 27, 33, 132, 139, 156,
        171, 291, 292, 341, 346, 385,
        396
Banis, H., 388, 403
Banning, K., 237, 265
Banspach, S. W., 140, 142, 176
Baranowski, T., 36, 150, 165, 171
Barbé, F., 190, 191, 220, 226
Barbour, K. A., 173
Barefoot, J. C., 86, 115
Barnard, M. U., 330, 344, 353
Barnard, N. D., 29, 33
Barnes, H., 401
Baron, R. M., 278, 292
Baron, R. S., 252, 263, 316, 324, 325
Barondess, J. A., 302, 320
Barrera, M., 253, 258
Barrett, D. C., 140
Barrett, J. J., 399
Barsky, A. J., 301, 313, 320
Barth, R. P., 130, 142, 333, 347
Bartkowski, J. P., 281, 292
Bartkus, D., 305, 319
Bartlett, S. J., 148, 169, 171
Bartolucci, A., 395, 399
Bartrop, R. W., 239, 258
Basen-Engquist, K., 140
Basset, A., 214, 220
Bates, M. E., 46, 74
Battista, R. N., 92, 114
Baum, A., 235, 258, 372, 375
Baum, D., 344, 346
Bauman, A. E., 159
Baumann, B., 303, 320
Baumann, K., 163, 168, 175
Baumann, L. J., 303, 306, 309, 320
Baumeister, R. F., 251, 258, 270, 292
Baumgartner, M., 388, 402
Baumrind, D., 127, 139
Baxter, J. E., 31, 36
Beck, A. T., 53, 67, 74, 241, 258
Beck, N., 398
Beck, S., 347
Becker, A. B., 395, 399
Becker, D., 337, 354

Caldwell, E., 70
Calfas, K. J., 103, *116*, 149, 157, 158, *172*, *178*, *179*, *180*
Calle, E. E., 13, 14, *34*
Cameron, K., 330, *346*
Cameron, L., 300, 302, 304, 306, 308, 309, 310, 315, 316, *320*, *321*
Campanelli, P. C., 86, *110*
Campbell, M. K., 99, *118*
Campbell, S. M., 22, *40*
Campbell, T. L., 382, 394, 395, 396, 398
Cannon, W. B., 234, *259*
Canter, R. J., 208, *227*
Caporaso, N. E., *114*
Capper, A., 31, *34*
Carey, G., 313, *327*
Carey, K. B., 49, 52, 53, 67, 70, 84, *108*, 249, *259*
Carey, M. P., 249, *259*
Carey, T. S., *171*, 346
Carey, W. B., 212, *221*
Cargill, V. A., *144*
Carithers, T., 159, *173*
Carleton, R. A., 158, 164, *172*, *176*
Carlin, J. B., *116*
Carlson, L. E., 241, *259*
Carmack, C. L., 241, *259*
Carney, P., *399*
Carney, R. M., 342, *346*
Carr, C., *109*
Carroll, J. L., 208, *225*
Carroll, K. M., 53, 56, 63, 67, 69, *71*
Carroll, M. D., 21, *35*
Carskadon, M. A., 184, 186, 207, 213, 214, 216, *221*, 228, 230
Carter, B., *401*
Carter, W. B., 418, *419*, *420*
Carver, C. S., 245, 265, 311, *321*
Casagrande, M., 185, *221*
Caslander, B., 214, *220*
Caspersen, C., *174*
Cassel, J., 254, *259*
Cassell, C., *145*
Castro, C., 162, 163, *175*
Catania, J. A., 131, *139*, *140*, *144*
Cater, W. R., 340, *348*
Cathey, M. A., 203, *229*
Catz, S. L., 237, *258*
Cauley, J. A., *170*
Caust, J., *116*
Cavazos, L., 307, *320*

Cavill, N. A., 149, 150, *171*, *172*
Cayeux, C., *265*
Cecil, H., 132, *139*
Celesia, G. G., *221*
Cetel, M., 209, *223*
Chaisson, R. E., 333, *352*
Chaitman, B., *174*
Chalmer, B. J., 274, *298*
Chandler, H. M., 279, *292*
Chandler, S. H., 207, *222*
Chaney, E. F., 394, *401*
Chaney, J., 388, 391, 396
Chang, G., *71*
Charleston, J. B., *37*
Charney, D. S., *224*
Chassin, L., 85, 87, *109*
Chatters, L. M., 275, 282, 285, *292*
Chavez, C. T., *420*
Cheadle, A., 31, *34*
Chemelli, R. M., 196, 214, *222*
Chen, D., 169, *179*
Chen, J. H., 132, *144*
Chen, X., 87, *119*
Cherek, D. R., *67*
Cherry, N., 85, *109*
Cheskin, L. J., 148, *171*
Chesney, M., 345, *346*
Chesson, A. L., Jr., 192, *222*
Chetrit, M., 214, *220*
Chewning, B., 129, *139*
Chilvers, M., 100, *112*
Chinn, A., *220*
Chisholm, D. J., 242, *261*
Chisolm, W. A., 16, *36*
Choi, K. H., 133, *140*
Choi, W. S., 86, 88, 89, *117*
Chopra, D., 270, *292*
Chou, S. P., 44, *68*
Christensen, A. J., 248, *259*
Christensen, N., 337, *351*
Christian, B. J., *421*
Christiansen, A. J., 382, 396
Christophersen, E. R., 212, *222*, 336, *348*
Christopherson, V., 373, *375*
Chwalisz, K., 383, 392, 397
Ciaranello, R. D., *221*
Cirignotta, F., 195, 199, *221*, *226*
Civic, D., 129, *140*
Clark, B. L., *173*
Clark, D. O., 161, *181*
Clark, L. A., 313, *327*

DiMatteo, M. R., 329, 330, 331, *347,*
350, 353
Dinges, D. F., 191, *224*
Dischler, J., 331, *346*
Dishman, R. K., 156, 163, *173, 175*
Ditto, P. H., 310, 317, *321*
Dixit, S., *174*
Dixon, D. W., 301, *322*
Dodson, M., 237, *260*
Doghramji, K., 200, *222*
Dohrenwend, B. P., 237, *260*
Dole, V. P., 61, *68*
Doll, R., 75, *110*
Dollard, J., 312, *321*
Donahue, B., *67*
Donaldson, M., 333, *350*
Donham, R., *69*
Donnelly, D., 23, *38*
Donovan, D. M., 47, 49, 50, 53, 68, *69*
Donta, S. T., 167, *173*
Doraiswamy, M., *171*
Dorfman, S. F., 93, 94, *110, 111*
Dorr, N., *421*
Dorwaldt, A. L., *118*
Doswell, W. M., 127, *140*
Dotson, C. O., 153, *178*
Dougherty, G. E., 316, *325*
Douglas, J. M., 132, *142, 144*
Doyle, W. J., *321*
Dreon, D. M., 14, 15, *34*
Drew, J. B., 256, 262, *294*
Drewes, A. M., 184, 185, 204, *222*
Drewnowski, A., *36*
Drotar, D., 336, 352, 389, 393, *397*
Druley, J. A., 391, *397*
Dubach, U. C., 333, *347*
Dubbert, P. M., 156, 159, 163, 164, 165,
166, 168, *173, 173, 175, 176,*
177, 240, *266*
Dubin, L. F., 279, *296*
Duff, R. W., 316, *324*
Duivenvoorden, H. J., 246, *264*
Dunbar, J. M., 343, *347*
Dunbar-Jacob, J., 345, *347*
Dunkel-Schetter, C., 256, *260*
Dunn, A. L., 159, *171, 173, 176*
Dunn, C., 57, *67*
Dunne, M., 336, *353*
Dunning, E. J., 345, *347*
Duran, R., *143*
Durbe, G. A., 161, *177*

Durkheim, E., 254, *260*
Dusseldorp, E., 345, *347*
Duvall, R. C., *40*
Dworkin, S. F., 361, *375*
Dwyer, K. A., 314, *327,* 345, *347*
Dyer, A. R., *34*
Dymtrow, D., 332, *352*

Eagleston, J. R., 289, *297*
Easterling, D., 310, *324*
Eckerdt, J. R., 103, *110*
Eckhardt, S. G., 103, *110*
Ecklund-Johnson, E., *399*
Edwards, D. A., 85, *109*
Edwards, K. J., 212, *222*
Edwards, M., 95, *120*
Egan, K. S., *38*
Eggleston, P., *354*
Eid, N., *401*
Eigen, H., 386, *401*
Eisdorfer, C., 234, *260*
Eisinger, R. A., 100, *110*
Eitel, P., 240, *261*
Ekholm, B., 333, *350*
Eklerling, L., 330, *347*
Elashoff, R., 103, *112*
Elder, J. P., 158, 164, *173, 176, 179*
Elliott, G. R., 234, *260*
Elliott, P., 17, *34*
Elliott, T., 382, 387, 391, 392, 393, 394,
395, 398, 399, *402*
Ellis, A., 282, *292*
Ellison, C. G., 275, 278, 280, 281, 282,
288, 292, *294*
Ellison, R., 31, *34*
Ellsworth, N., *34*
Elmer, P. J., 166, *173*
Elmquist, J. K., *222*
Elward, K., 161, *173*
el Zein, H. A., 16, *33*
Emmons, R. A., 272, *293*
Endicott, J., *68*
Endres, R., 339, *354*
Eney, R. D., 336, *347*
Engel, C. C., *173*
Engel, G. L., 408, *420*
England, R., 204, *226*
Engle, M., *70*
Ennett, S. T., 44, *68*
Ensing, D. S., 289, *296*

Epstein, L. H., 29, *34*, 36, 149, 153, *174*, 330, 340, 337, *347*, *348*
Epstein, S., *174*
Erbaugh, J., 54, *67*
Erhardt, L. R., *346*
Erickson, D., *420*
Erickson, L., 281, *298*
Erickson, M. T., 388, *400*
Erikson, E. H., 127, *140*
Ernst, N., *37*
Escobedo, L. G., *108*
Esmundo, E., 89, *115*
Espelage, D. L., 336, *352*, *401*
Espeland, M. A., *37*, *41*
Esrey, K. L., 15, *35*
Estline, E., *220*
Ettinger, W. H., *41*, 161, *171*, *178*
Etzwiler, D. D., 332, *352*
Evans, D. E., 344, *348*, *351*
Evans, E. E., 336, *348*
Evans, J. C., 301, *319*
Evans, M. C., 18, 22, 39, *40*
Evans, W. J., *174*
Everett, F. M., 210, *229*
Everett, S. A., *145*
Everly, G. S., 234, *260*
Evers, K., 342, *352*
Ewing, R., 169, *174*
Exline, J. J., 280, 288, *293*
Eyler, A. A., *175*
Eysenck, H. J., 85, *110*

Fabsitz, R. R., 22, *40*
Faigle, M., 133, *140*
Fairfax, J. L., 131, *140*
Falgout, K., 289, *296*
Falloon, I. R. H., 80, *110*
Falvo, D., 332, *348*
Faraco, J., *225*
Farkas, A. J., 86, 88, *117*
Farkas, G., *347*
Farquhar, J. W., 158, *174*
Farrell, M., *74*
Fass, R. J., 409, *420*
Faucette, N., 149, *174*, *179*
Faucetter, F. N., 152, *177*
Faull, K. F., 188, *221*
Faust, D., 336, *354*
Faust, R., 98, *110*
Fay, G., *401*

Feely, M., 338, *352*
Fegan, M. F., 252, *267*
Fehrenbach, A. M., 386, *398*
Feifel, H., 238, 246, *266*
Feigelman, S., *144*, *145*, *145*
Feigenbaum, S. L., 203, *230*
Feinglos, M. N., 239, *266*
Feldman, E. B., 16, *35*
Feldman, P. J., *265*
Feldman, R., *36*
Felice, M. E., 126, *140*
Fell, R., *220*
Felman, H. A., 158, *172*
Felton, B. J., 410, *420*
Fennerty, F. A., 330, *348*
Ferber, R., 212, 213, *222*
Ferreira, M. F., 240, *260*
Fertel, R., *261*
Fetro, J. V., 130, *142*
Fiatarone, M. A., 160, *174*
Ficca, G., *220*
Fichtenberg, C. M., 107, *110*
Fielding, D. M., 342, *346*
Fiese, B. H., 392, *398*
Figgs, L. W., 77, *108*
Figueroa, J., *347*
Fillingim, R. B., 303, *321*
Fimrite, A., *33*
Findley, L. J., 191, *220*, *222*
Fine, M. A., 303, *321*
Fine, R., 390, *397*
Fineberg, N. S., 17, *41*
Fink, P., 301, *321*
Finney, J. W., 46, 52, 68, *71*, 249, *263*, 336, *348*
Fiore, M. C., 78, 93, 94, 96, 98, 101, *110*, *111*, *117*, *120*
Fireman, P., *321*
Fiscella, K., 384, *398*
Fischer, I. A., *118*
Fischer, M. E., 166, *177*
Fischer, W. A., *146*
Fischman, M., 45, *68*
Fishbein, M., 132, *140*, *142*, 305, *319*, *322*
Fisher, E. A., *34*, *37*
Fisher, E. B., Jr., 83, 95, 96, 100, 103, *111*, *112*
Fisher, J. D., 131, 137, *141*, *142*
Fisher, L., *400*
Fisher, W. A., 131, 137, *141*, *142*

Fiske, S. T., 310, *322*
Fiske, V., 384, 398
FitzGerald, S. J., *178*
Flaxman, J., 92, *111*
Flay, B. R., 87, 100, *111*, *120*
Flegal, K. M., 21, 22, 23, *35*, *40*
Fleming, M. F., 57, 63, 65, *74*
Fletcher, B., 62, *73*, 247, *266*
Fletcher, G. F., 155, *174*
Flewelling, R. L., 44, *68*
Flor, H., 386, 398
Flora, J. A., *118*, *174*
Flynn, B. S., *118*
Flynn, P. M., 49, 69
Foege, W. H., 12, *38*
Foerg, F., 69
Folkman, S., 235, 237, 243, 244, 245,
       246, 247, 248, 260, 263, 311,
       323, 381, *400*, 409, 410, 413,
       414, 415, 420
Follmann, D., 30, *34*
Folmar, S., *37*
Fondell, M. M., 129, *143*
Fong, G. T., 130, *141*
Fontaine, K. R., 169, *171*
Fonte, C., 81, *116*
Forchammer, H., *119*
Ford, D. S., 131, *140*
Ford, E. S., *38*, *263*
Ford, G. F., 399
Fordyce, W. E., 385, 398
Foreyt, J. P., 28, *35*
Forsyth, L. A., *175*, *176*, *177*
Fortmann, S. P., *110*, 158, *174*, *181*
Foster, G. D., 14, 28, *41*
Foster, M., 382, 396
Fowler, A., *37*
Fowler, G., 96, *118*
Fox, M. K., *174*
Francis, L. J., 281, *293*
Franckowiak, S. C., 169, *171*
Frank, L. D., 169, *179*
Frank, N., *227*
Frank, R. G., 391, 393, 394, 396, 397,
       398, 399
Frankel, B. G., 274, *293*
Franklin, B. A., 165, 166, *174*
Franklin, C., 127, *141*
Franklin, F. A., *40*
Frankowski, R. F., *116*
Franks, P., 382, 384, *398*

Fraser, E., 157, *181*
Fraser, M., *345*, *346*
Frazier, P. A., 278, *297*
Frederickson. L., 219, *222*
Fredman, L., 254, *265*
Freedman, M. A., 126, 127, *145*
Freedson, P. S., *178*
Freeland, K. E., *346*
Freeman, D. H., 287, *296*
Freeman, K. A., *223*
Freidenbergs, I., *420*
Freidman, J., *264*
Freidman, R. H., 163, *174*
French, J. R., Jr., 254, *263*
French, S. A., 31, *35*, *36*
Frerichs, R. R., 314, *319*
Freud, S., 282, *293*
Freund, A., 343, *350*
Frey, D. L., 28, *41*
Frey-Hewitt, B., *34*
Frid, D. J., *172*
Friday, J., 25, *37*
Friedland, G. H., 342, *348*
Friedman, L. S., 87, *111*, *402*
Friedman, R., *175*
Friedson, E., 315, *322*
Friend, R., 240, *261*
Frieske, D., 344, *352*
Friman, P. C., 213, *223*, 336, *348*
Fritz, S., 399
Frolkis, J. P., 333, *348*
Fry, C., 410, *421*
Fry, J. M., 185, *222*, *227*
Fryd, V., *119*
Frymoyer, J. W., 364, *375*
Fuchs, S., *225*
Fuller, R. C., 271, 284, *293*

Gaddy, J. R., 200, *222*
Gade, J., *222*
Gagnon, J. H., 134, 135, *142*, *143*
Galanter, M., 281, *293*
Galbraith, J., *144*, *145*
Gallagher, J. C., 19, *39*
Gallagher-Thompson, D., 390, 399
Gallo, L. C., 238, *260*
Gallup, G., 290, *293*
Gallup, G., Jr., 271, *293*
Gamble, G. D., 18, *39*
Garcia, M. E., *173*

Gardner, C. O., *114*
Garma, L., *220*
Garner, W., *262*
Garrett, V. D., 238, *258*
Garrison, C. Z., *140*
Garron, D. C., *265*
Gartner, J., 280, *293*
Garvey, A. J., *120*
Gary-Seville, M. E., 255, *260*
Gatchel, R. J., 357, 358, 359, 363, 364,
    365, 366, 367, 368, 370, 372,
    375, 376, 377, 378
Gauger, L., 198, *223*
Gavin, D. R., 49, *68*
Gavin, L., 340, *350*
Gaw, V. P., 333, *347*
Gawin, F., *67*
Gay, P. C., *225*
Gayle, H. D., 123, *145*
Gebski, V. J., *113*
Geiss, S. K., 343, *348*
Geller, B. M., *118*
George, C. F., 192, *223*
George, L. K., 278, 281, 282, 284, *293*
George, V. A., 240, *261*
Gerace, T. A., 240, *261*
Gerhardt, P. R., 75, *115*
Gerrard, M., 136, *141*
Gerstein, F., 343, *351*
Getsy, J. E., 191, *224*
Gianno, G. A., 76, 79, *112*
Gibbons, F. X., 136, *141*
Gibson, E. S., 336, *354*
Gibson, R. W., 100, *112*
Giffen, C. A., *115*
Giger, J., 395, *399*
Gijsbers van Wijk, C. M., 318, *322*
Gil, K., 373, *376*, 388, *402*
Gilbert, A., 337, *348*
Gilbert, G. G., 153, *178*
Gilbert, J. R., 336, *348*
Gilderman, A., *110*
Giles, W. H., 333, *349*
Gillis, D. E., *180*
Gilpin, E. A., 86, 88, 89, 97, *117*
Gilson, B. S., 418, 419, *420*
Gingras, J. R., *33*
Ginsberg, H. N., 16, *35*
Giorgetti, M. M., *174*
Giovino, G., 89, *108, 109, 112*
Girard, J., *118*

Gislason, T., 190, *225*
Glantz, S. A., 90, 107, *110, 112*
Glaser, R., 239, *261, 262, 400*
Glasgow, R. E., 80, 95, 97, 102, 103, *112,*
    115, 331, 340, *348*
Glass, D. C., 300, *324*
Glassman, A., 86, *112*
Glore, S. R., 18, *35*
Glover, E. D., *110, 114*
Glovinsky, P. B., 201, *229*
Glueckauf, R. L., 382, 392, 395, *399,*
    400, 401
Glynn, K., 85, *113*
Go, B. K., 387, *397*
Gochman, D., 305, *322*
Goel, P. K., *38*
Goetsch, V. L., 239, *261*
Goff, D. C., 301, *322*
Goggin, K. J., *176*
Gold, A. R., 193, *223*
Goldberg, A. M., 193, *228*
Goldberg, A. P., 29, *34*
Goldberg, D. P., 417, *420*
Goldberg, J., 25, *37*
Goldberg, R., 31, *34, 116*
Goldberg, R. J., *322*
Goldberger, A. L., 248, *265*
Goldenberg, D. L., *229*
Goldschneider, K., 359, *376*
Goldstein, D., 339, *348*
Goldstein, E. D., 336, *347*
Goldstein, G. L., 339, *347*
Goldstein, H., 75, *115*
Goldstein, M. G., 93, 94, *110, 111,* 163,
    174
Goldston, D., 343, *350*
Gollub, E. L., 132, *144*
Gomel, M. K., 100, *112*
Gomella, L. G., 409, *420*
Gonder-Fredrick, L. A., 340, *348*
Goode, K., 390, *402*
Goodey, E., 241, *259*
Goodkin, F., 316, *327*
Goodman, J., *349*
Goodrick, G. K., 28, *35*
Goodwin, R. K., *72*
Gordon, A. S., 87, *108*
Gordon, E., 318, *325,* 384, 390, *402*
Gordon, G., 300, *323*
Gordon, J., 52, 63, 70, 93, *110,* 156, *177*
Gordon, L., *67*

Gordon, W. A., 414, 415, *420*
Gordon-Larsen, P., 22, *35*
Gore, S., 238, *261*
Gorey-Ferguson, L., *399*
Gorfinkle, K., 343, *351*
Gornemann, I., 132, *138*
Gortmaker, S. L., 152, 154, 160, *174*
Goswami, M., 195, *223*
Goulding, P. M., 214, *224*
Gowda, M., 279, *293*
Graf, A., 183n
Graham, E. A., 75, *120*
Graham, J. W., 87, *108*
Graham, S., 100, *112*
Grande, F., *37*
Grandits, M., *173*
Granovetter, M. S., 316, *322*
Grant, B. F., 44, 53, 68
Grant, J. D., *113*
Grant, J., 395, *399*
Grant, M., 49, *72*
Graubard, B. I., 21, *37*
Gravestock, F. M., 336, *353*
Gray, J. A., 313, *322*
Gray-Ray, P., *143*
Green, C. J., 417, *421*
Green, J., 255, *261*
Green, L., *116*, 136, *141*, 339, *343*, *351*,
        354
Green, P. J., 384, 390, *402*
Green, S. B., *115*
Greenberg, B. G., 301, *328*, 361, *378*
Greenberg, M., 339, *350*
Greenfield, S., 343, *348*
Greeno, C. G., 240, *266*
Greenwood, M. A., *294*
Gregg, E. W., *178*
Gregor, F., 330, *346*
Grenyer, B. F., 409, *421*
Griebel, M., 210, *229*
Griffin, K. W., 240, *261*
Griffin, W. A., 384, *401*
Grigg-Damberger, M., *222*
Grim, C. E., 17, *41*
Grimm, R., Jr., *173*
Gritz, E. R., 81, 88, 89, 93, 94, 103, *109*,
        110, *111*, *112*, *114*, *115*, *120*
Grobe, J., 81, *116*
Grochocinski, V. J., 218, *225*
Gross, A., 335, *348*
Grothaus, L. C., 77, 95, 99, *110*, *119*

Grotzinger, R., 307, *320*
Grover, S. A., 15, *35*
Gruen, R. J., 237, 247, *260*, 263, 410,
        420
Gruman, J., 344, *354*
Grumet, F. C., 196, 214, *226*, *227*, *228*
Grunberg, N., 235, *258*
Guarino, A. P., *173*
Guberman, A., 198, *221*
Gudas, L. J., 336, 343, *349*
Guenat, E., *265*
Guijarro, M. L., 278, *295*
Guild, M., 18, *35*
Guilleminault, C., 190, 191, 194, 196,
        197, 198, 200, 207, 209, 210,
        213, 214, *222*, *223*, *224*, *225*,
        226, *227*, *228*
Gulati, V., 69
Gulyani, S., 228, *229*
Gunnar, R. M., 301, *322*
Gunnersen, A., *119*
Guthrie, J. F., 13, *35*
Gutmann, M., 303, *325*
Guyatt, G. H., 166, *177*
Guyton, A. C., 302, *322*
Gwadz, M., 129, *144*
Gwaltny, J. M., *321*

Haaga, D., 102, *109*
Haan, N., 244, *261*
Haber, D., *143*
Hacker, K. A., 127, *141*
Hagglund, K. J., 393, 397, 398, *421*
Hagino, O., *227*
Hahn, M., 333, *350*
Haire-Joshu, D., 96, 103, 104, *111*, *112*
Hajek, P., 95, *120*
Haldeman, G. A., 333, *349*
Haley, W. E., 390, 399, *402*
Halfon, N., 344, *349*
Hall, J. A., *353*
Hall, J. E., *173*
Hall, P., 49, *70*
Hall, S., 92, 102, *112*, *113*
Hall, W., 92, *108*
Hallet, A. J., 278, *295*
Halperin, S., 249, *259*
Halpern, C. T., 129, *141*
Hambidge, C., 31, *33*
Hambidge, M., 31, *33*

Hamilton, N. A., 240, *260*
Hamilton, P. J., 77, 101, *117*
Hammersley-Maercklein, G., 343, *348*
Handmaker, N. S., 48, *68*
Handy, S. L., 169, *174*
Hannan, P., *173*
Hannay, D. R., 301, *322*
Hansell, S., 300, *324*
Hansen, C. A., 343, *350*
Hansen, L. M., 184, *222*
Hansen, M., *119*
Hansen, W. B., 87, *108*
Hanson, C. L., 340, *349*, 388, *399*
Hanson, S., 337, *349*
Hardesty, P. H., 281, *293*
Harkins, W., 374, *377*
Harlan, L. C., 21, *35*
Harlan, W. R., 21, *35*
Harper, D. C., 387, 388, *399*
Harris, A. H. S., 270, 272, 280, 290, *293*, 297
Harris, B. A., *174*
Harris, R. C., 274, *293*
Harris, W. S., 279, *293*
Harrison, J. A., 136, *141*
Harrison, J. S., 137, *140*
Hart, B. L., 302, *322*
Hart, G. J., 134, *142*
Hartmann, K. A., 303, *323*
Hartse, K. M., *222*
Harver, A., 302, *322*
Harvey-Berino, J., 14, 30, *35*
Hasin, D. S., 44, 51, *68*
Haskell, W. L., 29, *41*, 156, 158, 161, *171, 174, 175, 176, 178, 180, 181*
Hasselblad, V., *120*
Hasson, A., *72*
Hastie, R., 256, *261*
Hatch, J. P., 129, *143*
Hatsukami, D. K., 84, 86, *110, 113*
Hatziandreu, E. J., 78, *117*
Hauck, W. W., *144*
Hauri, P., 185, 204, *223*
Hauser, R. A., 198, *223*
Hauser, S. Y., 343, *349*
Havas, S., 30, *36*
Hawkins, D., 204, *223*
Hawkins, E. H., *69*
Hawkins, L. N., 387, *397*
Hayduk, R., 214, *226*
Haynes, R. B., 332, 336, *348, 349*

Hays, K. F., 148, *174*
Hays, L. M., *350*
Hays, R. B., 134, *142*
Hays, R. D., 249, 265, 330, 336, 339, 342, *350, 351, 353*
Haysford, J. R., 342, *349*
Hazsard, A., 335, *349*
He, J., 190, *223*
Heady, J. A., 301, *319*
Heath, A. C., 82, 83, 84, 85, *113, 115, 119*
Heath, G. W., *175, 176*
Heatley, S. A., *110*
Hebert, J. R., *40*
Hebert, P. R., 28, *37*
Hecker, B. L., 305, *322*
Hedeker, D., *111*
Hedner, J., 191, *227*
Heeren, T., 163, *174*
Hegsted, D. M., 15, 17, *36*
Heider, F., 304, *322*
Heimendinger, J., 31, *33, 36*
Heitmann, B. L., 21, *38*
Heitzmann, C. A., 252, *261*
Helgeson, V. S., 255, *261*
Hellerstedt, W. L., 127, *141*, 240, *261*
Helsted, J., *119*
Helzer, J. E., 51, *72, 112*
Hengeveld, M. W., 301, *327*
Henggeler, S. W., 64, 68, 72, 386, 388, *403*
Hening, W., 199, *224*
Henley, M., 343, *348*
Henningfield, J., 84, *113*
Henretta, J. C., *350*
Henry, J. L., 242, *261*
Henshaw, S., 126, *145*
Hergenrather, K. C., 133, *144*
Herman, S., *171*
Hermann, C., *351*
Herskowitz, R. D., *349*
Herzog, A. R., 276, 284, *295*
Hessling, R. M., 136, *141*
Heurtin-Roberts, S., 317, *322*
Hewitt, W. E., 274, *293*
Hibbard, J. H., 255, *261*
Hibbard, M., *420*
Hibbert, M., *116*
Higgins, P., 204, *220*
Higgins, S. T., 56, 62, 67, 69, *73*
Hilgard, E., 312, *323*
Hill, A. B., 75, *110*

Hill, A. K., 303, *326*
Hill, H. A., 98, *113*
Hill, J. O., 13, 28, 36, *38*
Hill, N. S., 211, *223*
Hill, P. C., 273, 283, 289, *294, 297*
Hill, R., 102, *113, 118*
Hiller, L., 375, *376*
Hillman, D. R., 211, *224*
Hilsenbeck, S., 103, *110*
Hilyer, J. C., *176*
Hiroto, D., 236, *262*
Hirschman, R. S., 85, *113*
Hobbs, S. A., 343, *348*
Hoberman, H. B., 253, *259*
Hobfoll, S. E., 252, *262*, 380, 382, 396, *399, 400*
Hobson, J. A., 188, *223*
Hochbaum, G., 305, *323*
Hochberg, M. C., 415, *419*
Hockemeyer, J., 242, *262*
Hodson, L., 16, *36*
Hoff, K. E., *223*
Hoffman, C., 394, *399*
Hoffman, J. A., 49, *69*
Hofstetter, C. R., 151, *180*
Holder, H., 46, 56, *69*
Holliday, J. E., 239, *261, 262*
Hollingsworth, Z., 195, *220*
Hollis, J. F., 102, *112, 113, 120*
Holm, G., 242, *258*
Holmbeck, G. N., 391, *399*
Holmes, E., 103, *112*
Holmes, T. H., 236, *262*
Holroyd, K. A., 235, 245, *262, 266*
Honda, Y., 194, *224, 226*
Hook, R. J., 336, *348*
Hopkins, D. P., 100, *108*
Hops, H., *402*
Horan, P. F., 133, *140*
Horn, J. L., 52, *73*
Horne, J. A., 186, *228*
Horne, R., 342, 343, *349*
Horowitz, M., 236, *262*
Horst, L., 127, *141*
Horton, E. S., 13, *39*
Horton, T., 383, *399*
Hosemann, R. A., *172*
Hosmer, D., *116*
Hospers, H. J., *118*
House, J. S., 94, *113*, 250, 253, 254, *262, 263*, 276, 284, *295*

Houston, B. K., 245, *262*
Houston-Miller, N., 103, *119*
Hovell, M. F., 151, *179, 180*, 343, *347*
Howard, B. V., *37*
Howard, K. I., 45, 65, *69*
Howze, E. H., *175*
Hoyt, W. T., 269, *295*
Hu, F. B., 15, 16, 36, *111*
Hu, P. N., 129, *143*
Huba, G. J., 314, *319*
Hubbard, R. L., 62, *73*
Huber, A., 64, *69*
Hublin, C., 194, *224*
Hudes, E., *138*
Hudson, S. V., 303, 316, *323, 324*
Hudson, T., *399*
Huerta, R., *260*
Hughes, A. R., *114*
Hughes, G., 95, *113*
Hughes, J. R., 84, 86, *113*
Hukins, C. A., 211, *224*
Hull, M., *175*
Hummer, R. A., 275, *294*
Humpel, N., 168, *174*
Humphrey, F. J., II, *224*
Humphreys, K., 44, 58, 65, *69*
Hundleby, J. D., 87, *113*
Hunt, G. M., 62, *69*
Hunt, M. K., *40*
Hunter, J., 129, *144*
Hunter, S. M., 89, *114*
Hursch, C. J., 187, *229*
Hurt, R. D., 96, 110, *114*
Hurwitz, T. D., *222*
Huss, K., *354*
Hussein, M., 239, *264*
Hutcherson, M. K., 136, *141*
Hutchinson, S. J., 335, *349*
Huxtable, K., 339, *354*
Hymowitz, N., 95, *113, 116*

Idler, E. L., 274, *294*, 303, *323*
Iizuka, S., 185, *227*
Ilich, J. Z., *38*
Ingham, I., 301, *323*
Ingham, R., 137, *146*
Ingram, K. M., 409, *420*
Ironson, G., 242, *263*
Irwin, M. L., 157, *174*
Ishi, K., *228*

Kleinman, J., 317, *323*
Klem, M. L., 28, *38*
Klepp, K. I., 152, *175*
Klerman, G. L., 313, *320*
Klesges, R. C., *120*
Kliewer, W., 386, 388, *400*
Kline, L. R., *224*
Klinnert, M., 340, *350*
Knehans, A. W., 18, *35*
Knopp, R. H., *37*
Knuiman, M. W., 240, *263*, 417, *420*
Kobrin, S., *118*
Kocsis, A., 255, *261*
Koenig, H. G., 269, 274, 280, *294, 295, 296*
Koepsell, T., *34*
Koeske, R., 337, *354*
Kogan, E., *67*
Kohl, H. W. I., *173*
Kohn, L., 333, *350*
Kolata, G., 135, *143*
Kolb, J. W., *293*
Kolbe, L. J., *36*
Kolk, A. M., 318, *322*
Kolody, B., *174, 179*
Kolterman, O., *349*
Koman, J. J., 49, *69*
Konen, J. C., 242, *258*
Koocher, G. P., 336, *349*
Koop, C. E., 107, *114*
Kop, W. J., 239, *262*
Koren, G., 333, 339, *350, 351, 352*
Korhonen, H., 100, *114*
Kors, M. B., 330, *347*
Koskela, K., *114*
Koskenvuo, M., 194, *224, 263*
Kostis, J. B., *41*
Kotagal, S., 213, 214, *224*
Kottke, T. E., 92, 93, 100, 101, *114*
Koulack, D., 185, *224*
Kovacs, M., 343, *350*
Kowaleski-Jones, L., 129, *143*
Kozlowski, L. T., 81, 85, *114*
Kraaij, V., 345, *347*
Kraemer, H. C., 156, *175*
Krahn, L. E., 194, *229*
Kraiczi, H., 191, *227*
Krainz, S., 384, *401*
Kramer, J. C., 343, *348*
Krantz, D., *172*, 264, 372, *375*
Krauss, M., 90, *115*

Krauss, R. M., 16, *37*
Kravitz, R. L., 330, 335, *350, 353*
Krawiecki, N., 335, *349*
Krebs-Smith, S. M., 24, 25, *37, 40*
Kreuter, M., *118*
Kribbs, N. B., 191, 193, *224*
Kris-Etherton, P. M., 16, *35*
Kristal, A. R., 29, *37*
Kristeller, J., 101, 103, *112, 116*
Kritchevsky, D., 14, 16, *35, 37*
Krnjevic, K., 189, *224*
Kronholm, E., *263*
Krosnick, J. A., 87, *114*
Kruger, D. F., 409, *421*
Krummel, D., 19, *37*
Kruse, W. H., 339, *350*
Kruszon-Moran, D., *350*
Kryger, M. H., 190, 194, *223, 225*
Kubicki, S., 204, *228*
Kubzansky, L. D., 314, *323*
Kuczmarski, R. J., 21, 22, 27, *37, 40*
Kuller, L. H., 19, *40*
Kumanyika, S. K., 22, 28, 34, *37, 38*
Kumar, S., 338, *352*
Kunkel, E. J., 409, *420*
Kunz, S., *265*
Kupfer, D. J., 218, *225*
Kurusu, T. A., 270, *298*
Kurylo, M., 379n, 382, *398*
Kushi, L. H., 18, *38*
Kutner, B., 300, *323*

Labarthe, D. R., 301, *322*
Lachman, M., *174*
Lacroix, J. M., 301, *326*
Laffrey, S. C., 303, *323*
Lagergren, J., 299, 318, *323*
La Greca, A., *112*
Lagus, J., 95, *116*
Laing, B., *173*, 251, 256, *262*
Lamke, C., 86, *117*
Lammers, G. J., 196, *226*
Lamparski, D., 337, *354*
Lancaster, T., 96, 98, 102, *114, 118*
Landis, K. R., 95, *113*
Lando, H. A., *115, 120*
Lane, C., 382, *400*
Lang, W., 28, *38*
Langefeld, C. D., *350*
Langenberg, P., 36, 100, *120*

Mariotti, M., *220*

Markakis, G., 151, *176*

Markides, K. S., 280, *294*

Marks, E. C., *174*

Markus, H. R., 318, *324*

Marlatt, A., 93, *110*

Marlatt, G. A., 52, 54, 63, 69, 70, 156, *177*

Marmot, M., *33*, *265*

Marrero, D., *112*

Marsden, J., *74*

Marshal, S., *176*

Marshall, E. S., 343, *349*

Marshall, G. A., 50, *67*

Marshall, G. D., 343, *347*

Marshall, J. R., 14, *39*

Marshall, S., *179*

Marshall, S., 390, *397*

Martier, S. S., 49, 72, *73*

Martin, B. R., *67*

Martin, J. A., 126, *145*

Martin, J. E., 103, *116*, 281, *292*

Martin, J. L., *34*

Martin, K., *401*

Martin, M. E., 301, *327*

Martin, N. G., 83, *115*

Martin, R., 252, *263*, 300, 315, 316, 318, *324*, *325*, *327*

Martinsen, E. W., 167, *177*

Masi, A. T., 203, *230*

Maslach, C., 131, *143*

Masoro, E. J., 14, *38*

Massoth, D. L., 361, *375*

Mast, E. E., *108*

Masters, K. S., 280, *294*

Mathews, T. J., 126, *145*

Maticka-Tynedale, E., 136, *143*

Matkovic, V., 18, *38*

Matloff, J., 86, *117*

Matsi, D., 339, *350*

Mattes, R. D., 23, *38*

Matteson, D. R., 127, 128, *143*

Matthews, K. A., 238, *260*

Mattick, R. P., 92, *108*

Mattlar, C. E., *263*

Matusi, D. M., 336, 339, 344, *351*

Mayer, T. G., 357, 368, 369, 370, *376*

Mayfield, D., 49, *70*

Mayman, M., 281, *297*

McAfee, T., 99, *110*

McBride, C. M., 77, 95, *110*, *119*

McCaffree, K., 130, *141*

McCall, P. L., 281, *292*

McCallum, D. M., 240, *267*

McCann, K. L., 28, *39*

McCann, M., *72*

McCargar, L. J., *33*

McCarley, R. W., 188, *223*

McCarron, D. A., 18, *38*

McCarthy, W. J., 89, *115*

McCaul, D., 331, 340, *348*

McCaul, M. E., 60, *73*

McCrae, R. R., 245, 247, 248, *263*, 300, 313, *321*, *419*, *421*

McCreath, H., *38*

McCubbin, H. I., *401*

McCullough, M. E., 269, 270, 273, 274, 277, 280, *293*, *295*, *298*

McCurley, J., 29, 34, *35*

McDade, E. A., 86, *115*

McEachran, A., 218, *225*

McEwen, B. S., 285, *295*

McGill, C. W., *110*

McGill, T., *70*

McGinnis, J. M., 12, *38*

McGinty, D., 188, *225*

McGloin, J., *142*

McGovern, P. G., *322*

McGrath, E., 88, *115*

McGrath, P., 375, *376*

McGraw, S. A., 158, *173*

McGuire, M. T., 28, *38*

McGuire, W. J., 312, *325*

McIntosh, M. J., *421*

McKane, W. R., 18, *38*

McKay, G., 252, *259*

McKay, J. R., 49, *70*

McKenney, J. M., 339, *351*

McKenzie, T. L., 151, 152, *174*, *176*, *177*, *179*

McKeown, R. E., *140*

McKinlay, S., 158, *172*

McKnight, G. T., 236, *258*

McKusick, L., 133, *145*

McLaughlin, C. R., 129, *143*

McLaughlin, T. L., *113*

McLellan, A. T., 51, 61, 70, *74*

McLellan, B. Y., *180*

McLeod, G., 49, *70*

McMahon, K., 274, *295*

McMahon, P. T., *67*

McMahon, S., 307, *320*
McMurry, J. F., 409, *421*
McNamara, C., *70*
McNamara, M. E., 204, *225*
McQuaid, E., 340, *350*
Meagher, R. B., Jr., 417, *421*
Mechanic, D., 392, *400*
Medrano, M. A., 129, *143*
Meehan, J., 196, *228*
Meichenbaum, D., 330, 333, 334, *351,*
354
Meischke, H., *322*
Mellinger, G. D., 184, 202, *225*
Mellins, C. A., 388, *403*
Mellins, R. B., 344, 348, *351*
Melzack, R., 359, 360, 364, *376, 377*
Mena, A., *260*
Menaghan, E. G., 129, *143*
Mendelson, M., 53, *67*
Mendicino, A. J., 89, *109*
Mercer, G. W., 87, *113*
Mercury, M. G., 240, *266*
Meredith, C. N., *174*
Merisca, R., *353*
Mermelstein, R., 92, 94, 100, *109, 115,*
237, 253, 259
Merritt, R. K., 86, *117*
Messe, M., *353*
Mesters, I., 337, *354,*
Metz, K. F., *170*
Metzger, D. S., 61, *70*
Meulman, J., 345, *347*
Meydrech, E. F., 163, *173*
Meyer, D., 303, 304, 306, *324, 325*
Meyer, K. A., 18, *38*
Meyer, P. S., 301, *322*
Meyer, R., *71*
Meyer-Bahlburg, H. F., 129, *144*
Mezzich, J., 317, *325*
Miaskowsi, C., 374, *377*
Michael, M., *70*
Michael, R. T., 134, 135, *142, 143*
Michaels, S., 134, *142*
Michell, L., 78, *116*
Michie, S., 185, *227*
Mickelson, K. D., 383, *400*
Middaugh, S., 375, *377*
Midence, K., 333, 343, 345, *351*
Miele, G. M., *68*
Mignot, E., 196, 214, *226, 227, 228*
Milby, J. B., 46, 61, 62, *70, 72*

Milgrom, H., 336, *346*
Milgrom, P., 373, *377*
Miller, J. C., 186, 197, *226*
Miller, J. D., *226*
Miller, J. H., 17, *41*
Miller, J. J., 388, *402*
Miller, K. A., 203, *239*
Miller, K. S., 129, 130, 137, *140, 143,*
146
Miller, L., *140*
Miller, L. C., 133, *143*
Miller, L. G., 336, 339, 342, *351*
Miller, N. E., 312, *321, 325*
Miller, P., 301, *323*
Miller, S. M., 244, *263*
Miller, T. Q., 278, 279, *295*
Miller, W. R., 47, 48, 52, 53, 55, 56, 57,
65, 68, *70, 71,* 270, 271, 272,
281, 283, 286, 289, *295*
Milley, J. E., *349*
Millon, T., 53, *71,* 417, *421*
Mills, K. M., 161, 162, *177, 180*
Milman, L., *401*
Minuchin, S., 383, *401*
Misovich, S. J., 131, 137, *141, 142*
Mistry, S. K., 329, 331, 338, *351*
Mitchell, J. E., 86, *113*
Mitchell, J. P., 255, *264*
Mitchell, W. D., *353*
Mitchison, G., 189, *222*
Mitler, M. M., 186, 197, *226*
Mittelmark, M. B., 87, *116, 173*
Mizuno, K., 185, *227*
Mobily, K. E., 161, *177*
Mock, J., 53, *67*
Moen, P., 390, *401*
Mohr, J., *421*
Mokdad, A. H., 13, *38,* 239, *263*
Moldofsky, H., 204, *226*
Monarch, E. S., 360, 361, 363, 366, *377*
Monjaud, I., *34*
Montagna, P., 199, *226*
Monteiro, M. G., *74*
Monti, P. M., 69, 84, *108, 116*
Montoya, I. D., *73*
Montoye, H. J., 155, *177*
Montserrat, J. M., 190, *226*
Mookerjee, A. L., 333, *352*
Moore, D., 279, *297*
Moore, J., 133, 137, *140, 143*
Moore, J. A., *33*

Pirie, P. L., 86, *116, 117, 173*
Pi-Sunyer, F. X., *34*
Pitetti, K. H., 165, *178*
Pitson, D., 208, *220*
Pitt, L. C., 388, *403*
Pless, I. B., 316, *325*
Poehlman, E. T., 13, *39*
Polatin, P. B., 369, 370, *375, 376*
Polissar, N., *401*
Pollack, L. M., 134, *142*
Pollock, S. E., 411, 412, 414, 415, *421*
Pomerleau, C. S., 81, 82, 83, *117*
Pomerleau, O. F., 81, 82, 83, *117*
Pope, C. R., 255, *261*
Pope, M. H., 364, *375*
Popkin, B. M., 22, *35*
Poppen, P. J., 136, *144*
Porkka-Heiskanen, T., 188, *227*
Posner, S. F., 103, *116*
Powell, K. E., *175*
Powell, L. H., 273, 283, 285, *296*
Powell, N. B., *228*
Powell, T., 269, *297*
Powers, D., 390, *399*
Prabucki, K., 387, *396*
Pratt, M., 148, *171, 172, 178*
Prescott, C. A., *114*
Pressman, M. R., 185, *227*
Presson, C. C., 85, 87, *109*
Prevost, F., 185, *224*
Price, R. K., *113*
Priest, R. G., *226*
Prior, M., 388, *400*
Prochaska, J. J., 149, 151, 156, *178, 179*
Prochaska, J. O., 53, *71,* 99, *109, 117,*
        118, 136, *144*
Prochaska, J., 342, *352*
Prohaska, T. R., 310, *326*
Propst, L. R., 279, *296*
Pruitt, L. A., 163, *175*
Psaty, B., *34*
Pucci, L. G., 88, *117*
Pullar, T., 338, *352*
Pulte, D. E., 103, *110*
Putnam, J., 25, *39*
Putnam, R. W., 157, *176*

Quade, D., *116*
Quera-Salva, M. A., 191, *223*
Qui, X., *226*

Quigley, L. A., 69
Quittner, A. L., 336, 338, 339, 340, 341,
        352, 382, 386, *401*

Raab, E., 317, *325*
Rachlin, H., 82, 84, *117*
Racioppo, M. W., 418, *420*
Raczynski, J. M., 32, *38, 40,* 70, 176,
        183n
Rae, D. S., 45, *71, 72*
Raether, C., 31, *36*
Raglin, J. S., 167, *178*
Rahe, R. H., 236, *262*
Rahn, J. M., 240, *266*
Raia, J., 331, *346*
Rajgopal, D., 389, *400*
Rakowski, W., *174*
Ralph, M. R., 184, *227*
Ramanathan, L., *229*
Ramirez, G., *116*
Ramos-Bonoan, C., *348*
Ramsay, L. T., *175*
Ramsey, D. J., 301, *322*
Ramsey, T. B., 253, *258*
Rand, C., 329, 336, 339, *346, 352, 354*
Rao, S. N., 333, *352*
Rapoff, M. A., 329, 330, 331, 336, 337,
        339, 340, 342, 343, 344, 345,
        347, 348, 353
Rapoport, D. M., *226*
Rappaport, N., 237, *259*
Rapuri, P. B., 19, *39*
Rashidee, A., 333, *349*
Rasmussen, J., 392, *400*
Ratcliff, K. S., 51, *72*
Rausch, J. L., 86, *117*
Rawling, P. J., 242, *261*
Rawson, R., 64, 69, *72*
Ray, L. A., 280, *294*
Raynor, H. A., 149, *174*
Raynor, W. J., *265*
Razani, J., *110*
Reams, P. N., 129, *143*
Rechtschaffen, A., 185, *227*
Redd, W. H., 343, *351*
Redding, C., 342, *352*
Redline, S., *228*
Redmond, W. H., 88, *117*
Reed, G. W., 13, *36*
Reeder, S., 300, *320*

Scharloo, M., 306, *326*
Schatzkin, A., 21, *37*
Scheier, M. F., 245, 265, 311, *321*
Schenck, C. H., 201, 217, *225, 228*
Scherrer, J. F., *119*
Scheuler, W., 204, *228*
Schinkel, A., *349*
Schleifer, S. J., 333, *353*
Schmidt, C., 49, 66
Schmidt, H. S., 193, *222*
Schmidt, R. F., 359, *377*
Schmidt, S. E., 63, *72*
Schmitz, K. H., 169, *172*
Schneerson, J. M., 198, *222*
Schneider, S. J., 49, 69
Schneiter, P., *265*
Schnoes, C., *223*
Schober, R., 46, 54, *72*, 301, *326*
Schoenbach, V. J., *113, 116*, 254, 255, *265*
Schoenwald, S. K., 64, 68, *72*
Schopp, L., *398*
Schottenfeld, R., *71*
Schreck, R., 75, *118*
Schreiner, P. J., *38*
Schroeder, D. R., *110*
Schubert, N. M., *224*
Schuller, D. E., 193, *222*
Schultz, M. A., 207, *229*
Schultz, R. M., 343, 344, *351*
Schulz, A. J., 395, *399*
Schulz, R., 381, 382, *402, 403*
Schumacher, J. E., 46, 62, 70, *72*
Schuster, C. R., *73*
Schwartz, A. R., 193, *223, 224*
Schwartz, C. E., 248, *265*
Schwartz, J. M., 333, *348*
Schwartz, R. S., *174*
Schwarzer, C., 245, 246, *265*
Schwarzer, R., 245, 246, 251, 254, 256, *265*
Scully, J., 237, *265*
Seal, D. W., 132, *139*
Searcy, P., 68
Secker-Walker, R. H., 88, *118*
Seefeldt, T., *399*
Seeley, J. R., 86, *108*
Seeman, M., 279, *296*
Seeman, T. E., 279, 283, 284, *296*
Seematter, G., 240, *265*
Segal-Andrews, A. M., 389, *400*

Seibert, R., 210, *229*
Seidel, K. D., 22, *41*
Seidman, S. N., 134, *144*
Seifer, R., 216, *221*
Selby, V. C., 156, *177*
Sellers, D. E., 38, *322*
Sellers, E. M., 82, *116*
Selye, H., 234, 235, *265*
Selzer, M. L., 49, *72*
Sepsis, P. G., *180*
Sergis-Deavenport, E., 333, *353*
Serufilira, A., *138*
Seybold, K. S., 273, *297*
Shahabi, L., 273, 283, *296*
Shahar, E., 191, *228*
Shapera, W., *399*
Sharma, M., 341, *353*
Sharpe, S. J., 18, *39*
Shaten, B., 95, *116*
Shattuck, A. L., *37*
Shedler, J., 281, *297*
Shekelle, R. B., 15, *40*, 239, *265*
Sheldon, S. H., 207, *228*
Shema, S. J., 276, *297*
Shenton, M. E., *118*
Shepperd, B. T., 131, *140*
Sher, A. E., 193, *228*
Sherbourne, C. D., 249, *265*, 330, 342, *350, 353*
Sheridan, J., *261*
Sherman, S. J., 85, 87, *109*
Sherrill, K. A., *294*
Sherwood, A. R., *118*
Shew, M. L., 127, *141*
Shewchuk, R., 382, 387, 392, 393, 394, 395, *398, 402*
Shields, C. G., 382, 384, *398*
Shiffman, S., 81, 84, *117, 118*
Shifren, K., 344, *352*
Shigley, L., 183n
Shintani, T., 209, *228*
Shipley, M. J., 101, *117*
Shirley, A., *145*
Shope, J. T., 86, *110*
Shoptaw, S., 69, *72*
Shorter, E., 301, 319, *326*
Shrout, R. E., 237, *260*
Shuckit, M. A., 49, 58, *72*
Sicher, F., 279, *297*
Siddiqui, O., *111*
Siegel, D., 131, *143*

Steiger, A., 184, *229*
Stein, E., *40*
Stein, P., *346*
Steinberg, D., 19, *40*
Stenberg, D., 188, *227*
Stenner, K., 137, *146*
Stephens, M. A. P., 380, 391, *396, 397*
Stephens, R. M., 135, *146*
Stephens, R. S., *67*
Stephens, R., *142*
Stepnowsky, C., *220*
Steptoe, A., 238, 239, 242, 246, *259, 265*
Sterman, M. B., 188, *229*
Stern, E., 207, *229*
Sternbach, R. A., 372, *377*
Stetner, F., *112*
Stetson, B. A., 156, *173*, 240, *266*
Stevens, V. J., 28, *37, 112, 113*
Stewart, A. L., 161, 163, *177, 180*
Stinshoff, D., 204, *228*
Stitzer, M., 60, *73, 120*
Stoddard, A., *40*, 333, *347*
Stokes, J. P., 253, *266*
Stokols, D., 160, *176*
Stoller, E. P., 300, *327*
Stone, E. J., *38, 39*, 152, *177*
Stone, N. J., 17, *40*
Stoohs, R., 209, *223*
Storer, B. E., 14, *40*
Stores, G., 194, *229*
Story, M., 22, 31, *35, 40*
Stout, J. C., *400*
Stout, J. K., 281, *298*
Stovel, K. W., 388, *403*
Strack, S., 238, 246, *266*
Stradling, J. R., 208, *220*
Strain, J. J., *353*
Strawbridge, W. J., 276, 277, *297*
Strecher, V., 99, *113, 118*, 341, *354*
Streicher, P., 185, *229*
Stretch, V., *120*
Strickland, B. R., 88, *115*
Strikmiller, P. K., *177*
Strohl, K. P., *225*
Stroud, M. W., 409, *421*
Strum, R., 65, *73*
Strunk, N., 127, *141*
Strychacz, C. P., *293*
Stuart, E. M., 409, *420*
Stueve, A., *143*
Stump, T. E., 161, *181*

Stunkard, A. J., 36, 164, *172*
Subar, A. F., 21, 24, 25, *33, 37, 40*
Suchindran, C., 129, *141*
Suhan, P. S., 333, *348*
Sullivan, C. E., 210, 229, 280, *294*
Sullivan, M. J., 383, *400*
Sullivan, P., *114*
Suls, J., 247, 252, 263, 266, 315, 316, 324, 327, 382, 384, 390, *402*
Suminski, R. R., *178*
Summerson, J. H., 242, *258*
Sumner, A. E., *173*
Sumner, W., 89, 104, *118*
Sung, H., 394, *399*
Surwit, R. S., 239, *266*
Susser, M., 98, *118*
Svarstad, B., *353*
Svendsen, K., *173*
Svendsen, L., *222*
Svetkey, L. P., *33*
Swan, P. D., 240, 251, *260*
Swindells, S., 409, *421*
Swindle, R., Jr., 249, *260*
Szymusiak, R., 187, 188, *225, 229*

Taagholt, S. J., *222*
Tabak, G. R., 157, *177*
Talen, E., 160, *176*
Tan, T. D., 337, *354*
Tanaka, J. S., *353*
Targ, E., 279, *297*
Tarter, R. E., 49, *73*
Taylor, C. B., 103, *119*, 156, 158, 161, *174, 175, 176, 181*
Taylor, D. W., 336, *354*
Taylor, G., 101, *118*
Taylor, S. E., 310, 316, *321, 322*, 382, *397*
Taylor, W. C., 149, 165, *172, 178, 179*
Teitlbaum, L. M., 49, *67*
Telch, M., *118*
Telesky, C., 300, *320*
Tellegen, A., 313, *327*
Tennen, H., 204, *220*
Teran-Santos, J., 191, *229*
Terri, D., *296*
Terry, R. B., *34*
Thannickal, T. C., 187, 196, *229*
Tharps, D., 300, *326*
Thatcher-Shope, J., 343, *354*

Van Heel, N., *173*
Van Hemert, A. M., 301, *327*
Van Horn, L., *38*
van Koningsveld, R., 129, *139*
Van Mechelen, W., 150, *171*, 239, 266
Van Treeck, D., 18, *35*
Vargas, P., *354*
Varni, J. W., 333, 337, 348, 353, 388,
    403
Vaughn, C., 80, *114*
Vaux, A., 252, *262*
Veith, A., *398*
Velez, C. N., *143*
Velez, R., 345, *351*
Velicer, W. F., 99, *117*
Ventura, S. J., 126, 127, *145*
Verboncoeur, C. J., *180*
Verbrugge, L. M., 318, *327*
Verstraete, D. G., 332, *352*
Vessey, J. T., *69*
Villetard, K., *33*
Vincent, M. L., *140*
Vinicor, F., *38*, 263
Vinokur, A. D., 382, *396*
Violani, C., 185, *221*
Vitaliano, P. P., 240, 266, 385, *403*
Vittinghoff, E., *140*
Vogt, T. M., 95, 102, *112*, *113*, *120*
Vollmer, W. M., 17, *33*, *41*
Vollrath, M., 249, *266*
von Bertalanffy, L., 409, *421*
Von Frey, M., 359, *377*
Von Hoff, D., 103, *110*
Von Korff, M., 344, *354*, 369, *377*, 395,
    403
Vraniak, D. A., 389, *401*
Vuchinich, R. E., 48, *74*

Wadden, T. A., 14, 28, *41*
Wade, S. L., *350*
Wadley, V. G., *399*
Waff, D., *399*
Wagener, M. M., *421*
Waggoner, C. D., 237, *259*
Wagner, D. J., 331, *346*
Wagner, E., *34*
Wagner, E. F., 86, *108*
Wagner, E. H., 77, 95, *110*, *116*, *119*,
    160, *172*, 344, *354*, 395, 395, *403*
Wakefield, M. A., 100, *108*

Walco, G. A., 374, *377*
Walid, R., 194, *225*
Walker, E. F., 80, *119*
Walker, J., 315, *327*
Walker-Thurmond, K., 13, *34*
Wall, P. D., 359, 360, *376*, *377*
Wallace, D., 38, *70*
Wallace, R. B., 161, *177*
Wallander, J. L., 383, 386, 388, 399, *401*,
    403
Waller, J., 22, *41*
Wallston, K. A., 314, *327*
Walsh, R., 271, 272, *297*
Walster, E., 381, *403*
Walster, G. W., 381, *403*
Walters, A., 199, *224*
Wan, C. K., *325*
Wan, T., 303, *327*
Wanstall, K., 336, *353*
Ward, C. H., 53, *67*
Ward, D. M., *64*
Ward, K. D., *120*
Wardlaw, G. M., *38*
Wardle, J., 22, *41*
Ware, J. E., Jr., 343, *348*
Warnecke, R. B., 100, *120*
Warner, A., 61, *68*
Warner, K. E., 90, 104, *120*
Warner, T. D., 136, *141*
Warren, C. W., 129, *145*
Washburn, R. A., 162, *180*
Wasserheit, J. N., 122, 123, *145*
Waters, K. A., 210, *229*
Watkins, K., 344, *352*
Watkins, P., *296*
Watson, D., 302, 303, 313, 317, *325*,
    327
Watts, J. C., 313, *324*
Weaver, M., 395, *399*
Webber, L. S., *114*
Weber, S., *230*
Webster, P., 92, *108*
Wechsler, H., *36*
Wegner, E. L., *325*
Weinberger, M. H., 17, *41*
Weiner, B., 256, *265*
Weiner, E., 271, *297*
Weinman, J., 342, 343, *349*
Weinstein, A. G., 336, *354*
Weinstein, N. D., 136, *145*
Weinstein, P., 373, *377*

Weinstein, R. S., 131, *143*
Weintraub, J. K., 245, 265, 311, *321*
Weisberg, J. N., 359, 364, *376*
Weisenberg, M., 373, *378*
Weiss, L. H., *146*
Weiss, S. T., 314, *323*
Welch, A., 250, *260*
Welch, M. A., *350*
Welch, S., *74*
Welk, G. J., 151, 152, *180*
Weller, S. S., 317, *328*
Wellington, E., 251, *266*
Wells, B. L., 164, *176*
Wells, K., 65, *73*, 249, *265*
Wendell, D. A., *143*
Wenner, W. H., 207, *229*
West, C. A. C., *399*
West, R., 95, *120*
Westermeyer, J., 317, *328*
Westoff, C. F., 121, *139*
Weston, A. T., 151, *181*
Wetter, D. W., 92, 93, *120*
Wetterberg, L., 216, *227*
Wheeler, E., *294*
Whelton, P. K., 28, 30, *37, 41*
Whitaker, D. J., 129, *146*
Whitaker, R. C., 22, *41*
White, D. P., *225*
White, E., *37*
White, F. A., *399*
White, H. R., 46, *74*
White, I., *33*
White, K. L., 301, *328*, 361, *378*
White, N. E., 410, *421*
White, T., *111*
White, Y., 409, *421*
Whiteman, M., 87, *108*
White-Means, S., 389, *403*
Whitlatch, C. J., 393, *396*
Whitlock, E. P., 102, *120*
Whitney, C. W., *228*
Who, J., *114*
Whyte, J. J., *36*
Wiebe, D. J., 240, *267*
Wiebe, J. S., 248, *259, 264*, 382, *396*
Wiecha, J., *174*
Wiesemann, S., 344, *348, 351*
Wiet, G. J., 210, *229*
Wigal, J. K., 245, *266*
Wigand, J., 91, *120*
Wilbourne, P., 55, *70*

Wilcox, K., 388, *403*
Wilcox, S., 163, *175*
Wiley, J., 133, *145*
Wilhelm, B., 185, *229*
Wilhelmsen, L., 255, *264*
Wilkinson, C., 63, *72*
Willemsen, G., *265*
Willenheimer, R. B., *346*
Willett, W., 23, *41*
Willett, W. C., 15, *36*
Williams, A., 342, *348*
Williams, C. D., 103, *116*
Williams, D., 102, *109*
Williams, D. A., *173*, 373, *376*
Williams, D. R., *295*
Williams, F., 361, *378*
Williams, J. M., 281, *298*
Williams, M., 343, *349*
Williams, M. A., *180*
Williams, O. D., *38*
Williams, P., 155, *181*
Williams, P. T., 29, 34, *41, 174*
Williams, R. B., 86, *115*
Williams, R. L., 187, *229*
Williams, S. S., 137, *146*
Williams, T. F., 301, *328*
Williamson, D. F., 21, *41, 108*
Williamson, G. M., 255, 259, 382, *403*
Willie, J. T., *222*
Willis, K. L., 132, *142*
Willis, L. A., 135, *146*
Wills, T. A., 250, 251, 252, 259, *267*
Wilner, B. I., 240, *266*
Wilner, N., 236, *262*
Wilson, C., 101, *118*
Wilson, D., 339, *354*
Wilson, D. G., 253, *266*
Wilson, G. T., *36*
Wilson, M., *401*
Wilson, P. H., 242, *261*
Wilson, W., 331, *348*
Wimbush, E., 157, *181*
Winett, R. A., *144*, 157, *176*
Wing, R. R., 14, 28, 29, 34, 35, 36, 38, 39, *41*, 255, *267*, 337, *354*
Wingood, G. M., 132, *146*
Winkelstein, M. L., 333, *354*
Wirtz, P., *67*
Wise, M. S., 213, 214, *229*
Wish, E. D., 49, *69*
Wister, A. V., 161, *181*

SUBJECT INDEX

Chlamydia, 123. *See also* Sexually
transmitted disease
Cholesterol, serum
and coronary heart disease, 15
and fiber, 17–18
and physical activity, 149
Chronic disease, 330. *See also* Patients,
adaptation to chronic illness
children and, 331, 388
and smoking cessation, 103–104
role of major dietary factors in
(table), 12
variables of, 412
Chronic pain. *See* Pain
Cigarette smoking. *See* Smoking,
cigarette
Circadian rhythm, 205–206, 215–219
Clinical Practice Guideline, 92
Clinics
group smoking cessation, 102
Cocaine, 54, 63
Cocaine Anonymous, 59, 61
Commission for the Accreditation of
Rehabilitation Facilities, 365, 370
Commitment, 127–128
Common sense model, 304–306
Community Health Activities Program
for Seniors, 163
Community Intervention Trial for Smoking Cessation, 100
Compliance, to medical regimen
vs. adherence, 331
defined, 331, 332
Conditioning, and smoking, 83–84
Condoms, 134, 136–137
female, 132–133
and interventions for sexual risk,
132
Continuing Survey of Food Intakes by
Individuals, 23, 24, 26
Coping, and stress, 235, 410. *See also*
Stress; Social support
defined, 243–244
and family support, 388–389, 391
future research on, 249–250
and health, 248, 307
individual differences in, 246–248
measurement of, 245–246
models of, 244
religious, 289

Coronary heart disease, 165, 330. *See also*
Cardiovascular disease
and high serum cholesterol levels, 15
and medical regimen adherence,
336
and social support, 255
and spirituality, 280
Counseling
and drug abuse disorders, 61–62
CRA Plus Vouchers program, 62
Crisis exploration, 127–128
Culture, 411. *See also specific race*
differences in physical activity, 159–
160
and family support, 389–390
and pain, 372–373
and symptom perception, 317
Cystic fibrosis, 339, 341

Daily Stress Inventory, 237
Department of Health and Human
Services, U.S.
Depression, 195, 277, 381
and coping, 249
and exercise, 167
and sleep disorders, 218
and smoking, 86, 87, 102–103
Diabetes, 330, 409
and behavior, 80
and diet, 12
and medical regimen adherence,
332, 335, 336, 339, 343, 344
and smoking cessation efforts, 103–
104
and stress, 239
Diagnostic Interview Schedule, 51
Dietary Approaches to Stop Hypertension, 18
Dietary behavior, 9–10. *See also* Dietary
intake; Obesity
dietary change intervention outcomes, 27–28
environmental interventions, 31–32
factors that influence, simplified
depiction of (figure), 11
individual interventions on, 27–30
Dietary intake, 9–33. *See also* Dietary
behavior; Obesity
and alcohol, 19
and energy intake, 13–14

Gate-control theory, of pain, 359–360
Gay men
    and high-risk sex, 124, 133–134
Gender, 411. *See also* Women
    differences in physical activity, 148–
        149, 154
    and family support, 390–391
    and pain, 373–374
    and smoking, 78
    and social support, 255
    and substance abuse, 54–55
General Health Questionnaire, 417
Genetics
    and smoking, 82–83
Guide to Community Preventive
    Services, 154
Gulf War Veterans Illnesses, 167–168

Harm reduction
    and sexually transmitted disease, 64–
        65, 66
    and smoking cessation, 10
Hassles Scale, 237
Health. *See also* Behavior, health-care
    seeking; Medical regimen adher-
    ence; Pain management; Patients,
    adaptation to chronic illness;
    Spirituality, and health
    and coping, 248–249
    and social support, 254–255
    status indicators, 335–336
    and stress, 238–240
Health belief model, 305
Health-care seeking behavior. *See* Behav-
    ior, health-care seeking; Medical
    regimen adherence; Pain manage-
    ment; Patients, adaptation to
    chronic illness
Health Education Authority of the
    United Kingdom, 149
Health status indicators, 335–336
Heartburn, 299–300, 306, 307, 311, 316,
    318–319
Hemodialysis, 341, 382
Hispanic Americans
    adolescents, 129
    teenage pregnancy, 126–127
    and substance abuse, 54
Homelessness, 129

Human immunodeficiency virus (HIV),
    123, 124
    and adolescents, 131
    harm reduction policies for, 64–65,
        66
    interventions for, 133
    perceived risk of, 135–138
    substance abuse and risk for, 54
Hypertension, 165, 330
    and calcium, 18
    and medical regimen adherence,
        336, 344
    and obstructive sleep apnea, 191
    and physical activity, 156
    and sodium, 17

Identity crisis
    in adolescence, 128
Idiopathic hypersomnia, 215
Illness
    defined, 361
Imprisonment
    for drug crimes, 54, 66
Insomnia, 201–203. *See* Sleep; Sleep dis-
    orders
    cases of, 202–203
    in children, 211
    defined, 201
    therapy for, 202–203
Intensive intervention (smoking), indica-
    tions and components of (table),
    105
Interpersonal Support Evaluation List,
    253
Inventory of Social Supportive Behaviors,
    253

Joint Commission on Accreditation of
    Healthcare Organizations, 365

Kleine–Levin syndrome, 215

Latino Americans. *See* Hispanic
    Americans
Life Experiences Survey, 236

National Health and Nutrition Survey, 86
National Heart, Lung, and Blood Institute, 158
National Heart Attack Alert Program Coordinating Committee, 301
National Institute on Drug Abuse, 59
    principles of effective drug addiction treatment (exhibit), 60
National Institutes of Health, 19, 64, 273
    Office of Behavioral and Social Sciences Research, 282–285
National Livestock and Meat Board, 26
National Osteoporosis Foundation, 18
Native Americans
    and obesity, 22
    and smoking, 78
Nebulizer Chonolog, 339
Needle exchange, 64–65
Negative affect, 313–314
Neuromatrix model, 360
Neuromuscular disorders, 210–211
Nicotine, 81–82, 83–84. *See also* Smoking, cigarette
    gum, 96
    patches, 96
    pharmacological interventions for, 95–97
Nociception, 361
Nursing services, 371
Nutrient intake, 22–23

Obesity. *See also* Dietary behavior; Dietary intake
    and cancer risk, 14
    and children, 22
    and dietary behavior, 11–14
    and energy restriction, 14
    epidemiology of, 21–26
    and increased morbidity, 13–14
    intervention outcomes, 27–28
    and minority groups, 22
    national rates for, 21, 33
    and women, 21–22
Office of Behavioral and Social Sciences Research
    physical health report of, 283–284
Olive oil, 15, 16
Organizers
    and medical regimen adherence

Osteoporosis
    and alcohol, 19

Pain, 357–375, 385. *See also* Pain management
    acute, 362
    assessment of, 363–366
    biomedical reductionism theory of, 358
    biopsychosocial model of, 360–361, 363–367
    chronic, 362, 370–372, 418
    cultural factors, 372–373
    gate-control theory of, 359–360
    historical overview, 358–361
    mental deconditioning interaction with physical (figure), 367
    neuromatrix model of, 360
    vs. nociception, 361
    and pain management, 364, 366–367
    pattern theory of, 359
    pervasiveness, 357
    recurrent, 362
    self-report of, 364
    specificity theory of, 359
Pain management, 364. *See also* Pain
    of chronic pain, 370–372
    and communication, 372
    critical elements of, 368–369
    primary care of, 368, 369
    secondary care of, 368, 369
    Step Care Framework, 369
    techniques, 366–367
    tertiary care, 368, 370–372
Parasomnias, 200–201
Partner Safety Beliefs Scale, 137
Patients, adaptation to chronic illness, 405–419. *See also* Behavior, health-care seeking; Family support; Medical regimen adherence; Social support
    biopsychosocial model, 408–409, 414
    and cardiovascular disease, 413–414
    characteristics of ideal model, 408–409
    domains of, 406–407
    domains of patient adaptation to chronic illness (exhibit), 406

ABOUT THE EDITORS

Editor-in-Chief

Thomas J. Boll, PhD, is director of the Neuropsychology Institute in Birmingham, Alabama. For 32 years, he was a professor at several universities and medical centers, including the University of Washington; the University of Virginia; Chicago Medical School; and, for the past 20 years, the University of Alabama at Birmingham (UAB). He was a professor in the Departments of Psychology, Pediatrics, and Neurological Surgery. He is board certified in clinical psychology, clinical neuropsychology, and clinical health psychology. His research investigations in the areas of health and human behavior include issues related to heart and lung transplantation and chronic pediatric illnesses, including congenital cytomegalovirus, low birthweight, seizure disorders, and learning disabilities. He has written on various aspects of educational and curriculum design for health psychology and was the founding chairman of the Department of Medical Psychology at Chicago Medical Center and the first director of clinical training for the Medical Psychology Program at UAB. He was the chair of the Doctoral Curriculum Committee at the Arden House Conference, which set the curriculum for health psychology doctoral training programs.

Volume Editors
James M. Raczynski, PhD, is professor and dean of the College of Public Health (COPH) at the University of Arkansas for Medical Sciences (UAMS). Before joining the faculty in the COPH at UAMS in 1992, he was at the University of Alabama at Birmingham (UAB) for 21 years, where he served as professor and chair for the Department of Health Behavior, School of Public Health; professor and chief for the Behavioral Medicine

Unit, Division of Preventive Medicine, Department of Medicine; and director of the UAB Center for Health Promotion. His research has focused primarily on chronic disease risk factor identification and health promotion and disease prevention methods. In recent years, his interests have focused on primary prevention approaches, particularly within African American and other underserved communities. He is the coeditor of the *Handbook of Health Promotion and Disease Prevention* (1999).

Laura C. Leviton, PhD, is a senior program officer of the Robert Wood Johnson Foundation in Princeton, New Jersey. Before joining the foundation in 1999 she was a professor at two schools of public health: University of Pittsburgh and University of Alabama at Birmingham. She received the American Psychological Association's 1993 award for Distinguished Contributions to Psychology in the Public Interest for her work in HIV prevention and worksite health promotion. She has served on an Institute of Medicine Committee to evaluate preparedness for terrorist attacks and on the Center for Disease Control and Prevention's National Advisory Committee on HIV and STD Prevention. She was president of the American Evaluation Association in 2000 and is coauthor of two books: *Foundations of Program Evaluation* (1991) and *Confronting Public Health Risks: A Decision-Maker's Guide* (1997).